JUVENILE DELINQUENCY

JUVENILE DELINQUENCY

Its Nature and Control

BY

SOPHIA M. ROBISON

Assistant Director, Juvenile Delinquency Evaluation
Project of the City of New York

Holt, Rinehart and Winston, New York

85159

To the memory of Judge Kenneth D. Johnson, Dean of the New York School of Social Work, Columbia University, a courageous fighter for the rights and the welfare of all mankind.

May, 1963

Copyright © 1960
by Holt, Rinehart and Winston, Inc.
Library of Congress Catalog Card Number: 60–7980
27528–0110
Printed in the United States of America

Preface

IN A FRESH ATTACK ON THE PROBLEM OF JUVENILE DELINQUENCY, THIS TEXT proposes to re-examine the field as it has been staked out by a variety of scientists and technologists. Part I looks critically at the processes of labeling behavior which, in the past, have assumed that delinquency is a *state of being* that, like a disease, can be identified and treated. Part II is concerned with the efforts to explain delinquency in terms of individual or family characteristics, the sociological concepts of ecology, role, class, the psychological and anthropological approaches in explaining behavior. Parts III and IV describe and evaluate official and unofficial agencies for dealing with delinquents in institutions or in the community. Part V outlines general proposals for preventing delinquency.

Our main sources are: (1) published and unpublished documents and deliberations of various organizations which have assumed responsibility for dealing with the legal, the treatment, or the preventive aspects of delinquency; (2) official statements of standards set by commissions and conferences concerned with dealing effectively with delinquency. In evaluating causal theories and the programs of institutions and agencies, the author draws upon her personal experience in social work practice and in social research.

Each trained observer reacts to events from his own perspective—that is, from the specific bodies of knowledge which for the convenience of study have been labeled sociology, psychology, anthropology, and so forth. He often forgets that the original groupings of such events were made by men acting on different assumptions. New ways of looking at events are constantly arising. As new instruments extend the range of our senses we are able to re-inspect the old groupings. When a considerable number of such re-readings are at hand, old labels no longer serve and old boundaries are obliterated. New fields are explored, staked out, expanded, and labeled. In short, the theoretical indoctrination of the early explorers, subjected to reorientation and cross-fertilization, determines the current field of study. So it is with delinquency.

Instead of an exhaustive catalogue of numerous studies and summary of many works, this text discusses in considerable detail only those studies which, in the opinion of the author, have made major contributions to our understanding of delinquency. To instructors who miss references to some of their favorite theories, the author says: "Mea culpa." Other textbooks, to which she acknowledges a debt for the parts of the field which they have plowed more exhaustively, will be good supplementary references. Students with special interests in some one aspect of delinquency should consult the major bibliographies. Cabot's includes almost a thousand annotated entries on researches published in the thirty-year period between 1914 and 1944.[1] Two publications of the Children's Bureau cover the period from 1939 to 1954.[2] The United Nations International Review of Criminal Policy, No. 13, October 1958, contains a topical bibliography of current technical literature on juvenile delinquency in the United States and in various European countries. *Sociological Abstracts* is an indispensable quarterly publication for keeping up with relevant current research both in the United States and abroad.

To supplement his reading the serious student will observe for himself what goes on in a court or an institution. Like the stock market broker, he will examine the official statistics on the rise and fall of delinquency in his own community to see whether the crests and the troughs are associated with changes in the ethnic and socio-economic composition of the population, with changes in police procedure, with general social crisis such as war and depression, or perhaps with a combination of these and other factors.

In summary, this text seeks to alert the student to the assumptions—both explicit and implicit—which underlie the many conflicting pronouncements on the characteristics of delinquents, the causes, treatment, and prevention of delinquency. The purpose, in what may appear to be a critical approach to much current theory and practice, is not to tear down but to try to penetrate the fogs. Because the nature of social problems, and consequently their treatment, must change as the conditions and our knowledge of what is important shifts, no textbook can legitimately lay claim to final answers. It can and should, however, point the way to better definitions, new insights into cause, and more effective ways of dealing with so persistent a social problem as juvenile delinquency.

Our hope lies in the fresh attacks that today's students will make. Armed

[1] Philippe S. De Q. Cabot, Ph.D., *Juvenile Delinquency, A Critical Annotated Bibliography*, New York, H. W. Wilson Co., 1946.

[2] *Bibliography on Juvenile Delinquency*, 1953, and Otto Pollak and Norman Johnston, *Studies in Juvenile Delinquency: A Selected Bibliography, 1939–1954*, 1956, Washington, U. S. Children's Bureau.

with what knowledge there is, they can begin to look at the problem afresh, re-examine its forms and the efforts at its control, and so renew the search for more effective solutions.

No author of a textbook which ranges across a field as broad as juvenile delinquency can rightly claim that the product is a result of his single-handed efforts.

My initial interest was stimulated by university teachers in the social sciences. Special acknowledgments are due to Professor Robert M. MacIver and Drs. Chaddock and Ross at Columbia University. Dr. MacIver's philosophy, and his books *Community* and *Society* have been a major influence on my thinking in the field of sociological research, and both are frequently referred to without specific credit in this text.

Dr. Neva R. Deardoff, Director of the Research Bureau of the Welfare Council, permitted me to use the facilities of that organization in the preparation of my thesis, "Can Delinquency Be Measured?" Among the consultants on that study, Dr. David M. Levy and Dr. Ralph Hurlin were especially helpful. Dr. Gordon W. Allport of Harvard University, Monsignor Paul H. Furfey of the Catholic University of America, and Dr. Thorsten Sellin of the University of Pennsylvania who worked with me on an assignment to evaluate the Cambridge-Sommerville Survey widened my experience and knowledge. Dr. Edward E. Schwartz and Helen L. Witmer of the Children's Bureau at various times have made it possible for me to have direct contact with systems of juvenile court reporting, to experiment with establishing a Central Register, and, as technical consultant, to assemble facts on delinquency for the 1950 White House Conference.

My associations as the Research Director of the Harlem Project, 1943-46, with Dr. Marian E. Kenworthy, Dr. Viola W. Bernard, The Hon. Judge Justine Wise Polier, Dr. Ernest Osborne of Teachers College, Dr. Jacob Theobald, then Associate Superintendent of Schools, Dr. Wayne Wrightstone of the Bureau of Research were particularly helpful in appraising the role of the school in an underprivileged community. Dr. Irving R. Lorge of the Bureau of Psychological Research at Teachers College introduced me to the intricacies of IBM tabulations.

I am also deeply grateful to the National Probation and Parole Association for its generous permission to use and to quote liberally from its journals, Year Books, guides, manuals, special studies, and reprints of articles inspired by it, which have appeared in magazines that have suspended publication.

Over the years E. Franklin Frazier, Kenneth R. Clarke, James R. Dumpson, Lester Granger, and Otto Klineberg have made me intensively aware of important issues with respect to Negro-white relations as they affect behavior. Professional contacts with Dr. Joseph Bram of New York University, with Dr. Clarence Senior, and with Joseph Monserrat and Leonard Covello of the Puerto Rican Labor Office have alerted me to the adjustment problems of Puerto Ricans and Italians.

As a staff member of the National Probation and Parole Association in 1955, I was put in touch by Dr. Will Turnbladh, Stephan Kneisel, Sherwood Norman, and Sol Rubin, the legal consultant, with issues and practices in courts, probation, and detention services across the country.

Fifteen years spent in supervising the theses of scores of students in various schools of social work—Columbia, Smith, Yeshiva and Adelphi—and twenty years of active participation in professional organizations and committees concerned in one way or another with social problems have extended the peripheries of my knowledge. Specific references will be found in the text.

As always, librarians have proven to be most willing and diligent pursuers of details in references. In particular, I wish to record my gratitude to Mrs. Grace G. Bermingham and Mrs. Margaret M. Otto of the New York School of Social Work, Miss Felicia Fuss, in charge of the Russell Sage Collection at the College of the City of New York, and Miss Armine Dikijian, librarian of the National Probation and Parole Association.

In the early stages of the manuscript the volunteer services of my friends, Mrs. Ceevah Rosenthal Blatman, Miss Jeannette Gevov, Mrs. Elsa Loeb, Dr. Bessie B. Wessel of Connecticut College, Dr. Robert R. Holston, who introduced me to General Semantics, were particularly helpful in discussing and organizing some of the material. I am grateful to Dr. Olga Lang of Swarthmore for her help with Russian references.

Professor William J. Goode of Columbia University, Sociological Editor of the Dryden Press under whose auspices this textbook was initiated, guided me through the first three drafts of the manuscript with skill and patience. Dr. David S. Milne of San Diego State College, Dr. Clarence C. Schrag of University of Washington, and Professor Dorothy R. Blitsten of Hunter College.

I owe a special debt to Professor F. James Davis for his critical reading of two versions of the manuscript and to Mrs. Hermine Popper for her skillful editing of the final version.

New York City
January 1960

S. M. R.

Contents

85159

PART TWO

Theories of Cause

PART THREE

Primary Legal Agencies for
Dealing with Delinquents

PART SIX

Conclusion

PART ONE

WHAT IS DELINQUENCY AND WHO ARE THE DELINQUENTS?

CHAPTER 1

What Is Delinquency?

THE CELEBRATED MAN IN THE STREET, OR T. C. MITS AS HE HAS BEEN CALLED,[1] assumes that juvenile delinquency, like most adult crime, is clearly defined by law. In consequence he believes that the rise and the fall in juvenile court statistics reflect the actual increase or decrease in antisocial behavior. But unlike the term "crime," which usually refers to specific acts—theft, murder, assault—the legal term "delinquency" is an umbrella for a wide variety of socially disapproved behavior that varies with the time, the place, and the attitudes of those assigned to administer the law. Moreover, there exist many extralegal definitions, put forth by a variety of "experts"—parents, teachers, psychiatrists, social workers, preachers, sociologists, judges—that are often inconsistent and sometimes mutually exclusive.

Yet one cannot deal intelligently with the phenomenon of delinquency unless one can define the problem and its extent. In an effort to arrive at a working definition this chapter discusses some of the major sources of confusion and misapprehension as to the nature and incidence of delinquency.

The Nature of a Social Problem

How we define a problem and how we deal with it depends first of all upon whether we regard the problem as purely personal or as social, i.e., having broad implications for others than ourselves. When a condition or a situation becomes the concern of many, it is labeled a social problem.

[1] Lillian R. and Hugh Lieber, *The Education of T. C. Mits*, New York, W. W. Norton, 1944.

A striking example is the recent shift from individual to social concern for family problems. Relations between husbands and wives and between parents and children were formerly considered the responsibility of the individual family. However, as the evidence piled up that many families were experiencing similar difficulties and that harmonious relations between parents affected the development of children's potentialities, family problems—in addition to their legal aspects—came to be recognized as appropriately the concern of the community.

The shift is revealed in a study of Greenwich Village, New York City, in the decade from 1920-30.[2] An examination of a large number of the statistical cards of the clients of a family agency between 1920-25 showed not a single notation of family conflict. In marked contrast, the clients who came to the agency after 1925—the year which initiated the founding of the mental hygiene movement—were frequently recorded as suffering from marital disharmony and conflict between parents and children. It is hardly likely that these conditions did not exist before 1925. A likelier inference is that they escaped attention because before 1925 no one had suggested that such problems were the proper concern of the agency.

Actually, the misbehavior of young people had come to be recognized as a social problem—that is, as delinquency—somewhat earlier when, with the expansion of the urban industrial economy in the late nineteenth century, individual families were no longer able to cope with it by themselves. The notion that parents had a "natural right" to control their children gave way before the superior right of the state to protect the public welfare. And juvenile courts came into being to perform the state's new function.

The question remained, what misbehavior should be considered delinquent behavior? And the answer, it soon became evident, was not simple or invariable; it depended upon the indoctrination and orientation of the individual who gave the answer, and this in turn depended upon the time and the place in which he lived, as well as on what past generations had thought and done.

Perhaps one reason why even today in America, where concern for delinquency is paramount, no consistent view of it has yet been arrived at is that no one institution or set of experts has been granted the sole right to its control. In this respect delinquency differs from illiteracy, sin, or illness: public schools were established to counteract illiteracy, the churches to curb sin, and our systems of medical care, doctors, and hospitals, to deal with and prevent illness. In the field of delinquency, however, while the police and the juvenile courts are charged with enforcement of the law, the law itself, as well as the attitudes of its administrators, is affected by the views of others in the com-

[2] Caroline Ware, *Greenwich Village, 1920-1930: A Comment on American Civilization in the Post-War Years,* Boston, Houghton Mifflin, 1935.

munity, most notably the lay public, and the mental health professionals—psychologists, psychiatrists, and social workers.

The Lay Attitude

The man in the street is concerned chiefly with behavior that interferes with his property, his person, and his rights. He believes that the official label of delinquency is attached only when the behavior is really harmful and has occurred repeatedly. He is not aware that, on the contrary, a large proportion of young people are referred to the courts for behavior which is not clearly defined or which might go unnoticed in many communities. Or that, as we shall see in our discussion of juvenile court procedures (Chapter 15) a considerable proportion of the cases which come before the court are dismissed, i.e., there is no finding of guilt.

Nor does the man in the street realize that delinquency statistics are often affected by the kinds of agencies available in the community to deal with deviant behavior. The fact that in large communities there is a juvenile court that sits every day is undoubtedly one of the reasons why *officially recorded* delinquency is so much higher in urban than in rural areas. Conversely, children whose parents make reparations for their misdeeds, send them to boarding school, or refer them to mental hygiene clinics, are not likely to be counted as official delinquents.

The lay person tends to think of the delinquent as inherently "bad." Often he forgets that in the process of growing up he too indulged in behavior which might have earned him the label "delinquent" had there been anyone around to apprehend him. He rarely considers his own pilfering, souvenir collecting, truancy, raids on neighborhood storekeepers' or farmers' property, disobedience to parental proscriptions, and so forth, as delinquency. Rather he thinks of such acts as incidental and infrequent transgressions, usually occurring in the company of peers who shared his standards of appropriate conduct under the circumstances. He sees little resemblance between today's apprehended delinquent and himself in his youthful unapprehended transgressions, whether alone or in the company of his "gang."

To remind the reader that behavior which may acquire the official label of delinquency also occurs in situations where it is not recorded, we refer to two important studies which followed the first systematic examination of the extent to which official statistics measure delinquency.[3]

In 1946 Porterfield[4] asked 337 students, a sample of those attending

[3] Sophia M. Robison, *Can Delinquency Be Measured?*, New York, Columbia University Press, 1936.
[4] Austin L. Porterfield, *Youth in Trouble*, Austin, Texas, Leo Potishman Foundation, 1946.

three colleges in Northern Texas, to record their delinquent behavior in their high school days. These reports were compared with the offenses with which 2000 delinquents in the Fort Worth Juvenile Court were charged. The comparisons showed striking similarities in behavior but great dissimilarities in the results. Although about 43 per cent of the collegians said they had been truants and almost 15 per cent had run away from home, not one was arrested for such offenses in his pre-college days. In contrast, these two offenses accounted for 43 per cent of the boys brought before the juvenile court in the Fort Worth area. Thefts accounted for 27 per cent of the boys in court; but in spite of the fact that almost one half of the collegians admitted petty thievery of one kind or another—money, tools, bicycles, automobiles— none of them had been apprehended.

Among the girls, none of the college students had been brought to court, although almost 9 per cent admitted petty theft and almost 2 per cent said they had shoplifted. Yet petty theft accounted for 4 per cent, and shop- lifting for 11 per cent of the town girls before the court. Less than 3 per cent of the college girls acknowledged illegal sexual offenses—and none had been apprehended. But similar behavior was the charge in almost 12 per cent of the girls' cases before the juvenile court.[5]

Nor did the behavior that the college students reported represent isolated instances. Each of the respondents was able to recall at least eleven occasions on which he or she might have been apprehended as an official delinquent.

Similar evidence is provided in Short's recent study in Seattle, Wash- ington.[6] High school boys and boys who had been committed to the state training schools from the same geographical area, in answering an anonymous questionnaire, revealed little difference in their reports of either the type or the frequency of delinquent acts. In testing whether the high school students who said they were willing to be interviewed reported less serious behavior than those who wished to remain anonymous, Short observed that the students who acknowledged homosexual relations and the violation of hunting and fishing laws were least willing to be interviewed.

The findings of these systematic studies are consistent with the mem- ories which most of us have, though we may repress them. Informal inquiry among one's classmates or guests at a party ordinarily turns up plenty of evidence of the occurrence in "good" families of stealing, shoplifting, malicious mischief, and assault on siblings or friends. This behavior might easily have brought those involved to the attention of the juvenile court if there had been anyone concerned enough to report it.

[5] *Ibid.*, p. 41.

[6] James F. Short, Jr., and F. Ivan Nye, "Extent of Unrecorded Juvenile Delin- quency: Tentative Conclusions," *Journal of Criminal Law, Criminology, and Police Science*, Vol. 29, no. 4 (Nov.-Dec., 1958), pp. 296-302.

The pertinent question is: At what point and why did our present respectable friends decide to mend their ways? The answer to this might resolve another public misapprehension: that delinquency is simply the first step on the road to adult crime (a heritage from the classical view of crime, discussed in Chapter 5). Before we can identify the youthful misdeeds that are, in fact, threats to the future of the individual and of society, we will need to develop new methods of case finding. One possible approach would be to interview a cross-section probability sample of the population. If we can follow the subsequent careers of those who acknowledge youthful behavior which might have earned them a juvenile court record, we may be better able to identify that kind of behavior which should concern us because it is a signpost of danger.

The Legal View

It has been said that if there were no law there would be no crime. Those who hold this view usually insist that studies of delinquency, like studies of crime, should concern themselves only with officially apprehended and labeled delinquents. They consider it impractical to extend the designation "delinquent" to those who do not come within the purview of the juvenile court even though their behavior might under other circumstances have been referred to the court. They say, in effect, that unless the thief is caught he is not a thief; and unless a young person is brought before the juvenile court he is not a delinquent. But even if one were willing to confine one's study to officially apprehended delinquents one would be confronted by definitions which are neither precise nor uniformly applied.

Ambiguities in Official Definitions

Juvenile courts differ with respect both to the age limits and to the kinds of behavior over which they exercise jurisdiction.

AGE LIMITS. Since it is generally assumed that a child under seven is incapable of willfully committing an offense, in most United States jurisdictions children under the age of seven are not brought to court as delinquent. The upper age limit of juvenile court jurisdiction, however, varies considerably across the United States. Such variation to some extent reflects inconsistencies in the definitions of adulthood. All societies mark the transition from childhood to adulthood with accompanying ceremonies; within our society adult status is marked by such "privileges" as leaving school, entering gainful employment, and obtaining a marriage license without parental consent; but the age at which a youngster attains this status is anything but uniform.

Attainment of the sixteenth birthday makes one ineligible for juvenile court consideration in seven states—Vermont, Connecticut, New York, and Maryland in the Northeast; North Carolina and Georgia in the Southeast; Utah in the West—and in Puerto Rico and the Virgin Islands. Seventeen is the maximum age for juvenile court jurisdiction in six states—Maine, Massachusetts, and Delaware in the Northeast; Kentucky and Louisiana in the Southeast, and Missouri in the Midwest. Eighteen is the upper age limit in approximately half of the states, including Alaska and Hawaii. In some courts the upper age limit for girls is higher than for boys, despite the fact that the age of consent to marriage is usually lower for girls than boys.

KINDS OF OFFENSES. Like age jurisdiction, the descriptions of delinquency also vary in different states. In eight states there is no definition. The judge determines whether or not the defendant is a juvenile delinquent. In contrast, some juvenile court codes include such specific proscriptions as, for example, violation of railroad laws (hitching rides on the back of streetcars or buses), misuse of transfers, failure to pay fares, violations of corporation ordinances, including selling without a license, turning on a water hydrant, and so forth (see Chapter 15 for a more complete list). Certain court codes mention many types of behavior which would not be punishable if the offender were an adult—such as associating with vicious or immoral persons, frequenting policy shops, gambling places or saloons, and so forth. In some juvenile courts, smoking cigarettes or the use of tobacco in any form constitutes delinquent behavior.

Desertion of home or ungovernable behavior account for a fairly large proportion of cases before the juvenile court, but are not applied uniformly either to types of behavior or to the sexes. *Desertion of home* may mean simply one young person staying away from home one night. In other instances, it may refer to repeated wanderings, or spending the night in a lodging house with associates assumed or known to be disreputable. *Ungovernable behavior,* a widely used label, covers all types and degrees of unsatisfactory relationships between the child and his parents, or his school, or community. One child may be labeled ungovernable because his parents cannot control his pilfering of family pocketbooks. A girl may be unwilling to account for her evening whereabouts or for the choice of her boy or girl companions. Sometimes the term "ungovernable" refers to the boy or girl who refuses to get up in the morning, help with the household chores, spend his money as his parents think proper, or go to bed at what they consider a reasonable hour. Still other young people are labeled "ungovernable" because they vent their anger on their younger brothers and sisters; or, conversely, because, as a younger brother or sister, they resent the assumption of authority which an older child in the family is allowed to wield. Girls guilty of sex offenses are customarily designated as ungovernable, or as having deserted their homes.

Thus, ungovernable behavior may at times embrace some aspects of truancy, stealing, running away from home, violent temper, impertinence, general uncooperativeness, and sex offenses. It is a complex rather than a homogeneous concept.

It is important to ask who attaches the label "ungovernable." Like stubbornness, it implies a two-way street; no one can be stubborn or ungovernable alone, but only in reference to the demands of another person. It is of special interest that in the cases of girls brought before the courts the petitioners are, in the main, their parents, whereas the police are the chief petitioners in the case of boys. This discrepancy is in large part a reflection of the strict view which is taken in our society concerning sexual activities among girls. In a heterogeneous population, representing diverse cultures, the amounts and the kind of obedience demanded of children will necessarily vary. Thus the wide range of parental standards, wisdom, and skill in governing children has a bearing on the reporting, as well undoubtedly as on the occurrence, of deviant behavior.

In essence, then, there are many times when even the official label "delinquent" is a value judgment differently applied to the behavior of boys and girls of varying ages and varying backgrounds. It reflects not only the roles of the male and the female in different cultures but also different standards of adulthood.

The Mental Hygiene Approach

In the mental hygiene view juvenile delinquency, like all behavior, is an expression of the individual's need. The same behavior may and often does have different significance depending upon the individual. If the behavior is socially disapproved, it calls for re-examination of the reasons for the individual's conduct. For example, stealing may be one person's way to gain attention by using the proceeds to buy approval of his peers; or it may be the way by which a child seeks the attention of a parent, who will feel disgraced by the disapproved behavior of his offspring. On the other hand, kleptomania—the compulsive theft of items of little intrinsic value—stems from much deeper psychodynamic needs of the individual. In the mental hygiene view, each of these three forms of stealing calls for very different treatment.

A child's truancy may not be officially registered, but if it continues it may point to mounting difficulty. It may represent a resistance to school that can be dealt with by the school, or a plea for help in meeting the requirements of daily living that requires a more basic approach. The label "truant," then, is not a diagnosis and, as psychiatrists point out (see Chapter 10), to deal with it as a routine act of "delinquency" may obscure the real problem.

To judge certain acts as simply right or wrong is to miss the fact that the concepts of right and wrong are rarely static. Mores—society's informal method of control—change with time. For example, there is much less concern today about girls who smoke and drink than there was in former times. Some aspects of delinquency are like masturbation: In the guidebooks of the past, the clergyman and the teacher almost uniformly condemned masturbation; to the former it was sin, and to the latter a step on the road to insanity. But we now know that practically everyone in the process of heterosexual development has at some time or other indulged in some form of masturbation, and concern with it has markedly receded in recent years.

The change of perspective has come about because of the mental hygiene point of view, which insists that the child must be seen as a whole. The "whole" child engages in many types of activities. He is rarely delinquent all the time, and when he does misbehave, his actions must be judged within the relevant context.

The crucial question is: What is the relevant context? Even within the broad framework of the mental hygiene approach there are widely varying emphases, as Part III of this book will illustrate. But they meet in agreeing, as does the author, that delinquency is a matter for treatment rather than punishment, and that it cannot be successfully prevented or intelligently treated unless the causes behind it are understood.

Delinquency Defined

One limitation to our ability to deal constructively with delinquency is that our customary language structure determines the formulation of our ideas and theories. We use the term "delinquent"—as we sometimes use the term "love"—as though it were a simple concept, whereas it actually embraces complex patterns of behavior. The either-or formulation—delinquent-non-delinquent, loved-rejected—is not truly descriptive of degree, quality, or context.[7] It is therefore reasonable that when the old words no longer serve we should go back to the happenings themselves and search for the meanings hidden underneath the labels.

Delinquency, it is clear, is many things to many people. To assume that

[7] Nathanial F. Cantor, "Dynamics of Delinquency," *American Journal of Orthopsychiatry*, Vol. 10 (1940), pp. 789-94. Cantor points out the fallacies of the Aristotelian view and suggests emphasizing the interrelated processes of growth and development.

the label "delinquent" is defined or applied uniformly is as naïve as it would be to assume that divorce statistics accurately and uniformly reflect the incidence of marital discord. The fact that the experts cannot agree on a definition, however, does not mean that the phenomenon cannot be explored, or that its extent cannot be measured. The necessary approach is to examine delinquency in as many as possible of its aspects in order to determine what it is and equally important what it is not. Since there is ample evidence that the official records are not representative of the universe of delinquent behavior, this text considers delinquency as *any behavior which a given community at a given time considers in conflict with its best interests, whether or not the offender has been brought to court.*

Summary

The antisocial behavior of young people came to be recognized as a community problem at the point at which a large number of individual families were unable to cope with it by themselves. Although the community assumed responsibility for this problem, loosely defined as delinquency, it did not, however, assign the major responsibility for its control—as it had with education, health, and morals—to one set of agencies.

One explanation may be that the definitions of delinquency vary with the points of view of the people who feel challenged by it. Specifically, the lay public is chiefly concerned with its discomfort or the losses it may sustain. In his prescriptions for dealing with today's youthful transgressors, the layman generally fails to remember that but for the grace of God, his family's attitudes, or the neighborhood in which he was reared, he himself might very well have been labeled delinquent. Conclusive proof of this hypothesis, as tested by Porterfield in Texas and Short in Seattle, Washington, awaits more refined research methods similar to those employed by Kinsey in his studies of the incidence of various forms of sexual behavior in America.

Those who accent the legal or law enforcement point of view regard delinquency as apprehended behavior which conflicts with the law in the particular community. Theirs is an untested assumption that the characteristics of those who are referred to the law enforcement agency differ significantly from those who are not apprehended. The offenses for which young persons are brought before the juvenile courts, however, reveal a wider variety than those for which adults are referred to court. Furthermore, labels such as "ungovernable," "incorrigible," "desertion from home," "association with undesirable companions," do not refer to behavior which has uniform meaning and significance. Nor are the age limits of juvenile court jurisdiction the same throughout the United States.

From the mental hygiene point of view, advanced by psychiatrists and representatives of social agencies, all behavior, whether approved or disapproved, is symptomatic of the individual's needs. The proponents of this approach are rarely concerned with the affixing of an official label of delinquent, because, in their opinion, the label frequently obscures the real problem whose discovery and treatment is their goal. In consequence, they do not limit their concern to those young people who have been officially apprehended.

When we study the various forms of delinquency in the subsequent chapters, let us bear in mind the ambiguity inherent in the official definition. And when, as in the next chapter, we consider the incidence and the extent of the various forms of delinquency, let us ask whether those who have been caught represent a good sample of all those who misbehave.

CHAPTER 2

Is Delinquency Increasing?

THE EXTENT TO WHICH OUR ATTENTION IS CALLED TO A PROBLEM USUALLY determines our concern with it. When the newspapers report an increase in juvenile arrests, the bench, the pulpit, and the desk not only view these statistics with alarm but usually proceed to tell us who and what is to blame. We would do well to stop and ask: "Where do the figures come from? What do they really mean? How do they compare with those of other countries?

Until the end of World War I it was impossible to obtain comparable data for juvenile courts even within a single state, let alone for the United States as a whole; and until 1930 there was no organized effort to establish uniform statistics on adult crime. While we have made some progress, there is still a long way to go before we can make reliable pronouncements on the incidence of crime or delinquency in the United States. As Sellin has said: "We might well hang our heads in shame—our statistics on crime and delinquency are probably the least reliable in the Western world."[1]

The two major roadblocks to bringing order into delinquency statistics are: (1) the inconsistencies, as noted in Chapter 1, in identifying the delinquent; and (2) the insistence on state's rights, even in the impersonal area of statistical reporting. To appraise the statements of those who view the figures with alarm or of those who insist that their efforts have decreased the delinquency rate, these factors must be taken into account. Try as we may, we cannot make such an analysis sound like a case story. The social scientist must be willing to pay as close attention as the engineer and the physical scientist does to the language of numbers. There is one comfort,

[1] Quoted in Robert Wallace, "Crime in the United States," *Life*, Vol. 43, no. 11 (Sept. 9, 1957), p. 49.

however. One does not need to be a mathematics major to understand what the figures say.

The two official sources of delinquency statistics in the United States today are the Children's Bureau and the Federal Bureau of Investigation. A brief history of their efforts and accomplishments in this aspect of their work should help to provide an understanding of what is involved in the attempt to provide an adequate statistical picture.

The Children's Bureau Series

In May 1923 a joint committee of the National Probation Association[2] and the Children's Bureau recommended setting up a reporting system on juvenile courts which would:

1. Furnish an index of the general nature and extent of the problems which are brought before the court officially and unofficially.

2. Show the extent and kinds of service given by the court in such a way that significant trends in methods of treatment and important facts with reference to scope and volume of work might be brought out.

3. Point out significant causal factors, to throw light on possibilities of correction and prevention.

4. Show the extent to which service given by the court has been effective in correcting social problems, according to some definite measure of success or failure, to the end that possibilities and limitations of methods might be revealed and necessary changes or reinforcements indicated.

These clearcut and reasonable objectives were adopted by the Children's Bureau after extended research. In 1914 Flexner and Baldwin had shown that there was as yet no statistical basis for well-founded comparisons between different courts and different communities,[3] and in 1918 a nationwide questionnaire-survey of courts hearing children's cases revealed such chaos that it was impossible to obtain even comparable data for courts within a state.[4]

Number of Courts Reporting

The number of courts which over the years have agreed to report to the Children's Bureau increased from 42 in 1927 to 1549 courts located in 41

[2] In 1947 the name of the organization was officially changed to National Probation and Parole Association.

[3] Bernard Flexner and Roger N. Baldwin, *Juvenile Courts and Probation*, New York, Century, 1914.

[4] Evelina Belden, *Courts in the United States Hearing Children's Cases* (results of questionnaire-study covering the year 1918), No. 65, Washington, U. S. Children's Bureau, 1920.

states in 1955, the year when a new plan for collecting statistics was put into operation. While the initial goal had been eventual complete coverage in all the states, the Bureau pursued no systematic plan to bring juvenile courts into the system. Thus only those courts which expressed interest in the project, or were conveniently reached by the Children's Bureau field staff, joined in the reporting series. In consequence, the figures for 1946-49,[5] 1950-52,[6] 1953,[7] 1954,[8] and 1955,[9] were based on varying numbers of courts whose procedures were not always uniform.

Methods of Tabulation

When the series began in 1927, each of the cooperating courts forwarded to the Bureau (1) a card for each case disposed of by the court, and (2) a card for each child discharged from supervision during that year. Tabulations of the essential data were made by the Children's Bureau, and forwarded to each reporting court.

With the coming of World War II a cut in the Children's Bureau appropriation forced the abandonment of individual tabulations for each court. Instead the Bureau began to advocate state-wide reporting systems. Under this plan, the individual juvenile court would furnish to the appropriate state office information on each case with which each court dealt. The state office would then consolidate the data and supply the Children's Bureau with an annual report on the number of cases dealt with in each court in the state which had agreed to cooperate. However, by 1959 only eight states—Massachusetts, Rhode Island, Connecticut, New York, Ohio, Indiana, Missouri, and Utah—had so far assumed the responsibility for reporting to the Children's Bureau on a state-wide basis.

Limitations of the Series

As a result of these changes, the number of courts reporting as well as the breakdown of data in the Children's Bureau Series have varied, sometimes from year to year. It is therefore difficult, and often impossible, to trace changes in such factors as source of and reason for referral throughout the series.

5 Children's Bureau Statistical Series No. 8, *Juvenile Court Statistics, 1946-49*, Washington, Federal Security Agency, 1951 (413 courts).
6 Children's Bureau Statistical Series No. 18, *Juvenile Court Statistics, 1950-52*, Washington, U. S. Dept. of Health, Education, and Welfare, 1954 (458 courts).
7 Children's Bureau Statistical Series No. 28, *Juvenile Court Statistics, 1953*, Washington, U. S. Dept. of Health, Education, and Welfare, 1955 (666 courts).
8 Children's Bureau Statistical Series No. 31, *Juvenile Court Statistics, 1954*, Washington, U. S. Dept. of Health, Education, and Welfare, 1956 (937 courts).
9 Children's Bureau Statistical Series No. 37, *Juvenile Court Statistics, 1955*, Washington, U. S. Dept. of Health, Education, and Welfare, 1956 (1549 courts).

Moreover, from the beginning, the official reports have drawn attention to the incomplete coverage of the juvenile court statistics on which the series is based. For example, I. Richard Perlman, Chief of the Juvenile Delinquency Statistics Section, notes: "They can never reflect the entire delinquency problem, since many difficult children are dealt with by individuals and agencies without recourse to the court."[10] Each of the Bureau reports remarks on the varying role of the juvenile court in different communities and the different ways in which communities deal with behavior they consider serious. The 1939 report noted the anomalous position of courts in communities in which the court had held wider powers before the passage in 1935 of the Social Security Act, which made the public agencies responsible for the welfare of large numbers of dependent and neglected children as well as those in danger of becoming delinquent. "The juvenile court is only one instrument in a unified and comprehensive child welfare program for the treatment of delinquency as a form of social maladjustment requiring specialized treatment."[11]

Related Studies of the Children's Bureau

The variations in the juvenile court statistics spurred the Children's Bureau into probing factors in various cities which might explain some of the apparent contradictions. To this end the Bureau undertook several studies either directly or in cooperation with other organizations.

The early Children's Bureau studies included a compilation of juvenile court laws,[12] the formulation of a Standard Juvenile Court Act,[13] studies of the structure and function of juvenile courts in various communities,[14] and an analysis of the courts' changing role.[15]

In addition to studies focused on the juvenile court, the Children's Bureau examined the detention facilities for young people awaiting disposition of their cases in the juvenile court,[16] as well as the institutions and training schools to which the court committed young people who in its opinion needed to be removed from their own homes. The experience and

[10] I. Richard Perlman, "Reporting Juvenile Delinquency," *Journal,* National Probation and Parole Association, Vol. 3, no. 3 (July, 1957), pp. 242-49.

[11] "Children in the Courts," Washington, U. S. Children's Bureau, 1938-39, p. 2.

[12] Gilbert Cosulich, *Juvenile Court Laws of the United States,* New York, National Probation Association, 1939.

[13] *A Standard Juvenile Court Act,* New York, National Probation Association, 1926. Revised in 1928, 1933, 1943, 1949, 1959 (forth coming).

[14] Bernard Flexner and others, *The Child, the Family, and the Court,* No. 193, Washington, U. S. Children's Bureau, 1933; and *Juvenile Court Standard,* No. 121, Washington, U. S. Children's Bureau, 1934.

[15] Alice Scott Nutt, "The Future of the Juvenile Court as a Casework Agency," *The Child,* Vol. 4 (July, 1939), pp. 17-22.

[16] Florence M. Warner, *Juvenile Detention in the United States,* Washington, U. S. Children's Bureau, 1933; see also Chapter 21.

knowledge gained from these and other studies provided the broad base for the 1940 White House Conference on Child Care and Protection.[17]

As we shall see in the later discussion of the community's efforts at preventing and controlling delinquency, in the decade from 1940 to 1950 the Children's Bureau turned its attention to projects which emphasized the essential oneness of delinquency with other problems in the community. This new emphasis reflected the fact that delinquency had begun to be regarded as only one aspect of a child's behavior, intricately interwoven with his personality, his family, and the availability of wholesome outlets in the community, regardless of color, parentage, or area of residence.[18]

e 1955 Plan for Reporting Delinquency Statistics

Currently, in response to the demand for better statistics, the Children's Bureau has initiated a plan for collecting juvenile court statistics from a scientifically chosen representative national sample of courts.[19]

On the basis of its population estimates, the Bureau of the Census has selected 230 areas which it considers representative with respect to geographic location, population density, economic characteristics, and racial composition. In these areas 502 juvenile courts have agreed to collect information on specified items and send it to the Children's Bureau.

It was anticipated that beginning with 1957 this sample would provide more reliable data not only on trends but eventually on such important aspects as costs, reasons for referral of children to the courts, kinds of services provided by the court, and disposition of cases which come before it. Simultaneously, the Children's Bureau recommended an extension of the state-wide reporting system.

> The Children's Bureau is emphasizing to State agencies that the national sample data will furnish the basis only for national estimates of delinquency, not for State estimates. Because of the importance of reliable delinquency estimates for States and for local communities, the State agencies will be encouraged to seek reports not only from the courts in the national sample but from all the courts in their States.[20]

Despite the valiant efforts of the Children's Bureau, however, the presently available juvenile court statistics, "when taken by themselves, can-

[17] Elsa Castendyck, "Juvenile Courts in the Light of the White House Conference," *Yearbook*, National Probation Association, 1940.

[18] See *Children in the Community: The St. Paul Experiment in Child Welfare*, No. 317, Washington, U. S. Children's Bureau, 1947; and *A Community Plans for Its Children: Final Report on the Newport News, Va., Project*, No. 321, Washington, U. S. Children's Bureau, 1947.

[19] See *The American Statistician*, Vol. 8, no. 2 (April-May, 1954), pp. 5-6, for a description of the design of the sample area.

[20] Communication from I. Richard Perlman, May 28, 1956.

not measure the full extent of either delinquency, dependency or neglect. In regard to the extent of such problems, they may be *particularly misleading* when used to make comparisons between one community and another. They do, however, indicate how frequently one important community resource, the juvenile court, is utilized in dealing with such cases."[21]

Not all apprehended juvenile offenders, it should be noted, come before the juvenile courts. Young persons charged with federal offenses are otherwise handled. Statistics on juveniles charged with violations of federal statutes and arrested by the United States probation officers and marshals are compiled by the Federal Bureau of Prisons. These reports show for each judicial district the age, sex, race, offense, type of detention, and final disposition of each juvenile delinquent. In those cases for which the court orders commitment, the length of the sentence is also given.

Juveniles charged with violating federal statutes may elect to be tried under the Federal Juvenile Delinquency Act. If their cases have not been diverted to state or local authorities, the administrative offices of the United States courts, rather than the Federal Bureau of Prisons, assemble the data.

Estimates of Annual National Volume of Delinquency

Periodically, the Children's Bureau issues statements on the number of delinquents in the United States. In 1930 their estimate, based on the reports of 92 courts, was 200,000 delinquents. In 1950, based on reports from 458 courts, the estimate rose to 435,000; and in 1956, based on returns from approximately 83 per cent of the courts in the national sample, the estimate was 450,000, or 2.2 per cent of all children aged 10 through 17.[22]

Table I illustrates some of the difficulties in interpreting delinquency statistics. No satisfactory explanation has been offered, for example, of why, with the exception of the war years, the delinquency index was less than 100 up to 1950, whereas it has more than doubled since (while the population estimates have increased by only about 25 per cent). The sources of the statistics themselves are limited: the case count for 1940 to 1954 is based only on 200 courts, since these were the only ones that reported continuously during those years; and the census data becomes inevitably less accurate as they move away from the years—the first of each decade—when the census is taken.

A similar change in police arrest data (see Chart I) for 1940-50, the only period for which the method of collecting data remained the same,

[21] Children's Bureau Statistical Series, No. 31, p. 12. Italics added.
[22] Children's Bureau Statistical Series No. 47, *Juvenile Court Statistics, 1956*, Washington, U. S. Department of Health, Education and Welfare, 1958, p. 1.

TABLE I

TREND IN JUVENILE DELINQUENCY CASES DISPOSED OF BY JUVENILE COURTS,
UNITED STATES: 1940-57.
Index: 1950 = 100

Year	Juvenile Delinquency Cases	Child Population of U.S. (10-17 Years of Age)	Year	Juvenile Delinquency Cases	Child Population of U.S. (10-17 Years of Age)
1940	71	110	1949	97	100
1941	80	109	1950	100	100
1942	89	107	1951	106	102
1943	123	105	1952	119	105
1944	118	102	1953	134	109
1945	123	101	1954	141	112
1946	105	100	1955	154	116
1947	94	100	1956	186	119
1948	91	100	1957	215	127

SOURCE: Children's Bureau Statistical Series No. 52, *Juvenile Court Statistics, 1957,* Washington, U. S. Dept. of Health, Education, and Welfare, Table H, p. 8. Data for juvenile delinquency cases are based on the reports of 200 juvenile courts, and on the national sample for 1955, 1956, and 1957. Estimated child population is based on *Current Population Reports,* Series P-25, Nos. 98, 146, and 170, Washington, U. S. Bureau of the Census.

was cited by Schwartz[23] and later by Perlman[24] as reflecting "some common determining factor, perhaps 'delinquency,' however defined." According to Perlman:

> The similarity cannot be accounted for on the grounds that police arrest data include a large proportion of the cases referred to court, for *police fingerprint arrest records* embrace only a small proportion of those cases referred to juvenile court. From this similarity in trends we can have some confidence that national data on juvenile delinquency do show the general direction of the *volume* of delinquency, even though the *extent* of the change is not precise.[25]

Volume of Delinquency in Specific Communities

Of more immediate concern than the *over-all* estimates, are the changes in the amount of delinquency in the *local* communities. Here is where the impact of delinquency is felt and where measures for dealing with it must be devised.

[23] Edward E. Schwartz, "Statistics of Juvenile Delinquency in the United States," *The Annals,* American Academy of Political and Social Science, No. 261 (Jan. 1949), pp. 9-20.
[24] I. Richard Perlman, "Reporting Juvenile Delinquency," pp. 242-49.
[25] *Ibid.,* pp. 242-44.

CHART I

COMPARISON OF JUVENILE DELINQUENCY CASES DISPOSED OF BY JUVENILE
COURTS, WITH POLICE ARRESTS OF CHILDREN UNDER 18, 1940-51.
Index: 1940 = 100

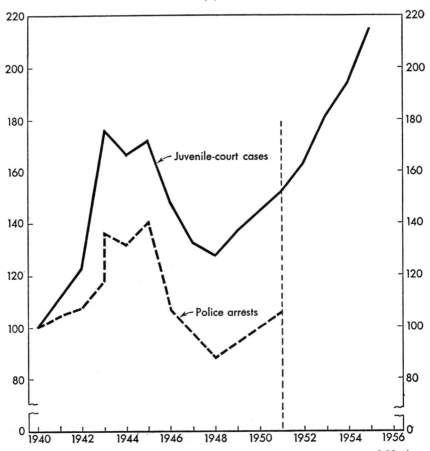

SOURCE: Police arrest data from section on fingerprint arrest records in annual *Uniform
Crime Reports*, Washington, Federal Bureau of Investigation; Juvenile court data
from Children's Bureau Statistical Series No. 37, *Juvenile Court Statistics, 1955.*

Although one can control more factors in comparing figures from a
single community than for the country as a whole, the rises and falls in
the individual communities are puzzling unless one knows how and whether
the administrative procedures may have been changed.[26] In Bridgeport, Connecticut; Akron and Columbus, Ohio; Des Moines, Iowa; Indianapolis,
Indiana; Grand Rapids, Michigan; Norfolk, Virginia; and San Antonio,
Texas, juvenile delinquency appeared to decline after 1943. To determine
whether increases reported by half the courts in 1954, in comparison with
1948-49, may have represented an actual higher rate, one would need to

26 See, for example, the description of "unofficial" procedures in Chapter 15.

examine the changes in law enforcement practices and/or in juvenile court procedures in both years. Obviously, *rates* can be fairly accurate only in a census year, when population figures most nearly correspond to the actual number of residents in a community.

We cite below the challenging figures for two communities, Jersey City and New York City, where we know some of the factors which affected at least the official registering of antisocial behavior. In New Jersey, 18 is the upper age limit of juvenile court jurisdiction; in New York, it is 16.

JERSEY CITY. The changes in the statistics for Jersey City are especially challenging. Without a doubt the decrease from a total of 1974 delinquents brought to the court in 1930 to a total of 684 in 1954 (incidentally, the same number that were reported in 1935), represents mainly a marked change in procedures. In February 1931 the Police Service Bureau was constituted in the Board of Education by the then Mayor Hague who believed it was best to keep children out of the juvenile court. Without taking this fact into consideration, the spectacular decline in delinquency figures might lead an unwary stranger to choose Jersey City as the ideal place to assure the rearing of law-abiding citizens.

Using the 1950 population aged 10-17 as a base, the 1956 delinquency rates per hundred were .003 for Jersey City, .04 for Hackensack, and 7.2 for Newark.[27] It seems evident that Jersey City's Police Service Bureau drains off cases which, in neighboring communities, become a matter of court record.

NEW YORK CITY. Erratic changes in the official incidence of juvenile delinquency in New York City also suggest that factors other than the actual incidence were at work in the three decades from 1903 to 1936.[28] In spite of the addition of the categories of truancy, waywardness, and disorderly conduct to the delinquency count, the estimated official delinquency rate per thousand children dropped from 12.5 in the first decade to 6.1 in the third decade. The statistical low points in the New York City delinquency statistics were 1904 and 1920-25. In 1956 approximately as many cases (10,000 in round numbers) were referred to the children's court as in 1904, although the city's population had more than doubled in the interim. At the close of World War I, community controls on youthful behavior were said to have been relaxed. One might therefore have anticipated a rise rather than a fall in the delinquency statistics in the period 1920-25.

The explanation offered in the official reports for the decline of 1000 juvenile court cases in 1920, in comparison with 1919, is the deterrent activity of settlement houses, community centers, parent-teacher associations,

[27] Children's Bureau Statistical Series No. 47, *Juvenile Court Statistics, 1956,* Table 2, p. 15.
[28] J. B. Maller, "Juvenile Delinquency in New York City," *Journal of Psychology,* Vol. 3, no. 3 (Jan. 1937), pp. 1-25.

and the setting up of a probation system. Chief Justice Franklin Chase Hoyt of New York City's juvenile court offered another possible partial explanation in his 1920 report. He said that he thought the inclement weather during the first three months of 1920 explained why 1400 fewer cases were brought to court in those months than in the same period in 1919. It is possible that the drop in 1920 in the number of arrests for trespassing on railroad property, peddling, and selling newspapers in the subway actually reflected a decrease in those types of behavior. As we shall see when we discuss the effect of changes in police regulations on arrests, however, an equally plausible explanation of the total drop is a difference in enforcement policies.

These erratic changes in the statistics for Jersey City and New York City (quoted because we know the local situations) as well as the complications introduced by the fact that some cities exclude and others include "unofficial" cases, cast doubt on the validity of the Children's Bureau prediction of 785,000 delinquents in 1960. The estimate suggests that between two and three children out of every hundred at risk will be known, in any one year, to the juvenile court. This over-all figure is, however, deceptive. It does not differentiate between serious and trivial behavior, or between those whose cases are dismissed and those who are removed from their parents' custody. Nor does it, in some large communities, reflect the actions by voluntary agencies which, to differing degrees, may drain cases that would otherwise come to official attention.

The FBI's Statistics on Delinquents

Although the major interest and concern of the FBI is with the adult criminal, for the seven states and two Possessions in which the juvenile court jurisdiction terminates at age 16—Connecticut, Georgia, Maryland, New York, North Carolina, Vermont, Utah, and Puerto Rico and the Virgin Islands—the FBI *Uniform Crime Reports* provide some supplement for the Children's Bureau figures discussed above. Like the Children's Bureau, the FBI is apt to allege, especially at budget time—the end of the fiscal year—an alarming increase in juvenile delinquency. We shall examine below the basis for these pronouncements.

The Offense and Arrest Series

The FBI since 1930 has issued two series: the Offense Series, based on *complaints*, and the Arrest Series, based on reports of *arrests* forwarded to Washington by the local police.

The Offense Series covers Part I offenses, i.e., criminal homicide, rape, robbery, aggravated assault, burglary, larceny, and auto theft reported to the police as occurring within their jurisdiction. If police investigation establishes that these complaints are groundless, they are not included in the published tables.

The Arrest Series includes both Part I and Part II offenses. The long list in Part II includes: assaults which are not of an aggravated nature, carrying or possessing weapons, forgery and counterfeiting, embezzlement and fraud, buying and receiving stolen property, prostitution, commercialized vice and sex offenses, driving while intoxicated, violation of road and driving laws, parking violations and other violations of traffic and motor vehicle laws, drunkenness, disorderly conduct, vagrancy and gambling, violation of narcotic and drug laws and liquor laws exclusive of federal violations, and all other categories of state or local laws for which no other provision has been made.

Population Base for Tabulation

Not only are many more offenses included in the second series but the geographic area covered by the two sets of reports is not identical. In the *Uniform Crime Reports* for 1957, for example, the number of offenses reported by the police are classified by geographic region and state for the 1473 cities which in 1950 had 2500 or more inhabitants. But only part of the Offense Series is used to project trends on the basis of changes from 1956 to 1957 for the country as a whole, i.e., the figures for the 445 cities which in 1950 had populations of 25,000 or over.[29]

In contrast, the data in the Arrest Series on incidence and on trends cover 1220 of the 1473 cities which transmitted comparable reports for 1956-57. The percentage increase for cities with populations over 25,000 was 3.9 in the total, but 8.1 for persons under 18.

It should be noted that there may be several arrests of suspects in connection with a single offense, and also that a considerable proportion of persons who are arrested are not convicted. Hence, the arrest statistics do not correspond to the actual incidence of crime and delinquency. "The information in the table does not present total arrests in the U. S., but is limited to usable information received from reporting cities."[30]

Nor do all the arrests in the 1473 cities with 1950 populations over 2500 represent crimes of equal magnitude. In 1957 drunkenness and driving while intoxicated accounted for 42 per cent, or 2,068,677, of the arrests; disorderly conduct and vagrancy together accounted for 15 per cent.

[29] *Uniform Crime Reports for the United States, 1957*, Vol. 28, no. 2, Washington, Federal Bureau of Investigation, 1958.
[30] *Uniform Crime Reports for the United States, 1955*, Vol. 26, no. 2, Washington, Federal Bureau of Investigation, 1956, p. 111.

In contrast, crimes against property accounted for a little more than 10 per cent, and crimes against the *person* for approximately 5 per cent of the total. In 1957 criminal homicide, including murder and manslaughter, was the charge in 3245 or about 0.1 per cent of all the arrests.[31]

Statistics on Juveniles

To highlight the incidence of crime among juveniles, the FBI has prepared special charts. In Table II we have abstracted the base figures on arrests for all crimes against property, which, as we noted above, accounted for 10 per cent of the 2,068,677 arrests reported to the FBI in 1957.[32]

TABLE II

ARRESTS FOR CRIMES AGAINST PROPERTY REPORTED BY 1473 CITIES, CLASSIFIED BY NUMBER AND PERCENTAGE OF PERSONS UNDER 18 YEARS OF AGE, 1957

Crimes Against Property	Arrests		
		Persons Under 18	
	Total	Number	% of Total
TOTAL	223,140	105,897	47.4
Auto theft	29,121	19,682	67.6
Burglary	51,398	28,179	54.8
Larceny	102,476	52,550	51.3
Robbery	11,820	3,124	26.4
Embezzlement and fraud	16,168	454	2.8
Receiving stolen property	3,869	1,249	32.3
Forgery and counterfeiting	8,288	659	8.0

SOURCE: *Uniform Crime Reports, 1957,* Table 42, p. 115, and Fig. 14, p. 116.

The charts which are based on percentages in each offense category suggest that serious proportions of the offenses against property are attributable to young persons. They do not, however, give the numbers in comparison with the population at risk, which is accurately known only for the date at which the official United States Census is taken.

Possibly the high percentage of young persons arrested for burglary (54.8) and larceny (51.3) can be explained by the fact that they are less skilled than older men in evading detection and apprehension. The number of arrests for auto theft is obviously affected by the increasing numbers of cars in use each year. Moreover, even auto thefts must be variously interpreted. Many juveniles steal (or, as they phrase it, "borrow") cars for joy

[31] *Uniform Crime Reports, 1957,* Table 41, p. 114.
[32] *Ibid.,* Fig. 14, p. 116.

rides and then abandon them. The older thief, on the other hand, is more likely to steal a car to sell it or make a getaway in connection with another crime. That almost one third of the arrests of those accused of receiving stolen property is charged to persons under 18 is in part a reflection of the extent to which youths are used as accomplices by adults.

These statements are not to be interpreted as suggesting that auto theft, robbery, larceny, burglary, and so forth, are not serious offenses. The intent, rather, is to suggest that *figures issued by the FBI cannot always be interpreted as evidence of an alarming incidence of offenses for any particular age group in any specific category of offense in an intercensal year.* Thus they offer an unsound base for statements reflecting increase or even decrease in comparison with previous years.

The FBI itself states that it does not assume responsibility for the accuracy of its figures. It is acting only as a service agency in publishing figures as submitted by the contributing agencies. It comments further: *"Caution should be exercised in comparing crime data for individual cities because the differences in the figures may be due to a variety of factors. Such comparisons are not necessarily significant even though the figures for individual communities are converted into terms of the number of offenses per 100,000 inhabitants."*[33]

Among the factors which the 1957 report lists as affecting the incidence of crime are the size of the city; the composition of the population with respect to age, sex, and race; the business activities of the population; the educational, recreational, and religious facilities; the number of police, their qualifications, and their methods of appointment; the policies of the prosecuting officials and the courts, and the attitudes of the public toward law enforcement problems.

Recommendations for Establishing Better Statistics

In 1946 the Attorney General's Conference on Crime and Delinquency recommended the following: (1) the establishment of a uniform unit of count, either case or individual; (2) comparable age limits; (3) a careful statement by each agency regarding the limitations of its published data; (4) an explanation of any assumptions or methods which give rise to apparent contradictions or discrepancies with the reports of other agencies.[34]

More recently, a Consultant Committee on Uniform Crime Reporting, chaired by Peter J. Lejins, was appointed by J. Edgar Hoover, Director of

[33] *Ibid.*, p. 97. Italics in the original.
[34] Report of the Attorney General's National Conference on the Prevention and Control of Juvenile Delinquency, held at Washington, D. C., 1946.

the FBI, to make recommendations for improving the Bureau's reports.[35] The committee recognized the Bureau's handicap in obtaining complete coverage because unlike the situation in other countries, the cooperation of the local police with the FBI *has been and continues to be* entirely on a voluntary basis. In consequence it is always difficult and sometimes impossible for the FBI to obtain either complete coverage from all police departments or the inclusion of some items which, for reasons of public relations, a local community may not wish to report.

The major recommendations were:

1. To issue one *Uniform Crime Report* a year instead of two.

2. To substitute for the present reports on Part I and Part II offenses, three reports on: (a) offenses as they become known to the police, to cover the general tabulations of U. S. crime statistics; (b) selected offenses, as the basis for calculating the crime index; and (c) offenses which are of special importance to the work of the police department.

3. To analyze crime data on three geographic bases as established by the U. S. Bureau of the Census in its 1950 tabulations: (a) standard metropolitan areas; (b) urban; and (c) rural.[36]

4. To calculate crime rates in intercensal years based on annual population estimates of the U. S. Bureau of the Census.[37]

5. In demonstrating trends, to make comparisons on a wider basis than that afforded by the *previous* year's figures.[38]

The committee rejected the suggestion of a sampling procedure (such as the one adopted by the Children's Bureau in their Juvenile Court Statistical Series) in favor of continuing the present attempts to get more complete coverage.[39] The consultant committee also rejected the proposal of the International Juvenile Officers Association at its annual meeting in Milwaukee in May 1958, which would have broadly extended the uniform crime reporting system in the juvenile field. It was the considered opinion of the consultant committee that these recommendations "would take the Uniform Crime Reporting Program outside of its originally planned and presumably observed scope, which is a policy matter for decision by the FBI, itself."[40]

When the responsibility of the two Bureaus, FBI and Children's Bureau, for reporting on juveniles is clearly stated in official documents, there will be less public misunderstanding of the meaning of the statistics on juvenile delinquency.

Until then, the two official series remain, as Perlman says,

[35] *Uniform Crime Reports for the United States,* Washington, Special Issue, Federal Bureau of Investigation, Nov. 1958.
[36] *Ibid.,* p. 30.
[37] *Ibid.,* p. 32-33.
[38] *Ibid.,* p. 38.
[39] *Ibid.,* p. 39.
[40] *Ibid.,* p. 43.

. . . the best statistics relating to juvenile delinquency now available and, as such, give some insight into delinquency trends.

Current efforts to improve these data are salutary and will unquestionably increase their value. Although these two series will never measure juvenile delinquency to the complete satisfaction of everyone, they can, if extended and improved, define more accurately the size of the problem with which communities and agencies must deal. They can provide much more information than we now have about the children—why they were referred to court and how their cases were handled; the number, qualifications, and salaries of staff; the availability of detention and diagnostic facilities; a basis for studying the effectiveness of treatment.[41]

Summary

There are two official sources for figures on the extent of delinquency in the United States. Since 1927, the Children's Bureau has intermittently collected annual data from an increasing number of courts. Tabulations by age, sex, nationality, color, place of abode, and source of referral were last published in the 1936 report. The changing role of the juvenile court in large cities, changes in administrative procedures, as well as in age jurisdiction, have made it increasingly difficult to achieve the main objectives of the Children's Bureau Series, i.e., an index of the nature and extent of delinquency, trends in volume, and some clues as to cause. The Bureau's estimates of delinquency ranged from 200,000 in 1930 to a forecast of 785,000 cases in 1960, based on the new plan of soliciting reports from a representative national sample of 500 courts in 230 counties across the country.

Publications of the Federal Bureau of Investigation provide supplementary statistics on offenses and arrests of some individuals under 18. Issued annually since 1930, these statistics cover only the arrests for *certain* offenses of which records have been forwarded to Washington. Like reporting to the Children's Bureau, the forwarding of records to the FBI Central Bureau is entirely voluntary. A consultant committee has recommended to the FBI changes in its reporting system so that both scholars and the community at large will have a better understanding of the meaning of the statistics.

With the forthright recognition on the part of both the Children's Bureau and the FBI of the need to improve both our definitions of delinquency and our methods of reporting and recording it, we can look forward in the next decade to better yardsticks for measuring the extent of the problem, both before and after we have attempted to deal with it.

[41] Perlman, *Reporting Juvenile Delinquency,* p. 259.

CHAPTER 3

Juvenile Delinquency in Foreign Countries

CONFRONTED WITH OUR OWN STATISTICAL SHORTCOMINGS, PERHAPS WE CAN get some perspective from comparisons with the statements on delinquency from other countries. At the First United Nations Congress on the Prevention of Crime and the Treatment of Offenders held in Geneva in September 1955, statistics were presented on the volume of juvenile delinquency for certain countries.[1] The data included material which had arrived at the office of the General Secretariat by February 1, 1955.

It is difficult to interpret the marked differences in the figures for countries as similar ethnically and culturally as Denmark—in which less than 1 per cent of actual crime is attributable to juveniles—and Sweden and The Netherlands, which report much higher delinquency rates. It is equally difficult to explain why countries as culturally diverse as Spain, Turkey, France, and Algiers report similar percentages of delinquents. The authors of the report suggest that rates of juvenile delinquency in the Anglo-Saxon countries may be the highest of all because "these countries attach particular importance to delinquency and its detection."[2]

Although each of these countries defines delinquent behavior much more precisely than we do, the authors of the report take pains to note the

[1] Report of the First United Nations Congress on the Prevention of Crime and the Treatment of Offenders, section entitled "Juvenile Delinquency Statistics," Bureau of Social Affairs, Department of Economic and Social Affairs, New York, The United Nations, 1955.
[2] *Ibid.*, p. 7.

limitations of the statistics. Those limitations to which they call special attention also apply to our statistics:

1. The figures refer only to crime (including delinquency) which has been detected. In the words of the official document: "even the crime which is detected depends just as much on criminality as on the social and economic structure of each country, on the relations between the police and the public, the efficiency of the police, geographical, cultural, climatic and other conditions."[3]

2. The figures for males and females in each age group are not always given separately, "although it is well known that some ages are more sensitive than others to crimogenic circumstances."[4]

3. ". . . the choice of the year 1950 as a basis of compariosn has a definite effect on the indices of comparison depending on whether the year 1950 was a good or bad year for crime in that particular country."[5]

We must wait for the next United Nations Congress on Crime and Delinquency, planned for 1960, for more up-to-date reports on most European and Asian countries. There are, however, a few additional sources which throw some incidental light on the fluctuations in juvenile delinquency abroad. We cite below the 1955 data for Canada; 1958 data for England and Wales; 1956 data for France and Algiers; and pre- and post-war studies in Germany. We conclude with some comments from the Soviet press on the situation in the USSR today. We shall refer in Chapter 25 to the kinds of institution for delinquents provided by some countries abroad. Our concern in the present discussion, however, focuses mainly on the changes in the extent of delinquency in the selected countries.

Canada[6]

The 1952 Juvenile Delinquents Act of the central Parliament in Canada defines the juvenile delinquent as follows: "Juvenile delinquent means any child who violates any provision of the Criminal Code of any Dominion or provincial Statute, or of any by-law or ordinance of any municipality, or who is liable by reason of any other act to be committed to an industrial school or juvenile reformatory under the provisions of any Dominion or provincial statute."[7]

[3] *Ibid.*, p. 5.
[4] *Ibid.*, p. 6.
[5] *Ibid.*, p. 7.
[6] Based on Paul W. Tappan, "North America," *Comparative Survey of Juvenile Delinquency*, Part I, New York, United Nations Department of Economic and Social Affairs, 1958.
[7] Quoted in *ibid.*, pp. 6-7.

85159

While, according to a Canadian correspondent,[8] only the more serious types of offense generally bring young people to court in Canada, practice with respect to holding children charged with delinquency for court hearings varies from province to province. At one extreme are provinces which issue formal charges in every instance in which a delinquent act is alleged to have occurred. In other provinces, formal charges are withdrawn if it is established that the appearance of the juvenile in court might prove damaging to him or to his family. In the province of Saskatchewan, where a social investigation is ordered when delinquency is reported, the chief probation officer decides whether proceedings shall be instituted. Thus the court "is considered a tool in treatment" rather than "an obligatory jurisdictional process."[9] As a result, sometimes as few as 10 per cent of those who are reported to have committed delinquent acts appear in the Saskatchewan court. Tappan suggests that because of the strong English tradition in Canada, "there is a greater measure of due process in the ascertainment of offenses before delinquency adjudication can occur."[10]

In the whole of Canada, whose 1955 child population under 16 was estimated at less than 3 million, the number of delinquents declined slightly from 1947 (8265) to 1955 (8187). The ratio of delinquent boys to delinquent girls was about 8 to 1, in comparison with our ratio of 5 or 6 to 1. The Canadian figures differ markedly from ours also in respect to the different types of offenses. Both in 1947 and 1955 juvenile offenses against property accounted for much more than half the total in Canada (almost 60 per cent in 1947 and 70 per cent in 1955), in comparison with the FBI figure of 47 per cent in the United States in 1957.

England and Wales

As in Canada, the statistical and interpretative reports for Great Britain are based on data for the whole country, in contrast with our fragmented data.

In Table III the nonindictable delinquent offenses, which roughly account for 40 per cent of the total, are the nuisances, the minor and insignificant offenses such as playing games in unauthorized places, violating traffic laws, cycling without a light, mischievous behavior, and so forth.

In the nonindictable category, boys outnumber girls 20 to 1, reflecting no doubt a wide difference in types of behavior considered appropriate in England for each sex. There are relatively fewer girls in Great Britain brought

[8] A. J. MacLeod, Director, Criminal Law Section, Ministry of Justice, Dominion of Canada.
[9] Tappan, *op. cit.*, p. 6.
[10] *Ibid.*, p. 7.

TABLE III

JUVENILE OFFENDERS, ENGLAND AND WALES

CLASSIFIED ACCORDING TO SEX, AGE GROUP, AND TYPE OF OFFENSE, 1958

Sex and Age Group	Total	Class of Offense	
		Indictable	Nonindictable[a]
TOTAL	85,506	51,775[b]	33,831[c]
Total boys	79,933	47,678	32,255
under 14	37,120	26,050	11,070
14-17	42,813	21,628	21,185
Total girls	5,673	4,097	1,576
under 14	2,450	2,033	417
14-17	3,223	2,064	1,159

SOURCE: Statistics Relating to Crime and Criminal Proceedings, England and Wales, for the Year 1958. Presented to Parliament by the Secretary of State for the Home Department by Command of Her Majesty, July 1959. London, Her Majesty's Stationery Office.

[a] Excluding motoring offenses.
[b] Ibid., Chapter V, p. x.
[c] Ibid., Chapter VIII, pp. xxvi and xxvii.

to court for indictable offenses (mainly larceny and breaking and entering)—1 girl to 10 boys—in comparison with the 1 girl to 5 or 6 boys in United States statistics.

Classified by age group, in the *indictable* group, boys under 14 (26,050) outnumber those over 14 (21,628). Among the *nonindictable* offenders, girls as well as boys over 14 outnumber those under 14.

In comparison with the 1958 population estimates of approximately 7 million boys and girls (8-17 years of age) in England and Wales, less than 1.3 per cent are delinquents. If the basis of comparison is *indictable* offenses, a little more than 0.7 per cent were so accused in 1958.

The reports issued by the British Home Office also tell us what was done about the young persons guilty of the more serious, i.e., the indictable, offenses. Excluding cases which were disposed of in the higher courts, the dispositions of offenders under 14 years of age in 1958 were as follows: 40 per cent were discharged; 5 per cent were committed to approved schools; 35 per cent were placed on probation; and the remainder were fined or otherwise disposed of.

In contrast, among the indictable offenders over 14 years of age (in round numbers, 24,000) 28 per cent were discharged, 10 per cent committed to institutions, and 34 per cent were placed on probation. The total commitments in the year 1958 add up to approximately 3800 for England and Wales, or less than 2 in every 2000 in the population at risk.

In Scotland for 1956, in the estimated total of 15,000 delinquent youths

7 to 17 years in age, approximately ⅗ were guilty of crimes (8907), including attacks on persons, destruction of property with or without violence, forgery, and crimes against currency. The other ⅖ had committed such offenses as drunkenness, running away, violation of traffic laws (chiefly with bicycles). Boys outnumber girls 15 to 1 in crime and 25 to 1 in offenses. Less than 8 per cent of the total were committed to institutions. Half were fined and the rest were "warned or admonished."

Delinquency Trends, Great Britain and United States, Compared

Chart II, issued in January 1955, compares the reports of the British Home Office with those available for the years 1938-53 for the United States.[11] As the accompanying release notes:

> Reports from Britain reveal that a marked decrease of delinquency in England and Wales has been taking place at a time when the trend in this country [the United States] has been decidedly upward.
>
> The Children's Department of the British Home Office bases its trend on the yearly count of persons under the age of 17 found guilty of indictable offenses. Delinquency in England and Wales reached its highest point in 1951. The downturn began slowly in 1952, when the number of persons under 17 found guilty of indictable offenses decreased by about 3 per cent from the preceding year. This was followed by the sizable drop of 14 per cent between 1952 and 1953, making for a total decrease of a little more than 18 per cent for the 2-year period 1951 to 1953.
>
> The decrease in the delinquency *rate*, which gives a more accurate picture of the relative extent of delinquency than do the raw numbers, was even slightly greater. The rate shows the number of delinquents (8 to 17 years old in England) in proportion to the size of the total 8-to-17 age group. During the 2-year period mentioned, while the number of delinquents was decreasing, the population group from 8 to 17 years old was increasing. There was a decrease of 7 per cent in the delinquency rate between 1951 and 1952, and a further decrease of 16 per cent between 1952 and 1953, making for an over-all decrease of 22 per cent. In other words, the delinquency rate of England and Wales dropped more than one-fifth in 2 years.
>
> Throughout the forties and up until 1951 the delinquency trend in this country was roughly similar to that of England, with minor variations. In both countries there was a rapid increase following the entry of each into World War II, a decline following the war, and a new rise as the "cold war" began and worsened into the Korean War.
>
> In 1952, however, as the British rate began to drop, delinquency in

[11] "News Notes on Juvenile Delinquency," U. S. Children's Bureau, Dept. of Health, Education and Welfare, Feb. 21, 1955, pp. 9-10.

CHART II

DELINQUENCY TRENDS: BRITAIN AND UNITED STATES[a]

Index: 1938 = 100

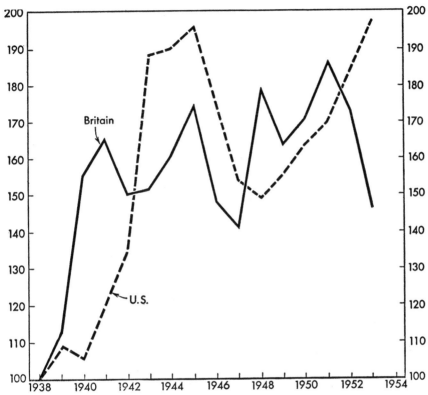

SOURCES: British trend—*Criminal Statistics, 1953,* and *Sixth Report on the Work of the Children's Department,* both published by the Home Office; U. S. trend: unpublished data furnished by the Children's Bureau, Jan. 1955.

[a] Rate based on the number of juvenile court cases in proportion to the population of relevant age group (8-17 for Britain, 10-17 for the U. S.).

this country continued to climb and in 1953 reached its highest point so far.[12]

A 1953 report lists some of the reasons why the United Kingdom statistics may not reflect either the comparative or the actual incidence of delinquency in England, Wales, or Scotland.[13] Mack suggests that increases in juvenile delinquency in comparison with the previous peak in 1917, during World War I, may reflect social changes which have made the English public

12 *Ibid.,* p. 9.

13 John A. Mack, *Family and Community,* Carnegie United Kingdom Trust, 1953: see also "A New Approach to Juvenile Delinquency," a review of Mack's report by Sophia M. Robison, *Autonomous Group Bulletin,* Vol. 10, no. 1 (Autumn 1954), pp. 24-32.

more willing to bring young offenders into the court. He suggests also that increased efficiency of the police organization may have encouraged the reporting of offenses which would previously not have been reported. In his picturesque language, "the new broom of police reorganization has moved silently from area to area and stirred up a dust of petty crimes, which had been hitherto swept below the carpet."[14]

Although the number of juveniles in the United Kingdom found guilty of violence against the person increased threefold between 1938 and 1951, the absolute numbers were only 116 and 349. The latter is less than one per cent of all juveniles found guilty of indictable offenses in 1951. While the figure for sexual offenses among juveniles doubled between 1938 (475) and 1951 (951), it accounts for barely 2 per cent of all juveniles found guilty.

It is perhaps salutary, Mack adds

> . . . in view of the tone of much of the ephemeral writing on the subject to draw attention to these things. The present order of magnitude of juvenile delinquency in Great Britain, in so far as it can be seen through the dust of the statistics, indicates no catastrophic decline in moral standards, no terrifying upsurge of aggressiveness and violence. The main question is *why the present upward movement, and the long-term upward trend which it confirms should be happening at all in a period when there has been a greater attempt to apply remedial and preventive measures than ever before.*[15]

A recent communication from W. J. Bohan of the Home Office confirms Mack's prediction of a long-term upward trend in England, in spite of the relatively lower rate of delinquency in comparison with the United States.

> I am replying to your letter of 2nd July about recent statistics of juvenile court cases in this country and the problems of teddy girls and juvenile gangs.
>
> I enclose a copy of the Criminal Statistics for 1956; this is the most recent statistical information we have available. The figures for 1957 will not be published until the late autumn but the indications are that juvenile delinquency in this country is continuing to increase. The Home Secretary disclosed in a recent speech that the number of youths and girls between fourteen and seventeen found guilty of indictable offences during the first nine months of 1957 was 25% higher than in the corresponding period for 1956. The increase for those between seventeen and twenty-one was 27%.
>
> We have not been able to trace the particular news reports [in New York papers] about teenagers and gang violence that you mention, but

[14] Mack, *op. cit.*, p. 46.
[15] *Ibid.*, p. 51. Italics added. In comparison with 1938, the index for both girls and boys has risen more sharply since 1956 for indictable offenses. *Statistics Relating to Crime and Criminal Proceedings for the Year 1958, op. cit.*, p. xl.

I hope you will find the enclosed newspaper cuttings of interest. They include reports of Mrs. Skillings' report to her local probation committee which was I understand quite brief and its substance has been adequately reported by the press.[16]

The *London Times* reference to Mrs. Skillings' annual report reads:

GIRLS "FASCINATED BY TOUGHS"

Reason for Increase in Offences

Mrs. P. L. Skillings, Croydon woman probation officer, says in her annual report that the town is facing a new type of problem—teen-age girls who are "fascinated" by gangs of young toughs.

Three times more girls were brought before Croydon juvenile court in the past 12 months than in the previous year. "In many cases the girls have been closely associating with youths and men in groups where a general lack of conformity to law or to decent standards of living is approved," she says.

Flamboyant Dress

"These are the young men who rarely work and who often make themselves conspicuous by their insulting behaviour, by creating nuisance or by causing wilful damage. By these habits and by their flamboyant dress they build themselves a reputation for 'toughness' and for being 'wide boys' whom nobody can control. They have leaders who demand obedience, and they have café headquarters.

"Many girls in their teens, of widely differing background and education, seem to be fascinated by these groups. In going about with or being the chosen girl friend of a youth of this reputation the girls seem to find satisfaction far beyond any they can find in more normal teenage pursuits. They also know they can find temporary shelter with some members of the group if they run away from home."[17]

Croydon, located southeast of London, has a population of 250,000. Normally it has a lower rate of juvenile delinquency than many other thickly populated areas.

Subsequent clippings from the English press suggest that in normally peaceful suburbs both boys and, at an increasing rate, girls are getting into trouble. They not only disturb the peace but have become wantonly destructive and even violent. In Liverpool, where the police have been particularly cooperative with the schools and the organized social agencies, Waddington writes:

[16] W. J. Bohan, Home Office, Children's Department, Horseferry House, Thorney Street, London, S.W.1, letter dated August 12, 1958.
[17] *London Times,* April 19, 1958.

There are indications that within the next decade Liverpool could become the scene of a wave of juvenile crime comparable to that which has so shocked America.

There is nothing abnormal about this type of delinquency. Such delinquents are people reacting with absolute normality to certain conditions which are to be found in well defined central areas of large cities. They believe as strongly in their own way of life as other citizens. They will defend it even more vehemently. These people form the "Minority Groups" which in America are racial in origin. Minority feelings are growing up in Liverpool even in areas where no racial differences exist. Neighbourhoods situated close to the heart of the city are becoming less and less integrated with the life of the city.[18]

We should note that the delinquency is not charged to *racial* minorities as is so often the case in the United States.[19] Waddington's explanation is similar to that of Mack, Jephcott, and Carter discussed in Chapter 8.

France and Algiers

According to the official reports for 1956,[20] delinquency in Paris has decreased since 1949, but it has increased in the provinces. The comparable figures for Paris are 5253 for 1949 and 2983 for 1956. For France as a whole they are 11,795 in 1949, and 14,778 in 1956.

While the 1956 totals are 400 higher than the 1955, the size of the population base in each year is not given. According to the United Nations *Demographic Yearbook* for 1956, France's 1955 population aged 7-18 was almost 7 million.[21] This gives an approximate ratio of 2 delinquents in each 1000 at risk. As in the United States, delinquent boys outnumber girls 6 to 1.[22]

Table IV classifies the juvenile delinquents by type of offense and age group. According to the table, and consistent with normal expectancy, offenses against property account for roughly 68 per cent of all the boys' cases in comparison with 55 per cent of the girls'. As in the United States, action in morals cases was registered for a much smaller percentage of boys (5) than girls (18).[23]

[18] J. R. Waddington, Warden of the Victoria Settlement, Liverpool, "Good Neighbors Can Lead These Liverpool Outcasts Back to Useful Society," *Liverpool Post*, March 6, 1958.
[19] The anti-West Indian Riots reported in the September 1958 press are chiefly protests against economic competition.
[20] *Rapport Annuel de la Direction de L'Education Surveillée*, Ministère de la Justice, 1957.
[21] *United Nations Demographic Year Book, 1956*, Statistical Office of the U.N. Department of Economic and Social Affairs, Eighth Issue, XIII, 5.
[22] *Rapport Annuel, op. cit.*, p. 12.
[23] *Ibid.*, based on Tables 1-5, pp. 11-14.

TABLE IV

DELINQUENTS IN FRANCE AND ALGIERS CLASSIFIED BY TYPE OF OFFENSE,
SEX AND AGE GROUP, 1956

Type of Offense	Total	Boys	Girls	Age Groups	
				Under 16	16 to 18
TOTAL	14,778	12,932	1,846	7,556	7,222
Against persons	2,440	2,162	278	978	1,462
Against property	9,926	8,894	1,032	5,607	4,319
Against morals	983	649	334	417	566
Other	1,429	1,227	202	554	875

SOURCE: *Rapport Annuel de la Direction de L'Education Surveillée,* Ministère de la Justice, 1957, Table 2, p. 12.

The official figures for delinquents in 1956 (3189) in Algiers register a continuing annual decline since 1952 (4362). As in France, the older age group (16-18) predominates among both the boys and the girls arraigned in court. For each group it accounts for about half the offenses.[24] With respect to the different offenses, those against property decreased from 643 in 1951 to 575 in 1952 and to 448 in 1956.[25]

Charges against morals—7 per cent of the French total in 1956—accounted for less than 4 per cent in the Algerian total. In absolute numbers charges against morals were brought against 120 boys but only 3 girls.[26]

Both in France and in Algiers the political unrest and economic difficulties of the last few years do not appear to have affected the delinquency rate. In contrast, the fluctuations in delinquency statistics in Germany for the somewhat fragmentary currently available data is much more marked. The latest *Demographic Yearbook* does not include data on delinquency in Germany. We draw, therefore, in our discussion below on a variety of other sources.

Germany

Although Germany published statistics which showed double the number of girl sex delinquents between the beginning and the end of World War I, World War II statistics showed a marked decline in the incidence of sex offenses.[27] There was, however, a rise in offenses against property and persons

[24] *Ibid.,* Table 7.
[25] *Ibid.,* Table 9, p. 15.
[26] *Ibid.,* Table 8, p. 15.
[27] Liepman Moritz, *Krieg und Kriminalitat in Deutschland,* Stuttgart, 1930. A series of monographic studies on the effect of war on the economic and social life of belligerent and neutral countries published under the auspices of the Carnegie Endowment for International Peace.

in large cities. Gangs became more numerous, more violent, and more destructive. Young persons were reported engaging in such fraudulent enterprises as collecting funds for nonexistent charities and impersonating war heroes.

Commenting on these apparent differences in the two war periods, Sellin says: "statistics of juvenile court cases fail to indicate the real rise in delinquency. The post-war depression and the inflation period reaching a climax in Germany in 1923 made law enforcement completely illusory."[28]

According to more recent data on delinquency in the West German Republic for the year 1953, people under 18, a group which accounted for about 5 per cent of the total population, were responsible for 10 per cent of the reported crimes.[29] Theft was the major cause of arrests of persons under 21. Unlike the situation in the United States, in Germany theft was more commonly reported for girls than for boys. Girls outnumbered boys in the category *einfache Diebstahle* (simple theft). However, males predominate in the ratio of about 2 or 3 to 1 in *schwerer Diebstahl* (more serious theft).

The USSR

It is interesting to note that the first industrial revolution in the USSR was not followed by a let-down in delinquency. In 1921 when famine and pestilence raged, about 800,000 of the 8 million homeless children in Russia were labeled delinquents. A subsequent decline in juvenile delinquency was attributed to the state's effort to bring about social salvation along with economic rehabilitation. Assuming that the Marxian hypothesis is correct, i.e., that crime and delinquency are rooted in the structure of competitive class society, Wile wonders why juvenile delinquency increased so markedly during the first five-year plan in 1929-33.[30] Using 1931 as the base year (100), the index rose from 128 in 1932 to 165 in 1933 and 185 in 1934, perhaps reflecting the liquidation of the Kulaks in 1932. In spite of increased economic security (for some classes, but not for all), the enhanced social welfare, increased educational facilities, better standard of living, and a more widely disseminated culture, stealing and plundering accounted, Wile says, for two-thirds of juvenile delinquency in 1934. Hooliganism and poor conduct, on the other hand, diminished.[31]

To stem an unanticipated rise in juvenile delinquency in 1936, the

[28] Thorsten Sellin, "Child Delinquency," *The Annals,* American Academy of Political and Social Science, No. 229 (Sept. 1943), p. 163.
[29] *Bekampfung der Jugend-Kriminalitat,* Wiesbaden, Bundeskriminalamt, 1955, pp. 55-62.
[30] Ira S. Wile, "Present Problems of Mental Health in Russia," *Mental Hygiene,* Vol. 22, no. 1 (Jan. 1938), pp. 25-56.
[31] *Ibid.,* p. 43.

Commission of Justice urged criminal prosecution for those 12 years or older, if they were found guilty of violence, assault, or murder. Previously, according to the law of 1935, their parents had been designated as neglectful. Henceforth, these young persons were required to appear personally in the criminal court, subject to all measures of criminal punishment.

General Comments in the Soviet Press

For information on the last few years, we have no official statistics and must rely instead on excerpts from the Soviet press. These reflect an increasing concern with the incidence of delinquency, and their suggestions for coping with it sound very similar to some of those advocated in the United States.

A 1954 article suggests that adolescents between the ages of 12 and 15 whose mothers cannot supervise them are better off if they participate in actual work rather than roam aimlessly about the streets after school.[32] Another article entitled, "This Cannot Be Ignored," gives details of street brawls very similar to those of our gangs.[33] Occasional reference is made to the preferential handling by the police and the militia of misbehaving children of prominent citizens.[34]

A March 1955 item on "Style and Its Devotees" refers to the new phenomenon of the "playboy."[35] Characterized as a "worthless parasite," he is recognized by his special type of slang, his manners, his flashy clothes, and impudent looks. His goal, contrary to that of a Marxian society, is to get as much out of life as possible. He is "servile to anything foreign," that is, "to the tastes and morals of the gilded bourgeois youth." There are several playboy types: the young man who extorts money from his parents, blackmails and intimidates his father; the boy who steals when he is short of money; the boy who stabs a fellow-student while drunk.[36] "The main responsibility for this situation is laid not at the feet of the schools and the Young Communists League, but with the parents."[37]

Commenting further on the situation the press cites, "What Readers Say About Playboys": "A certain group of people have broken away from the great, shining, fervent life of Soviet youth, and are actively spreading views alien to Communist ethics. While playboys are few in Soviet Russia, the phenomenon should not be neglected: 'All our young people must participate in useful social activity.' "[38]

[32] "No Child Should Be Without Supervision," *Current Digest of the Soviet Press*, Vol. 6, no. 30 (Sept. 8, 1954), pp. 26-27.
[33] *Current Digest*, Vol. 7, no. 5 (March 16, 1955), p. 23.
[34] "Nepotism," *ibid.*, Vol. 7, no. 43 (Dec. 8, 1954), p. 22.
[35] *Ibid.*, Vol. 7, no. 4 (March 9, 1955), pp. 15-16.
[36] *Ibid.*, Vol. 7, no. 11 (April 27, 1955), p. 13.
[37] *Ibid.*, Vol. 7, no. 4, p. 16.
[38] *Ibid.*, Vol. 7, no. 11, p. 13.

Judging by the excerpts from the Soviet press in 1957 and 1958, the chidings in the articles quoted above have not brought about the desired result—more character training of Soviet youth by the Young Communist League and other authorities. Almost every month there continues to be some reference to delinquency in the Soviet press.

The Offenses

Apparently the older adolescents are committing crimes of violence, including rape and murder. The punishment is severe. It may be as much as fifteen years at hard labor for robbery, as in the case of three boys, all young workers in the OZERO paper combine in Moscow,[39] or in the case of two boys under 19, who were guilty of armed robbery in Baka.[40] A student in the Kartek Equipment Operator's School found guilty of murder was sentenced to death by shooting.[41] A like penalty was the fate of a truant who, as a vagrant in the company of two comrades, went to his grandmother's apartment, robbed, and killed her.[42]

As in the United States, automobiles and bicycles are the targets of young Russian thieves.[43] But most of the complaints relate to idlers, stilyaga, translated as zootsuiters or playboys. They are described as repulsive young men wearing "ultra-modish" jackets, trousers which are too short and too tight, and displaying "eccentric" neckties. They have an air of "self-satisfied stupidity." They have girl companions whose coiffures are described as "à la garçon—pitiful bristling short-cropped hair."[44] The title of this article refers to the hero of a famous nineteenth-century novel Oblomov—a son of a landlord who had very little education and idled away his days on his parents estate.

Another article entitled, "One Cannot Pass Over This in Silence,"[45] reports a discussion which occurred at a City Party meeting and at a Soviet "Action" on the subject of hooliganism and disturbing the peace. The complaint is against some clubs which had been assigned the responsibility for providing constructive leisure-time activities, but which had instead become purely commercial enterprises. The factories, offices, and educational institutions are chided because they appear to tolerate loafing, drinking, and rowdyism. One superintendent is criticized for reinstating an upper-grade student who had been expelled for unseemly conduct in school. The upshot of the

---

[39] "Robbers," *ibid.*, Vol. 9, no. 1 (Feb. 13, 1957), p. 24.
[40] "Hand to Hand Combat with Armed Robbers," *ibid.*, Vol. 9, no. 1, p. 25.
[41] "Sentence Upheld," *ibid.*, Vol. 9, no. 22 (July 10, 1957), p. 24.
[42] "Murderers Shot," *ibid.*, Vol. 9, no. 30 (Sept. 4, 1957), pp. 21-22.
[43] "Car Thieves," *ibid.*, Vol. 9, no. 15 (May 22, 1957), p. 23.
[44] "The Mikofas of Modern Times," *ibid.*, Vol. 9, no. 6 (March 20, 1957), p. 32.
[45] *Ibid.*, Vol. 9, no. 16 (May 29, 1957), p. 30.

discussion at this meeting was to declare the parents responsible for the upbringing of their children and the schools and City Party committees for
directing their graduates to suitable jobs.

Adverse comments on the character training programs of higher educational institutions seem to echo some of the complaints in America which are
lodged against our schools. One complaint is that students are not punished
for cutting classes, avoiding difficult tasks, or drinking.[46] The Party is held
responsible for its apparent complacency about the lack of ambition, slack
habits, disorderly conduct, and offensive language of some young people.
Many high school graduates create disturbances in restaurants, hotels, and
theaters. They live off their parents, is the tenor of an article entitled, "Concern About Communist Upbringing of Young People."[47]

Two reports of speeches by Khrushchev, in April and June 1958, emphasize widespread drinking and disorderly conduct. At the Thirteenth Young
Communist League Congress, talking on the need to "Train Active and Conscious Builders of Communist Society," and on "Youth, Education and Work,"
he said: "I have heard that here and there the organization of young people's
evening parties starts with a phone call to the militia [police]. (*Laughter in
the audience.*) But why do you need a militiaman to subdue the hooligans
. . . ? The public can play a decisive role, it can and should through the YCL
expose idlers, hooligans, and drunkards, without waiting for them to make
trouble. . . . Intoxication of young people is intolerable."[48]

Khrushchev went on to assure his audience that the reason for his comments was not that excessive drinking was a *great threat* to Communist society,
but "on the principle of putting out a fire when you see sparks." He deplored
the reference to "heroes" who boast of having fallen into the sobering-up tank
"as if they had been to the theatre." He suggested, as one remedy, stamping
out "illicit brewing" (sounds like our Kentucky stills) and, as another, to
"keep the streets clean, establish new park areas, protect forests and rivers
from poachers" (the program of some of our Youth Camps).

Parents' Responsibility

Today in the USSR the task of upbringing of youth is not left to the
state, the Party, the YCL, or the school, as it was, in theory, in the past;
the family's share of responsibility is growing. No doubt this new direction
reflects the growing conviction that, even in a Communist society, the family
has a crucial role. One finds recurring reference to parental neglect, over-

[46] "Character Training of Students at Higher Educational Institutions Is Poor,"
ibid., Vol. 9, no. 4 (March 6, 1957), pp. 40-41.
[47] *Ibid.*, Vol. 9, no. 9 (April 10, 1957), p. 34.
[48] *Ibid.*, Vol. 10, no. 17 (June 4, 1958), p. 19.

indulgence, or failure to instill proper standards of conduct. For example, in discussing the case of a gang member, a fifth-grade student in an evening school, accused of robbery, a reprint from *Tadzhikistana*[49] states that the boy had been committed to a children's labor colony and was released in June 1956 at his parents' request. The boy's mother works in a school lunchroom, and his father, to whom his mother is not married, is a dispatcher for the railroad dining car service. His parents had thought that they were fulfilling their duty by providing plenty of spending money without concerning themselves about their child's other needs, such as the need for guidance. The final comment is that the crime was "the pernicious consequence."

This excerpt is particularly interesting to us not only because it reflects a universal recognition of parental responsibility but because of what it reveals about the Soviet method of dealing with the delinquent. In America, it is not permissible to identify the juvenile delinquent by name, nor would the details of the marital relationship of the parents be revealed unless the story was a sensational one in which such details were brought out incidentally in the court trial of an older boy.

Another article in *Tiesa*, a Lithuanian paper, dated January 12, 1957,[50] blames a father who spoiled his son from the time he was a little boy. The father took the boy to parties, let him taste liquor, and so forth. Even as he grew older, the father did not insist on the boy's working. The son was convicted of assault and robbery and sentenced to fifteen years in prison.

In the case of Oleg Lvov, 16, found guilty of killing a schoolmate who knew that Oleg had robbed a neighbor's house and who had threatened to blackmail him, the reporter[51] blames the parents, (1) for not having reported the killing to the police; (2) for having, when they found out about the theft, ordered Oleg to throw the stolen articles into the Moscow River and *forget about it*. The parents are described as *intellectuals*—the father is an assistant professor and the mother a secondary school teacher.

Several other stories reflect the growing emphasis in the USSR on family responsibility. For example, "About Upbringing: Origins of Crime,"[52] presents the opinion that blind mother-love prevented a mother from investigating the habits of her son's companions, and from knowing that he carried a hunting knife. The boy's father is also blamed *because he abandoned his family* and considered that he had discharged his duty by regularly paying the alimony installments. This is a far cry from the early Soviet attitude toward family responsibility. In the same articles, a note justifying the parents has a familiar ring, very like the excuses of English and American parents who

[49] *Ibid.*, Vol. 9, no. 5 (March 13, 1957), p. 26.
[50] "Fruits of Poor Upbringing," *ibid.*, Vol. 9, no. 6 (March 20, 1957), p. 41.
[51] Y. U. Yilenova, *ibid.*, Vol. 10, no. 14 (May 15, 1958).
[52] *Ibid.*, Vol. 9, no. 13 (May 8, 1957), p. 33.

grew up in poverty. The author comments: "They [the parents] have a justification: 'We had a hard life; let our children have it easy.'"

Echoes of America

Another explanation for the recent upsurge in juvenile crime—the public castigation of people in high places—also sounds familiar to American ears. It is suggested that the anti-Stalinist campaign "produced a painful trauma for impressionable young souls."[53] One reaction of youth is cynicism, obviously a deadly enemy to any successful promotion of a cause. The Russians have coined a term for these disillusioned youth—*Nibonicho*—which means, "they believe in neither God nor the devil."

Addressed to the need for inculcating good examples, there is another article which reminds us of some sectors of the American public who lay the blame for delinquent behavior on the mass media (see Chapter 10). Leonid Sobolev decries the abundance of "spy stories" among the adventure books for Soviet children:

Of the 46 books only five describe adventures which are not related to the hunt for spies, subversive agents and mere bandits. . . .

It is common knowledge that the essence, the heart of adventure books is a search, a mystery, a struggle. But must one really only search for murderers and struggle against subversive agents? Is it possible that there are no secrets that need unraveling which lie outside the vicious circle. . . . Of course not! . . . They can argue with me that the stories about spies and saboteurs, thieves and bandits stir the youth to vigilance. This is an important and sensible consideration . . . but . . . not *all* adventure literature should be devoted to it. . . . As for vigilance, I am reminded of a response of a young reader. "A spy is very easy to recognize. He wears a good grey overcoat and has a predatory look!"

The criminal sabotage bent of modern adventure literature carries within it still another danger. . . . There is no hero whom young people would like to imitate. . . . This hero should be thoroughly noble, brave, frank, honest, resolute. And this is the kind of hero our adventure literature lacks. One recalls with regret the remarkable Brigadier Gerard, the main character in Conan Doyle's books.[54]

Another echo of America's woes with the problem of recidivism and rehabilitating institutionalized delinquents is the complaint concerning the difficulty of securing employment for former inmates.[55] Distrust of the rehabilitative processes is as prevalent apparently in the Soviet Union as it is

[53] "Youth and the Young Without Youth," *ibid.*, Vol. 9, no. 27 (Aug. 14, 1957), pp. 12-14.
[54] *Ibid.*, Vol. 9, no. 25 (July 31, 1957), p. 11.
[55] "Second Offense," *ibid.*, Vol. 9, no. 6 (March 20, 1957), pp. 42-43.

in the United States in spite of official disapproval of this type of discrimination.

One surmises from other sources that the competition for advancement in the Soviet Union is similar to that in middle-class American and British families. The Russians, like the Americans and the British, appear to be deeply concerned with the opportunity their children will have to enter higher educational institutions, the one road in the USSR to professional advancement. A common thread also stresses the importance of constructive affection, good example, and proper control even in a "noncompetitive society," which we will see developed in more detail when we discuss the psychological approach to understanding and controlling delinquency in America (Chapter 6).

Summary

Unlike the United States statistics on delinquency, those collected by the United Nations Division of Social Welfare from various countries abroad and from Canada reflect much more restricted definitions of delinquency. The chief concern in most countries is with offenses against property; offenses against persons rank second. Fluctuations in Germany's statistics appear to reflect changes in the socio-economic conditions since World War I. In the United Kingdom, Mack believes the rise in delinquency statistics has reflected administrative procedures rather than different incidence. But currently there seems to be an increase in actual disruptive behavior.

We have quoted at length from the current Russian periodicals to show their growing concern with juvenile delinquency. We detect the possibility that the Soviets do protest too much in their oft-repeated comment that, of course, these accounts of hooliganism, drinking, assault, and so forth, do *not* describe common occurrences. Perhaps the way the comments are phrased reflects some concern with censorship. Yet the fact that they are reprinted for foreign as well as domestic consumption suggests that the phenomena are not rare.

From the American point of view, we may infer that in some ways the current Soviet philosophy of family responsibility, and their emphasis on useful work, industry, honesty, and so forth, reflect values similar to ours.

CHAPTER 4

The Central Register

Delinquency Rate and Illness Rate

THE AVAILABLE STATISTICS ON DELINQUENCY IN THE UNITED STATES RESULT in what might be called a "general illness rate." An undifferentiated illness rate, however, is of little use as a measure of a community's need for specific preventive or therapeutic facilities. Obviously, if the increase in the illness rate is due to smallpox or tuberculosis, the problem is quite different—both from the individual and the public health point of view—than if the increase were due to chickenpox, measles, or the mumps.

The current official methods of labeling deviant social behavior are as unenlightening as a public health procedure would be in which classification was based solely on rashes or fluctuations in temperature. Just as there are many kinds of rashes and many different implications in temperature fluctuations, so there are many kinds of misbehavior, and disturbances of varying seriousness that may express themselves in the same symptomatic act. Today's juvenile court procedures are often apt to treat behavior having "smallpox" implications for "chickenpox"—and vice versa—because we have no satisfactory definition of the phenomena that we are supposed to be measuring.

To make headway in clarifying our definitions of delinquency, we need to take a leaf from the public health book and develop a system of good case finding, which will provide an index of the prevalence of clearly identified behavior entities. Perhaps the reason that the common cold still defies explanation and control is because its characteristics have not been isolated from those of other respiratory infections. Its course may run from a day or two to several weeks. It may have disturbing or trivial accompaniments. Treatment varies from doing nothing about it to dosing with antibiotics. Explanations of its cause include overfatigue, getting one's feet wet, sitting in a draft or in the path of a sneezer, or even suffering a psychosomatic reaction to emotional crisis. Delinquency, like the common cold, appears to have eluded effective and discriminating definition.

Continued reiteration, however, of the shortcomings of existing statistics as a measure of juvenile delinquency in the absence of a more positive approach is fruitless. The cautious consumer of statistical material is inhibited from using the data, whereas the overzealous partisan uses them in disregard of their limitations. Delinquent behavior exists. It is a threat both to the individual and the community. It must be dealt with.

To arrive at a program of treatment, prevention, and community interpretation, a measurement of delinquency must be devised. Until the illness can be effectively defined, the most practical course of action is to reconcile the statistics on juvenile delinquency with the popular conception of the term. This can be done by expanding the coverage of juvenile delinquency statistics to include all children referred or known to any agency because of behavior which would be a violation of the law.

The Central Register in Practice

Defined

The Central Register of delinquents is such a device, designed to include the names not only of children referred to the courts but of all children in the community who are referred to agencies for behavior similar to that which might have brought them to the court's attention. Three cities have established a Central Register—the District of Columbia, New York City, and Los Angeles.

In the District of Columbia

The project in Washington, D.C., was proposed by the Statistical Division of the Children's Bureau as a test of the Central Register idea.[1] Under joint sponsorship of the Children's Bureau and the Council of Social Agencies of the District of Columbia, for the period June 1943 through May 1944, all the public agencies of the District having responsibility for dealing di-

[1] This project was initiated to test the proposal advanced by the author of this book and Neva R. Deardorff in a 1937 memorandum to the agencies in New York City. The author served as consultant in setting up the Central Register in the District of Columbia in 1943 and in New York City in 1950.

rectly with delinquent children, excluding those providing long-time institutional care, participated in this registration.

Each agency submitted reports on each child under 18 years of age who was referred because of alleged delinquency, that is, juvenile misconduct which might be dealt with under the law. No attempt was made to impose a uniform definition of delinquency upon the agencies or to influence intake policy or practice. The identifying data—name of child, name of parents, address, age, sex, and race—as well as the administrative data—reporting agency, date, source, and reason for referral to the agency, method and date of disposition of the case—were reported. If there was more than one registration for the child, or a registration for more than one child in a family, the cases were grouped so that it was possible to get an unduplicated case count by families, by census tract.

The analysis of the registration revealed that:

1. Less than half of all children registered for delinquency were known to the juvenile court.

2. The juvenile court registrations included duplication amounting to 25 per cent, since the basis of the court count is cases rather than children.

3. The juvenile court cases differed from those reported by the other agencies in several respects:

a. In monthly reports, *changes* in the juvenile court figures paralleled those of the receiving home, but were quite different from those of the women's bureau of the Police Department.

b. With respect to *residence*, the children reported by the court included a large proportion from the northwest section of the city—chiefly traceable to traffic violations, which were reported to the court, but not to the other agencies.

c. With respect to *characteristics* of the children, the court series included larger proportions of boys and older children, but fewer white girls than were known to the noncourt agencies.

d. With respect to *offenses*, 99 per cent of traffic violators, 75 to 80 per cent each of the categories of stealing, assault, and acts of carelessness and mischief, 24 per cent of sex offenses, but only 5 per cent of truants were reported to the juvenile court.

e. In both series—court and noncourt—the highest *concentrations* of cases occurred in areas of low median rental and large Negro populations, all areas with high incidence of social pathology.

Thus this Washington, D.C., project was a clear-cut demonstration that:

1. The juvenile court statistics were insufficient as a measure of juvenile delinquency in a community in which it was not the only agency dealing with socially disapproved behavior.

2. One quarter of the young persons under 18 were known to two or more agencies and 5 per cent were reported by three or more in that year. This fact calls for an analysis of the operation of different agencies in the community.

3. Of the young people reported to the register, 21 per cent were identified as belonging to families in which one or more of their brothers or sisters were also reported for delinquency. This suggests a need to examine the family settings and the community services that have been provided.[2]

In the opinion of the United States Children's Bureau, "The Central Register for communities which provide many services for children is a manageable project, and can be an important factor in study and evaluation, the first step in effective community action toward the treatment, control, and prevention of juvenile delinquency.[3]

Between 1954 and 1958 an unduplicated case count of children between the ages of seven and eighteen known to the Police Juvenile Bureau and the juvenile court was made in Washington. Comparisons of the estimated population at risk in each of the five years with the children referred to these two agencies reveals some startling facts.

1. Although there was a decided increase in Washington's total child population, the percentage of delinquents decreased from 26.8 in 1954 to 19.1 in 1958. The white child population decreased from 62,000 to 52,000 but the ratio of white delinquents to estimated white child population hovered between 14.6 and 16.3 per thousand. (The one exception was 1956 in which it rose to 18.2.) Although the comparable Negro population increased from 69,000 in 1954 to 93,500 in 1958 the number of delinquents per thousand declined steadily from 37.1 in 1954 to 21.2 in 1958.

2. The delinquents who resided outside the district (mainly in the suburbs) varied from approximately 10 to 14 per cent of the annual total.

3. By 1958 approximately one third of the delinquents who resided in the district had appeared more than once in the Register.

4. About 20 per cent of 4800 district residents dealt with by the police reappeared in the court. In contrast, only 6 per cent of the 1376 nonresidents were referred to the juvenile court for subsequent offenses.

5. Classified by race, sex, and type of offense the five-year total reveals striking differences. Traffic offenses predominate among the complaints against white boys and girls. Among the nonwhites, stealing is the most frequent charge against boys; ungovernable behavior and stealing account for three fourths of the cases of Negro girls.

[2] For additional data see Neva R. Deardorff, "Central Register of Delinquents," *Probation,* Vol. 23, no. 5 (June 1945), pp. 141-47.
[3] Edward E. Schwartz, "A Community Experiment in the Measurement of Juvenile Delinquency," *Yearbook,* National Probation Association, 1945, pp. 157-182.

The report suggests that the marked decline in the Negro ratio may be associated with the increased institutional commitment of Negro children and their removal from the community, made possible because of the expansion of the Children's Center Facilities. In 1953 Negro children in institutions accounted for 68 per cent (409 out of 600). In contrast, in 1958 Negro children occupied 762 of the 930 bed capacity or 82 per cent.

Recent reports from Lincoln, Nebraska, suggests that this community also plans to establish a central register as part of its delinquency control program of "Casefinding, Reaching Out Casework and Referral."[4]

In New York City

Six years after the first Children's Bureau demonstration, the New York City Youth Board also set up a Central Register for Delinquents. Initially both the public and private agencies agreed to report all cases coming to their attention for behavior which might have brought them to the juvenile court.

Analysis of the first two years' operation, 1950-52, showed that in the first year about 40,000 names were registered, between 7000 and 8000 of them known to the juvenile court. There was about 13 per cent duplication in the first year's roster, and 11 per cent recidivism in the second year.

The analysis of characteristics of the young persons included in the Register showed that:

1. Boys predominated.
2. The modal age group was 13-15.
3. The principal reasons for referral were stealing and truancy.
4. The figures from the voluntary agencies, which in the second year accounted for less than 5 per cent of the total, showed an uneven geographic distribution, partly as a result of selective intake policies with respect to type of case and religious affiliation.

Although the analysis of the first two years' data revealed wide differences with respect to area of residence, sex, age, color, and religious affiliation of the registrants, the Research Bureau of the Youth Board decided in March of 1953 that subsequent analysis would be limited to: (1) volume of cases by health area of residence (the health area, a combination of census tracts accounting for a population of 25,000, is the basis of New York City health statistics); and (2) cases known to the Bureau of Attendance, Children's Court, Magistrate's Court, Juvenile Aid Bureau, and the Bureau of Identification.

The total figures by health area for each of the five boroughs of New York City and rates per 1000 of 1950 population are available for 1953 and

---

[4] Lloyd L. Voight, Director, "Need for a Community Program for Troubled and Maladjusted Children," Lincoln Youth Project, Aug. 1958, and subsequent correspondence.

1954.[5] In June 1958, a mimeographed report listed the areas with rates above 45.0 in comparison with the 1957 population estimates. For comparison purposes the earlier report includes health area tabulations of the 1950 census data on population by ethnic groups—white, Negro, Puerto Rican, and others —percentage of overcrowded dwelling units, and median income for families and unrelated individuals. For 1957, the report utilizes the interim census figures for New York City by health areas.

The New York City Youth Board Central Register shows that the juvenile court figures account for less than 12 per cent of the total. However, analyses have not been made of (1) the differential nature of the behavior; (2) the characteristics of the individuals; (3) the agency treatment and outcome. Nor do the reports, which are based on offenses rather than individuals, distinguish, as they might, the families that contribute more than one child a year to the count.

It is of interest, however, that even within the expanded coverage no health area in New York City had, in the course of a year, more than 3 out of 100 children included in the register. Thus the vast majority of the children in New York were not identified as delinquent, either officially or unofficially.

If the Central Register were used as the original plan intended—i.e., like the public health service compulsory reporting of certain illnesses—it would provide a genuine case finding device. The next steps would be a thorough study of the individual in trouble, his cultural milieu, and his family background. Properly used, the Central Register, like the public health reporting of illness, could lead to identification of trouble spots and experimentation with more effective methods of control of delinquency.

The Basic Essentials of a Central Register

A Central Register which will achieve community-wide knowledge of the incidence of delinquency has three essential ingredients.[6]

1. It will include all children at risk in the community who are in conflict with the law. This implies cases other than those which "find themselves" by referral to the court. There are at least three seeing eyes to detect disapproved behavior—the police, the school, and the agency.

[5] "Juvenile Delinquency Rates and Socio-Economic Characteristics for New York City," research department, New York City Youth Board.
[6] See Sophia M. Robison, "Wanted, an Index of Crime and Delinquency," in Robert E. Seliger, Edwin J. Lukas, Robert M. Lindner (eds.), Contemporary Criminal Hygiene Source Book, Oakridge Press, 1946, Chap. 4. pp. 74-89.

a. The *Police Department* is ubiquitous and is charged with responsibility for uncovering violations of law, destruction of property, and generally undesirable behavior of the entire community, including children. Police officers are not only the chief source of referral to the court; they are also one of the best informed groups in the community concerning delinquent behavior which is never known to the courts.

b. Since the *schools*, public, private, and parochial, have almost the entire child population under observation during a term of years extending into the period of adolescence, teachers are in a strategic position to report instances of antisocial behavior without stigmatizing themselves or the children.

c. If the child's conduct is satisfactory at school but unsatisfactory at home, his *parents* may appeal to an unofficial agency such as a private child welfare agency or child guidance clinic for assistance in managing him.

2. It will assemble information on these "found" cases. This includes:

a. a description of the behavior which was considered sufficiently serious to bring the child to the attention of the agency, and

b. sufficient identifying data to indicate characteristics which might be useful in community planning for treatment and prevention.

3. It will involve agreement on the part of each cooperating agency to notify the Central Register:

a. when it accepts a child for care; and

b. when it terminates its services. Termination notice should include a statement of the reason for closing, an estimate of the progress made, and the condition of the case at the time of closing.

The Contributions of a Central Register

There are six ways in which a Central Register would clarify both a community's understanding of and its attack upon the problem of delinquency.

1. The register would provide an operating definition of delinquency consonant with accepted usage of the term rather than one limited to apprehension by the court.

Each community could determine the extent and the types of all behavior which, in the view of responsible persons, calls for attention from established agencies. Grades of seriousness, frequency of recurrence, length of "onslaught," degrees of contagion in the form of gang behavior, or the confinement of the symptoms to a single individual, would be points for study and investigation.

2. The register would make it possible to evaluate the treatment services

of the community, in connection with the various types of behavior, which in turn would point up inappropriate and uneconomical practices.

As we shall see in later chapters, in many communities the juvenile court plays an anomalous role because it is no longer the sole arbiter of the fate of "bad" children, where other agencies are also providing services for children in trouble. In some communities, however, whether or not there are psychiatric and medical clinics, child placement services, and caseworking staffs, the juvenile court still continues to be regarded as the chief source for treatment as well as for the correction and prevention of delinquent behavior. In such a setting all too frequently the judge and his staff are expected to play roles inappropriate for the new script.

3. A community-wide roster would provide a mechanism for classifying cases into those which need handling by the court procedure and those which need social agency treatment.[7] Many juvenile courts are in the difficult position of attempting to reconcile their authoritative role—implied in the community's demand for protection from the delinquent child—which requires quick and decisive action to bring about compliance and conformity with what the community regards as socially accepted behavior, with the mental hygiene emphasis on preserving the best interests of the individual child in the light of his capacities and needs implied in the juvenile court philosophy (see Chapter 14).

4. As a device for community-wide accounting, a Central Register would reveal:

a. the relative distribution of delinquent children in various sections of the city as well as among the various groups in the population;
b. gaps in services as well as inappropriate and uneconomical use of resources, both agency and personnel, if the delinquent's needs are largely for *environmental* treatment; or
c. if the problem is largely in the parent-child relationship, the need for psychiatric and child placement facilities, in the light of the community's provision for services to all such children.

5. With such data as a base, the community can score itself with regard to:

a. the over-all conditions which make for decent living, and high morals; and
b. the presence of special stimuli to undesirable behavior on the part of certain subgroups.

It can then seek to provide adequate shelter, health, and recreation, and the basic requirements for the maintenance of family life.

[7] See the writings of Thomas Eliot and Grace Abbott and recommendations of the White House Conference for 1940.

For example, because of differences from the dominant group in race, creed, or color, equal opportunities *for* service as well as equal access *to* service have frequently been denied to some groups in the community. Moreover, members of minority groups are often apprehended for behavior that is disregarded in a member of the majority group. And as will be noted in subsequent chapters, the handicap of socio-economic class differences, which may and often does cut across these lines, needs to be counteracted. No one has yet determined the psychological importance of such factors in precipitating revolt against organized social patterns.

The over-representation of certain ethnic groups which we will note in juvenile court statistics suggests that these lines of investigation are also important in appraising the *community's* responsibility for generating unhealthy and undesirable behavior. It is well known that Negro children in particular must generally learn to face the problems of living in an "ascribed" role, both as Negroes and as Americans. It is surprising that they do not express more aggressive behavior than is revealed in official statistics. Similarly, the "zoot-suit" incidents involving Mexican children in the early 1940s in many California communities seemed to be responses to positive deprivations suffered primarily because these were the children of America's less privileged citizens.

6. A community device like the Central Register will ultimately make it possible to conduct continuous and systematic research into delinquent behavior, based on better general knowledge than is now available in the official statistics. With a reservoir such as the Central Register, problems of representative sampling would be at a minimum, and manageable research projects could be formulated.

From a laboratory or clinical point of view, study might begin with an abstract definition of juvenile delinquent behavior. With agreement as to its definition, the research project might investigate all the instances which meet the agreed-upon definition regardless of where they may be found—in the records of the courts, social agencies, schools, or police.

If experts could agree on the choice of relevant factors, great progress might be made in extending our knowledge of delinquency. For example, a committee of psychiatrists, psychologists, penologists, and child welfare consultants might jointly decide how much and what kind of overt behavior was dangerous for the individual's development and the community's welfare. If all cases meeting these specifications were the subject of careful study, the characteristics of the families and of the young persons who presented this combination of symptoms would be revealed. Plans for treatment which promised greatest success could be inaugurated and studied under controlled conditions.

Another alternative which has been suggested to the Youth Board is to select for study the hard-core families, i.e., those whose members appear again and again in the register. Holding constant the factors of residence, ethnic group, and socio-economic status, one might proceed to ascertain which characteristics or determinants are associated with what kinds of behavior—and eventually to differentiate the deviant from the conforming members of the families studied.

Summary

As a basis for better measuring the volume and incidence of juvenile delinquency than that offered by the juvenile court statistics, the operation of the Central Register is described in this chapter.

Set up originally as a pilot project at the initiation of the Children's Bureau, the District of Columbia Central Registration demonstrated its practicality and its effectiveness in supplementing the somewhat skewed figures of the juvenile court operations in Washington, D.C., in 1943. As a result, the device was recommended by the Children's Bureau to local communities which desired to appraise the relative roles of the court and other community agencies in dealing with delinquency. To date, some form of Central Register is in operation in New York City and in Los Angeles. It has been revived in Washington, D.C.

Intermittent publications of the New York City Youth Board give rates by health area based upon all the cases reported to the Bureau of Attendance, the Police Department, and some other agencies, instead of juvenile court figures alone. To date, however, these publications do not discriminate with respect to the character or the agency's disposition of the case, and thus have not added to our understanding of the nature of the problem or the characteristics of the delinquents. They have merely provided the basis for larger rates than those formerly based on juvenile court statistics alone. More productive use of the Central Register data will be forthcoming if imagination, energy, and resources can be provided for formulating appropriate hypotheses for testing.

PART TWO

THEORIES OF CAUSE

CHAPTER 5

Classical, Neo-classical, and Clinical Approaches

UNTIL THE JUVENILE COURT WAS ESTABLISHED, CHILDREN IN TROUBLE WITH the law were treated as adult criminals. Then as now, both the definitions and the explanations of crime to a large extent arose from the philosophic and scientific concepts of the day. Thus, in Puritan New England, the belief that a heretic was possessed by the devil in the form of a witch justified burning or drowning him.

We know that philosophic systems represent attempts to integrate current scientific theories into a unified pattern. Yet we frequently forget the tentative and ephemeral nature of much that is labeled scientific knowledge. Often the theology of one age is regarded as mythology by the next. All organized bodies of knowledge were made for a particular time and context, and none can rightly claim either universal or eternal application. So it is with formerly respected explanations of crime and delinquency.

Many advances in knowledge result from new ways of looking at what has probably always existed. A new way of looking at the physical universe may in turn grow partly out of improved techniques of observation. What we see with the new techniques is thus largely determined by what we have been prepared to see. The object identified by a new device may be recognized under its old or familiar label; or, as new knowledge grows, the old label may be replaced and the data assigned a new significance in the hierarchy of knowledge. Often, however, the old knowledge does not disappear, but hangs on as a residue, coloring what comes after.

Similarly, each successive link in the chain of casual explanations of crime and delinquency has reflected not only the observer's viewpoint and the popular theories of his time but the technical equipment for seeing and interpreting what he looked at. Each explanation has seemed entirely reasonable until challenged by newer ways of looking at the problem. But its adherents have not always abandoned it in the light of newer developments. Thus even today in the study and treatment of delinquency there are elements of the earlier view of children in trouble as simply youthful versions of adult offenders. And long outmoded causal theories of crime continue to color both our thinking and our actions in relation to delinquency.

Following the terminology of criminologists, we shall refer to the causal theories of crime as classical and neo-classical. The former was concerned with the form of the crime. The latter shifted emphasis to examining the biological and physiological characteristics of the criminal, and paved the way for the emergence of many clinical studies. Stress on the role of intelligence coincided with two developments: the invention and application of objective tests of intelligence, and the establishment of juvenile courts. Current explanations of delinquency which stress psychiatric, sociological, and cultural factors are discussed in subsequent chapters.

The Classical School—Emphasis on the Crime

Beccaria's Study

Cesare Beccaria has been acknowledged as the founder of the classical school of criminology. His *Crime and Punishment*, published in 1764, was intended as an antidote to the arbitrary imposition of penalties according to the whim of individual judges of the day. Beccaria, like his contemporaries, had embraced the doctrine of free will and its corollary that each individual is morally responsible for his acts. Thus, the punishment should fit the crime, i.e., be appropriate to the moral guilt, whether the criminal was rich or poor.

Assuming that everyone prefers pleasure to pain, Beccaria said that no one would engage in criminal acts unless he anticipated that the pleasurable consequences would outweigh the painful ones. Therefore, the logical way to prevent crime would be to impose penalties painful enough to deter it. The degree of punishment must be severe enough to outweigh the pleasurable effects of the crime. Because children and the insane were incapable of intelligent judgments as to the consequences of their acts, they were to be exempted from punishment. Presumably the latter were to be removed from society for its protection.

Some of the implications of this approach persist today in the imposition of definite time limits for imprisonment and in like retribution for like crimes.

Neo-Classical School—Emphasis on Physical Characteristics

Lombroso's and Goring's Studies

The next step toward causal theories of crime was taken by another Italian, Cesare Lombroso (1836-1909). Influenced, no doubt, by the increasing emphasis on physiological, sociological, and anthropological approaches to understanding individual behavior, Lombroso shifted the focus from the *criminal act* to the *criminal himself*. Instead of regarding the individual as an entirely free agent, in accord with the moral philosophy of the classical school, the neo-classicist considered him the product of hereditary social forces, some of them beyond his individual control.[1]

In his search for explanations of crime in the physiological characteristics of the criminal himself, Lombroso believed that he had "discovered" a criminal type. The criminal, he said, could be recognized by his protruding ears, abundant hair, sparse beard, enormous frontal sinuses and jaws, square and protruding chin, broad cheekbones, and so forth.

Lombroso's pronouncements stimulated other research. Some of his disciples went further than the master, maintaining not only that there was a born criminal type but that this type could be subdivided into recognizable subgroups, with specific physical stigmata for thieves, murderers, and so forth.

Perhaps the most important reaction to Lombroso's theories were the studies of the English criminologist, Goring (1870-1919), who tested this hypothesis that physical stigmata play a dominant role in crime. Goring compared various physical measurements of 3000-odd English prisoners with those of Cambridge and Oxford graduates. When he found that the postulated anatomical differences did not distinguish the two groups, Goring criticized Lombroso's circular reasoning, i.e., his assumption of a causal relationship between the high incidence of stigmata and criminality in a prison population without testing his findings on a noncriminal population. As a result, Goring began to suggest that some other factor, possibly intelligence, was more significant. Meanwhile, other neo-classical criminologists, following Lombroso's and Goring's leads, sought to see whether there were, perhaps,

[1] See Paul Popenoe, "Twins and Criminals," *Journal of Heredity*, Vol. 27 (1936), pp. 388-90, a summary of four German studies of criminal behavior in twins which suggests that heredity plays an important role; compare with Healy and Bronner, *New Light on Delinquency and Its Treatment*, New Haven, Yale University Press, 1936, discussed in Chapter 6.

some biological characteristics—glands, body structure, and so forth—which differentiated the criminal from the noncriminal.

Glands and Delinquency

For a short time in the 1920s, the glands were thought to hold the key to delinquency. At the Boston Institute of Endocrinology, the possibility of a positive relationship between excess glandular functioning and delinquency was tested on 100 inmates of the Massachusetts Reformatory for Women; but it was not supported by the findings.[2]

Somewhat extravagant claims that excess glandular secretions were the cause of crime were made by Schlapp in 1924. He predicted that an examination of convicts would reveal that one third were suffering from emotional instability—another name, in his opinion, for glandular or toxic disturbance. Schlapp and his associate Smith suggested that the thief and the murderer suffered from a disturbance in gland cells and nerve centers.[3]

These authors, however, did not take into consideration that crisis situations may disturb the ordinary body functions. For example, if the examinations were made at the time of arrest the glandular disturbances evidenced in excessive perspiration, flushing, trembling, stomach ache, or even inability to control the eliminatory and excretory tracts might not be the cause, but rather the effect, of the situation.

Body Structure

Another set of theories stemming from the neo-classical school related crime and delinquency to body structure. This explanation is akin to the concepts of inferior and superior races which were playing so large a part in determining America's immigration policies between 1880 and 1924. None of the proponents of race superiority seemed embarrassed by the fact that there was neither a satisfactory definition of race nor an explanation of the way in which traits are inherited.

In pre-Hitler Germany, Kretschmer[4] advanced a hypothesis that related body type to certain psychological phenomena. He linked schizophrenia to the asthenic body—long, angular, and lean. Manic behavior he thought to be characteristic of the pyknic type, exemplified by the stocky body and the fleshy smoothness of trunk and limbs of the Mediterranean peoples.

[2] Allan W. Rowe and Miriam Van Waters, "Physical Associations with Behavior Problems," *Endocrinology*, Vol. 19 (1935), pp. 129-43.
[3] M. G. Schlapp and E. H. Smith, *The New Criminology*, New York, Liveright, 1928; see also Louis Berman, "Crime and the Endocrine Glands," *American Journal of Psychiatry*, Vol. 12 (1935), pp. 215-38.
[4] Ernest Kretschmer, *Physique and Character*, translated from *Koerperbau and Charakter* by W. H. Sprott, New York, Harcourt, Brace, 1925.

Current emphasis on the relation of body structure to crime and delinquency appears in the studies of William Sheldon,[5] of the late Professor Hooton of Harvard,[6] and of the Gluecks.[7]

According to Sheldon, the mesomorph (the muscular type) is more vulnerable to delinquency than the ectomorph (the nervous, wiry type, characterized by small face, sharp nose, fine hair) or the endomorph (the fat, soft, round type). Temperamentally, the mesomorph—the somatonic type—is the active, dynamic, voluble person who springs to action at the drop of a hat. The endomorph, or visceratonic type, is the relaxed, comfortable, "jolly good fellow" who refuses to get excited, while the ectomorph, the cerebretonic type, is characteristically the introvert intellectual who "eats his heart out."

This analysis, in which the physique is regarded as *the* factor determining the individual's behavior pattern, gives no consideration to the role of diet and environment in the development of body types.[8] Probably because the incidence of pure body type is rare, and because the application of Sheldon's indices requires an elaborate code, relatively little use has been made of this device in explaining delinquency.

Pursuing a long interest in the relation between body type and delinquency, the Gluecks have elaborated some of their data in *Physique and Delinquency*.[9] In this volume they present certain physical factors that differentiate the delinquent from the nondelinquent. There is some evidence, however, against their hypothesis that the physique of a baby or first-grader determines his future body build. According to Dr. Willard Olson, there are at least two distinct patterns of growth among school children. In the first group, growth proceeds rapidly and symmetrically, i.e., bones, teeth, learning ability, and so forth, proceed at about the same rate. In the second group, bones and teeth may grow at one rate, learning ability at a slower or faster one. When dental age, carpal age, height and weight age, reading age, and mental age are growing normally—at the average rate or better—the likelihood of good adjustment with a plus margin for meeting life situations exceeds that of the slow grower. Slow growth of the organism as a whole appears to be accompanied by reading and behavior difficulties.

Olson cautions that there are still unsolved problems in understanding the relationship between growth and behavior adjustment. "The student of

[5] W. H. Sheldon, Emil M. Hartl, and Eugene McDermott, *Varieties of Delinquent Behavior,* New York, Harper, 1949.

[6] E. A. Hooton, *The American Criminal,* Cambridge, Harvard University Press, 1939.

[7] Sheldon and Eleanor Glueck, *Unraveling Juvenile Delinquency,* New York, The Commonwealth Fund, 1950. See also Chapter 6.

[8] Ashley Montagu, "The Biologist Looks at Crime," *The Annals,* American Academy of Political and Social Science, No. 217 (1941), pp. 46-58.

[9] Sheldon and Eleanor Glueck, *Physique and Delinquency,* New York, Harper, 1956.

child development," he says, "is struck by the *individuality* of growth curves and by the *futility of setting any standard* in terms of group averages or in terms of considerations extrinsic to the individual child."[10]

Dr. Norman C. Wetzel, a Cleveland pediatrician who has distinguished seven hereditary types of size, weight, and stature, warns that expected growth patterns may be disrupted by glandular and emotional disturbances. Such disturbances are usually most pronounced during puberty or at its onset.

Since we do not yet know the role of such obscure factors as internal tensions, glandular imbalance, and emotional insecurity, which no doubt change as the child grows older, we cannot at present predict body build at maturity with any certainty.

In summary then, the theories of Beccaria, Lombroso, and Goring paved the way not only for the biological explanation of crime and delinquency but for physiological investigation. The recent studies of Hooton, Sheldon, and the Gluecks expand Kretschmer's postulation of a relation of body type to behavior.

Goring moved beyond Lombroso to become a progenitor of the clinical school, which came to look upon crime and delinquency as rooted primarily in the psychological characteristics of the individual. Although Goring suggested that intelligence might be the factor which differentiated the criminal from the noncriminal, his investigation was handicapped by the lack of objective measures of intelligence. The development of intelligence tests stimulated the clinical approach to understanding crime and delinquency.

The Clinical Approach

Intelligence and Delinquency

The early decades of the twentieth century gave rise to several studies, mainly by psychologists, of the incidence of high and low intelligence among delinquents' families. To appraise these studies of the relation of intelligence to delinquent behavior, one needs to know (1) how intelligence is measured, (2) the reliability of the measurement, and (3) how effectively intelligence can be factored out as a cause.

HOW INTELLIGENCE IS MEASURED. The first scale of general intelligence was devised by Binet in France. It was assumed that the tests measured inborn intelligence. While the individual's store of knowledge would increase as he grew older, his "brightness" would remain relatively constant. The tests were arranged by age and their results expressed in terms of mental age. A child's

[10] W. C. Olson and R. O. Hughes, "Growth of the Child as a Whole," in Barker, Kounin, and Wright (eds.), *Child Behavior and Development*, New York. McGraw-Hill, 1943.

MA says that his performance is equal to an average child's at that age. The IQ is the ratio of the child's MA to his CA. An IQ of 100 means that the MA and CA coincide. The higher the IQ the brighter the individual; the lower the IQ the more marked the retardation.

RELIABILITY. Since the questions on the tests for each age obviously must grow out of the normal life experiences of the persons tested, the original questions in the Binet tests needed to be changed before they could be used for American children. Terman standardized his scale on nearly 3200 children in 11 states and 17 communities. He used 100 boys and 100 girls for ages 6 through 14 and 50 boys and 50 girls for those below 6 and above 14. When, however, these tests were given to children in other sections of the country—in the South, for example—the scores did not show the normal distribution, but lumped toward the lower end of the curve. This striking difference raised questions concerning the meaning of the results; for it was not reasonable to assume that whole groups of persons living in certain sections of the country were natively less well endowed.

Following this line of questioning, children were tested after a lapse of time in which they had been exposed to certain environmental changes. Otto Klineberg's rigorously scientific studies of Negro children who had been transferred from Southern schools revealed a considerable increase in IQ for each additional year of attendance in a New York City school.[11] Other evidences of marked changes in IQ were furnished by retests of white children transferred from orphanages to individual foster homes, showing average increases of 20 per cent.[12] Even more definitive were studies under the auspices of The National Education Association, demonstrating that even children of mentally deficient parents could achieve average intelligence scores when placed in foster homes which provided proper educational opportunities.[13]

The results of these and other studies cast doubt on the hypothesis that feeblemindedness is an inherited trait. Further doubt has been cast by the psychiatric theory that behavior is not always consciously directed (see Chapter 6); for if this is true it is hardly likely that the usual forms of delinquent behavior are more apt to occur among the less intelligent strata of our population.

FACTORING OUT INTELLIGENCE. The development of various types of intelligence tests and their fairly widespread application made it possible to test the relation between intelligence and delinquency.

[11] Otto Klineberg, Negro Intelligence and Selective Migrations, New York, Columbia University Press, 1935.

[12] Lucille Lazar, unpublished Master's Thesis, Teachers College, Columbia University, 1926.

[13] Barbara S. Burks, "The Relative Influence of Nature and Nurture upon Mental Development," a comparative study of foster parent-true parent child resemblance. Yearbook, National Society for the Study of Education, Part I, 1928, pp. 219-316.

The early application of measures of intelligence to apprehended delinquents did show a higher percentage of low IQ's among them than among the general population. In 1926 Healy and Bronner estimated that 37 per cent of the delinquents tested in their Chicago and Boston studies were in the subnormal range. They concluded *at that time* that delinquency was five to ten times more likely to occur among the mentally handicapped than among the normal group.[14] Subsequent inquiries, however, cast doubt on this finding.

A study published in 1929 compared the IQ's of delinquent boys and their nondelinquent siblings.[15] The comparable median scores were 86 and 75. This small difference favoring the delinquents, and the spread of the scores, suggested that the IQ's of delinquents, in general, resemble those of nondelinquent individuals *in the same socio-economic strata.*

Sutherland, concerned with appraising the incidence of feeblemindedness in delinquents, assembled the findings of psychometric studies of inmates of 145 juvenile institutions and 82 reformatories in the years 1910-28. He found that the average percentage of the inmate population designated feebleminded in studies from 1910 to 1914 was 45 in the juvenile institutions and 44 in the reformatories.[16] The comparable percentages in the 1920-28 studies were 17 and 26.

How we interpret this significant decrease in the average percentage of feebleminded inmates of institutions for delinquents depends on the weight we assign to the following considerations:

1. As a result of the army Alpha tests developed early in World War I, our evaluation of intelligence levels in the general population as a basis of comparison had been downgraded by the time of the second study. At the same time, in recognition that intelligence comprised at least two types—the manual and the cognitive, or what Dewey called the "thing" and the "idea" thinkers— new tests had been devised to distinguish specific abilities. In other words, the methods of testing had changed in the second period.

2. Improved methods of screening feebleminded children in the school population since World War I had led to segregating them in special classes or institutionalizing them apart from the general delinquent population, thus excluding them from the statistics.

An outstanding example of the application of specific ability tests to delinquents in institutions is John Slawson's study[17] of 1543 delinquent boys

[14] William Healy and August J. Bronner, *Delinquents and Criminals—Their Making and Unmaking,* New York, Macmillan, 1926, pp. 151-74.

[15] William M. Butcher, Jane M. Hoey, and J. A. McGuiness, *A Study of Problem Boys and Their Brothers,* Albany, N. Y., The Crime Commission, 1929.

[16] For a summary of these studies of intelligence and delinquency see Harry M. Shulman, "Intelligence and Delinquency," *Journal of Criminal Law and Criminology,* Vol. 41, no. 6 (March-April 1951), pp. 763-81.

[17] John Slawson, *The Delinquent Boy,* Boston, Badger, 1926.

committed to four institutions in New York State: the New York House of Refuge on Randall's Island in the East River, the State Agricultural and Industrial School at Industry, the Hawthorne School at Thornwood, and the Berkshire Industrial Farm at Canaan. Slawson used tests and questionnaires to reveal the psychoneurotic and physical traits and environmental conditions of the inmates. As a control, he used groups of New York City school children of similar nationality, age, and socio-economic status. His major findings concerning the relation of intelligence to delinquency were:

1. Eight out of ten delinquents did not achieve scores comparable to those of the unselected public school children in abstract verbal intelligence.

2. Nonverbal intelligence and mechanical aptitude were not correlated with delinquency. Almost one third of the delinquents either reached or exceeded the Thorndike norms on nonverbal tests. On the Stenquist tests of mechanical aptitude, the delinquents' scores were about normal.

3. There was no relation between IQ and the number of arrests or the seriousness of the offenses charged.

Slawson's findings stimulated a number of studies reappraising the validity of intelligence tests. Among their severest critics today is Ferentz, who does not consider the IQ an adequate measure of a person's ability to function in society. On the contrary, he feels that social functioning and capacity for development are as important as the IQ in classifying a person's mental efficiency.[18] In his opinion, if there is no evidence of social pathology the usual system of classifying a child as defective is destructive, and often leads to the child's being "socialized into mental deficiency."

The preponderance of current evidence does not support the proposition that there is a significant causal relationship between delinquency and low IQ. Instead it is more accurate to say that, if IQ scores are related, by and large, to educational opportunities, then the likelihood of being apprehended *officially* as a delinquent is greatest in the most deprived socio-economic groups.

Complexes of Factors

The many attempts to factor out single traits such as intelligence of one type or another, of which the studies quoted above are significant examples, were soon replaced by efforts to study complexes of factors in large numbers of cases. The groundwork had been laid by Healy when, in 1915, he had distinguished 138 factors, which he classified into fifteen major categories, in a few more than 800 cases brought before the juvenile court from 1909 to

[18] Edward J. Ferentz, "Mental Deficiency Related to Crime," *Journal of Criminal Law and Criminology,* Vol. 45, no. 3 (Sept.-Oct. 1954), pp. 299-307.

1914.[19] On the average, Healy had said, one major and two minor factors appeared significant in each case. The most frequently recurring factor was "mental abnormalities and peculiarities" (55 per cent), with "defective home conditions" (20 per cent) next in order. "Defects of heredity," noted in 502 instances, was the most frequently recurring minor factor.

Reckless,[20] regrouping Healy's factors as social, intermediate, and individual, concluded that the latter occurred twice as often in the total as the social factors, and more than three times as often as the intermediate factors (mental conflict, improper sex experience and habits, unsatisfied interests, mental shock, use of stimulants and narcotics).

Burt, like Healy, studied the syndromes of many factors in individual case studies. He identified 170 such factors, which he grouped into nine categories.[21] In a comparison of the incidence of these factors among 200 children referred to the London juvenile court and 400 pupils in London schools with no juvenile court records, the most striking difference was the nature of parental discipline. Defective discipline—i.e., parental indifference and vacillation, disagreement between parents about control of their children, and overseverity—occurred about seven times more frequently in the delinquent group than in the nondelinquent.

Burt identified one other factor which, though he disregarded it in 1925, today would be considered highly important: 23.5 per cent of the delinquent boys had been deprived of a mother's affection, in comparison with 1.5 per cent of the control group. Among the girls, the comparable figures were even more striking: 36.5 per cent for the delinquents and 0.5 per cent for the nondelinquents. Burt did not attach particular significance to this finding because at the time of his study, as Mack points out,[22] the theories of child development did not stress the crucial importance of the physical and emotional closeness of mother and child in infancy and early childhood.[23] Thus, although the facts were there, the insights necessary to interpret them and comprehend their significance had not yet been developed.

Burt's study, like others which dealt with a variety of individual characteristics, encouraged investigations of an ever-increasing number of factors by psychologists, sociologists, and other professionals. Unfortunately, however, pursuit of the many possible combinations of characteristics in indi-

[19] William Healy, The Individual Delinquent, Boston, Little, Brown, 1915.

[20] Walter C. Reckless and Mapheus Smith, Juvenile Delinquency, New York, McGraw-Hill Book Co., 1932, pp. 198-99.

[21] Cyril Burt, The Young Delinquent, fourth rev. ed. (Bickley, Kent, University of London Press, 1945; first printing, 1925).

[22] John A. Mack, Family and Community, Carnegie United Kingdom Trust, 1953, p. 63.

[23] Harlow's studies with monkeys of the nature of love suggest that the male parent may be an adequate substitute for the mother if he holds the infant properly and is sufficiently "warm and cuddly."

viduals has not so far produced satisfactory explanations of delinquent behavior. Burt's conclusion that defective discipline distinguished the delinquent, and the lack of maternal affection which he found but did not emphasize, might have suggested that the nature of the family offered a more fruitful line of inquiry. And in fact, with the impetus of the psychiatric insights described in the next chapter, the focus of delinquency research did soon shift to a fresh and more promising attack in the search for causes: the investigation of the socio-psychological aspects of family life, which is discussed in Chapter 8.

Summary

Through the years, the prevalent philosophical and scientific theories of behavior of each era have largely determined the definition and explanation of crime and delinquency, whether the explanation was individual responsibility (Beccaria, Lombroso, and the early Goring), glands (Schlapp and Berman), body structure (Sheldon, Hooton, following Kretschmer, and more recently the Gluecks), or low intelligence (Sutherland, and the early Healy studies).

Healy's and Burt's studies of many factors in the individual delinquent in comparison to a control gave impetus to other investigations which, however, were largely unsuccessful in differentiating the delinquent from the non-delinquent.

The growing recognition of the importance of the primary group and the face-to-face relationships in the family shifted the search for cause to a new direction.

CHAPTER 6

Psychological Approaches

THE ADHERENTS OF THE CLASSICAL AND THE NEO-CLASSICAL SCHOOLS, AND also to a certain extent the clinical school, of criminologists assumed that all behavior was consciously directed. If they agreed with Beccaria that crime was the deliberate choice of the criminal, they could justify punishment but insist, as he did, that it be meted out without favor—as symbolized by the blindfolded figure holding the scales.

Even the subsequent efforts to show that biological, physiological, or intellectual attributes might explain delinquency did not take into account the possible unconscious basis of many acts. It was Freud's demonstration that our behavior is not always consciously motivated that gave fresh impetus to the search for cause or causes of crime and delinquency. While it is now generally recognized that behavior is often not consciously directed, opinions still differ as to *why* some individuals appear to act rationally while others seldom do. Or why, to bring the point closer to home, some adults and some young people defy the moral and ethical standards of their society.

In their contacts with people in trouble, psychologists, sociologists, and social workers have utilized the ideas and many of the practices developed by the psychiatrist. They have inquired: How and why did this person get to be the way he is today? What can we do to help him find his way back to a useful life in society? Because today much of our thinking on delinquency and many of our devices for helping delinquents—in case work, counseling, child guidance, group therapy in the community, or care away from home in an institution—are based on the applications of psychiatric principles, an understanding of this thinking and these devices depends on a knowledge of the basic tenets of Freud and those of his followers who have been interested in understanding or helping delinquents.

Psychiatry's Contribution to Understanding Delinquency

The nuclear assumption common to all psychiatric explanations of behavior is that whether the behavior is *good* or *bad*, it is always the individual's reaction to a situation as defined and interpreted by *him*, and *not* as someone else might describe it. If it is agreed that no situation appears exactly the same to any two observers, then, the psychiatrists believe, the individual and his needs *as felt by him* must be the focus for study and understanding.

Freud's Contribution

Freud's theory was built largely on his experience with persons confined in insane asylums. His three main tenets were:

1. The parents' reactions determine whether a child will develop feelings of security or of frustration, and whether or not he will learn to cope with reality. Unless his parents help him dispel the hostile fantasies which arise as a result of his early deprivations, the child's later reactions are likely to be colored by fear, aggression, and even irrationality. However, *too much* as well as *too little* parental attention and solicitude will prevent the child from learning how to meet life's vicissitudes outside the family circle.

2. While his parents' attitudes and his cultural milieu supply the environment in which and toward which the child reacts, there are forces within the child himself which largely determine *how* he reacts both to his parents and his environment.

3. If the various behavior manifestations of an individual appear to be contradictory, the key to the riddle lies in unconscious mental processes and motives which often have devious ways of expression. To solve the riddle of the meaning of the symptoms, the psychiatrist must search in the irrational and unconscious areas of the mental life of the patient.

Although some of Freud's followers disagreed with some of his interpretations and started schools of their own,[1] in the main they agreed on the following premises:

1. The human being is not a passive recipient of experience. He is the actor who selects, eliminates, and adapts both internal and external forces to his own use.

2. There is no such thing as a chance reaction to either internal or

[1] For an exposition of the various schools of thought, see Ruth L. Munroe, *Schools of Psychoanalytic Thought*, New York, Henry Holt and Co., 1955.

external situations. The meaning of any behavior is always specific in terms of the individual's needs. Regardless of whether the reaction is or is not socially acceptable, it is a signal that the individual is trying to solve a problem.

3. The patient's solution of a conflict may take various forms. He may submit or fight; he may try to propitiate with good behavior; he may deny that there is a problem; or he may invent a more pleasing reality.

4. Alleviation of symptoms will not cure psychiatric disorders; the disappearing symptom is likely to be replaced by another. Attack on the symptom is like the old-fashioned method of prescribing medicine to reduce fever instead of regarding the fever as the body's own healing process.

5. An appeal to the patient's reason is not sufficient to cause him to change his ways.

Freud's major contribution to the therapeutic process was to replace the usual appeal to logic by identifying and making use of an *attitude* that develops in the relationship of the patient to the analyst. This process is called "transference": the patient reacts to the therapist as though he were the natural parent. An affectionate reaction to the analyst is a *positive* transference and a hostile reaction is a *negative* transference; both have therapeutic significance. In either case, the patient's attitude toward the analyst reflects his earlier relations with one or both of his parents.[2]

For various reasons the Jungian, the Adlerian, the Horney, and the Sullivan schools have paid relatively little attention to delinquency. On the other hand, Aichorn, Friedlander, and Eissler in Vienna, and more recently, David Levy, Healy and Bronner, Jenkins, and Erikson in the United States have felt challenged to explain the aggressive delinquent. In meeting this challenge each, in his own way, has built on Freudian premises.

Aichorn's Contribution

Aichorn, who was not a physician but a psychologist, applied Freud's theories to redirecting the behavior of aggressive delinquent boys in Vienna in the 1920s. His classic volume, *Wayward Youth*,[3] describes delinquents as boys who are unable to accept either restraint or authority. They are unconcerned about the feelings of others and often show utter disregard for other people's property. As Aichorn unravels their story, some of these boys have had *too little* and some *too much* love—too much in the sense that its effect was smothering.

To change the destructive behavior of the boys in his institution, Aichorn had to prove to them that there were adults in the world who really cared for children and wanted to help them grow into useful, happy adults. If

[2] Erik Erikson, *Childhood and Society,* New York, W. W. Norton, 1950, p. 196.
[3] August Aichorn, *Wayward Youth,* New York, Viking Press, 1935.

their natural parents had not overprotected them by the wrong sort of affection, or, at the other extreme, had been able to separate their disapproval of bad behavior from their regard for their children (in other words, not say continually, "I won't love you any more"), the likelihood is that these boys would have been able to accept the appropriate community or adult controls on their behavior.

Aichorn had many enthusiastic disciples both abroad and in the United States who elaborated on various aspects of his methods of treatment. Some followers of Aichorn such as Friedlander and Eissler, mentioned below, have been interested in developing theory. Others, whose views will be discussed in subsequent chapters on psychiatric clinics and treatment centers (see Chapters 17 and 24), were more concerned with practical applications of theory.

Friedlander's Explanation

According to Kate Friedlander, the differences between delinquents and nondelinquents are quantitative rather than qualitative.[4] Tolstoy's description of his feeling on the verge of adolescence[5] offers dramatic evidence that thoughts and impulses acted out by the delinquent and the criminal occur also to well-adjusted people:

> Somewhere I have read that, not infrequently, children of from 12 to 14 years of age—that is to say, children just passing from childhood to adolescence—are addicted to incendiarism, or even to murder. As I look back upon my childhood, and particularly upon the mood in which I was on that (for myself) most unlucky day, I can quite understand the possibility of such terrible crimes being committed by children without any real aim in view—without any real wish to do wrong, but merely out of curiosity or under the influence of an unconscious necessity for action. There are moments when the human being sees the future in such lurid colors that he shrinks from fixing his mental eye upon it, puts a check upon all his intellectual activity, and tries to feel convinced that the future will never be, and that the past has never been. At such moments—moments when thought does not shrink from manifestations of will, and the carnal instincts alone constitute the springs of life—I can understand that want of experience (which is a particularly predisposing factor in this connection) might very possibly lead a child, aye, without fear or hesitation but rather with a smile of curiosity upon its face to set fire to the house in which his parents and brothers and

[4] Kate Friedlander, *The Psychoanalytical Approach to Juvenile Delinquency*, New York, International Universities Press, 1947.

[5] Leo Tolstoy, *Childhood, Boyhood and Youth*, translated with an introduction by C. J. Hogarth, New York, Dutton, pp. 128-29.

sisters (beings whom he tenderly loves) are lying asleep. It would be under the same influence of momentary absence of thought—almost absence of mind—that a peasant boy of 17 might catch sight of the edge of a newly sharpened axe reposing near the bench on which his aged father was lying asleep, face downwards, and suddenly raise the implement in order to observe with unconscious curiosity how the blood would come sprouting upon the floor if he made a wound in the sleeper's neck. It is under the same influence, the same absence of thought, the same instinctive curiosity—that a man finds delight in standing on the brink of an abyss and thinking to himself, "What if I were to throw myself down?"—or in holding to his brow a loaded pistol and wondering, "What if I were to pull the trigger?"—or in feeling, when he catches sight of some universally disliked personage, that he would like to go to him, pull his nose hard and say, "How do you do, old boy."

The main difference between socially adjusted people like Tolstoy and antisocial people is that the former have overcome their inclination to antisocial behavior. Because they had received sufficient gratification in their relations with their parents, they were able to repress the disapproved impulses and develop a social conscience, which, in psychiatric terminology, is called the *superego*. The properly functioning superego sets up restraints which help to counterbalance the demands of the *id* (inner impulses). In this way, the individual develops a sense of his own worth, an *ego*.

Although the process of psychoanalyzing adults reveals the ways in which many early antisocial impulses were modified and character was formed, only longitudinal studies can reveal the factors within the individual, the family, and the environment which bring about the social adaptation of the "charming toddlers," all of whom underneath are "little savages."

As has been emphasized by psychiatrists of every school, the primary factors in the child's development are the attitudes of his parents toward him at each stage of his development. These attitudes are determined not only by the parents' personality structure but by the pressures of the environment. Unfavorable environmental factors in the case of young persons with antisocial character formation may precipitate antisocial behavior.[6] In some instances only a slight provocation is sufficient to produce a delinquent reaction. In such cases the young person who feels frustrated is likely to react in a hostile manner against the situation, environmental or personal, which has imposed the frustration.

From this point of view, truancy, running away from home, waywardness, stealing, prostitution, are all forms of hostility, some of them more appropriate for boys and some for girls. To remove the environmental cause, however, rarely results in changing the underlying antisocial character forma-

[6] Friedlander, *op. cit.*, p. 165 ff.

tion. New frustrations and new conflicts are likely to create anew the anti-social behavior reaction.

According to Friedlander, the chief distinction between neurotics and delinquents is that the neurotic has an abnormally severe superego. There are some delinquents who are also neurotic; for example, the kleptomaniac, and the criminal whose sense of guilt impels him to seek punishment for his disapproved behavior. In such cases the outlet for the impulse which is repressed by the superego assumes a disguise which is unrecognized by the conscious mind; the symptom behavior represents a compromise between the desire and the repressing force.[7]

Eissler's Explanation

Eissler[8] does not agree with Friedlander that some delinquent behavior is neurotic behavior. Delinquency, unlike the neurosis or the psychosis, is, in his opinion, a reaction to the *value systems* of the individual societies. For example, if the usual pattern of behavior in a society is reserved, then excited or hyperactive behavior will be considered abnormal. Conversely, if hyperactive behavior characterizes a whole group of people, then extremely reserved behavior will be considered abnormal—though not necessarily delinquent.

Delinquency, then, according to Eissler, is abnormality, involving a basic conflict with the value system prevalent in the society in which it occurs. Delinquency is aggressive behavior, which defies the established values in any given society. Eissler calls outwardly directed aggression "alloplastic," and inwardly directed aggression "autoplastic."

Levy's Classification

David M. Levy[9] suggests that aggressive delinquents fall into three main categories, each with an appropriate treatment.

1. In the first group are those whose delinquent behavior appears to be mainly the result of environmental situations, in which the mores of the group offer no incentive for behavior which would meet the standards of the community outside of the particular groups. Examples are children born and reared in prison or those living in slum areas in which gangster influence is dominant. This may represent a fairly large group of children, for whom

---

[7] *Ibid.*, p. 143.

[8] Kurt R. Eissler, ed., *Searchlights on Delinquency* (anniversary volume in honor of Aichorn's 75th birthday), New York, International Universities Press, 1949.

[9] David M. Levy, "On the Problem of Delinquency," *Yearbook*, National Probation Association, 1932-33, pp. 95-110.

the principal treatment would obviously involve amelioration of their living conditions.

2. The second group is composed of children whose delinquency stems mainly from unsatisfactory parent-child relationships regardless of the socio-economic status of the family. Appropriate treatment for this group is clearly not manipulation of the extra-familial social environment, but must be directed to the parents to help them understand the meaning of the asocial behavior of their children. In this process parents are helped to recognize how their own feelings and attitudes may have precipitated the undesirable behavior.

3. In the third group, which Dr. Levy believes is the smallest, he posits that delinquency stems from an internalized condition which, although it may have originated in faulty child-parent relationships, has reached the stage where the children are "sick." They need to be specially treated and perhaps isolated from the rest of the community.

Levy's hypothesis has never been tested. If it were we might well be on the road to a better and more effective differential utilization of our treatment resources.

Jenkins' Classification

Another classification, which has been tried out on an occasional institutional population, is that of the psychiatrist, Jenkins.[10] Jenkins, who, like Levy, deplores the confusion in the definition of delinquency, suggests a bimodal classification which describes reaction patterns as: (1) adaptive, i.e., goal-directed behavior; (2) maladaptive, i.e., frustration behavior. These two types correspond to the American Psychiatric Association classification of dysocial and antisocial reaction.

Jenkins describes the *adaptive* delinquent as on the average more muscular, more venturesome, less suggestible, and more rebellious toward adult authority than law-abiding young people. Jenkins' institutional studies show that as a rule this type of delinquent comes from a disorganized home, in which parental supervision is lacking. Because he usually lives in a neighborhood in which other delinquents live, he is daily exposed to examples of delinquent behavior. His loyalty to his group makes him feel guilty if he informs on them.

The *maladaptive* delinquent is described by Jenkins as hostile, vengeful, explosive, cruel, defiant, deceitful, boastful, selfish, jealous, destructive, and obscene. He does not learn by experience. He has few feelings of guilt and

[10] Richard L. Jenkins, "Motivation and Frustration in Delinquency," speech at the 33rd annual meeting of the American Orthopsychiatric Association, March 16, 1956.

little sense of group or individual loyalty. He has ordinarily been grossly neglected by his mother in his infancy.

In Jenkins' opinion, these differences in background call for very different treatment approaches. The adaptive (goal-directed) delinquent, who uses delinquent techniques to obtain money, possessions, prestige, or desired experiences, represents a *social* rather than a psychiatric problem. He needs help from socialized adults to develop an occupational adjustment which will net him group approval. The maladaptive delinquent, however, must have his sense of guilt aroused to develop an enlightened self-interest, which should be supplemented with some external controls.

Jenkins' system of classification has been applied in studies at the New York State Training School for Boys in Warwick, New York,[11] and at the Michigan Child Guidance Institute.[12] Its feasibility has also been tested on the population of a residential school for delinquents in Kent, England, where Lewis[13] found more than three fourths of the inmates were emotionally deprived children whose parental discipline had been sporadic, who had been reared in dirty and disorderly homes, and who had been associating with other delinquents.

In spite of the difference in emphasis, through each of these explanations of delinquency there runs the common thread of agreement with Freud. Aichorn, Friedlander, and Eissler share the belief that behavior is largely determined by early childhood experience. If parents have shown real affection accompanied by reasonable methods of control in early childhood, the chances of persistently hostile aggressive behavior in youth are minimized. Levy and Jenkins emphasize the role of the physical environment more than is customary in strictly Freudian explanations. Friedlander, however, agrees that such reality factors as overcrowding, poverty, and large families may affect the time and peace of mind available to the mother to help in socializing her children's instinctive drives.

When we discuss the various types of child guidance clinics, we will see that they also differ among themselves in their concern with the influence of these reality factors in the child's immediate family or in the community. Likewise, in our discussions of institutional treatment, we will note that psychiatrists like Block and Gardner, or psychologists like Bettelheim, Redl, and Papernak, concern themselves in varying degrees with the importance of environmental or social class factors.

[11] R. L. Jenkins, H. H. Hart, Sidney Axelrod and P. I. Sperling, "Prediction of Parole Success: Inclusion of Psychiatric Criteria," *Journal of Criminal Law and Criminology,* Vol. 33, no. 1 (May-June 1942), pp. 38-46.
[12] R. L. Jenkins, "Fundamental Patterns of Maladjustment (the Dynamics of their Origin)," Springfield, State of Illinois, 1946.
[13] Hilda Lewis, *Deprived Children,* New York, Oxford University Press, 1954.

Major Research Based on Psychiatric Concepts

The few psychiatrists and clinical psychologists who have devoted any attention to delinquency have been concerned in the main with developing or using theory to explain behavior rather than with testing it. A notable exception is Healy and Bronner's classic study, *New Light on Delinquency and Its Treatment*,[14] because, as its title indicates, it is concerned with both theory and treatment. We will refer to it again in our discussion of psychiatric clinics.

New Light on Delinquency and Its Treatment

This study is the outstanding investigation of the dynamic psychological components in delinquency. Healy and Bronner, the former a psychiatrist and the latter a psychologist, worked with a clinic team attached to the juvenile court in three cities. Under the auspices of the Institute of Human Relations at Yale, they set out to study *family interrelationships* rather than the individual as the focus of their research. To explain why so often one member of a family became delinquent while another did not, they decided to investigate whether the child-parent relationship might have a different meaning for each sibling.

They began by defining the delinquent as a potentially serious offender who could be recognized on the basis of his already repeated delinquent behavior. To be eligible for the study, the families of the delinquents had also to have a nondelinquent child, not more than two years older or younger and of the same sex as the delinquent. In eight families the matched pairs were identical twins. Families which were ineligible for the study were (1) those in which the delinquent was subnormal in intelligence, (2) those in which English was not spoken, and (3) those who were not willing to accept the clinic's offer of help.

This approach was unique in another way. Although the term had not yet been coined, this was "action research." Healy and Bronner believed that one could not really know, much less understand, the dynamics of family interrelationships in a single interview. Consequently, they offered these families a counseling service which would bring them into normal contact with the research staff. In this way, it would be possible to test the hypothesis that the clue to delinquent behavior was in the nature and the quality of the

[14] William Healy and Augusta Bronner, *New Light on Delinquency and Its Treatment*, New Haven, Yale University Press, 1936. Reprinted in 1957.

parent-child relationship. To test this thesis in different types of communities (different with respect both to ethnic groups in the population and to provision for services), guidance clinics were established in connection with the juvenile court in Detroit, Boston, and New Haven.

Using the criteria outlined above—a delinquent with a nondelinquent sibling not more than two years apart in age, of normal intelligence, in an English-speaking family which agreed to come to the clinic for help—the research team succeeded in collecting data on 105 families in the three cities. Some were in comfortable financial circumstances and others had marginal incomes. There were some families of old American stock, and some recent immigrants. Some families were regular in their church attendance, others seldom went to church. Discipline was lax in some families and, in others, strict. And yet in each of these families there was a nondelinquent as well as a delinquent child.

Among the children, there were no marked differences with respect to mental capacity, educational achievement, or physical prowess. Thus, no one of these factors in the children or their families could be considered the cause of the delinquent behavior.

The clinics' contacts revealed that *the only way in which the delinquent differed from his nondelinquent sibling was in the nature of the relationship to their parents.* In 91 per cent of the cases the delinquent child *felt* thwarted and rejected, even though in many instances the parent or parents were unaware either of their own role in the delinquent's concept of himself or of his feeling toward his family.[15]

To illustrate the divergencies in the emotional experiences of the delinquents as compared to the controls, the authors cite three family situations in detail. In one, the German-born father died when the delinquent was three years old; in another, the natural parents and the stepfather were native-born. We quote below the third record, in the form in which the data are presented in the text.

MAC KAY

Scotch-Irish, fairly intelligent, honest parents. Hered. neg, Fa. 38, sickly, intense worker, irritable, great rages, terribly disappointed in U.S. M. 36, unhappy with husb., high temper, over-cleanly, outside employment. Lost property, now tenement in poor district, 4 chrn. Wm. oldest, always much contention abt him, F. whips, M. scolds, says he is like his F., boy snarls but parents curiously ambivalent towards boy. F. fonder of other chrn who are controlled, well-mannered.

[15] *Ibid.*, p. 122.

William—b.1916	James—b.1918
Delqy began at 7. Excess, stlg for yrs. Truancy. Slept away from home for days. Burglaries with companions. Took autos. Became leader of very notorious gang.	Never delqt.
Unhappy pregy. Normal birth, large baby, nursed long but cried much. Hard to manage. Rupture and opern at 3. Appendicitis at 11.	Normal pregy and birth. Smaller, nursed shorter time, quiet baby, abscess of jaw at 4, 2 mos. in hosp.
4 in. short, fair nutr.; strong; infected tonsils. Firm small features, often hard, sullen, aggressive expression.	3 in. short, good nutr.; fair strength; infected tonsils; defec. vision. Pleasant features, friendly expression, passive.
I.Q. 90. Fair sch. work, 1 yr behind. Always hated sch. teachers.	I.Q. 105. In same grade as bro. Fond of sch.
Personality: Very active, restless, impetuous, high-strung, varies quick enthusiasms with being unhappy and non-coop. Much pleasure in leading others. Bitter, cynical abt dishonesty and "pull" everywhere, even in courts. Sometimes well mannered. Befriends unfortunate boys, generous to beggars. Writes terribly vindictive letters even to F. Hates scouts, clubs, scornful of church. Self confident, secretive, suspicious that people "gyp."	Personality: Slow moving, a few good friends, brings them to house. Always friendly and placid. Bookworm. Desires education. Likes clubs, wants to be priest. Always reliable, model boy.

Contrasting Emotional Experiences

Sure for many yrs. that he is rejected and hated; in turn hates all authority. Disgust at family friction and circumstances. Wants love (nice to little sisters). Jealous of bro's standing in family. Once in burst of confidence to us told of long hating F. enough to kill him, of wanting his M's love tho she "snooped" on him; after all he cannot believe that she loves James better, tho F. does.	Satisfied with family relationships tho some contempt for F. when he occ'ly drinks. Avoids family fracas by reading and doing sch. work. Always secure in feeling loved.[16]

[16] Ibid., pp. 125-26.

To illustrate the *interpretation of the meaning of delinquency* to the delinquent, Healy and Bronner cited several other cases, of which we quote below the Laner case, in which, on the surface, all the factors seemed to be favorable.

LANER

F. 50, mechanic, good earner. M. 50, motherly, very good manager and housekeeper. Parents mixed ancestry, came from eastern Can. province. Both healthy, strong characters, high standards, religious, happy marriage, forging ahead, thrifty, intent on chrn having best possible educ'n. Own home. All boys in magazine distributing business under charge of eldest who organized it. Extraordinarily fine ambitious family with much good feeling between them. 4 chrn; 2 eldest boys preparing for college, one younger than Geo. regarded as very promising and somewhat favored on that account. All chrn big, strong, good looking.

George—b.1915	*Donald—b.1914*
1 yr ago stole fancy skates. More recently forged and collected on check found in office when delivering magazines, also later opened envelopes in another office and took money. Bought play things mostly.	Always honest, tho knew about skates and kept silent.
Normal dev, history. Long nursing. Always seemed healthy, but fatigues more easily than bros. Overweight for 3 or 4 yrs. Craving for sweets.	Norm. dev. history. Long nursing. Always healthy. Careful eater.
Norm. ht. 50 lbs overwt, high-pitched voice, retarded sex dev. etc. (Bros all early puberty) Diag. by thoro endoctrine study, hypopituitary. Defective vision, no glasses.	Big, strong, stout within normal limits. Good features. Wears glasses.
I.Q. 108 (later 116). Very rapid alert worker. Pleasantly responsive.	I.Q. 99. Very serious worker. Especially good in mech'l tests.
1st yr. H.S., poor marks, well liked.	2nd yr H.S., taking technical course, doing very well.
Personality: Active but tires easily, impulsive, changeable, pleasure loving, talkative, care-free, frank, different from bros in these respects, even-tempered. Worked in bro's business since 9, little time for companionship.	Personality: Active, steady, quiet, planful, studies hard, reserved, inarticulate, ambitious. Worked in bro's business since 10, little time for companionship.

Interpretations: For 2 or 3 yrs mainly on acct endocrine disorder Geo. has felt inadequate to meet high ambitions of family who have tried to spur him on. Has felt different and isolated in fam. circle. Attempt to get substitutive satisfactions thru stlg money for young boyish possessions which according to family standards were silly and useless. . . . Felt thwarted in normal desires and impulses, fond of sports but no time to indulge. Worked outside sch. for yrs, didn't have such privileges as other boys. Christmas coming, wouldn't have much. Revengeful display of impulsive aggressiveness; he would get things anyhow. . . . Strongly felt discriminated against; younger bro., "a popular hero," favored. Discouraged abt. it. Hostile attitude for a time; knocked his bro. about. Then ephemeral floundering aggressive impulses to get compensatory satisfactions thru having his own pleasures.[17]

While Healy and Bronner's study contributes to the understanding of the problem of delinquency and suggests conditions under which treatment is likely to succeed,[18] the authors state that their findings do *not* answer the important question—*why the delinquent sibling chose aggressive behavior* as his method of expressing dissatisfaction in his parental relationships.

It would be interesting to know what happened subsequently to both siblings in these 105 families. Unfortunately, however, little research in the field of delinquency builds in as orderly a fashion on the work of its predecessors as does research in the physical sciences; and the Healy-Bronner studies have never been followed up.

The Glueck Studies

Without question the most ambitious studies directed to the etiology of delinquency are those of Eleanor and Sheldon Glueck, a lawyer and a social worker. When their earlier studies[19] of children referred to the Judge Baker Foundation Clinic attached to the Boston Juvenile Court revealed discouraging results from the work of the clinic they decided to tackle the antecedent problem—that of causation.

In *Unraveling Juvenile Delinquency*,[20] which was begun in the early 1940s, the Gluecks used matched pairs to discriminate between the characteristics of delinquents and nondelinquents with respect to a series of factors which were assumed to be related (1) to the family, and (2) to individual characteristics of the delinquent.

[17] *Ibid.,* pp. 137-38.
[18] *Ibid.,* Chapters 10-13.
[19] Sheldon and Eleanor Glueck, *One Thousand Juvenile Delinquents: Their Treatment by Court and Clinic,* Cambridge, Harvard University Press, 1934.
[20] Sheldon and Eleanor Glueck, *Unraveling Juvenile Delinquency,* New York, The Commonwealth Fund, 1950.

The delinquents in this study were boys who had been committed by the Boston juvenile court to the Lyman School for Delinquents. The controls were boys of the same age, ethnic group, IQ, and area of residence, who had not been officially designated delinquents.

When the Gluecks were asked why their research design did not build on the work of Healy and Bronner, which was familiar to them, they replied[21] that they were not equipped to offer clinical services as Healy did. It was necessary, therefore, to confine their investigations to institutionalized delinquents, and to use as controls (or, in a stricter sense, as comparisons) nondelinquent Boston school boys. In both instances the Gluecks' subjects were, so to speak, a captive group: The institution arranged for the interviewing and the testing of the delinquent boys; and the cooperation of the Boston school system made it possible to interview and to administer the various physical, psychological, and educational tests to the school boys on school premises.

The Gluecks' study plan included elaborate and painstaking investigations of the backgrounds and characteristics of each of the 500 matched pairs. There was one psychiatric interview, and many psychological tests, including the Bellevue-Wechsler and the Rorschach (ink blot) Tests. Anthropomorphic measurements were taken and physical examinations made.[22] School record cards were carefully analyzed.

As a result of the investigations, the principal characteristics that differentiate the delinquent from his control are described by the Gluecks as follows in a popular volume:

> *Physically,* in being essentially mesomorphic in constitution (i.e., solid, closely knit, muscular); *temperamentally,* in being restlessly energetic, impulsive, extroverted, aggressive, destructive (often sadistic)—traits which may be more or less related to both their bodily structure and their erratic growth pattern with its physiologic correlates or consequences;
>
> *In attitude,* in being hostile, defiant, resentful, suspicious, stubborn, socially assertive, adventurous, unconventional, nonsubmissive (or ambivalent) to authority;
>
> *Intellectually,* in tending to direct and concrete rather than symbolic, abstract intellectual expression and in being less methodical in their approach to problems;
>
> *Socioculturally,* in having been reared to a far greater extent than the nondelinquents in homes of little understanding, affection, stability, or moral fiber, by parents usually unfit to be effective guides and protectors or desirable symbols for emulation; and under conditions unfavor-

[21] In a conversation with the author in 1940.
[22] See discussion of body types, Chapter 5.

able to the building of a well-balanced and socially adequate character and conscience (superego).

It is particularly in the exciting, stimulating, but little controlled, and culturally inconsistent environment of the urban underprivileged area that such boys readily tend to give expression to their untamed impulses and their self-centered desires by "kicking over the traces" of conventionally dictated behavior.[23]

The Gluecks conclude that: "These tendencies are apparently anchored deeply in body and mind and essentially derive from malformations of personality and character during the first few years of life." This is, however, a conclusion which, most psychiatrists would agree, could hardly be revealed in one psychiatric interview.

The Gluecks note that there were exceptions in each of these categories; i.e., there were ectomorphic rather than mesomorphic, and introverted rather than extroverted, delinquents; and there were nondelinquents who had been reared in immoral and criminalistic homes. Although they admit that a study of these atypical groups might lead to modifications of their hypothesis, nevertheless they claim their description of characteristics which appear to distinguish delinquents from nondelinquents is: "a giant stride in the study of causation that should be of great help to the clinician who has to deal with the individual case."[24]

As might be expected in view of the monumental effort and amount of money invested in this study by this noted team of investigators, there have been many reactions to these findings—some laudatory, some critical.[25]

Some of the criticisms are the following:

1. The factors which the Gluecks call the attributes of delinquents are those which observation of court procedures and careful perusal of probation records reveal *are likely* to determine commitment to an institution. For example, if a judge knows that the boy before him comes from a broken home, that his mother works, that the boy is aggressive and often truant, he is likely to order commitment. Thus the Gluecks' definition of a delinquent excludes boys whose antisocial behavior results in probation instead of commitment, even when the behavior may have been identical. It also obviously excludes those whose antisocial acts never reach the attention of the court.

[23] Sheldon and Eleanor Glueck, *Delinquents in the Making, Paths to Prevention,* New York, Harper, 1952, pp. 185 ff.

[24] *Ibid.,* p. 187; see also Chapter 12 for Pierce's discussion of the need for distinguishing between a definition and an empirical proposition.

[25] See Morris Ploscowe, Paul W. Tappan, Marion E. Kenworthy, E. Wesley Duperius, Robert M. Lindner, Justine Wise Polier, Henry W. Holmes, Edwin B. Wilson, "A Symposium on *Unraveling Juvenile Delinquency,*" *The Harvard Law Review,* Vol. 64, no. 6 (April 1951), pp. 1027-41; also, Sol Rubin, "Illusions in a Research Project Using Pairs," *The American Journal of Sociology,* Vol. 57, no. 21 (Sept. 1951); and Shaplin and Tiedman, "Comment on the Juvenile Delinquency Prediction Tables," *American Sociological Review,* Vol. 16, no. 4 (Aug. 1951).

2. The Lyman School population is not representative of the various ethnic groups in the total population presumably at risk of delinquent behavior. Only 37 out of 500 have American-born parents; there are no Negroes;[26] and there are only 9 Jewish children out of an estimated contemporary Boston Jewish population of 10,000 families.[27] This disproportion points up a serious shortcoming in the research design.

3. The techniques used in obtaining the data or synthesizing them may have subtly diluted the contributions which each member of the team might otherwise have made. No member of the team except the Gluecks was permitted to know the findings of any other member. Furthermore, proponents of the Rorschach Test as a diagnostic instrument point out that the tests were originally standardized on a quite different group of young people from those included in the Glueck studies, and may not be appropriate when applied to children brought up in slum areas.[28]

If these criticisms are valid, the Gluecks' conclusions add little of value to those of Healy and Bronner, whose study was methodologically superior (1) because they used siblings, and thus were able to hold constant the many environmental factors; (2) because their definition of the delinquent made it possible to cover a much wider range of antisocial behavior than did that of the Gluecks; and (3) because their sample, unlike the Gluecks', was representative of the population at risk.

Prediction Studies

The prediction scales developed by the Gluecks on the basis of the study outlined above are being subjected to a variety of tests on different populations. Among the subjects are some of the cases in the Cambridge-Somerville Youth Survey,[29] and some residents of the Hawthorne Cedar Knolls School.[30]

Another test of the Gluecks' predictive tables when applied to children who have not yet become delinquents is currently under way at the New York City Youth Board.[31] All boys who entered the first grade of two public elementary schools in the academic year 1952-53 are the subject of this

[26] There is no reference to Negroes in the index of the study.

[27] See Appendix B, pp. 297-304, of Glueck, *Unraveling Juvenile Delinquency*, for a complete list of cases.

[28] Dr. A. Schachtel, in a conversation with the author.

[29] Richard Thompson, "A Validation of the Gluecks' Social Prediction Scale," *Journal of Criminal Law and Criminology*, Vol. 43, no. 4 (Nov.-Dec. 1952), pp. 451-71.

[30] Selma Glick and Bertram Black, "Recidivism at Hawthorne-Cedar Knolls School," Research Monogram Number 2, New York, Jewish Board of Guardians, 1952; and Sidney Axelrod and Selma Glick, "Application of the Glueck Social Prediction Table to 100 Jewish Delinquent Boys," *The Jewish Social Quarterly*, Vol. 30, no. 2 (Winter 1953); see also Chapter 28.

[31] Ralph W. Whelan, "An Experiment in Predicting Delinquency," *The Journal of Criminal Law, Criminology, and Police Science*, Vol. 45, no. 4 (Nov.-Dec. 1954), pp. 432-41.

study. Situated four blocks apart, these schools serve neighborhoods with large proportions of Negro and Puerto Rican families. Out of the 236 children on whom data were originally obtained, 224 remained in the study in 1954. Negroes accounted for 58 per cent of the group, Puerto Ricans for 18 per cent. Among the 24 per cent who were white, about one-half were Jewish. Clearly this group was quite different in its composition from that on which the Gluecks' original prediction scales were built.

Five weighted scores were used in the Youth Board study to determine the proneness to delinquency. They related to: (1) the discipline of the boy by his father; (2) his supervision by his mother; (3) the father's affection for the boy; (4) the affection of the mother for the boy; and (5) the cohesiveness of the family. The data for construction of these five scores were derived from interviews conducted with the children's parents in their homes, interviews with teachers, and collateral information from social agencies to which the families were known.

Marked on this scale, approximately one third of the 224 boys achieved a failure score of 250 points or more—the cutting-off point between potential delinquency and nondelinquency. A little less than half (31) of the high-chance delinquent group were referred for treatment to the child guidance clinic. The research design called for annual follow-ups to determine whether, how, and when a boy in either the treated or untreated group begins to show the first signs of delinquency.

In the spring of 1956, some children were added from the entering classes in the two original schools as well as older kindergarten children in two neighboring schools, to provide a group which was somewhat more like that in which the scales had originally been developed.[32] The Youth Board group, however, still differed from the Glueck group in that Italians instead of Irish and English children predominated among the white children and, four years after the project was set up, the children were still six years younger than those in the Glueck study.

As of the 1958 follow-up,[33] 70 per cent of the boys who had then been observed for six years were considered normal; about 17 per cent had been problems in school, and 30 per cent were showing either neurotic or predelinquent symptoms. Negro and Puerto Rican children were overrepresented in the negative categories of school problems and predelinquent traits. With respect to the prediction scores, almost 93 per cent were reacting in conformity with the prediction.[34]

[32] *Delinquency Predictions—a Progress Report, 1952-1956,* Research Dept., New York City Youth Board, July 1957, Table 2, p. 10.

[33] Maud M. Craig, "Six Years of a Validation Experiment on the Glueck Social Factors Prediction Table of Juvenile Delinquency," speech delivered at American Association for the Advancement of Science, Washington, Dec. 28, 1958. Mimeographed.

[34] *Ibid.,* p. 8.

Despite this apparent confirmation of the Gluecks' scales, Mrs. Craig notes that "it is much too soon to reach any definite conclusions on the validity of this instrument." This type of research presents many problems. There is difficulty not only in holding on to the families but in retaining a well-trained staff. *Without the assurance of such a staff,* it is difficult to evaluate data collected from such a wide variety of sources as police, school, and parents (usually mothers), each of whom may have many reasons for not cooperating fully. In these respects both the Gluecks' original investigation and Healy and Bronner's study had many advantages not shared by the current Youth Board project.

A New Direction in Delinquency Research

Erikson's Approach

Combining the disciplines of psychiatry and anthropology, Erik Erikson has recently[35] set forth a provocative new approach to understanding delinquency.

He sees antisocial behavior as a result of crises which the child faces in the process of developing his sense of identity. He suggests that the way in which the child experiences these crises will largely determine his adult adjustment.

When the child first becomes aware as a tiny infant that he and his environment are separate, he realizes that he is dependent on persons and objects for the satisfaction of his needs. If his environment proves trustworthy, i.e., if he can depend upon it to supply his needs, he will have jumped his first hurdle toward adult security. Subsequent crises arise before he goes to school. How far has he a right to be himself? Can he exercise initiative and imagination? Can he accomplish what he sets out to do?

At adolescence boys and girls, facing increasing physiological and social demands, are again unsure of themselves. Each asks himself again and again: Will I grow up to be the kind of adult I want to be and that others want me to be? For a psychologically healthy adulthood, the youth must achieve a firm sense of *ego identity*, i.e., "a persistent sameness within oneself and a persistent sharing of some kind of essential character with others.

The opposite of ego identity is *ego diffusion*. The sense of diffusion, a characteristic of adolescence, has many aspects which irritate or worry

[35] Erik Erikson, "The Problem of Identity," *Journal*, American Psychiatric Association, Vol. 4, no. 1 (Jan. 1956), pp. 56-121; see also Helen L. Witmer and Ruth Kotinsky (eds.), "New Perspectives for Research on Juvenile Delinquency," a report of a conference on the relevance and interrelation of certain concepts from sociology and psychiatry for delinquency, Washington, U. S. Children's Bureau, 1956.

adults, most of whom have long since forgotten their own adolescent waverings. If the adult misinterprets the adolescent's behavior, he may unwittingly drive him into delinquency.

Erikson cites several readily recognizable ways in which adolescent ego diffusion manifests itself.

1. The adolescent's sense of time is diffused. One moment he is desperately eager to act, the next he appears almost unable to move. Erikson suggests that these opposite reactions flow from the adolescent's basic distrust of his ability to fulfill his desires.

2. Adolescents are preoccupied with how they look to themselves and to others. This makes them seem both vain and touchy. Advice and criticism do not seem to penetrate their defenses against a feeling of shame at being exposed, or their doubts about their autonomy.

3. As a corollary of the adolescent's vacillation and preoccupation with looks, some assume poses and roles—for example, being fat or being "bad"—which are directly at variance with their parents' aspirations for them. Erikson believes the adolescent must be granted the right to experiment in his search for what he wishes to become. Some highly gifted youths go through a period of "work-paralysis" which Erikson interprets as reflecting a deep sense of uncertainty about their potential.

4. The sexual behavior of adolescents is usually rather selfish. They cannot conceive that they may have both male and female interests. They are thus unable, until the adolescent crisis resolves itself in a firm sense of ego identity, to develop true intimacy with another human being.

5. Because in emancipating himself from his parents he cannot allow himself to depend on older persons for guidance, the adolescent typically has trouble with the question of authority, i.e., who bosses whom and when? He must learn both to lead and to be led under appropriate circumstances.

6. In order to firm up their own sense of themselves, adolescents tend to be uncompromising in their prejudices and belligerently loyal to the ideas and values of their own group. There is a tendency to total commitment and to commitment to extremes.

As Erikson points out, there are, of course, biological as well as social factors which at each stage will influence the child's development. However, to achieve a firm sense of himself and his environment, he needs to be sure that the people who mean most to him value him highly.

It is not too difficult to see a connection between these characteristics of adolescence, as described by Erikson, and some delinquent behavior. As an individual, the delinquent may be experimenting with a role which he is just trying out or dreaming about, as in Tolstoy's reminiscence. Unfortunately, the adult does not know it is an experiment and often takes it more seriously than the adolescent himself. This may, if other circumstances reinforce the tendency, confirm the youth in a negative role.

Erikson sees a connection between the adolescent's experimenting with fantasy and reality and some delinquent behavior. In comparison with their parents' own youth, children today lack opportunities for creative and meaningful participation. Mechanical devices, spectator sports, and the sedentary aspects of much of modern living have deprived these young people of natural stepping stones to adulthood. As a result some have turned to delinquent behavior as an alternative while others withdraw to fantasy.

Gang membership, as we shall see in Chapter 9, often helps the vacillating youth to act. It reinforces his sense of identity. His assignments in the gang overcome the feeling of work paralysis, and as a gang member he can safely assert his masculinity and his defiance of authority.

Erikson's suggestions for preventing some of the negative results of the adolescent crisis in a machine-dominated urban middle-class society are:

1. A psychological moratorium (endorsed also by Fritz Redl, whose ideas are investigated in Chapter 24) should be declared by the adults involved in the adolescent's life. Between childhood and adulthood, it would be appropriate for the young person to try out various patterns of identity to find that which suited him best and also to experiment with different work roles. The significant adults—parents, teachers, clergymen—have to learn to be less fearful that the trial role, of which the adult may disapprove, is destined to be the youth's final choice.

For the middle-class boy and girl, college life away from home often provides such a moratorium. Removed from the pressure of the family, youths can decide what they want to do. Forestry camps (see Chapter 19) also offer some opportunity, as does military service under peacetime conditions.

2. A truly imperative need, definitely recognized by detached workers with boys' groups (see Chapter 29) is to provide opportunity—which the simpler rural society offered almost automatically—for adolescents to achieve recognition in useful work.[36] Various kinds of work apprenticeships might be developed if the unions would not object. It has recently been reported that such an apprenticeship plan has been worked out in Philadelphia with the cooperation of the unions.

3. Adolescents should be encouraged to consort with their peers *without* adult direction. If adult direction can be kept at the merest minimum, peer groups will provide opportunities for all kinds of experimentation that should contribute to healthy adulthood.

As Witmer points out,[37] these challenging ideas of Erikson "derive from

[36] Some such opportunities are currently offered the Israeli youth in their settlements and in the defense army.

[37] Speech by Helen L. Witmer at the Tenth Anniversary Conference, New York City Youth Board, Waldorf Astoria, October 8, 1957.

theory and clinical observation. They await demonstration." Like the causal explanations discussed earlier in this chapter, they represent "that middle phase that looks backward to what has already been learned and forward to what has yet to be proved."

Summary

The psychiatric explanations of delinquency stem from the pioneering work of Sigmund Freud, who substantiated the role of the unconscious in determining the individual's behavior. He is credited also with developing a method, the use of transference, to replace the reliance on logic as a motive force in changing behavior.

Among the psychologists Aichorn has built on Freud's theory. Among the few psychiatrists who have so far been concerned with delinquents, Friedlander and Eissler have developed their own explanations, and Jenkins and David M. Levy have offered challenging typologies. Jenkins describes two basic types of delinquents—the adaptive, whose behavior is goal-directed, and the maladaptive, whose behavior represents response to frustration. Each type has different social and physical characteristics and each calls for a different approach. David M. Levy differentiates the social pathological delinquent from the child whose delinquency reflects a disturbance in the parent-child relationship and the one whose delinquency is mainly due to some inner psychological disturbance in the child himself. Each of these types, too, calls for a different treatment approach. The extent to which this is recognized in our practice will be discussed in later chapters.

Psychiatric studies of the cause and treatment of delinquency based on clinical material in which the definition of the problem, the choice of the method, and the inferences from the data meet the criteria for adequate evaluation are few and far between. While the studies of the Gluecks and of Healy and Bronner represent the most notable examples of efforts in this direction, that of Healy and Bronner appears sounder in method and design.

Efforts of the New York City Youth Board to validate the Glueck prediction scales based on *Unraveling Juvenile Delinquency* pose many questions with respect to comparability of populations, method of selecting samples, and the adequacy of the information assembled.

Erik Erikson, whose training includes psychiatry and anthropology, offers a new way of looking at individual as well as group delinquency. He suggests that delinquent behavior occurs because of gaps in personality development of all young people, healthy and unhealthy alike. At adolescence the youth re-experiences the insecurity and diffusion of identity which is the lot of most infants. The significant adults often fail to understand the infant's need for security, the growing child's need for acceptance, and the adolescent's need to experiment in many ways and to divorce himself from adult control. As a consequence, the adults' reactions to a young person's behavior may precipitate his choice of a negative role. In other words, the youth may become a delinquent in response to society's expectations. In suggesting change in our accustomed responses to the adolescent, Erikson advocates more provision for useful and important work experience for the adolescent in our highly mechanized society.

CHAPTER 7

Sociological Approaches:
I. Ecology, Role, and Class

IN THE LAST FOUR DECADES SOCIOLOGISTS HAVE BEEN INCREASINGLY INTER-
ested in applying the concepts of ecology, class, and role to an understanding
of such socially deviant behavior as delinquency. In discussing the major
studies which have used these concepts singly or in combination with others
as relevant explanations for delinquency, we confine ourselves here to
explorations of individual delinquent behavior. The applications of these
newer sociological concepts to group delinquency, exemplified by the troublesome anti-social gang, are considered in Chapter 9.

Ecology and Delinquency

Ecology, as the student of plant and animal life will recognize, is concerned with the effect of the physical surroundings, especially the soil, climate,
and sunlight, on the growth and development of organisms. Assuming an
analogy in human development, Burgess and Park in the 1920s applied the
ecological approach to a study of Chicago.[1] Using the Loop area as a nexus,
they schematized the city's expansion by a series of concentric circles, and
studied the spatial distributions therein of a variety of social phenomena.
These studies were the logical precursors of later studies by Shaw and others

---

[1] Robert E. Park, Ernest W. Burgess, and Roderick D. McKenzie, *The City, The
Ecological Approach to the Study of the Human Community*, Chicago, University of
Chicago Press, 1925.

that related delinquency to the growth of the city. The ecological explanation of delinquency was an important contribution of the so-called Chicago School, which though subject to the criticisms discussed in this chapter, provided a useful body of information and still exerts a hold in delinquency theory.

Breckenridge and Abbott's "Delinquent Neighborhoods"

The first spot map of delinquents antedates the work of Shaw, Park, and Burgess. Breckenridge and Abbott,[2] as pioneer social workers, who had fought for the juvenile court, were appalled by the increasing stream of delinquents in Chicago in the early 1900s. To highlight the geographic concentration of delinquents, they spotted on the city map the residence of each child who appeared before the juvenile court in the ten-year period between the court's initiation, in July 1899, and June 30, 1909. Their tabulations made note of the number of times each individual was arraigned, his sex, age, and color.

In describing the areas of concentration as "delinquent neighborhoods," Breckenridge and Abbott wrote:

> The region from which the children of the court chiefly come is the densely populated West Side, and the most conspicuous centers of "delinquency" in this section have been the congested wards which lie along the river and the canals—a large tenement and lodging-house district lying between two branches of the river and between wide and unsightly stretches of railroad tracks, and enclosed by a dense, semi-circular beltline of manufacturing and commercial plants.[3]

In their opinion the slight variation in the numbers of children from this neighborhood who were referred to the court over the ten-year period reflected changes either in the law or in the attitude of the community toward the court, rather than actual changes in the incidence of the behavior itself.[4] They called special attention to the temptation that the railroad tracks offered the children. It was their belief that the railroad company's fluctuating policy—insufficient supervision followed by periods of too strict supervision—went far to explain the variation in the number of arrests.[5]

Shaw's "Delinquency Area" Theory

In the 1920s, to test the relation between the geographic base and the occurrence of delinquency, Clifford R. Shaw, a probation officer, plotted on

[2] Sophonisba P. Breckenridge and Edith Abbott, *The Delinquent Child and the Home*, introduction by Julia Lathrop, New York, Russell Sage Foundation, 1912.
[3] *Ibid.*, p. 150.
[4] *Ibid.*, pp. 22 ff.
[5] *Ibid.*, p. 33.

the map of Chicago the geographic distribution of truants, juvenile delinquents, and adult offenders, covering the period from 1900 to 1927.[6] Shaw's
procedures differed somewhat from those of Breckenridge and Abbott. He
translated the number of delinquency petitions in each of the series he used
into: (1) *area* rates for each of the 110 square-mile census tracts; (2) *zone*
rates for census tracts grouped in concentric semi-circles a mile wide, considering the Loop area as the center of the city; (3) *radial* rates, i.e., rates
along the main thoroughfares which radiate from the Loop to the outskirts
of the city. Shaw's main findings were the following:

1. The area rates of school truants, juvenile delinquents, and adult
criminals vary markedly. In general, the nearer a given locality is to the
center of the city the higher will be its delinquency and crime rate.

2. The differences in rates reflect differences in community backgrounds.
High rates occur in the areas characterized by physical deterioration and
declining population.

3. The main high-rate areas of the city—those near the Loop, around
the stockyards and the South Chicago steel mills—are characterized by high
rates over a long period, notwithstanding the fact that the ethnic composition
of the population has changed markedly.

4. Delinquents living in areas of high delinquency rates are the most
likely to become recidivists, and among all recidivists, they are likely to
appear in court at least three times as often as those from areas with low
rates.

Shaw concluded that the decrease in delinquency rates from the Loop
to the peripheral areas of the city proved that delinquency was primarily
a function of the change of an area from residence to business. He described
such a changing area as interstitial.

Subsequently Shaw and McKay applied the same technique to the
distribution of delinquency cases in Philadelphia, Richmond, Cleveland,
Birmingham, Denver, and Seattle.[7] In spite of many differences in these
cities, as for example the relative percentages of foreign-born or Negroes in
the population, Shaw claimed that the configuration of the data followed the
pattern in the Chicago study, i.e., that the delinquency rate decreased from
the general business district to the periphery of the city.[8]

Applying a similar process with the cooperation of the New York State
Crime Commission, Shulman[9] studied the spatial distribution of young male

[6] Clifford R. Shaw, *Delinquency Areas*, Chicago, University of Chicago Press, 1929.
[7] Clifford R. Shaw and Henry D. McKay, "Social Factors in Juvenile Delinquency,"
in *Report on the Causes of Crime*, Vol. 2, no. 13, National Commission on Law Observance and Enforcement, Washington, 1931.
[8] *Ibid.*, p. 187.
[9] *The Youthful Offender: A Statistical Study of Crime among the 16-20 Year
Age Group in New York City*, New York, the Subcommittee on Causes and Effects of
Crime, 1931.

offenders in New York City. He distributed the addresses of the 16- to 20-year-old male offenders in New York City in 1929 according to residence, and calculated health area rates for comparable age groups in the population. Shulman described New York City's delinquency areas as follows:

1. [They are] . . . primarily areas of decreasing population.
2. A majority of these areas of severe delinquency are central rather than peripheral, being located in congested areas combining commerce, manufacturing and housing rather than peripheral residential areas.
3. . . . . delinquency throughout the city is in general distributed in irregular zones, most dense in Manhattan Borough and with certain exceptions less dense toward the peripheral suburbs.[10]

SHORTCOMINGS OF SHAW'S STUDIES. Although the findings of these and many subsequent delinquency area studies appear to agree with those of Shaw and McKay, their conclusions are subject to question for the following reasons:

1. Shaw's delinquency rates included in their numerators the considerable proportion (30 to 40 per cent) of cases before the juvenile court which were later dismissed, i.e., cases in which the allegations were not sustained. This process is similar to including in a disease rate all persons whose illness may have been mistakenly diagnosed.
2. No attention was paid to the differential distribution of the police in various sectors of the city, which obviously affects the rate of apprehension of delinquents.
3. In many communities in which there are unofficial agencies to which misbehaving young people may be referred, the official juvenile court figures understimate the amount of deviant behavior in the community. If these agencies cater to special groups in the community, such as one or another religious group, they will deflect the children of these groups from court attention.
4. Communities differ with respect to the ethnic homogeneity of their population. This in turn affects the extent to which the mores of the dominant population coincide or conflict with those of the newcomers.

The way in which provisions for dealing with antisocial behavior by different ethnic groups, can affect official registration of delinquent behavior is illustrated in the official statistics for New York City in 1930. Despite an estimated equal distribution of New York City's 1930 population, the ratio of officially delinquent Catholic children to Jewish children was 3 to 1, and of white Catholics to white Protestants, 7 to 1.[11]

Yet when one considered the variety of offenses included in the juvenile

10 *Ibid.*, p. 126.
11 Sophia M. Robison, *Can Delinquency Be Measured?*, New York, Columbia University Press, 1936, Appendix C, Table 52, p. 228.

court code, it was hardly reasonable to assume that any one ethnic or religious group had a monopoly on all these types of behavior. As a matter of record, when the unofficial Jewish cases were tabulated, the total rose to almost 1000, or almost twice the number known to the court or the police. Neither the Catholic nor the Protestant Big Brother organizations assigned *professional* staff to the courts. In consequence they were not able to siphon off cases of children of their faith from the court's official rolls, as the professionals from the Jewish agencies could and often did.

5. The use of the concentric residence zones is inappropriate in many cities because of the irregular outlines or the geographic configurations due to bays and rivers. The concentric zones in New York City, for example, would be significantly altered depending upon the choice of the base center of population growth—the Battery, Harlem, or Brooklyn, each of which was an early center of the city's population. The fact that the geographic center of New York City is a cemetery in the Borough of Queens suggests that a delinquency area *zone* map is inappropriate in New York City (unless the dead rise).

6. Shaw's assumption that all immigrant groups break up in the first area of settlement is not supported by the facts. For example, the Chinese community in New York City appears to be remaining intact, perhaps because other immigrants have not sought to replace them.

Ghetto patterns, moreover, are not uniform. Negro ghettos, Italian ghettos, and Jewish ghettos impose different types of restrictions and controls on their inhabitants and, as we shall see in Chapter 11, not all ghetto inhabitants act alike. The major problem may not be the ghetto aspect but rather the mixture or the conflict of one culture with another, and the pressure upon the young generation to conform to the standards of their peer group rather than of their parents.

7. The most disturbing contradiction to Shaw's theory is that his figures for Chicago do not support it, either quantitatively or qualitatively. Application of the tests for significant differences to area and zone rates in the Chicago study revealed that the only mathematically significantly different rates were those for the two extremes: the Loop area (which covered three census tracts) and the district furthest from the center of the city, which covered many times that number of census tracts. Only the Italian group in Chicago had a higher rate of delinquency, both in the earlier and later periods, than might be expected on the basis of the percentage of its child population in the total.[12] A striking contradiction to Shaw's predictions was the consistently high rate of delinquency among the Chicago Negroes regardless of where they were living.

Apparently, the significance of the interstitial area—marked by high

12 *Ibid.*, p. 172.

density of population, low family income, inferior housing, and civic neglect—needs to be re-examined. An interstitial neighborhood inhabited by one immigrant group produces quite different behavior from that inhabited by another. The "residuum of the defeated, leaderless and helpless," which Shaw says is characteristic of interstitial areas and responsible for delinquency, does not appear to have produced a disproportionate number of delinquents among the children of the earlier immigrant groups who have remained in the area.

It should be noted that Shaw himself later used the case study method in The Jack Roller[13] to supplement his ecological approach. The insights thus acquired became the basis for the area project approach to the control of delinquency (see Chapter 27).

As might be expected, in the decades following Shaw's delinquency area studies and Robison's critique, sociologists began to suggest other ways of looking at the relationship between crime and delinquency in an interstitial area or a slum. Reckless, Lander, and Whyte all went into the slum to learn, if they could, what variables (besides those suggested by Shaw) might affect the patterns of behavior in such an area.[14]

Variations in Self-Concept in Delinquency Areas

Reckless and his associates[15] asked why some boys who live in high delinquency areas appear to develop a resistance to delinquent behavior, even in the most adverse social setting. The sixth-grade teachers in each public school in the sixteen Columbus census tracts which contributed the greatest number of white delinquents to court or police records agreed to cooperate in the search for answers. Each teacher nominated two sets of boys as (1) those least likely to get into trouble, and (2) those most likely to become known to the court or the police. The teachers then gave the reasons for their selections.

The thirty teachers listed 192 boys (about half the sixth-grade pupils in their schools). Some listed only one or two boys, others a much larger number. The average was six. Of the original list, 108 boys were interviewed and tested. While some of both sets of nominees were already in trouble, search of the records revealed that the "good" boys—the potentially insulated ones—

13 Clifford R. Shaw, The Jack Roller, Chicago, University of Chicago Press, 1930.
14 See also next chapter for discussion of Jephcott and Carter's study of slum families in England.
15 Walter C. Reckless, Simon Dinitz, and Barbara Kay, "The Self Component in Potential Delinquency and Potiental Non-Delinquency," American Sociological Review, Vol. 22, no. 5 (Oct. 1957), pp. 566-70; and Walter C. Reckless, Simon Dinitz, and Ellen Murray, "The Self Concept as an Insulator Against Delinquency," American Sociological Review, Vol. 21, no. 6 (Dec. 1956), pp. 744-46.

had been involved in fewer or less serious offenses than the potentially delinquent nominees of the teachers.

Interviews with the boys and their mothers showed agreement in major items. Supplementary tests provided scores for each boy in the delinquency vulnerability and social responsibility scales developed in the Gough California Psychological Inventory.

The average delinquency vulnerability score of the insulated, or "good," boys was lower and their social responsibility score was higher than the corresponding scores for the "bad" boys. The good boy did not expect to be brought to court, he wanted to avoid trouble, he liked school, he wanted to conform to his parents' standards, and he usually considered these reasonable.

The mothers of the good boys knew *how* and *where* and *with whom* their children spent their leisure time. They also saw fewer occasions which demanded physical punishment than did the parents of the bad boys. Perhaps naturally, the mothers' descriptions of the home situations and the standards of punishment and bickering were more flattering than those of the boys. The mothers were less satisfied than their sons with the role of the father. The nominees made no distinction between their parents' attitudes, but "the mothers pictured their hubands as being relatively aloof and rigid in their affections and relationships with their sons."

Reckless concluded that if the boy conceives of himself as a socially acceptable individual, and finds his opinion fortified by the belief of his parents and teachers, he is likely to be a good boy regardless of the type of neighborhood in which he lives. Reckless writes that at age 16, well over 95 per cent of these boys had no court record and were planning to continue school.[16] Tests of the measures applied to 1000 Akron 6th–9th grades in 1959 discriminated the "good" from the "bad" in various subgroups (Edwin Sively's forthcoming thesis).

Slums, Delinquency, and Anomie

When Lander sought an explanation of his findings in a delinquency area study of Baltimore in 1939-42, he turned to the concept of anomie.

The word "anomie," derived from the Greek "anomia," originally meant "lack of order." As introduced by the sociologist Durkheim in the nineteenth century, it came to refer to a social milieu in which the collective control by the community of its members has broken down. This breakdown not only liberates the individual from the moral authority of the community but results in a personal disequilibrium which may manifest itself in a variety of anti-social behavior patterns, including suicide. In his famous study of

[16] Frank Scarpitti, *A Follow-up Study of Good Boys in High Delinquency Areas*, M. A. Thesis, The Ohio State University, August 1959.

suicide in France, Durkheim used the concept of anomie as one explanation for the fact that suicide rates appeared to be higher for urban than for rural dwellers, for men than for women, and for single than for married people. In each of these categories—urban, male, single—the adherents of the Protestant denominations (the outgroup in this largely Catholic country) predominated.

Lander, in his study of official delinquents in Baltimore, had started out to see if he could establish a relationship between certain socio-economic variables and the delinquency rate in each of 155 of Baltimore's 157 census tracts.[17] He used the 1939-42 juvenile court appearances as the numerator in the delinquency rate. The denominator was the number of persons of comparable sex and age in the 1940 census. Lander's socio-economic variables were census tract data on (1) characteristics of individuals, such as nativity, color, and number of years of school completed, and (2) characteristics of households such as home ownership, median rental for area, percentage of overcrowding, and substandard conditions.

The first step was a simple correlation of each variable with the delinquency rate. When Lander plotted his results in scatter diagrams, using the delinquency rate for the x-axis and each of the seven variables for the y-axis, he found that the relationships were not uniformly linear. For example, while the delinquency rate for Negroes was high in areas in which Negroes accounted for less than half the population, the rate leveled off as the proportion of Negroes in the population increased. Five of the seven correlations were curvilinear.

In the second step Lander tested the possible interaction among each of the seven socio-economic variables and delinquency. The partial correlations showed that only two of the seven variables (the percentage of home ownership and ratio of nonwhites to whites in each census tract) appeared to be positively associated with delinquency.

The third step, factor analysis—a statistical device which makes it possible to isolate configurations of the variables—yielded two sets of clusters. The first, which Lander called "economic," included the characteristics of individuals, median number of years of school completed, and three of the variables related to housing—median monthly rental, substandard condition, and percentage of overcrowding. The second cluster, which Lander called the anomic, included the delinquency rate, the percentage of owner-occupied homes, and the ratio of nonwhite to white population.

From all of these analyses, Lander concluded that the anomic rather than the economic factors explained the differences in area delinquency rates.

CRITICISMS OF LANDER'S THESIS. This interesting suggestion that the anomie explains the higher delinquency rates in areas where Negro popula-

[17] Bernard Lander, *Toward an Understanding of Juvenile Delinquency,* New York, Columbia University Press, 1954.

tions exist, but in a minority, and rented rather than owned homes prevail, rests, however, on somewhat shaky ground for the following reasons:

1. As has been noted earlier, official statistics of delinquency (with which he worked) are not an adequate index either of its extent or its seriousness.

2. Official delinquents are few in any one census tract in the course of the year. They may, as a matter of fact, be typically contained in one small section of the tract in which there may not be a large proportion of Negroes or rented homes.

3. Home ownership has very different implications, as Lander himself concedes, in different communities. Not only are there many communities in which well-to-do white families prefer to rent rather than to own apartments, but home ownership has an economic basis. Recent studies have shown such a high turnover in owned homes that one cannot assume, as one formerly did, that home ownership is an index of stability. It may instead be an index of shortage in rental housing, as it certainly was during World War II.

4. There is the possibility that Negro offenses are more apt to be subject to official attention when they occur in predominantly white communities than when they are directed against other Negroes in predominantly Negro communities. Thus not anomie but isolation would explain the lower official delinquency rate for Negroes in areas of large Negro population.

Another and important critique of Lander's study is that of Greenwood,[18] who congratulates Lander for his statistical sophistication, but questions the circular reasoning involved in using the concept of anomie to predict delinquency.

The Slum as an Organized System

A somewhat different conclusion from Lander's was reached by William Foote Whyte[19] who, as a research fellow at Harvard University just before World War II, went to live in the North End of Boston. There Italians from Southern Italy and Sicily had replaced the earlier immigrants from Genoa and Ireland. The few Jews remaining in the area in the late 1930s were mainly the proprietors of small dry goods stores. The *paisani* settled on certain streets, and brought along with them the *feste* of their patron saints as well as the tradition of reciprocal help.

As a participant observer, Whyte set out to study the genesis of various

[18] Ernest Greenwood, "New Directions in Delinquency Research, A Commentary on a Study by Bernard Lander," *The Social Science Review,* Vol. 30, no. 2 (June 1956), pp. 147-57.
[19] William Foote Whyte, *Street Corner Society (The Social Structure of an Italian Slum),* enlarged edition, copyright 1955 by the University of Chicago Press.

forms of racketeering and its political implications in "Cornerville." His collaborator, "Doc," a long-time resident of the community and a frequenter of the settlement house, cautioned Whyte to act naturally, not to ask who, what, why, when, and where—all questions to which a reporter would wish answers. If one asked such questions, Doc told him, people would "clam up" on him. If, however, he was accepted because of his friendship with Doc, he would learn the answers in the long run without having to ask questions.

In his day-to-day observations, over a period of about three years, Whyte encountered highly structured relationships in this slum area. He was able to see the ways in which the impact of the group determined whether the individual would conform to the predominant mores of the "in" or the "out" group. He concluded that far from being the disorganized area that it might appear to outsiders, this Boston slum was a highly organized society. We shall return to a discussion of some of Whyte's other findings in the next section of this chapter.

Role and Class as Explanations of Delinquency

Concern with the possible relation between an individual's behavior and his class status has increasingly overshadowed the previous emphasis among sociologists on the slum as a primary precipitant in delinquency. Moreover, many of these sociologists have turned the spotlight on the role (ascribed or achieved) which an individual plays in the social system as a conditioning factor in behavior. From this point of view, although different motives may precipitate similar behavior, the individual's basic personality pattern is formed by the socialization processes centered in the family in each subgroup in a particular society. While role and class are obviously interrelated, they are sometimes discussed in the following pages as though they were separate aspects of behavior.

The Basic Roles

Granted that social systems change in different ways and at different rates of speed, the four basic positions or roles in the family, those of father, mother, son, daughter, are universally associated with some system of specific functions—i.e., obligations and rights. In this sense, as Linton puts it,[20] a role is a pattern of behavior which corresponds to a system of rights and duties which are associated with a particular position in a social group. If the various social roles are clearly defined and articulated, the group can and

[20] Ralph Linton, "Status and Role," *The Study of Man,* New York, Appleton-Century, 1936.

probably will function as a unit because, in the main, the goals of the individual and of the collective group do not conflict. Thus status and role expectations, in simple, self-contained societies that are left undisturbed, combine in defining for the individual how he shall behave.

Initially, each of us learns our role or roles in living up to the expectations of parents and siblings. Subsequently we learn to conform to the expectations of persons outside the primary group, i.e., teachers, ministers, friends, colleagues, and so forth. In most societies, the "ascribed" status results from the facts of sex, age, and class. There is, however, also an "achieved" status, one which may be earned through one's own efforts or those of other persons. Both types of status vary appreciably in different societies.

Industrialization brought about not only the growth of cities, with what Clifford Shaw calls their "interstitial areas," but also changes in the roles of individuals. In rural communities and towns which were small enough for everybody to know everybody else, it was comparatively easy for parents to induct children into performing clearly labeled functions appropriate for their present roles as well as preparatory for their future roles. In today's more complex industrialized communities, however, many mothers have added bread-winning to their duties, and conversely some men have added housework to theirs. Such changes in function have been speeded up by the impact of new groups with differing conceptions of role and class, and by wars and economic crises which have interrupted and interfered with the pursuit of orderly living.

With respect to the former, America, as the haven of the oppressed from many lands and the open-sesame to wealth for the adventurous foreigner, has become the home of successive waves of immigrants who have brought with them codes of behavior often at variance with those of the earlier comers. With respect to the second disrupting factor, in the last one hundred years Americans have lived through the Civil War, the Spanish-American War, the Mexican War, World War I, World War II, the Korean War, and now the "cold" war. In between they have weathered the economic depressions and recessions of 1872, 1893, 1907, 1919, 1929, 1946, 1949, and 1957. The wars, the busts, and the subsequent booms have had some effect on class lines and perhaps have created greater competition for the rewards of achievement. Our special concern, however, is with the effect of these economic shifts on our ideas of "proper" and "improper" behavior for boys and girls, rich or poor.

Role Determinants in Delinquency

Chapter 1 pointed out that some of the specific *forms* as well as the *amount* of recorded delinquent behavior varied for boys and girls in our society. These differences are underscored by marked discrepancies in the ratio of apprehended boys to girls, on the average, 5 or 6 to 1. Rarely are boys accused of irregular sex activities or ungovernable behavior—the main reason for referring girls to court. Boys, however, are more often truant, and more often apprehended for stealing. Yet there is no reason to assume that girls are inherently more honest than boys. It seems more likely that only that behavior of girls is officially labeled delinquent which is inconsistent with the female role as defined by conventional American society and reinforced by the mothers.

Tangential evidence of the major role of the mother in the official labeling of girls as delinquent has recently been offered by Wattenberg and Saunders.[21] In their study of cases known to the Youth Bureau of the Detroit Police Department, they found that recidivism among the girls was significantly associated with friction between the girls and their parents or the school representative. In comparison with the boys, the behavior of the girls was more frequently affected by their relationships within the home, particularly with their mothers.[22]

Grosser suggests that appropriate role-function of the male and female explains the widely different incidence of stealing among adolescent boys and girls. He analyzed 200 cases of boys and girls referred to the Boston Juvenile Court in 1949 for stealing, using as his frame of reference the hypothesis of Parsons and Merton that deviant behavior is at least in part a product "of selective adherence to accepted social norms and occurs in areas of specific structural strains in a social system. . . . Since delinquent behavior never exhausts the total range of behavior of an offender, it was assumed that it would tend to be integrated with other role-appropriate behavior in the same sense that any specifically selected action pattern must be integrated."[23]

Following this line of analysis, Grosser differentiated three types of stealing patterns which he describes as follows: (1) role-supportive, i.e., stealing oriented toward the acquisition of objects for utilitarian purposes; (2) role-expressive, i.e., stealing oriented toward the commission of the act in its social context; (3) symptomatic, i.e., stealing equivalent to neurotic substitute gratification. Stealing in the cases of boys brought to the Boston court appeared to be predominantly role-expressive; i.e., it expressed their idea of the male adolescent's role. In contrast, stealing among the girls was predominantly utilitarian, role-supportive.

This difference, Grosser feels, reflects the concern of adolescent boys

[21] William W. Wattenberg and Frank Saunders, "Recidivism Among Girls," *Journal of Abnormal and Social Psychology*, Vol. 50, no. 3 (May 1955), pp. 405-406.
[22] See Toby's comments on the broken home, Chapter 8.
[23] George Grosser, "A Study in the Sex Specificity of Juvenile Delinquency," a speech delivered at the August 1955 annual meeting of the American Sociological Society in Washington, D.C., based on the doctoral dissertation: *Juvenile Delinquency and Contemporary American Sex Roles*, Cambridge, Harvard University Press, 1952.

and girls with the roles society expects them to perform. If a girl steals, she does so most often to acquire clothing, jewelry, or trinkets which she hopes will enhance her appeal as a female. When a boy steals, the act itself in some degree enhances his prowess as a male. To put it differently, stealing indulged in by a girl is not an end in itself, but only a means to an end. But when a girl steals, her behavior conflicts with the norms of her other relationships. Ordinarily, she will not acknowledge the thefts to either boy or girl companions, and of course hides them from her family. The boy, on the other hand, can boast of his exploits, since they are consistent with the other accepted features of the masculine adolescent role, usually expressed in nondelinquent activities.

This conflict between acts and roles, in Grosser's opinion, explains the reported higher rate of sex offenses among girls than among boys in the official statistics. Grosser rejects, as we do, the explanations of the difference in delinquency rates among boys and girls as "due to the innate moral superiority of women or the differential environmental pressures on boys and girls." Such explanation, he claims, fails to take account of the different actions of boys and girls who are exposed to similar environmental pressures.

While one may agree with Grosser that the consideration of the social roles is important in understanding the type of behavior labeled delinquent, one needs also to take into account the social response of adults to a girl's behavior when it takes the form of sex irregularity or disobedience, and the differing social roles of both boys and girls in varying ethnic groups.

For example, Italian girls rarely appear in juvenile court statistics in the large centers of Italian population in the United States. This may reflect the pressure in Italian families for conforming sex behavior and obedience, which makes it difficult for their girls to indulge in this type of protest. That the lid is not so tightly held on the behavior of the Italian boys seems to be reflected in the higher rate of various offenses reported officially for them.

Role, Class, and Education

It has been generally assumed that the reason children from working-class families drop out of school proportionately more frequently than middle-class children is that they have lower IQ's. There is, however, some evidence that both role and class may also be factors.[24]

In an eight-year follow-up of the school careers of the 5677 Pennsylvania boys in the sixth grade in 1926, the fathers' occupation noted in 2158 instances was compared with the IQ of the boys. The study concluded that chances of continuing education beyond the high school level are much more

[24] Elbridge Sibley, "Some Demographic Clues to Stratification," *American Sociological Review*, Vol. 7, no. 3 (June 1942), pp. 322-30.

highly correlated with the father's occupational ratings than with the boy's intelligence quotient. "At the college level the most intelligent boys have only a *four* to one advantage over the least intelligent, the sons of men in the highest occupational category enjoy an advantage of more than *ten* to one over those from the lowest occupational level."[25]

More recent evidence of the relation of class to formal education is offered in Davie's analysis of the plans for schooling of all the 16-year-olds in New Haven, in the school year beginning September 1949.[26] Davie's findings showed positive correlation between social class and continuation in school after the sixteenth birthday. The family's place in the social scale was determined by several factors—residential area, income, nationality, occupation of head of family, inclusion in social register, social club membership, and indices of delinquency and dependency of area of residence.

By the time they were 18 years old, 30 per cent of the 3800 New Haven youths had already left school. Slightly more than 50 per cent were still in high school, 10 per cent were attending private schools, and the remainder were either in liberal arts colleges or higher vocational schools. Those who had already left school were mainly residents of areas with the lowest class ratings.[27]

Supplementary interviews showed clearly that the parents in the upper economic classes considered college training essential for their children. Furthermore many of them preferred to send their children to private secondary schools rather than to public high schools. In marked contrast, the parents in the lowest socio-economic group who were interviewed regarded the expenditure of money for education beyond high school as unnecessary and impractical.

Whyte's comparison of "corner boy" and "college boy," in his study of Cornerville already referred to, points up the interlocking effects of role and class as determinants not only of educational patterns but of other forms of behavior. The corner boy, who typifies the majority of Cornerville's youthful population, is often a truant, sometimes a member of a gang; the college boy, even though also a slum dweller, is more likely to adhere to the standards of middle-class behavior. The key difference between the two is in their attitude toward higher education: the college boy, but not the corner boy, sees it as

[25] Harlan Updegraff, *Inventory of Youth in Pennsylvania,* Washington, American Youth Commission, 1936.

[26] James S. Davie, "Social Class Factors and School Attendance," *Harvard Educational Review,* Vol. 23, no. 3, Summer, 1953, pp. 175-85.

[27] This point is emphasized in a paper by Samuel Stouffer, entitled "The Study of Social Mobility: Some Strategic Considerations," delivered at the September 1957 annual meeting of the American Sociological Society, Washington, D.C. See also Stouffer's "Social Forces That Produce the Great Sorting," College Entrance Exam. Bd., Col. Admissions, No. 2, pp. 1-7 (undated).

the royal if difficult road to getting ahead. Whyte points out[28] that even if the parents of the slum dwelling college boy do not recognize his potential, his teachers often do. Because his teacher picks him out as college material, the college boy begins to be set apart from his fellows as early as the ninth grade.

The college boy behavior pattern calls for savings and investments, while the corner boy's life fits a spending economy. To finance his education and launch his business or profession, the college boy who lives in the slums must save his money and cultivate thrift. The corner boy, on the other hand, must share his money with his companions; if he is thrifty, he jeopardizes his position in the corner gang. While the corner boy may not consciously spend money for the purpose of acquiring influence over his fellows, his behavior must fit the action pattern of his group. Chick, the college boy, sees money as a means to advance himself. Doc, on the other hand, needs money to maintain his position in the corner gang.

The respective attitudes of the college and corner boy toward social mobility are also different. Chick judges men according to their capacity for advancing themselves; Doc, according to their loyalty to their friends. While each wishes to get ahead in his chosen sphere, the roads are different. The college boy does not tie himself to a group of close friends. He is prepared to sacrifice his friendship with those who do not advance as fast as he does. In contrast, a network of reciprocal obligations from which he is either unwilling or unable to break away ties the corner boy to his group.

As Doc somewhat poignantly says, the corner boy is not unaware of what he needs to do to advance himself, but he usually cannot act on it:

> I suppose my boys have kept me from getting ahead. . . . But if I were to start over again—If God said to me, "Look here, Doc, you're going to start over again and you can pick out your friends in advance," still I would make sure that my boys were among them—even if I could pick Rockefeller and Carnegie. . . . Many times people in the settlement and some of the Sunsets have said to me, "Why do you hang around those fellows?" I would tell them, "Why not? They're my friends."
>
> "Bill, last night at home my brother-in-law was listening to his favorite Italian program when my nephew comes in. He wants to listen to something else, so he goes up and switches the dial—without asking anybody. . . . I'm in a tough spot here, Bill. They want to do everything for these kids, and if I try to discipline the kids, they jump on me. . . . But that was too raw, I got the kid aside, and I gave him a lecture. Bill, I was really eloquent. But then at the end of it, I said, 'But don't change too much, kid. Stay the way you are, and you'll get ahead in the world.' "[29]

[28] Whyte, *op. cit.*, p. 96.
[29] *Ibid.*, p. 107.

Individual Delinquency as a Middle-Class Phenomenon

It is worth noting that Doc, although a corner boy, was obviously not himself a delinquent. Nor is Whyte implying that delinquency is a phenomenon confined to the slum (as a literal reading of the ecologists would lead us to believe). Differences between working-class and middle-class delinquency are the subject of study by Albert Cohen, building on the work of Parsons whose contribution to the theory of masculine protest in the genesis of aggressive and anti-social behavior is linked with the family and occupational systems. Cohen agrees with Parsons that the middle-class family, more than any other type, is characterized by the isolation of its children from socially significant male adults. He sees the delinquent behavior of the middle-class child as a result of blocked opportunities to play the male role.[30]

In middle-class families, it is the mother who transmits the traditional canons of good behavior. As a result, the middle-class boy who attempts to assert his masculinity must do so by protests against his mother's standards of goodness, which emphasize feminine virtues. To assure himself of his masculinity, he must therefore be "bad." The mother, says Parsons,

> . . . above all focuses in herself the symbols of what is good behavior, in conformity with the expectations of the adult respectable world. When he revolts against identification with his mother in the name of masculinity, it is not surprising that a boy unconsciously identifies "goodness" with femininity and that being a "bad boy" becomes a positive goal. There is a strong tendency for boyish behavior to run in anti-social if not directly destructive directions, in striking contrast to that of pre-adolescent girls.[31]

Cohen believes that a masculine identification in general is clearly easier for the working-class than for the middle-class boy. The prolonged period of the middle-class child's financial dependency upon his parents in comparison with that of the working-class boy is an additional handicap to emancipation. Even if he does earn some spending money, the former is not regarded as sharing the responsibility with the breadwinner.

> In brief, not only must the middle-class boy overcome an early feminine identification and prove his maleness; even the opportunities to assume the legitimate signs of maleness are likely to be denied him.
>
> Male delinquency in families which are culturally middle-class is *primarily* an attempt to cope with a basic anxiety in the area of the sex-

[30] Albert K. Cohen, *Delinquent Boys: The Culture of the Gang,* Glencoe, Ill., the Free Press, 1955.
[31] Talcott Parsons, "Certain Primary Sources and Patterns of Aggression in the Social Structure of the Western World," *Psychiatry,* Vol. 10, no. 2 (May 1947), p. 172.

role identification; it has the primary function of giving reassurance of one's essential masculinity.[32]

Summary

Shaw's studies and those of the many followers of the ecological approach to understanding social problems pointed up the differences in the spatial distribution of officially apprehended delinquents. While these studies were an important first step in describing some of the characteristics of delinquents they tell us little about the nature of the behavior or the forces that are responsible for it.

Reckless, in a study of "good" and "bad" boys in public schools in Columbus, Ohio, delinquency areas, finds the differential in a slum area in the insulating process which protects some boys. The good boys' self-concept, reinforced by the opinions of the reference groups they admire—teachers, parents, and so forth—protects them at least up to the sixth grade in school from being delinquent, even though they live in a high delinquency area. Tests of the effectiveness of this protective armor are offered in other grades in Akron and in a follow-up study in Columbus.

Lander's efforts to link anomie to delinquency area theory, although admirably sophisticated from a statistical standpoint, is an example of the fallacy of imputing a causal relationship to a descriptive factor which is part of the definition of the phenomena to be explained. As he himself points out at the end of his study, and as Greenwood agrees, a very different study design is necessary if one wishes an empirical test of the relation of anomie to delinquency. In his study of Cornerville, Whyte questions the prevalent view of the slum as disorganized.

Turning to the evidence of a relation between individual antisocial behavior patterns and class and/or role, a variety of sociological studies on the subject is examined. Grosser highlights the marked differences in rates of stealing among girls and boys (without regard to class identification) as a direct reflection of their ascribed roles in our society. Stealing, he believes, is much more frequent among boys because for them it is role-expressive rather than merely role-supportive as in the case of girls. Updegraff and Davie add empirical evidence of the significance of the parents' socio-economic status on the opportunity for educational achievement, which in our society is one high road to upward social movement. Whyte adds another dimension to his enlightening analysis of the complex organization of life in a slum by pinpointing how the corner boy adjusts his behavior to a goal which is quite different

[32] Cohen, op. cit., pp. 166-67.

from that of the college boy, even though they may both be residents of a slum area.

We conclude the discussion of role and class with reference to Cohen's thesis, building on Parsons, of the varying significance of the male role (parental and filial) in the working-class as opposed to the middle-class family. Cohen's interesting thesis provides a new direction to our thinking about the relation between class norms in American society and the antisocial gang as a cultural subform (see Chapter 9).

CHAPTER 8

Sociological Approaches:
II. Family-Centered Research

INEVITABLY, AS THE PSYCHOLOGICAL APPROACHES DESCRIBED IN CHAPTER 6 gained currency in England and the United States, they began to influence the work of fellow-scientists. If, as the psychological school believed, the early relationships between parents and child were a central influence on the future development of the child, then the search for causes of delinquency could profitably be turned on the family—its characteristics, and the socio-psychological aspects of family life—as the seedbed of delinquency. Here sociologists found a productive new field for research.

Family Characteristics

The sociological approach stems from Cooley's original formulation of the importance of face-to-face relationships in the primary group (the family) as determinants of character and group behavior. Such deviations from normal family settings as broken homes, working mothers, and insufficient income to provide for basic family needs have been examined repeatedly for their bearing on delinquency.

Broken Homes

Concern with the broken home as the explanation for delinquency has persisted over the years. The Children's Bureau juvenile court series often draws attention to the incidence of broken homes in the official statistics, pointing out, for example, that in 1928, 29 per cent of all boys and 48 per cent of all girls brought to the courts in the series were not living with both parents. The percentage would have been higher if the basis of determining the incidence of broken homes had been limited to its occurrence among institutionalized children (who over the years account for 10 to 18 per cent of those brought before the court). In 1923, for example, the Census Bureau estimated that almost one out of two (46 per cent) children in institutions came from broken homes. In a study of 341 delinquent girls at the Whittier State School in California, Mathews found that more than half were reared in broken homes.[1] Sullenger[2] found that about 51 per cent of the 1135 delinquents reported in 1930 in Omaha came from broken homes.

One of the most careful investigations of the relation between the broken home and delinquency was that of Shaw and McKay, who interviewed the families of 7278 boys aged 10-17 in twenty-nine Chicago schools, representative of the total range of delinquency areas in 1929.[3] They found that the over-all rate of broken homes in the population of each of the schools did not correspond with the delinquency rate of the area in which the school was located. When, however, they compared the incidence of broken homes in the various ethnic groups represented in the school population, the rate was highest for Negro boys with Mexican, native-born white American, Polish, Italian, Greek, and Jewish in descending order. As might be expected, the rate of broken homes generally increased with the age of the boys.

When both age and ethnic group were held constant, the comparable ratios of broken homes for the delinquents and the school populations were 1.18 to 1 in the total, but 1.30 to 1 for Negro boys. From their experience as probation officers, Shaw and McKay suggest that the formal break in the family may not be so crucial as the cumulative effects of family discord. In fact it is possible, they suggested, that where there is great tension, an actual break may prevent the occurrence of certain types of problems. This investigation shows how necessary it is in testing any hypothesis to define one's variables clearly.

The author of this book has also called attention in the past to the wide variety of situations, each with quite different implications for the children, which are grouped under "broken homes," pointing out that the effect of a home broken by the death of a loved parent is not likely to be the same as that of a home deserted by one parent, or one which may be formally intact but is daily and nightly rent asunder by quarreling parents.

[1] Julia Mathews, "A Survey of 341 Delinquent Girls in California," *Journal of Delinquency*, Vol. 8 (1923), pp. 196-231.
[2] T. E. Sullenger, *Social Determinants of Juvenile Delinquency*, Omaha, Nebraska, Douglas Printing Co., 1930.
[3] Clifford R. Shaw and Henry D. McKay, "Social Factors in Juvenile Delinquency," in *Report on the Causes of Crime*, National Commission on Law Observance and Enforcement, Washington, 1931, pp. 276 ff.

In the decade following the Shaw and McKay study, less attention was paid to the possible connection between broken homes and delinquency. However, one investigator, Monahan, has recently studied the rate of broken homes in Philadelphia court cases.[4] Monahan, as well as many probation officers, differs with Shaw, McKay, and the author by stressing the destructive influence on the child's development of the absence of either parent from the home, whether through death, desertion, separation, or divorce.

In analyzing 9000 juvenile delinquency cases referred to the Philadelphia court in 1954, Monahan found that one third of the white boys and three quarters of the Negro girls came from broken homes. Among white delinquents, broken homes were more characteristic of girls than of boys. And broken homes were twice as prevalent among apprehended delinquents as among the general population of Philadelphia.

Monahan's findings, however, do not confirm his hypothesis because: (1) the percentage of serious offenses of boys and girls from broken homes was *less* than that of young persons from intact homes; and (2) the increase in the percentage of delinquents from broken homes did not parallel the percentage increase of broken homes in Philadelphia for the same period.

We suggest, instead, that the incidence of broken homes in the official statistics is not a causal but a descriptive factor.[5] It is more likely to be causally related to (1) other factors which influence the referral of the case to court, and (2) the size of the Negro population, in which separation occurs more frequently than in white families.

Some testimony on this possibility is offered by Toby's recent analysis of Essex County, New Jersey, statistics.[6] In commenting on the findings of Shaw and McKay that broken homes did not appear to be a causal factor, Toby suggests that they would have been on firmer ground if they had cross-checked their data for the variables of sex, age, and race. Because in general, in our society, greater control is exercised over *all young children* and *all girls,* Toby thought it would be reasonable to expect that, in that part of the population with a large number of broken homes, and therefore presumably less supervision than the norm, the rate of delinquency will be higher among preadolescent boys and among girls.[7]

Unfortunately, this refinement of the variables is not directly possible,

[4] Thomas P. Monahan, "The Delinquent Child and the Broken Home," paper presented at the meeting of the Eastern Sociological Society, New York City, March 25, 1956.

[5] For a review of the literature on broken homes, see Harry M. Shulman, "The Family and Juvenile Delinquency," *The Annals,* American Academy of Political and Social Sciences, No. 261 (Jan. 1949), pp. 21-31; and P. M. Smith, "Broken Homes and Juvenile Delinquency," *Sociology and Social Research,* May-June 1955.

[6] Jackson Toby, "The Differential Impact of Family Disorganization," *American Sociological Review,* Vol. 22, no. 5 (October 1957).

[7] *Ibid.,* p. 508.

since the census does not cross tabulate age, sex, and race. As a substitute, Toby calculates delinquency rates for offenses which he describes as offenses against family life—running away and incorrigibility—for boys and girls in three age groups: under 11, from 11 to 13, and 14 and over, in comparison with other offenses. For information on family composition, he relies on 1950 census data on the marital status of heads of households and on the whereabouts of children under 17. His findings on the first point, the relative rates of delinquency, are as follows:

1. Like the delinquency rates in other urban communities which report to the Children's Bureau, the rates for girls in the Essex County, New Jersey, 1952-53 series were markedly lower than those for boys.

2. However, girls accounted for a larger proportion of the Negro than of the white total.

3. Younger boys accounted for a larger proportion of the Negro than of the white male total.

4. Classified by age group, the younger *white* male "offenders against the family" represented 11.7 per cent of the total white male delinquents in comparison with 7.4 and 7.9 in the age groups 11-13 and 14-15, and only 4.2 among those 16 and older.

5. Among the *nonwhite* male delinquents the comparable figures were 18.5, 8.1, 8.3, and 4.5 for each age group.

The significant differences were clearly those between the younger and the older offenders, between the younger white and Negro boys, and between the white and Negro girls.

Toby's study of the differential family types, as recorded in the 1950 census for Essex County, substantiate marked differences in white and Negro family characteristics. Specifically:

1. Relative to their proportion of the population, four times as many nonwhite women as white women were not residing with their spouses—a crude index, to be sure, of family stability.

2. Comparison with regard to the residence of the child showed 91 per cent of the white but only 71 per cent of the Negro boys classified by the census as children of the head of the residential household.

3. Of the nonwhite children, 13 per cent were living in the homes of grandparents, in contrast to 5 per cent of the white children.

Clearly, the Negro children in this New Jersey county were disproportionately concentrated in homes regarded as "broken" because they did not follow the modal pattern.

Other challenging evidence suggests, however, that this modal pattern is not precisely relevant to working-class Negro families. James Weldon Johnson, in a conference on illegitimacy in the white and Negro population about 25 years ago, called attention to the reversal of the usual breadwinning role in Negro and white households, and its effect on family stability. Because under slavery Negro men were mainly agricultural or unskilled laborers, while many of the women—as cooks, nurses, and so forth—had closer contact with the white households, the Negro woman after the Civil War had greater educational and economic advantages than the man. As the main breadwinner, she was, like the white male, freer to leave a spouse if she no longer loved him. (In the Negro community, the woman who alienated another woman's partner was the counterpart of the white man sued for alienation of the affection of another man's wife.)

As a consequence, Johnson pointed out, the structure of the Negro family has many matriarchal characteristics. Often the grandmother plays the role of the mother while the natural mother carries the responsibility of breadwinner which in the white family is normally carried by the husband. It is therefore possible that a home broken by the absence of a father may not have the same significance for the Negro child as it does for the white.

Toby's conclusion concerning the evidence of a sex and age differential, in the statistics at least, in the relationship of delinquency and broken homes, is as follows:

> On the basis of the foregoing examination of age- and sex-specific delinquency rates of Negro and white children and of urban and rural children, the conclusion seems justified that family disorganization is of greater causal significance in the delinquency of *girls* and of *preadolescents* than of *adolescent males*. It is even possible—although my analysis provides no direct evidence on the point—that family disorganization is of negligible causal significance in the delinquent behavior of male adolescents. This possibility certainly deserves further consideration in view of the fact that male adolescents constitute the heart of the juvenile crime problem—not only as far as numbers are concerned, but also as regards the seriousness of the crimes committed.

We may conclude that the available evidence to date does not confirm a causal relationship between delinquent behavior and the broken home for two main reasons: first, because children who reside in households whose pattern is not the modal one for middle-class white families are the ones most apt to be apprehended and labeled delinquent; and second, because the data do not reveal the differential significance of the family situation in the emotional reaction of the child.

Working Mothers

Another stereotype which, like the broken home, has been advanced as the cause of delinquency is the mother who is gainfully employed outside her home. It is generally assumed that a young child needs his mother's attention or that of an acceptable substitute to assure his proper emotional as well as physical development. Careful studies have indicated that very young children reared in institutions, despite excellent physical care, are handicapped in achieving mature and well-rounded personalities.[8] Goldfarb's findings along these lines are based on his study of the comparative development of New York City Jewish children placed in an orphanage as infants and those who spent their first year or so with their natural mothers and were then reared in individual foster homes. Whether this negative finding would hold for Negro or rural children has not been tested. It may be postulated, however, that children whose mothers cannot for some reason give them all the care and attention they need may get some of this satisfaction from other consanguinal adults in the household or from older siblings. Thus, for example, descriptions of Hutterite methods of child rearing, in which parents work in the fields, stress the responsibility of older siblings in child raising.

In a later examination of the statistical findings in their study *Unraveling Juvenile Delinquency,* the Gluecks have made comparisons of the relative frequency of working mothers among delinquents and nondelinquents.[9] They believe they have evidence of a "deleterious influence" on the family life and on the children of certain mothers working outside the home, especially in relation to delinquency. Reporting that their study revealed that the mothers of delinquents worked more sporadically than did the mothers of nondelinquents, they conclude that this means these mothers were less effective with their children. They hypothesize that the mothers of the delinquents may represent a "different breed," a group of women who wish to avoid the responsibilities of housework and child rearing. In contrast, they infer, tentatively of course, that the steady employment of the mothers of the control group reflects their steadfast desire to provide a more adequate income for their families. These inferences, however, seem vulnerable, for reasons which have already been discussed in the last chapter.

The increasing trend in gainful employment of women with children and the increasing concern in our society with the centrality of the mother-child relationship in the socialization process, has stimulated conferences to discuss these two aspects of life in urban America today.

At the National Manpower Conference in 1959,[10] a staff member of the Laboratory of Human Development in Harvard's Graduate School of Education took issue with the Gluecks' inferences that the effects of sporadic em-

[8] William Goldfarb, "Infant Rearing and Problem Behavior," *American Journal of Orthopsychiatry,* Vol. 13, no. 2 (April 1943), pp. 249-65.

[9] Sheldon and Eleanor Glueck, "Working Mothers and Delinquency," *Mental Hygiene,* Vol. 41, no. 3 (July 1957), pp. 327-52.

[10] Arden House Conference on Manpower, Harriman, N. Y., October 1957.

ployment are more harmful than those of steady employment.[11] Maccoby suggested instead that the differential factor in delinquent behavior of the boy might not be the mother's work pattern but "something about the family characteristics which led both to the mother's sporadic employment and her child's delinquency." To support her assertion, Maccoby referred to the Gluecks' description of the *other* characteristics of the mothers who worked irregularly: many had been delinquent, some had had husbands who were emotionally disturbed and whose work habits were poor. Neither parent in the majority of these families had displayed self-respect or affection.

In support of their conclusions, the Gluecks had compared the delinquent and nondelinquent groups with respect to the quality of parental supervision.[12] Maccoby proposed, instead of the Gluecks' two-way correlation, a three-way comparison—i.e., employment status of the mother, the quality of supervision of the child, and the percentage of delinquents. On this basis, 19 per cent of the boys whose mothers were regularly employed and whose supervision was rated good were delinquent. On the other hand, 32 per cent each of those whose mothers were housewives and of those whose mothers worked occasionally were in the delinquent group.

Maccoby interpreted these differences as follows: "If the mother remains at home but does not keep track of her child, he is far more likely to become a delinquent than if he is closely watched. Furthermore, if a mother who works arranges adequate care for the child in her absence, he is no more likely to be delinquent than the adequately supervised child of a mother who does not work."[13]

The deliberations of the conference concluded that we do not know either the psychological or the social factors in the husband-wife or the mother-child relationship which may offset the effects of the actual break in the child's experience that occurs when his mother works outside the home.

It seems reasonable to conclude, on the basis of the evidence so far presented, that more definitive studies are needed before we can say *when* and *under what conditions*—the child's needs, the home setting, and the parent-child relationship—working mothers are a precipitating factor in either delinquent or disturbed behavior of a child.

Poverty

Poverty has been another perennially popular explanation for delinquency.[14] Before the serious student accepts it as a definitive cause, however,

[11] Eleanor E. Maccoby, Ph.D., "Children and Working Mothers," *The Child,* Vol. 5, no. 3 (May-June 1958), pp. 83-89.
[12] Sheldon and Eleanor Glueck, *op. cit.,* Table 3.
[13] Maccoby, *op. cit.,* p. 84.
[14] Ernest W. Burgess, "The Economic Factor in Juvenile Delinquency," *Journal of Criminal Law, Criminology, and Police Science,* Vol. 43, no. 1 (May-June 1952), pp. 29-42.

he needs to scrutinize the concept of poverty as an independent variable. Poverty is not a clear-cut concept. Defined in economic terms, it is an income level too low for a family of specified size in a specified community to provide for its minimum needs. In psychological terms, however, poverty is an unbalanced ratio between wants and satisfactions related to the standards of the group of which the individual feels himself a part. Unfortunately, the terms in this ratio do not lend themselves to precise measurement.

Differences in standard of living—for example, whether one owns or rents one's home, maintains a savings account, buys insurance, invests in a college education for children—as well as the skill and ingenuity of the homemaker in adjusting ends to means, are all indicators of a feeling of poverty, or, conversely, of a feeling of sufficiency.

Independent of the size of income is the individual's feeling of his group status, or, in sociological terms, his reference group. Financial limitations often do not interfere with the ability to work out emotionally satisfactory and socially approved adjustments. There are well-adjusted poor people (using the term in the sense of a low economic group) and badly adjusted well-to-do people who, when their incomes are reduced from $100,000 to $10,000 a year feel themselves so poor that suicide is the only solution. To the residents of lower Park Avenue in New York, Locust Street in Philadelphia, the Gold Coast in Chicago, and Nob Hill in San Francisco, people who must live in Williamsburg, Brooklyn, South Philadelphia, or the stockyard section of Chicago are poor. Nevertheless, in America today, with the Social Security provisions for the general welfare, most of the residents of these areas have food, sufficient clothing, and some kind of shelter.

The 1955 estimates of the distribution of income indicated that about 50 per cent of the 42,800,000 families in major cities in the United States had incomes under $4500 and 23 per cent under $2500.[15] A modest but adequate income for a family of four was estimated by the Bureau of Labor Statistics to vary from $3812 in New Orleans to $4454 in Washington, D.C.[16] On this basis, at least half the families in the United States can maintain "minimum standards of health and decency."

The current Children's Bureau juvenile court reports do not indicate the economic status of the families of the children who come before them. But even in earlier studies, like that of Breckenridge and Abbott for the years 1899-1909, at least one fourth of the families of the Chicago delinquents were not classified as poor. In Robison's 1930 study of delinquents known to the probation department of New York City's juvenile court, one fourth of the families had incomes under $25 a week, and another fourth had incomes

[15] Income Distribution, March 1955, Sample Survey, Current Population Report, Bureau of Census, Consumer Income Series, No. 22, p. 60.
[16] Living Costs in Large and Small Cities, estimated in sample studies by National Industrial Conference Board, 1951. (Chicago, $4185; Houston, $4304; New York, $4083; San Francisco, $4263.)

over $50.[17] Translated into the purchasing power of dollars today, this means that three quarters of these families had incomes exceeding $50 a week, and of these a quarter had incomes of over $100. Healy and Bronner's early studies in Boston and Chicago designated a little fewer than one third of the homes of delinquents referred to the juvenile court as poor; and their 1936 study, *New Light on Delinquency and Its Treatment*, which included many poor families with both a delinquent and a nondelinquent sibling, leads us to conclude that we have no definitive measures of the relationship of poverty to delinquency.

Family income has an important bearing on whether a child's delinquent behavior will be *officially* recorded. In relating economic status to crime and delinquency, Sutherland comments: "First, the administrative processes are more favorable to persons in economic comfort than to those in poverty. So that if two persons on different economic levels are equally guilty of the same offense, the one on the lower level is more likely to be arrested, convicted and committed to an institution. Second, the laws are written, administered and implemented primarily with reference to the types of crime committed by people of lower economic levels.[18]

As we noted in Chapter 1, Texas college students acknowledged behavior in their precollege days which went unapprehended, although it was similar to that for which considerable numbers of Texas children had been brought to court. Of course, if the delinquent behavior involves murder, as in the Leopold-Loeb case, reported in May 1924, or the case of the three Brooklyn boys in the summer of 1954, action will be taken regardless of the economic status of the family.

It has been generally noted that in well-to-do neighborhoods there are fewer police to apprehend young people who may be engaging in antisocial behavior; and if the police do see them, they are more apt to consider the behavior of the well-to-do child as a prank than as a threatening act necessitating court referral (see Chapter 14).

The appropriate inference from the available data, on the basis of our present understanding of the nature of cause, is that whether poverty, broken homes, or working mothers are factors which *cause* delinquency depends upon the meaning the situation has for the child. It is of interest to note that Healy changed the focus of his early researches in delinquency to an investigation of the emotional satisfactions which the family provides, in different measure to its individual members, as clues to good or bad behavior. We shall

[17] Sophia M. Robison, "Can Delinquency Be Measured?", New York, Columbia University Press, 1936, p. 32.
[18] Edwin H. Sutherland, *Principles of Criminology*, Chicago, Lippincott, 1939, p. 179.

see in a later chapter, that no other factors appear to be so important in precipitating delinquent behavior.

Challenges to Middle-Class Concepts of Family

Toby's analysis of the high incidence of broken homes in Negro families in Essex County, like Johnson's comment on the breadwinning role of the female in the Negro family as one result of slavery, should give us pause when we generalize about family norms. The appropriate question is *whose* norms? Jephcott and Carter, investigating slum-dwelling families in an English town, give a further jolt to our middle-class assumption that ours is the ideal, or even the normal, family type.[19]

Class Differentials in a High Delinquency Area

The investigators' original plan was to compare the living patterns of families living on "black" (delinquent) streets with those of families residing on streets on which there were no delinquents ("white" streets). Observation of the actual distribution of families on the streets, however, did not reveal a concentration of any one type of family so that one would be justified in calling a street "black" or "white." The original plan therefore was revised so that all 325 families resident in the high delinquency area were interviewed and classified according to their prevailing practices and ideas. They appeared to fit into three major types: (1) "rough"—72 families; (2) "respectable"—59 families; (3) "medium"—94 families. The medium group differed from the respectable group mainly in their more easygoing tolerance of the rough group. The two extreme groups, although in the same socioeconomic category, differed in several important ways described below.

RESPECTABLE versus ROUGH FAMILIES. 1. Although they had less income than the rough group, which often had three or more adult wage earners, the respectable families were much better managers of their money, much less extravagant and wasteful.

2. The respectable families planned for the future and sacrificed immediate pleasures in anticipation of future gains. The rough families lived almost entirely in the present.

3. The respectable families cherished their privacy, while the rough families liked popping in and out of each other's houses, and enjoyed gossiping and "neighboring."

4. The respectable families chose their friends carefully and usually

[19] A. P. Jephcott and M. P. Carter, *The Social Background of Delinquency,* privately printed, 1954. Obtainable on loan from the University of Nottingham.

participated in or cooperated with community organizations in the schools and elsewhere.

5. The parents' ties with their children in the respectable families continued through adolescence, whereas in the rough families the children were cut loose from the family group much sooner.

While these five differentiating characteristics of the rough and respectable families have been observed in American society, the unique contribution of Jephcott and Carter has been to point up the differences in the meaning of "family" in the two types. The fact that they may exist side-by-side in a slum bears in important ways on our concern with conformity to the standards and goals set largely by middle-class urban industrial society.

THE MEANINGS OF "FAMILY." As Jephcott and Carter see it, the respectable family is synonymous with parents and children who share living quarters and eat their meals together, and so forth. The rough family, in contrast, is an extended family including many persons who may or may not live under the same roof. The sexual behavior of the mates and the decorum in the household may be free and easy. There is often open quarreling and even exchange of blows between men and women, women and women, adults and children, and between children.

The attitude of the rough families toward personal possessions does not encourage caring for them or teaching children the difference between "mine" and "thine." Yet the parents may want more personal possessions for their children, to make up for deprivations of their own youth. In contrast, the respectable family appears to want for its children more educational and cultural advantages rather than more *things*. The respectable family usually, unlike the rough family, strives to orient its children to the future rather than to the present.

DELINQUENTS IN ROUGH AND MEDIUM FAMILIES. Recently John A. Mack has reported on Jephcott and Carter's findings in detail, and described his own action research in Bristol, where he has developed a program that takes their studies into account.[20] According to Mack, these rough families, who contribute more than their share of delinquents, are not an aberration or a defective form of the model prescribed by society; they are *sui generis*. He suggests that they represent the survival of an earlier family structure—one form of the extended family with three generations and collateral kin living under the same roof or in close proximity. They have survived on their own terms by pursuing objectives and maintaining values which run counter to those of the wider society today. To quote:

> Note how communal these people are, as in the pre-industrial farm town; how limited their social range—they are very much part of the

20 John A. Mack, *Delinquency and the Changing Social Pattern*, The Fifth Charles Russell Memorial Lecture, Glasgow, University of Glasgow, 1957.

street, but they are practically self-contained in relation to the larger society; how resistant to influence or censure from outside, like any closely knit mining village; how complacently unaware they are of being delinquent or falling short in any way. There is something here that cannot be explained away. They may be a defective form of something, but that something is certainly not the modern family unit as we know it.[21]

Try as they have to change the ways of these families, ministers, teachers, probation officers, and youth workers have been largely ineffective because *what they have to offer meets no need recognized by the families themselves.* In the main these families see nothing wrong with their own way of life. An analogy might be the hard road of the missionaries' efforts to convert the heathen. And perhaps, as in the case of missionaries, the most effective propaganda is through the children.

Mack suggests that the only effective way of reaching the rough families is through their contacts with the children of the medium families. And if, as sometimes happens, these medium children also adopt delinquent patterns, Mack feels that this is usually a temporary phase, which he calls "nonpathological social recalcitrance."

He quotes J. B. Mays, leader of a boy's club in Liverpool's dockland (an area with a social tradition of crime) to illustrate his suggestion that the delinquent behavior of medium children is generally a part of the growing-up process. In Erikson's terms (see Chapter 6), this may be the experimenting which is typical of adolescence. Almost half of the eighty 16-year-old boys in Mays's club, a cross section of the better behaved boys in the area, said they had been in court. Most of the others admitted committing more or less serious indictable offenses without being caught. "For them it had been part of growing up in the city. They had no feelings of guilt about it. They enjoyed getting things on the cheap. Many of them looked on shoplifting as a normal method of getting additional pocket money. They enjoyed the excitement. 'It makes you sweat. . . . You have to prove you didn't have cold feet.' "[22]

But the important point is that most of these Liverpool boys grew out of this behavior; they became more aware of the risks they were running and more anxious not to upset "Mum." Obviously these boys belonged to the medium families, and in the main supported the standards of the wider society. From the English standpoint, Mack concludes, these medium families are the core of the community.

The contribution of Jephcott, Carter, and Mack is their challenge to the

---

[21] *Ibid.,* p. 12.
[22] Quoted in Mack, *op. cit.,* p. 6.

stereotypes of family structure which are usually applied in studying the inhabitants of slum areas in relation to delinquent behavior.

Summary

In the 1920s the possible effects of poverty, broken homes, and working mothers began to replace physical or mental characteristics of the individual as a major consideration in studies concerned with the causes of delinquency. Comparisons were made, and continue to be made, sometimes using control groups. The resulting correlations, however, have so far identified mainly descriptive rather than causal factors. Further progress in this promising field of study depends on (1) defining clearly the factors that are to be studied; and (2) developing a hypothesis which simultaneously takes into account the individual, the various family constellations, and the milieu.

Meanwhile, Jephcott, Carter, Mack, and Mays in England have thrown new light on family-centered research by challenging the accepted stereotype of family structure. They suggest that the presumed disorganization of family life in slum areas may be a middle-class fiction—the result of projecting one's own ideas of a normal family into a situation which has an entirely different conception of order. What appears as a delinquent way of life to middle-class society is, they suggest, "normal" for the rough families which live side-by-side with respectable poor families who adhere to conventional middle-class behavior.

CHAPTER 9

Sociological Approaches: III. The Gang

THE AGGRESSIVE ANTISOCIAL GANG WAS DESCRIBED BY REFORMERS LIKE Jacob Riis[1] in New York in the early part of this century and by sociologists like Frederick Thrasher[2] in Chicago in the 1920s. In the last decade and a half social workers who have been concerned with redirecting the gang's activities into more useful channels have had an opportunity to observe and to study and sometimes to assist the gang member to more socially approved behavior. Recently, Albert Cohen[3] has made an important contribution to theory by directing attention away from the *description* of gang behavior to its *explanation* by the application of sociological insights. These various approaches to the antisocial gang as a special manifestation of delinquency are the subject of this chapter.

The Nature of Gangs

Association with one's peers is a normal phenomenon of youth which begins in preadolescence. The degree of organization, the type of activities, depend upon such factors as age, intelligence, community environment, and the moral standards of the boys who join. The group frequently acts as a

[1] Jacob A. Riis, *How the Other Half Lives,* New York, Scribner, 1939.
[2] Frederick M. Thrasher, *The Gang,* Chicago, University of Chicago Press, 1927.
[3] Albert K. Cohen, *Delinquent Boys: The Culture of the Gang,* Glencoe, Ill., The Free Press, 1955. See also Chapter 7.

counterforce to the usual conservative social sanctions which control the individual's behavior.[4]

The Gang as an "Autonomous Group"[5]

Gangs exist among adults as well as among adolescents. In familiar conversation reference is often made to "the gang" that goes bowling, plays bridge, and exchanges visits in each other's homes. A distinguishing characteristic of such groups is that they have no set platforms, programs, or official membership requirements. They arise as a spontaneous combination of individuals loosely banded together in pursuit of common interests, which may be intellectual explorations or social activities.

When occasionally autonomous groups develop into formal organizations, the relation of the individual to the group changes.[6] The activities originally performed by volunteers are often gradually delegated to a professional staff. While membership dues provide financial support, their payment does not necessarily result in active participation by all members in the program. In contrast, the autonomous group has no constitution, no regular dues, and no staff. In varying degrees each member determines his own role, with leadership depending upon the focus of interest at a specific time.

The boy gang is a special variety of an autonomous group in that its activities are predominantly antisocial and its relationship to other groups is often hostile. While the usual social club is indifferent to nonmembers, it will cooperate actively with nonmembers when occasion demands. Hostility is expressed only in socially approved ways, i.e., in contests, debates, and so forth. In the antisocial gang, however, hostile acts against nonmembers parallel the ingroup-outgroup dichotomy of our society.

This hostility is an old phenomenon, especially in the big city. Jacob A. Riis's description of gangs in the last two decades of the nineteenth century has a strongly familiar ring:

> Along the waterfront, every corner had its gang, not always on the best of terms with the rival in the next block, but all with a common purpose—defiance of law and order. . . . The gang members were the American-born sons of English, Irish, and German parents. . . . The first long step in crime taken by a half-grown boy fired by the ambition to have standing

[4] Paul Hanley Furfey, *The Gang Age: A Study of the Pre-Adolescent Boy and His Recreational Needs,* New York, Macmillan, 1928.

[5] For data on autonomous groups, see issues of a quarterly by that name, published by the Committee on Autonomous Groups, which since 1945 has been concerned with reporting scientific and practical developments in the study of small groups. It may be contacted through Maria Rogers, Secretary, Hotel Park Sheraton, New York 22, N. Y.

[6] The Child Study Association of America and the League of Women Voters began as autonomous groups.

in his gang was usually to rob a "lush," i.e., a drunken man who had strayed his way likely enough asleep in a hallway.[7]

As today, the gang names were picturesque: Hell's Kitchen Gang, Floaters, Pugilists, Hell Benders, Moonlight Howlers, and so forth. One gang specialized in stealing baby carriages and depositing the babies on the sidewalk. More ominous activities were blowing up a grocery store because the proprietor resisted the demand for a gift, and trying to saw off the head of a Jewish peddler. Nor were policemen safe from attack, frequently the officer was beaten with his own stick. Whole neighborhoods were terrorized so that often no one dared testify against atrocities.

In two ways the gang activities highlighted in today's news accounts differ from those in earlier accounts. The ethnic groups to which the members belong, i.e., the gangs of Irish-German origin have been largely replaced by Italians, Negroes, Puerto Ricans, and Mexicans. Negroes and Puerto Ricans currently predominate in New York, as Mexicans do in the Southwest and West. Moreover, because there has been little new residential building in central cities since World War I, the latest gangs have moved into the formerly insulated sections of New York City instead of being confined to the other slum areas. In other words, the newcomers have "invaded" respectable neighborhoods, or neighborhoods inhabited by earlier immigrant groups.

This invasion has probably occurred in all large cities. Certainly the current antisocial activities around the University of Chicago appear to reflect in large measure the essential conditions which Thrasher's classic study of gang activity in the Loop Area revealed. The destruction of community property and attack on outgroups provided an opportunity for adventure while it simultaneously conferred status otherwise beyond the reach of a slum dweller.

Thrasher pointed out that the constructive aspects of gang membership—group loyalty, desire for status—were socially approved. Group attachments, a phenomenon of adolescence, served a variety of functions; (1) identification with the peer group as part of the weaning process; (2) opportunity for adventure and excitement unavailable to the individual alone; (3) a vehicle for concerted action (whether the goal is constructive or destructive); (4) opportunity for heterosexual contacts, i.e., meeting members of the other sex under conditions offering group protection to those who may be shy.

Gang Statistics

Although careful studies of court cases would probably reveal that breaking and entering, malicious mischief, and violation of corporation ordinances usually involve more than one boy, juvenile court statistics today rarely reflect

[7] Riis, *op. cit.*, pp. 217 ff.

membership in destructive gangs, perhaps because gang members are difficult to corral. Despite the lack of official statistics on gangs, however, the problem is an important one. Like stealing, gang membership appears to be mainly an activity of boys, perhaps because, in Grosser's terms (see Chapter 7), it is role expressive. When there are girl gangs, they usually play an auxiliary role. They hold the weapons before the fights and conceal them afterward because they cannot be searched by male officers.

Harlem Gangs

Two projects in the last few years have added considerably to our knowledge of gangs: the Harlem Project and the Welfare Council Street Club Project, both in Harlem, where the problem of gang behavior has demanded increasing attention. We cite below what we have learned about gangs from these two related endeavors. Chapter 29 will analyze the effectiveness of these projects.

When the efforts of the recreation director of Junior High School 120 in Harlem failed to draw the neighborhood gangs into the after-school programs, he sought them out in their own bailiwick.[8] With the aid of the police, Sachs identified twenty gangs in the school district which covered about 160 square blocks. The gangs were not evenly distributed. The members came mainly from those sections of Harlem in which considerable numbers of young persons were brought to the attention of the juvenile court or the Bureau of Attendance of New York City's Board of Education.

Four of the twenty gangs in the area were singled out for special attention in the Harlem Project. The Jay-Bees, The Gay Blades, The Royals, and The Knights ranged in size from approximately 35 to well over 100 members. Although the boys reported that none of these gangs was originally organized for antisocial purposes, when the project began each had a history of violent gang warfare, weapon carrying, stealing, rape, truancy, and some use of narcotics. Each gang had a definite meeting place—a candy store, bakery, or occasionally the hangout of an adult gang. Each appropriated a distinctive name, and wore an insigne on the jackets.

Size and Structure

No one knew exactly how many boys belonged to the gang. Each appeared to have a satellite following of younger boys, Tiny Tims, Kids, Midgets. Some had allies in their own age groups in other sections of the city.

---

[8] *The Role of the School in Preventing and Correcting Maladjustment and Delinquency: A Study in Three Schools*, report on the Harlem Project by the Research Committee, mimeographed Dec. 1947, printed Feb. 1949.

Some maintained connections with "Senior" adult gangs. Like other groups, gangs can only perpetuate themselves by the addition of new members. How these members were chosen, however, is not entirely clear. In some respects the process appeared to be somewhat similar to "tapping" in a fraternity. Seldom, however, did a boy who was told to join a gang dare to refuse. Boys who might never previously have been involved in any serious antisocial behavior reported that they were forced to join. Stories of boys who refused gang membership and who paid the penalty by being pushed off the roof were current knowledge at the time of the Harlem Project.

Each gang had a president, vice-president, and war counselor who planned the strategy, distributed the weapons, and often led the attack. A light-up man was responsible for the club's arsenal of weapons. While the president played a central role in coordinating the group's activities, the rivalries and hostilities were settled by a dictatorial procedure rather than through mediation and reconciliation. Playing according to the rules was rare.

Typical Activities

Each division had special-interest subgroupings—some liked to put on dances, others to play baseball together, or to fly pigeons. "Underlying these subgroupings was a complex network of inter-relationships which included cliques centralized around one dominant boy, pairs and triangles which sometimes interlocked and isolates who were on the fringe of the group. Some boys stood out in their subgroups because of their influence and power; others were distinguished by their popularity."[9]

Most of the gangs spent relatively little time in destructive activities. The boys in these four gangs just hung around. Their talk about bets, gang fights, individual exploits, boys in jail, girl friends, movies, was interspersed with horseplay, kidding, teasing, playing cards, pool, or stickball. When they stole, a commonly accepted practice, it was usually petty items, such as cigarettes, sodas, small articles of clothing. There was some purse-snatching, some breaking into stores, and some armed robbery.

Occasionally a boy said he stole to support himself. But most boys thought it was smart to steal whether you needed the article or not. They were not ashamed of stealing. If they didn't steal an article they felt that someone else would. "You have to take what you can get because nobody else is going to give you anything. Swiping stuff is all right as long as you follow the Eleventh Commandment: 'Don't get caught.' "[10] If they needed money for food or for the movies, it was cricket to steal, mug, or occasionally extort

[9] Paul L. Crawford, Daniel I. Malamud, and James R. Dumpson, *Working with Teen-age Gangs*, New York, Welfare Council of New York City, 1950, p. 11.
[10] *Ibid.*, p. 16.

lunch money or carfare from children on their way to school or on the school playgrounds.

Drinking, smoking reefers (marihuana), and gambling—acts of escape—appeared to provide release from tensions. Truancy was a form of escape. The boys felt that in the big schools the teachers did not know or care about them, and when they did return to school after an absence, they were often not welcome.

Although few sex offenses were reported among the younger boys, all appeared to be contemptuous of girls. In their eyes girls were objects of sexual pleasure rather than persons whose feelings were to be respected—"you take what you want from them. When they get off the beam and don't act right, slap them around so they'll know who's who."[11]

Fighting usually started because someone's reputation needed to be defended—"if you don't fight back you are a no-good punk and you never want to be a punk."[12] The gang members were almost always armed. They had their home-made bombs and collections of loot for warfare. One boy actually came to school with his gun concealed inside the cover of a fairly thick book after he had cut out the pages.

A gang boy injured in a fight was always assured of revenge. Such revenge, however, might not solve his problem, as the following account reveals.

> Roy, a 17-year-old boy, who had come to a child guidance clinic for help at his mother's suggestion, was embarrassed in telling of his slow progress in school. He had repeated grades, had played hookey. When he reached 17 and could lawfully leave school, he did. His explanation for his trouble was that he got in with the wrong crowd of boys, all older, and all of them out of school.
>
> The episode for which he was picked up concerned a brewing gang fight. In preparation for it Roy had made a Zip gun which was in his pocket when the police picked up a group of 13 boys who were playing cards. Roy had intended practicing to shoot, but got sidetracked into the card game. None of the other boys happened to have guns on them at the time. Roy is on indefinite probation and has grave doubts as to his ability to keep out of trouble very long. He hopes that if he can keep clear for six months, the Air Force will take him. He has passed all his tests and only his probationary status stands in his way.
>
> As he sees the situation, "gang fights are coming up" and it is next to impossible to keep clear of them. This particular fight began at an evening party at which two Bronx boys were present. One started an argument which continued into the street. He pulled the trigger of the gun aimed at Roy's chest. When it failed to go off, he hit another boy

[11] *Ibid.*, p. 16.
[12] *Ibid.*, p. 15.

with it, and cut his chin. On the arrival of the police, the boy hid his gun. As soon as the police left everyone jumped on one of the Bronx boys and beat him up. The police returned, rescued the boy, sending him home in a cab. The Bronx gang thereupon began preparations for war; Roy's gang likewise. The police became aware of these plans when a boy caught Roy and turned him over to the police.

Although Roy acknowledged that the police raids did stop this particular war, he believes any time the police pick up and search a group of boys, it is likely that one of them will be carrying a knife or a gun. To avoid guilt by association is possible only if he isolates himself.[13]

Under these circumstances, Roy is indeed "trapped." If he violates his probation, he will be unable to enter the Air Force where he anticipates a more useful education than that he received in public school. Since attendance at night school is one of the conditions of his probation, he cannot afford to play hookey. If, however, he attempts to attend school without the protection of a gun, he believes he is laying himself open to attack from a rival gang. To lock himself up in his room for six months is, of course, an impossible solution.

Roy's story differed in one respect from that of many gang members whose parents know nothing of their activities. Roy's mother *did* know what was happening to him and sent him to the guidance clinic for help.

As among the rough families described by Mack (Chapter 8), the parents of gang members rarely ate with the children, nor did they generally know where their young people spent their leisure time. A Harlem boy in trouble with the police often stayed in hiding for several days at a time without notifying his parents of his whereabouts. When asked what his parents might say if they knew he belonged to a gang, the usual reply was either: "They would beat me up," or "They would hand me over to the police."[14]

Some of these gang boys, however, were good students and attended school regularly.

John, in the 9th grade of Junior High School, was easily identified as the ring leader in a fracas occurring directly outside of the school building shortly after school was dismissed. Several boys had been seriously injured. John's parents, in fairly comfortable circumstances, were shocked when notified that their only son was the gang leader. They knew nothing whatsoever about his activities. John's teachers also found it

[13] Case recounted by Dr. Stella Chess of the Northside Center for Child Development, Inc. See "Juvenile Delinquency. Whose Problem?" *Federal Probation*, Vol. 19, no. 2 (July 1955), pp. 29-33.

[14] Sophia M. Robison, Nathan Cohen, and Murray Sachs, "An Unsolved Problem in Group Loyalties and Conflicts," *Journal of Educational Sociology*, Vol, 20, no. 3 (Nov. 1946), pp. 154-62.

incredible that John was the gang leader because he was one of the best students in the school and had given no trouble at all in any of his classes. Informed that this episode might interfere with his graduation, John broke down and cried like a baby—behavior inconsistent with the gang's disregard of ordinary standards.[15]

John's combination of qualities, not usually associated with gang members, suggests that the reasons for joining gangs may be as varied as those for joining other organizations. Membership in a gang cannot be presumed to serve identical purposes for all its members any more than regular attendance at church is always synonymous with religious devotion.

Attitudes Toward Adults

The gang members classified adults in three categories: "authorities" were the persons who push them around—police, teachers, and sometimes parents. "Hoodlums" were the smart guys who got along by cheating, exploiting, and outwitting the other fellow—the number man, the pimp, and the racketeer. Some boys considered the police "hoodlums"—"the only difference between a gangster and most policemen is that the police are allowed to carry a gun and get away with what they are doing much easier. They rob, take money from people, they sell dope, they do everything, but they can get away with it."[16] "Suckers" were softies, weaklings who work for a living, and keep their noses clean—indulgent parents, easy teachers, and naïve do-gooders. "Authorities" were hated and feared, "hoodlums" respected; but "suckers" were looked upon with contempt.

Most of the boys hated the filth, poverty, and overcrowding of Harlem. For them, their fellow club members were the only persons in the world on whom they could rely.

Cohen's Analysis of Boy Gang Behavior

So far, we have been concerned with description. Albert Cohen's contribution to an understanding of the teen-age gang has been to attempt to *explain* gang behavior in terms of the class structure of American urban society. Cohen sees a wide gap between the relevant facts and the many concepts of the nature and causes of this and other manifestations of delinquency. In distinguishing between the adolescent gang member and the adult criminal, Cohen points to the following differences:[17]

[15] A case from the author's files.
[16] *Ibid.*, pp. 18 ff.
[17] Cohen, *op. cit.*, pp. 24-30.

1. Stealing has quite different significance for the delinquent gang than it does for the adult criminal. The difference is not just one of degree, but of kind. The gang's stealing is usually nonutilitarian. Stolen objects are rarely converted into cash. Unlike the adult criminal, the gang often steals "for the hell of it," and not for profit.

2. Delinquent gang activity has an element of malice and negativism, "dirty tricks that are done just for fun." Nor is hostility directed only toward adults. Gang members persecute persons of their own age; they often drive "good children" from the playgrounds and the gyms. Their escapades have an element of spite and flouting of ordinary community standards.

3. Unlike the adult criminal, who usually specializes in one form of crime and is careful not to engage in petty crimes that might lead to his detection, a gang member's stealing often goes hand-in-hand with other property offenses, malicious mischief, vandalism, trespassing, and sometimes truancy.

4. A "generalized protean orneriness" and "short-run hedonism" (pleasure-seeking)—acting on the spur of the moment, impatience with planning or postponing of activities, and disregard of consequences—all of which characterize gangs, are not usually part of adult criminal activity.

Middle-Class and Working-Class Standards

To explain why delinquency in the working class differs from that in the middle class, Cohen[18] singles out characteristics which distinguish the family unit in the two classes—planning and foresight, deferment of present pleasures for future gains, saving versus spending. To these characteristics, which Mack also uses to distinguish respectable from rough families, Cohen adds three others:[19]

1. The middle-class "ethic of individual responsibility" (reminiscent of Max Weber's *The Protestant Ethic and the Rise of Capitalism*) is in contrast to the working-class "ethic of reciprocity." An old proverb has it that "the poor help the poor." When the rich help, they do so prudently, with an eye to conserving their own assets.

2. Honesty tends to be conceived in more particularistic terms in working-class society. Concerned with their respective obligations to each other, poor people may be honest in their personal relations because they expect other people to be honest with them. By contrast, the middle-class doctrine is more characteristically each for himself, the devil take the hindmost.

3. The middle-class unlike the working-class family emphasizes sophisti-

[18] *Ibid.*, p. 78.
[19] *Ibid.*, pp. 88-93.

cation, good appearance, selling oneself, all of which makes for greater ease in social mobility.

These major differences in the standards and aspirations of middle-class and working-class families are reflected in the responses of the children to their respective environments. For children, according to Cohen, differ not only with respect to the cultural models in their social class but also in their response to the demands and expectations of their parents and the community representatives. They respond differently to the school, to their peer groups, to the withdrawal of parents' approval as expressed by denial of love or physical punishment, and to the use of force in dealing with "the enemy."

Specifically the educational process in the middle-class families is apt to be "conscious, rational, deliberate and demanding."[20] The family leaves relatively little to chance or just growing up. Because of the emphasis on what the child is to be or to become, he learns to take the long view and to discipline himself to meet his parents' expectations. He accepts parental budgeting of his time—which approves only those activities which help to advance his career. Ordinarily, as Mack noted also, the middle-class family cooperates with the school, the church, and other agencies to see that the child's time is not wasted and that he conforms to expectations with respect to school, play, and work. As a result of his family's expectations and pressures, the middle-class child seems to have a great need to earn his parents' love through his efforts and achievements. This is what Allison Davis calls "an adaptive or socialized anxiety allayed only by the avoidance or proscribed behavior," and what Margaret Mead calls conditional love.[21] In the working-class family there is less stress on effort toward long-range goals. As an infant, the working-class child is more likely to be picked up whenever he cries and fed when he is hungry, without a rigid schedule. As a young child, he has considerable latitude as to when, where, and how he sleeps, eats, dresses, and plays. His frustrations, therefore, are not the result of systematic pressure to master certain skills by a certain time, or at the cost, so to speak, of deferred goals.

Cohen questions whether the effects of physical punishment for wrong-doing, which is more common in working-class than in middle-class families, are as lasting or as deterrent as the threat in the middle-class family of the loss of the parents' love.[22] He points out that love in the middle-class family is likely to be systematically contingent upon achievement; whereas, because of the looser structure of the working-class home, the child there is less dependent upon the love of one or two adults.

[20] *Ibid.*, p. 98.
[21] *Ibid.*, p. 99.
[22] *Ibid.*, p. 101.

The two family types, as noted also by Mack, differ in their use of physical power and aggression. Middle-class children more often avoid physical combat. Rather than take off coats and use fists, they are apt to copy their parents' way of settling differences, i.e., through diplomacy and negotiation. Competitive sports, which require expensive equipment, are encouraged even among the young children in the middle-class group. They serve, Cohen suggests, as an approved outlet for aggression at the same time that they encourage discipline and training as a means for achievement.

If one credits these explanations of the difference in upbringing of children in the two classes of families, one can see why many working-class boys defy middle-class standards. Lacking access to the rewards of middle-class status because their families' aspirations and capacities make the achievements valued by the middle class difficult if not impossible, they turn to their peers, who will support them in group activities which reverse the middle-class standards.

These activities to be an effective substitute, however, must represent joint efforts to solve problems. Without group interaction, the solution of a persistent problem is likely to take a private or neurotic direction which can be more satisfactorily explained in psychogenetic terms.[23]

The Delinquent Subculture

Cohen believes that a delinquent subculture offers an effective solution to the problems of some working-class boys in conflict with middle-class norms.

There is general agreement among sociologists that a subculture arises as the result of efforts to solve problems and thereby relieve tensions. Problems are met and solved in terms of (1) the frame of reference of the persons involved, (2) the situations they confront, and (3) the pressure toward conformity. The first two determinants of a subculture are interdependent.

Since each individual is powerfully motivated to conform to the already established ways of thinking and acting in his group, cultural innovations can only emerge if there is "effective interaction with one another of a number of actors with similar problems of adjustment." The response of individuals to "exploratory gestures" initiates a process of "*mutual* exploration and *joint* elaboration of a new solution." The acceptable solution is not a compromise or the result of any one participant's contribution, but what Lindeman would call an integrated solution.[24] When new group standards are evolved as a result of a shared frame of reference, a new subculture emerges. "It is cultural because each actor's participation in this system of

---

[23] *Ibid.*, p. 71.
[24] Eduard C. Lindeman, *The Community: An Introduction to the Study of Community Leadership and Organization,* New York, Association Press, 1921.

norms is influenced by his perception of the same norms in others. It is *sub*cultural because the norms are shared only among those actors who stand somehow to profit from them and who find in one another a sympathetic moral climate within which these norms may come to fruition and persist."[25]

An individual's status depends upon the judgments of his associates which, in turn, reflect their frames of reference. People who do not or cannot meet the criteria of their associates may solve their conflict by banding together and jointly establishing "new criteria of status which define as meritorious the characteristics they *do* possess, the kinds of conduct of which they *are* capable." Cohen cites as specific illustrations of this general process the Oxford Group, Father Divine's Kingdom, and the Nazi Party. Although the ideologies and value systems of the Oxford Group and Father Divine's Kingdom may seem to have little in common with those of the gang of kids bent on theft and vandalism, the general principles are the same.[26]

Because the personnel of schools and social agencies by and large share middle-class standards of behavior, they are often ready to label the typical working-class child as nonconforming. Thus, the working-class boy who, for whatever reason, is either unwilling or unable to comply with the demands of middle-class society faces a problem of adjustment and is in the market for a "solution." For him, Cohen believes the delinquent subculture provides an answer. It is a way of dealing with problems which will give status to the working-class child who feels unable to meet middle-class standards.

Whether people of low status necessarily feel deprived, injured, or upset by their status depends on: (1) whom they measure themselves against; (2) whose respect or admiration they value. There will be no feeling of deprivation if, like the old English domestic, the standards of their level are taken for granted. If the standards of others present a threat, then redefining the insignia of the status position—as is done by the Holiness sect, which equates virtue with humility, simplicity, and poverty—offers a satisfying solution. Cohen suggests that the *reversal* of the middle-class standards in the delinquent subculture is a similar process.

Although sociologists are beginning to pay more attention to class differences in America,[27] the extent to which the working-class boy really subscribes to the standards of the middle-class boy has not been studied. The standards of the working class are obviously not all uniform, and there are working-class parents who have middle-class aspirations for their children. In consequence, some working-class people are "culturally ambivalent"; their apparent acceptance of working-class jobs and income is challenged by the

[25] Cohen, *op. cit.*, p. 65.
[26] *Ibid.*, pp. 66-67.
[27] See Milton M. Gordon, *Social Class in American Sociology*, Durham, N. C., Duke University Press, 1958.

bombardment of the mass media trying to sell them middle-class consumption standards.

An effective defense against this ambivalence is self-esteem. The crucial questions are: Is the working-class boy satisfied with his picture of himself and of his status? And to what extent does he evaluate himself by his own class standards, or does he wish to be like Whyte's college boy rather than his corner boy?

Confronted with middle-class norms the working-class boy faces three choices:[28]

1. To accept the challenge of the middle-class status system, and play the game according to middle-class rules.

2. To adopt a middle ground, the corner-boy response, which is not specifically delinquent, and "which does not so much repudiate the value of many middle-class achievements as it emphasizes certain other values which make these achievements improbable. . . . The corner-boy culture temporizes with middle-class morality."

3. To participate in the creation and maintenance of a delinquent subculture. This entails costs as well as gratifications.

> The delinquent subculture permits no ambiguity of the status of the delinquent relative to that of anybody else. In terms of the norms of the delinquent subculture, defined by its negative polarity to the respectable status system, the delinquent's nonconformity to middle-class standards sets him above the most exemplary college boy.
> The cavalier misappropriation or destruction of property, therefore, is not only a diversion or diminution of wealth; it is an attack on the middle class where their egos are most vulnerable. Group stealing, institutionalized in the delinquent subculture, is not just a way of *getting* something. It is a means that is the antithesis of sober and diligent "labor in a calling" . . . in the delinquent subculture, the stolen dollar has an odor of sanctity that does not attach to the dollar saved or the dollar earned.[29]

Since it is possible to do only one thing at a time, says Cohen, the need to choose may create conflict and guilt, and a choice that falls short of the boy's expectations of himself may create ambivalence.

In essence, while Cohen does not suggest that the delinquent subculture is the only road to delinquency, he believes that unless delinquency were socially accepted in the delinquent group, this subculture would not exist. For although the delinquent subculture gives status as *against* other children of whatever social level, it is status in the eyes of *fellow delinquents* only. Because outside the gang, the delinquent's status is low, the gang itself

[28] Cohen, *op. cit.*, pp. 130-31.
[29] *Ibid.*, p. 134.

tends to create a kind of sectarian solidarity. Benefits can be realized only in active face-to-face relationships.

There are two essentials for the status criteria in the delinquent sub-culture: (1) They must be standards the working-class boy can meet; (2) they must define merit in terms that are the exact opposite of middle-class norms. If these criteria sanction aggression against the middle-class norms and persons who exemplify them, they have the added advantage of being symbolically masculine. Concluding his exposition of the delinquent sub-culture, Cohen remarks: "The heart of the matter may be expressed in this way: the working-class boy has his problem of adjustment and his motivation to the formation of a delinquent subculture even if his masculinity is not threatened by an early feminine identification; the middle-class boy has his problem in the area of sex-role identification and a motivation to being 'bad' even if he is equipped to succeed in the area in which the working-class boy is handicapped."[30]

Some Reactions to Cohen's Theory

FROM AN EX-GANGLEADER. As a class assignment in a school of social work, an ex-gangleader, who succeeded in by-passing the corner-boy role and identified himself with the middle-class educational goals, realistically challenged some of Cohen's interpretations in the imaginary letter quoted below.

Dear Mr. Cohen,

I have just read your book and I must say that it was a struggle. Man, I had to look up so many words, for a while, I thought I was reading a dictionary rather than your book. You can scribble like crazy.

You say that our stealing was "non-utilitarian, malicious and nega-tivistic," and that it was no more than a valued activity to us. It was no doubt negativistic and malicious. You see, man, it's not that I'm against anyone else, I'm just "all for me." Our stealing did have a utili-tarian motive. Sometimes we stole something we actually liked and wanted and stealing always proved that we had "guts." Further, it was a way to get back at all those people who didn't trust me. And, you know, man, all those groups who didn't trust me weren't middle-class either. The last storekeeper I stole from used to stop waiting on a $1.00 customer to sell me a 2¢ cigarette so as to get me out of the store so I couldn't steal. Man, most of the time I didn't even have stealing on my mind. We never stole from Pop's store because he used to trust us.

You say that we're hedonistic and we didn't engage in long-range planning. The present was bleak enough. Why should we look to the future? Everytime I looked into my crystal ball, something happened on the inside. I just couldn't keep my mind on it. On week-ends, every-

[30] *Ibid.*, p. 169.

body "balled" in my neighborhood. They lived from week-end to week-end and there was a liquor store and a pool room on every other corner surrounded by churches. Another thing, man, we lived too fast, we were always on the run. You talk about "corner boy," you mean "corner men," don't you? We couldn't get a foot on the corner for the adults who were hanging around. The only time they wanted to see us around was when they wanted us to turn in a number for them or to deliver a message to Joe. A lot of these guys used to be missing from the corner for 90-day stretches. Now, I know why.

You talk about group autonomy, that is, self-government. It may have looked like that. Man, we lived by impulse, trying to live every minute to the hilt without rhyme or reason. We really had little choice about what we could do. We were governed by the few pleasures that we had left in life, finding things to do that nobody else thought we should do. As far as the in-group structure, I was the leader of my gang, The Tuxedo Junction Boys, and nobody, not even Gimbels, told me what to do. My boys were at my command. We trusted nobody else and, you know, man, nobody trusted us.

Now about our community, you are right when you said that the "presence of delinquency" can be accounted for by the "absence of constraint." Man, I knew more number-runners, prostitutes, dope pushers, bootleggers and pimps than you can shake a stick at. Where was the law then? They came around occasionally with a little black book and when they left everybody was happy, even the bulls. When they did make an arrest, it was because they had received so many calls or happened to be in the wrong place at the right time. . . .

The "racket guys" mentioned above were our models. Our reputation was based on what people said we did. Nobody but us. When we went to the "Y" or the Settlement House, they watched us like we were the "forty thieves." They watched our every move. Yes, there were some nice men there but they weren't interested in us. Man, we felt like we had on handcuffs everytime we went to one of those places. Usually, we lived up to our reputation and turned out the place. None of the guys our age gave us any resistance at these places. It was always the adults who finally put us out.

I became a track man in high school. I trained while being chased by cops. . . . Well, on that track team, I met some of those middle-class boys you talk about. Some of them excelled in sports and some didn't, but they made up three-fourths of the track team and trained like mad. We trained only when the coach was looking. Naturally, the middle-class boy was the team captain, his father was a faculty member. He was taking an academic course like me. Man, I had to really put down a plea to get an academic course. They told me "We think it would be nice for you to go to college if you want to but, perhaps your parents won't be able to send you." That was the extent of my vocational guidance. All my boys were taking a vocational course. (That's how we learned to improve on our zip guns.)

Well, one day my middle-class friend invited me to his home. His home was much finer but no cleaner than mine. His father and mother sat around talking with both of us. They seemed to feel sorry for me. But man, I didn't feel bad at all. I had on a crazy suit with my $23 blue suede shoes. As we walked through my friend's neighborhood, the cops seemed to be different. Their clubs had no notches in them. And, you know, man, they talked to civilians like they were people.

I didn't hear any swearing on the streets and didn't even see one fight. Man, the place was dead. It seemed to me the community was like a big family where people tried to get along but didn't sacrifice their individualism. The models my friend saw were engineers, teachers, doctors, etc. But this didn't bother me because I knew I could never become a doctor. Besides, if I did, my boys wouldn't feel right towards me.

Now back in my neighborhood when my mother told me to come home early at night or to avoid swearing or to respect adults, it sounded real weird. She worked nights and got home at 1 A.M. Now man, I wonder if she expected me to go home at 9 P.M. on my own. About swearing, how did she expect me to talk to my boys. Yes, I respect women, when I have no alternative. Otherwise, I'm trying to make out just like the other guys. I blame the girls, not the boys.

It was hard to be "good," real hard. If I was good in school they would tell me I was a nice boy and that I should stop hanging around with my own boys. When I finally got into the "Y," they wouldn't let my boys come in until they had paid their membership fees. You see, nobody trusted us. . . .

In my neighborhood I learned early that I only had three guys for whom to look out, "Me, myself, and I." Anything that is not nailed down in my neighborhood is "free property." You learn not to worry about losses; you just look for an opportunity to "do up" somebody else. Call the cops? What for, man? All they do is make a record of your losses and that's it.

I come from a good home. My parents loved me because they always told me so, fed me well and saw that I had a nice home. They were very busy working during the week and "balling" on the weekends. Both of them did a lot of preaching. My father could swing a mean belt. He didn't take anything from me even though I was his son. He taught me not to take anything from anybody. The only place he ever took me was to church. He loved me because if a big kid bothered me, my father always came to my defense, no questions asked. If someone swore in my presence, my father would curse them out. What a guy he was!

My mother never joined the PTA or visited the "Y" or the Settlement House. She felt that I was in good hands and depended on me to do the right thing when away from home. She always claimed to be tired or busy. She made up for it by buying me practically everything I asked for. Most of the time, my father didn't know she was spending so much money on me.

Your main point, Mr. Cohen, is that the "hallmark of the delinquent sub-culture is the explicit and wholesale repudiation of middle-class standards and the adoption of the very antithesis." You say that conformity to middle-class norms interferes with conformity to corner-boy norms. What's wrong with my boys? They treat me all right. They had better do so!

What have we done? We're just trying to have some fun. We don't want to be like those middle-class guys. We are no mamma's boys. We can take care of ourselves. You people are always trying to sell somebody something. We are not babies.

Why should I want to be like those guys? "To each his own" is my motto. Man, I got myself three crazy rags, two benny's, and three pair "bad" shoes. What else do I need? My mother gives me spending money and my broad loves me. Man, I'm living. You know, you talk like a square. You're getting me mad telling me I want to be like those guys. They are no better than I am. By the way, you got a smoke, man? Thanks, daddy. . . .

Analyzing these comments, we see that our correspondent takes issue with Cohen mainly on the following points:

1. The general orneriness of the gang member proceeds *more* from a *need for protection* from fellow gangs than from a desire to *harm* or retaliate against middle-class standards. The collective hostility of the gang is directed toward *other delinquent groups* which threaten their status and reputation. Naturally these groups are unlikely to bring the attack to the attention of legal authorities. Furthermore, the only way to prove prowess is to test it with formidable opposition and not by chasing boys who are "chicken."

2. Distrust, aggression, and rationalization are not antisocial reactions. They are imitations of the way the gang member's own father reacts when the boy is threatened. They are not, therefore, patterns of defying middle-class norms but appropriate behavior.

3. No doubt because of his social-work indoctrination our correspondent now sees the seat of the trouble in the failure of the family to lay the foundation for a stable personality through affection and guidance. Because our correspondent had both guidance and affection he could withstand, at the proper time, the temptations of the destructive gang.

Cohen leaves unanswered the questions suggested by the last point: Why do some lower-class youngsters never join antisocial groups, and why are others later able to give up these associations? Could it be, as the psychiatrists and our correspondent suggest, that boys who have parental affection are more able to cut loose as they grow older?

FROM FATHER MYERS. An Episcopalian priest, Father Myers,[31] in telling the story of his mission's work with a lower East Side gang of Negro and Puerto Rican boys, writes of the meeting at which the Knights decided to use St. Augustine's Chapel of Trinity Parish as their base. "The long patient struggle for the souls of these lads began that night. They were unaware of our love for their souls—such an experience was quite foreign to them. Most of them knew nothing of the love of God because they felt *unloved* and *unwanted by man.*"[32]

The vicar illustrates the rejection of these youngsters, whom he has come to love, in the stories of Ben and Willie, born out of wedlock to Fanny, who had been raped at fifteen by four white boys egged on by a druggist in a Southern town. Fanny, in the North, played the numbers, hoping to provide for her brood of bastards whom she periodically deserted. Then there was Chris, whose stepfather knocked out the boy's teeth when he came upon him unexpectedly on the night he married Chris's mother. Jerry's father used him as an unwilling accomplice in narcotics pushing. Tim's father had deserted, and he and his older brother lived with their mother and her paramour, whom Tim hated.

The vicar and the chapel staff work valiantly, in the face of what often seem insurmountable obstacles in the attitudes of the youngsters as well as of the community, to *love* rather than to *judge* these boys. This does not mean that they work alone; on the contrary, they use every resource in the community—police, settlement house, other clergy, and, when it is available, psychiatric consultation. We refer to this effort of Father Myers because we believe it is important to bear in mind the adolescent's need not only for *status* as described by Cohen but for constructive and accepting affection.

FROM SYKES AND MATZA. The sociologists Sykes and Matza query Cohen's concepts on quite different grounds.[33] While they commend Cohen for his description of the *content* of what the delinquent learns, they argue against the conception of a delinquent subculture for the following reasons:

1. Many delinquents who are caught or committed to an institution reveal feelings of guilt and shame. This would mean that, like John and our correspondent, they do not reject middle-class standards.

When delinquents protect certain persons from harm and attack, and

---

[31] C. Kilmer Myers, *Light The Dark Streets*, Greenwich, Conn., Seabury Press, 1957.

[32] *Ibid.,* p. 28.

[33] Gresham M. Sykes and David Matza, "Techniques of Neutralization," *American Sociological Review*, Vol. 22, no. 6 (Dec. 1957), pp. 666-70.

when they know the "right answers," they acknowledge the validity of society's norms.

Because the world of the delinquent is imbedded in the larger world, his occasional acknowledgment of a sense of guilt or shame, his approval of some conforming figures, and his differential selection of "victims" suggest that he is not wholly committed to a reversal of the standards of the dominant group—a necessary condition, in Cohen's terms, for a delinquent subculture.

To explain how it is possible both to accept and to violate standards, Sykes and Matza refer to Morris R. Cohen, who, in attempting to explain why men violate the laws in which they believe, suggested that values or norms are not categorical imperatives but rather "qualified guides" for action. For example, killing is not always forbidden. It is legitimate in war and in self-defense. Often the delinquent justifies his behavior by reference to codes which seem valid to him even though they are otherwise disapproved.

These justifications for defying the code have the effect of neutralizing the delinquent's normal inhibitions. While Sutherland[34] implies these techniques of neutralization in his "definitions favorable to the violation of law," he does not spell them out. Instead of believing that the delinquent "learns" and "accepts" a value system which reverses middle-class standards, Sykes and Matza advance the thesis that the delinquent uses one or more of the following five techniques of neutralization:[35]

1. *Denial of responsibility.* This is evident when the delinquent blames his parents or gives the impression that he is more sinned against than sinning.

2. *Denial of injury.* The delinquent describes his actions as mischief, or a prank: he "borrowed" the car, the fight was a private affair. This is not a gesture of complete opposition but an extension of the common practice of qualifying the norm.

3. *Denial of the victim.* The delinquent claims that his action was justified in view of the circumstances. He plays the role of avenger—the culprit being the homosexual, a minority group member "who doesn't know his place," an unfair teacher, a brutal police officer, a dishonest shopkeeper.

4. *Condemnation of the condemners* or, to paraphrase McCorkle and Korn, *rejecting the rejectors.* We will see this device operating in a state institution, in Chapter 23. The authorities are caricatured as hypocrites, corrupt, stupid, cruel. What is important is not whether these epithets are deserved but rather that they serve the delinquent's purpose in deflecting the otherwise negative sanctions attached to violating behavior norms.

5. *Appeal to higher loyalties.* The delinquent sacrifices the demands

---

[34] E. H. Sutherland, *Principles of Criminology* (revised by D. R. Cressey), Chicago, Lippincott, 1955, pp. 77-80.
[35] Sykes and Matza, *op. cit.*, pp. 667-69.

of the larger society to those of the sibling pair, the gang, or the friendship clique. The delinquent resolves his dilemma by violating the law. When two conflicting sets of norms are both believed in, role conflicts are resolved in violating society's norms.

One can hardly take issue with Sykes and Matza when they suggest that these hypotheses, like Cohen's, raise some unanswered questions: (1) how do such factors as sex, age, and ethnic group membership affect the use of the denial mechanisms; (2) how, for example, does the nature of the stimulus, i.e., individual or impersonal, call into action the technique of "denial of the victim"?

FROM BLOCH AND NIEDERHOFFER. Bloch and Niederhoffer[36] do not consider the antisocial gang as essentially the working class boy's revolt against the middle-class norms of school and community. Nor do they believe that the gang is indigenous only to slum areas. Instead they regard the gang as a normal manifestation of the fundamental striving essential for development and survival. As evidence of the universality of this drive, Bloch cites the tolerance of middle-class America to many "crimes" in the area of sex behavior—for example, the distorted phases of the normal behavior patterns of teenage dating, courtship, and college fraternity practices.

The behavior of the working-class gang member, they insist, differs only in degree from that of the middle-class clique. The clique, the peer group, or the club (words with less stigma than "gang") are all manifestations of the general grouping process at a given age level. In striving toward adult status the adolescent is seeking to establish his sexual, economic, and civic independence. He finds it difficult to fulfill each of these roles not only because of obstacles placed in his way occasionally by his elders but because of his internal psychological strains and because of the prolonged period of dependency in our society.

As Bloch puts it, "When a society does not make adequate preparation, formal or otherwise, for the induction of its adolescents to the adult status, equivalent forms of behavior arise spontaneously among adolescents themselves, reinforced by their own group structure, which seemingly provide the same psychological content and function as the more formalized rituals found in other societies."[37]

If, as Erikson suggests, we could find some really constructive work for adolescents, which would simultaneously fulfill their needs and those of the community in which they live, they would be able to more quickly achieve responsible adulthood.

FROM SHAPIRO. Like Bloch, a sociologist, and Niederhoffer, a police

[36] Herbert A. Bloch and Arthur Niederhoffer, *The Gang—A Study in Adolescent Behavior*, New York, The Philosophical Library, 1958.
[37] *Ibid.*, p. 17.

officer who has worked with gangs, Shapiro,[38] curator of anthropology at the Museum of Natural History, New York, suggests that true understanding of today's antisocial gang demands that one "view it in the multiple perspective of time, space and culture."[39] Shapiro would agree with Cohen that the criminal behavior of the adolescent who is overwhelmed by personal frustration and rebels is a personal problem. It is quite different from the *antisocial* behavior which arises out of the interaction of a group of adolescents. The latter is a *social* problem because, although the resulting behavior may be reprehensible from the point of view of society-at-large, it conforms with the values and standards of the world of gang members.

Shapiro would agree with other cultural anthropologists (see Chapter 11) that the struggle of successive groups of immigrants, liberated from the rigid bonds of inherited social class and challenged by the American goal of upward social mobility, has presented some snags for the second-generation adolescents. He grants also that rejection by the dominant group plays an important role in throwing the young aspirant back on the marginal units of the street society which satisfy the universal need for association with one's fellows.[40]

But he holds other forces in America, besides the influx of different immigrant cultures, partly responsible for prolonging the adolescent's revolt and dependency. Our child labor laws and compulsory school attendance, although based largely on humanitarian principles, have made it difficult for the reluctant scholars, as Shapiro calls them, to spend their time profitably in our highly mechanized city homes. They are "ripe for the life of the streets" with its gang associations. Their normally high spirits, energy, and eagerness for adventure set the stage for behavior that can readily take an antisocial turn.[41]

Unfortunately, however, we fail to recognize that the normal demands of physical development are held back until society provides opportunities for earning a living which were open to youths of sixteen and seventeen in the early days of America. Today's adolescents have the strength of men, but have not acquired the restraints that come from discipline and responsibility growing out of socially satisfying activities.

Thus Shapiro, like Bloch, Niederhoffer, and Erikson, see much of our present-day antisocial behavior as the *unintended* consequence of the major changes in our economy from a simple self-contained society to vast industrialized multi-ethnic urban life. The villain in the piece, they suggest, is

[38] Harry L. Shapiro, Ph.D., "Youthful Offenses in Modern Culture," *Bulletin*, New York Academy of Medicine, Second Series, Vol. 35, no. 62 (June 1959), pp. 341-56.
[39] *Ibid.*, p. 342.
[40] *Ibid.*, p. 353.
[41] *Ibid.*, p. 355.

not primarily the struggle between the *classes* as Cohen sees it. It is instead failure to provide for many physically mature youths to assume appropriate and rewarding roles, especially if they are members of minority groups. To be sure some of this struggle is also illustrated in some gang behavior, but the remedy involves more than a change in class structure.[42]

Summary

Membership in peer groups is a natural phenomenon—beginning in pre-adolescence and extending into adulthood. In adolescence particularly, the peer group provides protection and support in the weaning process. Not all gangs are antisocial, or destructive all the time. In big cities, the antisocial gang is not new. In the course of a century, the ethnic backgrounds have changed, and with them the neighborhoods in which they hold sway; but some form of violence appears to remain constant.

Various projects designed to cope with gang activity in New York City have added to our knowledge of: (1) the social characteristics of gang members in lower-class neighborhoods; (2) gang structure; (3) the way in which the gang member spends his time; (4) how he gets involved in rumbles. This knowledge, however, does not explain satisfactorily why membership in the adolescent gang offers esteem for behavior which would be frowned upon in other sectors of society.

Not all boys who join the delinquent gang do so for the same reasons, or to solve the same problems. One boy may join the gang as a protection, and another, like John, probably because the delinquent groups in his neighborhood happen to be of his own racial or ethnic group, with which he either wishes or is forced for his own protection to affiliate.

Albert Cohen's fresh look at the gang as a working-class phenomenon discloses marked differences between the activities of the adolescent gang and the usual adult criminal behavior. The differences call for quite different explanations, and for understanding of why, according to Cohen, the middle-class delinquent so rarely joins a destructive gang.

Cohen's delinquent subculture theory attempts to incorporate the new knowledge from sociological research, i.e., in arriving at a solution of his problem of status, the working-class boy needs the support of other individuals who are experiencing similar threats. Despite evidence that antisocial behavior does crop out in middle-class and upper-class sections of society, the antisocial gang, according to Cohen, is characteristically a working-class phenomenon and a rejection of the standards of behavior of the middle-class group.

[42] *Ibid.,* p. 356.

What distinguishes the gang behavior as a subculture is that it is acquired and practiced in groups rather than being independently contrived by the individual as a solution to his private problems. The possibility of association with others who also seek solutions to their problems is decisive to gang formation.

Cohen's thesis, though provocative, raises several doubts. One set, put forth by a young social worker who in his high school days was the leader of a gang, rejects the notion that gang membership is an attack on middle-class standards, and sees it instead as self-protective and, in the context, appropriate behavior.

Father Myers sees gang behavior as a response not only to low status but to deprivation of love and acceptance.

Sykes and Matza, in a formal analysis, question the hypothesis of a delinquent subculture on the ground that the gang member does not reject or reverse middle-class standards, but rather accepts them and rationalizes his deviant behavior by calling into play one or more of the five techniques to neutralize inhibitions. These ideas, as the authors note, need to be tested.

Bloch, Niederhoffer, and Shapiro caution us that to understand the antisocial gang we must see it in its proper perspective, i.e., as an unintended consequence of modern, multi-ethnic industrialized urban living. While we have postponed the age at which young people may assume economic responsibilities we have not simultaneously slowed up the processes of physiological maturity. Nor have we provided reluctant scholars with socially acceptable and rewarding outlets for their youthful energies and capacities.

The important implication that stems from these studies is the need for less emphasis on descriptive characteristics and more on understanding the sociological variables, role, function, and structure involved in delinquency. These sociological variables, in turn, need to be considered in conjunction with their psychological and cultural determinants.

CHAPTER 10

Sociological Approaches:
IV. The School and the
Mass Media

THERE IS A CERTAIN IRONY IN THE FACT THAT SOCIETY'S TWO PRINCIPAL channels for communicating knowledge have been held increasingly responsible for the apparent rise in juvenile delinquency in the United States in recent years. If knowledge is an absolute good, then the schools and the mass media should both be forces of good. How is it that, in the minds of many people—both professional and lay—they seem to have helped to breed evil as well as good? This is the question to which this chapter is addressed.

The School and Delinquency

The school, like the church, is a major institution to which the modern family turns for help in rearing its children in the way they should go.

The school today is expected to perform many functions which were formerly the exclusive province of the home. It is perhaps as natural, therefore, to expect the school to make up for the shortcomings of the modern home as it is for the school to complain that many of its difficulties with children are rooted in the home. Teachers have been heard to blame delinquent behavior on the neighborhood. In turn, parents complain that schools do not properly discipline children. Teachers familiar with the delinquency area theory discussed in Chapter 7 have said, "What can you expect of that child? He comes from a delinquency area." Some parents are disturbed by the fact that "the schools of today are nothing like the school that I attended." The implication is that they are not as good.

Whether or not all the demands that are currently made on the schools are justified is not the issue. They remain of interest because they represent an attempt on the part of the community to assign responsibility to the school for creating and therefore dealing with the problem of delinquency.

The establishment of a public school system followed the community's recognition that ignorance and illiteracy were not only the individual's concern but had social implications as well. Up to that time only the children of substantial citizens had the advantage of education, paid for by their individual parents.

In 1855, in his annual report, the New York City Superintendent of Schools wrote:

> Why not teach them [the youngest children] definitions while forming words in the spelling stick [a special device called a "syllabarium"]. Such a method may at the same time also be made somewhat of a means of moral training. To illustrate, D-r-a-y—dray—a low cart, a carriage of burden with two wheels. Take care when crossing the streets— for some drivers are careless. Do not be *street* boys—they are *bad* boys— they throw *stones, cut* and *break* things, and make marks with chalk on houses and fences and speak bad words—do not do so—be *good* children. To the want of due attention to this *all* important point, in our Primary Schools, may be attributed the frequency of those associations of *banded young ruffians* that so often disturb the peace of our city under various titles, so significant of their clanship, "Rock Boys," etc.[1]

Hannig adds, "I do not recall having heard mention of this procedure in our campaign against gang delinquency." It was not recognized in 1855, however, and it is not always remembered today by the proponents of reading and writing as a cure for crime and delinquency that these tools of learning do not have built-in devices to assure their proper use. Unfortunately, knowing the right does not always mean doing it.[2]

The use to which any tool is put depends not only upon the skill but upon the will and the needs of the user. In sociological terms, as Robert MacIver points out, technological factors do not explain *why* something occurs, but only the form which it assumes. The pen may be used to write a

[1] Quoted by William A. Hannig, "Our Public Schools: Looking Backward One Hundred Years," in William Jansen, *Annual Report, 1953-54*, N. Y. Board of Education, p. 23.

[2] Leah Levinger and Hyman Grossbart have illustrated this well in their unpublished study of the answers of one hundred delinquents at Hawthorne-Cedar Knolls Schools to the Wechsler-Bellevue question: "Why are laws necessary?"

slanderous letter or an "Ode to the Skylark." The instrument is indifferent to the aim of the author; or, as the German proverb puts it, "Paper is patient."

There is, then, no guarantee that education is an automatic corrective for either crime or delinquency. It may, as a matter of fact, suggest to the individual or child contemplating antisocial action a way in which he can carry out his intention. Jenkins (see Chapter 6) reminds us that confidence men make expert use of their knowledge, without guilt feelings, for objectives of which society disapproves.

The major premises on which the schools are held accountable for delinquency are: (1) that the discipline is lax; (2) that the children are not being adequately taught to read; and (3) that willful truancy is the fault of the school, and the first step in delinquency.

Lax Discipline

Progressive educational methods have been blamed for delinquency. Persons who firmly believe the biblical injunction, "He that spareth the rod hateth his son," often quote their own beneficial experiences of sessions in the woodshed or with a razor strop. They fail to remember, however, that frequently this type of punishment was accompanied by an underlying acceptance of them by their parents, which may have served as a cushion in more ways than one. While the Hutterite father uses the strap with vigor, he also comforts the child later and explains that the punishment was necessary to impress on him that he must avoid wrong conduct.[3]

While most people avoid painful experiences, many factors besides fear of punishment play some part in decisions to desist from antisocial behavior. Punishment may follow misbehavior so rarely in comparison with the number of occasions for which it was "deserved" that the culprit is willing to take the chance that his misdeeds will escape punishment. Psychiatric study discloses that for some people punishment provides relief for a sense of guilt, and so reactivates the cycle: delinquency–punishment–relief–delinquency. In other cases, punishment literally slides off the back, as something to be tolerated, because the antisocial act had its own rewards.

Refusing to recognize the operation of these different meanings and values attached to punishment by the miscreant, the advocates of the get-tough policy still insist that the stricter the discipline, the less the revolt. These adherents of extreme disciplinary measures do not ask whether automatic obedience to law or to custom is always a healthy manifestation.

The alternatives of freedom and restraint are not black and white. The need is to find, in school and out of it, a nice balance in the setting of limits

[3] Symposium: "Research in Behavioral Development in Collectives," 35th Annual Meeting of the American Orthopsychiatric Association, New York City, March 8, 1958.

which will permit reasonable freedom of action in a democratic society in the light of the general welfare.

School Retardation

The second general reason that the public school is held to be an ineffectual bulwark against delinquency is that it does not teach the 3 R's successfully. A very large proportion of the children in the New York City public schools cannot read, write, or figure adequately even after they have been in school for some years. This is acknowledged officially in a report used as a guide for supervisors and teachers:

> It can be expected that at least one-half of the entering class of the junior high school will score at reading grade levels below the seventh (with norms adjusted for age). Nearly one out of five entering students scores at fourth grade or below. . . . Nearly half of these elementary grade readers may be considered retarded readers—that is, they have the capacity to read better. . . . Practically all of the 10,000 to 15,000 children scoring below grade 5 are also retarded readers, many of them severely so, *although most of them are of normal or near-normal intelligence.*[4]

According to the Presiding Justice of the Domestic Relations Court: "It has been shown conclusively that there is a definite link between reading retardation and delinquency. Reading difficulties were reported for 75 per cent of the delinquents in the non-school part of the Children's Court; and 85 per cent of the boys in detention at Youth House are handicapped by being unable to read books appropriate to their grade in school."[5] Whether or not this statement implies a *causal* connection between delinquency and reading disability, it is clear that reading disabilities, as likely barriers to social and emotional adjustment, are apt to impede the rehabilitation of the delinquent. Reading was not so important a skill in the days when there were plenty of jobs which did not call for reading facility. Today, however, the child who is unable to read is definitely handicapped. Some such children may try to compensate by indulging in undesirable behavior.

Before a causal connection between reading disability and delinquency could be established, however, we would need to know more than we do today. For example, we have no evidence of how many retarded readers are *not* delinquent. Furthermore, there are indications that, of the children who attend school regularly today, there are proportionately no more nonreaders

---

[4] "The Retarded Reader in the Junior High School: A Guide for Supervisors and Teachers," Bureau of Educational Research, N. Y. Board of Education, June 1955, p. 9. Italics added.

[5] "Perspective on Delinquency Prevention," *American Journal of Orthopsychiatry,* Jan. 1955.

than there were formerly. Teaching methods today are as good as or perhaps better than they were formerly. Educational research directed at discovering the advantages of various methods of teaching reading has not shown that any one method is decidedly superior to another. Because more parents of our day have themselves gone relatively far in school, however, they are more critical than their parents were. Perhaps, too, the personal element of the interest of the teacher or the boy's identification of reading with the female role in certain classes of society and among certain cultural groups not formerly on the school rolls may be more important factors today than they were formerly in learning how to read regardless of the method employed.

Truancy

Besides complaints about pedagogy and discipline, the school is also occasionally blamed for willful truancy. Because one so often encounters the slogan, "Truancy is the first step in delinquency," it is worth while taking a fresh look at the label "truancy." We shall inquire (1) whether the conditions under which it is affixed are uniform, and (2) whether there are specific psychological, cultural, and socio-economic conditions which appear to be associated with this particular form of disapproved juvenile behavior, and which may be crucial in determining its occurrence.

HOW THE LABEL IS APPLIED. Delinquency cases in which the school is the petitioner are usually connected with delinquency. As with other manifestations of delinquency, however, the definitions of truancy are not uniform. They vary from time to time and from place to place. In striking contrast to America, the European delinquency statistics do not include truancy. Part of the explanation may be that European school systems often select students in their early adolescence for continued training, eliminating those who seem less likely to succeed. Furthermore, the age at which one is permitted to leave school is lower; in England, for example, school attendance is not compulsory beyond the fifteenth birthday.

In the United States, too, truancy was not always illegal. A feeble attempt at legislating against it in New York City dates back to the 1870s though even earlier, in 1852, the city fathers were deploring the lack of concern of parents especially of the numerous indifferent and poor inhabitants of the city in the decade preceding the Civil War. The Superintendent's Report quoted above notes that less than 8 per cent of New York City's children attended school regularly in 1855. (Cincinnati and Boston had twice as good a record with approximately 17 per cent regular school attendance, and Philadelphia claimed 13 per cent.) We are reminded that 1854 was a peak year for Irish and German immigrants, who crowded into New York's already overcrowded tenements, without central heating, indoor toilets, and so forth. Water was available usually only at a faucet in the rear court or at a public hydrant. Above Thirtieth Street, Irish and German immigrants lived in board or mud shanties with their dogs, goats, and pigs. The men got what work they could in the nearby quarries and "the German women, especially lived on the bones and rags which they and their children gathered all the day long throughout the streets of the city."[6] No wonder they were not sufficiently concerned with their children's school attendance records!

It was not until 1914 that New York State passed a compulsory Education law, and the New York City Board of Education established its Bureau of Attendance to enforce the provisions of the state law. School principals were given specific instructions to see that children aged 7 to 17 attended school regularly unless they were excused because they were ill, legally employed, or had been officially suspended. Teachers were supposed to notify parents or guardians when children were absent. And on the third day of *unexcused* absence the principal was instructed to report the case to the Bureau of Attendance. This bureau then investigated the case and initiated appropriate measures.

By the 1920s truancy had become a focal point of interest by students of delinquency and crime. A study by the New York State Crime Commission[7] proclaimed (without, however, using a control group to check) that delinquents began as school truants and came from slum areas. A second Crime Commission study[8] of an institution known as the Parental School, established especially to deal with the persistent truant in New York City, reported that chronic truancy, in a disquieting number of cases, was the first step in a criminal career. More than half the boys committed to this institution had come to the attention of the police and the courts in the six- to eight-year period following their release.

The findings of this study were also open to question: It is possible that the subsequent delinquent behavior was a *reaction to the experience in the institution,* which was eventually closed because of disclosures of the abusive measures employed by the head of the school. Furthermore, there is a question concerning the representative character of the boys committed to this school; they represented a highly selected group of truants. Boys from "broken homes," who had given evidence of not being amenable to the family's control —many of them children of immigrant Italians—predominated. To assume that this sample represented the universe of truants is another illustration of circular reasoning—putting into a situation unconsciously the very factors which one later pulls out and labels causes.

The findings of two later studies of truancy in New York City schools—

[6] Hannig, *op. cit.,* p. 24.
[7] The Crime Commission of New York, Subcommission on Causes and Effects of Crime, *Individual Studies of 145 Offenders,* New York, 1928.
[8] The Crime Commission of New York, Subcommission on Causes and Effects of Crime, *From Truancy to Crime, A Study of 251 Adolescents,* New York, 1928.

one in 1930 and the other in 1947—have wide applications in the effort to identify those who are labeled truant.

In 1930 the Bureau of Attendance of the New York City Board of Education made available to the author 25,000 records covering one year's truancy hearings. These were subsequently analyzed (1) to clarify the basis of the official label of "truant" in the delinquency count (a very small proportion of New York City truants were referred to the court); (2) to estimate the size of the problem in New York City; and (3) to discover whether or not there were any special characteristics such as age, sex, color, ethnic group, or progress in school which distinguished truants from other delinquents known to the juvenile court.[9]

Truancy was then defined by the Board of Education as absence for *three consecutive days* without a satisfactory explanation, and when this occurred, the young person's parents or guardians were called before the district truancy office for a hearing. The result was sometimes dismissal with a warning, sometimes an order to come back for a rehearing, sometimes a request that the child report for a specified period to the truant officer. Occasionally, if there had been more than one hearing, the child might be committed to the Parental School until he reached his seventeenth birthday, after which school attendance was no longer compulsory.

Analysis revealed that only about one third of the 25,000 hearings represented cases of willful truancy—children whose parents were unaware of the fact that they were not in school; the remaining two thirds were children who were unlawfully detained at home by their parents, children who wished to leave school to go to work, some who were working but had not secured employment certificates, and some who were distributing or selling "without a badge or a license." Some children were also included who had been ill, but who on their return to school had failed to bring the required written excuses.

The rate for *willful* truants per thousand school children in Manhattan, which was twice that for the city as a whole, may be partially explained (1) by the fact that the Bureau of Attendance operated differently in various boroughs of New York City; (2) by variations in the programs of the public schools; and (3) by differences in the ethnic and socio-economic characteristics of the population in the different boroughs which appeared to be associated with regularity of school attendance. On this last point some evidence is noted in the following section.

The second comprehensive study of truants in New York City, in 1947-48, revealed that the official basis for reporting absences *had been changed from three to five days of unexplained absence.*[10] The records no

---

[9] Robison, *Can Delinquency Be Measured?*, New York, Columbia University Press, 1936, Chapter 8.
[10] This policy was again revised in 1958.

longer officially noted the ethnic group or religious affiliation. Furthermore, school retardation could not be calculated because of a change in the school policy which resulted in practically a hundred per cent promotion policy regardless of academic attainment.[11]

It is clear from these studies that even in recent years, in a single city, truancy has not been subject to a single invariable definition. It is not, from year to year, a consistent legal entity, and statistics of truancy are only significant when they are analyzed in connection with other variables.

CHARACTERISTICS OF TRUANTS AND THEIR FAMILIES. Such variables include the meaning of truancy to the child and his family. Truancy, like running away from home, may represent the need of the individual boy for satisfaction in the face of thwarting situations at school or home. Home pressures for regular school attendance may vary with the relative emphasis that different ethnic groups place on formal education. Or truancy may be involved with sexual identification.

Thus, for each girl truant in the 1930 study, there were six boy truants; and for each child under ten years of age, there were thirteen over ten years of age. Among the persistent truant groups (those who had had more than one hearing in the year), Catholic children of Italian parentage predominated. White Protestant children were least frequently truant, with a ratio of one to twelve Catholics. Jewish children appeared in the ratio of one to four Catholics. Negroes appeared in the truancy count twice as often as they appeared in the city's population.

Classified by age-grade status, retarded children appeared in the truant group two and one-half times more often than they did in the total 1930 school population.

Truancy was reported much less frequently from parochial schools. Possible reasons may be that (1) these schools had other ways of handling the problem of truancy; (2) only a small percentage of the children who attended the parochial schools at that time were Italians; (3) the staff of the Bureau of Attendance, reportedly overworked, did not as carefully check attendance in the parochial schools, which did not receive state subsidies for every day of school attendance. As a matter of fact, the original reason for establishing the Bureau of Attendance in New York City was not to cure or to prevent truancy and its presumed concomitant delinquency, but to assure to the city the receipt of the state's per capita allotment, which was based upon each day of school attendance.[12]

[11] Alfred A. Kahn and Trude Lash, *Children Absent from School*, New York, The Citizens Committee for Children, 1949.
[12] The extent to which the apprehending machinery can affect a truancy rate and a "delinquency" rate is revealed in a comment of the Washington, D. C., school authorities. In discussing the possibilities of including truancy in an analysis of "delinquency," preparatory to setting up a Central Register in 1943, they commented that if notice of absence of children were reported to the parents each school day, the Washington mailbags would be unable to carry any other communications.

An interesting case study highlights the importance of sociological and psychological factors that operate in truancy. In 1945 the Harlem and the Mount Morris District of the Community Service Society agreed to study twenty persistent Negro truants in attendance at Junior High School 120 in Manhattan.[13] Departing from the agency's usual practice of waiting until clients come to ask for service, social workers visited the homes to offer help with the truants. They also interviewed the school authorities and the teachers to obtain their estimate of progress and achievement of each of the twenty boys. These twenty families were ready and willing to cooperate in the search for an explanation of the boys' persistent truancy. Some of them remained under the care of the Agency until there was improvement not only in attendance but in some of the other family problems.

The study revealed that truancy appeared to be a symptom of a complicated set of difficulties covering a wide range of disturbance in relationships as well as in the physical environment. All of the families lived in the Harlem slums, in railroad flats of four or five rooms, at rents between $28 and $38 a month. Their homes offered little privacy, minimum comfort, and were insufficiently equipped for any semblance of normal family living.

Eleven of the mothers were working as domestics, in factories or laundries, had married early or had had children out of wedlock when they were very young. Some of them were trying to meet their own emotional needs through promiscuous relationships. If the father was in the home, he did not assume much responsibility for the children. Often the child was shunted back and forth because of the unstable family pattern. The usual sibling rivalry was frequently accentuated by the several sets of children in the home.

Closely associated with the economic and living deprivations of these families were many health difficulties. The children's school health cards reported a history of rickets, bone disorders, rheumatic fever, mastoids, asthma, and suspected tuberculosis.

Added to the personal strain in adjustment was the fact that the parents were either Negro or dark-skinned Puerto Ricans, and came from low-standard rural communities, which made it difficult for them to adjust to New York City life. Following the pattern of their own childhood, the parents expected their children to go to work as soon as possible, at the expense of continuing school, in order to supplement meager family incomes.

However, even in this sordid background there were some positive factors. The mothers showed affection for their children, though they were not always consistent in setting limits of permissible behavior. The boys were of normal intelligence, and they appeared to be seeking an adequate manhood.

The fact that practically none of these children had been truants before

---

[13] Ruth Downing, Frieda Kuhlman, and Patricia Sachs, unpublished study of the Community Service Society in connection with the Harlem Project, 1945.

their transfer from the six-year elementary schools to the junior high school suggests that *the impersonal relationship with a half dozen teachers of specialized subjects in the junior high school, compared with contact with one classroom teacher of the elementary school, plus the breaking of friendships in the small neighborhood school and the pressures of adolescence,* brought the difficulties of these boys into sharper focus. As a result, they became increasingly insecure and retreated from the unaccustomed new school experiences. Despite their potential capacities, there was unusual fluctuation in school performance. The stammering and the exhibitionism of some boys, and the withdrawal of others, seemed to be symptomatic responses to their deprivations. The important finding, however, was that there was no evidence that *any* of them were engaging in antisocial activity in the community. *In not a single one of these cases was the persistent truancy the first step to delinquency.* Instead, it seemed to Downing, Kuhlman, and Sachs to be a signal of their need for help.

TRUANCY AS SCHOOL PHOBIA. A similar view of truancy as a signal for help, rather than as a self-explanatory legal entity calling for strict enforcement of school attendance regulations, is disclosed in a study made by Dr. Emanuel Klein.[14] In examining children referred to him at the Bureau of Child Guidance of the New York City Board of Education, Dr. Klein found that many of them were actually afraid to go to school. This finding, he felt, had important implications for treatment. To force these children to return to school without understanding the basis for their fear would not only fail to cure the symptom but would undoubtedly result in much more serious disturbances.

A study of fifty-three cases of school phobia referred to the Judge Baker Guidance Center in Boston concludes that it can become one of the most disabling disorders of childhood.[15] Almost invariably truancy was accompanied by psychomatic symptoms. The most typical picture was a child who vomited his breakfast and used this device to remain at home. The explanation usually given was that the child was fearful of being separated from his mother. The ways in which these children may be helped are the subject of current research at the Center.[16]

TRUANCY AS SCHOOL RESISTANCE. In dealing with problems of child welfare in the Gary, Indiana, schools, Mark Roser,[17] the Director of Child

[14] Emanuel Klein, "Reluctance to Go to School," in *The Psychoanalytic Study of the Child*, Vol. 1, p. 263, New York, International Universities Press, 1945.

[15] Paper presented at the convention of the American School Counselors Association, Washington, D.C., March 26, 1956.

[16] Samuel Wald, Pauline B. Hahn, Ellen Teasman, "Evaluation for Program of Early Intervention in School Phobia," paper presented at 35th Annual Meeting of the American Orthopsychiatric Association, New York City, March 6-8, 1958.

[17] Mark Roser, "The Role of the Schools in Heading Off Delinquency," *Yearbook*, National Probation and Parole Association, 1951, pp. 168-83.

Welfare of the Gary school system, has stated that truancy needs to be re-defined as school resistance, based on hostility.

The school may easily provoke hostility if, in its elaborate testing mech-anisms, it exposes children to a climate of negative, hostile emotions. The intellectually inadequate child, resenting his school experience, often ceases to learn and develops unhealthy social patterns which may be expressed in truancy, fighting, stealing, or illness. The amount of negative emotion that a child can tolerate varies both for the individual child and for the group to which he belongs. If his group approves of truancy, it becomes a protective device for his own ego.[18]

Inability to read, according to Roser, may be one expression of hostility to school. The relatively lower incidence of nonreading among girls suggests that boys may tend to identify reading and spelling as "sissy" activities. This feeling would be reinforced by the predominance of women teachers in the elementary schools, which some psychologists and educators regard as a serious hindrance to the boys' drive toward male identification. Roser further suggests that since boys are more apt than girls to identify with the aggres-sive drama of life as depicted, for instance, in television and comic books, they have an additional struggle in making sense out of spelling "c-a-t," when, in phantasy, they are out chasing robbers. Roser suggests tutoring by men, as well as emphasis on athletics or shopwork, as ways of undergirding masculine identity.

Other children, says Roser, may be afraid to learn because they have been so often called "stupid" that they have come to feel that they cannot learn. Their behavior accords with the picture of their personality that they have come to accept.[19]

It would be advisable, according to Roser, with whom we agree, to sub-stitute for the fictitious entity "legal truants" the concept of hostile children who dislike school and resist it for a variety of reasons. The syndrome "school resistance" would thus include low or impaired intellectual functioning, defective self-image, extreme character defects, growth conflicts, boredom, and unusual group or family patterns. To expect a child, frightened at the thought of school pressures, to attend school is as unreasonable as it would be to expect the child to go with a broken leg or a temperature of 103°.[20]

TRUANCY AS NEGLECT. A further reconsideration of the meaning of truancy is proposed by a committee of juvenile court judges who were assigned the responsibility in 1955 for revising the 1949 edition of the Standard Juve-nile Court Act. In commenting on whether or not truancy should be included in the description of behavior classified as "delinquency" and within the

---

[18] Compare with Cohen's analysis of the delinquent subculture (Chapter 9).
[19] See Erikson's discussion of ego-identity in Chapter 6.
[20] For a description of Roser's plans for combating truancy, see Chapter 28.

jurisdiction of the juvenile court, they remark: "Truancy as juvenile court jurisdiction is better defined as neglect than delinquency. The *Standard Juvenile Court Act* gives truancy jurisdiction in the following words—'any child who is neglected as to proper or necessary support or education as required by law.' "[21]

Thus, while no studies to date have proved that laxness of discipline or failure to teach the three Rs effectively have made the schools insufficient bulwarks against delinquency, there are indications that the public schools have been less aware than they should be of the *significance* of truancy, especially among the most economically and culturally deprived segments of our population. To prove a *causal* relation between truancy and subsequent other types of delinquent behavior, however, one would need to study what happened in later years to an unselected group of truants. This procedure has not been followed in any study so far published.

Mass Media and Delinquency

Sociologists have for some time been interested in the effect of the mass media of communication—the press, the movies, the comics, television—on the behavior of individuals. Teachers as well as parents have complained that even the radio interferes with good study habits of students who are not highly motivated. As a substitute for the concentrated grind necessary to master the textbook, listening to the radio can easily lead to phantasy. Some students have attempted to document the popular belief that sensational accounts of crime and delinquency stimulate more of the same. Whether or not this is true remains to be proved. We review below the meager evidence with respect to the effect of movies, the comics, and television on delinquency.

Movies

With the exception of the classic study of Blumer and Hauser,[22] most of the studies concerned with the relation of the movies to delinquency are based on samples too small to be significant. Blumer and Hauser interviewed 386 delinquent boys and 252 delinquent girls. They also assembled auto-biographical data to compare the interests of delinquents and nondelinquents in grade and high schools. The major findings were that only 10 per cent of the boys and 25 per cent of the girls thought that the movies had played a role in their delinquent actions. Perhaps because of these negative findings

[21] Sol Rubin, "Protecting the Child in the Juvenile Court," *Journal of Criminal Law, Criminology, and Police Science*, Vol. 43, no. 4 (Nov.-Dec. 1952), p. 431, fn. 13.

[22] Herbert Blumer and P. M. Hauser, *The Movies, Delinquency and Crime*, New York, Macmillan, 1933.

the moviegoing habits of delinquents received relatively little attention in subsequent studies.[23]

Comics

Because the comic book is directly aimed at young people, there has been much concern with the comics as a cause of delinquent behavior. The Hendrickson Subcommittee on Juvenile Delinquency of the United States Senate[24] sought to determine whether exposure to vividly illustrated comics had a direct effect upon disturbed and potentially delinquent youth and caused them to indulge in wild behavior. Because there are no definitive studies based on controlled experiments, the Subcommittee requested a considerable number of sociologists, psychologists, and law enforcement officers to testify. The resulting testimony expressed a variety of opinions, which unfortunately did not add up to definite conclusions.

The Director of the National Institute of Mental Health, Dr. Robert Felix, commented on an unnamed study which indicated that disturbance of sleep evidenced by motility for two or three nights suggested that seeing a movie was not a neutral event, and "that reading comics may well have similar influences upon children to those that have been demonstrated for the movies."[25]

According to Dr. Harris Peck, then psychiatrist of the Children's Court in New York City, horror comics might provide an additional thrust toward antisocial behavior. Discussing the difference between the effect of fairy tales and horror comics, Dr. Peck stated that there was some humaneness about fairy tales, whereas the horror comics "seem to enlarge on the most perverse aspects of the human conscience."[26]

It has been suggested that Grimm's *Fairy Tales,* so avidly read in former years by today's "older generation," are the equivalent of modern horror comics and the violent television programs. Yesterday's child, however, generally knew that the fairy lore and characters, unlike those in comics and television programs, were not flesh-and-blood people whom he might be tempted to imitate in action. Instead the fairy tale enabled the child to "work out" his relationships and his conflicts in fantasy. For example, the Punch-and-Judy pantomimes, certainly sadistic by adult standards, might offer a constructive outlet for aggressive feelings. On the other hand, an admittedly

[23] Mortimer Adler, in *Art and Prudence,* New York, Longmans, 1937, subjects the various studies on the effects of motion pictures under the auspices of the Payne Fund, of which the Hauser and Blumer study was perhaps the most ambitious, to a critical appraisal of their research and their conclusions.

[24] Robert C. Hendrickson (with Fred J. Cook), *Youth in Danger,* New York, Harcourt Brace, 1956.

[25] Quoted in *ibid.,* pp. 201-202.

[26] Quoted in *ibid.,* p. 208.

negative aspect of fairy tales and pantomimes was the possibility that the child might be tempted to retreat to the fantasy world when, from the point of view of his mental health, engaging in antisocial behavior might be preferable.

Dr. Frederic Wertham testified that there are thousands of children who spend about $60 a year on comic books, most of which glorify murder, rape, and obscenity. He reported seeing a boy in a slum neighborhood buy as many as fifteen comic books at one time. Moreover, he disagreed with the majority of the experts who believed that comic books have their greatest effect on maladjusted children. On the contrary, Wertham believed that the normal child was most drastically influenced by the comics. He based his opinions on studies which he conducted in the years 1945-46. Since, unfortunately, these studies have not been published, there is no way of checking his conclusions.

Although Dr. Wertham did not argue that comics alone were the cause of delinquency, he considered them, without any reasonable doubt and without reservations, an important contributing factor. In his opinion the horror comics did not affect the most morbid children, because these children are ordinarily wrapped up in their own fantasies. He drew an analogy of the effect of horror comics on children with essentially healthy instincts by alluding to the *Confessions of St. Augustine*. St. Augustine described his initial revulsion against the bloody spectacles of the gladiatorial arena of ancient Rome. But soon, drawn on by his friends, he became "unconsciously delighted with it, and kept on going." In like manner, Wertham believed, children who see women beaten up, or men and women shot and killed in the comics, become "unconsciously delighted."

Dr. Wertham took violent issue with the publishers of comic books who claim that the effect of the comics is to teach that "crime does not pay." Wertham commented that their emphasis is on physical maiming and the actual triumph of the evil over the good. He referred to one of the *Tarzan* comics in which twenty-two people were blinded, among them a beautiful white girl. The fact that the culprit was a Negro, Wertham believed, was an incitement to race hatred. Other comics, in his opinion, taught contempt of the police; such expressions as, "Friendship is for suckers . . . loyalty, that is for jerks," like the details of the "perfect crime" and the glorification of the "superman," did not, as the publishers claimed, encourage virtue.[27]

The Hendrickson Subcommittee collected additional evidence, citing the advertising of switch-blade knives and other deadly weapons. It was noted that purveyors of pornographic literature are customers for the mailing lists of subscribers to the comics. In the spring of 1954, crime and horror comics represented one fifth of the monthly output of comic book publications, and

[27] Quoted in *ibid.*, p. 214.

a gross annual revenue of approximately $18 million underscores the stake that big business has in this type of enterprise.

Business interests might well take comfort in the lack of consensus among the experts who testified before the subcommittee on the effect of the comics. There were strong feelings on both sides, with perhaps more persistent emphasis from Dr. Wertham on the negative. Even those who took the middle stand, however, were willing to acknowledge that the horror comic might adversely affect the child who was already disturbed, and since these are the children who probably need protection, it is well that there is concern for reasonable censorship of the publications which are so easily within their reach.

Television

A number of spot studies on the relation of television viewing to delinquency were conducted by the staff of the Hendrickson Subcommittee in Boston, New York, Chicago, Washington, Cincinnati, San Francisco, and Los Angeles. According to the Chicago study 80 per cent of the 4000 elementary school pupils interviewed were television viewers. Other studies showed that many children spent as much time watching television as they did attending school.[28]

In analyzing the content of these programs, sample studies by the National Association of Educational Broadcasters indicated that there were at least six acts or threats of violence per hour in the programs of the seven stations monitored during the first week of January 1953. During the children's hours—from 5 to 7 P.M. weekdays, and from sign-on time to 7 P.M. on weekends—in comparison with other programs there were more than twice as many threats or acts of violence per hour (15.2 as compared with 6.2). The amount of crime and violence in all the programs viewed in 1953 was considerably greater than in 1952. The crimes ranged from misdemeanors to all kinds of felonies, including murder. A study by the National Association for Better Radio and Television[29] indicated that in 40 per cent of all television programs especially designed for children, crime and violence were the dominating factors.

The experts interviewed, however, could give no *verified* evidence of the effect on children of viewing violent dramas. Some regarded the programs as an escape or as vicarious experience for children's hostile impulses. Others thought the programs represented fantasy that bore no relation to real life experiences, and would therefore not affect children one way or the other. Some testimony was offered the committee to the effect that such television

---

[28] *Ibid.*, p. 231.
[29] Quoted in *ibid.*, p. 240.

programs were positively harmful. Spokesmen for the American Medical Association objected strongly to the manner in which crime is brought before the eyes and ears of American children. A committee of the American Bar Association asserted that grave harm has resulted. It did not, however, offer proof.

Less definitive testimony from persons who deal with criminals and delinquents is summed up in the qualified statement of James V. Bennett, Director of the Federal Bureau of Prisons in the Department of Justice. In his words: *"some* of these programs do spur on the *unstable* person, the *rebellious* individual, the *unhappy* boy or girl, the *suggestible* child."[30] Heman G. Stark, Director of the California Youth Authority, reported that boys have mentioned that the techniques they used in crimes of violence came directly from a television program. He was equally concerned because many of the programs portray the law enforcement officials as either incompetent or corrupt.[31]

The Hendrickson Subcommittee on Juvenile Delinquency concluded that, *without a full-scale and scientifically planned study, positive answers on the effects on juveniles of horror comics and television violence would not be available.* Nevertheless, the industry was advised to take steps in the meantime to lessen the amount of violence and crime in their media. Parents were urged to be more discriminating in supervising the programs to which their children devoted their leisure time. One of the difficulties with censorship of the industry, however, in addition to the initial problem of defining "bad" and "good," is to square regulation with the vital issue of freedom of the press.

At a conference held in New York City[32] to plan combative action against juvenile delinquency, Charles Y. Glock of the Bureau of Social Research at Columbia University drew attention to the lack of any real knowledge of the role of the media of mass communication in delinquent behavior. While we do know, of course, that children look and listen, without long-range, carefully planned research, Glock reminds us, we will not know *under what conditions* and for *what types of children* any of the mass media affect behavior *either positively* or *adversely.*

Summary

This chapter has reviewed the sociological explanations of delinquency advanced by those who hold that the shortcomings of the school or the bad examples of the mass media are the individual villains in the delinquency

---

[30] Quoted in *ibid.,* p. 240. Italics added.
[31] Quoted in *ibid.,* p. 243.
[32] Called by Attorney-General Riegelman, at Town Hall, Sept. 1956.

picture. Parents blame the school for the apparent increase in delinquency because its discipline appears to be less strict than formerly, and its pedagogy to be less effective in inculcating the three R's. Truancy is often held to be the first step in delinquency. That this is not necessarily so is evidenced in the Community Service Society's study of twenty persistent Negro truants.

A more promising approach to understanding truancy is suggested by Mark Roser of the Child Welfare Department of the public schools in Gary, Indiana. Roser considers truancy a fictitious legal entity—it is, he says, more appropriately regarded as "school resistance," sometimes expressing the boy's protest against schoolmarms and "sissy" reading assignments. Occasionally, as in the Community Service Society study, truancy is the child's signal for help with other problems.

Today, television and the horror comics are held accountable for delinquency in much the same type of reasoning which formerly blamed the Nick Carter stories and the movies. There is, however, no consensus among the experts as to the effect on delinquency of *any* of the mass media of communication and no well-documented scientific study in this admittedly important field has yet been published.

CHAPTER 11

Anthropological Approaches

THE AMERICAN PEOPLE HAVE LONG BEEN CURIOUS ABOUT THE POSSIBLE relationship between religion, nationality or ethnic group, and crime. In earlier days they noted the heavy increase in crime that paralleled the waves of immigration which began in the 1880s and continued up to the onset of World War I. The Irish and Italian Catholics who swelled the criminal roles at the time were described by the press and the public as natural criminals, despite the fact that the so-called Wickersham Report on Crime and the Foreign Born[1] rejected outright the explanation of inherent criminality in either group. More recently, the Negro and Puerto Rican migrants to the Northern cities, and the Mexicans of the West and Southwest, have come in for their share of group castigation.

As a perhaps natural accompaniment of the desire to promote America for the Americans, each successive group seems to have forgotten that the Americans for whom America was to be preserved "include the descendants of a former generation of immigrants, against whom the same outcry of race was earlier raised as a basis of discrimination or exclusion."[2]

As sociologists note, the ingroup perennially reacts unfavorably to the outgroup. The more the outgroup differs in customs and traditions from the ingroup, the more violent the reaction is likely to be. If, in addition, the newcomers offer economic competition of sizeable proportions and seek to be part of the social life of the community, the outgroup serves as an even more likely scapegoat.

[1] *Report on Crime and the Foreign Born*, No. 10, National Commission on Law and Observance and Enforcement, Washington, 1931.
[2] *Ibid.*, p. 5.

161

A variety of social scientists—including sociologists, social workers, and anthropologists—dissatisfied with the popular explanation of the overrepresentation of certain groups at certain times in the statistics of crime in America, have turned to anthropological approaches to seek for answers. They have asked, for example: To what extent is erratic or deviant conduct of a member of an outgroup (1) actually conformity to a norm established in his own culture; (2) his method of striking out against the rejection he feels he has met as a stranger in a new home; or (3) a result of nonethnic factors—such as the socio-economic situation—that may be associated with his group at a particular point in time and place?

In examining these questions and some of the answers that have been put forth, this chapter has three parts: (1) a brief consideration of the meaning of culture and its bearing on the conception of national character, or national identity, as Erikson[3] prefers to call it; (2) the evidence of variation in the incidence of crime and delinquency in the subgroups—religious and ethnic—of our heterogeneous population; and (3) some of the explanations offered by sociologists and anthropologists for the difficulties faced by outgroups in conforming to prescribed standards of behavior in the predominantly White Anglo-Saxon Protestant (WASP) setting.

The Role of Culture

The term "culture," as used by anthropologists, refers to the nonorganic milieu which every human group creates as its design for living. It represents a configuration of folkways, and stateways, sometimes expressed as "patterns of culture"—a phrase brought into prominence by the late Ruth Benedict[4] and widely used by psychologists and other social scientists. Culture is a vehicle which channelizes the individual's drives in ways which are approved by the majority in his society.

Because culture prescribes what to do in a variety of circumstances, it plays a vital role in establishing the individual's feeling of security. Security in this sense is a feeling of being inwardly at home with, and outwardly accepted by, the group whose standards of behavior one accepts. The feeling of belonging provides a link with the past and a bridge to the future. Individuals who do not feel that they belong to a group often experience anxiety and indecision even when the external situation is not objectively threatening. Like a system of insurance, a cultural system computes the threats which may be avoided or neutralized if certain patterns are followed.

From the days when men first came together in a society, religion and

---

[3] Erik Erikson, *Childhood and Society*, New York, Norton, 1950, p. 244.
[4] Ruth Benedict, *Patterns of Culture*, New York, Penguin Books, 1934.

nationalism have been dominant cultural forces, acting as carriers of the value patterns of the society. Each has served to mitigate tension by offering ready-made and "correct" modes of behavior for the crises in human existence. Moreover, conflicts between religions or nationalities have been at the root of the world's great wars and social upheavals. It is not surprising, then, that these forces, and the conflicts among them, often come to the forefront in studies of the causes of crime and delinquency.

Although most of the studies cited below attempt to isolate religious and national—or ethnic—affiliation, it must be remembered that the two are inevitably intertwined. In Dr. Mordecai Kaplan's words, "religion is the highest expression of nationalism." Nor can studies of crime among minority groups, whether ethnic or religious, be understood unless they are examined for other factors that may have bearing upon the results.

Church Affiliation and Delinquency

There is a widespread belief, often concurred in by the juvenile court judges, that the falling off in church attendance, or the failure to adhere to one's religious obligations however they are defined, is one of the prime reasons for the apparent increase in lawlessness in this country.

Since the significance of religious affiliation differs widely among the denominations, the initial step in any scientific study is to identify the unit of measurement for each.

For Catholics the forms of religious observance are strictly defined. The observance of the baptismal and other sacramental rites, attendance at Mass and in the confessional, practices believed to be conducive to right living, are required of Catholics. For Protestants, on the other hand, the requirements vary, depending upon the denomination. Identification with the church may involve a ceremony in which one declares oneself a member or an adherent of a specific creed. At the other end of the Protestant scale, as among Unitarians and Congregationalists, a minimum in the way of formal affiliation may be required.

Among the Jews, each of the three major divisions—the orthodox, conservative, and reform—set different requirements for synagogue attendance, prayer, observance of holy days, and the dietary laws. At one extreme, the fundamentalist orthodox Jews are similar in many ways to the fundamentalists of other faiths; at the other, the many reform Jews and the few "Jewish Scientists," are, in the opinion of many people, agnostics and not easily distinguishable from Unitarians.

Despite these differences in the definition, content, and pattern of religious observance among Catholics, Protestants, and Jews, however, they all strive to indoctrinate their adherents against crime. If, then, attention to religion could prevent delinquency, one would expect to find a relatively lower incidence among groups of people who emphasize observance of the religious tenets. Yet studies of people identified as criminals or delinquents have never proved that, to any considerable extent, church membership has deterred them from behaving in disapproved ways.

In investigating the relation between religion, crime, and suicide, Porterfield comes to the reluctant conclusion that there is no demonstrable negative correlation in the Southern states for selected periods from 1930 through 1949.[5] As a matter of fact, in communities characterized as "depressed folk societies," which should theoretically be less given to suicide and crime than many urbanized industrialized groups, he found the highest correlation between number of congregations (even though their membership lists may be small) and homicide. Porterfield suggests that perhaps communities made up of depressed classes and color groups require more congregations than do those where class and race division are not sharp.[6]

The Role of the Sunday School

The Sunday School is, in most denominations, assigned an important role in instilling standards of right conduct as well as of belief. The curriculum of the religious school varies in the emphasis on Biblical history, on understanding and observing religious customs, or reciting a catechism. The methods of teaching may be rote, or may follow progressive educational principles. The teachers may be trained or untrained, and the school sessions may be held in the late afternoon, on Sundays, or every day. Secular and religious education may be combined as in parochial schools.

The principal studies testing the effect of Sunday School attendance on honesty have been those under the auspices of the Character Education Inquiry. In these studies by Hartshorne and May,[7] test results were very disappointing for the advocates of the Sunday School as a means of insuring ethical behavior; there appeared to be no connection between non-cheating and Sunday School attendance. Studies which compared the honesty of children in a school which had many parochial aspects with the conduct of children in a strictly progressive school favored the children in the progressive school setting. The correct inference from these studies is probably that there is no *automatic* transfer for either children or adults from the verbal teaching of moral and religious principles into the desirable overt behavior.

[5] Austin L. Porterfield and Robert H. Talbert, *Mid-Century Crime in our Culture*, Fort Worth, Texas, Leo Potishman Foundation, 1954, pp. 55 ff.

[6] *Ibid.*, p. 57.

[7] H. Hartshorne and A. M. May, *Studies in Deceit* (1928) and *Studies in the Nature of Character* (1930), New York, Macmillan.

Incidence of Religious Groups in Delinquency Statistics

Several studies have been made of the relative incidence of delinquency among Catholics, Protestants, and Jews in America. No doubt some of this interest is the result of the religious auspices and the financial investments of each of these major groups in a wide variety of remedial and preventive services. The value of these studies, however, is somewhat diminished by the fact that they are rarely concerned with the degree of observance of the adherents.[8] We offer below what evidence can be mustered on the statistics of deviant behavior among Catholics, Protestants, and Jews.

CATHOLICS. A recent study in a Catholic institution, which sheltered both Catholic and non-Catholic girls, suggests a relation between delinquency and a rejection of religion.[9] Some 162 delinquent girls under the care of the House of the Good Shepherd in Seattle were interviewed, both individually and in groups, given projective tests, and asked to write individual essays. The findings were as follows: only 2 per cent of the total group (25 per cent of whom were Roman Catholic) attended church regularly. Religious values had apparently not been integrated in their home life. The girls evidenced no positive feelings of love, reverence, or adoration for God; only a few said they believed in Him. Some who said that as children they had been forced to attend church were now hostile or indifferent to religion. In the group sessions, these girls revealed feelings of being unloved and rejected by their families. Many girls who had dominating mothers were emotionally confused. These findings actually suggest the interdependence of many factors in delinquent behavior.

Barnes and Teeters[10] refer to two studies (one in Germany and one in Holland) which show that Catholics tend to be more criminal than Protestants, and that Jews are the least criminal of the three groups. The authors suggest, however, that the fact that the Catholic population in these two countries is largely from the low economic levels, may account for their preponderance in the crime statistics.

The following incident, reported by a Catholic chaplain in an American state institution for delinquent boys, suggests that factors other than religious orientation govern delinquent behavior. Convinced that his sermons did not result in improved behavior among his charges, the chaplain decided to try visual education, and found a film depicting honesty as a virtue. He showed

---

[8] See Walter S. Monroe (ed.), *Encyclopedia of Educational Research*, rev. ed., 1950, for summary of case studies of present-day religious teaching.

[9] Sister M. Dominik, RGS, "Religion and the Juvenile Delinquent," *American Catholic Sociological Review*, Vol. 15, no. 3 (Oct. 1954), pp. 256-64.

[10] Harry E. Barnes and Negley K. Teeters, *New Horizons in Criminology*, 2nd ed., New York, Prentice Hall, 1951, Chapter 11.

it to the boys in the studio of an artist friend and was pleased at the boys' apparent attention and absorption in the film. The next day, however, the host told him that there was nothing left in the studio that had not been securely nailed down. Apparently the moral of the film had no effect on the boys' behavior. The priest concluded that he was dealing with a group of boys who were amoral, and for whom middle-class standards of behavior had no meaning. They could not be reached by sermons or even by dramatic presentations, neither of which corresponded to their ideas of the reality of everyday life as they experienced it.

WHITE PROTESTANTS. Dunn[11] cites statistics which indicate that Protestants are more numerous than Catholics in twenty-seven penitentiaries and nineteen reform schools. To evaluate these findings, however, it would be necessary to know the populations from which these penitentiaries and reform schools drew. Was their population, for example, largely from the South, where Negroes would predominate among the Protestants? If they were located in the North, did they serve communities with a relatively small number of Catholics in the population? Like the Jews, the Catholics of this country are largely concentrated in the big urban centers.

Two New York City studies, one in 1930, the other in 1952, show that white Protestants appeared in the delinquency and the truancy statistics much less frequently than would be expected on the basis of their numbers in the population.

On the whole, the urban white Protestant population is more characteristically a middle-class group than is the white Catholic or Negro population. Furthermore, as our analysis of the studies on class structure suggests (see Chapter 7), the form of protest by young people in the middle-class family in America, may be characteristically different from that in the working-class family, which in the largest urban centers is more often Negro or Catholic than white Protestant.

JEWS. There appears to be a general consensus that the incidence of crime and delinquency is relatively lower among Jews than among Catholics or Negro Protestants. William Kvaraceus[12] makes special reference to the low incidence of delinquency in the Jewish group. His study of 761 delinquent children known to the Children's Bureau in Passaic, New Jersey, indicates that Jewish children were only 2 per cent of the delinquents, although the Jewish population was estimated at 15 per cent.

While there are no official statistics on the religious affiliations of the

---

[11] C. V. Dunn, "The Church and Crime in the United States," *The Annals,* American Academy of Political and Social Science, No. 125 (May 1926), p. 200; and P. M. Smith, "The Church in Delinquency Prevention," *Sociology and Social Research,* Vol. 35, no. 3 (Jan. 1951), pp. 83-190.
[12] William Kvaraceus, *Juvenile Delinquency and the School,* Yonkers, World Book Co., 1945, Chapter 10, p. 102.

population of the United States, there are estimates of varying degrees of accuracy for the distribution of the Jews.[13] These estimates, plus a recent one for Jews in New York City, make it possible to draw some conclusion on the relative incidence of official delinquency among Jews in the major cities.

The centers of Jewish population in the United States are New York City (which accounts for between 40 and 50 per cent of the total), Chicago, Detroit, Los Angeles, and Philadelphia. Together, these cities contain about three quarters of the estimated 4 to 5 million Jews in the United States.[14] Since New York City has such a large proportion of the total Jewish population in America, it is of interest to compare the incidence of delinquency among Jews at various times, as registered in the New York City Juvenile Court. In 1930 the 1400 Jewish children known to the juvenile court represented one fifth of the court total, whereas the Jews accounted for roughly one third of the city's population at that time. In 1952 a study of the juvenile court records yielded only 226 Jewish families (in four of the five boroughs of New York City) in which any member was officially designated as a delinquent. This number was less than 3 per cent of the court's total for that year.[15]

This twenty-year decrease in officially reported delinquency among Jews cannot be accounted for by any marked decline in the proportion of Jews in New York City's population. According to the United States Census, the city's population grew from roughly 6.9 million in 1930 to 8 million in 1950. While the recent immigration has been predominantly Roman Catholic, Jews have accounted for some of the increase. And despite a shift of the middle and upper-middle classes of New York City's populace to Queens, Nassau, Westchester, and Northern New Jersey, according to estimates by the Health Insurance Plan, based on a study of 5000 families, Jews still accounted in 1955 for 26 per cent of the individuals and 30 per cent of the households in New York City.[16] On this basis, the incidence of Jews in the court is one tenth of what might be expected on the basis of their ratio in the population. These figures are consistent with those in a court study reported in 1954 by Dr. Mollie Harrower.[17]

[13] Sophia M. Robison, "How Many Jews in America?" *Commentary*, Vol. 8, no. 2 (Aug. 1949), pp. 185-92; see also E. M. Rosenthal, "5 Million American Jews," *Commentary*, Vol. 26, no. 6 (Dec. 1958), pp. 499-507.

[14] "Religion Reported by the Civilian Population of the United States," March 1957, and "Current Population Reports, Population Characteristics," Bureau of the Census, Series P-20, No. 79, Feb. 2, 1958.

[15] Sophia M. Robison, "A Study of Delinquency Among Jewish Children in New York City," in Marshall Sklare (ed.), *The Jews: Social Patterns of an American Group*, Glencoe, Illinois, The Free Press, 1958, pp. 535-42.

[16] Neva R. Deardorff, "The Religio-Cultural Background of New York City's Population," *Milbank Quarterly*, Vol. 33, no. 2 (April 1955), pp. 152-60.

[17] H. B. Peck, M. Harrower, C. Harari, M. B. Beck, J. B. Maryjohn, M. Roman, "A New Pattern for Mental Health Services in a Children's Court: Round Table 1954," *The American Journal of Orthopsychiatry*, Vol. 25, no. 1 (Jan. 1955), pp. 1-50.

Examination of the court's disposition of delinquency cases in 1952 and 1930 reveals marked differences in Jewish statistics. In 1930 almost two thirds of the Jewish cases, in comparison with about one third in 1952, were dismissed. In 1930 the most frequent offenses were running away, ungovernable behavior, and peddling and begging without a license; the latter accounted for almost 40 per cent of the Jewish delinquencies in Brooklyn in that year. In contrast 1952 statistics showed a higher incidence among Jewish children of offenses against property and persons.

There appears to have been a shift among the Jewish delinquents from peddling (usually this meant minding their parents' pushcarts) to more violent and aggressive behavior. Although the total Jewish delinquency in 1952 is still proportionately small, the offenses of Jews in 1952 are more nearly like those of the non-Jewish group than they were in 1930.

Analysis of the background characteristics of the 226 Jewish families with children known to the court, contradicts most of the current clichés about the characteristics of delinquents. The majority of the Jewish families in which there was an officially designated delinquent child were physically intact; the mothers were housewives, both parents were literate; the families were small, and the children had been born in wedlock. In general, the children were not retarded in school, and very few were reported as having reading problems. Nor is it meaningful to suggest association between the area of residence and the delinquent behavior referred to the court. In most of the 300-odd health areas in New York City in which there were Jewish delinquents, there was only one in the course of the whole year, and the largest number from any single health area was eight. These findings are duplicated in Leonard Schneiderman's unpublished study of 12 Jewish boys and 1 girl, arraigned in St. Paul, 1957-1958.

The studies cited above have indicated a relatively lower rate of crime and delinquency among white Protestants and Jews than among Catholics. Since religious affiliation has not been proved to affect the individual's disposition toward crime or delinquency, other factors associated with members of the various religious groups must be used to explain the differing incidence of delinquency and crime in these groups.

Thus, undoubtedly one of the reasons that most studies show a larger proportion of Catholic than non-Catholic in white American prison populations is because Catholics are concentrated in the working-class urban populations which contribute most heavily to criminal statistics. Similarly, the low incidence of Jews in the official crime statistics is at least in part due to the existence within the Jewish community of institutions that deal with deviant behavior before it becomes a matter of official concern.

Shifts in the groups from which *official* delinquents and criminals come suggest that religion is not a central factor in determining their rate of crime and delinquency, but rather that a variety of factors is influential. These include recency of immigration, the cultural institutions that serve the group, and the socio-economic situation in which it finds itself.

Ethnic Group and Delinquency

One of the problems in correctly assessing the cultural identity of the immigrant is that it is not always synonymous with his country of origin. Thus, in interpreting the label "foreign-born," one must make a distinction (not made in official statistics) between persons who may have spent only the first two or three years of life outside the United States and those who came to America after their habits and patterns of behavior were fairly well established. Many of the first group belong culturally in the category of second generation, in the same sense as young persons born in the United States of foreign stock.

The geographic base of the population does not always correspond with a homogeneous political, national, or ethnic group. The term *ethnic* appears to be most definitive because it stresses cultural ties and folkways which may characterize large segments of a population whose geographic origin may be, for example, Switzerland, Germany, or France.

Because each of us is "culture-bound," i.e., saturated with our own cultural patterns, we find it difficult to sense or to perceive that there are designs for living which are valid for other systems than our own. An American family pattern which may be considered typical by some is usually only an impression of something sensed by thinkers and writers for over a century as distinctly American—a phase of American character. Family customs, religious practices, attitudes toward schooling, recreation, money, government, and authority differ markedly in various societies. The "typical American pattern" represents just one end of a continuum on a scale of individual and social values.

Naturally, the point of time at which one studies the components of national character as well as the point of view of the observer will affect its description. We shall be able to understand our own definitions of national character better when we consider, as we do in the following section, the major cultural differences between us and those "strangers" with whom we share America, and many of whom we tend to castigate as inherently delinquent.

Chinese and Japanese in America

SOME CULTURAL PATTERNS. One extreme of child rearing is the American pattern of individualizing and consulting children. Another extreme is that of the Chinese and Japanese. From their viewpoint, according to Sister Frances Woods,[18] Americans by and large "spoil" their children and do not prepare them for the harsh realities of life. Most American parents demand neither respect nor obedience for themselves nor for representatives of authority. The informal relations between parents and children characteristic of American families are alien to Oriental and many other cultures.

Similarly, our emphasis on companionship in marriage, with divorce available for many families, is a peculiarly American trait. The traditional Oriental family does not stress romance. The girl automatically becomes a part of the husband's family, and since marriage is a family contract, divorce or desertion is rare. While undoubtedly there are many changes in the making in the new China and Japan, the Oriental family in America by and large still adheres to the older patterns.

Status accrues from quite different sources in American and Oriental culture. The ideal American type is the successful businessman. While the Chinese and Japanese desire sufficient means to meet their economic requirements, prestige in their terms is more intricately involved with family honor and learning than it is with material possessions.[19] And in so far as Confucian philosophy continues to guide Chinese life in America, age rather than youth is honored.

In America, in the ceaseless effort to keep up with the Joneses, economic considerations often determine not only the number of cars in the garage but family size. In the Oriental family in America, which still represents an extended family system, the greater the number of children, the greater the status. Each family unit is responsible for the education and socialization of its young. The family transmits religious values, performs the socio-economic functions, and provides for life's contingencies. The economic system is interwoven with the family structure.

A vivid portrait of the contrasts between the norms of American and Chinese culture, which still affect the first- and second-generation Chinese in America is found in Hsu's studies.[20]

With these differences between the cultural patterns and standards of the American and Oriental family in mind, it is interesting to examine studies of the relative incidence of delinquency in the Chinese and Japanese population in America.

DELINQUENCY—CHINESE. Recently in the New York City press, the principal and teachers of a school with many Chinese children commented on their good upbringing. With stay-at-home mothers, fathers who wielded

[18] Sister Frances Jerome Woods, *Cultural Values of American Ethnic Groups,* New York, Harper, 1956.
[19] *Ibid.,* p. 346.
[20] Francis L. K. Hsu, *Americans and Chinese: Two Ways of Life,* New York, Henry Schuman, 1953.

authority but also displayed affection, these children grew up in an environment apparently stabilized by their parents' adherence to their religious beliefs.

One would expect a low rate of delinquency in the first and second generations whose members remain in the Chinese community (1) because the rules of conduct are definitely formulated; (2) because they are observed by the old as well as the young; and (3) perhaps also because love is more abundantly and healthily available to the child in an extended family system, where children are an index of status and where there may be several adults who provide not only affection and love but the necessary controls.

West Coast studies confirm these expectations, emphasizing the tenacity with which the Chinese heritage is carried on by children born and reared in America.[21] This solidarity is supported by the custom of arranged marriages, as well as the cooperative nature of the Chinese village culture. According to Smith, difficulty occurs chiefly when Chinese children break with their age-old traditions before they have acquired strong roots in American ways. The exposure to American ideas in communities such as those on the West Coast, where the Chinese have more contact with the American natives than they do on the East Coast, threatens Chinese traditions. When the young Chinese have not integrated either their own or the American culture, their behavior may be contrary to our socially prescribed modes of conduct.[22]

Comparative studies of behavior patterns of native-born children of foreign-born Chinese parents in Vancouver, British Columbia, suggest that Chinese children born and educated there develop attitudes very similar to those of native-born children of European immigrant parents. These attitudes are basically like those of the old Caucasian stock in that community. The expression of the conflicts between parents and children varies with the individual child and the background of the parents.

The juvenile court statistics for Honolulu from 1914 to 1926[23] provide another illustration of what happens when Chinese children are subjected to unfamiliar standards of behavior. The Chinese have been in Hawaii longer than the Japanese and the Koreans, and are the most completely urbanized. Because their children have had greater opportunities for contacts outside the group, the delinquency rate among the Chinese children is the highest. On the other hand, the Japanese children have the lowest rate, in spite of the fact

[21] William Carlson Smith, *Americans in Process*, Ann Arbor, Michigan, Edwards Brothers, 1937, p. 2.

[22] *Ibid.*, pp. 211; 213; see also R. H. Lee, "Delinquent, Neglected and Dependent Chinese Boys and Girls of the San Francisco Bay Region," *Journal of Social Psychology*, Vol. 36 (1952), pp. 15-31.

[23] B. C. Hayner and Charles N. Reynolds, "Chinese Family Life in America," *American Sociological Review*, Vol. 2, no. 5 (Oct. 1937); and Walter Eng, "Cultural Factors and Juvenile Delinquency in Hawaii," *Focus*, Vol. 30, no. 5 (Sept. 1951), pp. 140-43.

that their parents exercise less rigid control over them than do the Chinese parents.

DELINQUENCY—JAPANESE. Studies of juvenile delinquency among the Japanese in Honolulu note its occurrence chiefly in the areas in which the Japanese have mixed rather indiscriminately with the rest of the population.[24] In an area which was 89 per cent Japanese in 1927-28, there were no cases of juvenile delinquency. But in an area in which the Japanese accounted for 28 per cent of the population, the delinquency rate was roughly comparable (33 per cent). The author concludes that the well-knit racial ghetto provides a more wholesome atmosphere for rearing second-generation Japanese than does the neighboring, culturally nondescript residential area. (Note the parallel with Lander's findings among Baltimore Negroes, Chapter 7.) Obviously the ghetto helps to enforce standards as well as to sustain its residents in times of crisis.

During World War II, Chief Probation Officer Holton of Los Angeles remarked that although the Japanese comprise one of the largest racial elements in California, in spite of their experiences in relocation camps they do not get into trouble—"You couldn't find three Japanese kids in a state correctional school at any time. There is one place where the parents and their own society exercise a control that is effective."[25]

American Indians

SOME ASPECTS OF RESERVATION LIFE. A special form of ghetto living has been imposed on the American Indian. The statistics on delinquent behavior among Indians suggest that life in the reservation does not have the sustaining force that ghetto living among the Chinese and Japanese in the United States, for example, appears to have exerted. We are indebted to the hearings of the Hendrickson Senate Subcommittee on Delinquency for a description of the conditions under which American Indians live and for data on the relative appearance of their young people in the juvenile courts in the states which have relatively small percentages of Indians in their population.

According to the 1950 United States Census, almost one fourth of the 430,000 Indians in the United States lived in Oklahoma. The other three fourths were scattered over 25 states. The remnants of the first Americans who are confined on the government reservations are in the main poor and neglected.[26] Regardless of whether or not they live on reservations, in North

---

[24] Andrew W. Lind, "The Ghetto and the Slum," *Social Forces,* Vol. 9, no. 9 (Dec. 1930), pp. 206-15.

[25] Robert C. Hendrickson (with Fred J. Cook), *Youth in Danger,* New York, Harcourt Brace, 1956, p. 267.

[26] *Ibid.,* Chapter 14.

or South Dakota, in Arizona, or New Mexico, more than half live in one-room log cabins without the sanitary facilities which are available even in some of the worst tenements in the big-city slums. The average annual family income—$300 among the Navahos and the Pueblos in New Mexico and about $1300 in North Dakota—is about one third that of the average non-Indian family income in the same areas. And the average life expectancy of, for example, Papago Indian babies in southern Arizona is only 17 years, compared with 69 years for the general population.

DELINQUENCY. The delinquent acts which bring the Indian boys to court, are, in contrast with those of non-Indian boys, rarely acts of violence or viciousness or offenses against the person. The most prevalent Indian offenses are drunkenness, petty theft, sex offenses, vandalism, and incorrigibility among the boys; among the girls, sex offenses, incorrigibility, and drunkenness.

The percentage of commitments to juvenile institutions in centers of large Indian population shows a marked over-representation of Indians. In South Dakota, where Indians account for 5 per cent of the population, 50 per cent of the training school population is Indian. In Nevada, the comparable percentages are 4 per cent of the population but 42 per cent in the state training schools. Why the proportions in Nebraska should be more nearly equal—a little more than 5 per cent of the state's training school population against 4 per cent in the total population of that state—we do not know.

Relatively little research has been directed to this sector of our population, which we treat almost the way in which we used to treat the mentally ill, hidden away in the dark wings of the old houses. Perhaps the reason for our neglect is also that, unlike the descendants of the immigrants from Ireland, Italy, and Poland, the Indians are dying out.

American Negroes

SOME CULTURAL PATTERNS. Many of the Negroes who have come to the Northern cities since World War I have been settled in the United States much longer than many white ethnic groups. Their dark skins and the accompanying restrictions on areas of residence, jobs, educational opportunities, and earning capacity, however, have given them some of the social characteristics of an immigrant group. Their migration in large numbers from the rural South to the urban North has, in addition, subjected them to unaccustomed ways of living and to the intensive competitive struggle for a livelihood.

Like their white brethren, Negroes are heterogeneous in many respects. The British West Indian family in Harlem is often quite unlike the American Negro in its standards and mores.[27] For generations there have been some upper middle-class Negroes who shared "white" values and standards for themselves and their children, perhaps even accentuating them in their own behavior. Franklin Frazier's pace-setting work,[28] like that of Allison Davis and John Dollard,[29] and the follow-up studies of John Rohrer,[30] provide abundant evidence of a wide range of family patterns among Negroes in all walks of life. And Rohrer agrees with Davis that not all Negro behavior can be interpreted as a response to white discrimination.

DELINQUENCY.   Studies of the incidence of delinquent behavior among Negroes usually make no note of the different types of behavior which bring young people into the court, or of the difference in the court's disposition of the cases. Some studies have pointed out that there are marked regional differences in the proportions of Negro and white girls referred to court for certain offenses.[31] For example, in comparison with white girls, very few Negro girls in the Southern courts which reported to the U.S. Children's Bureau were brought in for sex offenses; the majority were apprehended for stealing. These differences are less likely to reflect the actual or relative incidence of either sex behavior or stealing in the two ethnic groups, than to reveal the white community's differing concern for the misbehavior of white and Negro girls. The fact that a larger proportion of cases involving Negro than white children are dismissed may mean that Negro children are more often picked up by the police for trivial behavior.

Kephart offers evidence of the differential attitude of police toward Negroes. His interviews with and questionnaires distributed to policemen of all ranks in Philadelphia show that police are aware of the disproportionate arrest rate in Negro areas of Philadelphia. They attribute this "to the prevalence of low moral standards and a looseness in community organization, above which the Negro is making too little effort to lift himself."[32] More than half of the district patrolmen said they found it necessary to be more strict with Negroes than with white offenders. Patrolmen who practiced differential treatment toward individual Negroes also revealed unfavorable attitudes toward the Negro as a group. Because Negro offenders tend to resist

[27] New York School of Social Work, Columbia University, Master's Project No. 747 (1944), and No. 1801 (1945).

[28] E. Franklin Frazier, *The Negro Family in the United States*, New York, Henry Holt and Co., 1948.

[29] Allison Davis, and John Dollard, *Children of Bondage*, Washington, D.C., American Council of Education, 1940.

[30] John H. Rohrer, *Sociocultural Factors in Personality Development*, New York, Columbia University Press, 1957.

[31] Elsa Castendyck and Sophia M. Robison, "Juvenile Delinquency Among Girls," *Social Service Review*, Sept. 1943, pp. 253-64.

[32] William M. Kephart, "The Negro Offender: An Urban Research Project," *American Journal of Sociology*, Vol. 60, no. 1 (July 1954), pp. 46-50.

arrest more often than do white offenders, these two tendencies fortify each other.

Mexicans

SOME CULTURAL PATTERNS. Another section of American society which is increasingly charged with crime and delinquency is the largely Spanish-speaking Mexican in the West and Southwest. As in the case of the Oriental family, the culture of the Mexican differs in many ways from that of the middle-class white American. As a prelude to our discussion of delinquency among Mexican-Americans, we draw largely on Sister Woods' description of the Mexican family pattern as she knows it in the Southwestern part of the United States.[33]

Derived from a mixture of Indian and Spanish strains the Mexican family differs biologically and culturally from "the typical Anglos." The Mexican family is even more extended than the Oriental, including the godparents as well as relatives by blood and marriage. Religion is associated with all life experience, including such recreation as is provided by religious feasts, and is thus a much more potent force in the Mexican than in the typical white American family. For most Mexicans time is not money, and formal education is not the royal road to advancement.

Like the Oriental, the Mexican woman is traditionally confined to the home. She is responsible for bringing up the children and is expected to be submissive, faithful, devoted, and respectful to her husband. While she may not like her husband's infidelities, her position as a wife is unassailable, because divorce is unusual.

Traditional Mexican patterns of parent-child relationships are somewhat akin to those of the Orientals. They emphasize respect and obedience to parents and older siblings. In contrast to the American family, the Mexican father, who is feared and respected, pays little attention to his children. The mother, however, is more outspoken in her demonstration of affection.

Corporal punishment is customary in the Mexican family; but the oldest and youngest child are favored in the distribution of food and clothing, and are least often punished. As a result there are often quarrels and fights, and sometimes estrangement. In one family which reported a runaway boy to the juvenile court the mother requested that the boy be "kept in an institution." The family had neither the time nor the money to go out looking for him. "Mrs. S. wants Pedro held in the institution until he is 16 and maybe he will do better. The boy wants to go on the streets and sell papers, but Mrs. S. is afraid he will get into trouble and then the police will blame the father."[34]

[33] Woods, *op. cit.*, pp. 257-62.
[34] *Ibid.*, p. 288.

In the Mexican family, as in the Oriental family, boys are preferred to girls, and learn the pattern of male dominance from their fathers. The Mexican attitude toward adolescent girls is much more strict than toward boys. Pedro's sister, a 14-year-old girl who came home at 11 o'clock, instead of directly after school, was told by her father that the next time it happened he would lock her out all night. For a Mexican girl to have premarital sex relations is considered a family tragedy.

To most Mexicans, formal law generally appears to be arbitrary. While they do not treat it as something to be disregarded, they dislike getting involved with representatives of American law. It is difficult for the Mexican to understand why, in America, truancy or loafing on the street corners is regarded as delinquency. "In Mexico it is customary for men to idle on the street corner because the street corner is the poor Mexican's equivalent of the well-to-do American's club or the Englishman's pub."[35]

DELINQUENCY. If this account of the culture pattern of the Mexican who comes to the States is correct, one can readily understand why the Mexicans figure fairly prominently in the official delinquency statistics today in the Western and Southwestern states. No doubt their proximity to the mother country reinforces their cultural patterns and makes for greater resistance to American patterns. At the same time they are not as safely insulated from the disrupting effects of the American culture as first-generation Orientals tend to be.

An illustration of the way in which acculturation will probably be reflected in a declining rate of delinquency among Mexicans in the United States was provided by Judge Gilliam, a witness before the Hendrickson Subcommittee. Judge Gilliam predicted that although the current Denver crop of delinquents were predominantly Spanish-Americans, their rate would decline. The Mexicans, he said, "are going through the pangs of adjustment, of molding themselves into our culture, of establishing for themselves secure places in this new way of life that they have chosen. Once success has been achieved along these lines, our experience shows, the new group invariably becomes just as law-abiding as any other." As evidence of this expected change, the judge testified that: "among the 803 delinquents appearing in the Denver court in the year 1908-1909, there were 231, or a little more than one-fourth, listed as 'American.' Jewish parentage accounted for 166, roughly one-fifth; Irish for 116; Germans 98; Italians 97; and Scotch 20."[36] In the 1920s Italians outranked the other groups, possibly, as suggested by Judge Gilliam, because they were imitating the bootlegging activities of that era, which their parents considered legitimate. Currently the appearance of an Italian, a Jewish, or an Irish boy in this court is a rarity. These groups have become the most law-abiding in Denver.

[35] *Ibid.*, p. 288.
[36] Hendrickson, *op. cit.*, pp. 265-66.

Puerto Ricans

SOME CULTURAL PATTERNS. Somewhat akin to the Mexican immigrants in the Southwest and in California, Puerto Rican migrants to our metropolitan centers have found it difficult to adjust to the competitive urban life in a climate which is often unfriendly.[37]

Like the Mexicans, Puerto Ricans are ethnically a mixture derived from the early Spanish settlers, aboriginal Indians, and African Negro slaves. Unlike Mexicans, however, Puerto Ricans are American citizens, for whom the conflict between the standards of the old culture and the aspirations of the new is immediate and poignant. We are told that in Puerto Rico educational and job discrimination based on color is much less frequent than on the mainland. Thus, when Puerto Ricans settle in the United States, they react sharply to the additional problem of adjusting to our color line.[38]

The marked differences in cultural patterns of the Puerto Rican and mainland American white boy are summarized by Bram,[39] a sociological anthropologist who has specialized in studying Puerto Rican culture. Among the inmates at Warwick, Bram differentiated the Puerto Rican boys as follows:

1. The Puerto Rican boy makes a bid for adult status early in life. He cannot understand our emphasis on compulsory school attendance. Many of the 15- and 16-year-olds have been working in Puerto Rico. When they migrate to New York, they are compelled against their will to return to school.

2. The Puerto Rican boy who is conversant with the so-called seamy side of life is apt to be critical of the kind of reading material used in the New York City schools. Why read Longfellow's "Evangeline"? She has no prototype in actual life, she is not like the girls they know, and in their opinions such "fairy tales" are not appropriate diet for grown boys.

3. The responsibility of the adolescent male Puerto Rican resembles that of the husband in the continental pattern. The Puerto Rican boy plays the role of protector and ally of his mother. The Puerto Rican is preoccupied with the Spanish concept of dignity; in its defense even homicide is permissible.

4. The Puerto Rican does not place as much emphasis as the continental

---

[37] A. J. Jaffe, labor adviser to the Puerto Rican Government, estimates that about three quarters of all migrants from Puerto Rico to the mainland come to New York City because New York is the terminal airport. See Demographic and Labor Force Characteristics," in A. J. Jaffe (ed.), *Puerto Rican Population of New York City*, New York, Bureau of Applied Social Research, Columbia University, 1954, pp. 3-28.

[38] "The Attitudes of Puerto Ricans in New York City to Various Aspects of the Environment," Project No. 317, N. Y. School of Social Work, Columbia University, June 1953.

[39] Joseph Bram, speech delivered at the thirty-third Orthopsychiatric Conference in New York City, March 1956.

American on the value of the achieved as against the ascribed role, i.e., that given at birth. Nor, in Bram's opinion, has he unreservedly adopted the strong American incentive to advance in the social scale, as suggested in Tumin's study.[40]

5. Although there is relatively little difference in Puerto Rico in the status of dark-skinned or light-skinned children in the family, on the continent the dark-skinned children experience severe conflict due to the American reaction to color difference. Aware of the minority status accorded the American Negro, the dark-skinned Puerto Rican often clings to his native Spanish to distinguish himself. Bram suggests that the darker-skinned Puerto Rican, who is aware of discriminating attitudes on the mainland, is frequently less apt to migrate than his lighter-skinned brothers.

> Unlike many other groups of newcomers who come to the United States because of religious or political persecution, the majority of the Puerto Ricans come to New York to seek their fortunes, surely an approved American goal. Whether or not we welcome them appears to be a function not so much of their potential contribution, but rather of the nature of our labor demand and supply, the current housing vacancy rate, and the organized backing of persons already in the community who identify with them and are willing to help them in the difficult process of adjustment. Like most of our European ancestors, whether from Ireland, Germany, Italy, Sweden, Poland, or elsewhere, the newcomers from Puerto Rico, in general, do not come from the privileged groups of their native land.[41]
>
> One of the complaints made against the Puerto Ricans is that they fly here to get relief. The facts from the Department of Welfare as well as from other studies do not bear out this accusation. They come here seeking jobs, and come via air not because they are affluent, but because the competition of the airlines has made it possible to obtain passage very reasonably.[42]

Practically all studies of Puerto Ricans in New York City call attention to their unsatisfactory housing conditions. Since there has been relatively little new construction in New York City during the period of rapid expansion of the Puerto Rican population, it is clear that they, like other citizens, suffer from the housing shortage. Unlike other portions of the population, however, who can afford to pay high rents, the Puerto Rican newcomers have little

[40] Melvin M. Tumin, *Caste in a Peasant Society: A Case Study in the Dynamics of Caste,* Princeton, N. J., Princeton University Press, 1952.

[41] Sophia M. Robison, "Social Welfare Statistics on the New York Puerto Rican Population," in A. J. Jaffe (ed.), *Puerto Rican Population of New York City, op. cit.,* p. 45.

[42] *Ibid.,* p. 47.

mobility and little leeway in selecting available accommodations. The jobs which are open to them are mainly the low-paid, unskilled occupations.

Since one of their main reasons for wishing to come to New York City has been the supposed advantage of the schooling over that provided in Puerto Rico, it is of interest that 189 Puerto Rican parents who were interviewed in the Northside study[43] had little criticism of the public schools. The exceptions were the residents in the Washington Heights area, half of whom sent their children to parochial schools.

The Puerto Rican study sponsored by the Board of Education of New York City[44] initiated several special studies in the two school years 1954-56 to check the informal, off-the-record, negative opinions of school personnel with respect to attendance, truancy, and good behavior of Puerto Rican children in New York City schools. In the main the conclusions from these carefully designed studies contradicted the preconceptions of the school personnel. With regard to regularity of school attendance, the study revealed that, "For the Puerto Rican school population as a whole, the record of school attendance in New York City appears to be quite comparable to that of mainland children,"[45] even though the children are handicapped by unfamiliarity with English, the rigors of the northern climate, and the fact that school attendance is not compulsory in Puerto Rico.

DELINQUENCY. The record for truancy (as distinguished from absenteeism) is somewhat less favorable for the older than for the younger Puerto Rican youths. Among those who attend junior high school, truancy hearings occur proportionately twice as frequently for Puerto Ricans as for non-Puerto Ricans. Truancy in junior high school is more frequent in both groups than in elementary schools[46] (perhaps because the older child dares to rebel). It may, however, be more characteristic behavior of the Puerto Rican because there is less emphasis on formal schooling on the island than on the mainland.

Because there are no accurate figures on the number of Puerto Rican children in New York, we have only approximate data on their proportionate representation in the statistics of court referrals. For example, in 1950 delinquency petitions for Puerto Rican children in New York City's Domestic Relations Court accounted for 10 per cent of the total. In 1953 the percentage of Puerto Rican petitions was about 16. This increase, however, must be viewed against an estimated 100 per cent increase in the three years in the

[43] Manny Diaz, Earl Finch, Larry Gangaware, and others, "The Attitudes of Puerto Ricans in New York City to Various Aspects of Their Environment," Project No. 4317 of the New York School of Social Work, June 1953.

[44] J. Cayse Morrison, Director, *The Puerto Rican Study, 1953-1957, a Report on the Education and Adjustment of Puerto Rican Pupils in the Public Schools of the City of New York*, New York, Board of Education, 1958.

[45] *Ibid.*, p. 117.

[46] *Ibid.*, p. 120.

number of Puerto Rican children in the age group over which the juvenile court has jurisdiction.[47]

A more inclusive index of delinquent behavior than the juvenile court is the central register described in Chapter 4. In the year 1951-52 Puerto Rican youths who appeared in that register accounted for approximately 7 per cent of the total for whom the place of origin of the parent was known.

Later figures from the Juvenile Aid Bureau (see Chapter 13) show very little increase from 1957 to 1958 (9.7 and 10.3) respectively. Thus, one might safely say that the younger Puerto Ricans are probably not over-represented in the juvenile court and in the Juvenile Aid Bureau. In the youthful offender category, however, in 1958, Puerto Rican youths between the ages of 16 and 21 accounted for 27.3 per cent of the 1152 cases heard in the youth part of the special sessions court in Manhattan.

On the reasons for arrest, the data collected in the Puerto Rican study for School Districts 10 and 11 in Manhattan reveal relatively less serious behavior among the Puerto Rican than among non-Puerto Rican referrals.[48]

Thus, while one is handicapped in calculating rates, in intercensal years, especially in a highly mobile population like the Puerto Ricans, one concludes on the basis of the scattered data that the behavior of the older *adolescent* Puerto Rican youth is regarded with somewhat more suspicion than is accorded similar behavior of non-Puerto Ricans. As a consequence Puerto Ricans, along with Negroes, have replaced the Italian and Irish boys who a generation ago predominated in the probationary schools, the detention facilities, and the state training schools and reformatories.

Changing Cultures and Causal Theory

As we review these differences in the culture patterns of Chinese, Japanese, and Mexican immigrants, native Negroes and Indians, and migrant Puerto Ricans, we can see how they might well have precipitated conflict between the newcomers and the more firmly established earlier generations of white American immigrants. We see too how these differences have made it difficult for foreign-born families to exercise the usual control over their American-born or -reared children.

The fact that since 1900, the date of the establishment of the first juvenile court, with few exceptions the official statistics for delinquency have included a disproportion of children of foreign-born or migrant parents would indicate that recency of arrival is one important factor in vulnerability. The

[47] Robison, "Social Welfare Statistics on the New York Puerto Rican Population," p. 14.
[48] Morrison, *op. cit.*, Table 16, p. 121.

preceding survey of the culture patterns and delinquency records of our newest migrants and immigrants suggests, however, that it is not the only one. For although, in the main, each succeeding wave of immigrants appears to have pushed the preceding one from its ranking order in the official count, there are some exceptions. These exceptions—for example, among the Orientals (as among the Jews)—we believe reflect chiefly the self-insulating aspects of their culture.

The survey has also indicated how often among these groups (as again among the Jews) the offenses for which the second generation are apprehended are dissimilar from those of their parents. This finding is corroborated by Alida Bowler who studied the relationship between the offenses of first- and second-generation immigrants brought to the courts of Buffalo and Detroit. She noted that the offenses of the second-generation Americans were more like those of the native-born than they were like those of the foreign-born parent. For example, the rate of robbery among native-born sons of foreign-born parentage was four times that of foreign-born sons.[49]

Bowler suggests that there may be something in American attitudes, institutions, and conditions which molds the second generation into patterns of predatory lawlessness, in marked contrast to the respect for law normally revealed in the statistics of the parents' country of origin.[50] Other attempts to explain the overrepresentation of migrants and immigrants in statistics of crime and delinquency in cultural terms turn to (1) the concept of anomie; (2) the conflict of cultures; (3) our heritage of frontier mores; and (4) multiple causation.

Anomie and Nonconformity

Merton[51] suggests that anomie is the explanation of the pressures which American culture exerts upon some groups to produce socially nonconforming conduct. He points out that the pervasive materialism in American society is not paralleled by equal accessibility to opportunities for advancement. As a consequence, some economic and ethnic groups find themselves cut off from what seems to them to be legitimate access to these goals. With our excessive stress on success, members of these groups may resort to the most expedient, even though illegitimate, procedures to attain their ends. Expediency, or "success at any price," Merton believes, generates a state of normlessness or anomie which, in turn, incubates widespread nonconformist behavior.

In his view, some subcultures, like the Chinese and Jewish, have ways

---

[49] Alida C. Bowler, in *Report on Crime and the Foreign Born*, pp. 79 ff.
[50] *Ibid.*, pp. 157 ff.
[51] Robert K. Merton, "Social Theory and Social Structure," *Social Structure and Anomie*, Glencoe, Ill., The Free Press, 1949, pp. 125-49.

of counteracting the unequal access of youth in America to success. Both provide opportunities for their young people to succeed in ways which are approved by our culture. Because the stages in education of both Jews and Chinese are well-structured, the young people know the road that they are expected to travel. It is clearly more difficult, however, for Negro and other minority groups, such as Puerto Ricans, Mexicans, and Indians, who have not had experience in a competitive culture, to smooth the path to success for their young people.

A problem arises in translating Merton's concepts of anomie and nonconformity into indices which will show how they might produce delinquent behavior which, like suicide, might be taken as an index of social breakdown. In a special conference called by the Children's Bureau, Merton suggested that such hypotheses might be possible, but no one has so far come forward with specific proposals. Currently, however, new interest is being shown in a re-examination of Merton's ideas.[52]

Culture Conflict

Sociologists have been concerned with what they call "acculturation," i.e., the process which results when people with various norms come to live side by side in the United States.[53] These studies deal primarily with tensions which are evoked by bicultural loyalties. Some sociologists call this condition "marginality," and the plight of the individual caught between two cultures has been described as that of the "marginal man."[54]

Sellin,[55] writing in 1938, says that sociologists offer three explanations for crime and delinquency: (1) the conflict between acceptable norms of conduct held on the one hand by the old and on the other hand by the new culture; (2) shifts from rural to urban environment; (3) movement from a well-organized, homogeneous society to a disorganized heterogeneous one. In most studies, however, these three factors overlap.

With respect to the first explanation—the conflict in conduct norms— as Benedict so strikingly demonstrates in her first-hand study of our Pueblo, Dobus and Kwakiutl Indians, *each* "culture pattern" creates norms which stress *different* values.[56] Thus what may be considered normal in one group may be regarded as deviant in another. In most large cities, youth is con-

---

[52] See articles by Robert Dubin and Richard A. Cloward, and Merton's reply in *American Sociological Review*, Vol. 24, no. 2 (April 1959).

[53] See *Old World Traits Transplanted*, by Robert Park and Herbert A. Miller, Chicago, University of Chicago Press, 1925.

[54] Everett V. Stonequist, *The Marginal Man: A Study in Personality and Culture Conflict*, New York, Scribner's, 1937.

[55] Thorsten Sellin, *Culture Conflict and Crime*, New York, *Social Service Research Council*, Bulletin 41, 1938, p. 83.

[56] Ruth Benedict, *op. cit.*, Chapters 4-7.

fronted with competing norms of behavior due to cultural differentials against which he measures his own traditions. For the incompatible elements he must find a satisfactory solution. For example, the Irish, the Italian, and the Polish immigrant shared a common goal in coming to America—the enjoyment of economic advantages not available to them in the old country. Differences between these values and their own determined their adjustment to the American pattern of life and the American value system. The younger generation, whose values were not completely set, probably experienced more tension than did their parents who, firmly tied to their old-world ways of living, attempted to transplant these ways to life in America.

Thomas and Znaniecki suggest that norm violations increase when immigrants escape the sustaining force of their former ghettos and in the new country encounter groups with different mores.[57] The adjustment of immigrants coming from rural areas into urban centers has been complicated by *conditions* to which they were not accustomed. It was to be expected, therefore, that they would have trouble getting along in the new settings. As the more easily identifiable element they were more readily apprehended among the anti-social elements in the population.

In New York City the large number of Irish immigrants who settled in the Bowery during the 1850s, and later in the midtown on the West Side—known as Hell's Kitchen and Hell's Harbor—represented a serious threat to native New Yorkers. This threatening role was to some extent usurped by immigrants from Sicily who, at the turn of the century and up to World War I, poured into a city whose ways were very different from those at home.

It is not merely, says Pauline Young on the same theme, that a Pole or an Italian has come to America.[58] A villager has come to a great city. Had he moved to a large city in his native land, even though the language were familiar, he would still have met some of the difficulties he encounters in American cities. If, on the other hand, he had settled in rural America, the newcomer would have escaped one set of problems—those resulting from the "corroding" urban influences. By contrast to the rural American who moves to a large city, the city-bred European may find American urban life relatively easy.

Unfortunately, the effects of culture conflict are difficult to pinpoint, whether they are assumed to arise as a result of a shift from old to new cultures, from rural to urban environments, or from well-organized to dis-

[57] William I. Thomas and Florian Znaniecki, *The Polish Peasant in Europe and America*, 2 vols., New York, Alfred A. Knopf, 1927.
[58] Pauline Young, "Social Problems in the Education of the Immigrant Child," *American Sociological Review*, Vol. 1, no. 3 (June 1936), p. 420.

organized societies. The explanations referred to above do not specify *how* these factors give rise to criminality.

In general, the differences in cultural patterns are assumed to have been complicating factors which might lead to strife and emotional tensions between the foreign-born parent and the native-born child, which in turn would express themselves in crime or delinquency. There is little *concrete* evidence, however, either in the records of the juvenile court or other institutions dealing with delinquents, of the specific nature of such conflicts.

One of the reasons that there is so little evidence is that, until fairly recently, social workers in agencies supported by public funds were preoccupied with dealing with economic disabilities, and, since 1925, in privately supported agencies, with helping to adjust the psychological aspects of their clients' lives. Two reports of the Public Health Service in 1924 lamented the absence in agency records of material that revealed the attitudes of immigrant families toward American customs. Whether they felt antagonistic or satisfied with American conditions, and whether or not they were ready or eager to adopt American ways instead of continuing their native practices was not recorded.[59] Nor were earlier social workers concerned with cultural differences between themselves and their clients. For example, living arrangements which the native-born, middle-class caseworker would consider intolerable are not necessarily disturbing to a person accustomed to or unconcerned with sharing beds or living in slums. And unless the client mentioned them, they would not be noted in the record.

A hopeful sign today is that the curricula in schools of social work are including courses and field work experience which orient the student to perceive differences in his viewpoint and the client's culture, and to take them into account in dealing with tension situations.[60]

Frontier Mores

Elliott's "Crime and the Frontier Mores" [61] highlights the influence of our lawless frontier heritage on our current adult crime problem. Although she makes no reference to juvenile delinquency, her vivid descriptions of adult lawbreaking condoned in the expansion of our frontiers awake present-day echoes. These suggest a third way of looking at some aspects of juvenile misconduct. Numerous blatant examples of adult misconduct add fuel to the fires

---

[59] Mary Jarrett, "Factors in the Mental Health of Girls and Boys of Foreign Parentage," *Public Health Reports*, March and April 1924.
[60] Sol Weiner Ginsburg, M.D., *On Cultural Factors in Casework*, New York, National Travelers Aid Association, 1954, pp. 1-19.
[61] Mabel A. Elliott, "Crime and Frontier Mores," *American Sociological Review*, Vol. 9, no. 2 (April 1944), pp. 185-92.

of conflict in the values and goals of youth in some of the subcultures of our multi-ethnic population. Lawlessness in America, Elliott reminds us, has been one of the devices for social control. Criminals have not only been tacitly tolerated but they have been accepted and approved by some groups in American society. Some of those who helped to expand our frontiers and settle new territory were not hampered by strict codes of behavior.

Actually, the designation of behavior as antisocial, as well as the efforts to cope with it, differed in various frontiers. The travelers in the New England covered wagons brought along their puritan codes of behavior when they settled in the agriculturally fertile Middle West. The development of a caste system in Virginia attests to the persistence of English aristocratic ideas there. At the same time, both the South and the East condoned piracy, a characteristic type of illegal enterprise in America in the two hundred years from 1632 to 1827.

The Far West was the haven of many a horse and cattle thief from Nebraska and Kansas. They were joined by escaped burglars from the Eastern penitentiaries, counterfeiters and paroled convicts from Australia, and outlaws from Mexico. Together they sought new opportunities to carry on their illicit vocations among the less sophisticated, law-abiding settlers. Evidence of the disreputable background of many early Californians is found in folk songs. Elliott quotes:

> Oh what was your name in the States?
> Was it Thompson or Johnson or Bates?
>   Did you murder your wife
>   And fly for your life?
> Say, what was your name in the States[62]

Lynch law prevailed in the early settlement of the mining camps, in the opening up of the railroads, in the development of the lumber industry, and in the feuds between the cattle and the sheep men. Many of the current Wild West movies are not entirely fictitious in their portrayals of outlaw behavior in a frontier setting.

"As long as there were new wildernesses to conquer," wrote Frederick L. Turner, "any man with sufficient energy and initiative could make a living. No one bothered much about the general laxity in business honesty and financial integrity. In consequence, there was little restriction. If a man felt hampered by competitive forces, he could always 'go West.' Social controls were at a minimum and if the sound of the neighbor's axe seemed

---

[62] From Joseph Henry Jackson, *Anybody's Gold*, New York, Appleton-Century, 1941.

menacing, he could move further West." As the free lands were exhausted, however, "instead of moving when he heard the sound of his neighbor's axe, the son of the pioneer demanded—a muffling of the axe."[63]

The innumerable measures which have been adopted to regulate business, health, sanitation, education, and conduct reflect this demand. But in redefining old practices social legislation has, as Elliot points out, created new crimes. This was the obverse of its good intent, i.e., increasing the social conscience.

As we well know, the passage of a law does not automatically insure the conduct which the law is designed to promote. Without re-education of the people concerned and without their willingness to accept the new standards, legal sanctions will not be effective.

Elliot concludes: "Unlike our European cousins, we have had our most serious frontier problems within our own borders. In Europe, there has been much respect for law within national boundaries, whereas cultural conflicts have led to war, perhaps, instead of to crime."[64]

Multiple Causation

A fourth endeavor to explain crime and delinquency in the cultural vein, stresses multiple causation and calls for interdisciplinary cooperation. Some of the most promising work along these lines is exemplified in the writings of Lucien Bovet[65] and Erik Erikson, whose provocative ideas on the way our society contributes to the sense of ego identity or diffusion were outlined in Chapter 6. This approach, which embodies the insights of psychiatry and ethnology, is best described by the term "integrated."

Although the author of a theory may label it socio-cultural, he is usually fully aware of the pressure of genetic factors. Some stress the psychosomatic, i.e., the interrelation between organic and psychological factors; others, like Erikson, stress the ethno-psychologic interrelationship. By whatever name these new approaches may be called, they all reflect a concern with multiple causation and integrated treatment. They always regard the individual as an organic entity, subject to the laws which govern organic nature. Whatever the universal "drives" may be, they have been channelized through the cultural milieu from the moment of birth or perhaps even before.

The effectiveness of the application of socio-cultural viewpoint in dealing with delinquents awaits testing. So far, as Bram says, we lack real understanding of the many regional and subcultural variations in American life.

[63] Frederick L. Turner, *The Frontier in American History*, New York, Henry Holt, 1920, p. 32.

[64] Elliot, *op. cit.*, p. 192.

[65] Lucien Bovet, *Psychiatric Aspects of Juvenile Delinquency*, Geneva, World Health Organization, 1951.

In his opinion, with which this author agrees, the current psychiatric and sociological interpretations of delinquency are largely based upon untested assumptions about American cultural patterns in specific problem situations. There are no well-established frames of reference as to what is the normal conduct of various types of individuals, in various types of families, in different settings. While obviously such studies are difficult to carry out in a multi-cultural society, if we are to have an integrated, many-faceted theoretical and practical approach to juvenile delinquency, as one aspect of behavior, which must be viewed in its relative context or Gestalt, full-scale studies of our American culture are clearly essential.

Summary

This chapter has examined cultural factors in the lives of several ethnic and religious groups in the United States to explore some possible explanations for their changing representation in statistics of crime and delinquency at various points in time and place.

Increasingly sociologists, social workers, and anthropologists have considered the influence of cultural inconsistencies in the milieu on an individual's behavior. The theory has been advanced that culture, i.e., the ways of thinking and behaving which each parent generation attempts to transmit to its children, determines to a large extent the reaction patterns of the group members. The extent to which an individual holds to the patterns of his group may establish his feeling of belonging and security and enable him to control the expression of his aggressive instincts.

Religion is one of the major cultural transmission belts, and many people believe that the reported increase in the rates of crime and delinquency in the United States is associated with the falling off in religious observance. Back of this belief is the assumption that observant religious people adhere to the tenets of their faith. Since all faiths seek to indoctrinate their followers against crime, the incidence of Catholics, Protestants, and Jews in delinquency statistics should correspond with their proportions in the population if there is a direct relation between religious observance and delinquency. However, the unequal distribution of *apprehended* delinquents among the three major religious groups suggests that other characteristics account for the overrepresentation of certain groups in the official statistics.

Merton has sought to explain the deviant behavior of certain national or ethnic groups as a product of anomie and nonconformity. Another series of sociological studies sees it as the result of conflict between the succeeding waves of migrants and immigrants who have had difficulty in adjusting to established American standards and situations, many of which differed from their own. The problems of adjustment of the Chinese and the Japanese, who not only desire to have a place in the American socio-economic system but have wished also to maintain their own identity, are recognizably different from those of the Irish, Italians, and Poles, many of whom designedly lose their ethnic identity in the second and third generation. The adjustments of Mexican immigrants, and of Puerto Rican and Negro migrants, are complicated not only by wide differences in family life systems but by the rural-urban transition. Differences in skin color and language are additional barriers to easy socio-economic ascent in the United States.

Elliot suggests that our present-day gangsterism and political corruption are a direct heritage of the criminal behavior which accompanied the development of the American frontier and was tacitly approved. While the challenge of the frontier situation no doubt provided the opportunity and determined the form of the antisocial behavior, it is important to remember that not all or even a majority of pioneers, whether from New England, Virginia, or the Middle West, took the law into their own hands. As in the theories of culture conflict, we do not know what combination of circumstances within the individual, the family, and the milieu precipitated this antisocial frontier behavior.

None of the cultural studies has definitively delineated the actual combination of circumstances which, in families belonging to any ethnic group, appears to precipitate antisocial behavior. The ethnic characteristics outlined are therefore descriptive rather than causal.

In advocating an integrated interdisciplinary approach to understanding behavior deviation, the anthropologists' concern "for man and his works" emphasizes the interrelation between organic and cultural factors. In their continuing effort to understand how the personality grows and attains healthy development in different settings, they hope to learn more about how delinquent behavior has been caused and how it may be avoided. In the meantime, as Bram reminds us, we need more and better studies of the myriad subcultures in America as a preliminary to an integrated and many-faceted theoretical and practical approach to the causes of juvenile delinquency.

CHAPTER 12

Causal Theory: Its Problems and Its Future

UP TO THIS POINT WE HAVE REVIEWED ATTEMPTS TO EXPLAIN DELINQUENT behavior as the result of specific characteristics—biological, physiological, or intellectual—of the individual. We have presented evidence from sociologically oriented studies of such aspects of family living as bad housing, poverty, broken homes, and working mothers. We have examined studies which laid the blame for delinquency on inadequacies of the school, on the waning influence of the church, or the bad examples in the mass media of communication. We have looked at various psychiatric studies of faulty parent-child relationships as the mainsprings of delinquency. In most instances, the evidence in support of the underlying hypothesis, reasonable though it appeared to its advocates, was either contradicted by other studies or failed to take into consideration other relevant factors.

This chapter attempts to draw together the evaluations of causal theory to date as a basis for setting forth the new direction that research must take if it is to provide a sound basis for the detection, treatment, and prevention of juvenile delinquency.

Critique of Delinquency Research

We take off from Michael and Adler's monumental critique of the major causal studies completed before 1933.[1] Included in their analysis were

[1] Jerome Michael and Mortimer J. Adler, *Crime, Law and Social Science*, New York, Harcourt, Brace, 1933.

such studies of delinquents, already reviewed in this book, as those of Cyril Burt, the Gluecks, the early studies of Healy and Bronner, Clifford Shaw, H. M. Shulman, and John Slawson. Considerable space is devoted to explaining why the numerous studies of the relation between intelligence and delinquency, reviewed by Sutherland, and studies of the relation of body structure and delinquency, such as those of Lombroso and Goring and Berman and Schlapp's studies of glandular functioning, are not definitive. Truxal's study of recreation (see Chapter 28) is analyzed and found wanting from a research standpoint.

Michael and Adler conclude their analysis of studies designed to explain delinquency with the statement:

> The best pieces of research have been done by men who have more or less explicitly recognized the inconclusiveness of their findings with respect to their own research problems and the entire inadequacy of their research with respect to problems of etiology. . . . The assurance with which [some] criminologists have advanced opinions regarding the causes of crime is in striking contrast to the worthlessness of the data upon which those opinions (interpretations of descriptive knowledge) are based.[2]

Even though one may take issue with Michael and Adler's concept of appropriate research techniques for the social sciences, the painstaking nature of their research and its challenge to the field of criminology warrant review. As we shall see, most of their criticisms of the early studies unfortunately apply as well to the subsequent ones.

One must agree with Michael and Adler that the studies they reviewed provided only *descriptive* knowledge restricted to aggregates of individuals at a *particular* time and in a *particular* place. "No study satisfactorily differentiated the delinquent from the nondelinquent, nor any one type of delinquency from another in terms of individual factors or combinations of factors." Neither did any study "distinguish between the incidence of individual antisocial acts in a criminal versus a noncriminal group." Consequently, none of these studies materially advanced our knowledge of the causes of criminal behavior, "nor yielded conclusions relevant to the specific problems to which they were oriented."[3]

One must agree also that practically none of these studies, or those that followed, tested the validity of the data, or questioned the appropriateness of the scales or measurements used. When case histories were used, with the possible exception of Healy and Bronner's study of the Judge Baker Clinic, the items selected for observation were not always clearly defined, or if they

[2] *Ibid.*, p. 160.
[3] *Ibid.*, p. 9.

were defined, their reliability was often not validated. Because the conditions of observation were rarely uniform, it has been impossible, in the case of most of the studies, to repeat the observations to check their accuracy. This defect, Powers and Witmer point out, also characterizes the Cambridge-Somerville survey (see Chapter 28).

Frequently—as Greenwood indicated in the case of Lander's Baltimore study (see Chapter 7)—observation has not been distinguished from inference. Furthermore, in studies involving statistical techniques, investigators have used correlation measures which were not applicable to the kinds of distributions with which they were working. As we noted in connection with the delinquency area studies (Chapter 7), investigators have not been discriminating in applying correlation formulas or tests for statistically significant difference. As Keynes says:

> *Sensible* investigators only employ the correlation coefficient to test or to confirm conclusions at which they have arrived on *other* grounds. . . .
> If we have a considerable body of pre-existing knowledge relevant to the particular inquiry, the calculation of a small number of correlation coefficients may be crucial but, otherwise, we must proceed as in the case of frequency coefficients; that is to say, we must have before us, in order to find a satisfactory argument, many sets of observations of which the correlation coefficients display a significant stability in the midst of variation in the non-essential class characteristics of the different sets of observations.[4]

Although some of the recent studies of Grosser and Short, like that of Lander, show more sophistication in their statistical procedures, few students of delinquency have been critical of the nature of the data to which they have applied elaborate statistical measures.

The Nature of Science

Before we can begin to plan appropriate designs for an over-all investigation of the nature and causes of delinquency, we need to reflect on the nature of science and the concept of cause.

The Need for an Empirical Base

According to Michael and Adler, descriptive knowledge is the sum total of our accomplishment in research into crime and delinquency. But while *descriptive* knowledge may be a necessary preliminary, it is not scientific

[4] J. M. Keynes, *Treatise on Probability*, New York, Macmillan, 1921, Chapter 33. Italics in original.

knowledge. And without scientific knowledge there can be no solution to the practical problem of controlling criminal or delinquent behavior. Criminology, they go on to say, is not an independent science; it depends on both psychology and sociology, neither of which, unlike the physical sciences, is as yet fully developed as an empirical science.

Sellin agrees with Michael and Adler that criminology is a "bastard" science, grown out of the public's preoccupation with the social plague of crime. In order to be a criminologist, one must, he says, be "a psychologist, a sociologist, a psychiatrist, a jurist, or a political scientist with a specialized concern in a question which impinges on his broader interests."[5] This implies an impossible expertness for any one individual. Yet lacking these prerequisites one cannot arrive at valid generalizations, principles, or laws which have predictive values.

Sellin questions, however, whether Michael and Adler are correct in concluding that a field of knowledge which depends on other fields and is without an empirical base is necessarily unscientific. Such a definition of science implies that there is only one way for knowledge to be accumulated—i.e., the method of the physical sciences. As MacIver asks, is it not possible that differences in the nature of the subject matter in the two fields call for different approaches?

Observation of Physical Data

An important distinction between physical and social data, however, does exist, and has bearing on appropriate ways of observing and recording data in the two fields: As far as we know at present, the reaction of physical entities in a given situation does not depend on the attitudes of the observer. For example, although the values attached to a precious stone may vary in different societies, the attitudes of the observer do not apparently affect the stone's physical properties. These will be identical whether observed in Africa or America. If the instruments by which they are examined are equally reliable, it is possible to identify and classify diamonds in either country.

In contrast, similar types of behavior in Africa or America may not be similarly described (1) because of the differential interaction of the observer with the individual observed; and (2) because of differences in the value systems of the two countries. The behavior, for example, toward cows in India is totally unlike that in America. In India cows, as sacred animals, are allowed to clutter the streets, absorb the scanty food supply and, from an American point of view, make life very difficult. In America cows are not regarded as objects of worship, but perform an important national service

[5] Thorsten Sellin, *Culture Conflict and Crime*, New York, Social Science Research Council, Bulletin 41, 1938, p. 3.

in providing steaks or milk shakes. Killing a cow will have a drastically different impact in the two countries.

Interaction between the observer and the observed complicates the use of a control group in the social sciences. While the results of a controlled experiment are often effective in advising the farmer how to improve his crop yield, attempts to use controls in observing human behavior, as in the studies of the Gluecks and to a lesser extent (see Chapter 6) Healy and Bronner, are complicated. People, unlike crops, talk back and respond differently to the persons administering the tests. We have not as yet succeeded in devising foolproof methods to eliminate the human factor in social experiments.

Correlation is the usual substitute in the social sciences for the actual manipulation of the objects which is possible in the physical sciences. But unfortunately the incidence of the factors which we attempt to correlate in social situations is rarely known definitively for the normal population. In situations in which the use of correlation techniques illuminates some relationships, a further problem is how to put together in a dynamic whole those aspects of behavior which have been isolated for the purposes of correlation.

Empirical Proposition Versus Definition

Conant calls attention to the need for distinguishing between an experimentally testable assertion and a proposal to represent the observable facts by certain words or diagrams.[6] In spite of the deceptive similarity between these two formulations, which might conceivably be interchangeable in certain contexts, Pierce adds that, "under no circumstances, can a statement be simultaneously a definition and an empirical proposition. The terms are mutually exclusive.[7]

A definition *identifies* and refers to the *conformities* of objects, events, conditions, all of which are matters of objective confirmation. In contrast, empirical veracity properly applies only to the adequacy with which propositions describe *relationships* among types of objects, events, conditions, or processes which have been defined in terms that are *logically independent of each other* and *of the relationship predicated* in the proposition.

Defining a stone as a piece of rock of a given size and shape simply means that we have elected to call such an object a stone. We might have called it something else. An *empirical* proposition, on the other hand, might be that "under a specified set of conditions, a stone and some other object will fall the same distance in the same time interval." This statement represents an empirical proposition because it affirms a *relationship* between two

[6] James Conant, *On Understanding Science*, New Haven, Yale University Press, 1947, p. 48.
[7] Albert Pierce, "Empiricism and the Social Sciences," *American Sociological Review*, Vol. 21, no. 2 (April 1956), p. 136.

or more objects which have been defined in logically independent categories. Neither the stone nor the other object is defined in terms inherent in the proposition of their suspected relationships. The stated relationship can be verified or contradicted, independent of any logical connection between the items compared.

The important test of empiricism is that it is potentially refutable on nonlogical grounds. A proposition about the relationship of an individual's behavior relative to his presumed ends or goals is not empirical if the type of behavior is logically implicit in those ends or goals.

Pierce does not claim that nonempirical propositions have no use in science. As a matter of fact, he suggests that as illustrations rather than as proof they are appropriate in a historical (as opposed to a sociological) frame of reference. Nonempirical propositions may also be valuable as intermediate or preliminary steps in the process of empirical formulations.

Failure to distinguish between a definition and an empirically verifiable proposition is one of the shortcomings of *Unraveling Juvenile Delinquency*. The Gluecks' definition of a delinquent was synonymous with commitment to the Lyman institution. The authors enumerated as causal characteristics of delinquents those which influenced the judicial decision to commit a misbehaving boy to an institution rather than allow him to remain in the community. The characteristics they enumerated were not *causes*, but merely *descriptions* of certain types of young persons who, when they come in conflict with the law, are likely to be committed.

Basic Assumptions in Science Versus Technology

Sellin agrees with Michael and Adler that the field of criminology has two aspects. The first, concerned with information about the activities and the nature of criminals and their environment, is scientific. This scientific aspect is what interests us here. The second aspect—concerned with the ways in which criminals are officially or unofficially treated by social agents and agencies—is technological. This aspect we consider in Parts III, IV, and V.

The goal of the scientist is the discovery of *constants* in the *relationships* among certain defined facts. The technologist, on the other hand, is concerned almost exclusively with the *adaptation* of knowledge to the social needs of a given situation at a given time. Both activities, science and technology are necessary and in a sense interdependent.

According to Sellin, three basic assumptions underlie any science:[8]

1. that things are knowable;
2. that there is an orderliness in their interrelationships. Whether the

8 Sellin, *op. cit.*, p. 5.

orderliness is *revealed* or *created* by the mind is a question which, in some situations, is important. If it is the first, it assumes a reality external to the mind; if it is the second, it is more in line with the general thesis of this text which is that human beings create their own pattern of order, depending upon their indoctrination and conditioning.

3. While perception of these interrelationships is accompanied by intellectual satisfaction which is an end in science as in other branches of pure learning, the most important thing is the control over natural processes which science affords.

In the end, says Sellin, the social utility of science depends not on its scientific validity or the intellectual satisfaction it affords the scientist, but on its social *acceptability* which, in turn, is a function of tradition, custom, vested interests, public policy, and so forth. For example, while there is no proof that statutes designed to correct certain evils do so successfully, there is a notion that they protect the public and, as a consequence, they continue to be advocated as cures. One recalls that the Baumes Laws in New York State, which provide increasingly heavy penalties for recidivists, have not appeared to reduce the incidence of crime.

The Tentative Nature of Science

In taking issue with Adler's pronouncement that there can be no science of criminology because human behavior is voluntary and its effects are, therefore, indeterminate, and because scientific truths must be stated in absolute terms, Sellin reminds us that "a scientific law must always be considered as a *temporary* statement of relationships. As knowledge increases, this law may require modification. Even the natural sciences state all generalizations in terms of probability."[9] Mathematics and logic are exceptions, because they are not designed "to ascertain *truths* with respect to actual existences, but to trace the logical filiation of consequences which follow from an assumed *hypothesis*. If from this *hypothesis* we reason with correctness, nothing, it is manifest, can be wanting to complete the evidence of the result; as this result only asserts a necessary connection between the supposition and the conclusion."[10]

In contrast to mathematics and logic, the other sciences are founded on principles which may or may not correspond with "facts." Henri Poincaré is Sellin's authority for the statement: "They deal with what the logician refers to as 'moral' or 'probable' evidence; i.e., based on contingent facts, as com-

[9] *Ibid.*, p. 9. Italics added.
[10] Rudolf Carnap, "Logic," in *Factors Determining Human Behavior*, Harvard Tercentenary Publications, Cambridge, Harvard University Press, 1937, p. 113. Italics in original.

pared with 'demonstrative' evidence, illustrated in the mathematical sciences."[11]

Because *all* the conditions of a social science experiment can never be surely known (they may be forgotten or not recognized as essential) the social sciences can only say that *if* certain conditions occur, it is *probable* that a certain phenomenon will be approximately reproduced. Since, however, human behavior falls within the field of observable facts, Sellin avers that there can be no objection to the application of scientific method of study to these facts, even though the generalizations or laws drawn from the studies can be expressed only in terms of degrees of probability, characteristic of all sciences based on contingent data.[12]

As a result of the infinite variety of human behavior the data of the social sciences is complex, but not necessarily impossible to order. Instead it presents a special challenge to formulate a science of human conduct, good or bad.

Cause as Degree of Association

In abandoning the search for ultimate causes, science seeks instead to determine the degree of association between or among elements or facts derived from experience.[13] To say that the antecedent event is the cause and the subsequent event the effect refers to the usual *temporal* relationship between two sets of events. Research in criminology and delinquency causation has been directed almost exclusively to "a pursuit of these antecedents and the establishment of constants in their relations to criminal conduct."[14] Consequently, the conclusions of the largely impressionistic researches in criminology result only in suggesting hypotheses which, as Pierce notes, require testing before they can be considered relevant to a study of cause.

Nonlegal Definitions of Crime and Delinquency

The antecedent problem in a causal study is the definition of crime and the criminal, or of delinquency and the delinquent, in other than legal terms. Our discussion of the studies of the relationship of delinquency to the individual, the family, the home, the school, and so forth, has unfortunately shown that the criteria and methods employed generally offer a fragile basis for the generalizations produced.

Too often the study of delinquency is limited to circumstances of purely

[11] Henri Poincaré, *Science et Methode,* Paris, Flammarion, 1908, p. 249.
[12] Sellin, *op. cit.,* p. 12.
[13] *Ibid.,* p. 17.
[14] *Ibid.,* p. 18.

fortuitous nature based on merely external similarities in what is observed. Thus, for example, according to Catlin:

> The criminal norms, i.e., the conduct norms embodied in the criminal law, change as the values of the dominant group are modified, or as the vicissitudes of social growth cause a reconstitution of these groups themselves and shifts in the focus of power. Thus crimes of yesteryear may be legal conduct today, while crimes in one contemporary state may be legal conduct in another. This lesson of history makes it a safe prediction—an empirical generalization as well founded as any generalization in the natural sciences—that everything the criminal law of any state prohibits today, it will not prohibit at a given future time, unless complete social stagnation sets in, an experience unknown to the social historian.[15]

Yet, despite lip service to the extreme variability in the definition of both crime and delinquency, there have been few efforts beyond those of the present author, Porterfield, Short, and Nye to test empirically the adequacy of official juvenile court designations of delinquency as an index of the incidence of defined behavior in a population.

In commenting on Short's research, Albert Cohen remarked:

> A bane of delinquency study has been the tendency to treat delinquency as a homogeneous entity, and therefore delinquency-nondelinquency as a dichotomous variable. We all know that delinquency is not a clinical entity like smallpox; that it is, rather, a legal entity, comprehending a variety of different forms of behavior which may have many different kinds of cultural meaning and therefore motivations. The methodological conclusion has not, however, been drawn and acted upon. It is necessary, in studying delinquency, to break it down into elements, and to investigate empirically whether the propositions we make about [one kind of] delinquency are valid also about [another kind of] delinquency, etc. This study [Short's] with its detailed breakdown is a long step in this direction.
>
> In moving away from the idea of delinquency as a homogeneous something which one has or has not, one may move in two directions. One, the idea of delinquency as a continuous variable, various degrees of which are represented by different scale types, each scale type being a particular combination of delinquent actions. A sequence of scale types, corresponds to points along a continuum. The other is the idea of clusters or syndromes or, more modestly, patterns that tend to recur and which are correlated with situational, background or role constellations. These patterns may have elements in common, as a fever may characterize two different diseases, but there are nonetheless distinctive patterns, which are not points along a scale.

[15] George Catlin, "The Delimitation and Measurability of Political Phenomena," *American Political Science Review*, Vol. 21 (May 1937), pp. 255-69.

... it is to be hoped that the current enthusiasm about scaling will not leave us blind to the other possibilities. For example, do middle-class and working-class delinquency differ, and, if so, do they differ along a scale, like so many degrees of the same thing, or are they patterned, to be sure, but not in the sense of scale types? How about delinquents who operate in gangs and "individual" delinquents? Questions like these are important because our explanations must make sense of the facts about delinquency. An explanation that makes intelligible the delinquency of one group may not make sense of the delinquency of another group. But first, we must know how the delinquency itself varies. . . .

We need, therefore, techniques for investigating delinquency in the population at large. We should long ago have begun to exercise our ingenuity in devising ways of doing this; instead, we have spent more and more money trying to a better job of matching official delinquents with nondelinquents. But the best possible job is vitiated by the *fatal defect*.[16]

As the author of this text pointed out twenty years ago, the initial step in the direction of overcoming this defect was the development of a central register, described in Chapter 4.

This does not mean that studies based upon data about *apprehended* criminals and delinquents have no use. To be scientifically useful, however, scientific criteria must be applied to the selection and classification of these data independent of their legal form. It should be remembered that the *language* as well as the *goal* of the legislator and the administrator differ from those of the scientist. Consequently, before the scientist can use the *legal* categories either in crime or in delinquency, he must "process" them. To this end Sellin suggests that the concept of conduct norms be substituted for the ambiguous and inconclusive legal categories of crime and delinquency.

Conduct Norms as a Substitute for Legal Definitions

As was noted in considering anthropological explanations of delinquency, regardless of the variation in our biological inheritance, each of us is subjected to a lifelong process of absorbing and accepting ideas which are transmitted both formally and informally. Faced with the need to decide whether we should follow one or another course of action, our "choice" is ordinarily fairly automatic. When, however, we are confronted with a new situation which demands action and a balance of alternative interests, we select the alternative that appears to be most suitable at the time. In Dewey's terms, thinking (in contrast to rationalizing) occurs only at the moment of impeded action.

[16] Discussion at the September 1955 meeting of the American Sociological Society, Washington, D.C.

Our choice of action reflects the meaning of the life situation to us. Situations which recur frequently are, so to speak, socially defined, which means that the responses which they should evoke have been identified as norms, approved by the group. The individual's reaction to these norms is, in Sellin's terminology, appropriately labeled "conduct," a term that embraces all types of reactions. "*Antisocial* conduct" is, according to Sellin, an unscientific term because it belongs "to the language of social reform." "Normal" and "abnormal" conduct, on the other hand, are appropriate terms to refer to conduct which accords with or deviates from a conduct norm.

All of us must simultaneously harmonize our conduct with the norms of the many groups to which we belong—i.e., family, play group, work group, political group, or religious group. Each of these groups, in turn has its own set of conduct norms appropriate for its goals and its activities. Some norms may be contradictory to those of the group we grew up with and have incorporated in our personality. The more complex the culture, the greater the disagreement among the norms (see Chapters 9 and 11).

Because conduct norms characterize all social groups and are not confined within political boundaries or always embodied in law, their study affords a sounder basis for the development of scientific categories than a study of crime or delinquency as identified in the criminal law or the juvenile court codes. To develop such categories, however, requires a system for classifying norms.

A *conduct norm* may be regarded as a *rule* supported by sanctions which reflect the value attached to the norm by the normative group. Norms governing a specific type of life situation are *authoritative* to the extent that the group resists their violation. Thus the "resistance potential" of a norm, difficult though it might be to devise techniques for measuring it, might provide categories with universal application at least within a country.

Application of this concept of "resistance potential" to the legal norms of a state would produce a classification based entirely upon the degree of severity of the penalty assigned to crimes. Instead of comparison of *crime rates* of various states for *specific* crimes, one would compare rates of crimes with correspondingly severe *penalties.*[17] Thus, offenses with the same penalty would be grouped together regardless of any other characteristic of these offenses, a defensible procedure if both invoke the same degree of resistance by society. The most severe and the lightest penalties of the law of each state would form the limits of the scale for that state. The scale would be established by persons thoroughly familiar with the culture and the political values of the state in question. "Such scales of penalties," says Sellin, "would afford

---

[17] Sellin, *op. cit.*, p. 36. Also Lucille Clair, "A Survey of Dispositions of Major Felony Offenses in States Having Centralized Statistical Agencies," Project No. 4162, Aug. 1952, New York School of Social Work, Columbia University.

a sounder theoretical basis for the classification of crimes than the labels which are now found in the criminal codes."

To illustrate: because of the wide differences in the social values of the political groups in power in the United States and Soviet Russia, murder in the former and the malicious destruction of government property in the latter are similarly punished. "From a scientific point of view, it may be more important to know if violations of criminal law norms of a given strength of value are rare or prevalent, increase or decrease, than to know that a crime labeled as abortion or prostitution increases or decreases."[18]

Applying this concept to delinquency would mean that instead of studying changes in the *incidence* of acts of violence against persons, for example, we would study changes in the *proportion* of cases brought to the court in various communities in which the disposition was *dismissal* or *commitment*, the two extremes in penalties.

Sellin suggests other systems of classifying conduct norms in terms of "some other intrinsic quality of the norm measurable in degrees or on some basis on which norms, assumed to be different in kind, could be identified"; or, following a suggestion of Willard Waller,[19] on the basis of the type of social value which the norm protects. Neither of these ways of classifying conduct norms, however, is currently possible, because there is no scientific catalogue on which to base a study of combinations of norms or their relationships to other cultural phenomena.[20]

Violators versus *Conformists*

Another possible classification of conduct norms which Sellin proposes is an analysis of personality structure or growth process in different cultures which would distinguish the violator of conduct norms from the conformist.[21] This recalls Sykes and Matza's explanation of gang behavior in terms of techniques of neutralization (see Chapter 9).

The fundamental aim of sociological research, in contrast to psychologically oriented research on norm violations, is to isolate the personality elements which distinguish the violators from the conformists in various social contexts. The personality element in this sense is the meaning which an individual attaches to a social or cultural element when he is confronted with a particular situation, as for example it is revealed in a gang situation or in David Levy's and Jenkins's classifications (see Chapter 6). Says Sellin: "There is

---

18 Sellin, *op. cit.*, p. 37.

19 Willard Waller, "Some Sociological Aspects of the Definition and Classification of Crimes," a paper read at the Criminology Section of the American Sociological Society, Dec. 1955.

20 Sellin, *op. cit.*, p. 35.

21 *Ibid.*, p. 40.

no catalog of such meanings and the sociologist, generally speaking, probably knows infinitely less about them than does the anatomist about the structural elements of the human body."[22]

These meanings probably exist in characteristic configurations which operate as determinants of conduct depending upon the time and the circumstances under which one or more of the elements were introduced into the personality. In addition to the usual cross-sectional study, the genetic study would, Sellin believes, lead to the discovery of personality types more definitive than those currently described. This is in line with our suggestion that what is needed in order to understand how and why delinquents persist in or give up their disapproved behavior, is a Kinsey-type study of representative groups of citizens who would be willing to delve into their past to reveal the extent to which they had indulged in "delinquent" behavior in their private lives.

Sellin, in elaborating a fourfold classification of conduct norms ranging from no resistance to complete group resistance, acknowledges that it makes no allowance for the emotional significance of the norm to the individual, which determines the likelihood of his obeying or violating it.[23] Yet, as was pointed out in Chapter 6, knowledge of right conduct without emotional involvement in it will not assure approved behavior.

To provide for consideration of the emotional factors in behavior, Sellin suggests that "sociological research on norm violators should concentrate on persons who have violated norms (a) with high resistance potentials (b) incorporated as personality elements (c) which possess strong emotional tone. Offenders who have overcome the greatest and most pervasive group resistance probably exhibit more clearly than others the personality types which have significance for our research purposes."[24]

This formulation will be acceptable to the social worker and to psychiatrists who place the major emphasis on the meaning of the crime or delinquency to the violator. As noted in the study of twenty persistent truants (Chapter 10), truancy was merely a signal of the need for help; and as Healy and Bronner pointed out, the labels "stealing," "breaking," and "entering" do not reflect what the offender is trying to express through the delinquent act. Sellin agrees that the determinants of the behavior are not revealed in the labels, but "it is just these determinants which must be known and coped with if effective treatment is to be undertaken."[25]

The point emphasized by Sellin is that, although a criminal law with classifications which meet *all* the criteria of science is not within the realm of

---

[22] *Ibid.*, p. 41.
[23] *Ibid.*, pp. 42 ff.
[24] *Ibid.*, p. 44.
[25] Healy and Bronner, *New Light on Delinquency and Its Treatment*, New Haven, Yale University Press, 1936, p. 6.

possibility, if sociological analysis of criminal norms is to have any considerable scientific value, it must delve below the labels of the law. Thus, both typological classification as well as classification by "resistance potential" is necessary to arrive at universally valid generalizations. "These generalizations would describe the relationships between or among legal norms as samples of conduct norms, the relationships between legal and other conduct norms, the transition of norms from one category to another, the interdependence of norms and other cultural phenomena, etc."

Acknowledging the limitations of the details of the suggested plans for research in the scientific study of crime causation, Sellin concludes: "Ultimately, science must be able to state that if a person with certain *personality* elements in a certain *configuration* happens to be placed in a certain typical *life situation,* he will probably react in a certain manner, whether the law punishes this response as a crime or tolerates it as unimportant."[26] From the point of view of this text, this statement of Sellin's embodies the appropriate goal for research in delinquency as well as crime.

While a new research orientation has grown out of the structural-functional approach applied in different ways in the studies of Lander, Grosser, and Albert Cohen, the focus is still primarily on the *individual* rather than *simultaneously on the family and the community,* as suggested by both Sellin and MacIver. Healy and Bronner's *New Light on Delinquency and Its Treatment* opens the way for family-oriented research. Jephcott, Carter, and Mack, who concern themselves with differences in behavior within and between social classes (see Chapter 8), dramatically point up the need for pursuing this new orientation in causal research on delinquency. Says Mack:

> Forty years of progressive study and treatment of the young offender have been accompanied by a progressively higher incidence of official delinquency and a progressively greater confusion in the explanation of the problem. . . . This impasse may well be the aftermath of the tyranny of words. . . .
>
> As long as practically all researches continue to assume that juvenile delinquency is a legitimate field of research because it is a specific focus of related problems, the current confusion will not be resolved by more comprehensive researches into every aspect of "delinquency." In America as well as in England there is a preoccupation with tracing and treating delinquency as it occurs or threatens in the life of the individual child. This line of attack, however, is not likely to yield more knowledge about the problem.[27]

The one area of agreement in the various studies is the crucial role of some form of family disorganization—i.e., the failure of parents to give their

[26] *Ibid.,* p. 45. Italics added.
[27] John A. Mack, *Family and Community,* Carnegie United Kingdom Trust, 1953, pp. 3-5.

children the two things they need most: assurance of continuing love and acceptance and the moral discipline made acceptable by love. To date, however, most of the conclusions have been derived almost entirely from a study of *problem* families. Obviously, what we urgently need to know is how *ordinary* families manage to bring up their children in spite of the stresses and strains to which they, like their problem neighbors, are subjected.

An example of rewarding research in the health field, which might well be applied to delinquency, is the Newcastle-on-Tyne study over a period of ten years of the medical needs of a thousand families—one in six of the community's families in which a child was born in 1946. To date, the findings suggest:

1. That the normal competent family passes on the practices of good family living from generation to generation in complex and subtle ways.

2. That the strength and resilience of cultural traditions sustain community and family life.

3. That family well-being is also a function of factors in the community at large, specifically of informal community relationships which sustain families and individuals morally and socially.

Delinquency is only one indication that this fabric of family and community relationship has worn thin in many communities.

Summary

This chapter has reviewed a variety of concepts of cause in the social sciences. Michael and Adler's critique of the inconclusiveness and the ineffectiveness of most causal studies attempting to relate individual factors to delinquency appears to have been justified. Authors who have used statistical measures have not always understood their correct application as a description rather than as an explanation of a phenomenon.

Sellin's discussion of the nature of cause in the social sciences as similar to that in the physical sciences answers Michael and Adler's complaint that criminology cannot be a science because it depends upon sociology and psychology, neither of which is empirically based.

Albert Pierce's stress on the difference between a definition and an empirically testable proposition reminds us that research in the field of delinquency has not tested empirical propositions but instead, has largely described characteristics inherent in the definitions of delinquency, and has then proceeded to impute a causal significance to these characteristics. Thus research in delinquency has pulled out of the universe of events observations which fit the particular theories and then assumed that the observations were the explanations.

For more definitive answers to the why of delinquency, there must be initial agreement that neither crime nor delinquency corresponds to an entity or is coterminous with its legal definition. As a more satisfactory substitute for the legal terms, Sellin suggests the concepts of conduct norms and the resistance potential of the community to their violation, classified separately for each society.

Significant research in delinquency calls for settings which are natural rather than contrived, and in which we can observe empirically over a period of time the interrelationships (structural-functional and psychological) as well as the opportunities for learning and performance in terms of the culture and the technology of the family setting. If these natural situations include populations and circumstances which are fairly homogeneous and stable, it is more likely that our observations will yield clues to why certain people behave in specific ways in certain settings. The research design, however, calls for clearly formulated hypotheses which, as MacIver emphasizes, take into consideration the factors of interaction on four levels: individual, family, cultural milieu, and physical environment.

PART THREE

PRIMARY LEGAL AGENCIES FOR DEALING WITH DELINQUENTS

CHAPTER 15

The Police and Juvenile Delinquents

WHILE THE SEARCH FOR SATISFACTORY DEFINITIONS AS WELL AS EXPLANATIONS of delinquency continues, the community faced with a social problem makes what provisions it can to protect itself and deal with the troublesome child and his family. The major responsibility in this task, as the community's frontline defense against crime and delinquency, has been assigned to the police and the juvenile court.

The police officer stands between the citizen and the offender. What the officer does will depend on his interpretation of his own function, and on the various services the community provides, either through the juvenile court or other special agencies. Sociologically speaking, this involves a clear demonstration of the roles and functions of the various disciplines. Even if there is agreement among them, however, "that this far you go and no further," there are still psychological factors that will affect the way the individual, police, judge, probation officer, or social worker will react to any given situation. Some of these factors are illustrated in the hypothetical case of Johnny:

> Suppose Mrs. Smith calls the district station to report that Johnny, the 12-year-old next door, has just broken her window. The call is sent out to the officer on the beat, and he starts looking for Johnny.
>
> The officer knows this boy. He knows the child is a trouble-maker in the neighborhood, and that he fights with the other kids. And two or three times Old Doc Greeven down at the corner drug store said he thought the kid had swiped something—a $1.98 flashlight or a handful of comic books.

The officer, when he gets a chance, talks to Johnny and warns him about getting into trouble. Sometimes this works. Sometimes it doesn't. At any rate, you don't arrest a kid who broke a window or played ball in the street.

But suppose it was the window of a jewelry store? And suppose it was done in the middle of the night and a couple of watches are missing?

Then Johnny gets arrested. The officer on the beat brings him down to the district station and makes out a confidential juvenile report on the child in collaboration with the Juvenile Officer responsible for that district.

There's a Juvenile Officer responsible for each of the twelve police districts, and he studies and reports on cases of all arrested juveniles that are referred to him.

This officer compiles a complete record—a "case history"—on Johnny. To do this, he checks the boy's record in the juvenile file at Crime Prevention headquarters downtown. He checks up on the boy's home; he finds out if any other agency has tried to do anything for Johnny.

Finally he makes a decision. Should Johnny go to court or not? The Juvenile Officer gets all the help he can to make the decision. He discusses the case with many people before he decides. He also has the help of a lengthy study that lists 38 separate charges on which a child must be referred to court. But the Juvenile Officer has to make the decision. This decision—whether or not to send Johnny to court—is not in the nature of ordinary police duties. Traditionally, police aren't supposed to have anything to do with what happens to a criminal after he is arrested. That is up to the court.

But children under 17 present a different problem. Most people figure if a child gets half a chance and some decent direction, he might turn out all right—even after one or two offenses.[1]

The Available Data

In the course of a single year, police officers across the country probably encounter at least one million young people of juvenile court age who are either engaged in or suspected of delinquency. If the suspects were evenly distributed, this would mean roughly one out of every twenty-five people in the United States aged 7 to 18. But to apply this simple ratio of arrests to the total child population is misleading, for the size, the ethnic composition of the cities and towns, and the availability of the police all markedly influence which are likely to be apprehended as delinquents or suspects.

Because the individual states are autonomous, data on the operations of

[1] *Children in Trouble*, Annual Report, St. Louis Police Department, 1954, pages not numbered.

the police, which the central governments in some European countries collect automatically (see Chapter 3), are not available for the United States. Like our public school system, the set-up of our police, our health services, and our juvenile court system is by no means uniform from state to state or even from community to community within a state.

The most current and comprehensive sources on the functioning of the police in juvenile delinquency cases in the United States are: (1) a report of the combined deliberations of representatives of the International Association of Chiefs of Police and experts on the staff of the Special Delinquency Project of the Children's Bureau, hereinafter designated as the Lansing Report;[2] (2) a preliminary report of a Committee on Juvenile Delinquency of the International Association of Chiefs of Police and the Police Department of the City of New York under the chairmanship of Stephen P. Kennedy, Police Commissioner of New York City.[3] We shall refer to this document as the Kennedy Report.

Neither of these reports covers police practices in all communities. The Lansing Report represents about half of the 1300 urban areas with membership in the International Association of Chiefs of Police. All cities whose 1950 population was 500,000 or more reported, as did all but one city in the next largest category, 100,000-500,000. Least well represented are cities of less than 25,000 population and those in the Southern region. The Kennedy Report is based on replies from 153 of the 255 police jurisdictions polled in 1956 with respect to police practice in the juvenile field.

Factors That Affect Police Action

Legal Regulations

The police officer faced with the young person such as Johnny, whom someone accuses of wrongdoing or whom he apprehends in the act, has four choices:

1. He may dismiss the young person with a warning, as he does when he lets a suspected traffic offender off without a ticket. It is estimated that the police take no action in about one third of the juvenile cases that come to their attention.

[2] *Police Services for Juveniles,* Washington, U.S. Children's Bureau, 1954. Report of Special Conference under joint auspices of the Children's Bureau, the Special Delinquency Project of the International Association of Chiefs of Police, East Lansing, Mich., August 1953.
[3] *The Role of the Police in Juvenile Delinquency,* The Police Department of the City of New York, 1956.

2. He may decide that referral to an agency other than the court is appropriate. According to standard regulations, he prepares the family and the young person to accept his suggestion as a gesture of concern for their welfare and that of the community as well.

3. If he decides that he needs more information he may ask the parents to come to the police station or he may make a home visit. In either case, he tells the child and his parents that they are entitled to legal counsel and that, if they wish, they may refuse to answer any or all questions.

4. He will bring the offender directly to the juvenile court: (a) if the act would be a felony if committed by an adult; (b) if the evidence has serious implications; (c) if the immediate evidence contradicts the young person's denial of guilt.

In the large majority of all cases referred to court, the police are the petitioners. In some large cities almost three quarters of the petitions filed against children are signed by police officers. One can readily see how important it is to understand how the police officer interprets his role in estimating the extent and nature of officially reported delinquency.

Aside from the legal regulations sketched above, how the police action affects the recording of delinquency in the face of a suspected or actual crime depends upon three sets of factors: (1) Intangible factors in the reaction of the suspect, which in turn depend upon how the officer behaves, and how the suspect has been conditioned to behave when faced by a representative of authority. (2) Tangible factors in the physical set-up in the police department, i.e., whether or not there is a special youth division, and whether the officers assigned to that division have special qualifications. (3) Regulations concerning fingerprinting and confidentiality of record.

Reactions of and to the Police

The individual police officer's action depends upon how the suspect behaves when he is confronted by the representative of the law and how the officer interprets this response. For example, in witnessing a street fight, the officer will probably not interfere if he thinks the youngsters are just "letting off steam." On another occasion, however, he may decide to stop the fight. Depending on how he feels and the way the boys respond, the officer either tells them to "call it quits," or takes one or more boys into custody. The boys, in turn, may submit or protest violently.

Attitudes toward the police usually are conditioned by early childhood experiences. Many youths, like the ex-gangleader whose story is quoted in Chapter 9, regard the police as people to avoid. If one remembers the police as helping one at street corners, giving directions when one is lost, or even supplying carfare in an emergency, one will look upon the police officer as a helpful person. On the other hand, for young people whose only association is the warning whistle which means "Look out! Here come the police," the usual response will be avoidance or resistance. Unfortunately, there is testimony aplenty in the records of probation officers and of workers with gangs that most young people in trouble consider the police as an enemy.

Some young people seek to protect themselves by flight or evasion against what they surmise will be police hostility. Some youngsters openly try to provoke a counterattack. Whether the officer is able (1) to control his impulses to use physical force and at the same time (2) to exhibit the necessary firmness will depend on the extent to which he has been trained to react appropriately, i.e., to consider misbehavior not as a personal threat to his dignity but as the individual's way of expressing his hostility to adult authority.

Many police officers, like judges and other community representatives, share the points of view and prejudices of the ethnic group to which they belong. This undoubtedly affects their attitudes in labeling as antisocial the conduct of children with whom they deal. Some white policemen have frankly admitted their prejudices against Negroes.[4] No doubt some Irish-American policemen, who predominate in the police force in some large Eastern cities, also share the Irish-American prejudice toward Italian-Americans. The attitudes of the police toward ethnic groups are an important factor in designating behavior as officially delinquent.

The opinions and the actions of the police also reflect those of the larger community. It has been said that whether or not the police pick up shoplifters, subway turnstile-duckers, or even purse snatchers whom they may not actually have caught in the act, will depend on the time of the month—i.e., whether they need more cases to their credit—and on the pressure from the administration. Controversies aired at police meetings reported in the New York City press in the spring of 1958 suggest that administrative rulings and occasionally jurisdictional rivalries affect the activity of the police in bringing cases to court. The apprehension and referral of delinquents are not immune from such influences.

The Physical Set-Up of the Police Department

JUVENILE DIVISIONS. There is a special bureau, unit, or division, designated sometimes as crime prevention, youth aid, juvenile aid, juvenile control bureau, or juvenile division in more than three quarters of the police jurisdictions which cooperated in the Kennedy survey. They differ considerably

[4] See reference to Kephart's study of attitudes of Philadelphia police in Chapter 11.

with respect to the physical quarters, the rank of the officer in charge, and the number of training officers assigned.[5]

In some of the units the young person has to pass in front of the official police desk in order to see the juvenile officer. Some people object to subjecting a young person to this experience, especially if the station house is crowded.

In many units the commanding officer does not have a rank commensurate with that of the other deputies in charge of police divisions. This, in turn, affects the relationships of the juvenile officers with those in other divisions. The division known as the Juvenile Bureau in New Orleans is under the direct supervision of the superintendent of the police and has equal departmental status with other bureaus. In Chicago the director of the Crime Prevention Division is under the command of a deputy commissioner of police. The former Crime Prevention Bureau of the City of Detroit, established in 1944, was replaced in 1950 by the present Youth Bureau and operates through fourteen precincts, each commanded by an inspector.

The police commissioner of the City of Boston states that he has resisted establishing a separate juvenile aid division "although many demands have been made upon me by special groups of well-intentioned citizens to set up such a unit." He is unenthusiastic about the activities of a junior police force. In the field of recreation, he considers that the Boston Parks and Recreation Department is equipped to handle the recreational activities of the city. To assign the responsibility for work with youth to a special division would, in his opinion, appear to release the rest of the regular police force from any responsibility in that phase of the work.

SIZE AND NUMBER OF STAFF. As important as the rank of the officer in charge of the juvenile division is the size and the quality of the staff assigned to the special units. The usual unit is composed of 50 per cent policemen, 25 per cent policewomen, 10 per cent supervisors, and the remainder civilians. The number of personnel ranges from 1 to 239,[6] and the size of the unit appears to be independent of the size of the city. For the country as a whole, excluding civilians, there are slightly less than 4.4 police to 100,000 population,[7] and juvenile police make up 2.1 per cent of the whole force.[8] In New York City, among the 23,580 police officers on the force in August 1959, the juvenile division had 546 uniformed police personnel assigned to the Youth Squad.

[5] See Benjamin Fine, 1,000,000 *Delinquents*, New York, World, 1955. The chapter on police cites examples of good juvenile divisions in Cleveland, Chicago, Detroit, Houston, and Milwaukee.

[6] Kennedy Report, tables 86, 87, pp. 74, 75.

[7] *Ibid.*, table 89, p. 76.

[8] *Ibid.*, table 91, p. 76.

In some of the smaller jurisdictions, the juvenile officers serve on a part-time basis. In the larger ones, such as Cleveland, Chicago Park, and Newark, part-time officers supplement the services of the full-time staff.

The first women were attached to the police force in 1900, at a time when large numbers of young women were entering the business life of the community. Since then, in many cities policewomen have been assigned to work under executives in the uniform police divisions or in the detective bureau. Because the original policewomen were mainly concerned with problems of girls, policewomen continue to be assigned primarily to work with girls. If there are no policewomen available, the policemen are responsible for preventive and protective work with both boys and girls.

Special Qualifications for Juvenile Work

SELECTION AND TRAINING OF OFFICERS. Some police chiefs, such as Commissioner Sullivan of Boston, believe that all police officers should have some training for work with children, since all of them have contact with children. When one considers the million children who may encounter the police every year, this qualification certainly seems desirable and reasonable. There is, moreover, general consensus that all juvenile officers should meet the minimum requirements for appointment to the police force. These are: a high school education or its equivalent, good health, specified height and weight standards, and sufficient intelligence to pass required examinations.

Some jurisdictions require additional qualifications, i.e., evidence of personality and temperament requisite for constructive contact, as well as patience, understanding, and interest in young people. Opinions differ, however, as to whether the juvenile officer should be drawn from the ranks of the general police force or be independently recruited. A compromise suggestion made at the East Lansing Conference was recruitment outside the ranks of the force but assignment to regular police duties for the first six months.

A recommendation of the Juvenile Delinquency Evaluation Project of New York City was the assignment of special social work personnel to serve as consultants to the police in their work with juveniles.[9] This social work staff would have a relation to the police similar to that of police surgeons. Whether or not this recommendation will be acceptable to the police depends upon the recognition accorded to the need for special skills which the officer

[9] *The Police Department,* Interim Report No. 2, Juvenile Delinquency Evaluation Project of New York, Dec. 1956, p. 41. It is of interest that Commissioner Kennedy rose from the ranks and was assigned to one of the units of the old Crime Prevention Bureau, established under the direction of the then Deputy Police Commissioner, Henrietta Addition. See Sheldon and Eleanor Glueck, *Preventing Crime: A Symposium,* New York, McGraw-Hill, 1936, for a description of the program.

does not have and for which he ordinarily cannot be equipped without special training in a school of social work.

IN-SERVICE TRAINING AND ADVANCEMENT. Training after appointment, i.e., in-service training, was required in 70 per cent of those jurisdictions represented in the Kennedy Report, almost universally in the largest jurisdictions. The nature of the training, however, varied from reading assignments to attendance at specially designed training institutes. In almost half the jurisdictions, police officers were granted leaves-of-absence with or without pay to attend university, college, or police academy courses in juvenile work.

Among our special correspondents, officials in St. Paul's police department provide for special in-service training of and attendance by members of the Juvenile Division at a three-day institute at the University of Minnesota. The lieutenant in charge of the Juvenile Division is a graduate of the Delinquency Control Institute of the University of Southern California. Since 1955 the University of Minnesota has offered a ten-week course similar to that at the University of Southern California. Four members on the current staff of the St. Paul Juvenile Division have completed this course.

Chicago's staff of 150, assigned to thirty-eight units throughout the city from 8 A.M. to 12 midnight, are "indoctrinated in the sociological viewpoints of the causes and curative factors of delinquency by their interim attendance at in-training courses sponsored by the police department." Outstanding authorities serve as lecturers and instructors. They are supplemented by personnel from the family court, the state attorney's office, and the training schools for delinquents. No member of the department other than a juvenile officer can process juvenile cases. The police officer consults with the special officer who processes the case and decides whether to dismiss it, refer it to a local community agency, or to the family court.

Milwaukee provides a two-week training course in delinquency control for law enforcement officers in cooperation with the extension department of the University of Wisconsin. Each law enforcement officer accepted for training on the recommendation of his superior officer receives a full-expense scholarship, funds for which are contributed by the Allis-Chalmers Manufacturing Company of Milwaukee.

In a few states the police departments take advantage of opportunities for training offered by graduate schools of social work for police officers with the requisite academic background. In Southern California the Delinquency Control Institute is pioneering in offering special training for the correctional fields. In New York City several Juvenile Aid Bureau officers have completed their training in graduate schools of social work.

A major obstacle in the large city police force to retaining the men who have been specially trained is that promotion depends largely upon the number of arrests and convictions obtained. This condition penalizes a juvenile officer whose skill lies in being able to deal successfully with situations *without* having to take punitive action.

RELATIONS TO OTHER POLICE, SPECIALIZED AGENCIES, AND THE COURTS. The juvenile officer depends much more on using auxiliary services than do other members of the police force. Whether trained or untrained for his special assignment, the police officer who is responsible for helping young people must know how to cooperate with other divisions of the police, with representatives of other community services, and with the courts.

Considering the relatively small number of special juvenile police, it is evident that the majority of young people in trouble come initially to the attention of the regular police force. In some jurisdictions, the patrolman or the special detective squad continue their contact with the juvenile just as they would with the adult offender. In other communities, the regular police force hands over the young person to the juvenile officer, who then may take any of the steps outlined above for adjusting the difficulty.

Discussing the general run of cases referred to the Juvenile Aid Bureau in the New York City Police Department, Lt. Bernard Berkowitz (trained as a social worker)[10] has reported that about one sixth of all the children referred appear to be in need of specialized service. For those who require medical or casework service, the Juvenile Aid Bureau officer must choose the appropriate treatment resource in the light of the young person's major needs. The officer therefore needs to know the available treatment resources in the community. He must also be able to prepare the family or the client to accept referral—by no means a simple process. Often a family fails to see the need for help, and may therefore be ineligible for the services of an agency which accepts only clients who come voluntarily.[11]

If the juvenile officer has special training, one would expect him to be better equipped than the regular officer to decide whether it is necessary to refer a child to court. In general the available statistics support this assumption. They not only reveal that court referrals are relatively less frequent in the case load of the Juvenile Aid Bureau than in the regular police units, but that the judgment of special officers is more apt to coincide with that of the juvenile court judge. For example, a recent study in New York City shows a higher rate of dismissals by the juvenile court of cases referred by the precinct officer than in those referred by the Juvenile Aid Bureau officer.[12]

GENERAL COMMUNITY CONTACTS. In addition to their responsibility for protecting life and property, maintaining law and order, and locating runaway children, the juvenile officers, like other police, keep a lookout for community conditions likely to promote delinquency. They see to it that laws,

[10] Lt. Bernard Berkowitz, "The Juvenile Police Officer," *Focus*, Vol. 31, no. 5 (Sept. 1952), pp. 129-134, 148-49.
[11] See Chapter 28 for discussion of special services for resistive clients.
[12] *The Police Department*, p. 32.

ordinances, and regulations are enforced. In some of the larger cities the police have organized special traffic divisions to deal with youthful violators, in their sponsored safety education programs. In Fort Worth, Texas, the Juvenile Division sponsors bicycle racing and modified automobile clubs. The latter have attracted almost 2000 boys and girls to membership in fifty clubs. Milwaukee likewise works with bicycle violators. It conducts bicycle inspections and riding skill tests at twenty-four schools in the metropolitan area. Detroit encourages scouting, by sponsoring seventeen troops under the auspices of the department.

In patrolling bowling alleys, pool rooms, skating rinks, dance halls, bars, cabarets, candy stores, magazine stands which sell pornographic literature and various other types of establishments which attract children during the hours when they should be in school or at home, the police officer initially tries a friendly approach. If this fails, he may decide on court action or an appeal to the licensing agency. When the fault is not that of the individual establishment, the police representative calls it to the attention of some community planning body.

As might be expected, the scope of community responsibility of the juvenile unit varies with the size of the community. About half of the juvenile divisions in the largest jurisdictions are affiliated with at least one community planning or coordinating agency. In these jurisdictions the police serve on coordinating councils for delinquency prevention (see Chapter 27), on case conference committees, and on councils of social agencies, as well as other agencies in the community.

Fingerprinting and Confidentiality of Record

The practice of fingerprinting children varies from state to state. In some states only those suspected of serious offenses are fingerprinted. In others the practice covers all children taken into custody and suspected of an offense. Some states forbid fingerprinting except by order of the juvenile court. Those who advocate fingerprinting do so on the grounds that it is the most accurate method of identification and is widely used in industry, government, and so forth.

At the East Lansing Conference it was agreed that children should be fingerprinted *only* on court order in the following circumstances: when a child has been taken into custody as a suspect or as a known committer of serious offenses such as robbery, rape, homicide, manslaughter, or has a long history involving numerous violations of the law, or is a runaway and refuses to reveal his identity.

The conference recommended that (1) if the fingerprints are filed in local, state, or federal systems, they should have a "civil" identification and not bear any reference to the occasion when they were taken; (2) if it is proved that the young person who has been fingerprinted is not involved in the case, the prints should be returned to the court and destroyed.

The Lansing group emphasized the need for maintaining the confidentiality of police records as is done in the juvenile court, where only official agencies responsible for dealing with delinquents or those concerned with the child's welfare are permitted to inspect the records, and after the juvenile has reached the age of criminal responsibility, other police personnel are denied access to the records.[13]

The Police and Professional Social Casework or Group Work

Because delinquency is so general, there is apt to be a belief that one person's counsel is as good as another's. This notion must be examined from the point of view both of those entrusted with law enforcement (the police) and of the social work profession, dedicated to helping persons in various kinds of need.

Friendly versus Professional Relationship

If one is to understand the arguments for and against treatment activities by the police, it is important to distinguish a friendly from a professional relationship. A friend may advise on a personal basis but is often unable to discuss all the aspects of a given situation which are relevant to its solution. Friends are not expected to disapprove or to make comments which might upset or disturb the friendship. In contrast, because the professional person is not involved in a personal way he is able to view a situation of tension objectively. While expressing neither praise nor blame, regardless of any personal attachment, he will help the person in trouble weigh the negatives and the positives. One consults a professional not because he is a friend but because his *skill* and *equipment* enable him to advise and to assist one in arriving at necessary decisions in the most objective fashion. For example, doctors send members of their own families to other physicians even when the diagnosis indicates that the trouble lies within the specialty of the physician himself.

The Use of Authority

There is a special difficulty, however, in helping a person who resents authority of any sort—a characteristic of many delinquents.

[13] Lansing Report, 28-29.

Because the various connotations of the word "authority" are not always clearly delineated, there is some confusion as to its appropriate role in the helping process. There are both negative and positive implications in the use of authority. For example, authority expressed in the imposition of punishment, harshness, and rigidity obviously has no place in the helping process. Authority exemplified by such external symbols as a police uniform or a judge's robe, which may open the way for initial contact, does not automatically guarantee that the relationship will continue to be a helpful one. This will depend both on the attitude and on the skill of the person wearing the uniform or robe.

In this connection it is interesting to contrast the British and American attitudes toward a policeman's uniform. In many jurisdictions in the United States (though not in all), in order to avoid drawing unnecessary attention from the neighbors, the juvenile officer does not wear his uniform when he is visiting a family. British police officers, on the other hand, say that they always wear their uniforms when on duty. In their opinion, an officer's visit to a family does not reflect disgrace on them. The officer's uniform is as much a badge of honor as is that of the soldier. It is possible that the difference in the American and English reaction to a police visit reflects a difference not only in the self-concept of the police but in the attitudes toward law and order in the two countries. The English officer rarely carries a gun or pushes people around. In general, the English bobby is polite and helpful, and the English people appear to be more law-abiding than are we Americans, perhaps, because so many of us still adhere to the frontier mores described by Elliot in Chapter 11.

The positive aspects of authority as exercised by the helpful person are based on his greater competence in comparison with that of the person to be helped. It is this authority that enables the client to trust him and to accept help in a disturbing situation. Unless the professional person communicates a feeling of interest in the client, his offer of help is not likely to be accepted.

Social Treatment as a Police Function

The decision of the police officer concerning the guilt of a certain child is often a simpler matter than the determination of whether the child needs treatment and what that treatment should be. Many social agencies believe that only social work training enables one to decide on the need for help, and to provide the help skillfully. It is natural, therefore, that there should be considerable difference of opinion on the appropriate participation of the police officer in a treatment program.

Social agencies voice the following four objections to police as social workers:[14]

[14] See discussion on necessary training for probation officers, Chapter 16.

1. Police officers are neither selected nor trained to provide casework treatment. Such skills are developed in graduate study in a school of social work which provides supervised field work. Because most police officers do not have this training, their efforts are more appropriately directed to apprehending, screening, and making the best referral either to other agencies or to the court.[15] Even this limited function requires special qualifications.

2. Voluntary police supervision duplicates other services and is therefore wasteful.

3. A police department does not provide an appropriate setting for treatment.

4. If the community lacks adequate treatment facilities, the police department, in cooperation with other agencies, should use its influence to see that the community provides more services.

Arguments advanced by police departments which interpret their role as including social case work functions are:

1. Many families will not accept referral to casework agencies.

2. Some police departments have officers keenly interested in children and some who are trained in sociology or psychology, even if they are not caseworkers.

3. The police department can keep a close check on the activities of juvenile delinquents through the supervision program.

4. The community has not made enough provision either through probation officers or agencies to handle all the children with problems.

THE ENGLEWOOD EXPERIMENT. In 1954 the Chicago Police Bureau agreed to cooperate with the Juvenile Protective Association of Chicago in a project to provide casework service for families referred by its juvenile bureau.[16] The Englewood district, about seven miles southwest of the Loop, chosen as the area in which to explore the feasibility of the undertaking, has one of the highest rates of police and court referrals. Since 1950 its Negro population has increased from 15,000 to 50,000 and accounts for about one third of the estimated total population. With the moving out of the former occupants there has been deterioration of both business and residential units.

The goal of the project, financed by a grant from the Weiboldt Foundation, was to see whether the police and the social agencies together might prevent children referred to the police from developing into confirmed delinquents. The initial step was for both the police and social agency representatives to recognize their differing responsibilities and roles. With respect for each other's role in facilitating the welfare of children in trouble the treatment

[15] Some judges think police should not exercise even this judgment! This was the opinion of Sir Basil Henriques, retired Magistrate of London Juvenile Court, who visited the United States in 1957.

[16] G. Lewis Penner, "An Experiment in Police and Social Agency Cooperation," *The Annals*, American Academy of Political and Social Science, No. 322 (March 1959), pp. 79-88.

agency set up its own quarters outside of the police department and under its own jurisdiction.

In the course of three years of the project's operation, 204 families were referred for service. Obviously, not all accepted it; but three fourths of them did, through the reaching-out process. In the words of the sponsor this reaching-out process did not necessarily mean "a tireless pursuit of the body but rather the use of any method to reach the family psychologically. It required directness and the ability to deal with resistance immediately even by telephone if necessary."[17]

The research staff analyzed the records of 1 out of 2 of the 149 families which accepted service. In about half of these cases, the complaints registered with the police were offenses against property. The other half involved complaints of offenses directed against the person and complaints classified as directed against the self—i.e., running away, truancy, violating curfew regulations, or incorrigibility. More serious offenses were handled by the family court. Investigation of the family situation revealed that in about half of the families the problems were basically psychological. In one third of the families, problems were mainly economic or social.

While no precise tests were either planned or made of the results of work with these "left out, socially isolated, shy, discouraged and self-depreciating families . . . [their] responses covered the spectrum of attitudes from complete resistance to grateful acceptance of help offered."[18]

As a result of the project two recommendations were made:[19] (1) that the police department expand its juvenile bureau, increase its in-service training program, and develop a career service for officers in the juvenile division; (2) that six treatment centers be set up immediately to which the police and the schools might refer children who appeared to be developing behavior problems; these treatment centers to be staffed by trained and experienced workers who would provide both casework and group work services similar to those sponsored in street club programs (see Chapter 29).

This program is to be commended because it follows the principle of respecting the appropriate roles of the police and the social agencies.

Recreational Activities under Police Auspices

Recreational activities under police auspices are somewhat less controversial than casework services. About half the police department replying to the East Lansing inquiry reported that they conduct recreation programs for the following reasons:

[17] *Ibid.*, p. 84.
[18] *Ibid.*, p. 86.
[19] *Ibid.*, p. 87.

1. Recreational facilities in most communities are insufficient.

2. The police speak the language of the youngsters in underprivileged areas and hence can work effectively with them.

3. The programs reinforce the children's conception of the police officer as a friend.

One of the best publicized recreational programs under police auspices is that called PAL. The Police Athletic League was initiated in the 1930s by a New York City Deputy Chief Commissioner, who believed that recreation was a more effective antidote for delinquency than the services of trained caseworkers. This belief found support in the idea sequence: (1) Satan finds mischief for idle hands to do; (2) the police share America's passion for baseball and sports; (3) social work is unfortunately associated in the opinion of the public with charity for the incompetent poor.

In reply to the police argument that their role as recreation leaders contributes to a good relationship with young people, the social agency suggests that the child's conception of the police officer should rather result from his observation of the officer's conduct when engaged in activities *consistent with his major role* in controlling deviant behavior.

From the social work point of view there are four basic requirements for a community recreation program:[20]

1. Recreational facilities should be planned on community-wide basis in relation to community needs.

2. Participation of the police in providing recreational service should be determined through joint community planning.

3. Supervisors of such programs need to be trained in the field of recreation and should meet recognized standards. Without trained leaders and adequate programs, young persons can learn delinquent behavior on a playground.

4. The police, rather than providing the program themselves, should keep the community informed as to recreational needs, especially in underprivileged areas.

Taking issue with police departments which attempt to be all things to all people, the chief of police in Hilo, Hawaii, has said that it is about time that the police recognize that they should undertake only those activities which are directed at the effort to protect the public.[21] In his opinion the police have no responsibility for rehabilitating the offender, as this is the

[20] "Juvenile Delinquency and the Relationship of the Police to Social Agencies," National Social Welfare Assembly, January 1953.

[21] Anthony R. Paul, Chief, Department of Police, Hilo, Hawaii, "Crime Prevention—Where Do We Stand?" Report of Commission on Crime Prevention and Juvenile Delinquency to 65th Annual Police Conference of the International Association of Chiefs of Police, Miami Beach, Florida, October 30, 1958.

responsibility of the sociologist and the social worker. Nor is a police athletic league appropriate, because it is not *directed at the public, but an effort to channel the activities of youngsters.* This lies within the prerogative of park departments, recreation boards, and private agencies. To reject such a project, he feels, is no reflection on the need for the program.

There has been so much pressure on the police, says Chief Paul, that they have become a "'catch-all' for society's undeclared and unchanneled problems."[22] In his opinion, the mnemonic device, PIE, encompasses the main facets of an appropriate police program: *P* for patrol—in its broadest sense, the officer on patrol acts as a crime deterrent. *I* for investigation—a good investigational organization will discourage criminal acts. *E* for education—which means instructing the public in ways and means of safeguarding their persons and possessions to reduce the possibility of crime.

The English Police

Perhaps because the British people have traditionally shown less re-sistance to authority than do Americans, it is possible for English police to be helpful in a wider variety of services. Although some English magistrates deplore the American customs of permitting the police officer to judge whom to bring to court, the English juvenile courts permit and encourage representatives of the police to sit in on court proceedings, to observe the participation of the petitioning officers. The judges and the probation officers alike apparently also welcome the voluntary assistance of the London police in the rehabilitative process.

Attendance Centers under Police Auspices

An interesting and, from reports, effective volunteer service of London police was begun in 1956 at five attendance centers in the London area. Three police officers volunteer for about two and a half hours on twelve alternate Saturday afternoons to help boys referred to them by the juvenile court as one condition of their probation. These are youngsters who, had they been over 17, would have been convicted for felonies.

The Home Office arranges for the use of appropriately located and equipped school buildings. The Aylesworth Center, observed by the writer in late August 1957, was in charge of Inspector Philo, a police officer in his forties.

Inspector Philo stated emphatically that his program was not treatment but *punishment.* The aim of the attendance center is to impress the boys

---

[22] *Ibid.,* p. 7.

with the fact that they have broken the law, that they are "sinners," and that they must face the consequences: deprivation of their Saturday afternoon freedom (quite a severe punishment since most of the boys have jobs during the week). They are told, however, that the deprivation is intended to help them build character so that they will refrain from repeating the disapproved behavior. As Mr. Philo said, the program is ultimately designed to prove that the boy is not a "villain." In the inspector's opinion most of these boys have never been taught to face up to the fact that there are rules and regulations in society that they must obey.

The attendance center program often gives them their first notion of discipline. There are rules and regulations about the way the boys address the officers in charge—the officers are addressed as "Sir" and there is no answering back. A boy who disobeys any of the rules is assigned to such tasks as scrubbing, digging, and "other tasks of a less attractive kind." If he does not improve, he will be taken before the court which originally sent him to the center. When he satisfactorily completes the twelve sessions, a report is sent to the same court.

A new boy came into the center during the time of this writer's visit. He stood at attention with his hands behind his back while the officer in charge sat at his desk. The boy was told that he was there to be punished, that he was a "criminal," and that he must stand up and take his medicine. Did he understand that? Attempts to evade the rules and regulations would not be tolerated—he must attend regularly and his discharge would depend on his performance and cooperation with the program. He was to wear old clothes because the program was a vigorous one. While all this sounds pretty punitive, there was not a trace of punitive attitude in the conduct of the police who were carrying on the program.

At the end of the two-hour session, the boys showered. Great stress is put upon cleanliness. Before they left they came into Mr. Philo's office one by one. In the presence of the other two officers, when asked how they were getting along, they replied in monosyllables. An occasional comment on a boy's progress was favorable; a reminder that he should stand up straight, or that he needed to firm up was made in a matter-of-fact tone. At the end of the interview each boy, after being asked how things were going at home and whether or not he was working after school, was told how many sessions he still had to attend. He was then given two sheets to sign, indicating the time and day of his next attendance. The boys were impressed with the fact that they had to be punctual, and that if they weren't there would be consequences. The new boy was asked how far he had to come and whether or not he had carfare. When another asked to be excused a little early because he had to report to a clinic, Mr. Philo consulted his record and said he was pleased that the boy was getting medical attention.

Mr. Philo and his two assistants occasionally make home visits and have the cooperation of the parole officers and the schools which the boys are attending.

According to Mr. Philo, out of the 43 boys who had been assigned to the center during its first year and a half of operation, only 3 had gotten into difficulty again. On the whole the program's success is probably due to careful selection of police officers for the volunteer activity and a capacity to understand the thinking and action patterns of the English working-class boy. Perhaps the English police are better able than middle-class social workers to recognize the meaning, language, and attitudes of these boys in trouble (see Chapter 17). Thus the program is based upon recognition of the culture pattern of the English in respect to:

1. The role of the police.

2. Respect for authority. It is "British" to admit when one has done wrong (even though one may not understand the underlying reasons for one's doing wrong).

3. The identification of the British people with the ideals for which they stand. There was some intimation that people who do not share these ideals are in some way inferior.

The attitude toward young persons in trouble is that their families have not done the right thing by them, that is, given them sufficient teaching as to the proper respect for adults and their role in society. In Mr. Philo's opinion, there is currently a certain softness in the British character and an unwillingness to face the challenge of pioneering experiences.

There is little reliance on the use of psychological tests and the psychiatric interpretation of behavior. Mr. Philo commented that he thinks Americans have become too psychological in their approach. In answer to an observation that three of the twelve boys were left-handed and that one was a bed-wetter, Mr. Philo said he thought that had no psychological significance. Whether the boys with whom the program is unsuccessful have special problems is a subject which would need further study.

Summary

As the front line of the community's defense against crime and delinquency and as the petitioners in the cases of four out of five young persons referred to the juvenile court, the police largely determine the extent to which behavior deviations of young people in a given community will be officially registered.

It is estimated that the police have contact with about one million children a year. The number of their contacts in an individual city, however, is not in direct ratio to the size of the city, largely because of differences in the definition of the delinquency, the composition of the population, the assignment of the police, and the regulations governing their activity.

The police officer who confronts troublesome children has several alternatives: he may let them go with a warning or he may refer them to the court, or to a community agency. In some communities, the officer personally assumes responsibility for their redirection. The choice depends not only upon the responsibility assigned to the police in that community but upon the individual officer's understanding of the nature and significance of behavior and the availability of alternate services for the young person's care.

Despite official regulations for dealing with young people, the police officer always exercises individual judgment in his decision to dismiss, apprehend, detain, or refer a child to the juvenile court. To conform to the juvenile court philosophy, the police officer, like the judge, must be specially equipped to understand the significance of the behavior rather than to react aggressively to the behavior itself. The important issue is to assure that when the police officer is faced with aggressive young people he will act responsibly both to the community and in the best interest of the offender.

To facilitate this process, departments in the larger cities in which the commissioner recognizes the preventive role of the police have set up special juvenile divisions. These are manned by officers, usually specially chosen and sometimes trained to deal with juveniles whom they apprehend.

Where juvenile officers provide casework and recreational services, social agencies have raised several objections. One objection is that the officer's basic training does not automatically equip him with the necessary skill. Other objections are that the authoritative auspices of the police services may interfere with the client's ready acceptance of help. The role of the police, it is suggested, is not to engage in therapy but to make the community aware of its responsibility for developing the needed services under proper auspices.

This position of the social agencies with respect to the major role of the police, i.e., the need for proper direction and the recognition that something needs to be done about helping, rather than aggravating, the trouble, meets with considerable support in some police jurisdictions.

From the sociological viewpoint, any institution—the church, the school, the court, or, as in our present discussion, the police—provides the most effective service if its various functions are: (1) clearly defined; (2) appropriate in the light of its primary role. If a community has developed other agencies which provide social casework or group work services, it is sound policy for the community to insist that each agency play its own role instead of taking on that of another. Thus the balance of favor in the argument in the United States as to whether the police should provide casework and group work services under its own auspices is that the police should adhere to their special function—protection of the community. In Britain, where there has been less resistance to authority, the success of police attendance centers may indicate that this qualification does not apply with equal force.

Naturally, the qualifications for the police include behavior on their part which will not aggravate the difficulties of youthful offenders. It is also generally agreed that to discharge their responsibilities to young people the police need training, and specially trained officers should be available either at the court or in the precinct.

CHAPTER 14

The Development of the Juvenile Court and Its Legal Underpinning

AS AN INTRODUCTION TO THE JUVENILE COURT AS THE OFFICIAL AGENCY FOR dealing with delinquents, this chapter presents the theories of its legal origin and its relation to other courts; outlines the major questions of constitutionality in respect to the customary procedure and types of admissible evidence; and describes efforts to extend the juvenile court philosophy in dealing with young people beyond the age jurisdiction of the juvenile court.

Legal Origins and Relation to Other Courts

Forerunners

As with many other institutions, we are inclined to take the juvenile court for granted as though it had always existed. In consequence, we are sometimes more critical of its shortcomings than appreciative of the enormous contribution of its approach in dealing with delinquency.

In a simple society formal institutionalized procedures are not necessary to deal with deviants because the deviant is usually the exception and because the individual family or clan usually takes matters into its own hands. The establishment of the juvenile court and the differentiation from adult courts illustrate one way in which a complex society attempts to institutionalize its controls over its members.

Before the establishment of the first juvenile court, in Chicago in 1899, England, Australia, Canada, and Switzerland had laws which mitigated or modified the severity of the criminal laws as applied to juveniles. In the matter of arrest, detention, and trial, a delinquent child was subject to practically all the criminal procedures applicable to adult offenders. For example, for centuries children in England were, like adults, hanged for setting fires and condemned to death for murder. As late as 1833 a child of nine who broke a glass and stole two pennies' worth of paint was condemned to death.[1]

The first modification of court procedure in the United States occurred in 1870 when separate hearings were required for the trial of juvenile offenders in Boston. In 1877 New York's Society for the Prevention of Cruelty to Children prohibited the placing of any child under sixteen "in any prison or place of confinement, or in any court room or in any vehicle in company with adults charged or convicted with crime except in the presence of proper officers."[2] Indiana in 1891, New York in 1892, and Rhode Island in 1898 all made various provisions for the trial of juveniles. Summing up the situation before the establishment of the Chicago Juvenile Court, Lou, the classic historian of the juvenile court, writes:

> . . . persistent efforts were made in various states to save offending children from the horrible ordeals to which children of tender years were subjected in the criminal courts in the last century. We know that in some places there was juvenile probation, there were separate hearings for children and there was institutional care for children.
>
> What was lacking was the conception that a child that broke the law was to be dealt with by the state not as a criminal but as a child needing care, education and protection. Whatever solicitude for the welfare of children had been professed in these early laws, children who came into conflict with the law were tried for the commission of a specific crime and were treated as adults with all the formalities of the criminal law and constitutional safeguards in order to vindicate the dignity and majesty of the state. . . . Despite the various beneficent efforts in a number of states to save offending children, numberless children in the country as a whole were indicted, prosecuted, and tried as ordinary criminals and imprisoned in reformatories and penitentiaries.[3]

The First Juvenile Court

The story of the birth of the juvenile court is told by the first chief probation officer of the Cook County Juvenile Court.[4] In the 1890s settlement

---

[1] H. H. Lou, *Juvenile Courts in the United States*, Chapel Hill, The University of North Carolina Press, 1927, p. 14.

[2] *Ibid.*, p. 17.

[3] *Ibid.*, pp. 18-19.

[4] T. D. Hurley, *Origin of the Illinois Juvenile Court Law*, 3rd Ed., 1907.

workers in Chicago were deeply concerned with the plight of children for whom no appropriate institutional care was available. An unending stream of children seemed to be coming before the criminal court from the crowded sections of Chicago during its period of rapid industrial growth. The "Ladies of Hull House," as Jane Addams and Julia Lathrop were called, convinced that something could and should be done to help these unfortunate children, set to work to mobilize the social conscience of the community.

> In Chicago it was the social and civic organizations, notably the Chicago Women's Club and the Catholic Visitation and Aid Society—that first urged a juvenile law. The Women's Club actually had a bill drafted in 1895 for a separate court for children and a probation department, but their legal advisers told them it was unconstitutional, and they abandoned it. They and many other organizations kept up the agitation. Hull House, under its peerless leader, Jane Addams, interested itself in the plight of the thousands of children then in the jails.[5]

In 1898 the Governor of Illinois appointed Julia C. Lathrop as a member of the Board of State Commissioners of Public Charities. Miss Lathrop informed the board that 575 children charged with offenses had been confined in the county jail. Furthermore, in the preceding twenty months, almost 2000 boys had been committed to Chicago's House of Correction. Concerned by this disclosure, the Chicago Bar Association, at its annual meeting on October 22, 1898, charged a committee of five of its members "to investigate existing conditions relative to delinquent and dependent children and to cooperate with committees of other organizations in formulating and securing such legislation as may be necessary." Judge Harvey B. Hurd, a member of the committee, was unanimously appointed a subcommittee of one to prepare a bill to be presented to the legislature the following January. Judge Hurd was assisted in the formulation of the bill by Dr. Hastings H. Hart, superintendent of the Illinois Children's Home and Aid Society, the superintendent of schools, the county jailer, and a state representative, John C. Newcomer.

After several revisions a bill, introduced as the Bar Association bill, passed with only one dissenting vote in the senate and became law on July 1, 1899. Officially styled "an act to regulate the treatment and control of dependent, neglected, and delinquent children," the bill created no new or special courts. In all sections of Illinois, outside of Cook County, it conferred upon circuit and county courts jurisdiction in cases arising under the law. In counties with a population of 500,000 or over (Cook County was the only one), the bill provided that the circuit court judges designate one or more of their number to hear all juvenile cases in a separate courtroom, with its own

[5] Charles L. Chute, "The Juvenile Court in Retrospect," *Federal Probation*, Vol. 13, no. 3 (Sept. 1949), p. 4.

records. The court called "The Juvenile Court," brought under one jurisdiction all cases involving delinquent, neglected, and dependent children.

The new and important contribution was the concept that the child who broke the law was not to be regarded as a criminal but as a ward of the state. He was to receive the same care, custody, and discipline formerly accorded the neglected and dependent child. The proceedings were divested of almost all the features attached to a criminal proceeding. For the terms "arrest by warrant, examination by a magistrate, holding for bail, possible indictment, and trial by jury," the juvenile court procedure substituted the terms "complaint, investigation, petition, informal hearing, adjudication, and disposition." This difference in terminology reflected the difference in the approach of the juvenile court.

Through the efforts of Judge Ben Lindsey, the second juvenile court in the United States was established in Denver in 1903. Its special contribution was that the Colorado law authorized the county courts to try persons who contributed to the delinquency and dependency of children.[6]

In rapid succession Pennsylvania, Wisconsin, New York, Maryland, California, Missouri, New Jersey, Indiana, Iowa, and Ohio passed juvenile court laws before 1905. Today juvenile court laws are on the statute books of all the states and territories. As later chapters will reveal, however, not all counties have effectively functioning courts.

The idea of the juvenile court, which in dramatic fashion captured the interest of the American public, has also strongly appealed to European countries, many of which have sent visitors to this country to study the operation of the court in the hope that it might assist them in dealing with their problems of delinquency.

Relation to Other Court Systems

Courts, as the judicial tribunals established by law to administer justice, have been traditionally classified as criminal or civil courts. The former deal with offenses against persons and property, determine guilt or innocence, and pass sentence on convicted persons. Civil courts deal with matters of equity, property, and personal rights. The juvenile court does not fall neatly into either category.

As Lou says, it is easier to describe the juvenile court than to define it. It is not a court simply because it is called so in the statute, nor because it has a separate courtroom. It is not a court of equity (or chancery), nor is it a common law court.

It is a statutory court and, therefore, its legal definition is to be found in the organic acts of the different states creating it, for statutory courts and

[6] School Law in 1899.

their procedure are usually arbitrarily defined and jurisdiction clearly specified therein. In general, we may say that a juvenile court is a court having special jurisdiction of a parental nature over delinquent and neglected children. It is not . . . a sort of simple tribunal dealing with minor and petty offenses committed by the youth of the community. . . .

[Its most essential features are:] It exercises chancery or at least quasi-chancery jurisdiction over delinquent, neglected and in some instances, dependent children, holding separate hearings for children's cases, and having the power to put children on probation. . . . Other features, important but not so essential, . . . are separate detention, special recording system, separate court room, and provisions for mental and physical examinations.[7]

Not all juvenile courts are separate and independent, i.e., created by special law for large cities or counties. The vast majority in the 2600 counties of the United States are *designated* courts, appended to other court systems—county, district, superior, probate, courts of common pleas, circuit, municipal, or courts of general jurisdiction. In such courts, the juvenile section consists legally of special sessions, divisions, or departments, served by one or more judges assigned from the courts or chosen especially to hear children's cases. Whether a juvenile court is separate, designated, or coordinated depends upon the historical evolution of the court system in the particular state. The important fact, however, is not the *type* of the court but the *fulfillment of its underlying purpose.*

Chancery versus Criminal Origin

It is perhaps natural that the establishment of the juvenile court and its early experimentation with procedure should generate considerable discussion as to whether it derived from criminal or chancery origins.

The arguments that the juvenile court is primarily of chancery origin are as follows:[8]

1. The juvenile court embodies the concept of welfare or balancing of interests. It stands for flexibility, guardianship, and protection rather than for rigidity and punishment.

2. Along with English common law, chancery jurisdiction and procedure were transplanted to America. In the English common law, the Crown is the *parens patriae,* the father of the country. In its modern equivalent, the state is the guardian of the social interests of the child and thus the ultimate parent. Sovereign states have assumed prerogatives and obligations of the Crown and still continue to enlarge their summary jurisdiction for the protection and

[7] Lou, *op. cit.,* 32-33.
[8] *Ibid.,* pp. 2-7.

care of individuals abnormal in person, i.e., the feeble-minded, the physically handicapped, the aged, the unemployed, or the unfortunate, destitute, and neglected. Following this line of reasoning, the juvenile court laws in the United States may be regarded as a logical extension of the principles of chancery in guardianship in the English court of neglected and destitute children to cover delinquent behavior as well.

In disagreement with this explanation Roscoe Pound suggests that the juvenile court was invented by a few socially minded judges who tried, after its establishment, to reconcile their invention, a direct offshoot of the criminal law, with historical legal dogmas.[9]

There are those who argue that the juvenile court is an extension of the common law principle of the age of criminal responsibility, i.e., that no person can be guilty of a crime unless he acted with a guilty mind. A child under the age of 7 is considered incapable of felonious intent. Whether a child between the ages of 7 and 14—the upper age limit of the English court— can be considered criminally responsible would depend upon his ability to understand the nature and the consequences of his misconduct, which in turn would be a function of his psychological condition. In Sutherland's opinion the main issue is "whether or not the state as a policy, desires to stigmatize those who offend against the law as being criminal and to prescribe different methods of treatment in order to achieve the end in view. . . . Responsibility does not necessarily go with punishment, for the juvenile court law recognizes responsibility but the weapons which it uses are reformation, protection and education rather than punishment."[10]

Lou concludes that juvenile court procedure has traces of both chancery and criminal law origin, and that its logical justification is the recognition that the older criminal courts did not succeed in preventing crime. In contrast the juvenile court, concerned with care and rehabilitation, attempts to replace the punitive and retributive attitude prevailing in courts of more general jurisdiction.

Despite this brave new hope of the founders of the juvenile court, however, the procedures in many juvenile courts, agencies, and institutions, still reflect punitive attitudes. As long ago as 1918 George H. Mead pointed out the conspicuous failure of the punitive approach to the law breaker: "This attitude of hostility toward the lawbreaker and this supposedly impartial and impersonal character of justice provide no principles for the eradication of crime, for returning the delinquent to normal social relations, or for stating the transgressed rights and institutions in terms of their positive social func-

[9] Roscoe Pound, *Interpretations of Legal History*, New York, Macmillan, 1923, p. 135.
[10] E. H. Sutherland, *Criminology*, Philadelphia, Lippincott, 1924, pp. 19-20, 307-308.

tions."[11] And, according to Roscoe Pound, the sociological school of jurisprudence which regards law as a living social institution does not need to cling to the ancient sentiments of vengeance which, in the traditional administration of criminal justice, have failed spectacularly to repress crime. Instead, the law needs to take account of social causes and social effects in respect to social conditions and social progress.

In an eloquent description of the juvenile court as the first legal tribunal where law and the social sciences work side by side, Lou writes:

> In place of magistrates, limited by the outgrown custom and compelled to walk in the paths fixed by the law of the realm, we have now socially-minded judges, who hear and adjust cases according not to rigid rules of law but to what the interests of society and the interests of the child or good conscience demand.
>
> In place of juries, prosecutors and lawyers, trained in the old conception of law and staging dramatically, but often amusingly, legal battles, as the necessary paraphernalia of a criminal court, we have now probation officers, physicians, psychologists, and psychiatrists, who search for the social, psychological, physiological, and mental backgrounds of the child in order to arrive at reasonable and just solutions of individual cases.
>
> In other words, in this new court we tear down primitive prejudice, hatred, and hostility toward the lawbreaker in that most hide-bound of all human institutions, the court of law, and we attempt, as far as possible, to administer justice in the name of truth, love, and understanding.[12]

Legal Questions Concerning Juvenile Court Action

Since the juvenile court is not a criminal court, the child within its jurisdiction is not charged with crime but is regarded as a ward of the state subject to its discipline and entitled to its protection. Since the court's purpose is not to punish but to rehabilitate, its intent is to understand and meet the child's needs. In so doing, the state may intervene to safeguard the child from neglect or injury and to assure his legal rights.

In most states the juvenile court act provides: (1) that the care, custody, and discipline of the children brought before the court shall approximate as nearly as possible that which they should receive from their parents; (2) that as far as is practicable, they shall be treated not as criminals but as children in need of aid, encouragement, and guidance; (3) that no child shall be denominated criminal by reason of an adjudication in the children's court, nor should such adjudication be deemed a conviction.

[11] Lou, *op. cit.*, p. 1, paraphrasing G. H. Mead, "The Psychology of Punitive Justice," *American Journal of Sociology*, Vol. 23 (March 1918), p. 590.
[12] Lou, *op. cit.*, p. 2.

Much has been written about the socialization of the procedure in the children's courts. Socialization is a variable term when employed to define the judicial processes of these courts. It has been explained as the process by which the purpose and goal of the children's court is best attained; that method which best frees the spirit of the children's court and permits it to serve the social ideal it was created to express. In establishing children's courts the aim of legislative bodies has been to formulate rules of procedure most likely to promote the benign and humanitarian purposes of these tribunals. To the judges of these courts plenary powers have been granted in order that they may cast off the shackles of formality that are inherent in conventional court procedure. Informality most nearly characterizes the course that is contemplated for the correct functioning of these courts.[13]

Right of Custody

The primary legal question is in most instances the right of a court to control the custody of the child. Since the court has the power to commit children to institutions upon the ground that the welfare of the child demands that the state assume control in the place of the parents, it is of vital importance to determine the nature and extent of the rights of parents to the custody of their children.

The argument advanced *in favor* of the right of the state to assume the custody of a child is based on the following premises:

1. That the legal definition of infancy is determined by the state: parental custody is merely a privilege or duty conferred upon the parent in the exercise of the police power of the state.

2. In theory all persons in the status of infancy are wards of the public. The public has delegated the power of raising and caring for them in sacred trust to the parents.

3. The parents representing the state and having custody of the children in trust owe a duty to the public to act as guardians of infant citizens.

4. The state can enforce that duty by deposing them as guardians and putting the infants at the common guardianship of the community, if the public good requires.

The *objection* to the right of the state to custody is based on the belief in the natural rights of parents, i.e., the parent is entitled to the control, custody, and education of the child against the whole world. In answer to this claim, it is argued that the parental right is not an *inalienable right*: it is subject to ordinary legislative power unless that power is limited by some con-

---

[13] "Legal Evidence in the New York Children's Courts," by Irving I. Goldsmith (former Supreme Court Justice; former member New York State Probation Commission; former chairman New York State Board of Parole), *Brooklyn Law Review*, Oct. 1933. p. 7, and fns., pp. 7-8.

stitutional prohibition. Thus, this natural right continues only so long as it is *properly exercised*. Today it is conceded that the main consideration is the welfare of the child, and in the matter of custody this principle should, and generally does, govern court decisions.

In some jurisdictions, the state may supersede the parental right of custody in cases of *neglect,* if there is proof that the state of neglect of the child is such as to come within the provisions of the law; *and* if the parent or legal guardian is incompetent or has criminally neglected to care for the child; *and* if the parent or legal guardian has failed to provide the training and education contemplated and required by both law and morals. In cases of *delinquency* the state need only show a condition of delinquency on the part of the child. Under the laws of most states it is not necessary to prove failure on the part of the parents.

The tendency in American courts has been to repudiate a "proprietary right" or interest in the custody of an infant. The American law seeks to compel the parents to perform as far as possible their duties to the public and their children. The state displaces the parents only when the welfare of the child *demands* it.

As a consequence of its noncriminal nature the juvenile court does not need to conform to certain constitutional guarantees usually contained in the Bill of Rights for the protection of persons charged with crime. Because of the seeming disregard of these constitutional rights, there has been considerable litigation, the bulk of it in connection with establishing the fact that the child has engaged in the specific act or behavior with which he is charged. Some judges believe that because its purpose is to act in the place of the wise parent, the juvenile court has jurisdiction over a child even if it cannot prove that in a specific instance the child was guilty of the behavior which brought him into court.

A case in point is reported by former Judge Kenneth D. Johnson of the Quincy Juvenile Court. A boy was brought to court on the petition of a woman who said that she saw him climb through the window of a loft building, enter it, and presumably make off with some property which did not belong to him. When the case was heard in court the investigating probation officer reported that this boy had terrorized many people in the neighborhood.

To check the evidence, during lunch recess the judge visited the home of the woman who had entered the complaint. Placing himself in the position from which she said she had observed the boy, the judge determined that it was impossible to see the fire escape from that window. Yet when the court reconvened, in spite of the fact that there was no proof that the boy was guilty of the alleged offense, Judge Johnson adjudged the boy a delinquent and ordered probation on the ground that all the reports of the boy's previous conduct indicated his need for the care and the protection of the court.

To those juvenile court judges who would automatically dismiss such a case, as they would in the adult court, Judge Johnson would say that the socio-legal evidence is, in his opinion, an appropriate basis for juvenile court action. Strict adherence to the long-established practice of the criminal courts, which requires proof beyond a reasonable doubt, is not necessary in the juvenile court. Some judges, especially those whose practice is not exclusively in the juvenile court, apparently either forget or are reluctant to admit that the child is not on trial for the commission of any crime but is before the juvenile court for correction, care, and protection.

Rules of Evidence

Questions of fact in the juvenile court are determined by *a fair predominance of the evidence*. The liberality of the procedure, described below as authorized in the New York State law, is characteristic also of the procedure now authorized in the children's court acts in most other states.

> The court may adjourn the hearing from time to time and inquire into the habits, surroundings, conditions and tendencies of the child to enable the court to render such judgment or make such order as shall best conserve the welfare of the child and carry out the purposes of this act.
>
> Where the method of procedure in a case or proceeding in which the court has jurisdiction is not provided in this act, such procedure shall be the same as provided by law, or *by rules formally adopted by the court within the scope of this act.*
>
> The court, if satisfied that the child is in need of care, discipline and protection of the state may adjudicate the child to be delinquent, neglected or abandoned and render judgment as provided in the act including placing the child upon probation, committing the child to a suitable institution, placing out the child or discharging the child to the Commissioner of Public Welfare.[14]

On the character and the weight of the evidence essential to sustain an adjudication, Goldsmith continues:

> There is a vast difference in the method of dealing with a case where the only problem before the court is the kind of care and correction needed by the child, and one where the custody and liberty of the *child is at issue.* In the former, which is the usual case of destitution or delinquency, where the need of care or correction is *admitted,* evidence of a clinical and social nature is all that the judge requires for a proper understanding of the child's condition and surroundings and the remedial action to be taken. More formal proof than the reports or statements of the probation officer, psychiatrist, physician and social investigator is *unnecessary* and was not intended by the law. This information is the very type of evi-

[14] *Ibid.*, p. 8. Provision formerly read: "if satisfied by *competent evidence*" (fn. 29).

dence which was contemplated by the children's court act and which makes it possible for the judge to reach an intelligent and satisfactory judgment in respect of the child's physical, mental, educational and moral needs. This procedure has been recognized as sufficient under modern children's court statutes and in no way conflicts with constitutional or legal rights.[15]

Goldsmith says that the amount of evidence required in delinquency cases *does not* depend upon whether the act would be a crime if committed by an adult. Nor does it depend on whether or not the child actually committed the act of which he is accused.

> . . . the modern children's court is a tribunal of civil jurisdiction and if the act charged is proved by a fair preponderance of legal evidence the child has not been deprived of any constitutional or legal rights. This is the general rule in *all* jurisdictions where the children's court act provides that the jurisdiction of the court shall be civil, and although the courts have felt it necessary to write at length in disposing of constitutional and legal objections, they nevertheless have been in accord as to this rule.[16]

> Competent evidence is legal evidence. In a court of criminal jurisdiction it means evidence in accordance with the rules of criminal practice and in a court of civil jurisdiction evidence in accordance with the rules of civil practice.[17]

A Case Illustration

The oft-cited case of the People *vs.* Lewis established a rule of procedure under the New York State act in cases where there is an issue of fact. According to the reviewing court record, the facts in the case were as follows:

> Arthur Lewis, fifteen years old, in company with a younger boy, broke into a store in Binghamton and stole twelve dollars. Afterward the two boys together with two other boys, made their way to Buffalo, by means of three automobiles stolen in succession. Brought home, each boy, in separate proceedings, was charged in Children's Court with juvenile delinquency. In this particular case the charge was based upon the theft of the money. No fault is found with the proceedings had prior to the hearing. The hearings in the four cases were held in succession on the same day. Each boy was examined separately in his own proceeding in the presence of his parents, relatives and friends. When so examined the other boys were not in the room. The entire testimony thus taken was apparently deemed evidence in each case.

[15] *Ibid.,* p. 9.
[16] *Ibid.,* p. 10.
[17] *Ibid.,* p. 13.

The course of the hearing in this case, then, was as follows: The boy, in company with his mother, sister and the family clergyman, appeared and their appearances were noted. They were advised by the judge that they might have the aid of counsel if so desired. The boy was then questioned by the judge. The other boys were thereafter examined in the manner above stated. All the testimony thus given appears in the record by question and answer. Each boy told substantially the same story. The testimony sustains the charge beyond any doubt. Indeed, there was full admission and no attempt at denial. The judge then inquired if anyone desired to speak on behalf of the boy. There was no answer. The boy was thereupon adjudged a delinquent child and was committed to the State Industrial and Agricultural School at Industry, N.Y.[18]

The Court of Appeals (two judges dissenting) in a second review reinstated the judgment of the children's court. It made no reference to a distinction between the two classes of delinquency and "inasmuch as the proceeding was not a criminal one, there was neither right nor necessity for the procedural safeguards described by the Constitution and statute in criminal cases."

Outlining the procedure to be followed in the children's court, the opinion is at considerable pains to make it clear that " 'a purely socialized trial' may be had in these courts. 'Hearsay, opinion, gossip, bias, prejudice, trends of hostile neighborhood feeling, the hopes and fears of social workers, are all sources of error and have no more place in the children's courts than in any other court.' "[19]

The rules of procedure outlined call for a *reasonably definite* charge and the application of customary rules of evidence which experience has indicated as essential for ascertaining the truth with reasonable certainty in civil trials. Finally, the finding of fact "must rest on the *preponderance* of evidence adduced under those rules."

This decision was of inestimable value not only because it went beyond the determination of the specific question with which it was concerned. It also set forth the correct procedure to be followed in the different classes of delinquency cases and in so doing established a clear and understandable rule to be applied not only to all proceedings in the children's courts of New York organized under the state-wide act, but for other juvenile courts to follow.

Extensions of the Juvenile Court Philosophy

The active proponents of the juvenile court philosophy have sought its extension to courts which deal with young people beyond juvenile court age.

[18] *Ibid.*, p. 14.
[19] *Ibid.*, p. 15.

They are especially concerned with the increasing frequency of arrests of youth below 20, the peak age in pre-World War II. There has also been agitation, especially in the large cities, to extend the jurisdiction of the juvenile court itself, regardless of its present upper limit, to cover the adolescent offender as well as the child.

There is, as Erikson reminds us (see Chapter 6), an understandable relationship between the increase in aggressive behavior during adolescence and the physiological, psychological, and emotional development of the young person seeking to emancipate himself from parental control. As Tappan so well phrases it, because of the adolescent's strength and sexual capacity that may endanger the community, he

> . . . can no longer be treated by the law as a child. Yet, treating him as an adult criminal in the courts, as is customarily done, is even less justified. It is evident that a punitive-retributive justice has failed to deter or reform the youthful offender or to protect the community from his illegalities. . . . It is out of a recognition of the failure of traditional methods, as evidenced in the crime rates of youth, that the movement has grown to deal with the adolescent separately and differently from the adult.[20]

Special Statutes

Among the various efforts to meet the challenge of the adolescent offender are the "wayward minor" statutes, which symbolize "the still surviving mores of complete filial subjection to parental will."[21] The earliest wayward minor statutes were those on the books of Michigan and Pennsylvania in 1915, and New York in 1923. According to these statutes, a wayward minor is one who: (1) is resistant to parental control; (2) is in danger of becoming morally depraved; (3) has committed minor crimes which, instead of being prosecuted as felonies or misdemeanors, may be reduced to the wayward minor charge. These statutes save the individual from a criminal conviction.

A second type of special statute has to do with dispositions for the adolescent offender. According to the Idaho law, if the defendant has never before been convicted of a felony, the court may:

> . . . commute the sentence and confine the defendant in the county jail or, if the defendant is of proper age, in the state industrial school, suspend the execution of judgment or withhold judgment on such terms and for such time as it may prescribe, and in either event, may put the defendant *on probation in charge of one of the probation officers of the juvenile*

[20] Paul Tappan, *Juvenile Delinquency*, New York, McGraw-Hill, 1949, p. 231.
[21] *Ibid.*, p. 237.

court of the county in which the juvenile court is sitting or other probation officer or any other person selected and designated for that purpose.[22]

In short, the judge is given wide discretion and may use the facilities of the adolescent court with emphasis on probation.

Tappan states that neither the wayward minor statute nor the provision for probation has effected any great change in court powers. It has, however, concentrated attention on the policy of giving special consideration to youth and has thus established, in a way, a precedent for the development of more specialized judicial facilities.

As noted earlier, some of the older adolescents are cared for in those children's courts in which the upper age limit has been extended beyond 16 years of age. In Tappan's opinion, the facilities of the juvenile court, as well as the detention quarters or the institutions to which they may be committed, are not always appropriate for the more aggressive of the older adolescent offenders. He agrees, however, that young people are handled better in the juvenile than in the criminal court, and advocates two parts of the domestic relations court—one for children and the other for adolescents.

Specialized Youth Courts

Three communities have established specialized youth courts: Chicago, Philadelphia, and New York. The first such was established in Chicago in 1914 as the Chicago Boys Court. It is part of the municipal court "with power to try boys from 17 to 21 accused of misdemeanors and minor offenses." This court, however, has not been effective because of the inadequacy of the facilities within the court and of those provided by the community.

In 1915 Philadelphia established, as part of its municipal court, a special men's and women's misdemeanants division for minor offenders from 16 to 21 years of age. The lower age limit was subsequently raised to 18 to accord with the upper age limit of the juvenile court. The Philadelphia courts have more facilities for diagnostic work than the Chicago Boys Court; nevertheless, because of the lack of trained personnel and community facilities they, too, have been deemed ineffective.[23]

The first adolescent court in New York City was established in Brooklyn in 1935. It was followed in 1936 by a similar court in Queens, to serve "incorrigible male offenders from the age of 16 to 19," who before the establishment of these courts would have been exposed to the process in the criminal courts. The court's jurisdiction, however, is not limited to those in danger of becoming "morally depraved or disobedient to their parents' demands," but

[22] *Ibid.*, pp. 237-38. Italics added.
[23] *Ibid.*, p. 241.

extends to young persons who have been guilty of violence and misdemeanors, and who are spared the ignominy of a criminal record by the process of "reduction of these charges to the wayward minor offense." To be eligible for this court procedure, the young man must give his consent to a reduction of the charge and to a social investigation. A decision as to whether or not he is "corrigible" depends more upon the court's opinion of the character of the offender than it does on the specific act he has committed.

Since the legislative enactment of the city-wide Girls' Term Court Act in 1951, young women between 16 and 21 are tried on wayward minor charges—mainly for sex offenses—in the girls' term court, currently within the magistrates' court system. In Kings, Queens, and Richmond Counties, male adolescent offenders between 16 and 21 may be tried on wayward minor charges in the specially constituted adolescent courts. Misdemeanors and felonies committed by boys between 16 and 19 may be reduced to wayward minor charges and likewise tried in these adolescent courts. Hence at this point in the development of the young offenders laws and courts in New York City, the adult criminal courts have jurisdiction only over offenders above the age of 19 who have been *disapproved* for wayward minor treatment.

The Youthful Offender Act

The passage of the Youthful Offender Act in April 1943 provided for a youth part in the county courts of Kings, Queens, Richmond, The Bronx, and in New York County's general sessions as well as in the special sessions court of New York City. According to this act, a defendant over the age of 16 and under 19 who is recommended by the grand jury or the district attorney, and/or by the court, may be investigated to determine if he should be adjudged a youthful offender. If he consents, and is approved for investigation, a study by the probation department and the psychiatric clinic determine whether or not he may be tried as a youthful offender, either in open court or in chambers. If he is held to be a youthful offender, instead of being charged with the commission of a particular offense, he may be placed on probation for a period not to exceed three years, or committed to an institution under an indeterminate sentence, with a three-year maximum.

Tappan believes this procedure is a great improvement on that of the other specialized courts, because it provides for better protection of the civil rights of the defendant. According to the statistics of the general sessions court of New York County, Tappan says that about 30 per cent of the adolescent cases are accepted for youthful offender treatment, and 95 per cent of them are put on probation.[24]

[24] *Ibid.,* p. 246.

Criticism of Youth Courts

Tappan has two main criticisms of the youth courts regardless of their geographic location:

1. Their area of operation is not specifically defined or predicated upon definite and precise statutory evidence or conduct categories.

2. Appraisal of the adolescent court operation is not based on the facilities as they exist, but upon an idealized view.

Consistent with his objections to the juvenile court procedures in dealing with young people who have not committed specific acts, Tappan believes the court's role should be to urge the community to provide appropriate facilities rather than act as an "inexact and unjust substitute. By a proper legal selection of cases for its specialized treatment, the court can learn to apply its methods and treatment on the basis of empirically derived, pragmatically tested, and cooperatively shared experience."[25] In Tappan's opinion, the dubious distinctions between those who may or may not be given youthful offender treatment are inappropriately applied. The standards and the criteria are too vague to be entrusted to the discretion of a particular judge, district attorney, or probation officer.

Many issues remain unsettled in respect to volume of cases and the financial and other resources of the community.[26] This applies to the functioning of the juvenile courts as well as to the extension of the chancery principle to the older adolescent. At least, however, the legality of the chancery principle of the juvenile court has been firmly established.

Summary

We have briefly reviewed the events which led to the establishment in 1899 in Chicago of the first juvenile court in the world. As part of the judicial system, the distinctive nature of the juvenile court, whether it is independent and separate or a designated and coordinated court, has given rise to many opinions as to its legal origin. Today its procedure, aimed at protecting the child rather than punishing him, is recognized as having some roots in chancery and some in criminal procedure.

A primary legal question is the right of the court to control the custody of the child brought before it, vis-à-vis the rights of the parent and the state. With the constitutionality of the juvenile court upheld and its social goals

[25] *Ibid.,* p. 248.
[26] See Bernard Fisher, *For the Family in Court,* New York, Community Service Society, 1956, for a discussion of the need for review and consolidation of the many legal procedures to which families and youth in New York City are subjected.

approved, arguments in the second decade of its establishment arose concerning the necessity for evidence and its nature as a precedent to an adjudication of delinquency. Higher courts have not only sustained the constitutionality of the juvenile courts but, in distinguishing between action in a criminal court and that in the juvenile court, have outlined the procedure by which socio-legal evidence may be the basis of the juvenile court action. This procedure simultaneously safeguards the rights and best interests of both the child and the community.

Some proponents of the juvenile court philosophy have advocated its extension in setting up specialized courts to deal with adolescent offenders above the juvenile court age or wayward minors. Tappan objects to this procedure. He sees the danger of the inappropriate use of a social rather than a legal approach as a hazard to the civil rights of the individual. Further, he questions whether the facilities provided by these courts are adequate to serve the needs of those who come before them.

CHAPTER 15

The Juvenile Court in Action

THE JUVENILE COURT HAS JURISDICTION, I.E., A RIGHT TO SPEAK, IN CASES involving delinquency. In some juvenile courts the cases of dependent as well as neglected children are also heard. The distinction between dependency and neglect is chiefly financial. In the widest sense, of course, all children are dependents. Legally, a child is considered a *dependent* child if his family is unable to provide for his support. A *neglected* child is one who is not receiving the kind of care to which he is entitled, regardless of the status of his family.

In some states the children's courts have been assigned complete jurisdiction over mentally defective children, children held as material witnesses, child marriages, adoptions, paternity proceedings, adults contributing to delinquency of juveniles, other administrative functions (mother's aid, and so forth), desertion and nonsupport, truancy, property rights of children, destitution, neglected children, physically handicapped children. Our chief concern in this text is with the delinquency rather than with the dependency jurisdiction of the court, although the difference between the two is not always clearcut, and the judge's decision is sometimes influenced by the availability of appropriate community resources for treatment.

Juvenile Court Procedures

Jurisdiction

While in all states the juvenile court is assigned jurisdiction in the case of violation of a law or an ordinance, in some states it has concurrent juris-

244

diction with other courts for certain types of offenses, or over young people in certain age groups. In some states the juvenile court has no jurisdiction over murder or serious offenses. As a rule, the juvenile court law does not use the term "delinquent" but describes the circumstances or the conduct that may bring the child within its jurisdiction. Thus, unlike the courts for adults, the juvenile court has jurisdiction over acts and conduct "likely to endanger the morals or the health of the child himself or of others."

As Rubin says, "The definition of delinquency does not, however, stop there, but *starts* there." In addition to the violation of law or ordinance a child may warrant the label juvenile delinquent if he engages in:

immoral or indecent conduct
illegal occupation
(knowingly) associates with vicious or immoral persons
growing up in idleness or crime
(knowingly) enters, visits house of ill repute
patronizes saloon or dram house where intoxicating liquid is sold
patronizes, visits policy shop or gaming place
patronizes public poolroom or bucket shops
wanders in streets at night, not on lawful business (curfew)
(habitually) wanders about railroad yards or tracks
jumps train or enters car or engine without authority
habitually truant from school
incorrigible
(habitually) uses vile, obscene or vulgar language (in public place)
absents self from home without consent
loiters, sleeps in alleys
refuses to obey parent, guardian
uses intoxicating liquors
is found in place for permitting which adult may be punished
deports self so as to injure self or others
smokes cigarettes (around public place)
in occupation or situation dangerous to self or others
begging or receiving alms (or in street for purpose of)

Of course not every state, nor any state, has all these items in its definition of delinquency. However, the laws average eight or nine items in addition to violations of law. No juvenile court law confines its definition of delinquency to violations of laws and ordinances.[1]

Intake

In some communities the chief probation officer receives the complaint and screens the cases for filing of a petition and formal hearing. In other

[1] Sol Rubin, "The Legal Character of Juvenile Delinquency," *The Annals*, American Academy of Political and Social Science, No. 261 (Jan. 1949), p. 2.

communities, a referee, who may or may not be a lawyer, decides whether there are grounds for continuing with the case. In the children's division of New York City's Domestic Relations Court, all children brought to court for the first time by a parent or a guardian are referred to the bureau of adjustment, set up in 1935 when the volume of business before the court was heavy. A conference with the officer in charge helps the complainant decide whether he wishes to proceed with the case and file a petition, or whether some other agency in the community may more effectively handle the situation.

Official and Unofficial Cases

Not all the situations referred to the court are necessarily dealt with officially. Courts use unofficial procedures in different ways, depending upon the philosophy of the judge, the size of the staff, and perhaps precedents in the community. For example, in Jersey City very few cases have been handled officially since the establishment by the former Mayor Hague of the Police Service Bureau. The matter of official and unofficial court cases merits some discussion because it underscores the wide variation in practice, complicates attempts to estimate or compare relative incidence of delinquency in different communities, and is sometimes a cause for jurisdictional controversy between the police and the casework agencies.

Some of the confusion in the use of the term "unofficial case" is due to the fact that the term "unofficial" seems to imply that there is no court action. In reality the court does act but it is by "informal adjustment . . . without the filing of a petition." According to the draft of the 1959 Standard Juvenile Court Act, Section 2:

> Whenever the court is informed by any person that a child is within the purview of this Act, it shall make a preliminary investigation to determine whether the interests of the public or of the child require that further action be taken. If so, the court may authorize the filing of a petition; or may make whatever informal adjustment is practicable without a petition, provided that the facts appear to establish prima facie jurisdiction and are admitted, and provided that consent is obtained from the parents and also from the child if he is of sufficient age and understanding. Efforts to effect informal adjustment may be continued not longer than three months without review by the judge or the director.[2]

In reply to the suggestion that a case should be considered unofficial if there is no hearing, the legal counsel of the National Probation and Parole Association notes:

> There are, however, many cases which come to the attention of the Court, in which all of its facilities, *other than court hearing*, are involved,

2 *A Standard Juvenile Court Act*, New York, National Probation and Parole Association, rev. ed., 1959.

and in which the proper outcome is a dismissal. The distinction between these cases and cases proceeding to decree of probation or commitment is that there has been a final disposition without a hearing. There is no reason why such a proceeding should be considered less official than a decree arrived at after a hearing. The outcome has followed the preliminary decision of the court that a petition be filed and the case is therefore properly considered official.[3]

An unofficial case, then, is one in which a petition is not filed, but an officer of the court makes an investigation, either by means of an office interview or perhaps by a visit in the community to verify the facts of the complaint and to decide whether or not court action is needed. Even though on initial investigation the decision may be that no further action is necessary, such a case should be reported as an unofficial one.

The instructions for Michigan, which has adopted a system of uniform state-wide juvenile court reporting, give the following as an illustration of an unofficial case:

> A farmer complained to the court that three boys who lived in the neighborhood have torn down his haystack, with the resulting damage of $25.00. A county agent [in Michigan county agents perform the same services as probation officers in other states] went to see the boys, who admitted that they did the damage. The boys agreed to rebuild the haystack and to pay $3.00 apiece. The farmer was satisfied and, since no further court action was indicated, the case was dropped. These three boys are counted as three unofficial cases.[4]

To counter the claim that the court's action in such situations is an exercise of coercive authority without the protection of a procedure recognized by Constitution or statute, the Standard Juvenile Court Act gives the juvenile court the authority to "make a preliminary inquiry . . . and informal adjustment" *only* when the court is informed that a child is within the purview of the act.

Thus, unofficial casework is legal only if the information presented to the court is such that, if verified, the filing of a petition could follow. The juvenile court probation department is not given carte blanche to delve into any problem affecting children and families which comes to its attention. It must find its authority in the jurisdiction section of the juvenile court law. In contrast to proceedings following filing of a petition which may result in an authoritative order of the court, this phase of juvenile court work is distinguished from official cases in that the unofficial proceeding is *voluntary*. The court, through its probation department, may investigate without coercion.

[3] Communication from Sol Rubin, Dec. 1956. Italics in original.
[4] *Reference Guide for Michigan Juvenile Court Reporting,* Michigan Probate Judges Association, Feb. 1945, p. 10.

Unofficial casework is indicated where (1) the case is one in which the child and the family are cooperating in a disposition which does not involve commitment or change of custody; (2) where there is no question as to whether the delinquent act occurred; (3) where the offense is minor. Consistent with the voluntary character of the procedure in unofficial cases, the parent and child must be informed as early as possible that the proceeding is one which may eventuate in a petition and that the data obtained by the intake department is recorded in a suitably permanent manner.

Data from 300 courts which reported both official and unofficial cases in 1946—the latest date for which these facts are reported—reveal that more than half of all the juvenile delinquency cases were handled unofficially. While there appears to be a general tendency to reserve official hearing for older children and those brought to court on serious charges, the incidence of unofficial cases varies so widely that "it is frequently difficult to rationalize their differences in handling seemingly similar groups of children."[5] Thus, Cincinnati's Hamilton County labels less than 5 per cent of cases referred to it as official, in contrast to 90 per cent in Trumbull County (Columbus). On a state-wide basis official procedures are used in one quarter of Ohio, one half of Missouri, and almost 80 percent of Pennsylvania, of all courts reporting.

Screening procedure, as well as official or unofficial handling, however, can obviously be effective only if the court staff is equipped to make the proper decisions and the community is ready to offer the necessary help. It is plain that the primary requirement is a sufficient number of adequately trained probation officers assigned to this function. If the probation officer thinks a community agency can help in a particular case, he must have both the time and the skill to make the proper referral, i.e., to prepare the child or his parents for the service that the agency can give (see Chapter 16).

Filing the Petition

If the child does not go to a special intake department, he is brought by the petitioner to a clerk at a window labeled "petition desk." The clerk fills out the blanks in a formal petition and the petition is then handed to a court attendant who puts the case on the court calendar, i.e., schedules the case for a court hearing. If the hearing is set for the same day, the child and his parent may be asked to wait in a nearby room. If the hearing is set for some time ahead, the child may be kept in detention quarters (see Chapter 21) if there is any doubt that he and his parent will appear at the appointed time.

[5] Edward E. Schwartz, "Statistics of Juvenile Delinquency in the United States," *The Annals*, American Academy of Political and Social Science, No. 261 (Jan. 1949), p. 16.

The court has no authority to require the appearance of any individual at the preliminary hearing, since issuance of a summons under the juvenile court law can only follow the filing of a petition. A petition must be filed if the authority of the court is required in the preliminary investigation or if the court wishes to assume custody.

In the words of the 1949 Standard Juvenile Court Act: "If it appears that the child is in such condition or surroundings that his welfare requires that his custody be immediately assumed by the court, the judge may order, by endorsement upon the summons, that the officer serving the same shall at once take the child into custody."[6]

Procedures in referral vary considerably from court to court. In some, arraignment follows immediately after apprehension or referral. In others, social study always precedes a court conference. In still others, the preliminary social study or investigation, usually by the probation staff, and in the larger courts, psychological and physical examination and, if indicated, psychiatric study, not only precede but actually determine whether there will be a court conference.

The Hearing

Cases may be heard by the judge, referee, or probation officer. The hearing itself may be formal and legalistic, similar to that in the adult criminal court, or informal, as at a case conference. Whether the hearing is formal or informal, however, depends on the atmosphere in the court rather than on the participants. Although there is *no* need for an attorney, since in the intent of the Act the court represents the child, the parents are informed that lawyers may be retained. In a case involving more than one child, if one child is represented by a lawyer, the parents of the other children are advised of their rights likewise to be represented by an attorney if they so desire. Witnesses may be sworn, stenographic notes may be taken, and, although they are kept to the minimum, spectators may be present. As a general rule, the press is excluded in the interests of protecting the child. When the evidence or the discussion would be inappropriate for the children to hear, they are excluded from the courtroom.

Some judges prepare themselves ahead of time by reading the case study of the probation officer, which gives them a vantage point from which to ask questions if necessary to clarify the issues.[7]

[6] *Standard Juvenile Court Act,* rev. ed., 1949, Section 12, paragraph 2, p. 20.
[7] In California the probation officers succeeded in including a section in the Welfare and Institutions Code in which the judge must certify that he has read the probation officer's report before making any orders in the case.

Court Action

As noted earlier, children coming to the juvenile court are not *convicted* but are adjudged as delinquent, neglected, and, in some courts, dependent children. Of course, when the petitioner fails to make out a prima facie case of juvenile delinquency by a preponderance of credible evidence the petition is dismissed. Following the child's adjudication as a delinquent, the court has the choice of the following dispositions: (1) To place him on probation; (2) To remand him to an institution for a specified period of observation, after which time he will be returned to the court for further action; (3) To commit him to an institution or agency.

Juvenile court statistics indicate that with some variations, the courts dismiss or discharge between 40 and 50 per cent of all the boys' cases and about one third of all the girls' cases that come before them. Supervision by a probation officer is ordered in approximately one third of all cases. Commitment to an institution is usually more frequent in girls' than in boys' cases, the distinction doubtless related to the different type of offense and to the referral source (see Chapters 1 and 2).

Child Offenders Against Federal Laws

Cases of juvenile offenders against federal laws are referred to state authorities whenever possible[8] and are included in the United States Children's Bureau Juvenile Court Series on delinquents. Most of the young persons charged with violations of federal statutes and for whom responsibility is not accepted by local authorities are dealt with in the United States District Court under the Federal Juvenile Delinquency Act of 1938. This act made possible the use of procedures in these courts similar to those in the juvenile courts. At the same time, United States attorneys "at the request of the Attorney General inaugurated a procedure for handling unofficial selected cases of first offenders who appeared amenable to supervision."[9] Probably because of the lack of child welfare services, the Southern and Rocky Mountain states lead in the referrals to the federal courts, while the New England states refer the smallest number.

Young people whose cases are disposed of by the federal courts are included in the reports of the Federal Bureau of Prisons. In recent years, violations of the National Motor Vehicle Theft Act, larceny, and theft, are the most frequent offenses; in such cases the median age of these offenders, more

[8] Schwartz, *op. cit.*, p. 16.
[9] *Ibid.*, p. 17.

than 90 per cent of whom are boys, is 16½ years. The rate of commitment is approximately three times that in the children's courts.

Juvenile Court Judges

Administrative Responsibilities

Most of the juvenile court judges have broad administrative responsibilities in addition to their judicial ones. These responsibilities usually involve appointment of the heads of all court departments, as well as the appointment of the staff. In Michigan, for example, the judge of the juvenile court is a judge of the probate court as well, and is responsible for the selection and appointment of the probation officers and for the county agents, who report to the court as well as to the department of welfare. In some communities the judge also administers the detention facilities. The extent of the judge's responsibilities will depend, of course, on the volume of court business, the number of judges, and the size of the probation staff.

Unlike judges in the other courts, the judge of the juvenile court is appropriately responsible for many community relationships. In order to make the work of the court effective, the judge must maintain a wide range of community relationships, including the following:

> Maintaining of cooperative relations with police, schools, churches, social agencies, and institutions caring for children.
> Interpretation to the public of the major factors underlying juvenile delinquency, neglect, and non-support, the stimulation of community planning that will tend to prevent or mitigate these problems.[10]

While it is appropriate for the judge to make policy, both for the court and with respect to relationships between the court and the other agencies in the community, there is a difference of opinion as to whether the judge of the juvenile court should have all of the administrative responsibilities which are carried by many of them.

Since the judge is in the pivotal position in the juvenile court, we are interested in knowing (1) how he is chosen; (2) what qualifications are specified; and (3) how he actually sees his role in court.

Method of Selection

There are a variety of methods by which judges of the juvenile court are selected. Some are elected; some are chosen by their confreres on the bench;

[10] *National Probation and Parole Association News*, Vol. 34, no. 3 (Sept. 1955), p. 2.

some, in the large city courts, are appointed by the mayor. Sometimes the local bar association furnishes a list of candidates whom it considers suitable for appointment. If the court is state-wide, as in Connecticut, Utah, and Rhode Island, the judge is appointed by the governor. Appointments to the independent juvenile courts may be for life or for a period ranging from two to ten years. Where the juvenile court is a designated court, the judge may serve in rotation with other judges.

Qualifications

One of the moot questions is whether or not a judge of the juvenile court should be a lawyer. Though the emphasis in the juvenile court procedure is on social rather than on legal evidence, there seems to be consensus in this country that legal training is necessary. As might be expected, the Association of Juvenile Court Judges considers not only a law degree but practical legal experience a prerequisite, because one of the major functions of the court is the protection of the rights of parents and children. Some states specify qualifications such as character, personality, tact, patience, common sense, and understanding of the problems of families and children. In reality, however, in communities in which judges of juvenile courts are paid substantial salaries and tenure is assured for a considerable time, appointment is at the mayor's discretion and judgeships are likely to be used as political patronage rewarding service to the party in power.

In some of the large urban juvenile courts served by more than one judge, there is pressure to balance the number of judges who are Catholic, Protestant, or Jewish, so that when a vacancy occurs on the bench it is almost always filled by a person of like religious faith. According to the Gellhorn report: "Only a strongly independent mayor would dare to give a 'Protestant vacancy' to a 'Jewish judge' no matter how well qualified he might be, nor would he be disposed to supplant a 'Catholic judge,' if one of the seven were to retire, with one of another faith."[11]

A recent procedure which illustrates how citizens may take responsibility for securing a qualified juvenile court judge was the joint action of representatives of the League of Women Voters and ninety-odd community organizations which organized an Independent Citizens Committee in Westchester County. In line with what they considered appropriate criteria for a judgeship, they presented a list of qualified candidates, from which the two major political parties might make their nominations. The criteria known as the "Westchester Standards," were as follows:

[11] Walter Gellhorn, *Children and Families in the Courts of New York City*, New York, Dodd, Mead, 1954, p. 101. This is an excellent study of the laws and the way they are carried out in the children's court, the youth, and the family court in New York City.

. . . personal integrity, patience, freedom from political, racial, or religious prejudices.

. . . a man or woman having *membership in the Bar of the State of New York*, versed through experience in the rules of court procedures. As his previous education, training, and experience would ordinarily not be designed to fit him for the unique work of a Children's Court, he must be not only willing, but eager to learn. He (or she) must have true understanding of and sympathy with the problems of families and children and be temperamentally suited to deal with them.

. . . capable of conducting informal conferences of interested and contending parties in a kindly manner . . . the ability to question skillfully, to bring out pertinent facts as to events, personalities, and backgrounds, and to give proper evaluation to these factors . . . to deal understandingly, sympathetically, and patiently with children, parents, policemen, probation officers, representatives of health and social agencies, school administrators, and others.

. . . be ever mindful that the purpose of the Children's Court is to help, rather than to punish; that a child in trouble, though technically an offender against the law, is really primarily a neglected or disturbed child, who has the right to the State's protection and help. He should appreciate the importance of a child's religious background and the influence of religion in rehabilitation of the child. He should understand the value of psychiatry and other resources in determining the best way to help a child. He must be able and willing to work with all interested persons and agencies, in an effort to arrive at a considered judgment as to the best disposition of every problem presented to him.

. . . the vision and courage to point out the need for services not already available and to cooperate in their establishment.[12]

How the Judge Sees His Role

Studies of the juvenile court operation are usually concerned exclusively with the law, judges' qualifications, and the nature of the procedure; these are somewhat abstract frames of reference. As Maxine Boord Virtue remarks in her résumé of children's services in Michigan:

> What is the law? Words in a statute book, with decided cases and departmental regulations? The fearsome authority of the policeman on the corner with the courthouse and prison looming behind him? Unyielding and authoritarian application of naked force as distinguished from planning and carrying out of a program to help the child? Shall we, as has been suggested, "treat children as human beings instead of as court cases?"

[12] *National Probation and Parole Association News*, Vol. 34, no. 3 (Sept. 1955), pp. 1-2. Italics added.

... "the law" is the machinery provided by statute and case precedent for dispensing public services to persons under 21. This machinery is not viewed as in a vacuum, but at the point of impact. So viewed, the law is a means of bringing about the legitimate purposes of an organized democratic society for the benefit of the group and any affected member of it as an individual. Hence a child who is, or has, a social problem may be helped by one of the legal techniques, if appropriate; that is, a child is a legal problem because he is a social problem. For our purposes then the law is the legal machinery as it acts upon or for children.

Until the nature of this legal framework, and the way in which it is used, at the point of impact, are fully known and analyzed, the study of practices alone cannot result in a more adequate system.[13]

The procedures in the court depend largely, as Maxine Virtue reminds us, upon the way in which the law is interpreted, which in turn depends upon the judge's interpretation of his role and the setting in which he presides. Since the juvenile court law prescribes that the judge shall act in the best interest of the child and not primarily in relation to the determination of guilt or innocence, the way in which the juvenile court judge views his role is a decisive factor in the outcome of the case. Furthermore, because the decisions of the juvenile court judge are usually final, there is seldom an appeal, so that rarely does a higher court review a juvenile court case and reverse the judge's decision. In this sense, then, the juvenile court judge has more opportunity to "play the role of God" than is true of other judges.

The best way to know how the juvenile court judges interpret their role is to observe them in action.[14] The material which follows is based on a study conducted by two experienced graduate students in a school of social work, who, over a period of eight months, observed 219 sessions presided over by fifteen judges in a large city court. Among the 325 children whose cases were heard there were white and Negro girls and boys, and the offenses ran the gamut from truancy to murder.

Immediately after the court sessions the observers recorded not only the case situations but the reactions and the remarks of the judges to the court staff, to the children, and to their parents. Note was made of reasons which the judge gave for his decisions, on the assumption that these would reflect his opinions in regard to the nature and consequence of the child's behavior and the parents' responsibility.

Although all fifteen judges observed presumably met the preliminary qualifications for their appointments with respect to their legal background,

---

[13] Maxine Boord Virtue, *Public Service to Children in Michigan: A Study of Basic Structure*, Michigan Pamphlets No. 24, Ann Arbor, University of Michigan Press, p. 19.

[14] Ruth Cannon and Richard Steinman, "The Juvenile Court Judge in Action, A Content Analysis of His Roles," Project No. 4079, New York School of Social Work, Columbia University, 1952.

experience, personality, and interest in children, no two judges apparently conceived of their role in exactly the same way. Such difference is no doubt more characteristic of judges in the juvenile than in the criminal or civil courts, where the rules of evidence and the restrictions of the setting more or less prescribe the procedure and the judge's role. In criminal courts, for example, the judge usually reserves his comments until all the evidence is in and until he writes an opinion. In contrast, in the juvenile court, the judge more frequently interjects his opinion.

On the basis of their many observations, the students were able to identify, through analysis of their independently recorded observations, five more or less distinct roles apparently performed by the judges they observed. They were those of the parent, the counselor, the chancellor, the lawyer, and the antagonist.

THE PARENT JUDGE. In this role, the judge identifies with the parent more than with the child and regards the child's duties to his parents as paramount. Obedience, in this judge's opinion, is essential if the child is to be saved. Usually this judge does not look at the individual child in the light of his special individual needs but believes that, like a parent, he knows what is best for the child.

THE COUNSELOR JUDGE. The counselor judge is the opposite of the parent judge. His emphasis is almost exclusively on the unique individuality of each child. The counselor judge views the behavior of each child as stemming from a specific chain of experiences at home, in the school, in the community. He is therefore concerned with the dynamics of the interrelationship between the child and his parents. Ordinarily he insists upon seeing the complete history of the child ahead of time and considers the probation officer as a resource for supplementary information. The other court personnel—the psychiatrist, the psychologist—he regards as members of a professional team. To a considerable extent the counselor judge, in contrast to the parent judge, appears to be aware of himself and the extent to which he may be projecting his own needs in his relations with other persons.

THE CHANCELLOR JUDGE. While somewhat similar to the counselor judge, the chancellor judge is self-disciplined rather than self-aware. As the protector of the child, he balances the child's rights with those of the parent and the community. When difficulties arise between them he is the arbitrator. When he acts *in loco parentis* he symbolizes the benevolent parent since the court is set up to help the child and the law is the primary tool in that process.

THE LAWYER JUDGE. The judge who sees his role primarily as that of a lawyer rather than a chancellor likewise uses the law as a primary tool but he uses it differently. The lawyer judge regards the court as the appropriate set-up for administering the law—helping the child is but a by-product. In contrast to the others, the lawyer judge appears to have a stronger identification with the adult court. This approach symbolizes the concept of proceeding *against* rather than *in behalf of* the child.

THE ANTAGONIST JUDGE. The antagonist judge, represented by three of the fifteen visited, reacts personally in each situation so that it is difficult to classify his concept of his role. But because he appears, more often than not, to be hostile to the child, his role is designated as that of the antagonist.

While the application of these designations obviously disregards the variations in the particular reactions of individual judges at specified times, there appeared to be enough consistency in the behavior of each of the fifteen judges in the course of the eight months' observations so that they could be generally classified in one or the other of these five categories.

The Judges in Action

As the discussions below reveal, the role was also reflected (1) in the use that the judge made of the setting; (2) in the manner in which he approached the parents and the child and informed them as to their rights; (3) in the time he spent on the case, and (4) in the extent to which he individualized each situation before him.

THE SETTING. From the lawyer judge's point of view, a high-ceilinged, wood-paneled, austere courtroom may seem an appropriate background for the dignity of the law. To the young child, however, such a setting may be frightening. If he stands below the dais and has to stretch to look up to the judge, he can hardly feel sufficiently relaxed to respond easily to questioning. The presence of one or both of his parents, of court attendants or other persons of whose business he is ignorant, may easily disturb him. Aware of this possibility, some judges see children in informal settings. The judge's desk may be a table at which the child and his parents are invited to sit.

A judge's robes, like a priest's vestments, may serve as the symbol of his role. In this sense the robe serves to separate the judge from the child. Separation may be necessary and important in certain situations in which a person readily accepts the judgment on or control of his action when he accedes to the authority symbolized by the costume. The uniforms, for example, of the police, train conductors, firemen, and theater ushers enable them to perform their functions more smoothly because people ordinarily accept the authority of the uniform. Whether or not the juvenile court judge feels that he needs the authority of his robe depends upon his individual interpretation of his function. Only two of the fifteen judges observed wore their robes habitually.

APPROACH TO PARENT AND CHILD. Another important factor in the readiness of the child or his parent to accept the help of the court is the way in which he is greeted. In the courts observed, the judge's greeting varied with his concept of his role and naturally with his personality. The antagonist and occasionally the lawyer judges were noted to be brief and somewhat stern in their greetings. The counselor judges immediately greeted the child and his parents warmly but quietly, indicating that they were interested and wished to be helpful.

Since the hearing takes place in court, one expects some legalistic aspects, even though, according to juvenile court standards, these are to be minimized. All fifteen judges customarily informed the respondents that they had a legal right to be represented by counsel. Some, however, emphasizing the legal aspects of their role, put the child on the stand as they would an adult and in this manner attempted to get fairly extensive testimony, as illustrated in the case below of a lawyer judge:

Virginia and Elsie, two attractive, well-dressed 13-year-old white girls who had run away from their homes had been found two weeks later living in an apartment with two men. There was a slight delay before the judge appeared in the court and the girls and their parents, whom they had seen for the first time since running away, were already seated. As Virginia's father seated himself on the bench next to his daughter, he shoved her so hard that the sound could be heard throughout the courtroom.

The hearing began with the judge taking testimony from the policewoman who said that the girls had been found in the apartment with the men at a very early hour of the morning.

Next, the judge took testimony from Virginia herself. The judge began in an objective, judicial way but later changed to some of the lawyer's techniques, especially in his questioning. For example, he attempted to find loopholes in the girl's story, of which there seemed to be many. He also spoke rather sharply to her at times. If, however, the girl's reply was not clear, the judge would say sharply: "What? What did you say?" Or, "Speak up!" At one point when he noticed that Virginia was chewing gum he asked her to dispose of it.

At another point the judge warned Virginia not to look to Elsie for the answer to the question. What the judge wanted was the truth, not the story that the girls had concocted between them. When in reply to the judge's question Virginia stated that she and Elsie had been afraid to go home one night they stayed out until 12:30, the judge asked, "Afraid of what?" At first Virginia avoided answering the question and then said she was afraid of being punished. The judge asked how she would be punished, in the presence of her father, who at this point was leaning forward in his chair with ear cupped in his hand. Virginia seemed afraid to say. After the judge had repeated the question several times, Virginia said she was afraid of being scolded.

In response to further questions by the judge, the girl then told the story of their trip to the city. They had not originally intended to go but their hitchhiking brought them by a very circuitous road and took the entire night. Since they had only $2.50 between them, she said they looked for work along the way. At this point the judge asked: Where did they think two 13-year-old girls were going to find work today? The girls said that the chef in a highway diner where they had asked for work offered to drive them to New York City and help them to find jobs. On their arrival they were approached by two young men who rented the apartment in which they were found by the police.

To the judge's question whether they had had sexual relations with any of the three men, Virginia said "No." When the judge repeated the question and the girl's answer was the same, the judge warned Virginia that she would be subject to a medical examination; that in any event the truth would be ascertained. This remark was delivered in the tone of a threat. The judge extracted by testimony which man had been each girl's escort. When she was asked whether she knew that one of the men was married and that he carried a gun, Virginia replied, Yes, she had known it; and when she was asked what she thought of that, she said she hadn't thought anything about it. At this point the judge told Virginia that she should have shown more consideration for her parents; that it was cruel to run away and leave them for two weeks without letting them know where she was.

The judge then asked Virginia's parents what they thought could have motivated her behavior; they had nothing to say. The judge asked what could Virginia have been running away from. The mother could not imagine—they had a good home. To the question whether she ever beat the girl the mother said "No." The judge then addressed himself to the father, asking him if he could think of any reasons why she should run away, to which he replied that he could not. The father's only comment was to ask whether the police had apprehended the "party" who had taken the girls out of their home state. To this the judge replied, with a wry smile, that he didn't see how they could have in view of the fact that this was the first time that the girls had mentioned this man.

During the remainder of the hearing Virginia sat weeping silently in a chair to the right of her mother, who sat with her right hand up to her eyes like the blinder on a horse in order not to have to see her daughter.

Elsie then was asked to testify. She was a pretty, animated and extremely bright child who told much the same story as Virginia's. She spoke clearly, simply, answering all questions in a lady-like manner. Unlike her companion, she did not hang her head or act submissively, although there was no hint of bitterness or defiance in her manner. Her mother was not present as she was sick, and her father wept through most of the interrogation.

When Virginia acknowledged the policewoman's allegation that the girls had accepted $200.00 from the man who had originally driven them to New York, Elsie stated that she knew it was wrong but they had done it because they needed money. At this point the judge appeared to be angry as he asked if the girl was in the habit of ignoring whether or not a thing was right or wrong. Elsie shrugged her shoulders when asked if she had not known why the man was giving them the money, and said she had not. In reply to the question whether she had had sexual relations with the man, she said she had not, but when the man rented the hotel room and said he would return in a little while, the two girls had begun to suspect what they might be planning, had become frightened, and had run away. Later in the day they had "met" the two men on the street and had told them that they were 16 years old. In reply to the judge's question, Elsie denied having had sexual relations with the two young men, said they had merely sat up all of the previous two nights and had fallen asleep on the beds. As in the case of Virginia, the judge warned Elsie that the court would be able to find out the truth about this from the medical examinations which would be administered.

As in the case of the other girl, the judge's final questions to Elsie were: had she known that her escort carried a gun and that he was married? To which Elsie replied that she had asked no questions about the gun, but that he had shown her a picture of his wife who was expecting a baby. He had told her he was separated and planning a divorce. When the judge asked Elsie to step down from the witness stand, his tone was angry.

Next, Elsie's father was questioned. He said he and his wife were divorced. Elsie had lived with him for a while but he could not manage her. He freely admitted that he had hit her on several occasions and that she had tried previously to run away several times to her older brother who lived in a nearby city.

In remanding the two girls for study and investigation, the judge stated: While there still might be some hope for Virginia who seemed repentant, he did not have much hope for Elsie, who sat there as cool as a cucumber all through the hearing and apparently had no feeling of having done anything wrong.

Elsie's independent attitude appeared to disturb the judge, who, though he repeated that the girls were hurting their parents, made no reference to the fact that their behavior was possibly related to their unhappiness and a search for something more satisfying.

An opposite interpretation of his role was that of the counselor judge who reprimanded the court reporter for requesting a sobbing girl to stop crying as he could not hear what she was saying. This judge was as concerned with the emotional needs of the child as he was with securing precise evidence.

The case that follows is chosen from those heard by a chancellor judge who acts within the legal framework but does not overlook the needs of the child before him:

Listening to the mother of a 15-year-old boy charged with murder on the previous evening, the judge informed the mother of her right to request an adjournment in order to secure legal counsel. The mother stated she would like to do so but that she had no funds for the lawyer's fee. When the judge hesitatingly said that the juvenile court could not provide money for the fee the mother replied that she did not then know what to do. After a moment's hesitation the judge instructed the court officer to telephone the Magistrate's Court to ask whether they could obtain free legal counsel for the mother.

A situation in which the judge sees his role as an antagonist is the following:

An attractive Spanish woman came into court to complain about her daughter because she could not handle her. She had not brought the child with her, not having expected to appear before the judge that day. Without giving her any chance to speak, the judge suggested that she was probably solely to blame for the child's behavior. He noted she was carrying a Spanish magazine which he asked for, showing her his little knowledge of Spanish.

The judge then asked what work she did and when she told him she worked in sportswear, wanted to know to which union she belonged and her salary. After she had made reply, he said she had lied about the union name because he knew them all well and if she worked in sportswear she had to belong to a certain one. The lady became very upset but insisted on the one she had said. The judge then inquired about her husband, the child's stepfather. She said that he was a carpenter and got a low salary, which she mentioned. The judge again called her a liar and said he knew that carpenters got much more. The probation officer finally intervened and said that the father was not a union man. By this time the lady was too upset to be able to think in English, even having difficulty with the interpreter that they had got for her.

At no time was the judge apparently concerned with the actual behavior of the child and its meaning to the child. When the lady did try to explain, the judge interrupted her and she was never able to get her story across.

This Spanish woman was very attractively and neatly dressed in good taste and style. However, as she left the courtroom, the judge passed a remark about the high-heeled shoes she was wearing, and suggested that she couldn't have given her child very good care.

TIME DEVOTED TO HEARING. The length of time that a judge is willing to spend on a case reveals a great deal about his attitude and his approach to the delinquent. As they would in other courts, almost without exception the judges took the time to explain the nature of the proceedings to the respondents. Occasionally, however, a respondent was too confused or so limited in understanding that the judge became impatient. For example:

> In a case involving the age of legal consent, neither the girl and boy, nor their parents, understood English very well. When their case came before him the judge was still discussing the previous case with the probation officer. He looked at the two families, said not a word, wrote briefly on the petition, handed it to the appropriate court officer, and sat waiting apparently for the next hearing. There was an expression of complete bewilderment on the faces of the young couple and their parents as they were ushered out of the court. They obviously thought they were waiting for the proceeding to begin since no words at all had been exchanged with them.

While some of the judges hurried through the day, one counselor judge spent an exceptional amount of time with each case. In the case of a group involved in a gang fight, which most of the judges ordinarily hear as a unit after there has been a social investigation, this judge always sees each boy and his parents separately. The court attendants react to this procedure in varied fashion. One attendant commented: "Judge ——— gives us a lot of legwork. I don't mind because the kids get a break." Other attendants, however, were quite surly to this judge in contrast to their manner with other judges.

As a rule counselor judges are aware that the extent to which they give the child and his parents the feeling that they are concerned and wish to be helpful is related to the amount of time they are willing to devote to the case. Aware that what a child says will depend upon who is listening, they arrange to take extra time to hear the child's story separately. Occasionally a judge asked the parents to leave the courtroom.

In contrast, the judges who saw their role chiefly as lawyers did not talk to the child unless the parent was present, although they often talked with the parent when the child was not present. Apparently their reason for not seeing the child alone was that although the law gave them the right to act *in loco parentis,* they did not wish to convey the impression to the parent that they were usurping his role.

INDIVIDUALIZING THE CASE. Whether or not the judge is able to convey to the child that he sees him as an individual is a very important factor in the child's acceptance of help. We all react negatively to the feeling that we are just a number or a case. Some judges appeared to talk to the courtroom or to the air; they did not address the child directly or seem to expect an answer to their question. As an example:

> Two 14-year-old girls were picked up by two policewomen who charged them with theft from a street peddler and for stealing a pocketbook from

a nearby department store. One girl's case was disposed of immediately because this was apparently her first offense.

Because her companion had been in court on three former occasions there was a question as to whether she should be dismissed or put on probation.

The judge addressed one of them: "Rose, what are we going to do with you?" to which the girl made no reply, nor did the judge seem to expect one.

The policewoman appeared to be sorry for the girl and agreed with the judge that the fact that this theft had been reported by a policewoman rather than by the store detective might have a sobering effect on the girl. The girl's mother, however, markedly hostile to her daughter, turned her back on the girl who wept silently, attempting to put her head on her mother's shoulder.

Although the judge obviously intended to be kind when he asked the girl to leave the courtroom while her case was being discussed, he made several references, when she returned to the court, to the effect that the girl had been diagnosed as a mental defective.

A judge who individualizes each child who comes before him gives the child the feeling that he wants to understand what has been troubling him and to help him overcome the difficulties which cause his unhappiness and disturbance. To invoke this feeling such a judge tries to get the child to talk about himself at the very beginning of the hearing as an indication of interest in him as an individual. Other judges achieve this feeling of interest by asking that the younger children particularly be brought up to the bench beside them.

The Judges' Attitudes

TOWARD LAWYERS. As might be expected, the majority of the judges observed were respectful to the occasional lawyer who appeared in the juvenile court.

In a case in which two parents were each represented by lawyers, one lawyer stated that they were working jointly towards the same end, adjustment for the child and unity for the family. The judge, in a very courteous but at the same time professional manner, said that he considered the joint appearance of two lawyers unusual. He proceeded with the case following the relatively unstructured pattern of the juvenile court. At one point he interrupted the proceeding to inform the attorneys that he realized he was departing from the procedure to which they doubtless were accustomed but he wondered whether they would not agree to his proceeding in this fashion in view of the fact that this was the method that the juvenile court had found to be most efficacious in helping children and their families. The lawyers agreed.

In contrast, a judge classified as the antagonist type displayed his hostility even to attorneys in a direct, gruff, and uncivil approach.

In a case in which an attorney was defending a boy who had run away from a private institution and whose discharge the institution was requesting, the judge was very impatient. When the lawyer reported that the boy had been badly beaten the judge's response conveyed the attitude that the boy probably deserved it.

TOWARD PROBATION OFFICERS. The judges who respected the probation officer as a member of the team were ones who saw their role chiefly as counselors. One counselor judge always listened conscientiously and demonstrated a real give-and-take in his work with the probation officers with whom he discussed the case briefly before the respondent appeared in court. Whether or not he agreed with the probation officer, he conveyed the feeling that he was giving careful consideration to what the probation officer had to say, and that his decision was based on a weighing of the various aspects of the case.

Another counselor judge was observed always to include the probation officer as a member of the team, even though he was obviously aware of differences in the skills of individual officers. This judge was reported to carry a briefcase of records home with him and to come to court prepared with a knowledge of the situation described in the studies of the probation officers. Before entering the courtroom he would frequently inquire of the probation officer: "What do you think I should talk to this child about today?" For example:

In a case involving several burglaries which was brought for a final hearing, the boy had had a psychiatric examination, supplementing the probation officer's social history. When the judge asked the probation officer what he thought he should discuss with the boy, the probation officer said he had no idea. To this the judge suggested that in view of the fact that he believed his decision was to return the boy to his own home it would be wise to discuss with the mother her rigid and unaffectionate supervision of the boy; the probation officer said that he did not think this would be appropriate because, in his opinion in view of the kind of neighborhood in which the family lived, it was no wonder that the mother had to use strict discipline for her unruly son. The judge appeared to acquiesce.

When the judge told the mother that his decision was that the boy should go home, she seemed mildly pleased. When the boy came into the court later, the judge repeated his decision and the boy nodded his head solemnly; whereupon the mother, with considerable sharpness and somewhat subdued anger, said to the boy, "Thank the Judge." The boy said, "Thank you," very quietly. With a little hesitancy the judge gently told the mother that the boy did not have to thank him; that it made no difference whether he did or not; the important thing was, that the boy should understand what had been said to him. The mother made no comment.

After the mother and the son left the courtroom, the judge said, addressing the probation officer in a very mild tone: "You see, the mother is quite rigid with him; she won't let him grow up. To her he is still a baby and she wants to keep him that way." The probation officer, blushing slightly, agreed. Apparently the judge wanted to discuss the rigid behavior with the mother but had deferred to the probation officer's opinion that it should not be discussed.

There are many more illustrations of ways in which the counselor judge was aware of the contributions as well as the limitations of the probation staff. In his role as counselor he was careful not to offend the probation officer in situations in which he did not agree with him:

A 12-year-old boy involved in a third stealing episode appeared before a counselor judge for disposition of his case. The boy was accompanied by a social worker from one of the private child-care agencies which requested that the boy be permitted to continue in treatment with the agency instead of being committed to a state institution. The boy's mother, who accompanied him, also said that she wished to have him remain at home. The probation officer objected to this plan. He said that as a third offender the boy should be automatically committed to the state training school and requested the judge to make this disposition of the case.

At this point the judge interrupted the probation officer and said he would like to hear the social worker's opinion. The social worker replied that he felt that because the boy had shown some improvement during the time he was under the care of the agency, it would be helpful if the boy were permitted to continue with the treatment plan of the agency.

The judge, turning to the probation officer, asked him directly if he didn't think it would be good for the boy to remain under the agency's care since they had shown such an interest in him?

It was not, the judge said, that he did not think that the probation officer could also help the boy, but because the contacts had already been begun in the other agency, he thought it might be better for the boy to remain under said agency's care. He added quickly that he knew that the probation officer was very busy with his large case load and might find the intensive treatment which the boy needed an additional burden.

This judge realized how difficult it was to expect to secure intensive casework treatment for a boy when the court staff, regardless of their skill or lack of it, was so overworked.

The chancellor judge more characteristically looked upon the probation officer *as a member of the court*. For example, one chancellor judge, always very professional in his attitude toward the probation staff, did not call upon their services extensively but depended chiefly upon his own perceptions for his decisions.

TOWARD SOCIAL WORKERS. The case cited above illustrates a situation in which the relationship between the judge and the social worker, whom he recognized as more skilled in this instance than the probation officer, was a constructive one. As Judge Polier notes, however, it is not always easy for a judge to accept objectively the attitude of many social workers to judges. In her opinion, a judge who thinks of himself as socially progressive when he practices in the juvenile court must surely be taken aback when he finds that he is:

> . . . frequently looked upon as a legal anachronism in the field of child welfare. Coming directly from the practice of law he is often faced with the conflict between the broad powers with which he is entrusted and the carefully veiled condescension of the social work staff by whom he is surrounded. Confronted with this harsh reality, the judge might very well like to ignore the authors of his discomfort and their pronouncements. Instead, he must resist the temptation to substitute his judgment for that of experts in areas where a different type of scientific training is essential.[15]

Most of the counselor judges observed gave definite consideration to the opinions of those social workers whom they considered adequately trained.

TOWARD THE POLICE. As key people in the juvenile court proceedings, the police appear more frequently than lawyers, social workers, or attendance officers. There was no uniformity, however, in the way in which the various categories of judges approached the police. Some judges criticized them sharply, saying for example, in a case in which the officer had apprehended a boy on heresay evidence only, that the officer should know whether or not to bring a charge against a boy.

Another judge, in the chancellor category, was concerned about the way in which the police had handled children whom they had picked up. This judge detained a policeman after a hearing in order not to destroy the respect that the parents or the children might have for the police.

> In a very calm but nonetheless firm tone, the judge reminded the police that the children and their parents had certain rights and that the police must not jeopardize these rights. There was neither anger nor hostility

15 Justine Wise Polier, "The Children's Court—Its Relation to the Community and a Commentary on Some of the Problems," Speech at the New York State Welfare Conference, Nov. 28, 1950.

in his remark. His manner implied that he considered this interpretation to the police as part of his responsibility.

At times there appeared to be a subtle rivalry between the judge and the police officer, especially in an instance in which the police officer was a well-trained person from a special juvenile police unit.

A policewoman had filed a petition against two women whose sons had been involved in a theft. Her investigation revealed neglect in both homes. On the witness stand, the policewoman was eloquent and poised. The judge seemed somewhat irritated by this quality and seemed to feel acutely that she did not hold him in any kind of awe. He was cool towards any fraternizing aspects of her behavior. For example, when trying to arrange a date for a hearing, instead of referring to the calendar on the wall behind her, she reached for the calendar on the judge's desk, saying, "May I?" In the course of the case the judge became critical and picky. He found fault with what he thought was some omission in the presentation.

An occasional judge approached the police as though he needed their acceptance. He entered into personal inquiries and established a friendly contact by asking them if they knew so-and-so on such-and-such a beat. Some officers were apparently made uncomfortable by this approach.

TOWARD CONFIDENTIALITY OF THE HEARINGS. Most of the judges observed were fully aware of the importance of confidentiality of the hearings and were reluctant to admit visitors, except for very special reasons. The authors of this report, as students interested in the process, received special permission to attend sessions. They made only slight notes during the hearings, and disguised all the names so that the identities of the people involved would not be revealed.

Some of the judges, in discussing a case before them, refrained from mentioning the specific nature of the behavior, as for example in the case cited above which involved a boy accused of murder. During the court hearing this chancellor judge never once mentioned the offense. In another case which involved an adopted child, the judge made no reference to the child's adoptive status.

This caution against revealing data which might be harmful to the child is consistent with the exclusion of the press from the juvenile court in spite of occasional strong pressure to permit them to attend hearings. The most potent arguments against their admission are that these young people are not accused of crimes but are children in need of care and the protection of the court. Publicity attendant on the hearings could in no wise be helpful but, on the contrary, might very well harm the young person's subsequent adjustment.

Because, as far as is known, the literature provides no other such systematic study, we cannot state how typical are these observations of judges in one of the largest juvenile courts in this country. There is nothing, however, to prevent similar studies of the judge's concept of his role in other courts. Such studies should prove valuable if we could follow and analyze the subsequent developments in a sufficiently large number of cases.

An English Juvenile Court

Since an appeal from the decision of the juvenile court judge is infrequent, his efficacy is not put to legal test. This raises the question whether the juvenile court process requires the services of so many legally trained judges.

In London, the juvenile court in each district is presided over by a panel of three outstanding lay citizens called "magistrates"; each volunteers his or her services one day a week. One member of this panel assumes the responsibility for conducting the hearing. The petitioner, the juvenile, his parents, and the probation officer are given an opportunity to testify and to comment. The presiding magistrate asks for the recommendations of the probation officer and consults, of course, with his two associates before reaching a decision. Matters of law are interpreted or ruled upon by an attorney, who is salaried. The role of the attorney, however, is an advisory and supportive one rather than that of a leader.

The author of this book observed the hearings in twenty cases in London during August 1957. In her opinion, the decisions reached in this court were very similar to those which would have been arrived at by the majority of the lawyers employed full time in New York City's juvenile court. Whether they were any *more correct* is a matter on which we have no definitive evidence. For an explanation of the reason, we refer to Grünhut's analysis.[16]

Summary

This chapter has discussed the varying jurisdiction of the juvenile court with respect to age and type of offense. It has explained the intake process, as well as the official and unofficial handling of cases, filing of the petition, and the hearing procedure.

The descriptions of various methods of selection of juvenile court judges,

---

[16] Max Grünhut, *Juvenile Offenders Before the Courts in England and Wales,* New York, Oxford University Press, 1956; see also Norval Morris' review of it in *The Yale Law Journal,* Vol. 6, no. 6 (May 1957), and Mannheim's *Studies* at Cambridge University, Department of Criminal Science.

their qualifications, and responsibilities serve as a background for the observation of fifteen judges of a large urban court in action. If the observations in this study can be applied generally, it would appear that judges, like other people, bring to their courts, in addition to their specialized training as lawyers, their characteristic attitudes and orientation to life and to people. These different systems of evaluating people and behavior partly reflect their individual life experience. For some judges, what they have learned in their parents' homes, in church, and in their practice of law, constitutes almost their entire equipment for the juvenile court judgeship. Others appear to feel the need for additional knowledge.

The extent to which a judge's action in the juvenile court, in contrast to other courts, is governed by his awareness of the relation between his personal feelings and his professional objectives was the basis for the classification of judges, by trained observers, according to the predominant patterns which they display on the bench.

Recognizing the limitations of this study as an exploratory one aimed at supplementing the usual evaluations of juvenile court law, procedures, and the qualifications of judges and staff, the findings may be summed up as follows:

Among the fifteen judges, five different types were observed: (1) the *parent judge,* who sees himself primarily in the role of a good parent and draws chiefly from his own experiences and feelings; (2) the *lawyer judge,* who is apt to put more stress on whether or not the act occurred than he does on the nature and the needs of the offender, and who will draw from the supplemental personnel in the court only the data that he considers relevant to the legal facts of the case; (3) the *chancellor judge,* who follows a pattern somewhat like that of a lawyer judge but makes less use of the legal forms, and slightly more use of the supplementary information; (4) the *antagonist judge,* who ordinarily asks for little guidance from other members of the team, and whose court has an atmosphere of rigidity and rejection; and (5) the *counselor judge* who most nearly reflects the ideal of the juvenile court judge as envisioned in the Standard Juvenile Court Act.

An adequate understanding of the operation of the juvenile court requires both a knowledge of prescribed procedures and an awareness of the way in which they are actually carried out. The study just quoted opens up new avenues of investigation for the qualities needed for properly qualified key personnel, i.e., judges of the juvenile court. It provides evidence of the crucial role of informal processes, within the formally prescribed framework of the juvenile court, as a determining factor in the effective functioning of a social institution.

CHAPTER 16

Juvenile Probation

Carol's Story[1]

Two policemen in a squad car arrested Carol, at three in the morning. She was staggering drunkenly down past a row of cheap hotels in Illinois Street in Indianapolis.

She was a homely girl, her eyebrows were inexpertly plucked, her eyelashes were sticky with mascara and she was wearing ill-fitting "falsies." Her ears and fingernails were dirty. When first questioned, Carol claimed to be 17 and said she was walking home from a joy ride with some soldiers. She went on to recite a long history of sexual promiscuity in her own neighborhood and in downtown hotels.

In some American cities, Carol would be marked down by her own admissions as just another tramp. An overburdened mill of justice would grind out one more decision: "Two years in the State training school!"

Some onlookers might even have added "Good riddance!" But in Indiana things are different:

I am one of Marion County's 21 juvenile probation officers. My duties include investigating cases like Carol's before they are heard by the judge. I talked with Carol's mother and her older sister, with her school social worker and with several others; I got a full medical report on Carol. And I sat down at least half a dozen times for quiet personal talks with Carol herself. From the information I patiently dredged up, there emerged a girl altogether different from the tart walking on Illinois Street.

[1] Je're Merritt, "Wanted: Someone to Trust," *Woman's Home Companion*, Sept. 1955, reprinted by National Probation and Parole Association.

269

Carol, I learned, was not 17 but 14. She was the younger of two sisters. She had been an unwanted and resented child from the moment of her birth. Her older sister, Mae, was prettier and smarter than Carol and was the apple of her mother's eyes.

This mother brought Mae expensive clothes which the family could ill afford, let her stay out with men till any hour and waited up for her return to enjoy with Mae the intimate details of each date.

The climax came one day when a boy in her class invited Carol to the movies. The date meant a lot to Carol—it was her first. But what could she wear? Carol brooded all day, then she followed the only course she could think of and borrowed one of Mae's pretty blouses to wear with her own school skirt.

The movie was fun and so were the two sodas afterward at the neighborhood fountain. Carol hurried home all aglow, anticipating the same warm sharing of experience with her mother that always occurred when Mae came home from a date. Instead, both mother and sister pounced on her unmercifully, calling her a thief and worse. Her mother threatened to turn her out. Carol cried most of the night. The next day she stayed home from school, biting her nails into the flesh in rage. As the lonely hours at home passed, she felt more and more like a trapped animal. They'd called her a thief? All right, she'd steal! They'd called her a prostitute? She'd show them!

The medical report told the rest. Carol's feet had blisters on them the size of half-dollars following seven hours of walking off her rage and despair. When arrested she had been staggering not from drunkenness, but from pain and weariness. And despite her lurid stories of habitual sex misbehavior, the medical report left no doubt that Carol was still a virgin. Her false self-accusation was a troubled child's inexpert attempt to revenge herself on a mother she loved but who didn't love her.

When Carol appeared before Marion County's Juvenile Court Judge Harold N. Fields, my information gave him the actual facts, not the caricature Carol had created. And after talking half an hour with Carol, Judge Fields placed her on probation for truancy and curfew violation.

What Is Probation?

Defined

From the point of view of the general public, probation is sometimes associated with leniency, i.e., people are "let off" when they are put on probation; or contrariwise, probation is punishment, with the emphasis on discipline—"You're on probation now, your personal freedom is curtailed." From the point of view of the social worker, as illustrated by Jer'e Merritt's story, probation is social casework designed to help a young person who has been referred to the juvenile court for some form of disapproved behavior.

Probation is legally defined as one of several types of disposition the court may make after a young person has been adjudged a juvenile delinquent. When a court orders a child to be placed on probation, it may either suspend sentence or it may impose sentence and suspend the execution thereof, permitting the child to return to his family and community. The court continues its supervision, guardianship, and control through an agent known as a probation officer for as long a time as may be warranted by the facts of the case. Probation is frequently confused with parole, which refers more correctly to supervision after release from an institution.

As noted by the founder of the National Probation and Parole Association, either the child or his parents may be placed on probation. "Probation, as it relates to children, may be defined as a system of treatment for the delinquent child, or, in the case of the neglected or destitute child, for delinquent parents, by means of which the child and parents remain in their ordinary environment and to a great extent at liberty, but, throughout a probation period, subject to the watchful care and personal influence of the agent of the court known as the probation officer."[2]

In the 1949 edition of the Standard Juvenile Court Act the original statement on probation as "supervision in his home, or if not in his home, in the custody of a suitable person elsewhere under conditions determined by the court," was expanded to read: "Probation shall mean *casework* services during a continuance of the case. Probation shall not be ordered or administered as a punishment, but as a measure for the protection, guidance and well-being of the child and his family. Probation methods shall be directed to the discovery and correction of the child's personality and character, with the aid of the social resources of the community."[3]

Thus, from the viewpoint of the juvenile court's basic concern—the protection and well-being of the child—the negative aspects of apprehension are counterbalanced by the court's efforts in helping a young person overcome his difficulties. Describing probation in the children's court as a constructive approach to the treatment of the delinquent, Marion M. Brennan says that "the conflict with society frequently is both a blessing and a handicap. It forces the recognition of the existence of a problem often previously unrecognized or untreated."[4]

[2] Charles L. Chute, *Probation in Children's Courts*, No. 83, Washington, U.S. Children's Bureau, 1918, p. 7.
[3] Standard Juvenile Court Act, rev. ed., New York, National Probation and Parole Association, 1949.
[4] Speech by Marion M. Brennan, Assistant Chief Probation Officer, Domestic Relations Court of the City of New York, New York State Conference on Social Work, November 28, 1950.

Conditions

The conditions which the probationer must meet are explained to him and his parents, either at the time of the hearing or subsequently through the probation officer, so that they will understand their mutual responsibilities and duties. Occasionally a judge writes to the child and his family mentioning the name of their probation officer, the length of time and terms of the probation, when and where the child is expected to report, and any other limitations on his activities which may have been specified, as, for example, avoidance of public dance halls, or loitering on street corners, or staying out late at night, or using liquor or tobacco, or leaving the locality without the consent of the court. Sometimes the references are not specific but warn against bad companions and advise the probationer that he is expected to attend school regularly, obey his parents, and report regularly to his probation officer. Lenroot and Lundberg[5] caution realistically that the child should be told by the probation officer that because a particular type of behavior is not specifically prohibited does not necessarily imply that it is permitted.

History

Probation antedates the establishment of the juvenile court by about sixty years. A forerunner of probation was the common law practice of suspending sentence for an indefinite time during which the convicted offender was permitted to remain at liberty upon the condition of good behavior. If the conditions were violated, and if the original sentence had not been pronounced, the offender was returned to the court, sentence pronounced and carried out. If sentence had already been pronounced and the violator was returned to the court, the original sentence would then be put into effect.

The element added by John Augustus, a Boston shoemaker who is credited with introducing modern probation to compensate for the severity of criminal procedure in Massachusetts in 1840, was supervision during the suspension period. The idea occurred to him on an August morning in 1841 when he saw a wretched-looking prisoner being brought into court from the lockup. His suspicions that the man was a drunkard were confirmed by the clerk's reading of the complaint. Seizing the opportunity to talk to the defendant, John Augustus decided that he was not beyond redemption because he pleaded to be saved from the house of correction and promised

[5] Katherine F. Lenroot and Emma Lundberg, *Juvenile Courts at Work*, No. 141, Washington, U.S. Children's Bureau, 1925.

with great earnestness that he would never drink again. Persuaded by the man's apparent desire to reform, Augustus decided to come to his aid and with the court's permission he put up the necessary bail. The judge suspended sentence for a three-week period and the probationer signed the pledge.

Three weeks later, when the probationer returned to the courtroom with his sponsor, no one would have believed that this was the same ragged, trembling prisoner. The judge, pleased with the metamorphosis, decided not to impose the usual penalty—imprisonment in the house of correction. Instead, he fined the culprit one cent and costs, which, amounting in all to $3.76, were immediately paid. The prisoner remained industrious and sober and, as Augustus comments, was "saved by probation from a drunkard's grave." In his words, "Individuals and communities generally are but too prone to infer evil of a class if they but occasionally observe it in individuals."[6]

It was not until twenty years later, in 1861, that the Illinois legislature authorized the mayor of Chicago to appoint a commissioner before whom boys between the ages of 6 and 17 could be taken on charges of petty offenses. In 1867 the commissioner's authority to place the boys on probation was transferred to judges. In 1869 Massachusetts passed a law providing for supervision of juvenile delinquents by a state visiting agency, entrusting it for the first time to the hands of public officials rather than volunteers like John Augustus and those who followed him.

Probation for adults is not legally permissible in all types of cases. In some states it may not be granted for serious offenses, with the definition of "serious" varying from state to state. In some states it is available only to first offenders, and in others to courts with specified types of jurisdiction, or in counties of specified population.

Probation for juveniles, however, is provided for in the juvenile court acts of all the states and territories, as well as in the federal system. Some state laws, as for example Pennsylvania, make probation mandatory if the child is under 12 years of age. In some jurisdictions a certain period of institutionalization must precede probation, a practice which reflects a misunderstanding of the philosophy of probation. In line with its definition, granting probation should not depend upon the nature of the offense, but should be based on whether rehabilitation is more likely if the young person remains in the community than if he is removed from it. If commitment would be more constructive, probation is not appropriate. In either case, the decision should be based on the individual's need, although the court cannot ignore the effect and impact of that decision on the community to which the child returns.

[6] Quoted in Negley K. Teeters and John Otto Reinemann, *The Challenge of Delinquency*, New York, Prentice-Hall, 1950, p. 386.

Aim

Adequate probation service, according to Lou, "is the heart of the matter if the philosophy of the juvenile court is to be effectively implemented. . . . High-sounding principles, wise statutory provisions, progressive judicial pronouncement, efficient organization, elaborate procedure, perfect record systems and right prescriptions of treatment in which the child himself has too frequently been buried—will be useless and meaningless unless there is a fine personal touch pointing the way to good habits and building up the character of the child." Probation is the human side of the court's work in which the psychological and social implications of behavior play a central and important role. The probation officer is as concerned with justice in human relationships as he is with the preservation of life and property.

In attempting to reshape attitudes and behavior, the probation officer draws upon all forces in the community, as well as upon the positive potentialities of the child and his parents.

> Domination and emotionalism are two of the most harmful attitudes in probation work. . . . The problem of the child must be approached in an unbiased fashion and without the heavy hand of blind force. The probation officer must be objective and free from prejudice and emotional preferences. It is his task to get the facts, weigh them carefully and, on the basis of these findings, institute the necessary measures for the correction of the individual.
>
> In probation we must endeavor to wean the youngsters from a path of evil through sympathetic understanding and friendly guidance.[7]

Although today's terminology differs from that current in the twenties, the basic philosophy of probation today is essentially the same as that outlined by Lou and Van Waters.[8] Modern social work would be in full agreement with the main requirements for probation work mentioned by these pioneers— freedom from prejudice and emotional bias, refraining from the use of force, and the application of knowledge of behavior derived from the natural and social sciences. There would be no quarrel with the credo of the worth, dignity, and integrity of human personality, nor with the fact that it is the probation officer who is the generator in the rehabilitation process. The main difference between the earlier and present interpretations lies in the probation officer's approach to his task and the use he makes of his skills. Today's emphasis is *not on telling people what they should do, but on helping them*

[7] H. H. Lou, *Juvenile Courts in the United States*, Chapel Hill, The University of North Carolina Press, 1927, pp. 148 ff.

[8] Miriam Van Waters, "Force *versus* Knowledge; Some of the Problems of Probation," *Proceedings*, National Probation and Parole Association, 1923, pp. 155-64.

to plan for themselves and encouraging them in their attempts to carry out realistic plans—realistic, in the sense of being within the realm of possibility in view of the individual's capacity and his alternatives.

Social Casework and Probation Compared

Like the issues raised in the relation of social workers and police officers (see Chapter 13), there are differences of opinion as to whether social work can be effective in a court setting, and whether the usual training of the probation officer equips him for the delicate and often difficult task of helping people in conflict with the law. To weigh the evidence on this issue we present below the opinions of authorities on the aim of social work and the appropriate role of the social caseworker.

Social casework, Harleigh Trecker writes, is "a professional service rendered to people for the purpose of assisting them as individuals or in groups to attain satisfying relationships and standards of life in accordance with their particular wishes and capacities and in harmony with those of the community."

There are five basic assumptions underlying casework: (1) Every individual must be seen as a person of dignity and worth; (2) behavior, whether acceptable or unacceptable to the community, expresses a need of the individual; (3) an individual can and will change his behavior if the right help is given at the right time and in the right amount; (4) if the offer of help is given before the problem becomes seriously aggravated the response is likely to be better; and (5) the family is the most influential force in the development of personality in the crucial early years.

While social work is predicated on the possibility of change, it recognizes wide variations not only in the ability of individuals to change, but in the rate and the amount of possible change, depending upon the person and the environment. To a certain extent, therefore, every treatment problem, Trecker says, "is a problem in prediction, a problem in selection, and a problem in making the diagnostic judgment as to the extent of the strength which resides in a person and which strength can be used to foster change."[9]

The primary instrument in social work treatment is the social worker's insight, self-awareness, and skill in helping people to change. This is accomplished by acceptance and understanding. If a person in trouble refuses to accept controls which the social worker is personally powerless to alter, the social worker acquaints him with the consequences of his choice and explains that he cannot protect the delinquent from the negative consequences if he chooses to continue his disapproved conduct.

[9] Harleigh Trecker, "Social Work—Principles in Probation," *Federal Probation,* Vol. 19, no. 1 (March 1955), p. 9.

A professional relationship is essential if a bridge of understanding is to reach from the social worker to the individual and enable the latter not only to understand his difficulties but to decide what he wishes to do and can do to overcome them. This process involves both the caseworker and the client, because "participation engages, motivates and mobilizes the individual for change."

In the case of Carol, Jer'e Merritt, a probation officer trained in social casework, fulfilled the role of a sincere and interested helper. She made no prejudgments, accepted Carol despite her behavior, helped her to mobilize her strengths and assets, and to accept the necessary limits which society placed on her conduct.

Comparing the concepts of social casework and of probation, then, it is clear that their *purposes* are essentially the same. The tasks of the probation officer and of the social worker are, however, dissimilar in some respects: criteria for intake, the client's role, the agency's position vis-à-vis the client, the pressure of time, and the point at which the relationship is severed.

In a nonjudicial agency, the social caseworker enters the case at the request of the client. The client, therefore, has a voice in initiating the relationship. In contrast, the probation officer receives his case on the order of the court, following an official complaint. Thus neither the probation officer nor the probationer has any choice in initiating the relationship. The court is unable to limit or control its intake once its jurisdiction has been established. Such considerations as volume of work, lack of resources, accessibility or amenability to treatment, which an agency under private auspices can fall back upon in refusing service, are not available to the court. The clients are there and even though they have not come of their own free will, they must be served.

In much of current social work theory, there is the assumption, based on service to neurotics, that the caseworker cannot be effective in dealing with an unwilling client. Some progress, however, has been made with this type of client in the use of what has been called "aggressive casework," initiated by the Youth Board in New York City. This will be discussed more fully in Chapter 28.

Another approach to preparing the unwilling client for treatment is based on a hypothesis originally advanced by Dr. Donald Bloch, that hostile delinquent behavior may be a defense reaction against the intense anxiety aroused at the thought of the close contact between the delinquent and the therapist in a treatment relationship.[10] Experimenting in 1952 with a program to restore sailors and marines to active duty, Douglas Grant formed

[10] J. Douglas Grant, "The Problem of the Unwilling Client—A Hypothesis and Its Investigation," *Journal of Correctional Psychology*, Vol. 2, no. 1 (March 1955), pp. 10-12.

groups of 20 sailors and marines under the direction of a supervisory team of specially selected marines and a clinical psychologist as consultant.

For nine weeks all members of the group lived in closest proximity in their work, in their play, in their schooling, and in the group therapy sessions. It was hoped that the intensive contacts in the small group would arouse so much anxiety that the individual sailors and marines would eventually be willing to participate in a program of therapy which would bring about a change in their behavior. Thus, instead of waiting until the clients ask for help, the research team planned to introduce anxiety-producing procedures to accelerate request for treatment. The factors studied were: (1) the personality characteristics of the individual members; (2) those of the supervisory team; (3) the interaction of each member of the group in assessing the success of the plan.

After six months the men were followed up to see the effect of the program on their performance when they returned to active duty.[11] The results disclosed decisive differentials in the success rates. Obviously the odds would favor the men with the high scores on the social maturity scale. *But* among them *only* the men who were consistently and skillfully supervised responded favorably and were able to carry over the changed attitudes when returned to active duty. The program made no dent on the subjects with low social maturity scores, regardless of the quality of supervision.

The authors note two important implications:[12]

1. In the armed forces "the cost of military recidivism could be reduced by installing a Closed Living Group program with effective supervision for high maturity inmates."

2. Studies of *institutional* effectiveness need to consider all three factors: kinds of subjects, kinds of supervisors, kinds of programming.

We would add that these findings might also apply to therapy programs under court or other auspices, as for example Highfields (see Chapter 24).

Another dissimilarity between probation and social casework in a family or children's agency is the pressure of time imposed by the court calendar. Material must be available in time for the judge to render adequate decisions. Emotions likely to be aroused by referral to the court, together with the pressure for speed, may make it difficult to develop the kind of a relationship between the delinquent and the probation officer necessary for a dispassionate review of the facts and the circumstances which bring the young person into the court.

Furthermore, an investigation under court auspices sometimes results

[11] J. Douglas Grant and Marguerite I. Grant, "A Group Dynamics Approach to the Treatment of Nonconformists in the Navy," *The Annals*, American Academy of Political and Social Science, No. 322 (March 1959), pp. 126-35.
[12] *Ibid.*, p. 134.

in the curtailment of personal liberty, as when the court's decision is to commit the defendant to an institution. The ordinary social agency contact, on the other hand, rarely involves such curtailment.

A further difference between probation and social casework is that the caseworker in the family agency, for example, enters the case in a position to initiate treatment. In the court, however, the decision rests entirely with the judge who, by virtue of his status, may disagree with the probation officer's interpretation of the facts as indicating the need for casework services. Illustrations of such differences of opinion were cited in Chapter 15.

A final difference is that probation is not terminated at the will of the client but at the discretion of the court, which may not always coincide with the judgment of the probation officer. In contrast, in the usual social agency contact, clients either automatically terminate the agency's services by their failure to return for an appointment, or decide together with the social worker that the helping process has gone as far as it can, in which event the case is closed by mutual consent.

The Formal Steps in Probation

Social Study

The probation officer's aim in the preliminary investigation is to understand the child as an individual in his social situation in order to assist the judge in making an appropriate disposition of the case. It will be recalled that the implications of Carol's statements to the police were quite different after Miss Merritt was able to pierce the girl's tough and ugly outer shell.

While information regarding the social, emotional, physical, and psychological aspects are all significant, the focus in scope of the social study depend upon the purpose and function of the agency. For example, in medical social service, the focus is on helping the patient to get well more quickly, just as the visiting teacher's aim is to aid the child's progress in school. Since the first task of the probation officer is to determine the eligibility of the young person for the court's services as defined by law, his initial social study[13] is therefore concerned with ascertaining whether an offense has been committed, and whether the child is in need of court care. The answer depends on the investigation, and the adequacy of the investigation in turn depends upon the training and experience of the officer and the time allotted for the completion.

Having determined that the young person is eligible for court care, the probation officer's next task is to decide whether the child's need can be

[13] See discussion on the nature of social *versus* legal evidence, Chapter 14.

most effectively met (1) at home without court supervision; (2) with supervision or probation; or (3) away from home, either in a substitute family or in an institution. To perform this function adequately requires a social diagnosis.

Diagnosis

The process of determining the significance and relation of the findings to each other and to the client is called diagnosis. In probation, social diagnosis means assessing the main problem and the applicability of social controls. This process is illustrated in Miss Merritt's contacts with Nancy:

I first met Nancy while she was being held in detention at the Marion County Juvenile Center—after a long series of delinquent acts like excessive drinking with a crowd of older teenagers, persistent truancy from school, curfew violations and even suspicion of theft. Nancy was not yet 16. Basically an attractive girl, with dark hair and big brown eyes, her appearance was badly marred by an adolescent skin condition.

To me she was sullen and defiant, unwilling to talk, unwilling to look me in the eye. She answered my questions with monosyllables or a shrug of her shoulders. Almost anyone would feel annoyed and hurt by her obvious unwillingness to make friends but casework training teaches a probation officer to concentrate on the challenge hidden in such behavior. In Nancy's case, the challenge was great.

I learned that Nancy had tried three times to commit suicide—by slashing her wrists, turning on the gas and by an overdose of sleeping pills from a neighbor's medicine chest. The psychiatric report from the Child Guidance Clinic interpreted these suicide attempts as bids for recognition and affection.

I was afraid I'd never get through to Nancy. During her stay in detention, I dropped in to see her almost daily and took her for rides in my car. We'd stop at a drive-in for ice cream; Nancy always refused to go into a restaurant with me.

Then I took her to an understanding dermatologist who explained her skin condition to her and agreed to treat her. As we left him, Nancy remarked, "Let's stop at the drive-in on the way back and I'll buy you a cup of coffee." From that moment, I knew I was in. Still, it took weeks before Nancy trusted me with her whole story.

Her mother, she told me, had run off with another man three years before, when Nancy was 12, leaving behind a mountain of unpaid bills which her father was still struggling to pay off. Nancy had one brother, who soon quarreled with the father and enlisted in the air force, leaving Nancy and her father alone.

The father worked long hours. His wife's desertion, his son's anger, his debts, all bore down heavily upon him; he was totally unprepared for bringing up a troubled adolescent girl by himself. At first he did try but he just didn't know how. He began to retreat into a shell. Contacts between father and daughter gradually withered away.

It was during this period that Nancy ran wild—stayed out late, ran around town with an older and tougher crowd, drank beer until she was sick at her stomach. But that wasn't really much fun. Her suicide attempts followed. Then her school absences became more frequent.

"It does a lot of good just to blurt it all out," Nancy told me finally.[14]

Social diagnosis, however, does not immediately and automatically suggest the treatment plan, nor is it a one-time process. In the course of supervision of the probationer, the second step in probation, the diagnosis may change. The initial task, however, is to see the young person's problem as he defines it, and to find out what he wishes to do about it and what additional factors might influence the immediate problem or possible treatment. It is not necessarily the function of the probation officer any more than it is of the social worker in any agency to do something about everything that he sees diagnostically. Although it is important to see the situation as a whole, it is another thing to assume responsibility for doing something specific about a given area.

When I consulted the psychiatrist who had seen Nancy at the Child Guidance Clinic, he told me: "Nancy needs a mother-figure on whom she can depend, who can fill the gap in her life. We'll continue her visits here but you're the first person who has really got through to her and you can probably do a great deal for her."

Ordinarily a probation officer is careful not to take on a motherly role. But casework training gives you flexibility. I saw that this was the best way I could do my job as probation officer. Also I knew the Child Guidance Clinic would help me if necessary.[15]

Miss Merritt had the advantage of consultation with the psychiatrist at the Child Guidance Clinic (see Chapter 17) who helped diagnose the core of the problem.

Supervision

In ordinary casework the major goal in treatment is to help the client achieve the fullest possible measure of self-reliance, socially, emotionally, and financially. Because delinquent behavior is so often the result of faulty training, the probation officer may decide to concentrate on helping parents assume their proper responsibilities. In such cases he may work only incidentally with the delinquent himself.

---

[14] Jer'e Merritt, *op. cit.*, p. 8. Page references are to reprint.
[15] *Ibid.*, p. 9.

Because of the large number of cases for whom most probation officers are responsible (75-150), they have had to devise ways of seeing their probationers more or less en masse. In referring to a county in which a single probation officer was responsible for supervising several hundred children, Miss Merritt realistically says, "The most she could do was to shuffle their papers about as the flood of delinquency mounted around her."

Often the officer requires the probationer to report on a certain day in a specific school room. On such occasions the probation officer will ask for the child's school report, and may possibly check on his school attendance. This procedure obviously cannot be much more than a routine contact somewhat similar to the health examinations of the school doctor, who checks a whole line of children by asking them to stick out their tongues and pulling down their eyelids.

While home visits are definitely preferable, they too will be perfunctory if the probation officer has the usual heavy caseload. Probation officers have been seen to visit their clients in crowded tenement sections, calling up the stairwell to save themselves climbing stairs, to converse with a parent. The ensuing conversation is usually a series of questions. Is the child obedient? Attending school regularly? Faithful in his religious observances? This type of service is hardly likely to be helpful in effecting a change in a child's behavior. If the caseload of the officer is small enough (25-30) to permit relaxed and unhurried home visits, he is more likely to be able to help both the child and the family mobilize their strengths and their assets.

Use of Community Resources

Because of the nature of the situations that come to the court, the probation officer must be fully familiar with the various facilities which the community provides, in order to help in securing jobs, changes in school programs, tie-ups with recreational agencies, and necessary medical services. When the housing shortage is not too acute, he can sometimes assist families in moving to more appropriate quarters.

> To help girls like Nancy—and boys too—I make use of all the social resources our city provides. My youngsters take part in the city recreation program, in teen-age canteens, in a wide variety of church groups and in community centers where they learn to dance, to work cooperatively and to play games in a healthy, unselfconscious manner. Thus they build friendships with the opposite sex of a kind society accepts and approves.
> Ordinarily such programs by themselves are not enough to attract and hold children in trouble. They steer clear of any group programs. Like Nancy, they must have first of all a warm personal relationship

with an adult they like and can trust. When I helped Nancy join in organized group activities she could do it because she had me to bring her troubles to when difficulties arose. She could hash out with me the little quarrels and squabbles which might otherwise have thrown her for a loss. Nancy even brought her boy friends around to meet me and secure my approval.

I helped Nancy find out that there was a course for practical nurses where in one year she could earn her cap. That year is almost up and I wish you could see Nancy today. No longer sullen, defiant and unkempt, she now comes bursting into my office, tastefully dressed and well groomed, with smiling face and eyes asparkle, eager to share with me her latest news.[16]

In helping Nancy, Miss Merritt took her

. . . to her weekly appointment with the dermatologist. I helped her make up a clothes budget and spend it wisely. I taught her new dishes to cook for her father. I remembered her birthday with a small gift and sent her postcards during my vacation—all simple measures designed to give Nancy a feeling that she was liked and respected.

Soon she was coming to see me with her problems as she would have come to her mother. Boy problems, for example. Nancy didn't want to be a tramp; few girls do. But she did want to make friends and have fun.[17]

The dilemma of uneasy and rejected teen-agers such as Nancy has been described by Stephan H. Kneisel (formerly consultant for the National Probation and Parole Association) in unforgettable terms.

Most of these girls . . . are not driven by raw sex hunger but by an insatiable drive to try out their charms on the most fascinating of all creatures—boys. Unfortunately, their sense of personal inadequacy and worthlessness is so great that they are convinced their only hope of attracting boys is by offering their bodies. Many of them tell us frankly how lonely they were as children and how they lacked the knack of making friends with either boys or girls. Then suddenly and unexpectedly they begin to mature a bit—and wonder of wonders, older boys begin to take an interest in them for their budding charms.

The rejected girl's response is just what you would expect. She is willing to offer anything, so long as she can hold a boy's or a man's attention and remain important to someone.[18]

In addition to her responsibilities for cases like Nancy and Carol, Miss Merritt's typical week includes:

16 *Ibid.*, p. 10.
17 *Ibid.*, p. 11.
18 Quoted in *ibid.*, pp. 9-10.

. . . a high school boy on probation for stealing a car [who] phones me to say he's just got three F's on his report card and is quitting school tomorrow.

A boy of 11 who calls to say his mother is sprawled out drunk on the kitchen floor and there's nothing to eat for supper.

A girl probationer who drops in to tell me she's worried about her attractive, scatterbrained younger sister, who has taken to running around with an older man.

A boy who breaks in excitedly to say he can land a badly needed after school job as a messenger—if I can help him get a bicycle by tomorrow morning; he's stolen before, but he doesn't want to steal this time.[19]

Jer'e Merritt's story of probation service under Judge Hoffman in Indianapolis illustrates how the convictions of public spirited citizens and the leadership of a judge who recognizes the need for adequately trained probation officers can convince even conservative taxpayers' associations that good probation service is a necessity. Unfortunately, only a handful of juvenile courts have the services of a probation staff as well equipped as Jer'e Merritt.

Another attempt to make probation services effective is an experiment initiated in Provo, Utah, in 1956.[20] It was designed to enlist the cooperation of the whole community to help boys who have not benefited from the conventional services provided by an overtaxed probation staff. To be eligible for the program the boys must be between the ages of 13 and 17 and have been in the court on more than one ocasion for offenses against property— for example, burglary, car theft, shoplifting, or malicious mischief. As a condition of his probation status the boy must agree to attend the group sessions two hours a day, five days a week from 4 to 6 PM, for a period of time determined by the director of the program.

The program has two phases. Phase one is directed by Professor Empey, a sociologist. In addition to the group activities in athletics, handicrafts and auto mechanics, there is individual remedial school work and counseling. The distinctive aspects of Phase I of the program are the semiweekly guided group discussions, trips to community facilities, business and otherwise, and group discussions with carefully selected inmates of nearby prisons. These prisoners are interested in helping the boys, identify with them and help them face the reality of the consequences of continuing delinquent careers. This phase of the program is somewhat similar to that of Alcoholics Anonymous.

"The whole emphasis of the program is upon using the group as an instrument . . . other activities serve primarily to provide a community of

[19] *Ibid.*, p. 11.
[20] Lamar T. Empey, *The Provo Experiment in Delinquency*, Provo, Utah, Brigham Young University, May 1959.

experience, diagnostic information and a series of new experiences upon which group discussions can center."[21] Like the guided group interaction at Highfields the aim is to establish and maintain group norms with which the delinquent will wish to identify and become aware that there are alternative ways of looking at himself and society.

In phase two of the program, the boys are offered opportunities to channel the anxiety induced in the group discussion into useful activities. Opportunities are made available to serve as apprentices in service stations and so forth. Summer jobs are provided by the U.S. Forest Service. Through the participation of a professional and lay council, a variety of services—including the help of big brothers and the opportunity for discussions with the parents—are provided. The training and the experience on these apprentice jobs help the boy learn how to work and how to behave in school if he still attends. As he learns to maintain himself with a suitable job, he acquires conventional friends and will no longer need to resort to delinquent behavior.

The program is properly designated an *experiment* because its sponsors, including Judge Munroe J. Paxman of the Third Juvenile District Court of Utah, want proof of its effectiveness. They recognize that this means more effective diagnosis which will include the social as well as the psychological characteristics of the delinquents who participate in the various phases of the program. The sponsors hope to be able to compare various treatment methods with respect to the characteristics of the groups, the point of time at which they are introduced and how long they are maintained. And as a measure of outcome they plan to compare recidivist rates with the control group in the community.

Organization of the Probation Department

Although the juvenile court has been in existence for over fifty years and is recognized by every state in the union as an invaluable aid in providing needed services to disturbed and delinquent children, more than half of the 3000 counties in the United States have no probation service for juveniles. Among the juvenile courts that do have probation officers, not all the officers are full-time employees. Some have additional employment as sheriffs, bailiffs, clerks of the court, truant officers, welfare workers. According to the National Probation and Parole Association estimate, the 3700 currently employed are only one third of the number needed.[22]

[21] *Ibid.*, p. 3.
[22] Will C. Turnbladh, "Substitutes for Imprisonment," *The Annals*, American Academy of Political and Social Science, No. 293 (May 1954), pp. 112-15.

Appointment of Officers

In discussing the judge's role in the juvenile court, mention was made of his responsibility for choosing the court staff. If the probation staff is not under civil service, the judge may ocasionally respond to political pressure, and appoint probation officers who are not specially qualified for their tasks.

If probation officers have civil service status, they are appointed from eligible lists based on competitive written and oral examinations. A few communities have set up a voluntary merit system for the appointment of probation personnel. In some states the probation officers are employees of the state, serve on a statewide basis, or occasionally are assigned to one or more counties. In other communities probation officers are certified by state welfare departments or civil service agencies for local appointments. In Los Angeles the chief probation officer, who, incidentally, is as highly paid as the judge, is appointed by the county board of supervisors, probably because the probation department is independent of the court. In Alameda County and San Francisco, on the other hand, the judge appoints the chief probation officer, who in turn is responsible for appointing other members of the staff.

One of the shortcomings of the civil service system is the frequent stipulation that the candidate must be a legal resident of the state in which the opening exists. Such a residence requirement, as well as the principle of promotion from within the ranks, while a legitimate effort to protect the rights of workers, is also obviously an attempt on the part of those already employed to limit competition. This is a characteristic shared by other associations such as medical and legal societies, boards of education, labor unions, and so forth. Under the civil service system, tenure is granted unless the position is abolished—hardly likely in the field of probation. If, however, the officer is appointed by the judge, his tenure may be coterminous with that of the judge.

Qualifications of Officers

The stories of Carol and Nancy suggest how important well-qualified as well as well-trained probation officers are to the effective functioning of the juvenile court. Before 1913, when probation was put into the classified civil service system in New York State, "kindly ex-policemen or retired subway guards with political pull could be entrusted with the delicate task of analyzing a neurotic personality and advising the court about the factors which led to a broken home."[23] The requirement of a high school education as a minimum

23 Paul Blanshard and Edwin J. Lukas, "Probation and Psychiatric Care for Adolescent Offenders," New York, Society for the Prevention of Crime, 1942, p. 5.

for probation officers was initiated in New York State in 1928. Recognition of the need for better trained personnel, whether police, judges, or probation officers, to deal constructively with people in trouble has increased as the social sciences have taught us more about the difficulty of interpreting and changing behavior.

Addressing itself to the formulation of principles, the professional council of the National Probation and Parole Association, in consultation with administrators in the correctional field, lists the following as desirable experience and educational requirements for probation officers:

1. A bachelor's degree from a college or university of recognized standing or its educational equivalent with courses in the social sciences; and

2. One year of paid full-time experience under competent supervision in an approved social agency or related field (teaching, personnel work in industry, casework in an institution or correctional agency).

These educational minima, like those for other professions, apply to new appointees. For the majority of the old-timers a conciliatory statement adds that there are probation officers who have attained professional competence but who do not meet these standards. Similarly, there are persons teaching today whose native ability, character, and experience make them effective teachers notwithstanding their lack of a college degree.

As regards character and personality, the Association includes as essential: "Good health, physical endurance, intellectual maturity, emotional stability, tact, dependability, adaptability, resourcefulness, sincerity, humor, ability to work with others, tolerance, patience, objectivity, capacity to win confidence, respect for human personality, and genuine affection for people." One is tempted to say: "All this and heaven too, for $65.00 a week!"

In addition to these educational and personal qualifications, MacCormick feels that a good probation officer must have faith not only in his charge but also in his charge's desire to help himself: "I do not mean blind faith in individual probationers; it is not realistic to expect all of them to succeed. Putting a person on probation is taking a calculated risk. When one is dealing with the imponderables of human motivation, a decision to take that risk is likely to have components of hope and faith. Faith is a great spiritual power but there is no field in which 'faith without works' is more certain to fail than the probation field."[24]

Obviously, if as suggested in our discussion there is an essential similarity between casework and the probation process, in spite of the difference due to the court setting, the basic training for casework and probation should be the same. Two distinguished lawyers have recorded their opinions, shared

[24] Austin MacCormick, "The Potential Value of Probation," *Federal Probation,* Vol. 19, no. 1 (March 1955), p. 7.

by the faculties of many schools of social work, that training in a graduate school of social work is a prerequisite for effective probation work.[25]

A contrary view is that of the sociologist, Reckless.[26] He considers courses in criminology and in the field of juvenile and adult correction a better preparation for the probation officer than casework training. Although he does not claim that such courses cannot be given in schools of social work, he believes that the emphasis on psychiatry in schools of social work leaves little room in the curricula for background in sociological and criminological theory and practice. In his opinion university departments of sociology offer a more appropriate setting for training of probation officers. Many universities, however, look askance at the inclusion of practical training in an academic curriculum.

Reckless disagrees also with the requirements which call for field work for the probation officer simultaneously with classroom instruction and under skilled supervisors to help the student practice the theories and procedures expounded in the classroom. The field work supervisor attached to a school of social work is skilled as an *educator* and as a *practitioner*. He allocates definite time for discussion with the student and introduces cases illustrating different types of problem situations at the rate at which the student is prepared to work with them. Reckless, however, is satisfied to let the prospective probation officer learn to sink or swim without organized and planned assistance from a supervisor.

In-Service Training Programs

Since obviously not all the knowledge that a probation officer needs can be gained from his academic and field work experience, if he has not had specialized training it should be provided on the job. Like big industry, probation departments in the large courts have instituted training programs in the interest of more efficient functioning of their officers.

The Citizenship Training Group, Inc., which is affiliated with the Boston Juvenile Court, conducts an in-service training program with the cooperation of the presiding judge of that court and his probation staff.[27] This program includes a survey of the relevant statutes and procedures, field trips to correctional institutions and other agencies, training in work at the court, case-

25 Walter Gellhorn, *Children and Families in the Courts of New York City,* New York, Dodd, Mead, 1954; and Kenneth Johnson, "The Role of Social Work Education in Preparing Personnel for the Correctional Field," *Federal Probation,* Vol. 20, no. 3 (Sept. 1956), pp. 54-58.

26 Walter C. Reckless, "Training Probation and Parole Personnel," *Focus,* Vol. 27, no. 2 (March 1948), pp. 44-48.

27 George H. Grosser, "An Internship for Probation Officers," *Focus,* Vol. 28, no. 3 (May 1949), pp. 75-77.

work with individual offenders and their families, and group work with juvenile delinquents. It is designed chiefly for students in the second-year program of schools of social work or graduate students with some training in the social sciences.

Minnesota, New Hampshire, Ohio, Wisconsin and Pennsylvania all conduct in-service training programs under university auspices. Through its St. Lawrence University Institute, New York State conducts summer seminars for the training of personnel in the correctional field. California, however, appears to have taken the lead in recognition of the need for in-service training. In Los Angeles County newly appointed probation officers are given a one-year training course before being employed full time. They receive $150 per month, in addition to the G.I. allowance if they are veterans. When they pass the civil service examination at the end of their year's training, they are assigned as deputy probation officers. The University of Southern California and the University of California in Berkeley have both instituted extensive courses for probation and other correctional personnel.

Using grants which state departments have made available, some schools of social work are currently planning what are called "work-study" programs for probation and police officers. These arrangements permit officers to attend classes, acquire field work experience, and remain on the payroll of the organization which employs them. This plan makes it possible for persons with family responsibilities to obtain the necessary training without too great a financial sacrifice.

Currently, under the auspices of the Council of Social Work Education, the newly established division on training in the U.S. Children's Bureau is engaged in the process of setting up various training programs.[28]

Allocation of Work

The judge is usually responsible for outlining the duties of the probation officer. If the court employs more than two officers, one will be designated as chief and he in turn may have the responsibility for choosing his assistant. If the staff is fairly large, as it is in big cities, the chief probation officer may be assigned the responsibility not only for the immediate direction of his assistant but also for the supervision of the field officers and clerical staff.

In courts employing more than two probation officers, it is important that the three main functions of the probation department be clearly defined:

[28] Elliot Studt, Milton Chernin, et al., *Training Personnel for Work with Juvenile Delinquents*, Parts I-IV, No. 348, Washington, U.S. Children's Bureau, 1954; and *Perspectives and Guides in the Expansion of Social Work Education for the Correctional Field*. Council on Social Work Education, New York, 1959.

(1) To sift intake, which involves a review of the requests coming to the court and a preliminary decision as to whether the case should be referred to the court or dropped.[29] (2) If the decision is referral to the court, to make a preliminary investigation prior to the hearing in order to assist the judge in deciding on the appropriate disposition. (3) To supervise the probationer if the court decides that the young person is to remain under its jurisdiction. In the process of supervision illustrated by the cases of Carol and Nancy, the probation officer is the liaison between the court and the community in the interests of the child.

In some large courts, investigation is separated from supervision. In others, the officer who makes the investigation is also charged with responsibility for supervision. The advantages of combining the two functions in one person are that the process of investigation is really the first step in treatment. Even in an initial interview some sort of rapport is established between the officer and the probationer, and it is to the probationer's advantage if this relationship is not broken off through the assignment of another officer as supervisor. Miss Merritt was responsible for both investigations and supervision.

Those who propose separate assignment of the two functions believe that they require different emphasis and different methods of work. They assume that some officers are better qualified for investigations whereas others are more efficient in supervision. Given social work training, this argument, however, is groundless because the same skills are as necessary for an adequate case study as for supervision. The one difference might be that some probation officers function better with short-term assignments than under a continuing responsibility for extended care, especially if the situation demands a great deal of self-control by the officer when challenged by aggressive behavior.

To minimize travel time, many large courts assign the probation officer to work with persons residing in a specific territory. Some courts assign probation officers to probationers of the same race, religious affiliation, or sex. It is generally suggested that it is preferable to have a woman probation officer supervise older girls, whereas in the supervision of young children, the sex of the officer may be less important. Yet qualifications and training being equal, the sex of the officer should make no more difference in supervision than does the sex of the doctor treating sick patients. While overcoming initial resistance may be easier if the probation officer is of the same sex or race as the probationer, a caseworker's training should make it possible for him to serve any client irrespective of his religion, his race, or his sex.

[29] See Chapter 15 for description of various types of intake units, and reference to the practice of unofficial supervision in some courts.

Summary

This chapter has illustrated and defined probation as one of the principal methods available to the juvenile court judge in his decision to redirect a young person's antisocial behavior while he remains in the community.

The probation process has been defined as a reshaping and reconditioning of attitudes and behavior. It draws upon the social sciences to help the probationer mobilize his strengths and assets in the pursuit of his own needs without conflict with society. While there are acknowledged differences between probation and casework in a nonauthoritative agency, the helping process is essentially the same. It is based on the acceptance of the integrity of the client's individuality and his willingness to participate in the readjustment process. Perhaps the probation officer requires more skill than the social caseworker, since he is more often faced by the resisting and unwilling client than is the worker in an agency to which the client comes voluntarily.

The two main functions of the probation officer are investigation and supervision. He investigates in order to enable the judge to make the appropriate disposition, and he supervises the probationer after adjudication by the court. Officers responsible for investigations are not always responsible for the supervision of probationers. Allocation of the work of the individual probation officers is usually on a district basis.

Opinion differs as to whether probation departments should be under direct supervision of the judge, the usual set-up, or should be a treatment service administered independently of the court.

Opinions also differ as to whether probation is casework and what are the appropriate educational and training requirements for probation officers. According to some lawyers and social work school faculties, a college degree and at least one or two years of training in a school of social work are essential. Reckless, representing the views of some sociologists, holds that since probation differs from casework, special training in a school of social work, which usually emphasizes the psychiatric approach, is unnecessary. In his opinion, courses in sociology are preferable. Both groups agree, however, on a long roster of inner and outer qualities essential for probation officers. While both agree that in-service training is necessary, opinions vary as to its content. Several experiments are currently in process in different sections of the country and under a variety of auspices in efforts to meet the increasing needs for adequate probation.

CHAPTER 17

Psychiatric Services Available to the Juvenile Court

IN TUNE WITH THE GROWING EMPHASIS IN THE LAST THIRTY YEARS ON MENTAL hygiene, some courts, particularly in the large urban areas, are using psychiatric services to increase their effectiveness. In Chapter 6, which reviewed the theoretical basis of the psychiatric approach in understanding and explaining behavior, it was noted that although there is general agreement that all behavior, approved or disapproved, is a response to inner and outer pressures, there are differences of opinion as to the dynamics of these responses and consequently as to the best way to redirect them.

In this chapter we shall: (1) describe the kinds of clinic services available to juvenile courts across the country; (2) present the findings of the occasional studies of clinic services to the courts; (3) summarize some recent suggestions including the use of group psychotherapy for overcoming some of the more patent obstacles to effective individual psychiatric treatment in a court setting.

Auspices

Psychiatric services are available to the juvenile court (1) in clinics either directly under court auspices or limiting their services to referrals from the court; and (2) in community clinics whose services are occasionally called upon by the courts. Data on the *distribution* of these services is provided by a publication of the National Association for Mental Health.[1]

1 "Outpatient Psychiatric Clinics and Other Mental Health Resources in the United States and Territories," *Directory 1954-55*, The National Association for Mental Health, Inc., in cooperation with the National Institute of Mental Health, 1957. The subsequent financing of the Mental Health Boards has undoubtedly increased the number of clinics.

Clinics Attached to Juvenile Courts

To assist the judge of the Cook County (Chicago) Juvenile Court in deciding on appropriate disposition and treatment for the young persons who came to that court, Dr. William Healy established the first court clinic in 1909. Currently juvenile courts administer or have the exclusive service of psychiatric clinics in Boston, Buffalo, Pittsburgh, Philadelphia, Washington, D.C., and Essex County, New Jersey. Each of New York City's five boroughs and Westchester County has a court clinic under its jurisdiction. In the Middle West, there are court clinics in Cincinnati, Cleveland, and Toledo, and in the Far West only in Los Angeles, where the clinic is operated by the County Probation Office. The only southern court with a clinic is Jefferson County, Kentucky, in which Louisville is located. Each of these clinics has been in existence for some time.

Community Clinics

The current trend is for the court to use community clinics increasingly, although these too are not equally available in all states. Classifying the states according to the number of communities which report child guidance service or specify service to persons under 21, the rank order is: New York, 83; Massachusetts, 31; California, 27; Pennsylvania, 20; Michigan, 17; New Jersey, Ohio, and Wisconsin, between 11 and 13 each. Seven states—Arkansas, Idaho, Montana, Nevada, New Mexico, North and South Dakota, the Virgin Islands, and Puerto Rico—report no clinics exclusively for children. The remaining states have less than 10 clinics each. In most states only three or four communities are served by child guidance clinics.

New York City reported 49 psychiatric clinics which state specifically that they serve children. This number includes branches of central clinics such as those maintained by the Bureau of Child Guidance of the Board of Education.

The number of children served varies with the size of the community, the size of the staff, the number of days that the clinic is open for business, and whether its function is treatment or only diagnosis. In the large cities, clinic services are usually available five days a week. In the small cities, however, the services of a traveling clinic may be available only one or two days a month. According to current reports, the actual case loads of the clinics range from as few as 12 to almost 1400. The majority of the clinics in the 1952 Directory of the National Association for Mental Health reported less than 100 children under care in that year. This figure was not given for

1954-55. When a uniform reporting system is universally accepted we will have better data. In any case a directory listing carries no estimate of the quality of the service.

Aims and Methods of Treatment

Clinics differ not only in their auspices but in the personality, interests, and training of the clinic director and his staff. The nature of the problems for which they offer service and the technical methods employed also differ.[2] In the orthodox tri-discipline clinic—psychiatry, psychology, and social work— patients are treated by the psychiatrists. Nevertheless, plans for treatment are based on diagnostic formulation to which the psychiatrist, psychiatric social worker, psychologist, often a pediatrician, and sometimes an educator have contributed their thinking. In many clinics the treatment responsibility may be assigned to any one of the three disciplines according to the aims of the treatment, and the nature and severity of the personality problem.

The needs of the patient will dictate whether the *child is to be treated or his parent or both;* by which discipline each is to be treated; what the goals of treatment in relation to the psychic life will be; whether the direct treatment is to be enhanced by planned real-life experiences or even displaced by them.[3] For example, the psychiatrically trained social worker will be assigned the major responsibility (1) in those situations in which the child is preoccupied with reality factors; (2) if opening up the inner problems would be too threatening; or (3) if "role-playing" appears to be the appropriate therapeutic relationship. On the other hand, the clinic psychiatrist will assume major responsibility for working with the patient when the therapeutic goal is a more profound re-orientation of the personality. While the social worker also assists the patient in the re-orientation process, because the psychiatrist's goal is different, he uses different methods in handling the patient's dream material and associations.

As the psychodynamic study of the patient and his environment progresses the clinic team arrives at a tentative working diagnosis, a treatment plan, and treatment objectives. In the traditional child guidance clinic the child is assigned to the psychiatrist for therapy, and the parent—usually the mother—to the psychiatric social worker for casework treatment. Experimentation with other allocations of function has been carried out in many child guidance clinics. For example, in some clinics the child is assigned to

[2] *Psychiatric Social Work in the Psychiatric Clinic,* Report No. 16, Committee on Psychiatric Social Work of the Group for the Advancement of Psychiatry, Topeka, Kansas, Sept. 1950, pp. 1-5.
[3] Rose Goldman, "The Psychiatric Social Worker's Treatment Role," *Journal of Psychiatric Social Work,* Vol. 20, no. 2 (Dec. 1950), pp. 65-68.

the social worker and the mother to the psychiatrist. In others, either of two workers or two psychiatrists may be assigned to treat the mother, the other to treat the child. Regardless of the modifications of the original pattern of child guidance treatment, the psychiatric daignosis and psychotherapy are a primary responsibility of the psychiatrist.[4]

The procedure for referring children to the court or the community clinics varies. As a rule the probation officer, or his supervisor if the staff is large, inquires by telephone whether the clinic deals with the problem presented by the child and if so whether appointment time is available. The clinic usually asks that the request for service include a statement of the problem as the court or the referral agency (which may be the school, or the special juvenile division in the police department) sees it.

Whether the referral is to a court or community clinic it is always discussed with the client. The purpose of this discussion is to awaken his recognition of the nature of the problem and to ready him to take some action about solving it. Once the child is accepted by the clinic, the attempt is to make the necessary adjustments in his physical and emotional climate. His problem may be explained to his teachers and other adults who are involved.

The child himself is encouraged to participate in activities in which he is likely to have some success. To develop his potential talents he is directed to various community resources. In every possible way new outlets are sought for his energies and capacities. If his intellectual or physical disabilities appear to separate him from his peers, every effort is made to assist him to overcome this problem. To speed up progress in school, special tutoring or remedial reading is provided. Even plastic surgery is available if indicated.

In recognizing the psychological and environmental handicaps to which many young people are exposed in early childhood the clinics seek to spread the community's understanding of the need to deal constructively with the situations which caused the problem.

As Fink says, "It is only by taking full account of the role of the emotional factors in the development of personality and behaviour that any perceptible progress has been realized. Basic to all this is the belief that there can be no change in behaviour without a change in those elements which produce the behaviour."[5]

While the clinic still retains the title "child guidance" it realizes that its help is offered to both child and parent. Indeed, it has been learned that if help is to have any effect upon the child it must be directed to both parties; for despite the mother's initial insistence that the clinic *make over* her child, no real change takes place until the mother realizes that she is part of the

---

[4] *Psychiatric Social Work in the Psychiatric Clinic*, p. 4.

[5] Arthur E. Fink, Everett E. Wilson, Merrill B. Conover, *The Field of Social Work*, 3rd Ed., New York, Henry Holt, 1957, Chapter 9, pp. 259-66.

situation and must undergo change too. At no point, however, is it the purpose of the clinic to order the life of the parent. It has long since been learned that advice is entirely gratuitous unless it is related to the movement that is taking place within the client.

Unfortunately, in spite of all the clinic's specialized knowledge, it does not have all the answers to the riddle of personality. Nor has it developed sufficient skills to be of *help in every situation* with which it is faced. In the light of our present knowledge and skills there are many children and parents who present difficulties that the clinic simply does not reach. Because of the highly individualized character of the helping process there are no two clients to whom the same specific therapeutic skill can be applied.

Clinics attached to courts are considered by the court and the public as part of the front-line defense against delinquency. Despite this their efforts are subject to criticism within and without the setting in which they operate. There has been an increasing tendency for clinics to divorce themselves from court auspices. Part of the pressure has come because of the belief that clients associate the clinic with the authority of the court and are therefore apt to resist the help when it is offered. There have been some studies of the effectiveness of treatment under court auspices.

Effectiveness of Court Clinic Treatment

Study Results

The lack of success with children referred by the courts is highlighted in the Glueck study of the Judge Baker Clinic attached to the Boston court; by the Healy and Bronner report of their clinics which served the courts in Boston, Detroit, and New Haven; and by Dunham's study of the Wayne County Clinic in Detroit, which was not attached to the court but served it.

The Glueck Study of *One Thousand Juvenile Delinquents*,[6] (delinquents referred by the Boston Juvenile Court to the Judge Baker Clinic) yielded a recidivist rate of 88.2 per cent. In the controversy which followed the publication of these figures, the clinic's protagonists argued that it was being used for diagnosis only, and not for treatment; and that in many cases the clinic recommendations were not followed by the court.[7]

Since the recommendations of the diagnostic clinics appeared to be no more effective than the usual court recommendations in assuring a successful

---

6 Sheldon and Eleanor Glueck, *One Thousand Juvenile Delinquents*, Cambridge, Harvard University Press, 1934.

7 Henry B. Elkind, M.D., and Maurice Taylor, Ph.D., *"One Thousand Juvenile Delinquents: A Critique," Mental Hygiene*, Vol. 18, no. 4 (Oct. 1934), pp. 531-75; see also Thomas D. Eliot, "Suppressed Premises Underlying the Glueck Controversy," *Journal of Criminal Law and Criminology*, Vol. 26, no. 1 (May-June 1935).

outcome of the cases, some court clinics incorporated treatment as well as diagnostic services. In the three clinics set up by Healy and Bronner,[8] full services were offered to a group of delinquents, and an attempt was made to modify the factors in the family situation which appeared to be directly or indirectly responsible for the delinquents' behavior. Even so, 50 per cent of the children continued their delinquent behavior.

Dunham's study of the Wayne County Clinic[9] reveals that although the clinic over the years has increased the number of trained personnel on its staff, decreased the case load, and presumably provided more effective treatment skills, the recidivist rate of young people referred by the court and treated in the clinic has not abated. Furthermore, the services of the clinic have increased in expense, and from the point of view of the community have made little dent in the problem of delinquency.

Obstacles to Effective Treatment

In defense of the clinics serving the courts, whether attached or in the community, it may be argued that the type of case currently referred to them may be less amenable to help than those that they formerly dealt with. This hypothesis, however, has not been tested. It must also be remembered that the demand of the community is frequently for the psychiatrist to play the role of the policeman. The community is concerned with the actual behavior of the person, and not with what he thinks or suffers, the main concern of dynamic psychiatry. While the ultimate objective of psychiatry is the relinquishment of socially disapproved behavior by the delinquent, this is not its immediate objective.

Furthermore, unless the disapproved behavior is a result of psychological stresses, psychiatric treatment is hardly likely to cause its disappearance. Because much delinquent behavior is a reaction to social pressures and deprivations, psychiatry can only help the patients find compensation if they wish to do so. If a clinic is to be effective in reducing delinquency it must estimate the extent to which the delinquency is due to psychological causes. In other words, "delinquency is not a purely intrapsychic phenomenon; it involves social institutions as well as individual activities."[10]

In summarizing the obstacles to effective psychiatric work with delinquents, which inhere both in the attitude of the delinquent and of his family, Witmer reminds us that:[11]

[8] William Healy and Augusta Bronner, *New Light on Delinquency and Its Treatment,* New Haven, Yale University Press, 1936.

[9] H. W. Dunham and L. Adamson, "Clinical Treatment of Male Juvenile Offenders," *American Sociological Review,* Vol. 21 (June 1956), pp. 312-20.

[10] Helen Leland Witmer, *Psychiatric Clinics for Children,* New York, The Commonwealth Fund, 1940, p. 287.

[11] *Ibid.,* p. 293.

1. Some delinquents are too emotionally maladjusted to respond to psychiatric treatment. Healy and Bronner identified 18 per cent in this category.

2. The parents of delinquents are often impoverished, unhappy, discouraged. They are criticized by their neighbors for their discordant home life and neglect of their children. These are the children for whom Healy and Bronner suggested foster-home placement; but when they return home, the disapproved behavior usually reappears.

3. Since their own efforts at punishment were of no avail, many parents are hostile to their delinquent children and fatalistic about what can be done for them.

4. Since the clinic is serving the court, negative attitudes toward the court are apt to carry over into feelings about the clinic itself.

Other discussions of the difficulties facing effective use of court clinics draw attention to: (1) the referral process; (2) the attitude of the probation staff and the judge; (3) problems of diagnosis; (4) the realities—(a) the liabilities in the life situations of the court's clients and (b) the personal limitations of the therapist.

The Referral Process

As we noted earlier, the child referred to the court clinic usually feels that he has no choice—he must accept its service. He is apt to be uncommunicative because, as Peck suggests below, he is not used to talking about his problems, or may not even recognize that he has problems. If he agrees that he has problems he may be afraid that what he says to the psychiatrist will be used against him in the court. Furthermore, parents are often unenthusiastic about clinic services because they are apt to regard the clinic as being on the child's side rather than on theirs.

The Attitudes of the Court Staff

Hartwell, the assistant director of the Division of Mental Hygiene of the Michigan Department of Mental Health, sums up the attitude of the court and the clinic toward each other.[12] The court, he says, has three main complaints against the clinic:

1. The psychiatrist does not believe in punishment and appears to be unconcerned with society's welfare.

2. The clinic staff is apt to be critical and impatient in working with untrained probation officers.

[12] Samuel W. Hartwell, M.D., "The Guidance Clinic and the Court," *Federal Probation,* Vol. 12, no. 3 (Sept. 1948), pp. 3-7.

3. The treatment process is not only slow but seldom seems to help the delinquent child.

On their part, the staff of the psychiatric clinic voice two major criticisms of the probation officer:

1. He expects too much of the clinic which he often consults after instead of before he has decided on the treatment plan for the child.

2. He resents as criticism the efforts of the clinic to obtain better trained probation officers.

The greatest handicap to the clinic, however, is the judge who has no use for the philosophy of child guidance.

Under these conditions the services of a clinic, even if the probation officers are anxious for such service, are hardly likely to be helpful. The criticisms reflect the need for a better interpretation to the court personnel of the clinic's goals, its methods, and its limitations.

Problems of Diagnosis

Another serious obstacle to effective court clinic treatment, which applies too in out-of-court settings, is incorrect diagnosis. Anna Freud, Donald Bloch, and Harris Peck are eloquent on the subject of misdiagnosis in clinic practice.

Anna Freud is concerned about the careless and too frequent use by both clinicians and child welfare workers of "rejection" as the explanation for the troublesome behavior of children.[13] As Anna Freud explains, there are many degrees and types of rejection and it is important to discriminate between mothers who can be helped to cope with their attitudes and those whose rejection appears to be beyond control. Some mothers who consciously or unconsciously are unwilling parents leave the care of their children to others when they go out either to work or to travel. Others may desert their children, psychologically if not physically, because they are so deeply absorbed in their own problems. Each type of rejection evokes its counterpart in the reaction of the child. Some children habitually get lost. Others feel anxious and guilty and unworthy whenever their mother withdraws her attention. A mother who fluctuates between too much and too little attention may invite quarrels, physical reactions such as vomiting, or seemingly insatiable demands for affection from her child.

Anna Freud cautions against labeling as rejection the inevitable frustrations of life which everyone experiences. One must discriminate between the fantasies of rejection expressed by the child and the reality factors in the life situation.

[13] Anna Freud, "Safeguarding the Emotional Health of Our Children," *Case Work Papers, 1954,* National Conference of Social Work, Family Service Association of America, pp. 5-17.

Bloch[14] approaches the problem of diagnosis from a different angle, with the reminder that diagnosis "is not a fact but simply a more or less useful construct erected about that biological, psychological, sociological continuum called a human being." He defines delinquency as a pattern of *interaction* which focuses attention on modes of dealing with *interpersonal* situations. Accordingly, an awareness of the role of the "partner"—parent, teacher, judge, psychiatrist, social worker, police officer, or fantasy figure—is crucial in the treatment outcome.

The delinquent's characteristic response to the partner is conditioned by his earliest childhood experience and the way in which his parents responded to his needs. The delinquent whose parents rejected and punished him anticipates similar responses from the adult community. Thus he is not disappointed when the teacher upbraids him because he is truant or when the policeman uses his nightstick when he catches him in a compromising situation. If, on the other hand, the teacher, policeman, or judge does not respond to the delinquent's provocative behavior, the delinquent can and often does use aggression, flight, perceptual distortions, and misrepresentation as a defense. Occasionally, the delinquent punishes himself by self-mutilation. These devices are the delinquent's efforts to avoid dangerous intimacy and to prove to himself that hostility and aggression are the only types of relations possible for him.

The Realities

THE CHILD'S LIFE SITUATION. Reality factors, to which both Peck and Bloch call special attention, add obstacles to effective treatment of children referred by the courts. Instead of the customary refuge in diagnostic terminology, Peck, formerly psychiatrist at the New York Children's Court, suggests that we re-examine our views of the young person in trouble and reconsider whether the therapeutic and conceptual tools derived from psychoanalytic work with adult middle-class neurotics are appropriate. Among the latter, the psychodynamics are usually internalized; whereas in the lower socio-economic group, from which most apprehended delinquents come, they are acted out. Some of the behavior patterns characteristic of an "acting-out pathology" are therefore just normal reactions in certain socio-economic segments of American society.

If a delinquent were to tell the therapist what he was really thinking in the course of a session, he might speak as follows:

"What do you mean that you want to help me with my problems? What problems? I ain't got none, and if something *was* the matter, what would

14 Donald A. Bloch, "Some Concepts in the Treatment of Delinquency," *Case Work Papers, 1954,* National Conference of Social Work, Family Service Association of America, pp. 84-98.

you do about it—talk to me? I been talked at by bigger wheels than you and that includes principals, cops, teachers, judges, and a lot more. You think I'm bothered about school? What do you think I am, a fruit? Listen, lady, I'm getting along fine and I don't want no nosey social worker telling me what to do. Nope, I'm not worried about what's going to happen to me. In a couple of years I'll probably be in the army anyway."[15]

This reaction, Peck says, is no more psychopathic, amoral, pathological than that of many of this young person's friends in the classroom and the neighborhood who have not been referred to the court.

By definition, all delinquents have done something to get themselves into difficulty with the duly constituted authorities. The punitive attitude of the community is therefore a predictable, though not always a helpful, response. The misbehavior of the young person in the lower economic strata is probably a response to different kinds of frustration than those experienced by the middle-class child, who has generally more opportunities for acceptable compensatory activities.[16] In Peck's words the working-class boy before the court is "a suspicious, guarded, nonverbal, and negativistic 'client' who tends to translate his impulses readily into actions and who is more responsive to peer group pressures than to adult remonstrance. He tends to meet therapeutic overtures with either outright defiance or superficial conformity."[17]

Both Peck and Bloch agree that the staff in the clinic must come to grips with the problem of authority when dealing with acting-out behavior. The usual passive or covert indulgence practiced in some clinics is as ineffective as its opposite, the customary method of the probation staff in setting what are perhaps too strict limits for the probationer. To blame the client because he is unable to use the services offered by an authoritarian agency is to forget that most of the young people who come before the court have been unable to use the services of any type of agency.

PERSONAL LIMITATIONS OF THE THERAPIST. A difference in the class identification of the therapist and the delinquent child referred to the court may also interfere with effective treatment. The therapist who devotes himself to the task of trying to help aggressive, anti-authoritarian, acting-out persons, whether adults or children, must face squarely the fact that his choice of profession may reflect both his need to be omnipotent and the problems he himself may have in dealing with authority because his own parents were either extremely repressive or over-permissive.[18] Therapy, like social work, may represent a profession which offers help with one's own problem. The

[15] Harris B. Peck, "New Approaches in Treating Delinquents," *Casework Papers,* 1955, National Conference of Social Work, Family Service Association of America, p. 21.
[16] See Albert K. Cohen's description of delinquent subculture, Chapter 9.
[17] Peck, *op. cit.,* p. 22.
[18] Bloch, *op. cit.,* pp. 92-95.

desire to get such help may stand in the way of working with people who resist the idea that they need help and who find it difficult to accept anything from anybody.

There may be a panic reaction in the therapist, Bloch says, because of the forced intimacy in the treatment situation. If the patient will not accept help the therapist may be tempted to judge him as bad. On the other hand, there is also the possibility that work with the delinquent "may provide vicarious gratification of hostile, erotic and sadistic impulses often unrecognized." As a reflection of the anxiety which stems from his own feeling of helplessness, the therapist, according to Bloch, is usually only comfortable when he knows what ails everyone around him. His verbal or intellectual efforts to regain control in situations with acting-out delinquents are, as Peck has pointed out, usually ineffective.

The therapist therefore not only needs to be aware of his own problems but to help the staff of the clinic to withstand the "gaff" of the delinquent. This involves helping the staff to explore, understand, and deal with their emotional responses to the delinquent child's aggressive behavior.

The senior supervisor of the Bureau of Mental Health Services of the Domestic Relations Court of New York City[19] emphasizes these points made by Block and Peck. She reminds us that the psychiatric social worker in the clinic has to reconcile three different identifications. First, there is her identification with community culture, which is chiefly middle class; second, she belongs to a subculture, i.e., that of the helping professions, which, as Peck points out, may not agree in all its aspects with the community mores vis-à-vis antisocial behavior; lastly, she needs to recognize the culture of the client who comes to the court.

In describing the values of the majority of the young people who are brought to court, Mrs. Brenner emphasizes that her use of the term "lower-class" to describe the court clients is in a sociological frame of reference. It is a description and not a judgment. It is crucial for the clinician, be he psychiatrist, psychologist, or social worker, to recognize that the court's clients are "the most deprived, the most hurt, the most ill-nourished, and least well-serviced segment of the community."[20] They are often also members of an ethnic minority group.[21] This segment, most sociologists agree, has a set of values easily distinguishable from those of the middle class. If the clinic is to be effective, it *must* recognize the existence of these different value orientations.

To succeed, the worker must help the child before the court (usually

[19] Ruth F. Brenner, "Cultural Implications for a Child Guidance Clinic in a Court Setting," *Social Work*, Vol. 2, no. 3 (July 1957), pp. 26-31.

[20] Molly Harrower, "A New Pattern for Mental Health Services in a Children's Court," *American Journal of Orthopsychiatry*, Vol. 25, no. 1 (Jan. 1955), pp. 1-50.

[21] Brenner, *op. cit.*, p. 28.

there because, unlike the neurotic, he acts out his resistance to authority) to change his conception of authority as embodied in the community and the court. To be helpful, the clinician needs to *understand and accept* the reality of cultural differences and know how to deal with "the dynamics which provoke and stimulate the variety of responses, be they hostile and defensive, overdependent or manipulative."[22]

Group Therapy in a Court Clinic

To meet some of the obstacles to successful individual therapy outlined above, and to cope with the challenge of increasing numbers of young people referred to the court clinic for behavior which ranges from truancy to occasional murder, Peck instituted group therapy in the New York Juvenile Court Clinic program. He tested its use in three differently constituted groups described below.

In the first group were children who had failed to respond to six months of individual treatment in the court clinic. It was hoped that in their peer group they might be able to reveal and talk about ideas and feelings which they did not verbalize when they were alone with the psychiatrist.

The second experimental group was composed of young people at their initial referral to the court. Peck wished to observe the reactions of the boys to each other which would reveal their strengths and their potentialities. Too often, Peck says, therapists give only lip service to understanding the attempts that the individual makes to meet situations which overwhelm him and which may be unfamiliar to the therapist. The group interactions reveal assets as well as liabilities in the behavior patterns of the individual members.

The third group project concentrated on the problems of the retarded reader. Dr. Peck set up three experimental classes. In the first tutorial therapy group seven boys were instructed in reading and also participated in group discussions to help them understand what it was that was interfering with their ability to learn to read. A second group received only remedial reading instructions and a third only group therapy. The first group, in which the remedial reading was used to stimulate group discussion, showed the greatest progress in reading achievement.

Dr. Peck attributed the success of this group to the fact that it engaged the members in a collaborative endeavor with respect to matters "that are concrete, of real and current concern, not too threatening but yet linked to critical disturbances in other life areas . . . it provides the kind of semi-structured situation that is more tolerable to most delinquent youngsters than the usual amorphous contacts of therapy."[23]

22 *Ibid.*, p. 31.
23 Peck, *op. cit.*, p. 29.

Similar therapy groups of children referred to the court might be organized to discuss such problems as leaving school, finding a job, leaving home, or improving one's social contacts. The important point is the use of the young person's immediate concern as a method of establishing contact, and as a springboard for dynamically oriented assistance concentrated about a crucial life area.

Even when the intrapsychic conflicts are traceable to early experience, they are likely, Peck believes, to be discernible at many levels and in more than one area by the time the child is officially in trouble. Meaningful contacts with the psychiatrist within one of these areas provide an opportunity for therapy. If therapy succeeds, a significant change in the interpsychic structure will almost invariably come about.

This type of group therapy is neither a dilution of therapy nor the substitution of educational for therapeutic methods. Nor does its use mean that teachers and group workers are effective substitutes for clinic services. It does, however, in Peck's opinion, with which we concur, indicate that the clinical personnel should move out from their relatively isolated setting in the court and attach themselves to institutions in the community.

Bloch is critical of clinics which close cases as unsolvable because they reveal gross social pathology, or because the client does not seem to want help. In his opinion, social work's body of specialized knowledge, skills, and techniques, as distinguished from those employed in individual or group psychotherapy, have a vital role in helping "the more demoralized clients who come to the court and the clinic."[24] This is in line with current social work philosophy.

Summary

In reviewing the peculiarly American contribution in psychiatric treatment for delinquents, it has been noted that since the establishment of the first clinic set up by Dr. William Healy to serve the judge of the juvenile court in Chicago in 1909, seventeen courts in the United States have established clinics which either function directly under juvenile court auspices or limit their services to referrals from the juvenile courts. There were in 1955 (the last date for which nation-wide figures were compiled), in addition, almost 400 community clinics for children, of which about one fifth were in New York State. These psychiatric services are sometimes available to judges of juvenile courts for diagnosis and occasionally for treatment.

As noted in Chapter 6, a considerable number of refinements in both theory and practice have been built on the theories of Freud. Despite differing practices, however, there is agreement that each person selects, eliminates,

24 Bloch, *op. cit.*, p. 96.

and adapts to his own use both the internal and external influences in his environment, and that because the individual's reaction is always an indication of his attempt to solve a problem, treatment of symptoms is ineffective.

Application of these theories to practice in court or community clinic has shown that clients are not always ready to accept the help for which they seemingly ask. They cannot be persuaded against their will to conform to another's plan for the solution of their problems. Consequently, clinics have not always produced the results which the community desires, i.e., conformity to the community's standards. Because the recommendations of clinics in Boston, New Haven, and Detroit have yielded less satisfactory outcomes than their proponents had anticipated, attention has been directed to the reasons for their comparative failure. It has been pointed out that the court auspices often appear threatening and restrictive to both parents and children. Many judges as well as probation officers have not clearly understood the conditions of clinic services or their limitations.

Psychiatrists, critical of the role of the clinic in serving the court clientele, call for a more realistic examination of the nature of the behavior that brings a child to the court. Bloch considers delinquency a response in a two-person situation in which the delinquent's partner may be the parent, the teacher, the judge, the police, and so forth. To this partner the delinquent responds as he has learned to respond in his childhood experiences. Peck suggests that the behavior which the middle-class therapist and judge label delinquent may be normal behavior in the lower socio-economic group from which most of the court referrals come. In a sense, this point of view is similar to Cohen's delineation of the delinquent subculture.

Some obstacles to successful treatment are due to limitations within the therapist. To deal with the customary aggressive response in its various forms requires great skill on the part of the therapist. Persons who choose helping professions may, it is suggested, be seeking help with their own problems. The need of the therapist—psychiatrist, psychologist, or social worker—to come to grips with authority and to be able to help the young person in trouble to accept limits is one of primary importance in dealing with delinquents.

In questioning the applicability of the usual treatment methods which involve verbal communication, Peck suggests that group therapy focused on a problem of immediate concern to the members of the group (possible reading difficulties, problems in connection with dating, jobs, parents, and so forth) is more likely to reveal the assets and the liabilities of young persons in trouble. Bloch suggests that some of the new social work techniques, with emphasis on seeking out the client, may be more effective than individual or group psychotherapy, if the client is a member of the lower socio-economic group.

CHAPTER 18

Evaluations of the Juvenile
Court Today

PROCLAIMED AS "THE GREATEST ADVANCE IN JUDICIAL HISTORY SINCE THE Magna Charta,"[1] the juvenile court occupied a pivotal position in the first two decades of the twentieth century, when it was the only place to which children in trouble could be referred. Today, however, every large urban community has social agencies and occasionally clinics with personnel professionally trained to deal with young people's problems. In consequence, the half-century which has elapsed since the first juvenile court was established in Chicago in 1899 has witnessed not only questions of its constitutionality but criticism of its operations and effectiveness. To evaluate the juvenile court, therefore, one must consider its present role in comparison with the community situation in which it arose.

Critics of the juvenile court fall into two groups, those within and those outside the court. In the first group are juvenile court judges, who believe the court's services are not understood and frequently do not meet the standards established by such organizations as the National Probation and Parole Association, the Association of Juvenile Court Judges, and the U.S. Children's Bureau. The second group of critics raises questions about the relative roles of the court and the social agencies. They are doubtful that the training of the judge equips him to be helpful in situations other than those requiring legal skill. They lament the inadequate probation services and suggest, as the critics of the clinics do, that a court setting by its very nature negates treatment efforts.

[1] Roscoe Pound, "The Juvenile Court and the Law," *Yearbook,* National Probation Association, 1944, p. 13.

Criticism by Judges

Court Is Misunderstood

Judges Alexander, Schramm, and Wylegala are spokesmen for the judges who feel that the juvenile court still has an important role but one that is misunderstood and needs to be reinterpreted to the community at large as well as to the social agencies. Judge Alexander, of Toledo[2] reminds us that the juvenile court does not correspond to the ordinary idea of a court commonly accepted by both laymen and lawyers, i.e., a place to which people go or are taken to get justice. Unlike the civil and criminal courts, the juvenile court emphasizes the *why* instead of the *what*. The traditional idea of administering even-handed justice by doing something *to* the individual is replaced by the idea of doing something *for* him. Furthermore, juvenile court investigations are social, not juridical. They are made in the field, not in the court, and while they may invoke the ultimate exercise of judgment, they are not judgmental.

Unlike other courts, Judge Alexander points out that the juvenile court has no fixed law to be applied to the finding of delinquency. Its exceedingly broad authority permits it to suggest a number of alternatives (some of which may be in the nature of trial and error), but the court's action is rarely the sole basis for treatment of the child. Just as the doctor does not mend a broken bone but brings the ends together so that nature can do the healing, so the court cannot make the delinquent go straight; he has to *want* to go straight. The task of the court, therefore, is to help the child mobilize his desire to improve by helping him change his attitudes and working with his family and the community to assist in this process.

Like Judge Alexander, Judge Schramm of the juvenile court of Pittsburgh believes that:

> Juvenile courts are the least understood and the most misunderstood of the courts of our land. Their unique philosophy, procedures and approach are features that not all segments of the population, even of the legal profession and of the bench, have fully perceived as yet. In our traditional courts the emphasis is on "did you or did you not?"; not on "why, under what circumstances, and what can be done to help?"
>
> In the comparatively short 50-year period every state in the Union has made statutory provisions based on the fundamentals propounded by the originators of the Juvenile Court idea. It is in the *day-to-day carrying-out of those fundamentals that much yet remains undone.*
>
> Some courts by implementations have kept pace with experience

[2] Paul W. Alexander, Judge, Division of Domestic Relations and Juvenile Court, Toledo, Ohio, "Of Juvenile Court Justice and Judges," *Yearbook*, National Probation and Parole Association, 1947, pp. 187-205.

and have brought about progressive changes; some have been able to incorporate the findings of many fields of social and medical science into their processes of treatment and diagnosis. There are up-to-date models, aging models, and obsolescent ones.[3]

The Judge's Role

One of the major handicaps to effective operation of the juvenile court is that in the vast majority of the 3000 counties in the United States it is not a specialized court. Although all fifty states have passed acts empowering their cities and counties to establish juvenile courts, there are only 200 separate juvenile courts, the majority of them located in eight states. In more than 2300 counties the juvenile court is part of a court of general jurisdiction, i.e., circuit, district, superior or probate court. Because in such jurisdictions the juvenile court proceedings represent only a minor responsibility of the judge, it is hardly likely that he will have the appropriate special qualifications or the time to consider the kinds of evidence produced by the social investigation in children's cases.[4]

One of the reasons why judges of other courts may have little incentive to equip themselves for service in juvenile court sessions is that the judgeship requires comparatively much more work—law books cannot be consulted for answers to questions of human behavior.[5] Furthermore, the juvenile court judge is often beset by politicians who make the task of choosing and holding properly qualified probation staff difficult, if not impossible.

The custom in some areas of rotating judges to the juvenile jurisdiction instead of appointing special juvenile court judges suggests the lower prestige of the position. Likewise symbolic of the lower prestige is the smaller salary of the juvenile court judges. The juvenile court judgeship, therefore, is sometimes just a stepping-stone to other more lucrative and less demanding judicial positions.

Legal and Financial Handicaps

Social workers who complain of the backwardness of some juvenile courts need to remember that these courts are not self-made nor self-ruled.[6] They cannot automatically accommodate themselves to the wishes and desires of individuals and groups. Their performance must be appraised under the

[3] Gustav L. Schramm, Ph.D., "The Juvenile Court Idea," *Federal Probation,* Vol. 13, no. 3 (Sept. 1949), p. 22. Italics added.
[4] Alice Scott Hyatt, "Courts and Services to Delinquents," Technical Committee on Fact Finding, No. 8, White House Mid-Century Conference.
[5] Alexander, *op. cit.,* p. 198.
[6] Victor B. Wylegala, "Children's Courts, An Effective Aid to Social Agencies," *Child Welfare,* Journal of the Child Welfare League of America, Inc., July 1949, pp. 6-9.

laws which created them, not according to standards advocated for them by experts. Before juvenile court reform is possible, the laws under which they operate must be amended to conform with the new ideas.

Some sociologists agree with the judges cited above that because in many communities it still functions as it did initially, the juvenile court today does not always meet the needs of children in trouble.

> . . . at the turn of the century when the Juvenile Court appeared in America it was really the juridical answer of urban child welfare workers to the needs of big city children. Today, half-a-century later, that is still essentially what the juvenile court remains—the juridical answer to the delinquency problems of the great city. . . .
>
> Outside of those 200 big city courts, the juvenile court, in its dealings with children, is actually a kind of legal fiction. It has the name, it has a presiding officer—probate judge, common pleas clerk, or what-have-you—chosen without regard to his understanding of children. It has sundry sketchy documents called case records, compiled, of course, without benefit of any trained caseworkers, and sometimes not even compiled; a notebook in the judge's pocket may serve the purpose! In the eyes of the law and of the public in a couple of thousand jurisdictions that assemblage of characteristics plus some legally defined authority to deal with neglected, dependent, and delinquent children constitutes the juvenile court. . . .
>
> The 2,000 small town courts don't know what a psychiatrist looks like. There is no question about the facts. Item by item one can check down the Children's Bureau list of characteristics of a "standard" juvenile court and find the overwhelming majority of the juvenile courts in the United States below par on every count. Their judges, their facilities, their budgets, their procedures, their records, their personnel, their attempts at treatment, their guiding philosophies—all fail to measure up. The conclusion seems inescapable; the standard juvenile court, as child welfare experts define the term, is a big city court. The little fellows simply do not qualify.[7]

The substandard operation of nine out of ten juvenile courts is not due to crooked politics, rural backwardness, or public stupidity, but to the hard facts of insufficient clients and money. The vast majority of counties have less than 100,000 population with less than one case a week, and do not have the resources to support standard juvenile court operations. Often the judge will know the families whose children get into difficulty and so does not need the paraphernalia of the large court. "Rural counties cannot possibly raise the money to pay for such standards. If they could, it would be an outright waste of public money. Six days out of seven the high-powered specialists would be

[7] Lowell Juilliard Carr, Ph.D., "Most Courts Have to be Substandard," *Federal Probation*, Vol. 13, no. 3 (Sept. 1949), pp. 29-30.

playing checkers to pass the time. The delinquency business simply is not there. County by county, rural America does not produce enough juvenile delinquents to keep its juvenile courts running at big city tempo. . . ."[8] We have no evidence to contradict Dr. Carr.

Critics Outside of the Court

The second group of critics of the juvenile court, whose opinions are summarized below, include those who draw attention to the courts' failure to adapt to such new developments as changes in social philosophy, the growth of public welfare services, and the emergence of a professional role for social work.

It has been suggested that the original concept of the juvenile court judge was the product of the idealistic philosophy of the age which produced Ford and Rountree, Montessori, the Webbs, and Jane Addams.[9] It was quite consistent with this paternalistic philosophy to accord the juvenile court judge the broadly defined powers of a kindly and wise father prescribing for the good of his children. With our increasing knowledge of the complexity of human nature, however, we are less sure today than we were formerly that good will and common sense will help us to deal with social problems.

Enumerating the many changes in the social agency structure that have taken place in the fifty-year period since the first juvenile court, the former chief of the Children's Bureau[10] reminds us that the development of professional training for social work and the establishment of child guidance clinics occurred almost two decades after the establishment of the first juvenile court. In the early 1900s social agencies were advocating the removal of children from undesirable surroundings and placing them in institutions or foster homes. In exposing and attacking the depraved living conditions of the children who came to the court, the first juvenile court pointed the way toward public aid to dependent children in their own homes. Furthermore, the court's experience suggested the advantages of psychiatric, psychological, and social study of problem children as well as improved programs for detention, foster home, and institutional care.

The Roles of the Juvenile Court and the Social Agency

Because the juvenile court was usually the only public agency dedicated to the welfare of children in difficulty or in need, Lenroot points out that it

[8] *Ibid.*, pp. 30-31.
[9] Alan Keith-Lucas, "Social Work and the Court in the Protection of Children," *Child Welfare*, Journal of the Child Welfare League of America, Inc., July 1949, pp. 3-6.
[10] Katherine F. Lenroot, "The Juvenile Court Today," *Federal Probation*, Vol. 13, no. 3 (Sept. 1949), p. 9.

frequently assumed administrative functions in such fields as mother's pension and foster home care. Today in many communities social agencies exist which can carry on some of the functions originally performed by the courts or not at all. As a result, there is both confusion and honest difference of opinion as to what is and what should be the tasks of the juvenile court in the communities which support social agencies. According to one point of view, usually advanced by the representatives of the social agencies, the court's activities should be limited to those primarily judicial, leaving administrative or treatment services to the social agencies under public or private auspices.

DIFFERING CRITERIA FOR SERVICE. There are essential differences in the responsibilities of the juvenile court and of the social agencies. The juvenile court is mainly concerned with the protection of the rights of children. Social agencies were created to assist individuals and families to conform to society's laws in order to enjoy the maximum benefits of civilized living. The auspices of public and private social agencies differentiate them from one another and from the court. Social agencies under private auspices limit their services in the light of their resources, and select their clients from among those who come to them voluntarily. In this way they hope to add to our understanding of social problems and how to deal with them. In contrast, social agencies under public auspices must offer their services in a field prescribed by law. They must serve all those who apply and qualify for their services as defined by law, for as long a period as such persons wish to be served.

Because the services of the juvenile court are not voluntary, they are dissimilar in the following ways to those offered by social agencies, whether under public or private auspices.

1. Although the clients of the court sometimes concede the necessity for its services, rarely do they request them voluntarily.

2. Clients who come to the court must accept and conform to the court's judgment as long as they remain under its jurisdiction.

3. Most juvenile courts must depend on agencies outside of their jurisdiction to provide the services which they prescribe for their clients. The one exception is probationary supervision which, however, is not always directly under the court's jurisdiction.

In short, the laws under which a juvenile court in each community operates prescribe both the content of the procedure as well as the court's powers.

COMPARISON OF LEGAL AND SOCIAL WORK FUNCTIONS. The two functions of the court according to Keith-Lucas are:[11]

1. To adjudicate human rights when the rights of a child may be in conflict with those of his parents.

[11] Keith-Lucas, *op. cit.*, pp. 4-5.

2. To sanction and add dignity to personal transactions such as surrender, adoption, and voluntary transfer of custody.

Confusion results if the court attempts to carry out or to control the actual *care* of the children, or if social work steps in to determine that a particular parent is unfit to care for his children or should not be permitted to take some proposed action affecting his children's rights. Wherever human rights are at stake, both social work and the law are needed to supplement and to act as checks, each on the other. The court adjudicates the rights of the child as defined by those who believe that he needs its protection over and against the rights of the parents to exercise normal discretion in their child's upbringing. The judge needs to be an expert in the evaluation of the rights of the conflicting parties, and to be sure that all sides of a question have been thoroughly discussed. This is primarily a legal skill.

The social worker suggests the social plan for the child *after* the court has decided on the basis of the social investigation that such a plan is necessary for the protection of the child and does not interfere unwarrantably with his and his parents' normal prerogatives. The social worker's function is to help a child choose for himself an acceptable plan and to present it to the court as one which embodies the child's best interests.

A complication, however, is that there is no one gospel even among those who believe that psychology is a better tutor than law in planning for children's welfare. Some social agency representatives try to persuade the judge to disregard the court setting, his legal training, and his insistence on the evidence appropriate to a court of law, in favor of their plan for a child, based exclusively on clinical material. In their opinion, a judge's action merits approval not because he interprets the law and adjudicates conflicting human rights according to the ethics of his profession, but solely because he does what social workers want him to do.

Such a demand on the part of social agencies confuses the role of the law and that of social workers in the welfare of society. To ask the judge to function as the social worker may desire means demanding that he become by statute both judge and social worker. In such cases he would have the authority of the judge, but without the usual limits to the use of personal discretion. In essence he would have the responsibility of a practitioner in both fields, without being subject to the discipline of either.

Rappaport,[12] discussing the views of Wylegala and Keith-Lucas, believes that courts should adhere to their primary function, balancing the rights of children, parents, and the community. Instead of more emphasis on the formal legalistic aspects she suggests that the court consider improvements in the operations of the laws which are designed to protect the rights of

12 Mazie F. Rappaport, "Social Work at the Court," *Child Welfare*, Journal of the Child Welfare League of America, Inc., Nov. 1949, pp. 15-17.

children. In presenting the relevant facts to assist the court in reaching a decision, casework service helps clients to clarify their own purposes, desires, and needs, and to be able to live within the law.

While in a sense an advocate for the child, the social worker is *not* an official adjunct of the court; he may therefore bring to the community's attention unmet needs which press for solution. If the laws are bad or inadequate, no good can come when the social agency moves into the court's bailiwick, because the social worker does not have the training to adjudicate a case. On the other hand, if the court cannot or will not make decisions, chaos can result both for the client and the community.

In substance, Rappaport insists, and we agree, that it is essential for the court and the social agency each to remain within its own orbit, applying its respective skills in its own area of competence (hoping that it is "competence"!). A partnership between the juvenile court and the social agency would permit each to function as fully and as professionally as the nature of their auspices and skills permit.

THE RELATIONSHIP TO THE CLIENT. The relationship to the client is another of the major differences between the court and the social agency. The judge not only directs the staff working with individuals but, in his judicial capacity, also deals directly with them. In contrast, the agency executive cannot impose obligations upon individuals or enforce orders. He cannot exercise the rights of parents or guardians as the judge does automatically, unless these are specifically assigned to the agency.

The public welfare agency's legal responsibility is generally described in broad terms—to administer child welfare activities, advocate the enforcement of laws for the protection of specified groups of children, or take the initiative in matters involving the interests of children. Essentially, the authority of the agency, like that of the physician, "inheres in the professional knowledge and skill of its staff." The structure of the agency, like that of a good hospital "permits it to use this knowledge and skill to develop, expand and strengthen social services to individual children and, at the same time, to serve and strengthen family life."[13] In essence then, the nature of the juvenile court is primarily judicial and law enforcing, whereas that of the public welfare agency is primarily administrative.

TREATMENT IN A COURT SETTING. The adequacy of the treatment phase of the juvenile court, i.e., its probation service, is the one which is most often questioned, chiefly because the child's attitude toward the official status of the probation officer, which is a symbol of control and restraint, may, unless the officer is very skilled, interfere with the casework relationship. Chapter 16 has referred to the inadequate educational preparation of probation officers, many of whom do not meet the standards set by the National Probation and

[13] Wylegala, *op. cit.*, p. 7.

Parole Association. Moreover, even when the probation officers are adequately trained, it has been noted that too often the number assigned to the court is insufficient in comparison with the case load.

THE COMMUNITY'S ATTITUDE. The whole responsibility for the constructive use of the court, i.e., invoking authority, not in a punitive but in a limiting and constructive fashion, does not rest with the young person's attitude. It inheres, Judge Long points out, partly in the attitude of the community, which often regards the court as a residual agency, i.e., one to which cases "too special to be unique and perhaps too seemingly hopeless to be referrable to other agencies, are assigned."[14] The skills which such cases require are not often found either in the social work staff of agencies concerned with behavior or conduct disorders, or in the majority of the probation staffs. If the probation officers in the court were highly skilled and could be relieved of responsibility for helping children whose defects are of a less critical nature, Judge Long suggests, they would be vastly more effective in working with the really difficult and troublesome cases which most community agencies are now unwilling to accept.

Recommendations for Changes in Court Procedure

In the face of the criticisms both within and outside of the judiciary, recommendations for improving the juvenile court have been made by the judges, the standard setting organizations, and by social agency representatives.

By Judges

1. Some judges believe that the juvenile court should continue to develop as a children's agency and to encompass the wide range of services and facilities needed by those who come before the court for official action. Some judges even recommend that the court exercise jurisdiction over the children who are now handled unofficially, if there is any suggestion that their behavior may develop into delinquency.

2. Other judges suggest that the court should incorporate the new discoveries and the new techniques in diagnosis, prediction, and treatment.

3. Some judges call for improved cooperation between the court, the school, and the police. In Toledo the court no longer reproaches the school for unloading its failures onto the court, and the school does not hesitate to refer children to the court when, in its opinion, such authority is needed

[14] Donald E. Long, "The Juvenile Court and Community Resources," *Yearbook*, National Probation Association, 1940, pp. 24-33.

to assure the welfare of the child. The plan is based on mutual acknowledgment of respective roles and limitations.[15]

In Pittsburgh there is effective cooperation between the court and the police. Each has defined its role. Issues are clarified and a method for meeting them is arrived at by joint consultation. A liaison officer with the rank of inspector is assigned to the court. Because he channels all police contacts with the court, it is unnecessary for the arresting officer to appear in court or to bring children to the detention quarters. The petitioning officer discusses with the liaison officer his reasons for referring the child to the court and makes suggestions for appropriate action. When the court has disposed of the case the petitioning officer is informed of the action. In this exchange he often acquires a better understanding of the ways in which the community's facilities can be useful to children. Naturally, the effectiveness of this device depends largely upon the skill of the liaison officer.

By the National Probation and Parole Association

The point of view of the National Probation and Parole Association on the relation of the court to the community agencies has been publicly expressed in the statements made by its former executive, its legal consultant, and the advisory council of judges. Charles L. Chute maintains that the juvenile court should insist on complete jurisdiction over offenses belonging within the juvenile court which are now shared with other courts or are outside its jurisdiction. Such divided jurisdiction, he claims, is "inconsistent with the original purpose of the juvenile court, which seeks to protect all children who are in need of care and protection regardless of the offenses."[16]

Rubin suggests that the juvenile court avoid taking jurisdiction in most cases of neglected children, and that a study be made of the hodgepodge of behavior called "delinquent" which has no equivalent in acts which if committed by an adult would be referred to the criminal court.[17] The forthcoming 1959 revision of the Standard Juvenile Court Act, like the 1949 version, does not include dependency within the court's jurisdiction.

In order to improve the functioning of the judges assigned to the juvenile court, the advisory council of judges has prepared a handbook on juvenile court procedures which describes and illustrates the various processes and suggests appropriate standards and qualifications for other court personnel.[18]

[15] L. Wallace Hoffman, "Court-School Relationships," *Federal Probation*, Vol. 9, no. 3 (July-Sept. 1945), pp. 27-30.
[16] Charles L. Chute, "The Juvenile Court in Retrospect," *Federal Probation*, Vol. 13, no. 3 (Sept. 1949), p. 5.
[17] Sol Rubin, "The Legal Character of Delinquency," *The Annals*, American Academy of Political and Social Science, No. 261 (Jan. 1949), p. 3.
[18] Marjorie Bell (ed.), *Guides for Juvenile Court Judges*, Advisory Council of Judges, National Probation and Parole Association, in cooperation with the National Council of Juvenile Court Judges, 1957.

By Social Agency Representatives

The social agency critics who believe that the court's major role is judicial suggest that it should not administer services in communities in which welfare services are adequate. The court should retain responsibility for admitting children to detention quarters and for releasing them. The administration of the detention quarters, however, should be the responsibility of a local welfare agency. Moreover, the court should not continue to operate foster homes or institutions even if it has assumed that responsibility in the past. In this fashion the court would become a highly specialized instrument of the state, called into service only when necessary. The court's decision should be the "nature, extent and amount of services to be made available, as well as the administrative arrangements under which these are to be furnished."

Since adequate probation services are unavailable today in the majority of courts, policies need to be worked out for the administrative conditions under which casework services can be furnished to the court. For example, caseworkers might be assigned to the court to handle intake, as well as to make social investigations prior to the court's disposition. Following disposition by the court, however, treatment would be turned over to the social agency, whether the plan is to care for children in their own homes, or in foster homes or institutions. A policy which assigns distinct roles to the court and to the social agency involves decisions about where the records are to be kept, to whom the social worker is to be administratively responsible, and who is responsible for providing the technical supervision.

The process of differentiating the role of the court and that of the social agencies will vary in different communities. If the juvenile court has a well-worked-out treatment program, there may be little pressure to divest it of its administrative functions. On the other hand, in those communities in which the court may be fighting doggedly to retain full responsibility for treatment in spite of the fact that there are social agencies equipped and supported by the community and willing to assume these services, the pace of change will be slower.

The larger courts would no doubt agree to transfer some of their so-called nonjudicial functions if they could be assured that other agencies in the community would assume the responsibility and provide the necessary quality and permanence for the services. It was noted in reviewing the psychiatric approaches to delinquency (Chapter 6) that many social agencies have been unwilling to accept the responsibility for working with delinquents whose behavior does not conform to the neurotic pattern which makes them seek help. Other skills are needed to work with the non-neurotic delinquent.

Since no community has as yet provided all the types of services needed by young people in trouble, in many instances the juvenile court has tried to bridge the gap.

Keith-Lucas outlines a four-step process which provides full protection of the law to both parents and children and conforms to acceptable child care standards:[19]

1. The referral of a problem situation to an adequately staffed social agency for screening and for developing a plan which, if it involves the removal of a child from his home, would be referred to the court for sanction.

2. Provision by the court of a "legal next friend" or *curiae ad hoc* who would not participate in the judgment but would assure that all sides of the question have been presented and that the judge's decision does not overstep the limits of reasonable discretion, including the right of appeal when there is any question of a child's rights.

3. Consideration by the court of the agency's plan in terms of the evidence and the principles of equity, and approval or rejection of the plan.

4. A reopening of the case if either the parents or the agency request it.

This plan for juvenile court and social agency cooperation prescribes the court's participation in the area of child protection and simultaneously sets the legal framework within which social work can function. It involves submitting the judgments of social workers to democratic review and the participation of social workers in the legal process, not as suppliants, but on a full professional basis. It is in accord with the suggestions made by Rappaport for the more effective utilization of the skills of the judge and the social worker.

Tappan[20] is more critical than Rappaport of the procedure in the juvenile court and of the role of the social worker in that court. He would agree with the social workers that the treatment facilities available to most juvenile courts are inadequate to provide the individualized casework services which the courts would like to believe they are able to give. Tappan sees no point in the court's attempting to deal with problems which require intensive skill and time for their solution. In his opinion, it is not only ineffective but hazardous to subject young persons to the usual court procedure, unless the wielding of authority is necessary for the stability of a child or the security of the community.

In consequence, Tappan opposes the continuing expansion of the functions of the juvenile court.[21] Instead, he argues that the powers of the juvenile court should be limited and defined by clear statutory norms which

---

[19] Keith-Lucas, *op. cit.*, pp. 5 and 6.
[20] Paul W. Tappan, *Juvenile Delinquency*, New York, McGraw-Hill, 1949, p. 220.
[21] See Chapter 14, and *ibid.*, pp. 219-23.

express the official policy of the state as well as the self-imposed limitations of the court. Furthermore, he disapproves of informal probation and the unofficial handling of cases. The only basis for court handling should be definite and convincing proof of a commission of a specific offense.

Tappan's suggestions for courts dealing with delinquents or adolescent offenders involve changes in substantive norms, in procedural standards, and in administrative policy. He favors substantive norms to do away with the omnibus statutes and to restrain the courts from "either too broadly extending or too narrowly restricting the province of their action. He advocates procedural standards which are just and consistent and which include real proof of violation of substantive norms established by laws. This would eliminate incompetent and prejudicial hearsay evidence. In his opinion, the standard of proof required in the English juvenile courts and theoretically in certain American jurisdictions, and always in adult criminal courts, is not too high when one considers the implications of adjudication. Psychological, psychiatric, and medical facilities for clinical diagnosis should be part of the investigation and standard procedure in a court clinic. These services should be available and manned by trained personnel to assist the judge in making appropriate disposition and deciding on treatment. He suggests that there is too much use of commitment to mass congregate institutions with poor facilities and poor records of cures. Changes in the administrative policy of the courts would, he believes, make possible the maximum use of the specialized diagnostic and treatment resources in the community.

Improving Probation Services

Tappan disapproves of the use of the probation officer in the preliminary prehearing investigation, before it is determined that the behavior for which the young person has been referred to the court has actually occurred. He believes that the probation officer might be more effective if his efforts were confined to supervision. Regardless of the limitations on the adequacy of probation staff generally today, it appears to Tappan that the results of probation on the whole are more encouraging than those of institutional treatment. What the results might be if the probation staff were properly equipped is a matter of hopeful conjecture.

In judging the results of probation, MacCormick suggests that it is unfair to use courts which operate substandard departments. In the adult field, in which the offense is often more clearcut than in the juvenile field, the Los Angeles County Superior Court, which places between 40 and 50 per cent of the convicted cases on probation, claims 90 per cent subsequent satisfactory adjustment. The General Sessions Court of New York City which uses probation in a smaller percentage of cases—less than a third—claims a similar degree of success.

MacCormick in 1948 estimated that "based on actual performance over a term of years, a good juvenile court and probation service, operating in a community with adequate social resources and utilizing them fully, can put as high as 90% of its juvenile delinquents on probation the first time around, and 50-75% the second or third time around, and get as high as 75-80% success."[22] The authors, however, do not specify which juvenile courts meet their conditions.

Some evidence of the results of probation in the Allegheny County Court, one which undoubtedly has standards as high as any juvenile court, is offered in a follow-up of 280 delinquents who were placed on probation by that court in 1940.

Personal interviews were used to verify reported criminal records and the various factors in the social adjustment of the probationer, who was also questioned about the treatment that he received in the juvenile court. The measure of success was the absence of a subsequent criminal record. The results of Diana's study are as follows:[23]

1. About 20 per cent of those who had been before the juvenile court were charged with subsequent criminal offenses, including fornication, bastardy, rape, assault and battery, and burglary. Only 16 per cent of those were convicted of the crimes charged to them. And of those convicted, about one fourth were committed to penal institutions.

2. There was about one probation visit every three months in 84 per cent of the cases. The inference is that while the large majority of the probationers do not have criminal records, their apparent adjustment can hardly be attributed to treatment received on probation. When this hypothesis was checked statistically for the factors assumed to have the greatest significance in the probation process, it was found that only 14 per cent of those on probation received casework treatment, defined as following a plan which involved the client's understanding of his problem and willingness to participate in its solution on the basis of the record material. The rate of success in this group was unusually high.

It would appear that the probation officers expended most effort in working with offenders who demanded assistance. (These cases offer a basis for further research.) It is probable, Diana suggests, and we are inclined to agree, that *being on probation* may induce a positive change in behavior which

[22] Austin H. MacCormick, "The Community and the Correctional Process," *Focus,* Vol. 27, no. 3 (May 1948), pp. 65-68; 86-89.
[23] Lewis Diana, "The Treatment of Delinquents in Allegheny County—Evaluation of the Juvenile Court," University of Pittsburgh *Bulletin,* Vol. 50, no. 13 (July 10, 1954).

even if it is not accompanied by skilled services may serve a useful purpose for the majority of young people who come before the courts.

3. While subsequent criminality, as well as its absence, appears to be associated with many other factors *commonly used* to explain delinquent behavior, these associations are not necessarily causal. They reflect the orientation and preconceptions of the probation officer who selects those facts that *he* considers important. The *critical potentials* have not been isolated.

4. Of the probationers interviewed, 56 per cent reported that they considered the probation officer's interest and warm understanding helpful to them. The remainder were evenly divided between those who reacted negatively to the probation officer and those who made no comment. Some of those who reacted unfavorably believed that their offense was minor. Others thought that they had been treated unfairly in comparison with other young people guilty of the same offense.

Diana, from his experience as a probation officer, concludes that the most favorable factor in probation success is the interest and understanding of the staff. This is not necessarily synonymous with professional training in a psychoanalytical framework.

> Casework may attempt to formalize, standardize, ritualize, and routinize the display and exercise of warmth, sympathy, and respect, but these most important qualities are not inevitable results of training and instruction. The personality of the worker is paramount; casework recognizes this but loses sight of it in its schools.
>
> Correctional workers should examine and question the basic assumptions of a casework orientation. They ought to consider, for example, whether the social system itself should be investigated as a basic variable in antisocial behavior, and whether the correctional worker should become active in promoting fundamental social reform or reorganization. These and other questions are largely ignored and probably will continue to be ignored as long as those in the field are concerned primarily with behavior problems and psychodynamics.[24]

Diana agrees with Tappan on several points:

1. In advocating that the juvenile court's jurisdiction be restricted to definite cases of delinquency precisely defined and carrying penalties limited with respect to kind and time.

2. In contending that prehearing investigation sometimes results in decisions based upon distorted, unreliable, and irrelevant data. Instead, complainants and witnesses should be required to appear in court and be confronted by the child or his parents. Furthermore, the delinquent and his family should uniformly be informed of the rights they possess under existing law.

[24] Lewis Diana, "Is Casework in Probation Necessary?", *Focus*, Vol. 24, no. 1 (Jan. 1955), p. 8.

Despite the philosophy underlying the juvenile court procedure, the results, in Diana's opinion, are too frequently punitive, reflecting the nature of the offense and the bias of the court, since once a petition has been filed there is apt to be a presumption of delinquency.

3. In recommending that, assuming the social agencies agree, cases which present only social and behavior problems should be referred to social agencies rather than to the court.

Discussion up to this point discloses that Diana and Tappan question from the legal standpoint the functioning of the juvenile court in many cases which today come before it. The judges and social agency representatives, on the other hand, who do not question the juvenile court's *philosophy* but its *performance,* agree that probation staffs in the majority of the courts are inadequately equipped to give more than routine supervision.

State-Wide Courts

Diana's analysis of the Allegheny County record, suggests that the successes are not due to the provision of skilled casework service in the majority of the cases. To test what might happen if the courts were properly equipped, from the social work viewpoint, would require the provision of services which, as Carr points out, cannot be met in the majority of the counties in the United States.

In referring to the variation in juvenile court procedure, Carr underscores the paradox:

> . . . that the poor counties in scores of states do not produce enough delinquents to justify fully equipped modern courts. . . . This is the situation of the rich vs. the poor counties in Michigan. It is also the situation in Ohio, Wisconsin, Minnesota, Kentucky, West Virginia, and dozens of other states. . . . They could not possibly pay for such courts if the business were there and yet one case mishandled by their well-meaning but untrained officials may cost their states many times the cost of efficient service.[25]

Granting the cogency of Carr's arguments, the deduction is clear. If the small communities are to have adequate juvenile courts, they will have to combine resources and set up a state-wide system. An analogous need of small communities is the provision for hospital care. This, like proper juvenile courts, can only be adequately financed by cutting across county lines.

There is a precedent for state-wide courts in states which have large rural populations. Utah, for example, in 1908 established a State Juvenile Court Commission, divided the state into districts, appointed five district

[25] Carr, *op. cit.,* p. 31.

juvenile court judges, four of whom serve full time, and have the services of full-time probation officers.

In 1941 Connecticut established a State Juvenile Court with three full-time judges appointed by the Governor to serve the entire state. This plan superseded city police courts and justices who handled children's cases obviously without adequate facilities. In 1944 Rhode Island established a State Juvenile Court, with two full-time judges, replacing the twelve district court judges, all of whom had previously handled children along with criminal and civil cases. It does not follow, of course, that the large states should necessarily have a state-wide system.

If studies indicated that the problem of juvenile delinquency is handled better in the states in which the jurisdiction is state-wide, in comparison with those in which juvenile sessions are part of other court systems, there might be a basis for considering the further extension of the state-wide system.

Summary

The juvenile court, like any institution which has survived fifty years, needs to review its current functioning in the light of changes in the climate of philosophy and practice. In the first twenty-five years of its existence, the juvenile court survived criticisms as to its constitutionality. In the second twenty-five years, the development of professionalized social work and of public welfare services have given rise to criticisms of the court's performance and personnel.

One group of critics, which includes several judges, believe that the juvenile court is misunderstood. They are concerned because the standards of many juvenile courts do not meet those outlined in the model act. They claim that the demands of the juvenile court judgeship are more strenuous and less rewarding, in prestige and financial terms, than those of other judgeships. In addition, since so few of the juvenile courts are specialized, the major responsibilities of the judges who also serve in courts of general jurisdiction differ markedly from those demanded of a juvenile court judge.

Judge Wylegala points out that even if some juvenile courts might wish to meet the standards set for them by national groups, they could not do so without changes in the law under which they operate. Carr stresses that the substandard operation of nine out of ten juvenile courts is not due to crooked politics, rural backwardness, or public stupidity, but to the hard facts that the volume of juvenile delinquency in rural counties does not warrant the creation of separate courts and, even if it did, these communities could not afford them.

The second group of critics, in which social agency representatives predominate, contends that the idealistic philosophy popular when the juvenile court was established furnished a logical basis for a paternalistic concept of the juvenile court judge. With increasing knowledge of the dynamics of behavior, however, we are less certain today that good will and parental wisdom are sufficient basis for effective planning for children's welfare. The enactment of public welfare programs and the emergence of professional social work make it necessary to differentiate the contribution of law and social work to human betterment.

There are essential differences in the social and legal responsibilities of the juvenile court and those of the social agencies whether under public or private auspices. The services of the juvenile court are not voluntary; the clients who come to the court must accept and conform to its judgment as long as they remain under its jurisdiction. The court must depend on the social agencies outside its jurisdiction, to provide most of the services which it prescribes for its clients.

Not all the states, however, have assigned the local welfare agencies broad responsibility for children, or allocated the administrative responsibility in the same way, nor have they all made equally effective provision for the additional child welfare services in foster homes and in institutions for long-term or temporary care. In some communities the juvenile court has attempted to bridge this gap by providing such services under its own auspices. In communities which provide these services, the intake policy of the agency often excludes the resistive client. In still other communities, the court's treatment efforts are hampered because it is regarded as a dumping ground for cases which community agencies will not accept.

With respect to the social agencies' claim that their auspices are more appropriate for effective dealing with antisocial behavior of young persons, Judge Long grants that the major tool in casework treatment is the client's voluntary acceptance of the relationship with the caseworker and that a fairly large number of delinquents resist the offer of help. Aiding resistive clients to ask for help and to accept the necessary limitations which the community places on their behavior is usually possible only if social workers are skilled. Such services, however, are not always available even in well-staffed community agencies. If adequately trained probation officers were relieved of the responsibility for dealing with the less difficult situations they could help.

Tappan is critical of the procedure in the juvenile court, and opposes extending its functions to areas more properly in the domain of social agencies. He does not agree that a prehearing investigation is appropriate in juvenile cases unless the court has already determined that the behavior for which the young person is brought to court has actually occurred.

Because there is no objective method for measuring the results of juvenile probation, arguments in its favor are based on its reasonableness, i.e., rehabilitation in the community is more effective than removal from it; it costs much less than commitment; persons in direct contact with probationers have faith in it.

Diana's 1940 Allegheny study suggests that the occasional contact with the probation officer can hardly be responsible for the 84 per cent of the probationers who went straight subsequent to the termination of their probation period. On the basis of his analysis of the case records and of interviews, he believes that whatever success there is, is due to the personality and the interest of the probation staff. He is not sure, however, that the services must be provided only by persons trained as social workers. This conclusion is similar to Witmer's in her evaluation of the successful outcomes in the Cambridge-Somerville Survey (Chapter 28).

Diana, Tappan, and the judges, as well as the sociologists and social workers, have made a variety of recommendations for more effective operation of the juvenile court. Diana and Tappan believe that the court should require evidence and proof very similar to that which prevails in the criminal court. Some judges would like to see the juvenile court expand the jurisdiction which it now shares with other courts in some communities. Other judges think the court should extend its services to the so-called unofficial cases if there is any likelihood that the young people involved may become juvenile delinquents.

Social work spokesmen advocate a clearcut definition of the appropriate roles of the court and the social agency in the light of their respective professional competences.

Because neither the financial resources nor the amount of business in the majority of the states warrant the creation and the maintenance of a fully staffed juvenile court, a state-wide court and a state-wide probation system offer possibilities for more adequate services than are possible on the present county basis in the smaller states. With state subsidies, setting of standards, and the raising of salaries commensurable with the probation officers' responsibilities, more adequate services would be made generally available to the young people who come before the majority of the juvenile courts in the United States today.

CHAPTER 19

The Youth Correction Authority

WITH THE RECOGNITION THAT JUDGES ARE EQUIPPED BY TRAINING TO DETER-
mine matters of law but not to decide on the appropriate treatment program
for the young people who come before them, a special committee of the
American Law Institute established a project to find a way to separate the
judicial function, i.e., the determination of guilt, from the treatment function.
As a result of their investigations the Institute—a scholarly organization of
lawyers, law professors, and judges—recommended a Youth Correction Authority to control all post-conviction treatment.

Since this concept really represents a change in the function of the
court, it is appropriate at this point to describe the development of the
Authority in the five states—California, Minnesota, Wisconsin, Massachusetts, and Texas—that have adopted it in some form.[1]

The Model Act

The immediate impetus behind the Youth Correction Authority plan
was a study which described the disastrous effects on youthful offenders of
arrest and arraignment, detention in the Tombs (an abandoned jail for New
York's untried prisoners), and their experiences in reformatories and prisons.[2]
In response to this study the Model Youth Correction Act, drafted in 1940,
provided that with only minor exceptions all boys and girls convicted of
violations of the law in the age group between the upper limit of the local

[1] Bertram M. Beck, 5 States: A Study of the Youth Authority Program as Promul-
gated by the American Law Institute, New York, Community Service Society, 1951.
[2] Leonard V. Harrison and Pryor McNeill Grant, Youth in the Toils, New York,
Macmillan, 1938.

juvenile court and 21 years must be committed by disposition to a statewide panel to be known as the Youth Correction Authority. Its major responsibility was to provide a genuine study and rehabilitation program. To this end it would have the power to utilize any facility in the state as well as to construct new facilities if funds were appropriated. The authority could compel an institution to accept a youth if commitment was appropriate, and would maintain control of the delinquent minor until he was formally discharged.

The Model Act suggested that the governor of the state appoint a three-man commission whose members would serve for terms of three, six, and nine years respectively, and receive salaries for their service. They would be eligible for reappointment to a nine-year term. One of the members would be designated the chairman. The argument for a three-man commission was to assure that more than one point of view would be considered in any decision on a treatment plan. Provision was made for the right of appeal to a court of law, periodic review, and discharge at a specified age unless otherwise ordered by the court.

The proposed diagnostic process would require from one to two months' residence in a reception or diagnostic center. A team—psychiatrist, psychologist, social caseworker, physician, aided by teachers and supervisors in the center—would be responsible for planning individual programs. Assignment to an institution was to be on the basis of the individual's special needs and the institution's ability to do more than provide "a veneer over the custodial routines, the brutality and the homosexuality that pervade such unnatural societies of children in custody and of the adults guarding them."[3]

In short, the aim of the Model Act was to substitute treatment for retributive punishment, which seemed to be the rule rather than the exception once the young person had passed the age of juvenile court jurisdiction. It was "not a radical innovation but the implementation of the practice of private agencies approved by all students of the problem concerned with diminishing the burden of repeated criminality from which the public now suffers."[4]

The Adoption of the Youth Authority Plan

The American Law Institute engaged the services of John Ellingston to advise states which were considering the enactment of Youth Authority legislation in establishing appropriate programs. Although the authority in each of the five states that now have such a program has the responsibility for diagnosis, treatment plan, and the choice of the treatment facility, there

[3] John R. Ellingston, "Protecting Our Children from Criminal Careers," *Federal Probation*, Vol. 12, no. 3 (Sept. 1948), p. 34.
[4] *Ibid.*, p. 4, fn. 9.

CHART III

YOUTH AUTHORITY PROVISIONS

	American Law Institute, Model Act	California	Minnesota	Wisconsin	Massachusetts	Texas
Name	Youth Correction Authority	Youth Authority	Youth Conservation Commission	Division of Child Welfare and Youth Service in DPW	Youth Service Board	Youth Development Council
Statistical references	1940 Adopted American Law Institute	1941 chapter 937; Welfare and Institutions, Code Division 2.5, chapter 1	1947 chapter 595	1947 chapters 546, 560 (1949 chapter 376)	1948 chapter 310	1949 chapter 538
Administrative organization	3-man full-time board appointed by governor; 9 year staggered terms, board selects chairman	3-man full-time board appointed by governor; 2 from list of advisory panel (6 presidents of quasi-public professional associations), 4 year staggered terms, governor selects chairman	6 appointed by governor (3 public officials ex-officio; director of institutions, chairman of parole board, juvenile court judge), 6 year staggered terms, governor chairman	Division of DPW Board may appoint citizen committee with governor's approval to advise on programs and problems, DPW director selects division head	3-man full-time board appointed by governor from list of advisory committee on children and youth (15 appointed by governor), 6 year staggered terms, governor selects chairman	6 appointed by governor and 8 state officers ex-officio; DPW director is chairman
Age jurisdiction	16-21 from criminal or juvenile court	Discretionary, 16-21 from criminal or juvenile court	Minors convicted of crime, sentenced to less than life.	Minors sentenced to less than life, juveniles not re-	Juvenile court; children convicted of crime after juve-	Juvenile court

			Juvenile court commitments to trade schools	leased on probation	nile court waiver (under 18)	
Type commitment	Indeterminate	Indeterminate to 25, subject to maximum	Indeterminate to maximum	Definite (fixed by court), 1 year minimum; or indeterminate to maximum	Indeterminate to 21	Indeterminate to 21
Probation	Granted by authority	By court	By court	By court	By court	By court
Administration of facilities	Authority is mainly diagnostic; permitted to administer facilities	Manages institutions	Manages state trade schools	May be given management of treatment facilities	Manages institutions; may use other facilities	Manages institutions
Duration of control	To 25, Juvenile court commitments to 21; if over 18, 3 years. Unlimited control on approval of court may continue where release is dangerous	To 25 for felons; 23 for misdemeanors. Control may continue by court order but only to maximum for offense. Juvenile court commitments to 21	To 25, or maximum for offense, if shorter. To 21 for delinquents. Control may be transferred to another agency after 25 where release is dangerous	Unlimited, with approval of court. Jury trial on dangerousness may be demanded. Juvenile court commitments to 21	To 21; unlimited with approval of court. Boys 14-18 convicted of crime may be committed to board to 23, or punished as adult	To 21
Discharge parole	At any time	At any time	At any time	2 year minimum for felons, except with approval of court	At any time	At any time

SOURCE: Prepared by Sol Rubin, National Probation and Parole Association.

are differences in the number of committee members, the manner of their appointment, their qualifications, the delegation of major responsibility, and the age group over which the authority has jurisdiction. Chart III shows the current status of the authorities in these states.

To illustrate the operation of the Youth Authority some details of the California program, which was the first to be adopted, and of the Minnesota program, are presented below.

The California Youth Authority

The provisions of the California program, adopted in 1941, differ markedly from those of the Model Act, with respect both to age jurisdiction and to responsibility for engaging in preventive work. The power to place people on probation, one of the main aims of the act, was left to the courts of criminal jurisdiction. In 1942 and 1943 the title was changed from Youth Correction Authority to the California Youth Authority. The responsibility for preventive work was expanded when the authority acquired the task of administering, as well as using, the existing training school facilities. Although the authority is located within the state Department of Correction, the director of that department has no supervisory control over the functions expressly given to the California Youth Authority by law.[5]

WORK CAMPS. One growing element in the California Youth Authority Program is the use of work camps for delinquent boys, an outgrowth of the camps set up by Karl Holton in the 1930s in the Forestry Department of Los Angeles County.[6] Originally devised as a way to help transient delinquents earn carfare back to their homes, the camps were subsequently used to care for delinquents committed to them by the juvenile court and as an extension of the state's correctional schools.[7] Currently the boys are screened through the diagnostic clinic at the Preston School of Industry under the Youth Authority. The camps exclude the seriously delinquent, the feeble-minded, arsonists, and boys known to have serious sex problems.

After an orientation of about two weeks, the boys are grouped in teams of ten and assigned to a senior and junior counselor for supervision. Their work assignments are trail building, road mending, telephone line maintenance, and pulp wood production, for which they are paid approximately three dollars a month. Discussion groups in the evening provide opportunity for recreation and relaxation.

[5] Karl Holton, "California Youth Authority: Eight Years of Action," *Journal of Criminal Law and Criminology*, Vol. 41, no. 1 (May-June 1950), pp. 1-23.

[6] Karl Holton and D. R. S. Morrison, "Forestry Camps for Delinquent Boys," *Probation*, Vol. 19 (1941), pp. 111-15; and Heman G. Stark, "Forestry Camps for Delinquent Boys," *Yearbook*, National Probation Association, 1937, pp. 357-61.

[7] John Zack, "The Junior Probation Camps of Los Angeles County," *Yearbook*, National Probation and Parole Association, 1949, pp. 76-89.

The assets of the camp program are summed up by a member of the California Youth Authority as follows:

> Camps if properly operated are no less expensive than training schools. They should not be looked upon as a means of reducing the cost of dealing with delinquent youths. Neither should the camps be considered as a means for securing for the state cheap labor to take care of fire-fighting, reforestation, road building and other public work service. This work in conjunction with camps in the foothills and mountains should be so set up that it will be part of a rehabilitative program. If camps for older boys are properly organized and the right selection of youth is made for camp placement, the camps can be made profitable from a labor and a rehabilitative standpoint. Habits of work, improved health and character development through counselling and guidance will be the outcome of a well balanced camp program.[8]

Since California originated the camp idea, it has spread rapidly. Today California has 32, 23 of them all-year-round. Michigan has 12; Wisconsin 10; currently Ohio, Minnesota, Illinois, Washington are expanding their camp programs. The first camp in New York State was opened in October 1956 at Pharsalia. An additional camp was opened at Monterey in March 1958. This camp will provide for 60 boys sent from Elmira and Coxsackie. Only in California, Minnesota, and Wisconsin, of course, are these camps run in conjunction with a Youth Correction Authority.

As a rule a camp has provision for from 50 to 70 boys. The length of stay is not more than six months, at which time the boy is returned to the community and the supervision of the probation officer. The work projects are dedicated to conservation, park development, road construction, safety programs, and farming; these projects are supplemented by individual and group counseling, recreational, educational and religious programs.

Like the European institutions and the Provo experiment (see Chapter 16), many of the camps involve the boys in joint activities with the community. The work projects develop a sense of responsibility and their actual accomplishments bring the boys favorable recognition from the community. A further advantage of the camps is the greater flexibility than is possible in large-scale institutions. They also provide more opportunities for individual counseling, and from the point of view of the parents, there is less stigma attached to a boy's being sent to a camp than to an institution. Camp programs are reported to be successful in 80 to 90 per cent of the cases when there is selective intake and good supervision. The camps, however, are only one resource, and not appropriate for every boy; to be really useful they must

---

[8] O. H. Close, "California Camps for Delinquents," *Yearbook*, National Probation Association, 1945, p. 146; see also Allen F. Breed, "California Youth Authority Forestry Camp Programs," *Federal Probation*, Vol. 17 (June 1953), pp. 37-43.

be part of an over-all system with some form of well-thought-out and co-ordinated plan such as that provided by a Youth Correction Authority.

The Minnesota Program

In Minnesota, the six-man Youth Conservation Commission includes the director of public institutions and the chairman of the state board of parole. The Governor appoints the director, who serves full time. The three part-time members are a judge of the probate and of the juvenile court and a woman designated by the Governor. The commission is responsible not only for pre-hearing investigations but for supervision of probation in all the juvenile courts which do not have their own probation staff.

In 1949 the state legislature transferred the control of Minnesota's two training schools to the commission. While the members of the commission interview each prospective candidate for admission to a training school, the final decision takes into consideration the recommendation of its professional staff and an estimate of community attitudes.

The treatment and training programs of the three temporary diagnostic centers in the state have been revised. The Willow River Forestry Camp, established in 1951 to care for sixty boys, is modeled after the California camps discussed above. To supervise the thousands of young people now under its care in the probation and parole divisions the commission's staff has been increased from nine to fifteen.[9]

Reviewing the results of the Minnesota Youth Commission, Reed says that a third of the youths have been placed on probation and treated either in their own or substitute homes.[10] He estimates that more than 80 per cent of this group have been able to make satisfactory adjustment. Furthermore, the commission's periodic review of the situation in the institution to which it has committed young people has expedited parole. In consequence the Home School for Girls at Saulk Center and the Red Wing Training School for Boys have been able to operate at sums considerably below their budget allotments. The Conservation Commission considers the suggestion of an Adult Commission for Minnesota a seal of approval on its services to youth.

Some Alternatives for Youth Authority Services

A few states have developed programs for special handling of youthful offenders other than a youth authority. New Jersey, for example, has differ-

[9] *Youth Centers: The Organization of a Community-wide Program,* Minnesota Youth Conservation Commission, Division of Prevention, St. Paul, 1952.
[10] George J. Reed, "Minnesota's YCC Program," *Focus,* Vol. 32, no. 2, March 1953, p. 49.

entiated its institutions to take care of different age groups and personality problems and also operates a diagnostic center at Menlo Park to which the courts, the state institutions, and other agencies refer young people for diagnosis. The service is headed by a psychiatrist and uses the clinical team approach. In 1960, Ohio will operate an even more extensive coordinated state-wide plan.

New York State's Reception Center at Elmira, after study, diagnoses all male offenders over 16 years of age who are sentenced to confinement in state institutions. The bulk of the young men are transferred from the Reception Center either to Elmira Reformatory or to West Coxsackie. This center has been in operation since 1945 (see evaluation of its program in Chapter 26).

As a result of a 1956 study, there is a proposal in the New York State Legislature to correct some of the inequities in the sentencing procedures in the New York courts by establishing a youth court in each county. The judges, assigned by the county court because of their special aptitudes for dealing with youth, would serve for a term of at least one year. On the basis of a preliminary investigation report, they would either release the youth on parole, detain him, or in exceptional cases, fix cash or security bail. Auxiliary court services would provide an early state in the rehabilitation process.

In Massachusetts a special commission to study and investigate the laws relating to certain youthful offenders[11] recommended to the Commonwealth that a Youthful Offender Division, to be known as the Youth Correction Authority, be established in the Department of Correction. This would assure a unified system of correctional controls and permit individualized correctional and rehabilitative treatment. The new authority would have power to transfer any inmate from one institution to another or to a forestry or work camp. It would administer a central reception and diagnostic center to be established with provisions for treatment as well. Its sponsors believe that this program would promote better use of existing personnel and attract the services of more highly qualified staff.

The Youth Service Board (the Massachusetts name for its original Youth Authority) would remain in control of the programs for offenders under 16, on the theory that the program for handling juveniles is mostly preventive while that for the youthful offender is rehabilitative, as is that of the Department of Correction in its handling of the adult offender.[12]

Instead of a special parts or special youth offenders court which would entail considerable additional expense and complicate the judicial machinery, in the opinion of the commission procedures of a noncriminal nature could be made available to any person between the ages of 17 and 22 who commits

[11] Report of Special Recess Commission on Youthful Offenders, The Commonwealth of Massachusetts, House No. 2790, Dec. 29, 1958.
[12] Ibid., p. 23.

any crime not punishable by death. The court in granting youthful offender status would make use of the proposed Youth Correction Authority for diagnostic study and recommendations. The court would be empowered to approve the recommendation and to impose sentence as it might deem proper.

Appraisals of the Youth Authority Program

Criticisms

In 1955 the American Law Institute revised the Model Act with respect to its sentencing, classification, correctional administration, parole, and community programs. A contributing reason for the change was the multiplicity of functions in those states in which the authority was responsible for both juveniles and youthful offenders.

It is to be expected that any proposal which interferes with functions which have formerly been considered the prerogative of any one group or groups will meet with opposition. Furthermore, if the proposal is adopted, opinions will differ as to its effectiveness. And so it has been with appraisals of the Youth Authority.

Possible reasons why most of the states have not adopted the basic tenets of the Model Youth Authority Act are: (1) the wide variations within the state with respect to the facilities provided; (2) the vested interests of the executives and boards of directors of the institutions; (3) the natural opposition of the judiciary to any proposal which would divest them of powers they have formerly enjoyed (even some of the most ardent promoters of the Youth Correction Authority idea have succumbed to judicial pressure); (4) the decision by some states that they would reject anything but the best and their failure to persuade the legislature to adopt the "best"; (5) public resistance because, although the interest of the public is mainly in behalf of juvenile delinquents, the Youth Correction Authority was designed initially for the treatment of youthful offenders.

In some of the states that have adopted Youth Authority legislation there is a wide gap between the proposals of the Model Act and the act adopted. Some have questioned whether the authority should have jurisdiction over the juvenile court age group. It will be recalled, however, that the upper limit of the juvenile court jurisdiction varies from 16 to 20.

According to Rubin, the Youth Correction Authority represents a "reorganization movement, concerned with renovation of the states' apparatus for dealing with juvenile delinquents or youthful criminal offenders, which attempts to create an agency drawing in highly responsible community representatives."[13]

The originators were not primarily concerned with the juvenile agencies which served almost exclusively residents of the local communities. Instead, the intent of the Model Act was to strip the *adult* courts of their power to designate the institution to which an offender should be sent. In each of the five states which have adopted the Youth Authority principle, the juvenile court still retains all its previous powers. The California law specifies that nothing in the Youth Authority Act shall be interpreted to change the powers of the juvenile court. The only exception is that the judge may not specify the training school to which he wishes to commit the child. Since in the majority of the states there is only one institution for boys and one for girls, the authority usually has little leeway.

Arguments for Extension

Arguing for the extension of the Youth Correction Authority plan to the younger age group, Ellingston writes:

> . . . the decision to extend the Youth Authority plan to include all committed juveniles was not made by the American Law Institute. . . . It was made by the stubborn and irreducible fact of the failure of existing industrial schools to provide delinquent children effective individual treatment aimed at their rehabilitation. In the main these schools for juveniles, like prisons for adults, provide custody and punishment-to-fit-the-crime. People who have discovered the chaotic and punitive nature of most correctional schools for delinquent children naturally feel that the place to begin applying the rational principles and procedures of the Youth Authority program is with these delinquent children.[14]

These comments foreshadow, in abstract terms, Tony's vividly described experiences in Chapter 22, as well as those noted by the participant observer at Ralston (Chapter 23).

Arguments Against Extension

Lejins calls attention to the seeming paradox presented by the authority of the criminal court to place any youthful offender on probation, and the jurisdiction apparently granted the Youth Authority to release wards to their

[13] Sol Rubin, "Changing Youth Correction Authority Concepts," *Focus*, Vol. 29, no. 3 (May 1950), pp. 77-82.
[14] John R. Ellingston, "Is the Youth Authority Idea Really Paying Off?" *Proceedings*, National Conference of Juvenile Agencies, Vol. 47 (1951), p. 79.

own homes under supervision of Youth Authority officers. In support of his opinion that the reform which the Model Youth Authority Act was supposed to accomplish has failed, Lejins writes: "The typical paradoxical situation is again with us; we again have first the decision by a non-expert as to what to do with the child, and then the opportunity to study what should be done. It is almost unbelievable but a fact. It goes without saying that all five states, in conformity with the pattern disclosed by this analysis, place the decision on probation in the hands of the lawyer-judge and take it away from the Authority, where the Model Act put it."[15]

In the opinion of the child welfare experts, to extend this program *would benefit only children officially labeled delinquent and retard the development of better services for all children.* Instead, they suggest revision of the Model Act and coordination of the efforts of all national organizations concerned with helping neglected and dependent as well as delinquent children.[16] This point of view supports the thesis that, to a large degree, the problems of dependent and delinquent children are similar in their origin, if not in their overt expression.

Summary

An attempt to improve the court's function by separating the judicial and the treatment role of the judge was advanced in the creation of the Youth Correction Authority program. The initial impetus was provided by study under the auspices of the American Law Institute of the shocking conditions to which youthful offenders in New York City in the late 1930s were subjected. California was the first state to adopt a Youth Correction Authority Act. The intent of the California act, passed in 1941, was to separate the process of diagnosis and planning for treatment from the determination of guilt, and to coordinate and improve the use of the state's facilities.

To date only four other states—Minnesota, Wisconsin, Massachusetts, and Texas—have adopted some form of Youth Correction Authority. New York State and New Jersey have made changes in their programs in order to correct some of the old abuses, in line with the Youth Authority idea; and Massachusetts is currently considering revisions of its original version of a Youth Authority, known there as the Youth Service Board.

The major explanations offered for the failure of the majority of the states to adopt the Youth Authority program are: (1) resistance on the part

[15] Peter Lejins, "Is the Youth Authority Idea Really Paying Off?" *Proceedings, National Conference of Juvenile Agencies,* Vol. 47 (1951), p. 92.
[16] Beck, *op. cit.,* pp. 11 ff; see also *idem., Youth Within Walls,* New York, Community Service Society, May 1950.

of the institutions, which heretofore have been autonomous with respect to their admission policies; (2) the objection of the judiciary to the separation of the treatment from the sentencing function.

In seeking ways to improve the institutional care of their charges some states—Michigan, Wisconsin, Illinois, Ohio, and recently New York—have followed California's lead in establishing work camps for certain offenders. Boys are sent to these camps either through reception centers or through transfer on the recommendation of youth authorities, in the states where these exist. With their work and counseling programs the camps provide more flexible settings for rehabilitation than do the large institutions. Furthermore, they are less threatening to the boys and to their parents. With the cooperation of the community they have been effective in the rehabilitation process. For their most effective use, however, they must be part of an over-all treatment program, centrally administered.

INSTITUTIONS FOR DELINQUENTS

CHAPTER 20

The Care of Delinquents Away from the Community

UNLIKE PROBATION, WHICH IS CARRIED OUT IN THE COMMUNITY, WHEN the court decides that the rehabilitation of the offender and the protection of society calls for his removal from the community, it uses its power of commitment.

Part IV reports on the number and characteristics of young people in the United States today who are receiving care as delinquents away from their homes, and outlines the variety of our institutional programs with respect to auspices, staff, and services, citing, for purposes of comparison, institutional practices in England and other foreign countries.

We review the institutional programs for delinquents as they reflect the rehabilitative philosophy of the juvenile court or the punitive philosophy of its forerunner, the criminal court. And we inquire into how far the addition of special personnel, educational, and clinical services and programs justifies the forceful removal of the delinquent from the community by counteracting the destructive effects of detention.

A common characteristic of most treatment devices is that their proponents tend to promote them as cure-alls. Today, for example, antibiotics, which are effective in certain illnesses, are sometimes applied to quite different ailments before their use has been sufficiently tested. Part of the explanation is no doubt an urgent desire to alleviate suffering. Gunther's *Death Be Not Proud* is a poignant record of a parent's desperate search to cure his son's brain tumor, which leads him to try even diet as a cure.

Sociological Approaches to Social Problems

In reviewing the development of society's approaches to the solution of any problem once it is recognized as a social problem, one can roughly distinguish four stages which to some extent overlap. The first stage is to crush the deviate; the second emphasizes attempts to deter the deviate and others from wrongdoing; the third is to provide custodial care for the deviate; and the fourth underscores rehabilitation and eventually prevention. For each of these emphases there has been a supporting theory.

Crush the Deviate

Because of the danger to the group which the deviate presented, in most primitive societies the usual solution of any social problem, including crime, was to crush the deviate. The rationale for this approach was—and still is, where it still exists—the belief in free will. If each individual has a choice and knows what he is doing, presumably he is responsible for his actions. If he does not control his behavior, he merits punishment and, as Beccaria believed (see Chapter 5), punishment should be equitably distributed and sufficient to deter the deviate.

The psychiatric point of view, however, rejects this position. It does not postulate free will and questions the prescription: "Let the punishment fit the crime." Instead it presumes a deep-seated need in each individual to punish others for conduct in which perhaps he himself would like to indulge.

Just as our knowledge of the meaning and underlying reasons for insanity has deepened our understanding of the ineffectuality of punishment in the treatment of the insane, so evidence mounts on the ineffectuality of punishment for many prisoners.

Deter the Deviate

The second approach in society's attempt to solve social problems also calls for punishment—not to destroy the wrongdoer, but primarily as a device for deterring him and others from further wrongdoing. Unfortunately, however, if a deterrent is to be effective, the standards of correct behavior must be universally accepted. But there is a wide variation in the opinions of various ethnic and socio-economic groups as to what behavior does merit punishment. We referred earlier (see Chapter 9) to Sykes and Matza's hypothesis of neutralization techniques used by people some of whose standards are different from those of the community, and which therefore make it "right" to be delinquent in certain circumstances.

An old but illuminating illustration of the inefficacy of even the death penalty as deterrent was the order in England to hang pickpockets publicly. The law had to be repealed. While the audience gazed at the pickpocket swinging from the gallows, his brother thieves had a heyday picking the pockets of the gaping spectators.

While undoubtedly the threat of punishment does deter some persons, what we do not yet know is *how* this threat operates, and how severe the punishment must be to accomplish this end. In spite of the mounting evidence of its inefficacy, however, preachers, judges, and teachers continue to call for increasing use of the rod. The vehemence with which the "anti-coddlers" assert that punishment is the cure for delinquency is consistent with the psychiatric explanation that it is the rousing of the anxiety of "normal" individuals that is behind much of the demand for control through punishment. Subvocally, this type of individual is probably saying to the community, "Please control this behavior so that my controls will hold."

Care for the Deviate

The custodial approach to the solution of a social problem was initiated when it was recognized that not all people are equally responsible for their behavior. Obviously, young children and mental defectives cannot be held responsible for all their acts. Thus, the emphasis in the attack on the problem shifted (1) to protecting the individual from himself since he is unable to control his behavior; and (2) to protecting the community from the consequences of his action.

For custody to be effectively applied, however, it is necessary to identify those who belong in this category; and—more difficult—to ascertain the length of time that such people should be kept in custody. Often community hysteria forces a person to remain in custody even though he has "served his term," and his reformation has been accomplished or he is at least unlikely to be a threat when he is released.

The form of the offense, or, in Sellin's terms, the community's resistance potential, usually determines the extent of the community's fear. Thus, although there is evidence that sex offenders and murderers are less likely to repeat their crimes than those who have offended against property, the former tend to be held much longer in custody. If the victim in a sex offense is a child, the community is apt to be very punitive, even though in all other respects the offender may be a law-abiding person. Yet study of his relationship with his parents and his wife often suggests that treatment rather than imprisonment would be appropriate.[1]

[1] Sidney Connel, Project No. 4163, New York School of Social Work, 1952.

If, as in a case described by the late Judge Ulman,[2] murder is accidental, the community's demand for severe punishment may be unwarranted. In the case cited, the consequences of the defendant's deed—the loss of his wife and the orphaning of his children—were, in the judge's opinion, sufficient punishment in themselves.

The community's attitude also sometimes influences a decision concerning parole, basing the decision upon the nature of the original offense rather than upon the offender's subsequent behavior. The prolonged refusal of the Chicago Parole Board to release the surviving member of the Leopold-Loeb affair, even after extensive psychiatric treatment and good conduct for many years in prison, was a case in point.[3] There is at least some possibility that the public's unconscious need to punish operates more severely when the offense is an expression of hostility against persons than when it involves property.

Rehabilitate the Deviate

In the fourth approach to the solution of a social problem, emphasis is shifting from custody to rehabilitation. The recognition that many maladjustments are reactions to social conditions, and not entirely the responsibility of the individual, has pointed to the need for change in those social conditions, and to an interest in cure. Cure, in turn, implies treatment rather than punishment. (The exception is the instance in which so-called "punishment" is actually appropriately designed as treatment.)

As noted above, however, institutional care has not been viewed as treatment, but instead has often been simply an expression of the law-abiding individual's unconscious need to protect himself by punishing the offender and removing him from society. Since the effectiveness of treatment and cure obviously depends upon the knowledge of the cause of the malady and the conscious use of appropriate treatment processes, we are faced today with a double-headed dilemma:

1. Can the institutions be effective for treatment when evidence suggests that so many of them are manned by people who consider them instruments of punishment?

2. How can the administrator balance his responsibility to society and to the deviant individual?

There is a vestige of each of these four approaches—crush, deter, care for, and rehabilitate—in today's institutions for delinquents. There is also, as Pansegrouw suggests,[4] another way of looking at our institutions for delin-

[2] Joseph N. Ulman, "The Trial Judge's Dilemma; A Judge's View," in Sheldon Glueck (ed.), *Probation and Criminal Justice,* New York, Macmillan, 1933, pp. 109-132.

[3] Meyer Levin, *Compulsion,* New York, Simon and Schuster, 1957.

[4] Nicholas Pansegrouw, Seminar for Social Work Teachers in Correctional Social Work, Berkeley, Calif., Summer 1956, under the auspices of the Training Section, U. S. Children's Bureau.

quents, i.e., as systems of social control. His analysis is worth quoting, even though any way of analyzing a social system obviously involves abstracting certain aspects of the totality and always reflects the orientation and indoctrination of the observer.

Institutions for Delinquents as Social Systems

In taking a fresh look at institutions for delinquents, Pansegrouw observes, it is important to see them as carryovers from the use of prisons. Viewed as a system, the prison is a device for dealing with adult members of society who violate the formally expressed social controls. As our discussion so far has pointed out, crime and delinquency are both socially defined phenomena. In consequence, one may expect that the controls for dealing with those who flout society's standards will reflect the power structure, the technological developments, and the value systems of the particular society.

Since American institutions for criminals and delinquents have their roots in their European forebears, Pansegrouw traces changes in methods for dealing with the social deviant as they have reflected changes in technology and in class structure of different European societies. Although the psychological drive to punish offenders is fairly constant, it has been most severe in those periods in which the social distance between classes has been the greatest. When there was a powerful elite, it punished the offender by banishment or mutilation as though he belonged to a different order of being. In inflicting punishment, it was assumed that the severity would deter others from similar acts.

As class distinctions became less marked in Western society following the industrial revolution, economic interest began to have an influence on the correctional process for adults. If one considers the offender as a potential consumer as well as a producer, methods for dealing with him, when he offends, will take a more moderate form. Thus in this period the drive to punish and to mutilate the offender was somewhat overlaid with attempts at his reform and rehabilitation.

In the simpler society, a correctional system that provided mass care for large numbers of persons was not only unnecessary but would have been economically impossible. With the growth of towns and cities, however, mass congregate prisons began to flourish. There adults and children alike were incarcerated with little regard for their health or rehabilitation. When the idle prisoner began to be viewed as an economic waste, the system of prison labor developed. But with the rise of labor unions, this system was protested as offering unfair competition. At the same time, with the emergence of John Doe from anonymity, more humanitarian theories began to permeate prison practice. In response to these developments, prison administrators readjusted their work program, so that the objectives became:

1. To meet some of the costs of running the institution by providing some of the necessities through the work program, at the same time cutting costs down further since the work-training program could be supervised en masse.

2. To retrain the prisoner for a productive role upon his return to society. While there is today a growing awareness that the use of force, expressed in formal controls and supported by the community's insistent demands for more severe punishment, is ineffective in rehabilitation, this realization is not always acted upon. For example, severe penalties are imposed in the Baumes Law in New York State for those guilty of a fourth offense, although they have not resulted in lower recidivist rates. Professional criminals apparently know that crime does pay and they figure that the chances of gain usually outweigh those of their apprehension.

Pansegrouw reminds us that law is not the enforcement of moral principles. Rather, it expresses the social needs of a given society at a given time in its development. Thus, law and morals are not coterminous, and formal controls are not always effective in changing patterns of behavior. Illustrative examples are drinking and speeding. In both instances the formal controls are primarily influential only in the immediate situation and usually only for as long as the individual remains within the effective jurisdiction of those who exercise the controls.

It is the *informal* social controls, i.e., those exercised through intangible and diffuse pressures from members of the group with which one identifies oneself, that tend to be incorporated into the individual's personal value system. The psychologists call this process internalization of values, the sociologists call it socialization—a process which is continuous throughout life. As we shall see in our discussion of the goals and the programs of the various institutions—public, private, education-oriented or treatment-centered—the crucial role of these informal controls is often ignored. Their relevance, for example, to the difficulty of effecting rehabilitation is underscored in the report of the inmate group described in Chapter 23, which, feeling itself punished by being banished from the community, felt a need to retaliate and to thwart the rehabilitative goals of the administration.

Summary

Although satisfactory causal explanations for the various forms which delinquency assumes in our society are not at hand, efforts to treat and control it cannot be postponed. Each of the four major approaches common to the solution of all social problems reflects to a certain extent the philosophy and causal theory in vogue at the time.

Initially, society's reaction to social deviation, of which delinquency is one illustration, was to punish the deviant as just retribution for his crime. The second approach was the use of punishment as a device to deter others from disapproved behavior, as well as to prevent its recurrence on the part of the delinquent himself. The third, custodial, approach came about when it was recognized that not all individuals, specifically young children and mental defectives, are answerable for their behavior. The shift from deterrence to custody had a two-fold purpose: the protection of the individual against himself, and the protection of the community against the consequences of the misdeeds. With the recognition that custody was not the whole answer, because society itself was partly responsible, the fourth approach emphasized rehabilitation and prevention. These four approaches were not self-limiting or mutually exclusive.

Viewed as a social system, our current institutions for delinquents, whose roots were in European prisons, reflect also the fairly rapid changes in the technology and class structure of America's highly industrialized urban, heterogeneous populations. Possibly because our American economy has been continually expanding, the mounting costs to the community of our institutions for containing and rehabilitating criminals and delinquents have not been balanced against their results in human terms. Nor has our institutional system always reflected an awareness that the informal system of controls, which operates differently in each subculture, is often more influential than the system of formal controls that the dominant society imposes.

CHAPTER 21

Temporary Detention Facilities

Charlie Goes to Jail

Twelve-year-old Charlie never could figure out how to behave on the nights when his father came home drunk and beat his mother. Sometimes he tried to protect her, and was beaten himself for his efforts. Sometimes he just cowered under the bedclothes. Finally, one night, he ran away. The policeman who found him sleeping in the entryway of a warehouse just across the county line from his home took Charlie to the station house and booked him as a runaway and "juvenile delinquent."

Charlie landed in a seven-by-twelve-foot cell heavy with the stench of unwashed prisoners of the past. It had no window, no washbowl, no table, no chairs—only four steel bunks with fetid, straw-filled mattress ticks. The dirty concrete floor was littered with the remains of comic books, parts of which had been torn off for toilet paper. A single unshaded 25-watt bulb provided the only light. When Charlie came in, three of the bunks were already occupied by older boys. They greeted him with sullen warnings to stop his whimpering or they'd "take care" of him in the morning.

After a few days, Charlie was sent home. There was no investigation of the problem which precipitated his running away. No one offered him or his family any help or guidance. You and I might agree that Charlie was more sinned against than sinning. And what he needed was shelter rather than custody. But technically he was a delinquent—he had run away from home.[1]

The literature on delinquency devotes relatively little attention to the problems of detention. As a theoretically short interim process between the delinquent's apprehension and the eventual disposition of his case, it may seem less important perhaps than other phases of a community's over-all program for dealing with delinquency. Yet it is an important link in the chain of society's efforts to deal with the young offender.

Since in the majority of instances, as in Charlie's case, it is the police officer who determines whether or not to hold a young person whom he has apprehended for subsequent court appearance, our chapter on the police might have included a discussion of temporary detention facilities and the circumstances under which it is appropriate for the police officer to deprive a young person of his liberty. Detention, however, is not only a concern of the police. Occasionally, detention facilities are used following adjudication if the judge wishes more information about the young person before deciding on a treatment plan. Thus, temporary removal from his own or a substitute home, either before or after a court hearing, may be a prelude to a longer sojourn in a training school or treatment center for delinquents. Their experience in detention may condition the reactions of some of these young people to authority and so either aid or obstruct the rehabilitative efforts of the long-term institution to which the court may commit them.

When and How Is a Child Detained?

Detention versus Shelter

The interim care of the neglected or dependent child is called "shelter," in contrast to "detention," the term which describes the care of the delinquent who is temporarily removed from his home either before or after court hearing. Many communities house dependent and neglected children in the same building as delinquents. The detention quarters may be attached to the juvenile court to provide easy access to and from hearings; in some cities, however, the facility is located at some distance from the court. As the National Probation and Parole Association surveys indicate, "if shelter and detention are combined, there is a temptation to use the detention facilities for temporarily unruly children in shelter care. If special provision is not made for children needing custody they are apt to be kept in 'cells' in the

[1] Ruth and Edward Brecher, "Jail Is No Place for Children in Trouble," *Colliers*, May 27, 1955; Reprinted by National Probation and Parole Association.

basements of the ordinary shelters," as in the midwestern detention "home" described below:

> From the outside, this "haven" for children in trouble—a three-story brick residence—looked inviting enough. Almost any afternoon you could see youngsters playing in the well-kept yard under the watchful eye of a kindly-appearing matron. But in the basement, an NPPA consultant found seven adolescent boys locked up in a room which was absolutely bare—no chairs, no benches, no tables. Nothing at all—just boys surrounded by walls, with windows too high to see out of and nothing to sit on except the floor. Some of the boys had been locked in that room for weeks, some as long as two months.
>
> Had they no activities whatever?
>
> Yes, the NPPA consultant was told, sometimes the boys were given a ball to play with.
>
> How about those youngsters playing on the lawn?
>
> Those weren't "delinquent" children, he was told, but "dependent" children who were being given temporary shelter. And the superintendent who ran the "home" couldn't let the "bad" children in the basement associate with the "good" children upstairs.
>
> So the good children ate in the dining room while the bad children ate off trays in their bare basement room. The good children had movies in the evening; the bad children stayed down in their hole. A teacher came in to give the good children lessons; the bad children got none.
>
> Oh, yes, there was one break in the routine. Twice a month, a women's group came in to lead hymn-singing parties. On these occasions, the bad children were allowed up to sing the praises of a kindly Father in Heaven who watches over every sparrow.[2]

Unfortunately this is not an isolated situation. The behavior of the superintendent reflects not only a lack of understanding of the feelings and needs of children but a lack of training as well. And the well-intentioned if naïve efforts of the visitors betoken the way in which even a city with a well-organized council of social agencies often closes its eyes to what is happening to "bad" children. Perhaps the community believes that the court takes proper care of its wards.

The Legal Basis

The juvenile court law in each state notes the conditions under which detention away from home is appropriate. In many states, the conditions conform to those stated in the 1949 revised Standard Act, i.e., "If it appears that the child is in such condition or surroundings that his welfare requires that his custody be immediately assumed by the Court, the judge may order, by

[2] *Ibid.*, p. 11. Page references are to reprint.

endorsement upon the summons, that the officer serving the same shall at once take the child into custody."[3] Further, a child who is found violating any law or ordinance, may be taken into custody without a warrant.

It will be noted that the Standard Act refers to a court order for detention. In most communities, however, the juvenile court is not in session after three or four o'clock in the afternoon, or on weekends. Under such conditions a police officer cannot secure a court order unless, as in Connecticut which will be discussed later in this chapter, the court makes a special representative available whenever it is not in session.

Role of the Police

Opinions differ as to whether it is proper for a police officer to remove a child even temporarily from his home without a court order. The Lansing Conference (see Chapter 13) decided that a police officer who places a child in secure detention without a court order should notify the court in writing stating the reason for his action. Some conference participants thought that the police officer might be given forty-eight hours' grace to make this report; others voted for a lapse of not more than two hours in notifying the court.

Whether the police officer takes a child into custody with or without a court order, he is supposed to notify the child's parents or guardian that their presence and that of their child may be required in court. If the police officer cannot locate the parents within a reasonable time, or if after consulting with them he believes that the child's interest or the safety of the community warrants detention, and the court is not in session, the officer may use the shelter or detention quarter designated by the court in accordance with written procedure.

In the opinion of the Lansing Conference far too many children were being unnecessarily detained by the police with detriment to the young people. Since the majority of these young people are subsequently released they could probably have been safely allowed to remain in their own homes pending court hearing. As Norman says: "The pity of it is that many of these children picked up for minor delinquencies do not require detention at all. As a result, they are thrown into contact with more sophisticated youngsters and pick up their first lesson in crime."[4]

The guide lines for the police officer, whose judgment and discretion largely determine not only which young people will be brought to court but also whether or not they will be detained, are unfortunately not as clear as those he follows in calling an ambulance for someone who is ill or injured.

[3] Standard Juvenile Court Act, rev. ed., National Probation and Parole Association, 1949.
[4] Sherwood Norman, "Detention Before the Hearing," *Alabama Correctional Journal*, Oct. 1958.

Since, unlike the emergency ward of the hospital, which is always open, many juvenile courts are not in continuous session, the officer who picks up a youngster after court hours must decide whether it is safe to let him remain at home until the court convenes.

This can be a crucial decision. Even the temporary deprivation of liberty of children or adults is an act which, in a democracy, needs to be surrounded by all appropriate safeguards. Moreover, temporary detention has a regrettable tendency to extend beyond short-term limits. In contrast to the ease with which bail is often available for well-known figures in the underworld, all too frequently youths who are arrested remain in detention for extended periods of time, because their families are unable to arrange for even small bail bonds and the court calendar moves slowly.[5] Overcrowding in the long-term institutions to which some youngsters are committed also tends to lengthen their stay in temporary detention.

Role of the Probation Officer

But the police officer and the judge are not the only ones who often detain young persons unnecessarily. Some probation officers clap young offenders into detention either in a panic-type reaction to the form of the offense, or to "teach them a lesson." More often, however, a probation officer detains a young person to expedite carrying out the officer's routine assignments. For example, in a recent survey on the West Coast, Kneisel observed that detention was sanctioned by the probation department as a means for getting information to be used in the social study of a child's case. If the young person was not detained it meant that the probation officer could not write his social history without making home visits, and it was frequently difficult to persuade the child or his parents to come to the court for the required psychological tests. When Kneisel suggested that the detention facilities should not be used in that way the probation staff protested that this would mean additional staff and cars if they were to produce the necessary records. Obviously, the probation staff regarded the detention facilities as an aid to diagnosis. In Kneisel's terms this was like the spider catching a fly, placing him in a web, then sucking him when it was convenient to do so. He had his victim where he wanted him.[6]

In Norman's opinion, with which we agree, detention should be regarded as a specialized type of care as important in the rehabilitative process as is hospital care for a child whose illness requires it, whether the illness is of long or short duration. Just as one does not expect a doctor to prescribe

[5] Interim Report No. 10, Juvenile Delinquency Evaluation Project of the City of New York, March 1958.

[6] Personal Communication, November 1957.

hospitalization unless it is needed, so children should be detained only under the following circumstances:

1. If it is necessary to protect the young person from his own destructive impulses.

2. If the detention experience will afford him opportunity to engage in meaningful activities.

3. If it brings the young person into contact with adults who not only like children but are also skilled in helping them to understand and deal with their difficulties.

Extent and Place of Detention

From time to time the U.S. Children's Bureau has been concerned not only with the kind of facilities provided for detaining children but with the extent of their use. Belden reported[7] that only 10 per cent of the more than 2000 courts studied in 1918 used separate detention facilities for children. According to a 1923 survey of the 200 courts which served areas whose population ranged from 25,000 to 100,000, almost 70 per cent of the children who came before them were held in jail. A simultaneous study of rural courts, which was made by the National Probation and Parole Association, showed almost universal use of jails for temporary custody of children.[8] A summary of returns from 380 courts in 1944 disclosed that well over half the young people who came before the court were detained, and that jails were still being used extensively.[9]

In 1955 Norman estimated that 200,000, or half of all children between the ages of 7 and 17, who appeared before the juvenile courts were held in some type of detention facility before their cases were heard. About 100,000 were held in county jails and police lock-ups, many of which, like Charlie's quarters, were substandard for adults. Additional thousands of children were confined in basement cells or behind bars in detention homes which offered nothing more than the "cold storage of physical care and custody."

To place a child in jail is clearly a contradiction of the philosophy which created the juvenile court. Yet about five sixths of the 3068 counties of the United States held juveniles in jails. While the available data are not complete, the Lansing inquiry revealed that the proportion of children detained by the police was higher in large than in small communities. In the

[7] Evelina Belden, *Courts in the United States Hearing Children's Cases*, 1918, No. 65, Washington, U.S. Children's Bureau, 1920, p. 49.

[8] Katherine J. Lenroot, "Progressive Methods of Care of Children Pending Juvenile Court Hearing," *Hospital Social Service*, Vol. 15 (1927), pp. 47-49.

[9] *Juvenile Court Statistics, 1944 and 1945*, supplement to *The Child*, Vol. 11 (Nov. 1946), Washington, U.S. Children's Bureau, Table 5, p. 5.

latter the police are apt to detain only the most serious cases. In the large communities the police may know less about the children whom they pick up and thus hold them to make certain that the young people will be on hand when their case comes before the judge. As a consequence of this practice, a greater percentage of children residing in larger communities is subsequently released without being referred to the court.[10]

Types of Detention Care

The National Probation and Parole Association, which has maintained a continuing interest in the proper use of detention facilities, has accepted invitations from numerous communities to study their detention problems and to make recommendations for staff and building.[11] As we shall see when we discuss criteria for evaluating institutions (Chapter 26) it is easy to be misled by external appearances. Recall, if you please, the pleasant exterior of the midwest detention "home" described by the Brechers. The studies of the National Probation and Parole Association in 1945 disclosed a distressing picture not unlike that found by Warner in 1932 in thirty eight states.[12]

Detention quarters, whether large or small, the NPPA has found, are generally poorly located and poorly designed for proper staff supervision. Many are undermanned. Only in rare instances is the staff trained to help children in trouble. While the effect of these deficiencies may be less depressing on older than on younger children or the young person who is detained before court hearing and soon released, it can be and no doubt often is very damaging for children detained while they await transfer to an institution.

Jails

The best that can be said for the experience of many young people detained in jail is that their keepers, like Margie's in the account below, are sometimes kindly.

Margie was a pert, blonde sixteen-year-old spending her 34th day in this overnight police lockup in a small southern town. The police who

[10] *Police Services for Juveniles* (Lansing Report), Washington, U.S. Children's Bureau, 1954.

[11] Sherwood Norman, "Detention," Part I, *Standards and Goals for Detention and Shelter of Children,* New York National Probation and Parole Association, 1954; see also *idem, Standards and Guides for the Detention of Children and Youth,* New York, National Probation and Parole Association, New York, 1958.

[12] Florence M. Warner, *Juvenile Detention in the United States,* Chicago, University of Chicago Press, 1933.

guarded her were kindly; they let her hang around the desk, and they supplied her with chewing gum and cigarettes. She had no place to take a bath, but she did have a washbowl where she carefully washed her clothes every night. There was no matron, and no other female prisoners.

Margie's alleged offense was taking $4 from a piggy bank in a home where she had been baby-sitting one evening. A judge in a nearby county had committed her to the custody of the State Welfare Department, and most of her 34 days in the police lockup had been spent awaiting transfer to some state institution. The judge later said he was astonished to learn she was still in jail. State officials said they were sorry, but Margie would have to wait her turn. There were five other girls in various jails and lockups, they explained, on the same waiting list.[13]

In New York State and in five others, Margie would not have been a juvenile delinquent, but a youthful offender or a wayward minor because she had already celebrated her sixteenth birthday when she was brought to court. While awaiting transfer to an institution in one of these states she might have been held in a girls' residence club or in the women's prison.

Other instances like that below, also reported by the Brechers, are not unusual.

The next time you read in your newspapers some account of a brutal crime committed by teen-agers, remember also this other side of the story. Remember the case of two teen-age Puerto Rican boys picked up one night last summer [1954] in Central Park in New York, and lodged in the Tombs Prison on a charge of having raped a fifty-one-year old woman. The charge later proved phony. But by the time the authorities established the facts, the youths—neither of whom had ever run afoul of the law before—had spent *five months and five days* in the Tombs.[14]

Foster Homes

Not all young people are as unlucky as Charlie, the boys in the Midwestern town, Margie in Virginia, and the Puerto Rican boys in New York. Knuckles, an obstreperous 16-year-old resident of Allentown, Pennsylvania, had a much more constructive experience with a foster family while he waited to be brought to court.

It took three burly policemen in a squad car to transport Mike (Knuckles) Smith to the home late one night last summer. It was Knuckles' birth-

13 Brecher, *op. cit.*, pp. 9-10.
14 *Ibid.*, p. 7.

day, and he had obviously been drinking. He was in an ugly, rebellious mood when he was picked up for disorderly conduct, disturbing the peace and striking an officer of the law. Knuckles was a big fellow, nearly six feet tall in his stocking feet; but the birthday he was celebrating was only his sixteenth.

"They'll never keep me in that can," Knuckles boasted on the way. "They ain't even got bars on the windows."

The three policemen exchanged glances. Their instincts urged them to take Knuckles to the county jail instead of to the pleasant suburban home where Mr. and Mrs. George Roth—"Mom" and "Pop" to Allentown's youngsters in trouble—keep house for juvenile delinquents. Mom and Pop didn't even have a gun; this boy could easily overpower them.

"It isn't going to work this time," one of the officers said in a worried aside as the car drove up to the Roths' door.

The Roth home, though its doors are kept locked and its windows are covered with specially designed screens strong enough to hold even kids like Knuckles, is not a jail. Knuckles appeared to sense the difference the minute he crossed the threshold. It wasn't what he saw or heard; it was what he smelled. By accident or design, Mom Roth's spick-and-span kitchen is right next to the admissions office; at almost any hour of the day or night, the first thing you notice when you enter is the comfortable aroma of Mom's Pennsylvania Dutch cooking. What Knuckles smelled was one of Mom's specialties—hot cinnamon-and-raisin buns.

Knuckles looked at Mom and Pop with a puzzled frown. It's hard to act tough when your mouth is watering, and you suddenly remember you've had nothing but a couple of greasy hamburgers since breakfast.

"Better lock this one up tight," the senior policeman warned, mopping his brow. "It was all the three of us could do to get him here."

Pop said nothing. Mom said, "My, you all must be hungry. Come on into the kitchen—I'll have coffee and a snack in two minutes."

The men and the boy sat down while Mom laid out the snack—Lebanon bologna, Pennsylvania head cheese, strawberry jam she had preserved herself, fresh bread, cinnamon buns. The coffee was hot and black.

"Our rules are pretty simple here," Pop told Knuckles. "First off, get yourself a real hot shower. Plenty of soap. When you've done, call me and I'll give you a shampoo. This is our home, you know. It's a clean home, and we aim to keep it that way. Tomorrow morning you can sleep late if you want to. But at ten, we all pile into the car and go to church together."

Knuckles, eating ravenously, nodded. His bluster was gone. For the first time in days, his stomach had a satisfied feeling. That hot shower sounded good. And Pop was the steady kind of adult Knuckles hadn't run up against in years—firm but friendly, a man you could trust to play square. Half an hour later, the police were on their way, convinced that Mom's and Pop's magic had worked once more. Knuckles was already asleep in a single room, snoring peacefully.

"What Mom and Pop chiefly accomplish," says Raven H. Ziegler, Lehigh County's chief probation officer, "is a change in the kid's attitude toward adults and authority. Mom and Pop don't pamper the kids in their care; but they don't reject them, either. They give the boy or girl a glimpse—often the first—of what decent, civilized, friendly American living can be like. You'd be amazed at how much even a few days of that can accomplish."

Not all the Roths' charges are six-foot toughs like Knuckles, of course. While we were there, the Roth "family" consisted of three fourteen-year-old girls brought in for shoplifting and for running away from home. All three were pretty as pictures, clean, neatly dressed and full of girlish vitality. Many communities still lock up such children in adult jails.[15]

The foster or boarding home was originally used as a substitute for institutions for young neglected or dependent children, whose own parents could not or did not provide proper care. In the 1930s Boston and Buffalo began to use foster homes for children who needed secure custody.[16] Unlike the usual financial arrangement in foster homes, boarding parents who provide temporary shelter or custody are guaranteed a flat sum with an additional per capita rate for each child in residence. Ideally, the number of children in a single foster-home shelter or custody at any one time should not exceed eight or ten.

Successful care requires well chosen and experienced foster parents who, like Mom and Pop Roth, can show affection without spoiling children. Some staff, in addition to the couple, is usually necessary for the smooth running of the boarding home. Provision must be made also for educational, recreational, and medical care. In the many small communities in which there are few children at any one time who cannot be returned to their own homes temporarily, the boarding home provides a flexible, constructive, and relatively inexpensive device which calls for no initial investment by the community in the physical plant.

Regional Homes

In communities which are not likely to have a tradition of foster care, if the population of the county is under 100,000 and fewer than 50 children

15 *Ibid.*, pp. 15-16.
16 Henry Lenz, "Juvenile Detention: Ten Years Use of Boarding Homes," *Yearbook*, National Probation Association, 1942, pp. 133-149; see also Sherwood Norman, *Standards and Guides for the Detention of Children and Youth*.

a year need secure custoday, Norman recommends, a small specially designed district detention home, strategically located with regard to a group of counties. Each county could pay a per diem varying with the county tax rate. Such a plan might well be tried in the form of a pilot project and, if successful, extended to all of the smaller counties throughout the states.[17]

Richmond, Syracuse, and three cities in Michigan—Detroit, Saginaw, and Grand Rapids—have established regional detention quarters which serve children who come from other communities in the state. All of Connecticut is served by three receiving centers, attached to the three branches of the state-wide juvenile court in Bridgeport, Hartford and New Haven (see Chapter 18). There are thirteen area offices distributed throughout the state. In the last seventeen years no child has been held in jail. Trained probation officers are on call twenty-four hours a day.

According to William MacKay, chief probation officer of the Connecticut state-wide juvenile court, which has jurisdiction up to age 18,

"The heart of the Connecticut system lies in the cordial relationship between these probation officers and the police.

"When a policeman anywhere in Connecticut takes a child into custody, his first step is to phone the nearest probation officer. In four cases out of five, the two agree that the child can be taken home, and his parents given a juvenile court summons. In these cases, the probation officer invariably visits the home the next day, and talks with both parents and child. He begins to collect the data which the judge will later need in disposing of the case. Even more important, he lays the foundation for counseling services which these children will get at home rather than in an institution."

At first, MacKay concedes, the police were leery about "just turning the kids loose." But as the system sank roots, they became increasingly enthusiastic. Few cops *like* to jail a kid, and the police could see for themselves that home supervision was really working.

Sometimes, of course, the child is so disturbed, or the home situation so intolerable, or the offense so serious, that detention is the only answer. In such cases, the probation officer authorizes detention—not in the local jail, but in the nearest court-operated detention home.[18]

The conditions with respect to detention appear ideal in Connecticut. The designation of a trained probation officer to decide whether or not a child should be detained is no doubt responsible for the relatively small number, 30 to 40 children, who were held in secure custody on an average day in the year 1955. In contrast, Philadelphia's imposing youth center described below has been overcrowded since it was opened.

[17] Sherwood Norman, *Standards and Guides for the Detention of Children and Youth*, Part 5, pp. 127-136.
[18] Quoted in Brecher, *op. cit.*, p. 18-19.

City Detention Homes: Selected Illustrations

PHILADELPHIA'S YOUTH CENTER. In Philadelphia, the decision to keep a child in detention is made after he has been taken into custody. The police officer brings each young person whom he apprehends to the Youth Center, where a representative of the court decides whether the situation calls for continued detention.

After placing a child in detention the police officer notifies the parents of the whereabouts of the child. He advises the parents that the child may be released to them if they go to the detention home and if the probation officer at the detention home decides favorably. (See Tony's account in Chapter 22.)

When the parents arrive at the detention home, the probation officer calls the boy, interviews him, and decides whether the child may be released to his parents pending a hearing. Regardless of whether a child is released or detained, a preliminary hearing is held the day following admission to detention to determine: (1) whether the police have a prima facie case; and (2) if a case is established, whether it could be handled on unofficial probation or should be referred to court. Regardless of this decision, the probation officer is responsible for deciding whether a period of punitive detention seems desirable. They call this "developing probation readiness."

The complaints of representatives of the schools, the police, and the court that the Philadelphia Youth Center does not hold the young people long enough suggest that these critics believe the purpose of the Youth Center is punishment or "training" rather than constructive custody for the shortest possible period pending the court's disposition of the case. Such use of the Youth Center as a facility for "shock treatment" to accommodate police and school personnel who want children "taught a lesson," and the fact that often over half the beds are occupied by children awaiting transfer to other institutions, tend to distort the function of the detention facility.

In going through the Philadelphia Youth Center, one can easily be over-impressed by the physical arrangements, the modern architecture, the pleasing decorative schemes, and the mechanical facilities. In a conducted tour through the center, a woman in charge of one of the household units, questioned about in-service training, mentioned jiujitsu. When asked why this was necessary she said they had pretty tough kids there and they needed to learn how to handle them. The remark suggests that, in spite of the usual in-service sessions, the staff may be more concerned with restraint than with helping. This may be due to the improper use to which the facility is put, a fact the administration readily acknowledges.

A person with the title of social worker but without professional training is in charge of the files on all children, and makes case summaries for social agencies that may request them. These files include a face sheet, a report of the physical examination, a social service exchange slip, and reports on the child's behavior made by the untrained supervising staff and especially assigned teachers, and occasionally a summary of the child's previous school record.

A psychiatrist visits the detention home daily to interview children who are referred to him. Since the psychiatrist generally does not have a social history, however, he can only screen for the most obvious pathology.

LOS ANGELES JUVENILE HALL. The Los Angeles detention quarters, in spite of a 600 capacity, is always overcrowded because the police sweep into custody anyone who violates the curfew law and are given forty-eight hours leeway to obtain a court order for those they have detained. An indication of the unsoundness of this practice is that the court finds further detention unnecessary in a large proportion of cases. The routine psychiatric screening, like that in use in Philadelphia, has been discontinued in Los Angeles. Lacking a social study made by trained caseworkers and psychologists, the psychiatrist usually noted only those cases which were so obviously in need of psychiatric help that they would have been automatically referred by the staff.

NEW YORK CITY'S YOUTH HOUSE. New York City's Youth House for Boys, whose new building was dedicated on March 1, 1958, has risen like a phoenix from the ashes of the old SPCC, which ran the New York City Shelter that formerly housed neglected, dependent, and delinquent children.

New York's Society for the Prevention of Cruelty to Children was established in 1875, two years after the Society for the Prevention of Cruelty to Animals. The metamorphosis of the SPCC was initiated by an investigation by the city's budget director when he disclosed that the city was actually supporting an organization with police power, but that it had no authority over the institution since the private board of directors was in no way responsible to the city. The SPCC staff which investigated complaints against the children and brought the cases to court had no special qualifications for this work. The best that could be said for them was that their intentions were good, if one were willing to grant that their ideas of what was good for children were sound.

Following a study of the dubious practices of the New York City Shelter, through a group of private citizens whose interests were spearheaded by Judge Polier of the juvenile court, the housing of neglected and dependent children was separated from that of delinquents. Quarters for the delinquent children were obtained on East Twelfth Street, and operations were turned over to a new Youth House board, appointed by the city.

The first program for boys was initiated under the leadership of Frank

Cohen, who also established a camp on Welfare Island for girls. Over the years, both the quarters for the girls, which were later moved to the Bronx, and those for the boys have been unduly taxed. This is partly because the police and judges often use them for purposes for which they were not intended, and partly because of a backlog of children destined for other overcrowded institutions. If New York City had a system like that in Connecticut, i.e., making probation staff available on call to decide whether a child's detention was warranted, the facilities would probably not be so crowded.

Nevertheless, as the consultants at the National Probation and Parole Association agree, the goal of the Youth House program is to make the experience in detention as constructive as possible. The house staff, the school staff, and the clinic staff all aim to change the belligerent child by proving to him that not all adults are hostile.[19]

As in Philadelphia, Youth House in New York City is used for study, and the probation department at the court often uses this facility instead of the clinic in the court itself. Opinions differ, however, as to whether such study and diagnosis represent a proper use of detention facilities. This author concurs with Kneisel's opinion[20] that:

1. No child should be detained for psychiatric study, even if there is prima facie evidence that the child's behavior brings him within the jurisdiction of the juvenile court, unless there is unmistakable evidence that the family relationship is so strained, the child so disturbed, and/or the neighborhood so aroused that the child undoubtedly would run away, get into new difficulty, or be in physical jeopardy if he were released. Unless these circumstances obtain there is no good reason why a young person should not be studied in an outpatient clinic.

2. The initial presenting picture, and/or the child's adjustment to his detention, should determine the type of study needed. The study may be by a psychiatrically oriented caseworker, by a psychologist, by a psychiatrist, or by a team.

3. When a study is appropriate and necessary, no child should be detained longer than five weeks. The maximum amount of time required for a social study is two weeks and for full psychiatric study not more than four weeks, but preferably three.

An argument in favor of study while the child remains in his own home is similar to that advanced by critics of Gesell, whose generalizations with respect to the young child's behavior are based on laboratory observations— surely an unnatural habitat. It is likely that the impressions which even a skilled staff get of a boy in detention may be considerably skewed by the

19 Frank Cohen, *Children in Trouble,* New York, Norton, 1952.
20 Personal Communication, November 27, 1957.

discomfort, if not by the threatening aspects, of the environment. Sociologists and psychologists would both agree that the individual's reaction is affected by the environment which is part of the situation. Others argue that the juvenile court should provide its own facilities even though those offered by the detention quarters may provide the court with more convenient access to the delinquent.

EXAMPLES OF GOOD DETENTION PRACTICE. In the last twenty years, more than fifty detention homes have either been extensively remodeled or newly constructed. Their plants have been renovated mainly as a result of plans and standards developed by the National Probation and Parole Association. In the more progressive communities, the services as well as the premises have been revamped. Rigid punitive measures, including solitary confinement, described in some of our excerpts above, have been replaced by a system of care based on controlled permissiveness, under the direction of a trained staff.[21] The Essex County Parental School, located in Newark, and the Buffalo Detention Department in Erie County, like the Connecticut system, employ trained social workers. These social caseworkers give each individual in detention an opportunity to find out what he really wants to do and to be. At the same time the social worker sets limits to help the youth control his aggressive impulses.

The detention facility in Dallas provides not only an extensive educational and recreational program but a modified form of group therapy. In several communities the young people in detention have access to such community resources as churches, movies, swimming pools, and high school gymnasia. Detention centers at the Child Training Institute in Toledo, and in Dayton and Richmond make extensive use of extramural facilities.

Suggestions for Improving Detention Care

Because the problem of detention will vary with the size and the character of the population and its social agency resources, the community should accept the responsibility for working out an appropriate plan. In a community which has some sort of council of social agencies—there are about 500 such councils in the United States—a citizens' committee initially attached to the social planning council might set itself the following agenda, suggested by Norman:[22]

1. Look into the numbers of children, the sources through which they come, and their length of stay in detention quarters.

[21] Elliot Studt, "Staff Guidance in a Detention Home," *Focus*, Vol. 30 (1951), pp. 12-17.
[22] Sherwood Norman, "Detention Before the Hearing."

2. Review the current intake practice to see whether detention is used as a convenience for the police or the probation officer, as a punishing device, or just for "cold storage," as Norman calls it.

3. Arrange for joint agreement of the police, the court, and the administration of the detention facility that an officer of the court be designated to assume the responsibility, whether or not the court is in session, for deciding whether detention is necessary.

4. Be reasonably sure that the children for whom the court orders detention fall in one or more of the following categories: (a) children who need secure custody because of inimical conditions in their own homes; (b) children who have run away or may be a menace to themselves or to the community, and (c) children who must be held as witnesses.

5. Make sure that the staff in the detention facility is properly equipped by personality and training: (a) to understand the various needs of children, and (b) to make the experience away from home as constructive as possible.

6. Review aspects of life in the community which create problems for which the community provides preventive and rehabilitative services which might decrease the need for custodial detention.

Summary

Detention before court hearing, i.e., deprivation of liberty, should be the decision of a representative of the court. It is, however, often used inappropriately by the police officer who may be afraid that a child he has apprehended will not be on hand when needed for court appearance. Occasionally, the officer uses detention "to teach a lesson."

It is estimated that half of the 200,000 children detained annually by police before court hearings are held in jails, a practice which is not only illegal but inappropriate from every point of view.

Unfortunately, even the communities that provide separate detention quarters for secure custody have failed, with rare exceptions, to staff them adequately so that the experience of being removed from his home will be a constructive one for the child. There is agreement among authorities that if the detention experience is not to be destructive the staff must be discriminating, understanding and helpful rather than punitive in its approach to young people in trouble.

Not only are many children unnecessarily detained before the court hearing but, in some communities, relatively large numbers remain in detention quarters after adjudication of their cases by the court. This occurs because institutions to which the court commits them may have no vacancy.

Many children remain in custody for extended periods of time. In such cases the onus is not on the police, or the probation staff, but on the community and perhaps on the institutions, some of which set up intake criteria which do not meet the needs of the children for whom the court seeks an institutional commitment. This is a question which will be discussed more fully in the chapters on institutional care which follow.

CHAPTER 22

Long-Term Institutions and Their Inmates

Tony Speaks

At the age of thirteen I was committed to a reform school. My first encounter with the law came when I was ten years old. Perhaps I was nine—I don't remember. Along with several other boys I was caught trying to take money from a cash register. The police took me to the old house of detention at Twenty-Second and Arch Streets and turned me over to an elderly man. He took my clothes, told me to get under a shower, handed me a suit of overalls, and told me to go upstairs to the third floor. The reason I was permitted to walk up to the third floor by myself was because the doors on the first and second floors were locked. I know—I tried them.

All this time, this old man did not say a thing to me. No one said anything to me. I was merely told to go here or there. My confusion was as great as my fright. I felt like a piece of wood being thrown about. Still without knowing what was to become of me, I was put to bed, and there I cried myself to sleep. The next morning my mother took me home. Not long after, there was a trial and I was released on probation. The probation officer checked on me at school and it seemed that everyone knew about this incident. A period of truancy and delinquency followed, and finally I was committed to the reform school.

It was the same old story. On my arrival I was asked my name, age, address, a few other questions, and that was all. No one explained what I was expected to do. I learned the hard way. Two or three nights later, I was reading a comic book in bed when a man came up and bodily ejected me. I was then ordered to kneel and read the book over and over again. Not knowing I was not supposed to read in bed, I protested, "But why? Why do I have to kneel?" "You'll do as I say and shut up!" said the man. How long I remained there I don't know. . . . I woke up in bed the next morning.

Several weeks later someone reported that I had been smoking. When I was brought before the supervisor who had ordered me to kneel all night, he asked, "Were you smoking?"

Having heard from the other boys of his meanness and my own personal experience, I was scared to death. "Yes, I was."

"Yes, you were what?" he barked.

"Yes, I was smoking."

"Yes, you were smoking what?"

"Yes, I was smoking a cigarette."

I didn't know that I was supposed to be addressing him as "sir." I was soon made aware of this! "Listen, dago, when you talk to me say, 'yes sir' and 'no sir' and put a 'sir' on the end of every sentence. Understand?"

"Yes," I hastened to reply. I wasn't being funny. I was just too scared to think and to know what I was saying. Before I could add the "sir" I was punched in the mouth. More hurt by the shock of a man in his position and of his age beating a youngster like myself, I yelled out in rage and cursed him.

Then he really lit into me, hitting me with what I thought was the back wall. And I continued to curse him until my sobs choked back my words. Another youngster washed the blood off me and tried to fix me up as best he knew how. Staring in the mirror at myself in disbelief— my face was a mess—I broke the mirror and yelled at the supervisor, "I don't know when or where, but I'm going to get you for this." He ordered me into the bathroom. I thought it was to get a shower and cleaned up. I got a shower all right . . . a shower of more blows. This time he knocked me unconscious.

How I hated this man—the very thought of him enraged me. When I was transferred to another division the supervisor was even worse than the first one. On one occasion he thrashed me so severely with a bamboo stick that I cried for hours.

Altogether I served thirteen months there and was released on probation. On returning to school, the principal's assistant personally greeted me. With a most insidious smile on his face, he said, "How did you enjoy your vacation?" "The same way you'll enjoy it if you monkey with me," I said. I was no longer a child. At the age of fourteen I was bitter, disillusioned and hateful. I had to get even. Someone had to pay for what had happened to me.

About a year later I was again arrested for stealing an automobile. The juvenile court ordered a complete physical and psychiatric examination. One was just as bad as the other. First thing on the agenda was a dental examination. A nurse who looked and acted like a mechanical robot came over to me, said, "Open your mouth," and jammed a tongue depressor in—all the while holding a conversation with the dentist. Angrily, I pushed her aside, saying, "What am I, an animal?"

She called the doctor who said, "All right, let's have no stuff out of you. Open your mouth." "Yeah, I'll open it—only to tell you to go to hell." I turned and walked out.

My interview with the psychiatrist terminated the same way. I walked out, despite her threats of reporting me. Since I felt they really didn't care, why should I? Only on very rare occasions have I felt that these people cared. They had a job to do, one they didn't seem to like very much, and that was all.

Once again I got fouled up with the law. This time I was sentenced to the house of correction for an indefinite period. Since I was only a juvenile I was supposed to be lodged in the Pennypack House as it is called. But I found myself placed in a cell among grown men. I didn't mind this too much since I felt more or less complimented by being placed with real criminals. But it did have its influence upon me.

Two incidents stand out in my mind. Foremost was a lieutenant whom I secretly admired and respected. One day while cooking coffee and eggs which were "procured" from the prison kitchen, another inmate and I were surprised by this lieutenant. This was really going to be bad for us. My friend, who was older, talked to the lieutenant, offered him a bribe, and we were permitted to go on with our activities. This may sound strange, but I would rather have gone to solitary confinement than to learn that this man was so easily influenced. [This is consistent with Sykes' idea that delinquents share the community's standards.]

The second incident was with a guard who cast all sorts of aspersions against me for associating and acting as though I liked colored people. I really blew up. Only the honesty of a guard who told the true account of what had happened saved me from the hole.

Well, I decided there wasn't going to be any more of this. I escaped from there with a new philosophy of life— With money you can do anything and get anything. Within a year all the money in the world wouldn't have cleared up the mess I had made of my life. I was sentenced to the Eastern State Penitentiary for twenty to forty years. My attitude didn't change—it got worse.[1]

And so the story continued in prison, until by a miracle, almost, through the chaplain Anthony's faith in human beings and in himself was restored.

The story is important because it is the account of his own experience

---

[1] Anthony J. Scoliri, Speech at Annual Meeting of The National Association of Training Schools, May 1957, Philadelphia. Copy given to author of this book "for whatever help it may be."

told publicly by a young seminarian. He tells it because he hopes it will help to change our attitude toward bad boys. As we read Anthony's story of his experience in one of our largest and richest Eastern states, we ask ourselves how far we have progressed since the days of those first houses of refuge described below.

Early Institutions

Houses of Refuge

Special institutions for delinquent children in the United States antedated the juvenile court movement by some seventy-five years. As in the case of the juvenile court, the impetus was furnished by small groups of people. The sorry plight of boys and girls confined with adult criminals in the jails of New York, Philadelphia, and Boston, the centers of urban population in the early 1800s, prompted visits to Europe to study ways in which juveniles were dealt with there. Thus the philosophy of these early American institutions is not indigenous to the United States. It can be traced to European educators among whom is Johann Heinrich Pestalozzi (1746–1827), who established a school for orphans at Neuhoff, Switzerland, in 1775. Students of education will recognize his name as a contributor of progressive educational ideas current today.

Believing in the possibility of reformation if children were not subjected to the horrible examples of vice and depravity in the American prisons of that time, the prime movers, who included the Quaker John Griscom, persuaded both men and women to subscribe the initial funds to establish reformatories to replace prisons. The first reformatory in the United States was called the New York House of Refuge, and located in New York City. Its board of directors was granted permission by the state to operate the institution, collect funds for its maintenance, and at the same time retain complete responsibility for its direction.

This combination of state approval and private subsidy, with later provisions for state subsidy, set the pattern for institutions caring for dependent and neglected children also. It established a precedent for institutions for delinquents controlled by private boards of directors but with a large measure of their support coming from public funds.

When it opened on January 1, 1825, the New York House of Refuge was housed in barracks in Madison Square Park, previously occupied by soldiers. It was closed in 1932, when the building it occupied on Welfare Island was condemned as unfit for the proper care of its inmates. Merged with the

New York State Vocational Institution at West Coxsackie, it was placed under the direction of the New York State Department of Correction.

Similar institutions were established in Boston in 1826 and in Philadelphia in 1828. Then in 1850 the influx of Negro children to Philadelphia, which occurred earlier than in New York (probably because of the former's greater proximity to the South) led to a further innovation in Philadelphia. Because of friction between whites and Negroes separate quarters for boys and girls were set up at some distance from the center of the city. The girls' institution subsequently developed into the well-known Sleighton Farms under the direction of Mrs. Martha Falconer, at Darlington, Delaware County.

The first institution under completely public auspices was a *municipal* reformatory for boys established in 1845 in New Orleans. The first *state* reform school for boys, located at Westboro, Massachusetts, in 1847, is now known as Lyman School for Boys, the locale of one of the Glueck studies (see Chapter 6).

The program of the first twenty-five years in these institutions naturally reflected the prevailing philosophy and educational practice of the era. Based on the belief that the individual's behavior was entirely within his own control, institutions emphasized strict discipline, inculcation of regular habits, and use of rewards and punishment. The specific regime of the individual institutions was usually a direct reflection of the ideas of its superintendent.

It is generally conceded that the Boston House of Refuge was unusual because of its first superintendent, the Reverend E. M. P. Wells. Expelled from Brown University because he refused to bear witness against his college mates in a student prank, Wells, as superintendent of the reformatory, did not ask a boy or girl to give information regarding another's faults. In fact, he is said to have been the first person to go on record against the utilization of stool pigeons, an integral part of many institutional settings today.[2]

Mr. Wells' system of classifying inmates according to whether they tried to do right or wrong is an intriguing example of a two-way classification of the individual's aspirations in respect to behavior. Each category had three subclassifications: (1) positively; (2) positively and regularly; (3) positively, regularly, and continually. Each of the subcategories carried a corresponding set of rewards and privileges for those trying to do right and for those trying to do wrong. Under this system, "The child was able to work himself out of a situation in which he had little freedom to a situation in which he enjoyed respect, honor and self-reliance."[3] According to Teeters and Reinemann, this probably marked the beginning of the modern system of classification.

[2] Negley K. Teeters and John Otto Reinemann, *The Challenge of Delinquency,* New York, Prentice-Hall, 1950, p. 345.
[3] *Ibid.,* p. 437.

Private Sectarian Institutions

Partly to offset the assumed religious propaganda of the early houses of refuge, whose direction was largely Protestant in line with the religious affiliation of the early settlers in the Eastern part of the United States, The Roman Catholic order of the House of Good Shepherd established institutions for girls in the early part of the nineteenth century, at about the time of the first influx of immigrants from Ireland. At the same time, the Christian Brothers assumed responsibility for parochial schools and for institutional care of delinquent Catholic boys. Protestant denominations also established private institutions for delinquent boys and girls; and after the major Jewish migrations at the end of the nineteenth century, the Jews in America began to build orphanages and training schools.

Although these sectarian institutions all raised—and continue to raise— a large part of their funds through sectarian channels, the early limitation of intake to members of their own religion was gradually liberalized, until today virtually all admit members of other faiths, though in varying numbers. The early emphasis on religious training has also been modified, especially in the Jewish and Protestant agencies, although the emphasis in the Catholic institutions has continued to be up to very recently[4] on religious practice and educational training.

Institutions Today

The thread of the four approaches to social problems described in Chapter 20 runs through the story of yesterday's and today's institutions. Because the early directors were primarily concerned with society's protection and people confined in institutions were theoretically society's enemies, their custody was usually regarded as a disciplinary measure.

We have come some way since then; just how far, the following chapters will attempt to show. The present-day institution for delinquents subscribes, at least superficially, to a philosophy of social responsibility for the re-education of the deviant as far as possible. In consequence, today's institution calls for much more elaborate provision for academic, vocational, and personality training, in addition to a program to inculcate better habits of daily living.

Since private institutions are largely supported by voluntary contributions, their policy is determined by boards of directors of their own choosing. (This does not, however, exempt them from official state and local regulation and inspection with respect to physical plant, medical and health care, and education programs.) To a marked degree they control the types of children

---

[4] See discussion of Lincoln Hall in Chapter 24.

for whom they agree to provide care. Most private institutions, moreover, enjoy wider latitude than do the public training schools in their choice of staff and the provision of special educational and training facilities. As a result they have generally had a greater opportunity for experiment and innovation, although this has not always guaranteed a superior program. In fact, in the Far West, the publicly supported institutions appear to be outstripping the private ones in many aspects of their program.

Although privately sponsored studies have made available a good deal of material on the programs of individual private institutions (see especially Chapters 24 and 26), there is no central source of over-all information on these institutions and their inmates. Thanks, however, to special studies of the Children's Bureau, published in 1956 and 1958, we have considerable information on the characteristics of the *public* institutions provided for the care of delinquent children.

Number of Institutionalized Delinquents

In each decennial census the people of the United States are classified according to where they are living at the time the census is taken. Those who are temporarily away from home, traveling, studying at college or schools, visiting, or receiving temporary care in hospitals, are counted as residents of their customary abode. Those who are not living in their usual abodes and are suffering from certain types of disabilities assumed to be hazards to themselves or to other members of the community, are counted as inmates of the various types of institutions in which they reside at the time.

Table V shows how the children under care in the institutions for delinquents were distributed in 1950. The table reveals some striking differences in regional distribution, auspices of institutional care, and the race of the 44,520 inmates in 1950. The relevant inferences are as follows:

1. The nine states in the Northeast contribute only slightly more (13,583) than the seventeen states in the South (12,387) to the 1950 total of institutional delinquents. The 7944 delinquents in the eleven Western states, accounting for about 18 per cent of the total, contribute the least.

2. Twice as many young people were being cared for in institutions financed completely from taxes (29,547) as were under care in institutions supported wholly or partly by private contributions (14,973).

3. Private care is not equally available in the various regions. Institutions under private auspices housed a little less than one half of the total training school population in the Northeast, the North Atlantic, and the West, but only about one sixth of the institutional population in the seventeen Southern states.

TABLE V

POPULATION IN TRAINING SCHOOLS CLASSIFIED BY AUSPICES AND
COLOR OF INMATES, EACH REGION, 1950

Region and States	Number of States	Total Training School Population	Public		Private
			White Inmates	Nonwhite Inmates	
TOTAL	49[a]	44,520	21,847	7,700	14,973[b]
Northeast	9	13,583	5,823	1,687	6,073
New England	6	2,438	1,666	134	638
Middle Atlantic	3	11,145	4,157	1,553	5,435
North Atlantic	12	10,606	5,201	1,556	3,849
East North Central	5	7,024	3,239	1,127	2,658
West North Central	7	3,582	1,962	429	1,191
South	17	12,387	6,461	3,938	1,988
South Atlantic	9	6,820	3,613	2,505	702
East South Central	4	2,911	1,393	828	690
West South Central	4	2,656	1,455	605	596
West	11	7,944	4,362	519	3,063
Mountain	8	1,688	1,177	88	423
Pacific	3	6,256	3,185	431	2,640

SOURCE: *Institutional Population*, U.S. Census of Population, 1950, Table 43 2C, pp. 155-161.
[a] Includes District of Columbia.
[b] Includes 3894 inmates of detention homes, and 3135 girls in homes for unwed mothers.

4. In the South nonwhites account for almost 40 per cent (3938) of the public training school population in comparison with 10 per cent (519) in the West, and slightly more than 20 per cent in the Northern areas. These wide differences no doubt partly reflect the concern of the communities to provide more varied types of care for white children than are usually available under public auspices, as well as the difference in income in the south available for private philanthropy. For private institutions figures for white and nonwhite population are not available.

Table VI shows the variation in the percentages of the nonwhite delinquents in public institutions by region. The most striking inference is the disproportionate overrepresentation of nonwhites on the mainland. For example:

1. In the Northeastern and North Central states nonwhites accounted for 7 and 5 per cent respectively of the population at risk in 1950, in comparison with 40 and 27 per cent of the 1956 training school inmates.

2. The figures for the Territories are almost equal, nonwhites accounting for 29 per cent of the inmates in 1956 in comparison with 31 per cent of the 1950 population.

TABLE VI

DISTRIBUTION BY REGION OF U.S. NONWHITE POPULATION UNDER 21 YEARS
OF AGE, 1950, AND IN PUBLIC STATE TRAINING SCHOOLS, 1956
(in percentages)

Region	Nonwhites Under 21	
	1950 Population	1956 Training School Population
United States	13	33
Northeastern	7	40
North Central	5	27
Southern	25	36
Mountain	6	13
Pacific	5	36
Territorial	31	29

SOURCE: Robert L. Rowland, Children's Bureau Statistical Series No. 48, *Statistics on Public Institutions for Delinquent Children, 1956*, Washington, U.S. Dept. of Health, Education, and Welfare, 1958.

These striking differences suggest that the labeling of the delinquent and what happens to him may be a function not only of the specific behavior but of the ethnic composition of the population as a whole.

We are indebted to the same source[5] for much of the information below on the location, capacity, personnel, and costs of public institutions for delinquents. Additional information is drawn from a special study of 109 public institutions made by the Children's Bureau, covering the year October 1952 to September 1953, and published in 1956.[6]

Some Characteristics of Public Training Schools

LOCATION AND CAPACITY. According to the Children's Bureau[7] the South has 57 institutions in comparison with 38 in the Northeast and 40 in the North Central states, and almost three times as many as the Pacific region (22). Institutions for boys are generally much larger than those for girls. One third (63) of all institutions accommodate more than 200 children. Texas has the distinction of having the largest institution: The capacity of

[5] Robert L. Rowland, Children's Bureau Statistical Series No. 48, *Statistics on Public Institutions for Delinquent Children, 1956*, Washington, U.S. Dept. of Health, Education, and Welfare, 1958.

[6] Children's Bureau Statistical Series No. 33, *Some Facts about Public State Training Schools for Juvenile Delinquents, 1952-53*, Washington, U.S. Dept. of Health, Education, and Welfare, 1956.

[7] *Directory of Public Training Schools for Delinquent Children*, Washington, U.S. Children's Bureau, May 1955.

the Gatesville State School for Boys is 900. California's Preston School of Industry reports accommodations for 700 boys. Out of 139 institutions that reported, 38 stated that they were overcrowded, about half of them being in the Mountain and a quarter in the Pacific regions.

RATIO OF STAFF TO INMATES. One measure of the efficiency of any program of care is the ratio of staff to inmates. In 1956[8] the national average was 2.6 children for each full-time staff person. The ratio was highest in the Northeast—one full-time staff person to 1.9 children, and lowest in the Territories and the South—one full-time staff person for 4.9 and 4.0 children respectively. A more meaningful ratio gives a breakdown of staff as administrative, treatment and educational, and maintenance. The comparable ratios are 1 to 20.4, 4.5, and 8.8. In general, girls' institutions employ larger numbers of staff than do institutions for boys. About 10 per cent of those institutions included in the 1956 survey (20) were coeducational.

SALARY SCALES. In 1952-53[9] salaries ranged from less than $1700 annually to more than $5200. The highest paid were superintendents; more than half had salaries exceeding $5200, and one fourth reported salaries over $7200. In descending order the modal salaries ranged from $4199 to $3200 for social workers; from $3699 to $3200 for nurses; from $3699 to $3199 for teachers; from $3199 to $2200 for recreation workers and day cottage personnel. Full room and board supplemented salaries of about one third of the day cottage personnel and nurses, and about one fifth of the superintendents.

PER CAPITA COSTS. The cost of maintaining the public state training schools in the United States and its territories in the year 1956 was estimated at $65 million. Of this amount, 87 per cent was used for current operating expenses; the remainder was spent for capital improvements.[10]

In absolute figures, the annual per capita operating expenses of public institutions in 1956 ranged from as little as $439 to ten times that amount. The median was slightly less than $2000. Consistent with staff-inmate ratios and lower salary scales, the median per capita in Southern training schools was the lowest, approximately $1200. The highest, approximately $2600, characterized the Northeastern region.[11]

Major Aspects of Institutional Programs

To actually understand life in an institution, whether for delinquents or for college students, it must be experienced. Each of us responds to a printed description in terms of the content of our previous experience. While even

[8] Rowland, *op. cit.*, Table 14, p. 35.
[9] *Some Facts About Public State Training Schools for Juvenile Delinquents, 1952-1953*, Table 21.
[10] Rowland, *op. cit.*, p. 13.
[11] *Ibid.* Table 16, p. 37.

a cursory visit is better than none, the structure of informal relationship which really determines what goes on in an institution is rarely evident without an extended stay (see Chapter 23). Furthermore, there are few publications which describe the operations of the public institutions for delinquents with more detail than the usual directory listing. Manuals issued by the individual states give the minima of location, name of superintendent, and admission policies, with occasionally a brief description of the services and facilities. Possibly because there is less room for experimentation in institutions under public than under private auspices, the professional journals carry few articles by the directors of public institutions describing their programs.

LIVING QUARTERS.   Institutions vary in the type of living arrangements provided for the inmates. Some are congregate, like the ones to which Tony was committed. Some are cottage plan, modeled on the Mettray System established in France in 1839. Camps such as those described in Chapter 19 are a recent development.

The congregate institution houses its population in dormitories, i.e., four or more in a room. There are rows of beds, bureaus, and sometimes chairs, spaced to conform to regulations of the state or local health departments. In most of the cottage plan institutions the buildings resemble the substantial suburban homes of 1900 or the fraternity houses on a state university campus. They are usually built of stone, stucco, or brick, combined with heavy beams of dark wood, and they are often set in spacious, well-kept grounds located, as a rule, some distance from the large urban centers. The population per room in cottage-plan institutions ranges from one to three. According to the 1952-53 survey only about one out of four of the 109 public training schools for delinquents had individual bedrooms. The dormitory pattern was the usual one in institutions for boys.

RECEPTION.   Many institutions of both types have reception units used to orient the newcomer, to observe him, and to administer tests and determine his appropriate living and school arrangements.

Directors of detention facilities have commented on the difficulty of fitting the newcomer into a program already under way. How effectively this is accomplished depends upon how aware the administrator is of the needs of young people, the meaning of their behavior in various settings, and how he uses controls. Problems similar in kind but not in degree face head masters of boarding schools to which middle-class families send children whom they cannot manage or control at home.

FOOD PREPARATION AND SERVICE.   According to the 1952-53 survey about one third of the public institutions had separate kitchens as well as separate dining rooms for each living unit. These arrangements were more usual in the girls' than in the boys' institutions, possibly because the cooking, serving, and so forth are considered part of the girls' preparation for future housekeeping. The slightly more than half of the institutions (57) which had centralized kitchen and dining rooms were for boys only.

The importance of food is often disregarded in institutions, whether the setting is a college, a camp, a hospital ward, or a training school for delinquents. Often keeping down per capita food cost outweighs the significance of the reaction of those fed to the quantity, variety, or quality of food, or the manner in which it is served. Some at the institutions for delinquents recognize the therapeutic value of palatable food and the importance, for example, of serving the same food to staff and children. There has been some recognition also of the need of adolescents for sweets as an energy source and as an antidote for some types of rebellious activity, especially on the part of girls.

HOUSEHOLD TASKS. In most institutions, the inmates participate not only in the preparation and serving of the food but in such other maintenance activities as laundry, mending, housecleaning, farming, horticulture, repairs, and so forth. The inmates' acceptance of responsibility and interest in acquisition of skills will often depend on the variety of experience provided, and the importance which the administration attaches to the different functions.

Some institutions pay their inmates in cash or scrip—others in credits toward time off for home visits—for services that, in a tight domestic labor market, they would ordinarily have to pay others for in cash.

The extent to which the needs of the adolescents are considered above those of the administration depends on the philosophy of the director, and his awareness that the institution exists to serve the needs of the young people rather than the convenience of the staff and the efficient and economical operation of the institution's household, piggery, or farm.

TIME SCHEDULES. Time schedules are obviously necessary in any setting which accommodates a number of people. Rising time, meal time, leisure time, bathing, and school schedules are as regimented in institutions for delinquents as they often are in the formal summer camps for well-to-do children. Bedtime in an institution is more apt to be set in relation to the convenience of the staff than to the needs of the young people. And, as in many hospitals, meal schedules may mean breakfast very early in the morning, and dinner or supper at 4:30 in the afternoon, to accommodate the kitchen and pantry staff. Schedules for washing, brushing teeth, baths or showers, and changing clothes are fairly rigid in most institutions.

Arrangements for physical and health care, as in colleges and boarding schools, include facilities and personnel for initial examination, and routine follow-up as well as quarantine for sick children.

CLOTHING. As has been sometimes remarked by visitors to institutions for delinquents, the young people whom they see loitering on the grounds, working on the farms, studying in the classrooms, playing on the ball fields, dancing on Saturday nights in the gym, especially in those institutions under private auspices, bear no mark of Cain on their foreheads. A group of college juniors, visiting in informal summer attire and unannounced at an institution for disturbed delinquent girls, were requested at the office to return to their cottages. The fact that the staff could not distinguish them from the inmate population was a severe shock to their feeling of superiority.

Of course one reason these college juniors were not immediately accorded the respect they thought their status demanded is that today delinquents do not wear uniforms. Gone are the days of the long black stockings and the recognizable uniformity of institutional clothes. The easy identification of the runaway, the economy of buying in wholesale lots, as well as an insensitivity to the young person's preferences—at least in respect to color, if not to style—were no doubt factors in the practice of insisting on institutional uniforms. The psychology of clothes is recognized today as an important factor in healthy personality development. Uniforms which bear some relation to one's role are not only tolerable but occasionally an asset, as in the case of sweaters with numerals or other insignia, or cap and gown. But the fact that these can be doffed as well as donned makes a great difference to the wearer.

STAFF. The staff of an institution which offers a rehabilitative and not just a custodial program includes representatives from many disciplines, ranging from management to maintenance. The more elaborate and the larger the institution, the more varied the staff. Unlike the directors of private institutions, the superintendent of the public training school is not completely free to select his staff, or to dismiss people whose attitudes are unsatisfactory. He is often plagued with the negative aspects of tenure in a civil service system, which sometimes protect people who have lost interest and ambition.

According to the 1952-53 survey there is considerable variation with respect to educational background, salary scales, number of working hours and the requirements for living on or off the premises. While as a rule the directors of larger institutions have their own cottages with full maintenance, appropriate quarters are frequently not provided for other staff members.

Some institutions employ a cottage mother, or cottage parents, and others put counselors in charge of groups of boys, either in dormitories or cottages. Because it is difficult to recruit adequate personnel not only for institutions for delinquents but for many others requiring residence on the premises, various devices such as eight-hour shifts are used, for example, by Bettelheim in Chicago (see Chapter 24). Long weekends for cottage parents in institutions located away from the city are the rule.

In our discussion of treatment centers we will see how important it is for staff to have some relief from the confinement of close living quarters, from constant association with people who are often competing with them for status in an institutional hierarchy, and from the seemingly insatiable demands of youngsters for attention and affection. Even parents need to get away from their children occasionally. The staff problem is a persistent and troublesome one, which calls for reconsideration of its status implications.

EDUCATIONAL PROGRAMS. The task of a teacher, in an institution for delinquents who are usually there against their will, is almost as demanding as that of the substitute parent. Besides the salary scales, the requirements, academic and otherwise, and the hours of work vary from institution to institution. This also applies to the curricula, whether academic or vocational, and the equipment, library facilities and teaching aids, which often do not meet the standards of the public school system. Occasionally an institution arranges to send its high school pupils to a community school.

On the assumption that these young people are entitled to an education whether or not they are in their own homes, as long as their families are part of the tax-paying community, some institutions have been able to arrange with local boards of education to provide teachers for the institution. Institutions which wish to provide specialized educational programs usually, however, establish and finance them from private funds.

In about 11 per cent of public institutions in 1952-53, psychological tests were used to judge the educational achievement of the young person, so that his assets rather than his inadequacies might be used as a foundation on which to build. About 80 per cent of the institutions replying that year to the Children's Bureau inquiry reported that educational achievement and IQ tests were part of their program. A little more than half routinely gave aptitude tests, and slightly less than half administered personality tests or psychiatric examinations.[12]

Return to the Community

The most frequent requirement for release from an institution is a stated number of months in residence. Less than 10 per cent of the institutions surveyed in 1952-53 mentioned earning a specific number of points. The majority considered adjustment in the school and conditions at home.[13] According to Children's Bureau estimates, almost 14,000 children were in after-care in December 1956.[14]

Opinions differ as to who should be responsible for after-care, and what its nature should be.[15] If most of the training school parolees live in one city,

12 *Some Facts About Public State Training Schools for Juvenile Delinquents, 1952-1953,* p. 34.
13 *Ibid.,* p. 37.
14 Rowland, *op. cit.,* p. 9.
15 Richard Clendenen, "After the Training School What?" *Yearbook,* National Probation and Parole Association, 1950, p. 65.

a social worker is usually assigned to supervise the parolee's readjustment to the community. Sometimes there is more than one such local office to serve the parolees of a large institution. A second alternative is a centralized after-care program for all training schools within the state, preferably separate from the state-administered adult parole system.

A third alternative is after-care service furnished by caseworking agencies in the local community. This plan has two advantages: It capitalizes on a wider variety of services; and it may help to wean the parolee from his conception of himself as delinquent.

The *disadvantage* is that since after-care is a minor part of a casework agency's services, it may be somewhat neglected in favor of more pressing demands. Furthermore, the caseworkers may not be sufficiently trained for this particular type of service.

After-care placement will not be effective unless there is preparation for the experience. Group discussion in the institution is sometimes used to anticipate facing such questions as: How do I apply for a job? Is it safe to list on a job application blank the vocational experience obtained in a training school? Problems, however, which reflect only the individual's personal needs cannot be profitably discussed in the group. They call for individual consultation to make clear the limits and the extent of the future relationship between the young person and the caseworker. None of these services will be effective without personnel with specialized training in after-care.

Foster Homes

For young people who for one reason or another cannot return to their own homes, several varieties of foster home placements have been used. A foster home, according to Williams,[16] is more appropriate for a young person who still has strong dependency needs than it is for the youth who is struggling to free himself from adult control. "Work" homes, a subcategory of foster homes, are useful for adolescents who cannot return to their own homes and who can perform some agreed-upon service for which they receive stated remuneration in addition to room and board. Some institutions provide group homes, usually city apartments which house a half dozen or so boys or girls who go out to school or to work. Ohio is planning a variety of interim homes in its five largest cities.

The Baltimore Plan

An interesting example of specialized after-care is provided by the Baltimore plan, described by Renee Berg.[17] The Maryland State Department of

[16] Herbert D. Williams, "Foster Homes for Juvenile Delinquents," *Federal Probation,* Vol. 13 (Sept. 1949), pp. 46-51.
[17] Renee Berg, "After the Training School," *Focus,* Nov. 1952, pp. 178-84.

Public Welfare exercises general supervision over the four state training schools. Until November 1949, parole throughout Maryland was the responsibility of the parole officers on the staff of each institution. In Baltimore, however, the protective services division of the Welfare Department has since that time been responsible for after-care of Baltimore residents.

The aim of the program, as described by Berg, is to assist the child in cutting his ties with the institution. The agency is instructed by the court to help "the child refrain from further delinquent behavior and to follow the instructions of his caseworker."[18] The caseworker, notified of an impending release from the institution, calls at the child's home to discuss practical details involved in his return. She sizes up the readiness of the family to take him back, and their ability to refrain from reminding him, at every fall from grace, of his commitment to the institution. If the home is not suitable, the caseworker will try to find a relative's home, or if that is impossible, a boarding home. This preparatory work may take as long as a month.

On the day the youth is released from the institution the caseworker meets him, shows him a copy of the court order, and discusses frankly the conditions of his release. She explains that although he may dislike the idea of supervision, he is not free to refuse it. If he is under 16, he is told that he must attend school, and if he is over 16 and wishes to leave school, he must obtain some form of stable full-time employment. He is also expected to abide by the regulations which his parents establish for home life.

There are several reasons, Miss Berg points out, why it is more difficult to help the delinquent than the nondelinquent child. In the first place the delinquent generally has a long history of conflict with the law. In the second place, parents of delinquent children are more likely to be sensitive about their failures than parents whose children have other handicaps. Third, whether or not parents blame the child and refuse to take their share of responsibility, they usually find it difficult to believe that the intent of the agency is not to belabor them with their own shortcomings.

Furthermore, although the symptomatic behavior that brings children to the court may be similar, no two children are alike in their needs. As Miss Berg says, accepting help is often especially threatening to the older adolescent. It is frightening for a boy who is approaching manhood to take help at a time when he is looking forward to being his own boss. The social agency in a way is going against the tide when it tries to help these young people feel close to their families precisely at an age when they should be getting ready to leave them.

The aim of the after-care services is to enable both the child and his parents to get along without agency help. The caseworker looks for incidents which signal the boy's or girl's growing ability to assume responsibility for

[18] Ibid., p. 179.

his or her behavior. Throughout, the child remains the center and focus of the service.

Summary

The first institutions for delinquents in the United States antedate the juvenile court movement by about 75 years. The houses of refuge, as they were called, emphasized discipline and habit training and followed the philosophy of their day. The goal of their modern counterparts, under public as well as private auspices, which may be sectarian or nonsectarian, is rehabilitation rather than punishment.

The exact number of young people currently in training schools for delinquents is not known. The 1950 Census tabulated approximately 45,000, of whom about *two thirds were in institutions under public auspices*. Boys outnumber girls three to one and nonwhites are represented in greater proportion than in the populations of the regions in which they reside, with the significant exception of the Territories.

The various types of institutions are not equally available in all sections of the country. They are dissimilar in admission requirements, capacity, living arrangements, programs for care in the institution, as well as assignment of and responsibility for care.

$$\begin{array}{c} \text{\bf CHAPTER 23} \end{array}$$

A State-Supported Institution

THE MATERIAL IN THIS CHAPTER IS BASED ON THE UNPUBLISHED DOCTORAL dissertation of a young man who spent a half year at Ralston, his fictitious name for an actual institution for juveniles in New York State.[1] Ralston may not be typical of institutions throughout the country. It is an end-of-the-line operation insofar as it has no choice but to accept boys referred by the New York City juvenile court. Furthermore, its population in the last twenty-five years has been swelled by large numbers of disadvantaged minority groups.

Life at Ralston

At the time of Robin's study, Ralston contained 350 boys, aged 12 to 17. Among them were a majority of Negroes and a scattering of Italian, Irish, Spanish, and Cuban stock. Those who came from large cities had been in the juvenile court on at least three occasions before their commitment, and many were known members of gangs. The others, rejected by the gang, were the sissies, the overprotected, the physically deformed, or the lone wolves. For the gang member, the Ralston experience was described as status raising. For the others, the court order and what followed was a degrading experience.

Reception

The grapevine picture painted by boys awaiting commitments in temporary detention quarters did not reassure those scheduled to go to Ralston. Stories told by the guards in the detention quarters and by some court attendants in order to maintain discipline reinforced street gossip about the

[1] Frederick Elliott Robin, "Reform School," unpublished doctoral dissertation, Columbia University, 1943.

program, the administration, the staff, and the food. Although the probation officers and the social workers in the detention quarters stressed the constructive aspects of the institution, most of the boys said they were in no way prepared for the actual situation when they arrived.

The handcuffed boy was brought to Ralston by the sheriff, and deposited in the administration building. His personal effects were checked and he was sent to the reception unit where, like a draftee, he received a complete issue of clothing. The period in the reception center was designed to orient him to his new life and, on the basis of a variety of tests, to provide the staff with the facts about the boy that they needed to plan his program of cottage, school, and recreation so that he might be prepared for eventual return to the community.

For nearly all of the boys the reception experience was one of emotional stress. This was not lessened by the highly regimented daily routine in the reception cottage. All the boys were awakened at 2:00 in the morning to go to the toilet. At 6:00 A.M. everyone arose to wash and dress. Before breakfast they were expected to tidy up their rooms and to polish the highly waxed floor. To any but a girl on a reducing diet, weekday breakfast would seem skimpy— a large bun and a glass of milk. The Sunday menu added cornflakes. Lunch at 11:00 A.M. was usually soup or spaghetti. Sunday dinner was roast lamb, mashed potatoes, string beans, and gravy.

Weekday mornings were given over to school and testing. On weekday afternoons, after some additional chores, the boys were taken to the reception field where they played baseball, football, or pitched horseshoes. Accustomed to smoking, which was not permitted in the reception cottage, they would then try to sneak a smoke. After dinner at 4:30 there were more jobs. These completed, they stayed in their rooms and read books furnished by the reception library. On Tuesdays and Thursdays they were permitted to go to the gym, box, punch bags, play ping pong and other games. At 8:00 P.M. they were locked in their rooms and at 9:00 the lights were turned out. A guard was on duty all night.

As one boy expressed it, the routine was like living by the whistle. Being told when to go to the toilet, when to eat, and when to sleep was resented by the boy who had lived his own way. On the other hand the overprotected boy away from home for the first time was acutely homesick. In general, the older and the more aggressive boy had less difficulty in adjusting to the first contact with his fellow inmates. There was some hazing, the older boys picked on the new ones, testing them to see if they would fight.

In the numerous bull sessions the most common topics in addition to cigarettes, clothes, women, and liquor were, "When will we get out?" the intricacies of the committee reviews, and the discipline reports which had been explained to them. The possibility of an escape was explored and all angles discussed. "Breeze" (escape) was the first word of Ralston's slang which the new boys acquired.

Among the factors that influenced what happened to the boys and made the goals of the administration more difficult to accomplish was the strain of the reception period. Their experience in this period intensified any undesirable traits—the abnormal sex life, for example, and the tendency to fight at the drop of a hat.

The Cottage Experience

When the time came to go to an assigned cottage, fear and anxiety replaced boredom. Exaggerated stories and rumors stressed the importance of saying "Yes, sir," and "No, sir," to the officer. The boys had heard of beatings, and of forced homosexual experiences. Although the weaker boys were the most apprehensive, even some of the older and stronger ones showed some anxiety. The grapevine advised that getting along in the cottage meant fighting back, learning the slang, and adhering to the group standards.

The society that had already formed in the reception center was certain to be cruel because the frustrating conditions of the reception experience reinforced the former gang experience of many of these boys. By virtue of its physical power and cohesion, the hardened delinquent group set the standards, values, and patterns for the general body of inmates in the cottages. The inexperienced, that is the non-gangster delinquent, found it difficult to reconcile the formal demands of the administration with those of his companions. In their conversations with the observer a few of the more hardened delinquents identified some of their fellow inmates as nice boys who were out of place at Ralston.

Boys were rated by their fellow inmates according to their ability to protect themselves and to resist homosexual advances. It was important to be shrewd in social situations to avoid being tricked or "jived." At the bottom of the role and status hierarchy was the scape goat, generally a physically weak boy. Isolated, nicknamed, and the butt of group ridicule, the scapegoat served to integrate the inmate group who displaced their aggressions and tensions on him.

For a new boy, entering a cottage was somewhat like coming into a class after it has been in existence for several sessions. In an institution for delinquents this disadvantage is magnified many times. Each new boy is a threat to the group already in the cottage. It is important therefore that the group test the new recruits to identify and exclude the types it rejects, i.e., the weaklings and the possible stool pigeons. Physical and mental coercion of the deviant was permitted. If it failed, isolation and exploitation were the alternatives. In the process of "johning" a new boy, the victim was lured or tricked into breaking institutional rules.

The formation of cliques and the development of positive and negative attractions among inmates was facilitated by the group's recognition of social types. In addition to the "john" (fool) these included: (1) the punk (homosexual), (2) the bulldozer or husko (bully), (3) the wolf or fiend (the highly sexed boy who may or may not indulge in homosexual relations), (4) the top lap (sycophant), (5) the rat (informer), (6) the bug (abnormal), (7) the fluter (miser).

The prized personal attributes were group loyalty, fighting ability, generosity up to a certain point, skill in debates, and familiarity with the techniques and lore of the underworld. The principal means of achieving status was through competition in either physical or verbal conflicts.

The antisocial mores of the majority of the boys were peculiarly adapted to an institutional setting which stressed dominant and subordinate relations. In its very set-up the administration appeared to the boys as the common enemy. As a result, if a boy was cooperative with the administration and established a reputation for "ratting" he would be isolated from his cottage group. If he tried to establish closer relationship with the administration for his own protection or to obtain an earlier release, he became a greater threat to the solidarity and welfare of the cottage group and his position was even more untenable.

Relations Between Staff and Inmates

Since the inmate code described above underscored social distance between the boy and the staff, there was little possibility of developing rapport between the two. In their unceasing fight against staff domination the boys presented a united front. This front was the chief weapon against the boy who cultivated the good graces of the officers. Though the common denominator was conflict, the attitude toward the various representatives of authority in the institutional set-up differed. Usually the boys conformed because they had to; but such conformity obviously represented no real change in their value systems—the goal of institutional treatment.

DIRECTOR. The director of Ralston, who was rarely seen by the boys, was seldom the butt of their hostility. His direct, hearty, sympathetic way of speaking gained him a measure of popularity. They were, however, suspicious of the "wheel horse" personnel with whom they had daily contact.

CLINIC PERSONNEL. The clinic personnel faced severe obstacles in attempting to help most of these boys. The widespread distrust of the clinic was engendered by the fact that its personnel constantly strove to affect a closer liaison with the individual boy than the inmate mores sanctioned. In consequence the boys tried to manipulate the caseworkers' professional objectives for their own ends.

The clinic personnel faced another obstacle—their relation with the resident staff. As nonresidents, the clinic staff was able to avoid close contacts with the problems, responsibilities, and vexations of institutional life. The nonresident staff member, looking in from the outside, found it easy to be critical. At the same time the institutional workers had less opportunity to mingle with the normal community, and were thus handicapped in replenishing their emotional reserves.[2] The result was friction.

The boys' hostility toward the clinic staff extended to the sponsor, the clinical staff member assigned to help each boy with his problems. Sometimes the sponsor was regarded as a stool pigeon. The boys spoke of "jiving" him. Because they realized that the impression they created on the members of the clinic staff would affect not only their work assignment but their length of stay at Ralston, they tried to make as favorable a case for themselves as possible. Instead of openly resisting, they usually conformed at least superficially.

The records, at the time of the survey, were accessible to the boys who worked in the offices. They told the participant observer that they looked up what was said about them in the case folders. These contained all the information that the institution had about the boy and his family, the results of the diagnostic tests, and the comments and recommendations of the various department members. Some said that the sponsors did not hold their remarks in confidence, but relayed them to the cottage masters. Others said that the sponsors appeared disinterested and neglectful. According to one: "Sponsors are no damn good. All they do is make you talk to them and then they write it down and try to frame you. They are all old men and old fogies." The boys would have liked to have someone young who could understand them. Most of them felt that the recreation worker more nearly filled this bill than any other staff member. As a matter of fact, the director of the athletic program had the least trouble with the boys, possibly because he had more in common with them than most of the other staff members.

The boys resented most the women sponsors. "How," one boy said, "can a guy talk about sex or jerking off or anything like that? A guy resents being under a woman." This remark is important for the insight it should convey into the role of the female in the lower socio-economic groups that predominate in institutional population. The boys said that they came to the initial meeting with their sponsors forewarned about what to do, e.g., how to cope with their foibles and how to manipulate these to their own advantage. Often a boy would attempt to play off the sponsor against the rest of the staff.

SCHOOL PERSONNEL. Whereas in the clinic the conflict between a boy and his sponsor was usually veiled and expressed only in words, in the classroom, with the support of the classmates, conflict between teacher and

2 See discussion of this point by Bettelheim and Papanek, Chapter 24.

pupil was often open, continuous, and at times on a physical level. In the clinic the actual clash of wills was sporadic because of the infrequency of face-to-face meetings; but in the classroom the issue could not be sidestepped because the institution clearly imposed obligations upon the instructor to maintain order and to prevent the boys from leaving the classroom even if he had to use force. Each of the thirty-one teachers employed at Ralston at the time of the study was called upon in different degrees to face the concerted opposition of a group of boys. The clinic worker could always terminate the interview. The teacher, on the other hand, was unable to retreat from impending conflict and had to meet its challenge throughout the school day.

Because many boys committed to institutions are retarded in school, and have developed a distaste for it, their opposition to the institution's academic program is not hard to understand. In many cases the Ralston boys' first contact with the law was because they had been truants. Since school attendance is compulsory up to age 17, except for very bright boys who have completed the 8th grade, the school was an integral part of Ralston's program. It claimed several hours in the daily schedule.

The woman teacher faced a special problem in the Ralston system. The male teacher could strong-arm some of the boys. The cross-sex attraction, strong in adolescence, combined with the boys' habitual resistance to authority, heightened the conflict between pupil and female teacher.

The observer reported symbolic and actual attacks he witnessed in which the female teacher was pressed to the wall, literally and figuratively. "The class sought to reduce her prestige, strip her of authority, halt classroom instruction and exploit her sex insofar as possible for personal satisfaction. The contest between class and teacher became a sort of sporting game tense with thrills and excitement."

In the unequal struggle between one woman and a dozen or more delinquent boys, the latter usually secured a marked advantage, especially if the class was composed of older boys. Obviously the teacher could not resort to corporal punishment and was afraid to use physical force lest the boys retaliate. This disadvantage reduced the teacher's bargaining position, leaving her with the alternative of persuasion through bribery, rewards and pleas for cooperation, or the use of disciplinary reports and the withholding of privileges. When the immediate situation got out of hand the teacher could call on the principal or one of the men teachers to restore order. None of these methods was particularly successful and each had its drawbacks. The first required the teacher to invent more and more privileges to keep the class pacified. If a teacher's inability to control her class was too often brought to the attention of the authorities, her position was obviously threatened.

The boys were rated on a competitive basis for good behavior in the class. Those with the highest scores were allowed to visit home for several days. A boy who saw that his score was low and the date of the final ratings was approaching was apt to misbehave again. He boxed or fought, shot missiles with rubber bands, threw books around, hung out of the window, smoked, patted the teacher on the hip or shoulder when she came into the room, or even masturbated in the classroom in front of the teacher.

The boys preferred male teachers "who would tell them what to do and if they didn't do it would smack them around until they did." This reliance on physical punishment as a means of control goes against the grain of the middle-class teacher's preference for nonphysical means of control. The participant observer made a study of the past and present women teachers in the institution and discovered that the only women able to manage their classes did so by the generous and frequent use of corporal punishment. Obviously they were the ones fortunate enough to be assigned to the lower grades where they often outweighed the average student by a hundred pounds.

The classroom relations of twenty-six male teachers revealed that half of them were preoccupied with preserving discipline. Over a prolonged period, the net effect of the class resistance was to wear down the teacher's pedagogical ambitions. In about a fourth of the classes the teacher had established fairly stable compromises in which the boys agreed to conform to the teacher's wishes if he did not demand too much from them. In speaking of one such teacher a boy said, "You don't try anything funny with him because he won't take any lip from you. When he is ambitious he may give you a history book, a writing pad, tell you to read a chapter and report on it. If he is very ambitious he goes around the class with each boy reading a paragraph aloud from the chapter. After that he gives a one-word test."

Most of the time, however, if the boys were quiet the teacher just sat through the fifty-minute period listening to his radio or reading. If a boy was unruly he was hit with a little rubber whip or sometimes with the teacher's hands. The current gossip about a teacher who used his hands was that he relied on the boxing matches in Madison Square Garden instead of classes in Teachers College for pointers on how to teach. The boys did not object to the system because, they said, he didn't drag them down to the office; they were satisfied because most of them didn't want to learn anything. But as one boy said: "The system is bad because it doesn't teach you anything."

About five teachers were regarded as regular guys. By making a special appeal to their class, and by using a little system of reward and privileges to encourage good behavior, these teachers were able to cover part of the prescribed curriculum. The rest of the time they used the class period for recreation, games, stories, and free periods when the boys might read magazines or listen to the radio.

There were three teachers who had been completely intimidated so that no power or authority of theirs could hold the clique of older aggressive boys who ran their classroom. These boys cooperated only enough to avoid investigation of their activities and punishment by the head of the school.

Because the boys knew the teachers' reputations before they were assigned to class, the patterns of interaction described above were almost predetermined. They were reinforced through repetition, and actually contributed somewhat to stability in the school. It is clear however that the setting offered little opportunity for any real educational accomplishment.

COTTAGE MASTERS AND WORK GANG SUPERVISORS. Commonly referred to as "the staff," the cottage parents and the work supervisors played a more important role in the boys' institutional life than either the clinic workers or the school teachers who saw them for only a small part of each day. The cottage parents were responsible for the boys during many hours, both while they worked and when they were supposed to be at leisure. In discussing the cottage parents with the observer, the boys remarked that they knew that the reviewing board placed considerable weight on their reports. In consequence, resistance to the cottage parents' authority was inevitably tempered by knowledge of their importance in the institutional hierarchy.

The boys defined a good officer as one who was just, tempered his commands with leniency, was not forced to rely upon institutional sanctions all the time, and most important of all, was basically sympathetic, willing to fight in their behalf. A good officer didn't play favorites, kept his promises, kidded around a little, and although he could beat up any boy, he didn't go around slapping them just for the fun of it. He remembered that he was a boy once and that anybody was liable to be bad once in awhile. He reasoned with you, gave you a fair chance, and didn't hold a grudge after you had taken your punishment.

The question of discipline is, as we have noted, one on which there is considerable difference of opinion. In the institutional setting, although the regulations officially frown upon physical punishment and in some states require that the institution shall report all instances in which corporal punishment is used, many of the boys do not react unfavorably to punishment if, in their opinion, it is deserved and properly administered. Many of the boys at Ralston told the observer that they believed corporal punishment was necessary. It should not, however, be administered by clubs, whips, or other instruments. Illegal blows, e.g., the rabbit punch, hitting below the belt, or "stomping" (jumping on a prostrate boy), were frowned upon.

If the officer was challenged by a boy, however, he must face his opposition boldly. Some of the bigger boys believed that if the officer was unjustly challenged by someone who was a streetwise fighter and physically strong, the other boys would come to the rescue of the officer. Personal courage on the part of the officer was admired.

The boys' definition of a bad officer was one who takes his job too seriously and insists on the letter of the law; who is arbitrary and capricious in his judgments, is unsympathetic, will not stand up for his boys; who doesn't know what's going on, beats up boys whether they deserve it or not, "is a mean, double-crossing son of a bitch who acts one way when he is sober and another when he is drunk"; who can't control the boys and so blames everything on them when it may be partly his fault, and relies almost entirely on the front office to support him.

Probably because there were so many more officers categorized as bad than as good, the boys had divided the bad ones into two subtypes—the "jeeps" and the "terrors." The jeep was stupid, ineffectual, and easily tricked. The terror, unlike the jeep, had little humanitarian impulse. He was harsh, brutal, and cruel, and loved power for its own sake. The observer noted the keen awareness among the boys of the psychological mainsprings of these two different types of behavior.

A new officer was handicapped usually because he insisted on showing his authority and was hesitant to accept the compromises that the older employees had granted as a vested right to the inmate group.

Most cottage parents and supervisors were rated somewhere between the good and the bad officers. A testing process, similar to that which determined a boy's role and status in the inmate society, established the staff member's reputation and set the pattern for relations with him. The test was the way he balanced humanitarian and authoritarian patterns. As one boy put it:

> "The boys always hope that a new man will meet the boys half-way, kid with them, talk with them, that he won't be too strict and follow the rules out to a T. With the new man, when he is on, the boys always take it easy at first. In a new man, they really want a leader, but they don't want one of these rats and everybody else. They feel around and take it easy to see how far they can go with him whether he is hard or easy. . . .
>
> "A good officer should be able to play with the boys and do what they like and be able to beat the heck out of them when they're bad and they know they done wrong. Otherwise they'll keep on doing it."

Relations Among the Inmates

The study indicated the way in which the boys rated each other. The stress on physical prowess, toughness, and resistance to authority without endangering the group were the prized characteristics. Another major influence on the structure of the inmate group was skin color. For many white boys, close association with Negroes of the same age came as a shock. Their parents, like the parents of some college students, supported these negative attitudes. In response, some of the white boys ran away. On the other hand there were white and Negro boys in Ralston who got along well and who were close friends. Tension and rebellion characterized the situation in some cottages. Each cottage worked out its own plans for dealing with the color problem.

Ordinarily the Negro group was unwilling to relinquish its superiority, and the white group was equally unwilling to accept a subordinate role. While direct intervention could moderate some of the overt aspects of race relations, it could not automatically change either attitudes or feelings. One boy commented:

> In our cottage they try to make us mix with the colored boys and we have to a little. This is brought about by the rule in most cottages that at one table there may be no more than about half of each color; it can't be all colored or all white. Or it can't be three of one color and only one of the other. But when we just sit around and play cards or something, and fellows can really be with who they want, the white kids stay by themselves, and the colored boys do the same. And sometimes, the colored fellows try to keep the white boys out of games or even out of the cottages. D-1 is now all colored and so is B-1. They hate white boys in those cottages.

There were numerous cases of racial tension on an individual and cottage basis which erupted into fights, with continual bad feeling between the white and the Negro inmates. While for the most part this state of affairs was brought on by the boys themselves, in some cases the officers were responsible. Some cottage parents were definitely prejudiced. One cottage parent encouraged the white boys to line up against the Negro boys in a pitched battle.

While the relationship of white and Negro boys varied with each cottage, there was generally a temporary armistice largely dictated by the dominant group. The size of the subordinate white group in any cottage was significant; as it approached that of the Negro group, tension mounted; race friction was greatest in those cottages having large minority groups of whites. Esprit de corps and feelings of ethnoculturalism and of the we-they variety developed to challenge the established ingroup.

Reactions of the Boys to Incarceration

Feelings of frustration and rebellion were intensified from the moment the boy set foot in the institution. In the all-embracing routine that prevailed, he felt circumscribed; no aspect of his life seemed free of regulation. The boys complained about the regulations and the quality and amount of food. They complained about the rules concerning smoking and what they might wear. They were upset because incoming and outgoing letters were censored and the contents often discussed with people for whom they were not intended. As one boy remarked: "You can write as often as you want as long as they are the right letters, because you're not allowed to write anything private to your parents or anything about the cottage life except that you're getting along good. If you write it's cold in the dormitory at night, it will be torn up and you'll have to write another one. If you write to your friend it will be torn up because you are not allowed to write to anyone but your relatives."

FOOD. Meals were served cafeteria style and additional portions were passed out by the cottage parents. The boys sat six at a table, and despite the rules, extra helpings were exchanged among them as currency in payment of debts. The food problem is a delicate one as feelings of dissatisfaction aroused by it may ramify in many directions and seep into officer-inmate and boy-to-boy relations. Some of the boys complained about the quality of the food, the way it was distributed, the fact that there were no desserts or that the portions were too small. One boy said, "they are trying to starve us out."

Within a few hours after entering the cottage his mates advised the new boy about what food to eat. There was a widely current belief that some boys excreted into the food. One remarked that although he had been in the cottage almost two months he had not seen anybody eat either the spaghetti or the dessert. Cornflakes, hash, and mashed potatoes seemed to be safe. One boy commented: "Everybody will tell you they mess around with the food —they jerk off, they excrete so that nobody will eat it." Another gave a different explanation. In his words, "the boys who don't like the job of washing dishes tell the other boys that something is wrong with the food—somebody blasted into the pudding or pissed into the peanut butter. The guy that I saw spit into the cocoa gotta beating."

A boy would say, "I wish I had some of what the officers got today." They were unhappily aware of the differences between what the officers ate and what they were given. Thus jobs in the officer's dining room, with possible pickings, were at a premium.

WORK. Work gang or workshop assignments were rated by the boys according to whether the officer was a jeep or a terror and whether or not the jobs were easy and carried a cash payment. Some jobs were assigned on a seniority basis, some were meted out as discipline for running away.

One boy, after careful deliberation, rated the jobs as follows:

"I think about the best slope-out [easy] job is the green house because all you have to do is water the plants, cut them and make sure they are all healthy. Another slope-out is in the chicken house where all you have to do is feed the chickens, collect the eggs, and kill the chickens.

"The hardest job of all is Mr. I's work gang where they shovel coal and help put out the fires, keep the grounds clean and do almost every sort of job. . . .

"The average boy has at least two or three jobs. If he's very very good, he'll have only one all the time he is up here. If he's bad, he'll have about five or six. The boys say if they don't like a man, they try their damndest to get away even if they have to breeze to get their job changed. If they don't like the officer, it doesn't make any difference if they get him into trouble."

RUNAWAYS. The problem of runaways is faced by all institutions. It is not necessarily negative in its implications although it is certainly inconvenient for the institutional staff. If there are many runaways the general public wonders about the program; if the same boy runs away persistently it is more likely to be understood as an expression of his particular problem and needs.

The participant observer interviewed 200 boys about their reason for breezing. September was the favorite month: March and April, during which marks were prepared had the fewest runaways. Running away was not sanctioned by the inmates when it was against the group's interest, that is, when the penalty for the individual's acts would be visited upon the group.

In explaining their reasons for running away, the boys said that the precipitating events were trouble with a particular officer, resentment of the committee's decision to refuse discharge, worry about personal or family problems, escape from punishment, or being bullied by other inmates. Sometimes the explanation was cumulative boredom and resentment—"I got sick and tired of it and fed up with having to do what I was told."

SEX PRACTICES. Sodomy was given by a few as a reason for running away. This, however, was an unusual reaction, since arrival in the institution almost required submission to sex practices that would not be approved or tolerated outside. This is a subject about which institution directors, staff, and boards (if they know anything about it) are usually silent.

The reception unit grapevine continually circulated rumors of sex practices, homosexual orgies, and rapes in the cottages. Fact and fiction in the lurid sensational details engendered fear in many newcomers that they would be forced into homosexuality. To the very young, and to the isolated delinquents who had little knowledge of sex, this information was a shock. Older boys who were aware of homosexual practices, even if they had not already participated in them, were far less concerned.

The housing arrangements strengthened the tendency of the inmate group to emphasize sex. There was practically no privacy in the cottage life. A boy was under the eyes of his mates and officers virtually every moment of his stay. Upon his entry into a cottage, the boy's role in a sex act was quickly determined.

The closest approach to group orgies occurred during the weekly movie in the gym. Oral acts or "handos" by punks as well as masturbation were common practices. It was reported that sometimes, when lights were turned on, an entire cottage group would be requested to leave the hall because eight or nine of its boys had been caught masturbating.

Physical force also played a part. The weak boys were overpowered by the group or, in return for protection from the older or stronger boys, had to grant them sexual favors. The boys brought with them to the institution the sexual mores and exploitative practices of the delinquent society from which they came. Unfortunately, by overlaying them with sadistic consequences, the institutional setting increased these practices. Because homosexuality represented the major source of satisfaction to the deprived inmates, the institution's attempt to suppress it was doomed to fail.

Kinsey's studies would support the urgency of the sexual needs of the young adolescent boy and the frequency of homosexuality in the general population. It is common knowledge also that this is a problem in many boarding schools and colleges. Some of the boys told the observer that they were able to consummate sex relations with girl-friend visitors whom they described to the administrator as their cousins or sisters.

PAROLE.   One of the explanations of the many runaways was unfavorable review by the committee which decided the date of the boy's release. When a boy knew that he had met the committee's standards and was returning home in a few weeks, he relaxed his hostile attitude toward the administration. When, however, the committee's decision was unfavorable, the animosity smoldering just below the surface flared up. It is reported that some of the worst riots in Ralston were engineered by ringleaders in revenge for unfavorable reviews of their progress. The virulence of these sentiments in their mildest form was expressed by an angry boy's wish to castrate all the male officers and rape all the female ones.

As the day of his release neared a boy counted the minutes until he was on the school bus starting back to the city. Often he jeered at and mocked those who remained behind. Sometimes he said he wished the place would burn down. As he neared his home he talked about the pleasures that he anticipated. He competed with the other boys in boasting how many pints of liquor he would kill, how long he would "lush it," how many women he would possess and how his future criminal exploits would exceed anything he might have done in the past. He was no longer afraid of being caught.

Evaluation of the Ralston Program

By the Observer

Unfortunately most of these boys return to the surroundings which fostered their precommitment activities. By virtue of their time at Ralston, their status and prestige among their friends and acquaintances is not diminished but enhanced. The Ralston experience, according to the observer, has chiefly been an introduction to the occupational risk of the professional criminal.

Subsequent discussion of the effect of such institutional treatment will reveal that this statement is not an exaggeration. The best that can be said for the small minority of boys who are able to survive the experience without contamination is that it has had little effect. For the majority of the boys who fall between these two extremes an experience like Ralston is likely to have exposed them to much harm. For most of them, release to the community represents a delicately shifting and precarious equilibrium, which may be easily upset by incidents in the crucial post-institutional period. Chance remarks of relatives or friends, the attitudes of neighbors upon their return home, or any one of countless fortuitous circumstances may help to decide an individual's fate when contrary predisposing forces seem to cancel each other out.

Cures at Ralston could be claimed only for the very small minority able to assimilate the "ethos" of the greater society through a particularly meaningful relationship with an individual officer. The majority of the boys experienced no change in their values or philosophical orientation. They learned only to accommodate by withdrawal through fantasy, which protected their personal will against boredom or invasion by the institution.

By the Boys

The boys with whom the observer talked were unanimous in expressing strong feelings of hate. They said they had not learned anything good. One boy who broke parole and was returned to Ralston expressed the sentiments of many others in saying: "This damn place is no good. Look at these hands, all chapped. That's the only thing you get out of the place. It's no good. All it teaches is things that the boys shouldn't know about. They don't know about punking but when they come up here, they learn. It doesn't teach you nothing." He continued by commenting on the language which the little boys picked up so quickly.

One boy said that when he got out he was going to rob and steal. Maybe this was just talk, but he certainly wasn't talking about being honest.

Another boy who was not a confirmed delinquent expressed his opinion of Ralston as follows:

"Ralston does teach a fellow to be careful about getting into trouble with the law but this isn't because it tries to teach that. It's only because in most cases, they don't want to come back to this place, and will try their best to stay out of trouble. I don't like the many months that must be spent here because I think only a few months are necessary to make the average boy realize the error of his ways.

"Thus far, I haven't seen any training of boys to be good citizens as long as I've been here. If that's what the school is supposed to be for then the most important part of our education here is most sadly neglected. So far, I haven't seen any part of the day set aside for training in any such thing as "citizenship." It seems to me that most of this time is taken up to make a boy more respectful to the superiors at Ralston.

"Most of the boys think it's punishment to be here, and hardly any of them think of it as a training school. Some of the boys think that all they had to do is spend time for doing something wrong and getting into trouble with the police. Most of them resent the whole thing.

"My idea is that they don't try to send a boy home early here. They try to judge a boy by the way he acts up here, but the boy will act differently when he returns to the city. Some guys resent being here and act bad up here, but when they get back to the city, they act differently altogether. From my experience, this place don't seem to help the boys. Maybe a boy has been good while he is at home and comes up here for some minor reason and mixes with other boys who know all the different kinds of rackets in and out and learns new tricks. When he gets out, he may become ambitious and try some of those new tricks he's learned. Usually the result is that he ends up in a place just like this or worse after a small amount of time. The only thing to do is give the boys a better chance and give the ones who didn't do much wrong a better kind of place, if they must be sent away. . . . I don't think this place is worth the money; perhaps they could make it worthwhile if they do a little weeding out of some of the boys and some of the officers. Right now, it certainly teaches one thing. It teaches you not to get caught."

Conclusion

Frustration and Boredom—The Obstacles

Assuming that the findings in this intensive experience of a skilled participant observer in an institutional setting correspond to reality as they do in many ways to Deutsch's findings (see Chapter 26), they have enormous bearing on the programs of other institutions which are much less favored in staff, plant, and financial support. One must recognize that, at best, the programs induce fantasy as an escape from boredom. The extent to which boredom bears upon the inmates is conveyed in the following outburst:

"Routine, routine, routine! They ought to change the name of this place to the Routine School for Boys. Everyday the same damn thing! After you're here a couple of months, you know exactly what you're going to eat every meal. I can tell you what we have each day, each meal, every week. The same in school and the same thing in the cottage . . . that damn routine. Get up at the same time in the morning and go to bed the damn same time every night. You got your special time to go to gym, special times to go to the Protestant Chapel. Just gets you mad to be told what to do every minute of the time."

Less emotional, but conveying almost the same sense of oppression is this statement: "The feeling of routine hit me in a week, maybe a little over. It's just lousy that's all, a dead life, knowing what you're going to do every minute of the time. I got so routiney I got to keeping a calendar to see how much longer this damn routine would go on. I still keep a calendar—eighteen and one half days before I go down for Christmas contest, fifty-nine before I go home. Maybe!"

The effect of boredom upon the individual often is to drive him to seek a different experience which will relieve the tedium of his daily round. Fantasy, our observer reminds us, is one form of accommodation on the psychological level. Accommodations on the behavioral level, i.e., overt attempts to create novelty in the institutional setting, usually involve infraction of the rules. Often conniving offers a way of making the best of circumstances in any group which operates under coercion. As one boy put it: "A lot of times I breezed just for the fun of it, for the excitement. Let me tell you, it's more fun than anything else up here. The only way to have fun is to break the rules."

The institution-wise inmates are those of average or better intelligence, who employ their knowledge of the organization and the psychology of its personnel for their own ends. They, together with the few boys mentioned above who appear to have been able, because of their youth and their fortunate experience with individual staff members, to come through unscathed, represent the only successes which Ralston can claim.

CHAPTER 24

Treatment-Oriented Centers for Delinquents

THE RECENT DEVELOPMENT IN THE UNITED STATES OF SPECIALIZED TREATMENT centers for delinquents has three roots: (1) dissatisfaction with the results of the usual large-scale institutional programs; (2) increasing awareness of the psychological mechanisms which precipitate delinquent behavior; (3) the conviction that treatment must be divorced from punishment.

Aims of Treatment

According to Freud, maladjusted character formation can be corrected if the young person relearns the social adaption which he should have learned at his mother's knee (see Chapter 6). Consequently, if the treatment setting provides better conditions than those which the child confronted in his family, he will develop the appropriate character structure, depending on his age and innate endowments. If he is obviously inadequate, i.e., feeble-minded or psychotic, the treatment aim is to protect society by rendering him as harmless as possible. Removing a normal person from the community, however, is justified only if it will help him to become a law-abiding citizen, and not because it satisfies an emotional demand of the community.

There may be a question whether attitudes formed early in life can be fundamentally changed. On the basis of experience in the Hawkspur Camp in England,[1] in Aichorn's School in Vienna,[2] and the Healy and Bronner

[1] W. David Wills, *The Hawkspur Experiment: An Informal Account of the Training of Wayward Adolescents,* London, Allen and Unwin, 1941.
[2] August Aichorn, *Wayward Youth,* New York, Viking Press, 1935.

clinics in the United States,[3] many students believe that delinquent behavior can be modified. One of the main reasons why the usual treatment is not effective with delinquents, psychologists claim, is that it fails to take into account the length of time it takes for a delinquent child to learn to react selectively to the personalities in the new environment and consequently to modify his behavior. Delinquent children are not impressed by expressions of good intentions on the part of the institution staff. Their former disappointments, like those of Tony and Carol, have made them suspicious of all adults. Because, as a rule, they were unable to suppress their infantile, instinctive urges to achieve satisfying love relationships with their parents, appeals to their "better feelings" are rarely effective.

As we noted in outlining the psychoanalytic approach to behavior, change is brought about through transference. When the elements missing in childhood—affection, acceptance, approval of the individual—are supplied, behavior can be redirected into socially acceptable channels. Repression or discipline, as we saw in the story of Tony and Ralston's boys, does not accomplish this goal. To discover the gap in the early stages of a child's development and help him relive the missing experiences in a positive way takes time, skill, patience, and the cooperation of both the person who is to be helped and his family.

Instead of flatly condemning institutions for delinquents, as do advocates of foster home care, a more enlightened approach is to examine institutional programs today to see whether they are oriented to meet the needs of the young delinquent in the light of current theory. Emphasis in such a program is either on individual or group therapy; this chapter presents illustrations using each type of therapy. The directors of all these institutions believe that young people can profit from the controls of institutionalized group living, even if they are not amenable to the usual large-scale programs of state institutions.

Treatment Centers Emphasizing Individual Therapy

Orthogenic School

The Orthogenic School,[4] established in 1944, occupies a remodeled stucco residence on the fringe of the University of Chicago campus. It was designed

---

[3] William Healy and Augusta L. Bronner, *Treatment and What Happened Afterward*, Boston, Judge Baker Guidance Center, 1939.

[4] Bruno Bettelheim, *Love Is Not Enough*, Glencoe, Ill., Free Press, 1950; and *idem.*, *Truants from Life*, case studies of four severely disturbed children at the Orthogenic School, Glencoe, Ill., Free Press, 1955.

for the care of seriously disturbed delinquents with many of whom individual psychotherapy had failed. The cost of care is approximately $4500 annually. Some scholarships are provided. The 40 children live in dormitories with space partitioned for a chest of drawers, a bed, and a chair. The personal belongings displayed in the cubicle and the condition of the walls reveal a good deal about the problems and the fantasy life of the children. Five dormitory groups house from 2 to 8 children each. Six would be the preferred number, but because of the physical plan it is not possible to arrange the groups in this fashion. In the four workshop programs, the number of children ranges from 10 to 12.

The school does not admit more than 10 children a year and usually not more than 3 at a time. In order not to disturb the already formed groups, admission is usually at the beginning or end of the summer and after the Christmas holidays—periods when children ordinarily experience changes in their school programs. The usual length of stay is from two to three months. As Bettelheim writes: "On the simplest level, how much an institution will be able to achieve for the juveniles under its care will depend to a large extent on the degree to which the staff of the institution and most of all its head remains insensitive to community pressure. Again and again I have seen youngsters kept behind closed doors because the community 'would not stand having him run around free.'"

The school is an open institution, i.e., doors are not barred. Whether a child should be in an open, semi-closed, or closed institution, and how long he should remain, depends, in Bettelheim's opinion, on a clear understanding of the child's underlying disturbance, and his type of defenses. Too often the nuisance value or the threatening nature of the young person's apparent symptoms overshadow his real problem. Bettelheim distinguishes three distinct types of disturbed children:

1. Children whose delinquency is mainly due to neurotic or psychotic disturbances.

2. Those whose underlying problem is expressed by copying the parental behavior.

3. Those known as delinquents because they conform with the mores of the community in which they grew up.

This latter group is sometimes described as illustrating delinquency due to socio-pathology and corresponds with David Levy's first classification discussed in Chapter 6.

Bettelheim is not in favor of country life as a year-round diet for city children.

Often community pressure places institutions out in the country because the community does not want to have these delinquents around, which it created. As a consequence, the city-bred youngster becomes starved for the, to him, tempting entertainments of the urban center to which he has been accustomed since childhood. Once he leaves the institution he will be unable to withstand any temptation, and he will be a fall guy for the first adults who offer him the pleasures he has missed so long; pleasures which seem good out of proportion to reality because of the day dreams which he spun about them due to the boredom of life in the institution.

Bettelheim, who is the pivot of the school's program, chooses as counselors young, vigorous, sympathetic, and open-minded students at the University of Chicago. In his opinion, training, experience, emotional maturity, and devotion in working with children are only starting points. Because of the incessant and pressing demands that delinquent children make on adults, the emotional well-being of the staff members is crucial. "Their therapeutic efforts," he writes, "continually drain the staff members of their libidinal energy, which must be continually replenished. Such restoring of libidinal energy to the staff members is essential if the institution is to serve its purpose."

A country setting is not likely to provide sufficient opportunities for the staff members to forget their work, enjoy a life rich in intellectual and aesthetic stimulation, and experience emotionally gratifying associations off the job. Such outlets are necessary if the store of emotional energy required for working with delinquents is not to run dry. The attitudes of a staff in a remote institution will reflect the consequences of the customary drab life, long working hours, short vacations, inadequate pay, and low professional status. Routine will characterize the life experience they provide for the children and, as the Ralston boys complained (though not in these words), Nothing is more devastating than routine to efforts to induce emotional growth and reaching out toward higher integration.

Bettelheim believes in permitting the staff, who work only thirty hours a week, to experiment in direct therapy and to learn by their mistakes. "If the cottage parents are to be responsible for the discipline, and the psychiatrist responsible for therapy, then discipline will win and therapy go out by the window." We will note that Goldsmith, at Hawthorne Cedar Knolls, does not believe this fiasco is a necessary result of leaving therapy to the professionals.

A visit to the Orthogenic School offers a challenging and exciting experience. The results of its treatment of these children have not, however, been made public.

Berkshire Farm for Boys *don't read*

Located in the foothills of the Berkshires on 1100 acres, the Berkshire Farm accommodates 150 boys, aged 12 to 16. They live in stucco cottages, with their cottage parents, who are on duty from 7:00 in the morning until 10:00 at night, when a night supervisor takes over. The usual dairy, barn, and farm buildings supplement the equipment for trade training. There is a gymnasium, a central kitchen and dining room, and an infirmary. Cabins for summer camping are located at the cove of Lake Queechy.

The present director, who is an experienced social worker, is assisted by a fully staffed clinic, a full time psychiatrist, a resident psychologist, and five psychiatric caseworkers under the guidance of a casework supervisor and a Protestant chaplain. There are two resident nurses, a part-time physician, dentist, and ophthalmologist.

The academic school extends from the fifth to the eighth grade. Five teachers work with boys who are ungraded and there are two teachers trained in remedial reading. For boys who have completed the sixth grade and are interested in agriculture, printing, carpentry, or mechanics, there are trade classes. High school students attend the community school.

Recreation includes athletics, physical training, camping, and group activities, all supervised by trained staff who are assisted by volunteers.

The career of Butch, described by the executive director,[5] illustrates some of the contrasts between the experience in a large congregate state institution such as that described in Chapter 23 and experience in a setting like Berkshire Farm.

> BUTCH. Butch's home life in a typical upstate New York community could hardly be termed typical. His mother was in and out of custody on morals charges. His father was emotionally unstable—brutal and alcoholic. "Butch," his two older sisters and two younger brothers were left without adequate care, food and clothing. When Butch was seven his father was sentenced to prison for armed robbery, his mother deserted the family, and an aunt took it over with the help of public assistance.
>
> When Butch's father was released from prison he resumed responsibility for his family, working as a laborer from 4 P.M. until midnight. The older sister, age 17, became the family's "mother."

Taunted by his schoolmates, Butch got himself into one serious scrape after another, including violent assault. When the police finally picked him up and brought him to the juvenile court, the judge could see no alternative

[5] J. Donald Coldren, "Berkshire Industrial Farm, Canaan, New York, Where Boys in Trouble Can Learn to Become Useful Citizens," undated.

except commitment to an institution. After clearing with the Berkshire intake staff, the probation officer informed Butch of the judge's decision that Berkshire Farm was the right place for him.

At first it was difficult for Butch to accept this new way of living. His resentment toward his own father, mother, brothers and sisters was directed toward the cottage "parents" and the other boys. But soon he learned that he could turn to "Mom" and "Pop" in times of disappointment. This developed into a real feeling of security. Eventually, through the patience and example of his cottage parents and his caseworker, Butch began to learn what the word "home" could mean to him. . . .

When Butch arrived at Berkshire, he was verbose and affable. He expected to get along by ingratiating himself with the staff in order to use them for his own ends. His gregarious attitude was a disguise to conceal his feelings of hostility and resentment.

To establish himself as a big shot, Butch instigated fights but took care to stand on the side lines pretending innocence. When this ruse failed, he tried running away and stealing. Instead of being punished as Butch expected from his past experience, "the staff and the caseworker helped Butch to understand the reasons for and consequences of his behavior. They told him that they understood why he had to be big stuff in front of the other boys and that their aim was to help him."

Butch began to realize, for the first time in his life, that the institutional staff understood *why* he behaved badly. Gradually he didn't need to fight the world around him any longer.

Of course this was no miracle cure. To change one's accustomed behavior is not easy for well adjusted people. Imagine how much more difficult it is for a boy like Butch or Tony. Each of the aspects of the institution's program had its special task and special role in helping Butch over the hurdles toward better behavior. Since Butch had always hated school it was hardly likely that he would suddenly become a model pupil. When he came to Berkshire, Butch was two years behind in his studies. When the testing program, to which he agreed scoffingly, revealed an aptitude in auto mechanics he was assigned to the auto shop. In spite of his aptitude, however, he came late to class, requested frequent permission to leave the room, resented attention which the instructor paid to other children, and often called them stupid.

When his behavior became distressingly disruptive in the classroom, his teacher, who was trained not only in elementary school instruction but also in individual child care, confronted "Butch" with the simple fact that she had responsibility to the other boys, too. She told Butch she understood it was not easy for him to share his association with her with other boys, but that he must learn to be a member of the group. This consistent, patient interpretation over a period of time seemed to help him. His writing improved, as did his arithmetic and social studies.

His class in auto mechanics gave him a start with the tools of the trade. He was visibly pleased when he helped reline the brakes on the farm tractor.

Like the classroom teacher, the man in charge of the work-training division was challenged in helping Butch.

Butch refused to report and loitered about near the work area. Other boys took him to task for his unwillingness to do his share. Gradually he began to work a little with the pickup crew on the truck. This crew was supervised by an older boy who drove the truck and who talked kindly to Butch. Again, this older boy was able to show Butch that getting along with the other fellows could be real fun.

During the period of greatest crisis in his cottage adjustment, Butch began to look forward to the outdoor work and ask for assignments that he preferred. These were given to him when this special attention did not favor him over another boy or interfere with the work program.

The recreation staff had to sell Butch the idea that reading comic books with titles like "Cases for the Morgue" was not the only form of recreation. Of course he might have been forbidden to read such comics and compelled to participate in the active sports, but this procedure would not have changed his attitude or established a healthy interest. "Instead, the group worker, a skilled employee responsible for the boys' leisure hours, continued to work with Butch and offer opportunities for participation. Ice skating, skiing, and sledding appealed to him. These were solitary sports. Other individual activities were arranged, and Butch took to goal shooting, throwing at targets—then two-man basketball, catch. Finally, he was persuaded to play on his cottage intramural basketball team."

Team play means getting along with one's fellows. But to get along with others means getting along with oneself. This is especially difficult for delinquents who, as Erikson points out (see Chapter 6), have not really accepted the role of bad boy as a permanent one.

The program at the Farm allows ample time for the boys to meet on their own grounds. As a result, Butch soon learned that he was not the only boy who had ever found himself in trouble. Some had been in less trouble than he . . . others in more. This provided him with food for thought. Maybe he wasn't "the worst guy in the world" after all.

As Butch developed a sense of security from the warmth and acceptance of the staff and his fellow students, his fear of failure was lessened. As meaningful relationships were formed, he became able to invest more of himself in his play. He began to learn what teamwork meant.

At Berkshire the chaplain was very much part of the treatment team. In helping Butch accept the help that religion might give him, the chaplain neither preached nor threatened. When he asked Butch to attend the Protestant service,

> the boy told him what his religious background had been at home. His mother, he pointed out, had been very religious. Yet look what she did to her family. His father did not believe in "preachy" stuff at all. Butch attended services with the other boys from his cottage. He also attended the weekday religious-education classes with his school class. God seemed so very far away to him. The Bible was like the dictionary. Why should he treat people kindly when they were always so mean to him? "Religion is for 'dopes.'"
>
> "If each person would find a way to feel good inside, people might not have so much unhappiness," suggested the chaplain. A short time later, Butch reported this to the chaplain: "Pop . . . you know, my cottage parent . . . trusts me! He left his keys in the car and the motor running when I rode to the store with him last night. He's one of those religious dopes, too. I warned him that I might steal his car. He said that he didn't think I would. I didn't." "Maybe religion does help people to feel good inside," the boy thought to himself.

This sketch of the rehabilitation of Butch selects from a long series of small incidents with teacher, caseworker, cottage parents, and the other members of the staff, which all together brought about the hoped-for result. We see in outline how different people in different phases of the Berkshire Farm program bring professional skill and experience to bear in rebuilding the personality of a boy. Butch is now living in a foster home, helping his foster father in his service station. He attends school regularly and is making good progress. He is second baseman on his school baseball team.

Neither the superintendent nor the board of directors of any institution, public or private, would claim that all their charges turn out as well as Butch did. Nor are they satisfied that they have all the answers. But most of them are searching for new and better ways to help young persons sent to institutions. Berkshire's after-care program under Martin Haskell's direction seems particularly thoughtful.

Hawthorne Cedar Knolls School[6]

Established in the early 1900s to provide residential treatment for delinquent boys and girls, the Hawthorne Cedar Knolls School, located at Thornwood, New York, about an hour from New York City, is one of several programs for treating delinquents under the auspices of the Jewish Board of Guardians of New York City.

[6] See Chapter 26 for evaluation of Hawthorne Cedar Knolls program.

In November 1959 the population was 200—147 boys and 53 girls—ranging in age from 8 to 18. The majority had been committed by the court because of aggressive delinquent behavior. During the last fiscal year about 140 children were admitted to care from about four times that number of applicants. The usual stay is eighteen to twenty-four months. About 10 per cent are non-Jewish. The fees range from $330 a month for children who are wards of the Department of Welfare to $5600 a year for those whose parents can afford to pay for them.

The resident staff includes the director, 35 cottage parents and child-care workers, and 29 maintenance personnel. The visiting staff includes a clinic director, an executive assistant, a chief psychiatric social worker, 13 social workers, a number of recreation workers, and a director of Jewish education. In addition there are 30 teachers and the principal.

About a dozen two-story stucco or stone cottages, each accommodating 20 children, face a broad, tree-bordered avenue. Behind each cottage is a garden, which the residents tend under the supervision of cottage parents. An administration building houses the synagogue, classrooms, workshops, and the administrative offices. The guidance clinic is located in a building of its own. A gymnasium, an infirmary, a swimming pool, and the Linden Hill School, which accommodates children with severe emotional disturbances, are fairly recent additions. The almost 300 acres in the rolling country of Northern Westchester provide ample space for a well-equipped farm and playing fields for the children.

Until 1925 or thereabouts, in conformity with the then prevailing ideas, the institution emphasized habit-training through quasi-military discipline. Bells rang to get up, to wash, to eat, to attend class, and for all other routine activities. The effect was to condition the young people to bell-ringing. When they returned to the community where there was no bell-ringing, their parents complained that beds were unmade, and baths were infrequent.

Boys at the early Hawthorne marched to and from meals, eaten in silence. The girls ate in their own building, and had to remove their shoes to go through the basement, in order not to scratch the polished floors. Hedges were trimmed closely and lawns nicely mowed. The bookkeeping disclosed the scrupulous care that not a penny should be wasted and that the property should be effectively maintained.

Today, in contrast, if one did not know that this was an institution for delinquents, one might think it was a coeducational boarding school, with its 200 boys and girls dressed in the informal fashion customary in suburban communities. They stroll about the grounds, sit on the steps of the houses, watch games in the gymnasium, dance together at Saturday-night affairs, go to the village, and visit one weekend a month at home.

The youngsters attend classes for half a day either in the morning or the afternoon. The teachers are supplied by the public school system of the community, and instruction is available through the second year of high school. Boys and girls able to continue beyond that point attend neighboring schools. The half day which is not spent in school is used for vocational assignments—for the girls, cooking, garment making, and commercial classes; and for the boys, work in the woodshop or the printshop, or assignments to the farmer, the plumber, or the painter.

As soon as possible after the young person has been accepted at Hawthorne Cedar Knolls (the first day is usually a Friday so that he will have the weekend free to become oriented) the new boy or girl is assigned a caseworker, who also keeps in touch with the child's parents, because their cooperation is necessary if the child is to benefit by the treatment program.

While the average length of stay is slightly less than two years, the severity of the individual's problems, his age, and his response to treatment determine when he will leave. The institution keeps in constant contact with the boy's family so that readjustment will be as smooth as possible.

At Hawthorne Cedar Knolls there is ample opportunity for meaningful contacts with accepting and understanding adults. According to the clinic director, the chief difficulty in offering help to persons who are upset is that the individual is frequently unwilling to acknowledge that he needs help. An added problem is the therapist's temptation to respond negatively to the aggressive behavior of the delinquent.[7] The case of John[8] illustrates the way in which Hawthorne Cedar Knolls works with a typical delinquent, whose overt behavior appears to be an inability to resist the temptation to steal automobiles. This, by the way, is a frequent symptom among the relatively few Jewish boys brought to the juvenile court.

> JOHN. The episode that brought John to court and culminated in his placement was "a classic." While he was riding a stolen car he stopped a police car and asked for a push. It is worth noting that he vehemently denied that he did this intentionally to get picked up. He was just too cocksure of himself.
>
> BACKGROUND AND INITIAL DIAGNOSIS. John, a 15-year-old boy of better than average intelligence, with good physical equipment, came to Hawthorne with a long history of car stealing. The first stealing episode occurred when he was about 13. He continued to steal in spite of the many drastic measures the family employed to rid him of this "bad habit." Projecting the blame on friends and neighborhood, the family uprooted itself and moved to the middle west.

[7] See Dr. Bloch's and Dr. Peck's comments on this point in Chapter 17.
[8] Based on case presentation by Hyman Grossbard, clinic director of Hawthorne Cedar Knolls School.

Life for John began anew in a good neighborhood with increased material things and gratifications. When, however, John resumed his car stealing and was brought to the attention of the juvenile court the family returned to New York. The car stealing became more frequent. . . .

John was described as a tough, sullen youngster who looked with contempt on school and those associated with it—it was "all childish stuff." He was arrogant, bitter and close-mouthed. He neither boasted nor was apologetic about his stealing. The repetitiousness of his stealing, his apparent lack of anxiety about it, his difficulty in establishing relationships and his apparent inability to learn from experience suggested the possibility of psychopathic personality. . . .

His history revealed that he was the oldest of three children of a lower-middle-class family with an indifferent, sadistic father and a neurotic domineering mother. The mother was full of praise of John's behavior as a child. He was so dependable and helpful that he was farmed out as a baby sitter; he was so good that at times she was afraid that he would turn out to be a sissy. Then unexpectedly things began to happen. Severe beatings, bribery, pleas for him to behave for the sake of the mother, did not bring any results, although the mother knew that he was a devoted son. . . .

INITIAL ADJUSTMENT AT HAWTHORNE. John went around with a chip on his shoulder, trying to give the impression that he knew it all. Even when superficially conforming, the staff felt if given the opportunity he would pull a "fast one." He seemed intent on annoying people and getting under their skin. He would lie brazenly and indulge in extreme projection. With his therapist he was guarded, laconic and hostile.

However, in spite of the façade of unconcern and poise that he attempted to preserve, one sensed extreme tension. The daring he demonstrated about car stealing which at first suggested the omnipotence of a psychopath, upon closer scrutiny emerged as the compulsive expression of a neurotic. Analysis of his behavior substantiated that we were dealing with a case of a compulsive stealing which John attempted to camouflage into dare-devil behavior. . . .

CRUCIAL MOTHER-SON RELATIONSHIP. Upon close analysis, John's irrational behavior began to assume meaning. He was basically a passive, dependent youngster with an extremely domineering, smothering mother and intimidating father. Fearful of annihilation he struggled for acceptance through submissive behavior. With dependence not sufficiently protecting nor satisfying, his need for independence was extreme. He had to resort to the dare-devil behavior to prove to himself his independence and strength.

This process of ambivalence and conflict was complicated by his mother who, on one hand, had to keep him as a submerged, dependent child, and, on the other hand, needed the image of the all-powerful son who could serve her as a husband substitute. Unconsciously, she encouraged his delinquency, car stealing, symbolizing to her the daring and strength which she admired. In spite of her protest, John sensed her partial tacit approval. Punishment was equated for him with strength and a sense of power which he so badly needed. The severe beatings of his father were utilized to square John's account of hostility toward his father. The sexual symbolic meaning of a car to a passive dependent boy of this type is of considerable significance. . . .

PLAN FOR THERAPY. It was obvious that John could not be treated effectively at home in close proximity to his mother. He showed the usual resistance of the delinquent to help which represents a threat to his image of himself. A preliminary thawing-out period preceding psychotherapy was necessary. . . .

During this period emphasis was placed on his general life experiences. Great discipline was exercised on the part of people who came into contact with him not to respond to his provocation. Opportunities for inviting punishment and using it as an armour against people were kept at a minimum. While his accomplishments were praised, few pressures and demands were placed upon him. His relationships with people were encouraged, particularly with his cottage parents who were able to take from him extreme hostility and aggression. . . .

CHANGES ARE NOTED. Gradually John seemed to gain more security with people and himself and thus was able to look at himself introspectively. His contact with his therapist became meaningful. There was outpouring of anxiety and reliving of past experiences. He began to gain insight into his behavior. He began to sense that his previous explanation of his car stealing, because he wanted to be a big shot or eager for excitement, was only a segment of the truth. He was not sure whether having a car would have given him sufficient excitement or solved his stealing problem; for if the wish for excitement, for a car, were fed only by the ordinary adolescent needs, the likelihood is that the ego would have been able to control, postpone or secure partial gratification through a legitimate way.

After a year and a half at Hawthorne, John is still a rather tense but friendly boy, with a fair control and understanding of himself and his relationship with people. He is realistic about his abilities and thoughtful in his plans for the future. He is still interested in automobile mechanics. Needless to say that there has been no recurrence of stealing.

While it may appear that John's rehabilitation was mainly the result of proper diagnosis and the contacts of the psychiatrist and psychiatric social worker, this is not the case. Every member of the staff, from the psychiatrist to the cook, played a calculated part in rebuilding his idea of himself as a responsible, law-abiding member of society.

STAFF INTERACTION. There are no second-class citizens at the Hawthorne treatment conferences.[9] This does not mean that the role of the clinician is identical with the role of the cottage parent. The fundamental idea of the team approach is that the child belongs to no one person but derives his health and strength from the combined efforts of all. Each staff member not only accepts his role but also his limitations. Satisfaction derives from success as a cottage parent or a maintenance man. There is no competition with the therapist, who also does not strive to be the key figure in the child's affection.

One of the problems in an institution emphasizing psychiatric treatment is, however, that the clinician is sometimes regarded by the other personnel as the person who gives permission for destructive behavior which interferes with the young person's discharge of responsibilities appropriately set by the cottage, the teaching, or the custodial staff. At Hawthorne Cedar Knolls, the clinician identifies himself with the structure of the institution, and realizes that the house parents and the school teachers must expect the appropriate amount of conformity from the child. At the same time the psychiatrist is permitted greater latitude in not demanding conformity, so that he can explore the child's problems.

In the last ten years, therapists have been coming to recognize the importance of the hour-by-hour management of the young person as an essential part of therapy. The therapist therefore has also assumed the task of explaining to the house parent, teacher, and the vocational counselor how unconscious motivation may influence their attitudes and their daily handling of the children. As adults learn to recognize and control these attitudes, in reaction to the surface behavior of the children, their tolerance increases.

STAFF SELECTION. Like other institutions sensitive to treatment needs, Hawthorne Cedar Knolls pays special attention to staff selection. In the early days, almost anyone who was willing could be assured of a job in an institution. The specialized institution today looks more closely at the personality qualifications of applicants. The staff member's ability to invest his energies in caring for children is as important as his receptiveness to new ideas and new ways of doing things. In interviewing applicants, a clinician and the administrator compare their impressions before the final choice is made. Needless to say, the conditions of employment, compensation, free time, and opportunities for professional advancement mean that today the task of house parent in a school like Hawthorne has improved considerably from the old days.

The Hawthorne School has experimented with the employment of pro-

---

[9] Jerome M. Goldsmith, "The Communication of Clinical Information in a Residential Treatment Setting," *Casework Papers, 1955*, National Conference of Social Welfare, Family Service Association of America, pp. 43-52.

fessionally trained persons as house parents, and recognizes that it is often difficult for these house parents to accept their role. The attitude of the therapist can, however, help them to function effectively if they do not regard the job as menial, and if the clinician does not so regard it. An effective way to resolve the rivalries which were created when there were two sets of supervisors—one for the child-care personnel and one for the clinical personnel—has been the establishment of unified supervision of both.

Lincoln Hall

Lincoln Hall, the new name for the N. Y. Catholic Protectory, founded in 1863 is run by the Christian Brothers, or more formally, the Brother of the Christian Schools. It is located about fifty miles from New York in lovely wooded country. On its ample grounds there are a farm, six baseball diamonds, and a pond. The plant is entirely modern—a residence for the brothers, a shop building, a gymnasium, barns and service buildings. Each of the eleven cottages houses 24 boys.

The intake process for Lincoln Hall is very similar to that for Hawthorne Cedar Knolls. Specifically, the intake staff summarize the court dossier for those boys whom the court refers. Then, if the intake committee decides to accept the boy he is visited at Youth House (see Chapter 21) and the Lincoln Hall program is explained to him. Each new boy spends the first two days in a Reception Unit during which time the necessary tests are administered and his placement decided.

HOME LIFE, FACILITIES, AND PROGRAM. There are two Brothers in charge of each cottage. A newly arrived Brother is usually assigned as the second prefect in addition to his full-time teaching schedule. The first prefect has full charge of the cottage and does no teaching except for religious instruction in each school day. All the Brothers at Lincoln Hall are college graduates, and several have graduate degrees. The following excerpts describing the program are taken from a report by Monsignor Furfey.[10]

> At Lincoln Hall the relationships between boys and prefects seem to be basically friendly; nevertheless one must not forget that this is an institution for problem boys. In spite of the friendly atmosphere, problems smolder beneath the surface. In understanding the boys' behavior, the prefects have certain special aids in addition to their opportunities to observe the boys day-by-day, such as the boys' case histories with their psychodiagnostic studies.
>
> Supervision at Lincoln Hall is therefore an informed activity. It involves a good deal of preventive work. It also includes education. Since

[10] Monsignor Paul Hanly Furfey, "Four Institutions Under Catholic Auspices," *Institutions for Delinquents*, Part II, Juvenile Delinquency Evaluation Project of the City of New York, Feb. 1958, pp. 1-72.

he is a religious teacher the prefect is able in his group lessons to discuss the moral principles that are needed to correct behavior disorders on the conscious level. Supervision also includes a good deal of informal, individual counseling. Finally, in understanding difficult cases, the prefect can turn to the psychiatric clinic and the social work staff for technical advice.

Lincoln Hall offers a wide variety of recreational opportunities. Play is obviously taken very seriously by the staff as an element in the treatment process. Probably [the boys] have at least as much time for play as the average boy living at home, and they have many more play facilities. In the afternoon there is a regular outdoor sports program which includes, according to the season, football, baseball, track, basketball, and swimming. In the evenings there is a study period, but plenty of time remains for choosing one's own sort of indoor recreation.

THE SCHOOL. Administratively, the school at Lincoln Hall is divided into two distinct parts. The academic classes are administered by the Christian Brothers or by lay teachers hired by them; the vocational classes, however, belong to the public school system of the City of New York and form part of the Bronx Vocational High School. In both parts the qualifications of the teachers are high. The eight vocational school teachers satisfy the standards of the New York Board of Education. Of the fifteen academic teachers, six are Christian Brothers; all of these latter have graduate credits and three have Master's degrees. Among the other teachers are two women who formerly taught in the New York City schools. Several of the lay teachers are now candidates, or planning to become candidates, for Master's degrees in remedial education.

To a rather surprising degree the boys are separated into homogeneous groups in the school. There is, first of all, a division between boys going to junior high school, senior high school, and continuation classes . . . for older boys who cannot profit by the academic program. . . . At the senior high school level there is a division between the vocational and the academic-commercial-vocational curriculum. Another division, in some cases, separates the juniors from the intermediates and seniors. Still another assigns to separate classes children of different levels of reading ability. Finally, for remedial reading, there are still finer breakdowns during certain periods. The remedial reading classes may sometimes consist of a single pupil. One very interesting class is the "tutorial" class, consisting of the twelve boys of third- or fourth-year high school level; these have two study periods and four tutorial periods a day.

A good deal of testing is carried out. Certainly enough raw data are available to give an accurate measure of the effectiveness of the school's teaching. Unfortunately, the school psychologist has made only fragmentary studies along this line. His time has been employed in working with individual boys rather than in making studies of the school program as a whole. Such data as are available are rather hard to interpret. They give a generally favorable, but imprecise, impression of the school's efficiency.

The shop courses offer the boys a choice of eight subjects, namely, industrial arts, printing, auto repairing, electrical work, barbering, upholstery, woodworking, and tailoring. . . . All boys, except a few of the more advanced high school boys, take two shop periods a day of forty minutes each and they rotate through four shops in the course of a year. As far as possible, a boy is allowed to choose the shop course he desires. . . .

RELIGIOUS SERVICES AND COUNSELING.   The current chaplain of Lincoln Hall, . . . Father Robert E. Moore, was a successful lawyer before studying for the priesthood. For six years he served on the State Commission of Correction; as a member of that body he used to visit and inspect the various prisons under State control. As chaplain, he conducts religious services, gives a certain amount of religious instruction, and does a great deal of informal personal counseling. This latter activity occupies a very large share of his time. He makes it his business to know every boy in the institution personally and to be concerned with his problem. It is the Lincoln Hall policy to have the chaplain participate in the various staff conferences and meetings at which the cases of individual boys are discussed. Thus he becomes an integral part of the treatment team.

CLINICAL AND CASEWORK SERVICES. . . . At Lincoln Hall the clinical and casework staffs are administratively distinct. . . . The clinic is headed by a psychiatrist who serves twenty-one hours a week, and the institution is now actively trying to secure another half-time psychiatrist. There is also a clinical psychologist who serves twenty-one hours a week, as well as a full-time educational psychologist who divides his time between school and clinic. The psychiatrist spends part of his time with individual boys; if he finds them accessible to therapy, they are treated by members of his staff. The balance of the psychiatrist's time is devoted to meetings, to in-service training, and to conferences with staff members. . . .

The social service staff, although it could profitably be expanded, is nevertheless large in comparison to many other institutions. . . . Moreover an increase of about 50 per cent in staff size is already authorized. . . . The full staff, as authorized, will consist of one administrative supervisor, three supervisors, and fifteen practitioners. Some of the workers on the present staff are untrained, but all of them have at least the experience which is considered an acceptable substitute for training in a school of social work when the qualifications of the staff are considered in reference to the reimbursement formula by the City's Bureau of Child Welfare. Moreover, it is now the definite policy at Lincoln Hall not to hire workers who lack a degree in social work unless they are willing to enroll at Fordham in the work-study program, by which a student obtains his social work degree in three years. . . .

It is indisputable that individualization is taken very seriously at Lincoln Hall and that program modifications introduced during the past few years have been selected with this goal consciously in mind. The small cottage groups and the small classes in the school encourage individualization. The growing importance attached to the clinical team and to the social service department reflect a consciousness of the desirability of treating the boys individually on a case-by-case basis.

The chief obstacles to individualization, according to Monsignor Furfey, seem to be three:

1. The lack of sufficient opportunities for the pursuit of special leisure-time interests. "By the very nature of institutional life, most of the activities of the children must be regimented to a certain extent. . . . In his leisure time however a child may be offered a choice of activities, and it is desirable to make this choice as wide as possible, for thus he is offered an opportunity to be himself, to express his own personality, and to escape the danger of becoming a robot."

2. The lack of flexibility of treatment imposed by the Barnabas system, "essentially a system for varying a boy's length of stay at the institution and the time of his home visits for disciplinary reasons."

3. The difficulty of agreeing on, and carrying out, an explicit treatment plan for each boy. "In the past it was entirely possible for the clinical staff, the social workers, the school teachers, and the home-life staff to work at cross purposes to the detriment of effective treatment. . . . At present a system is being introduced which will require adoption of a treatment plan by the staff and the notation of the plan adopted on the boy's record." The new system, however, may require additional staff time, and will definitely demand better communication between the various departments.

RETURN TO THE COMMUNITY. The aftercare of up-state boys is handled by the agencies which originally sent them to Lincoln Hall. New York City boys are taken care of by caseworkers from the Lincoln Hall New York City office on 22nd Street. The average aftercare period is about one year. New York boys visit the office about once a month where they are interviewed by a caseworker. An effort is made also to see the boy's parents about once in two months. Normally, the same caseworker who deals with the boy while he is at Lincoln Hall carries him also during aftercare. Workers have caseloads of about fifteen to twenty-five boys under aftercare in addition to their caseloads at the institution.

As the author of this study notes, the most striking fact about Lincoln Hall, as well as the three institutions for Catholic girls[11] is that they are

[11] *Ibid.*, p. 69. St. Anne, St. Germaine, and St. Philomena are under the auspices of the Order of the Good Shepherd.

constantly changing. The present-day Lincoln Hall is a far cry from the old Protectory which, according to the Brother-in-charge in the 1930s, practiced "Muscular Christianity."

All the Catholic institutions are being asked to accept children who are more and more disturbed and they, like the other institutions, are not automatically staffed to deal with the attendant problems. Staff shortages in Catholic institutions can, however, be more readily remedied than in institutions which are not staffed by members of a religious order. Moreover, they can be and are being sent for special training to man the increasing number of openings for their services. With increased staff, smaller units will be practical, and equally important, more attention will be paid to providing after-care which is more than token in quality.

As in the case of institutions of all kinds, Monsignor Furfey concludes, planned research with respect to successes and failures of the program is a sine qua non if tradition, guesswork, and rule of thumb are to be replaced by scientific method.[12]

Wiltwyck School[13]

The impetus for establishing the Wiltwyck School in the late 1930s was a request from Chief Justice Hill of New York City's juvenile court. He complained that there were no facilities for the care of Negro boys under 12 who were being referred to the court in increasing numbers. A group of public-minded citizens, including Mrs. Eleanor Roosevelt, raised funds to buy a residential school, which had previously operated under Protestant auspices at Esopus, near Hyde Park, New York. The expenses are partly met by a per diem allowance from New York City, supplemented by contributions from private sources. The current per capital cost is approximately $4500 a year.

The four main cottages, two-story affairs made of fieldstone, each house two groups of boys under the direction of resident counselors.

THE BOYS. Today the school is interracial, but the majority of the boys are Negro. About one third are committed through the New York City Department of Welfare, and the remainder come from the court. Like the Orthogenic School in Chicago, almost half of Wiltwyck's present population of about 100 have diagnoses either of psychopathic disorders, sociopathic personalities, or fairly serious neurotic disturbances. A few have impaired brain function. None of these boys would have met the admission criteria of Pioneer House described later in this chapter.

[12] *Ibid.*, pp. 69-72.
[13] See chapter 26 for evaluation of Wiltwyck Program.

THE STAFF. Dr. Ernest Papanek, its resident director from 1949 to 1958[14] and largely responsible for laying out its present program, combined training in education, psychology, and social work, and experience in Vienna with August Aichorn. The staff includes a psychiatrist, psychologist, psychiatric caseworker, an art therapist, and a specialist in remedial reading. Because many of the children are retarded in reading, tutoring by a remedial reading specialist is important. (In Papanek's opinion, some of the feeling of inferiority of these children is due to the fact that they cannot even read the things they would like to read—menus, directions, and so forth.) Religious education, on released time, is provided for the Catholic boys (about one fourth of the group) by the local priest; and for the Protestants by one of the school teachers who is an ordained minister.

Papanek insisted that there should be no punishment at the school. Instead, because young persons need to be helped to accept the consequences of their behavior, "penalties" related to the realities of the situation are imposed. If, for example, windows are broken and furniture destroyed, the boys learn to realize that this means school funds otherwise allocated must now be deflected for repairs.

Papanek agreed with Redl that the peer group is most important for boys of this age whose homes, in the main, have failed to furnish them the usual protection given to middle-class children. Because the director believed it is easier for boys to identify with a man counselor than with a woman, Wiltwyck employs counselors rather than house parents. As Papanek put it, the boys know the cottage institution is not their home. This aspect of the role of the counselor is well portrayed in the film The Quiet One.[15] Agreeing with Bettelheim that counselors need respite from the arduous demands of the boys, Papanek provided for both relief and night counselors.

THE NEED FOR A NEW LOCATION. Papanek also agreed with Bettelheim that it is important for both counselors and boys to be as close as possible to a metropolitan community which offers easy access to the kind of life to which they have hitherto been accustomed and to which they will subsequently return. Currently the school is searching for new quarters closer to New York City.

It is not surprising that the majority of institutions for delinquents in this country have been located in rural areas. Undoubtedly many of the founders themselves were country boys with a nostalgic remembrance of the beauties of nature, the virtues of fresh air, and the adage: "Early to bed and early to rise makes a man healthy, wealthy, and wise." This attitude was also

[14] Papanek resigned in March 1958; in September 1958 Nathan J. Levine was appointed acting executive director.
[15] See New York University Film Library for arrangements to borrow this film made at Wiltwyck by Athena Films in 1948.

evident in the development of care for dependent and neglected children, with the farming-out of trainloads of children in the vast open spaces of the West. The benefactors of those days were unaware of the traumatic effect of separation on children. Since no record of these placements in the far-away places was made, in subsequent years efforts of brothers and sisters to locate one another were as unrewarding as were those of slaves after the Civil War when they tried to locate members of their families who had been sold.

It is also possible that, in their lack of concern that parents should be able to remain in contact even with delinquent children, the directors of these institutions were expressing a rejection of parents. A similar phenomenon is the comment of many teachers that they could manage the children if there were no parents to interfere.

Children's Village

Located at Dobbs Ferry, Children's Village over the many years has changed its program to respond to the needs of certain New York City delinquents. In the last two and a half years the school has cut its population in half. Currently it cares for about 286 boys between the ages of 10 and 16. The average stay is approximately one and a half years. The young people presently under care present a variety of needs. Some need a simple routine with a minimum of personal entanglements and demands. Some, who must be removed from a highly charged home environment, need psychotherapy for themselves and their parents if they are to return to the community. A third group of children, who have too little control of their impulses, cannot manage to behave normally in their home-school-community environment. And a fourth group are children from "cultural islands" where the moral and ethical standards are at variance with accepted cultural modes. Their life at home has led to intrapsychic conflict as the child has been exposed to the more general standards of the American culture.

The institution does not accept children who cannot be trusted to be left alone, children who have homicidal or suicidal tendencies, or children who are chronic car stealers, fire setters, social deviates, or runaways.

THE PROGRAM. At Children's Village, treatment includes casework, psychotherapy, group work and recreation, offered both inside and outside the institution.[16] The academic and vocational program resembles that at Hawthorne Cedar Knolls and includes the full complement of testing and remedial curricula.

---

[16] James R. Dumpson and Joseph M. Linda, *New York City's Residential Treatment Programs*, report of the Committee on Services to Emotionally Disturbed Children, New York, Commission for Foster Care, May 1955, p. 14.

Ohio's Division of Juvenile Research, Classification, and Training

The new diagnostic center to replace the old Ohio Bureau of Juvenile Research has been assigned the responsibility for study and treatment of the approximately 2000 youths annually sent to it by Ohio's 88 Juvenile Courts. As in the old center on the grounds of the State Hospital in Columbus, the girls and boys are housed in groups of 10-15, according to age. Each group has all its own facilities for sleeping, recreation, and eating. The home-life staff works in three shifts with an overlap of about a half hour to permit communication in regard to details of happenings that might affect the succeeding shift. The staff-inmate ratio is 1 to 0.4, excluding maintenance workers.

The atmosphere on the day of the author's visit in late November 1959 was very relaxed. The girls were preparing for a dance with the boys. Many of them had their hair in curlers, a few were ironing, writing letters, or listening to the radio. The staff made no apologies for the disarray in the dormitory.

The new facilities for study and observation include medical facilities under the direction of a specialist in adolescent problems, a unit for emotionally disturbed youngsters, and closed-circuit TV for study and observation. The staff, directed by Dr. Paul Kirch, a psychiatrist, includes psychologists, social workers, educators, etc. Recommendations to the court include the use of placement facilities, to be expanded by small decentralized units in the larger cities, and work camps. Upon their implementation, Ohio will probably have the best state-wide diagnostic and treatment resources in the United States.

Treatment Centers Emphasizing Group Therapy

The Use of Group Therapy

Group therapy or group psychotherapy was originated by Dr. Pratt in Boston shortly after the turn of the century. A second spurt to institutional group therapy was the work of Slavson in the treatment of nonpsychotic children under the care of the various branches of the Jewish Board of Guardians.[17] Further impetus to group therapy was the dearth of individual therapists in the armed forces during World War II. And subsequent to the war, mental hygiene clinics, mental hospitals, correctional institutions, social agencies, and even private practitioners have increasingly incorporated group therapy techniques in their programs. There is, however, little standardization in techniques, which appear to be as varied as the practitioners. According to

[17] S. R. Slavson, *Child Psychotherapy*, New York, Columbia University Press, 1952; and *idem., Re-Educating the Delinquent*, New York, Harper, 1954.

McCorkle,[18] the descriptions of the group therapy process are largely impressionistic clinic reports of personal experiences in specific situations. The reader should remember also that *group work is not synonymous with group therapy*. Group work is the group counterpart of individual casework. Group therapy is the group counterpart of individual therapy.[19]

In 1950 McCorkle sent questionnaires to 267 correctional institutions to ascertain how widely group therapy was used. Among the 109 that replied, about 13 reported a group therapy program which was chiefly didactic or lecture discussion; another 6 institutions conducted group therapy programs which were psychoanalytically oriented.

The methods of selection of group participants varied. In some, participation was voluntary; in others, it was available to newcomers, or to people presenting special problems. Admission was usually determined by group therapists or by a classification committee.

The 19 institutions with group therapy programs considered it "a socializing experience which incarcerated delinquents need, want and can use." In their opinion social experience with peers and therapists is profitable if there is free discussion and examination of the problems of living in an institution. The atmosphere, however, must be a supportive, permissive, and nonpunitive one within which all participants are equals; and even in a penal institution the social controls must evolve out of the group interaction.

If the training in group discipline helps each participant to overcome his tendency to self-indulgence, the satisfactions derived from conformity with social rules will exceed those resulting from delinquent behavior.[20]

Pioneer House

Although discontinued because of lack of funds, the program of Pioneer House deserves mention as an interesting institutional approach to handling aggressive, disturbed young boys. With funds supplied by the Junior League of Detroit in the fall of 1946, Dr. Fritz Redl set up a resident program designed to continue the work begun in the Detroit Summer Camp Group Project.[21]

As Redl describes his program: it was not "to press or lure the aggressive child into simple surrender of his bad behavior" through premiums of special

[18] Lloyd W. McCorkle, "Group Therapy," Speech at Berkshire International Forum, 1951; and *idem.*, "Guided Group Interaction in a Correctional Setting," *International Journal of Group Psychotherapy*, Vol. 4 (1954) pp. 199-203.

[19] Gisela Konopka, *Group Work in the Institution*, New York, Whiteside, 1954; and *idem*, "The Group Worker's Role in an Institution for Juvenile Delinquents," *Federal Probation*, Vol. 15 (June 1951), pp. 15-23.

[20] See C. Gersten, "Group Therapy with Institutionalized Juvenile Delinquents," *Journal of Genetic Psychology*, Vol. 80 (1952), pp. 35-62; and K. I. Wollan, "Application of Group Therapy Principles to Institutional Treatment of Adolescents," *International Journal of Group Psychotherapy*, Vol. 1 (1951), pp. 356-64.

[21] Fritz Redl and David Wineman, *Children Who Hate*, Glencoe, Ill., Free Press, 1951.

reward or special love, or through exhortation by an adult friend, or by severe punishment. The purpose was to help him reveal the real problems which disturbed him and which he expressed in conflicts with adults, with the world around him, and with himself. Instead of trying to prevent the boy from acting out the symptomatic behavior for which he was sent to Pioneer House, the runaways, tantrums, stealing incidents, and so forth, actually furnished the very basis of the work with the child, and served as the core of clinical policies. The rapport which the boy established with the staff members and his emotional ties toward the group were not designed to help the boy to adjust to Pioneer House. On the contrary, his experience in Pioneer House was the gateway to adjustment to the outside world.

In addition to the director, the staff included a house mother, casework supervisor, group work consultant, and several field-work students from the Wayne University School of Public Affairs and Social Work. Teachers, chosen because of their interest in working with disturbed children, were assigned to special opportunity classes arranged by one of the Detroit public schools. There was constant cooperation between the school and the house in considering the boys' problems. As a matter of fact, progress in school served as the chief index of the boys' readiness to return to the community.

Pioneer House provided workshops, library, and recreational activities while community facilities were used for swimming, gymnasium, and camping. To minimize the institutional atmosphere, the boys were permitted to bring their friends to the house. The intent was, on the one hand, to avoid coddling, and on the other, to avoid over-stimulating or over-programming.

The age group, 8 to 11, was chosen on the assumption that this was the most promising time to reverse a bad start. Destructiveness, hyperaggression, stealing, running away from home, truancy, temper tantrums, lying, and rough talk were typical behavior. Bed-wetting, fears, and anxieties of various kinds were prevalent. The intensity rather than the type of behavior determined whether or not the child would be admitted to the group. The following were considered ineligible:

1. Children from overprotective backgrounds, who suffered from clear-cut compulsion or anxiety neuroses of clinical type. The aggressive behavior of the other children would be likely to frighten them into reinforcing their neurotic patterns instead of opening them up to treatment.

2. Children who were so sadistic that the welfare of the others would be jeopardized, and also those whose lack of reality insight and self-control would expose them to physical dangers on the street or in the handling of simple tools.

3. Children who could not share with the others, i.e., who obtained no satisfaction from group life, and who needed individual therapy more than they did group contact.

All parents had to agree to accept the fact that recovery would be slow and that a year might elapse before even partial changes were apparent.

The main assumptions of the service were:

1. That some children are too disturbed to make use of the "blessing" of a well-organized family life. "Before they can accept or digest the food of happy family life they need hospitalization and possible surgery, i.e., removal from their home."

2. That children who have grown up in high delinquency risk areas, have been neglected, and already show delinquent trends, do not usually respond to the interview or play technique which may be suitable for the treatment of clinical compulsion or anxiety neuroses. Interviews with such children are more productive when they are so close to the scene of daily life that "they cannot use their tricky alibi methods" and rapport can be established by the person who is a part of the group pattern of which the children partake.

These children do not have the value systems of those reared in the secure atmosphere of a protected middle- or upper-class home. (See Jephcott, Carter, and Mack's description of rough families in Chapter 8.) Living almost from babyhood in the so-called "open-door" neighborhood, their parental images have been displaced by the neighborhood gang. In Redl's opinion, the period of pre-adolescence is especially crucial in this process, because this is the time when children are "less submissive to parental demands and are searching for security through group alliances." The Detroit Summer Camp Group Project had demonstrated ways in which pre-adolescents reinforced each other in the wrong patterns of behavior.

Thus, the program at Pioneer House was designed "to combine in a repair shop on an all-year-round basis, the group psychological structure of the pre-adolescent gang and the pattern of youth groups with partial identification with an adult leader." Limits as to acceptable behavior were set because they provided important and essential supports in the educational and therapeutic program. In addition to casework, psychiatric interviewing, and psychoanalytic treatment when necessary, the group process was considered an essential part of the clinical task.

The group therapy at Pioneer House applied sound psychiatric thinking and experience to the wider frame of group life which for these children pervades all phases of their life.

Highfields[22]

Although not classified as a residential treatment center, Highfields, in New Jersey, makes effective use of group therapy for boys over 16, referred by

[22] See chapter 26 for evaluation of Highfields program.

the court. This program was initiated by Lloyd McCorkle before he was appointed principal keeper at New Jersey State Prison in Trenton.

An open institution without walls or bars, Highfields houses twenty boys, aged 16 to 17, the upper age limit of New Jersey's juvenile court. The judge gives the boys a choice of commitment to Annandale, the New Jersey institution for delinquent boys, or probation on condition that they agree to live for four months in Highfields and participate in the group therapy program.

The resident staff, consisting of the director-therapist, the cook and her husband, and a caretaker of the estate, are capable and dedicated to their task. In the readjusting or reconstructing of attitudes in correctional institutions the behavior of the authoritative figures is generally acknowledged to be most significant. The relationships between the staff and the boys at Highfields run the gamut from informal to formal, depending upon the role of the staff at the particular time. The staff members' awareness of the importance of their response is a large part of the effectiveness of the group setting.

The second major aspect of the Highfields program is the work which the boys perform daily on the grounds of the State School for Epileptics at Skillman. This work, for which they are paid 50 cents a day, serves as a testing and preparation for situations which each boy will face when he returns to the community. Many of the boys who come to Highfields have not worked before and not much production can be expected. The director underscores the importance of learning to work with and get along with each other, as well as how to take orders. It will be recalled that the majority of the boys brought to a juvenile court on serious charges have had trouble with authority figures. The report of the work supervisor to the director and the comments of the boys in the therapy sessions help the director to evaluate the boy's progress with his peers and his increasing ability to accept correction.

At the end of each day's work the boys return to Highfields, get their mail, receive telephone calls, and eat dinner. Evenings when there is no therapy group, they play cards or listen to dance music on the radio. Some boys just lie on their beds and read, others visit and talk. The usual hour for retiring is ten.

Unlike other institutions, recreation at Highfields is not compulsory. The one formal activity is the Saturday night movie at Princeton. Pick-up games, softball, football, checkers, playing practical jokes, pillow fights, and bull sessions are usual activities. The various forms of physical activity serve as vehicles to express hostility and aggression and to test the reaction of some of the other boys. Wrestling is a device that the rival leaders use to increase their status. Retreat from the group is expressed in absorption in listening to the radio. One of the boys remarked, "When John plays the radio he leaves Highfields and goes into a world of his own." Gambling for fun or for stakes is a favorite activity. When it is for fun, the boys use what they called "mouth money." For example, a boy will say, "You owe me a hundred thousand dollars," or "I'm in the hole fifty thousand dollars," and laugh.

The two major types of leaders are: (1) "The hand and foot" leader who stomps or forces his way and rules by fear, and (2) The leader who does not push people around and is often asked for advice.

Physical size is not always the determining factor in leadership. Traditionally at Highfields a new boy who attempts to assume the role of leader is stomped. Occasionally a friend, whom he may have met in the detention quarters, teaches him the ropes, but in the main he has to make his own way. The boy who chooses not to be part of the group is looked upon with some suspicion, and if he continues this behavior he is apt to be rejected by the group. The tradition of the group endorses socializing, and the fact that a boy doesn't socialize is sometimes discussed in the therapy session. The group therapy sessions, according to Walker,[23] can be classified according to their goals. In business sessions, for example, the group tries to help a boy identify his problem, see how he is working on it, i.e., whether he is moving in the direction of changing both his overt behavior and his attitudes. The leader uses various techniques, such as making the rounds, i.e., (1) asking the boys to discuss topics of interest; (2) polling the group for their opinions on the subject under discussion; and (3) checking the director's monthly report of his impressions with the group.

Situations which cause more strain than usual in a therapy session arise, for example, when a clique attempts to dominate a group, or there is a raid on the icebox, which carried to excess, means a scanty breakfast and lunch the next day.

Obstacles to Group Therapy

While the Highfields situation is exceptional in the small number of boys admitted, in the skill of the therapist, and in the cooperation of all members of the staff, McCorkle does not claim that a group therapy program, in itself, is a magic formula for success. The usual correctional institution discourages honest relationships with representatives of the world outside. To the inmates the therapist represents, initially at least, this hostile world.

In analyzing the process over a series of sessions it will be recognized that in the early stages the participants seek to test the therapist in every way possible. As a rule they are guarded and suspicious in response to his advances. If they are new to each other, it is natural that they hold back because

[23] William A. Walker, "A Participant-Observer Analysis of Group Process and Individual and Group Behavior at Highfields Project," unpublished doctoral dissertation, New York University, June 1958.

422 · INSTITUTIONS FOR DELINQUENTS

they do not know how much about themselves it is safe to reveal. The key to the therapist's success is his ability to continue to accept whatever happens in the group without aggressive retaliation. If he can hold out, the more hostile members will gradually be disciplined by the members of the group who show signs of recognizing that the leader really likes them and can help them.

The second stage in the group process is the point at which the participants begin to test one another, having satisfied themselves about the therapist. Warm and friendly relationships now replace the earlier hostility, so that the group becomes integrated, rather than an assortment of individuals.

As in the application of psychiatric theories to individual child guidance, so in the use of group therapy, different and occasionally contradictory theories are applied in practice.[24]

Regardless of the theory or the skill with which the therapist conducts the group, its success is limited because the setting emphasizes custody and discipline. The customary authoritative approach is antithetical to free discussion which is necessary to establish psychological insight and to help each individual to decide what he wishes to be and to do. The Highfields situation, however, minimizes the deleterious effect of the semi-custodial setting.

Summary

This chapter has discussed institutions for delinquents who have been considered appropriate subjects for psychiatric treatment. The aggression which is generally implied in the label delinquency is viewed mainly as a symptom of a malformation of character traceable in the Freudian theory to an affectionless childhood. Rehabilitation therefore involves a new experience for these young people who, unless they are feebleminded or psychotic, will, it is believed, respond to a therapeutic but not to a punitive environment. Convinced that the usual custodial mass approach is ineffective, some thirty-odd residential treatment centers have been established, most of them in the last two decades.

The programs of nine residential treatment centers dedicated to the specialized care of delinquent children are reviewed. Each of these centers— the Orthogenic School, Berkshire Farm, Hawthorne Cedar Knolls, Lincoln Hall, Wiltwyck, Children's Village, the Ohio Division of Juvenile Research, Classification, and Training, the former Pioneer House in Detroit, and Highfields—represents a particular way in which individual or group therapy is the

---

[24] Donald R. Cressey, "Contradictory Theories in Correctional Group Therapy Programmes," *Federal Probation*, Vol. 18 (June 1954), pp. 20-26; see also discussion of group therapy in a court clinic, Chapter 17.

main instrument of rehabilitation in an institutional setting. Except in their general orientation and insistence on treating rather than punishing their wards, no two of the programs are identical. While they are all small in comparison with state institutions, these centers differ in size, in location, type of plant, in the training of the director, the number and qualifications and type of staff. Some use cottage parents, others counselors. The academic and the testing programs as well as the remedial services differ in content and quantity. The costs may be as high as $5000 a year per child.

CHAPTER 25

Institutional Practices Outside the United States

BECAUSE THE BOARD OF DIRECTORS WERE SEEKING MORE KNOWLEDGE, AN International Forum on Institutional Practices was convened at Berkshire Farm (Butch's institutional home) in June 1951, with the joint sponsorship of the Division of Social Defense of the United Nations. Invitations were issued to about forty people known for their interest in the field of delinquency. Representatives of various foreign nations also participated. The fact that the conference site shut out the distractions of a large city, and that the participants were guests of the Berkshire Farm, undoubtedly contributed to the close interchange of ideas on some of the more difficult problems in institutional care. This chapter summarizes the descriptions of the various programs presented at the forum and supplements them with later reports of institutional practice in Sweden, Great Britain, India, Israel, Austria, and France.

General Points of Difference *know*

As might be expected institutions for the care of delinquents have developed along somewhat different lines in countries outside of the United States. Practice differs with respect to (1) the definition of delinquents; (2) the location of institutions in relation to population centers; (3) the size of the population and the ratio of staff to inmates; (4) the emphasis on academic *versus* other qualifications of the staff; (5) the use of discipline; and (6) the provisions for after-care.

Definition of a Delinquent

As noted earlier, one of our major problems is the lack of agreement as to which behavior is serious and which is trivial. In some Eastern countries, behavior which we consider delinquent is regarded as parental neglect. In most European and some Asian countries, children know from babyhood their place in the social system and what their expected roles in the family and in the system are. Perhaps this explains why, except in countries which are now experiencing rapid industrial change and an influx of diverse population groups, the problem of delinquency is nowhere as great as it is in the United States today.

Rural versus Urban Location

In contrast to many of the institutions for delinquents in the United States, institutions in other countries prefer sites either in or close to cities. This is the case in Argentina, Brazil, Chile, Colombia, Peru, and Uruguay.[1] Among the advantages are easier access to the boys' families, to schools, libraries, and museums, and more realistic apprentice training in the community shops during the time when the young person lives in the institution.

Like those in the Latin American countries, the Swiss institutions are also located for easy access to the community schools, which the inmates attend just as they would if they were living in their own homes. Situated a short distance from Geneva, the 35 boys at Les Ormeaux are able to secure apprenticeships in town and return to the institution at night. The town provides opportunities to learn jewelry making, watchmaking, photography, technical drawing, and electrical installation, rarely available in institutions in the United States.

This proximity to the city counterbalances the traditional isolation of the institution and supplements the restricted leisure-time and weekend recreational outlets not only for the wards but also for the staff. A further tie with the community is the participation of the inmates in such activities as scouting. In Swiss institutions, the boys, as members of the neighboring scout teams, attend the regular weekly evening and Sunday meetings. Sweden's institutions also encourage their wards to affiliate with local political youth organizations. The American superintendents at the forum commented on the possibility that the wards of these institutions had interests not usually displayed by the boys in America.

[1] Julius Altmann-Smythe, "New Approaches in Institution Treatment, The International Field," Document No. 8, Berkshire International Forum, June 1951.

Size and Staff

In comparison with institutions in the United States most foreign in stitutions are small. In Sweden, which like England has a centralized jurisdiction, the largest institution accommodates 82 pupils, and more than half house less than 30. The Swedes believe that a small institution has advantages over the American device of subdividing a large population into small groups in one facility.[2] The Swedes pride themselves on their determination to disregard cost in favor of the highest ratio of staff to pupils, i.e., three staff members to four wards.

Academic versus Psychiatric Training

The differing requirements for the staff reflect the emphasis abroad on *pedagogical* rather than *psychiatric* training. Instead of stressing professional and scientific background, the European administrator looks for dedication and warm interpersonal relations between staff and ward. The representatives from South America at the Berkshire Forum stressed the importance of the devotion of the staff to the well-being of the inmate as the basis for rehabilitation.

Use of Discipline

Physical punishment appears to be officially permitted in America to a much greater extent than in some European countries. In Latin America, for example, "corporal punishment is prohibited by law and a person violating such prohibition is subject to administrative penalty and/or prosecution under criminal law." The fact that it has to be prohibited by law indicates that it is probably practiced, even though not approved.

Practices in Selected Countries

Sweden

The most recent information on the Swedish institutions is contained in a special report made by Christina Ellwyn,[3] who was a participant at the Berkshire International Forum in 1951, and who has now returned to her native country.

Since July 1, 1954, a delinquent child in Sweden under 15, has been

[2] Paul Berthoud, "New Approaches in the Institutional Treatment of Juvenile Delinquents in Europe," Document No. 9, Berkshire International Forum, 1951.
[3] Christina M. Ellwyn, "The Treatment of Young Delinquents in Sweden," The Swedish Institute, Stockholm, Nov. 1958.

referred directly to a local Child Welfare Committee for "protective education." These committees of representative citizens are responsible for planning and supervising all the community's activities for the welfare and protection of children and youth. Although legal proceedings are permissible for delinquents between the ages of 15 and 17, the usual procedure is to consult the Child Welfare Committee. If, in their opinion, the offense is insignificant—obviously the result of mischief or thoughtlessness—prosecution may be waived. Thus, no offender under 18 is sentenced to imprisonment unless there are special reasons, such as the severity of the crime or insufficient resources available in the social welfare system.

YOUTH WELFARE SCHOOLS. The majority of the delinquents under 12 who need institutional care are assigned to one of the twenty-two "Youth Welfare Schools." These are unwalled institutions, which emphasize vocational education and social development. Therapeutic treatment is provided if necessary. All corporal punishment is forbidden.

The request for admission to a Youth Welfare School is reviewed by a school bureau committee of the Social Welfare Board. Each school has a local board responsible for the care and treatment of the pupils, its administration, and its finances. The staff consists of a director, one or more educators, several teachers, wardens, clerical, and domestic personnel. There is a visiting psychiatrist for each school. The clientele is differentiated according to sex, age, intelligence level, mental, and emotional characteristics.

A special survey made in 1952-53 revealed that most of the young people in these institutions came from homes with severely disturbed child-parent relationships. The parents had been either too severe, too uninterested, or too lax with their children. Most of the homes had little in the way of material or intellectual resources.

The pupils had not only been guilty of serious antisocial conduct, but gave evidences of immaturity, emotional disturbance, neurotic personality traits, maladjustment at home or on the job. The younger ones had difficulties in school and the older ones went from job to job and supported themselves through begging, gambling, or prostitution. Several children evidenced constitutional defects such as brain injuries or hormonal disturbances, and many of them were listless or unstable with low tolerance for frustration.[4]

The average time spent in these schools is about twenty months. During parole, which usually lasts about two years, boarding homes may be used and financial assistance given if necessary.

England

Because it presents an interesting method of handling delinquency in a society somewhat akin to ours, England's system of Approved Schools for

[4] *Ibid.*, p. 8.

offenders under 17 and of Borstals for those from 17 to 21 may be usefully considered here.[5]

A judge in the English juvenile court commits a young person under 17 to what is designated as an Approved School because it is inspected and approved by the Home Office. The institution retains jurisdiction until the charge's nineteenth birthday.

Remand Homes in England correspond to detention quarters in the United States. They are used for: (1) young people awaiting hearing or trial; (2) those in need of medical and psychological study as a preliminary to treatment plans; and (3) those who have been committed to an Approved School but are waiting for admission.

APPROVED SCHOOLS. Like the first cottage plans in the United States, England's system of institutional care was modeled after the French Mettray System. Following a series of government inquiries and acts, England today has a coordinated system for its reformatories and private schools. All of them are subject to official review in standard-setting, in supervision, and in accounting for the results of treatment.

The Approved Schools serve three different age categories: (1) those under 13 at time of admission who are called juniors; (2) the intermediates, aged 13 to 17; and (3) the seniors, those between 15 and 19 at time of commitment. There is more than one Approved School available for each of these three groups. The choice of the school depends upon a period of observation and study in Classifying Schools, two each for boys and for girls.

The Approved Schools are housed in a variety of settings—country mansions, remodeled reformatories, small cottages, and even army huts. While a minimum population of 50 and a maximum of 150 is considered desirable, because it provides sufficient variety in educational and recreational programs, some of the Approved Schools house as few as 6 boys who need special attention. The maximum number is 300.

Some of the Approved Schools maintain hostels for the older boys and girls who go out to work. The training program for girls is chiefly in domestic work. For the boys it includes carpentry, machine work, agriculture, and preparation for service in the navy. The period of training may be as short as six months or as long as three years.

BORSTALS. Designed to care for offenders between the ages of 17 and 21, the Borstals take their name from the Borstal Prison in Rochester, where Sir Evelyn Ruggles Bryce first experimented with separate treatment for young offenders. The inciting force for the Borstals was a report of the Department of Prisons on the failure of prisons to reform. The goal of the

[5] The English system is described in *Britain: An Official Handbook*, rev. ed., 1958, Central Office of Information, London, obtainable through the British Information Services, New York; see also John Gittens, *Approved School Boys*, London, H. M. Stationary Office, 1952.

Borstal is the all-round development of character, mind, and body consistent with the capacity of the young persons assigned to its care. Today the number of Borstals has increased, so that almost half of England's youthful offenders have the benefit of a training program which is flexible in its use of facilities both inside and outside the institution's walls.

The program of the fourteen Borstals (among them two for girls) is far wider than that provided in the ordinary prison. Although those for the older and more difficult offender are surrounded by walls, even they permit the inmate to go outside the walls. In Borstals that operate farms, some of the boys work for the neighboring farmers. The Borstal shops emphasize production rather than trade training. Some Borstals have camps to which boys are transferred when this type of discipline and hard physical work appear appropriate.

As a general rule release from the Borstal is possible after two years. Earlier release can be arranged if the commissioners are convinced that the Borstal training has served its purpose.

The term "license" corresponds with the term "parole" in customary use in the United States, to describe the period following institutionalization. "License" from the Borstal is based on a progress report which is reviewed by a visiting committee of the judges who make commitments to the institutions. It would be a good idea if the judges of juvenile courts in the United States were similarly required to visit and to study what happens to the young people they commit to institutions.

SUCCESS RATES. Despite the relative unavailability of psychiatric and psychological services in English institutions, their rates of successful parole far exceed those of American institutions. Using the criteria of freedom from re-arrest and imprisonment in the five years following release from the Borstals, the Home Secretary's reports show seldom less than 60 per cent success. In the Healy and Alper Study the Borstals attained as much as 84 per cent success.[6] By contrast, the Gluecks' study of 500 criminal careers chalked up less than 12 per cent for the Massachusetts reformatory inmates following their release.[7]

ADVANTAGES OVER AMERICAN SYSTEM. The English system appears to have several advantages.

1. It systematically replaces the hunches of the individual judges by treatment based on study and observation in a reception unit.

2. The program is oriented to developing the feeling of worth in the individual through a hard but interesting program which includes work,

[6] William Healy and Benedict Alper, *Criminal Youth and the Borstal System,* New York, The Commonwealth Fund, 1941; and R. Cowan, "Open Prisons and Borstals," *Criminal Law Review,* March 1955, pp. 169-172.

[7] Sheldon and Eleanor T. Glueck, *Five Hundred Criminal Careers,* New York, Knopf, 1930.

physical training, and planned recreation, in addition to some time for quiet contemplation, reading, and writing.

3. The system incorporates deliberate and long-time planning for release by fostering increasing contacts with the community outside the institution. The prison commissioner is responsible for the supervision of parolees, which he delegates to the Borstal Association for Men and to Aylesbury After-care Association for Young Women. And in the after-care period there is constant stimulation of the community to help in the rehabilitation process.

4. The devotion and the consecration of the Borstal personnel appear to be similar to that in the ministry.

5. No doubt the greater success of the English system is also partly due to the smaller size of the country, the greater homogeneity of the people, and the greater acceptance of authority. But the principal factor appears to be the centralization of care which permits coordination of the wide variety of services which are available in all parts of the British Isles. In America the inhabitants of most states and counties have access only to what the locality thinks it can afford. As in the parochial school system, the residents of a town or a parish are limited by that locality's wealth. Thus, the accident of residence limits Americans in their access not only to education but to rehabilitative service. In a centralized system of government, these are available to rich and poor alike, wherever they may have come from.

The Home Office is responsible for knowing what is going on in all English institutions and publishes periodic reports. In the United States evaluation reports are issued only at the discretion of the individual institution. The supervision which the state does supply extends mainly to administrative regulations of basic facilities for living and training. The state does not evaluate the outcome. As the data in Chapter 26 will reveal, we have a long way to go in most American institutions in spite of our enormous investment in plants and equipment for the care of juvenile delinquents. If the results in the Massachusetts reformatory revealed failures in 88 per cent of the cases, one may well wonder what the figures would be for institutions in less wealthy states.

A step in the direction of removing some of the more blatant inequities in America is the availability of federal funds to supplement the amount and the quality of care provided by states which claim they cannot afford to provide the facilities and the services their neglected, dependent, or delinquent children need. Although (under specified conditions with respect to standards and qualifications of personnel), the federal government has offered to match, in differing proportions, the state expenditures for relief and child welfare, not all the needy states are willing to make even this much investment. Some states fear federal control. Many of them appear to prefer to use their money for building highways and facilities which have more appeal to the voter.

The system of grants, moreover, has not been extended to services for delinquents, as proposed by the Eighty-Fifth Congress. Perhaps the diversity of our population makes it difficult for the many sectors to identify with parts of the population who seem strange and in a way responsible for their own set of miseries. Our laissez-faire philosophy may also be partly to blame.

The efforts of the supporters of social work to convince legislatures of the necessity for adequate appropriations have not been very successful. Money, however, is not the only problem. The main problem is to decide what we need to be concerned about—what is trivial and what is serious behavior and how to go about setting up an effective over-all plan which will make services as available to all who need them as they are in the public health organization of a well-managed city.

India

AFTER-CARE HOSTELS. The institutional approach to delinquency in India reflects that country's former colonial status. The state of Bombay has developed after-care hostels modeled on the English "probation hostel" system. Adapted for parole use, they serve as intermediate way stations for juveniles moving from treatment institutions back to their own community.[8] The largest of these, the Sheppard After-Care Hostel, accommodates 40 juveniles. This hostel is run by the Bombay Children's Aid Society, which is likewise responsible for the Chembur Children's Home and the David Sassoon Industrial School, in addition to providing after-care facilities for juveniles released from the latter.

Each hostel is managed by a probation officer whose supervisory responsibilities, as defined by law, are similar to those of the parole officer in the United States. One of his main responsibilities is to find suitable employment for the juveniles in his charge. If the inmates have jobs, they work in the community; otherwise, in the hostel. Those who have jobs pay for their keep, and those without give their services in exchange. All residents participate in the organized indoor and outdoor recreational activities and the vocational training programs. These vocational training programs offer at least three advantages: They (1) provide facilities for continuance of vocational training received in the institution; (2) broaden the vocational program and the completion of training; and (3) provide the opportunity for re-orientation of skills acquired in the institution to meet the new demands of industry in the community.

Thus, the after-care hostel in India serves as an *adjunct* to the treatment institution.

[8] Richard Paw-U, "New Approaches in Institution Treatment: The International Field," Document No. 11, Berkshire International Forum, 1951.

PROGRAM FOR "CRIMINAL TRIBES." Paw-U described another development in India's program, relating to its famous "criminal tribes": "In India certain groups have lived by criminal means since time immemorial. These groups or tribes are generally nomadic and unsettled in character, and they usually live by means of petty thievery, counterfeiting, armed robbery, pickpocketing, etc. Of course, the children of these tribes were indoctrinated in the cultural patterns of their elders and the predatory traditions were perpetuated."[9]

Ever since 1871 these criminal tribes have been officially identified as part of Indian culture. Realizing that it was ineffective to use the usual methods of dealing with them—first imprisoning them and then sending them back home—the central government established rehabilitation programs. Special acts empowered the state authorities to move these tribes, partly or wholly, to any place where they could be taught new norms of behavior. To inculcate new standards, school attendance is compulsory for children until they reach 18 years of age. In the common school, emphasis is on vocational training. Those too old for school are encouraged to work within or without the reservation, and extension classes are organized for further education.

Those who work are permitted to leave the reservation in the daytime, but required to spend the night within the settlement. Unless the parental situation is inimical to the child's welfare, he remains with his family; otherwise, he may be sent to a boarding school. Although the settlements are open institutions in many of the Indian states, their boundaries are marked by barbed wire fences. Some of them occupy as many as 500 acres; a few are established in villages. In describing this as an "enormous" program, Paw-U comments: "While it could not be directly adapted in most of the areas of the world, the philosophy behind India's approach to its criminal tribe has direct interest in considering the sociocultural aspects relating to the rehabilitation of children."[10] Under the new set-up, the tribes are now called "ex-criminal tribes" and the work with them is described both in government publications and in the *Indian Journal of Social Work*.[11]

Israel

COLLECTIVE SETTLEMENTS. Israel's institutional system is predominantly of the cottage type, with small dormitories staffed by youth leaders and housemasters. There are no fences and the prevailing atmosphere is informal,

[9] *Ibid.*, p. 3.
[10] *Ibid.*, p. 4.
[11] B. H. Mehta, "Ex-Criminal Groups in India," *Indian Journal of Social Work*, Vol. 16, no. 1 (June 1955); and P. N. Saxena, "Rehabilitation Work Among Ex-Criminal Groups in India," *Social Welfare in India*, New Delhi, Planning Commission of the Government, Sept. 1955, pp. 505-16.

as it is in the communal settlements. Instructors, and even headmasters, are called by their first names. There are no uniforms. The program is not standardized, but includes daily gymnastics, folk dancing, and communal singing. As in Latin America, the community's educational facilities are available when they are not provided by the institution. Wards are permitted to visit their own homes and the one disciplinary measure is deprivation of privileges. The provision of services from a part-time psychiatrist is an innovation undoubtedly due to American influence.

According to the report to the first United Nations Congress on the Prevention of Crime and the Treatment of Offenders,[12] the Israeli juvenile probation service uses the collective settlements for young people who are capable of profiting from elementary schooling and who show a willingness to work in agricultural trades.

RESIDENTIAL INSTITUTIONS. A little less than one fourth of the children on probation in 1954 were sent to residential institutions for children with slight behavior problems. The cost of maintenance in these institutions is paid from a special fund available to the juvenile probation service to supplement payments from the parents.

Israel has currently seven government institutions for delinquents, including one for girls and one for Arab boys. One institution is a semi-closed Borstal-like home for difficult boys, and one an observation home. As of September 1954, some 250 boys and girls were residents in these institutions. An institution for about 25 girls between 14 and 17 who showed serious problems was opened in 1956 under the auspices of the Welfare Commission.

The proper functioning of these institutions is hampered not only by lack of suitable staff but also by lack of special training in Israel for institutional staff. Difficult work conditions, inadequate housing facilities, low salaries, and long working hours are obstacles, as is the absence of facilities for individual psychiatric guidance and treatment. Too often young people diagnosed as psychopathic or suffering from severe behavior disorders, and sometimes even psychotic borderline cases, are sent to institutions for delinquents only because there is no other place available. Not equipped to cope with such problems, the group work program suffers. In July 1958 the Ministry of Health opened a ward of 40 beds for psychotic or seriously disturbed juveniles in Eitanim, a children's hospital outside Jerusalem. This first step in an expanding program provides a training center for Hebrew University students.

The fact that Israeli institutions for children are similar in many respects to those in the United States is undoubtedly traceable to their American auspices. The early child-care program of Hadassah (the Women's Zionist Organization) in Palestine was developed by Americans active in foster home

[12] Geneva, Aug. 22 to Sept. 23, 1955.

and institutional care for children in the United States. Since the establishment of the Jewish state in 1948, Israeli programs have benefited from the advice and assistance of United States experts as to the best methods of dealing with the severely disturbed among the new immigrant groups.

Another difficulty is the constant public criticism of the progressive re-educational approach in the "open" homes. This criticism, as Bettelheim and Redl point out in discussing the programs of treatment centers (see Chapter 24), not only creates insecurity in the staff, impairs initiative and interferes with consistent educational policy but often interferes with the best interests of an institution's wards.

Austria

We are indebted to a memorandum prepared by Mary Kohler[13] for the following descriptions of Austrian and French institutions for delinquents.

KAISER EBERSDORF. The one reformatory for boys in Austria, known as Kaiser Ebersdorf, which has been steadily used since the fourteenth century, is a large, dilapidated, and ill-equipped building, which in the United States would be regarded as obsolete because the inmates could not be segregated.

Nevertheless, Mrs. Kohler considers the treatment more individualized than is often the case in the United States. The boys have been ingeniously divided into groups of 20, each established in self-sufficient, separate apartments, within the huge building. The only contact each group has with the others is during school hours. Each unit is in charge of a young educator who lives with the boys. Some groups are permitted to go home for a day or two at a time, others never leave the institution because they are considered such poor risks that they merit maximum security. Some of the groups, while not released to their homes, go to town with their leader to attend motion pictures, concerts, or the opera.

KINDERHOFS. Another innovation in Austria for children who have no homes of their own are the Kinderhofs, or S.O.S. Children's Villages. Dr. Herrmann Gmeirer, a young physician, organized these after World War II as a compromise between the orphanage and the foster home. There are now five such villages in different towns in Austria, in each of which there are seventeen to twenty self-sufficient homes. Each home accommodates 8 to 10 children, who go out to school and participate in the life of the town as they would if they lived in their own homes. The housemother, who is carefully selected, is usually a single woman. She is provided with funds to manage

[13] Mary Conway Kohler, "An American Views Some European Approaches to Juvenile Delinquency," report to the Ford Foundation on her inspection tour in Europe in the summer of 1958.

the home and to provide for the children's needs as if they were her own. The system results in much less turnover than is characteristic of institutional staffs in the United States.

AFTER-CARE. Faced with a chronic shortage of funds and without an organized system of either probation or parole, Dr. Sepp Schindler, a young psychologist, has organized a group of 30 young volunteers, each of whom assumes responsibility for 1 or at most 2 juvenile delinquents. As they become more expert, through their weekly group discussions, they are assigned additional cases, but never more than 5 each. For each case they receive from public funds a grant of 50 shillings per month. Success has been claimed for all but 4 of the 50 boys in the first year's program, although many of them had previously involved in serious misconduct and some had served terms in a reformatory or prison. The fact that 3 of the failures occurred in the first month suggests there was something wrong with the selection of the boy for this type of treatment. In the fourth case deep therapy appeared to be called for. This Austrian innovation in after-care, although dictated by financial necessity, merits our further consideration.

France

The French, according to Mrs. Kohler, are both protective and realistic in their approach to young people in trouble. Their realism is expressed in their recognition, as M. Morelli, the French Deputy Minister of Justice, says, that the adolescent "is half adult, half child—a creature of romance, passion and impulse."[14] In consequence, they have a relaxed and realistic attitude and strive to prevent the emotions of young people from being unduly awakened. In marked contrast to the lack of censorship for adults, there is strict censorship for young people with respect to both films and books (see Chapter 10).

This realism extends also to the after-care program for boys released from the French correctional schools. Because the transition period is recognized as a crucial one, the French have established "semi-liberty" institutions. For a period of a few weeks to several months, the boy goes to work each day but returns at night to the institution. In this way he is given the support and encouragement he needs in the difficult period of reassimilation into his own home environment.

Both public and private correctional institutions in France offer vocational training since they consider the job as "the most important factor in the prevention of delinquency." Recognizing the important role of the police in combating delinquency and the need to prevent the results of hostility to the offender on the part of the police, the French Ministry of Justice has for

[14] *Ibid.*, p. 9.

many years operated a school for training all those who deal with young offenders—police magistrates, juvenile court judges, probation, parole, and correctional school personnel.[15]

Summary

Comparison of institutional practices in the United States with those in some other countries reveals differences in emphasis. Institutions abroad are more likely to be located in or near a city. The advantages are the accessibility to various types of schools, apprenticeship, and work opportunities, as well as to recreational and cultural activities. There is also closer contact between the institution and the community in all of the countries whose programs were described at the Berkshire International Forum. Administrators abroad prefer small institutions, and staffs trained in education rather than in psychiatric or psychological disciplines. Illustrations of practice in Swiss, Swedish, and South American institutions highlight these points of difference.

Summarizing these accounts of institutional experience abroad, Kahale stresses that no one program can be considered the solution for all countries.[16] The character of the population and its philosophy obviously define what behavior is considered delinquent. To be effective, treatment must therefore be related to the life of the individual country as well as to the nature of the offense. Programs in India, Israel, Austria, and France all reflect local attitudes and conditions, though the first two also show influences from England and America.

The English system of approved schools and Borstals appears to have attained an efficiency which might well be envied by the United States. Coordinated under the direction of the Home Office, the programs of the approved schools for boys and girls under 17 and of the Borstals for those from 17 to 21, offer opportunity for study of the young offender prior to commitment to one of a variety of institutions differing in size and in program. The English rate of success, as measured by the figures for recidivism, is six or seven times that in the Massachusetts reformatory reputed to be an example of good practice in the United States.

The centralization of the administration in the Home Office with responsibility for planning, allocation, and reporting on the outcome, makes possible an over-all appraisal of the various methods—which is practically impossible in the United States today.

[15] *Ibid.*, p. 10.
[16] George S. Kahale, "The Institutional Treatment of Juvenile Delinquency in the Middle East Countries," Document No. 10, Berkshire International Forum, 1951.

CHAPTER 26

Evaluating Institutions for Delinquents

IN CHAPTER 22 WE WERE REMINDED THAT REMOVING JUVENILE OFFENDERS from the community represented an extension of the use of prisons for the adult offender. Just as the proponents of the juvenile court advocated it as a better method than the criminal court for dealing with the offending child, so the first reform schools were ameliorations of prisons. To evaluate the various developments in institutional care for delinquents, we need to disentangle some of the strands taken over from the prison system. For to some extent today's methods of dealing with juvenile delinquents in institutions still show vestiges of the penal punitive accents in their custody, some of which inhere in the nature of the system.

In the "century of the child," the growing concern with the well-being of the lowborn as well as the highborn has prompted some modification of the punitive and custodial aspects of removal from the community. The successive changes in name from houses of refuge to reform schools, to training schools, to schools, reflect the shift in official philosophy. How great a change has actually taken place is difficult to measure with any certainty, but fortunately some criteria have been set forth for judging how well today's institutions are achieving their goal of re-educating the delinquent. These are listed and discussed briefly below.

Criteria for Evaluation

Physical Plant

One's first judgment of an institution is conditioned by the appearance of the buildings and grounds. When the sophisticated investigator, however, sees beautiful lawns, precisely trimmed hedges, massive buildings, shiny brass, polished floors, he will want to find out how much of the elbow grease is applied by young people for whom the decorative effect has little or no meaning. A Michigan institution notorious for its antiquated quarters and practices looks from the exterior like a well-kept estate. Meticulously kept grounds often suggest a director or superintendent who has his eye more firmly fixed on the reactions of the board of visitors than he has on the young people under his care. Orderliness per se is an adult need. Too often an overscrupulously neat institution means curtailment of freedom. A psychologist in a boarding school once remarked with respect to the disorder in the sleeping quarters, "These young people do not believe in the law of gravity; they throw things on the floor."

Director-Staff Relations

As in a home, whether rich or poor, the emotional climate of an institution is pivotal. Granting that the director is skilled and is concerned with creating and maintaining a rehabilitative rather than a custodial atmosphere, we look for answers to the following questions:

1. *Does the director communicate his philosophy to all staff members, and are there proper channels to assure its implementation?*

A good administrator cannot do the job alone. The task calls for a variety of auxiliary personnel—those in direct contact with the young people under care, in their living quarters, in their classrooms, in their work and special counseling. As the director of the Hawthorne Cedar Knolls School (see Chapter 24) says: the cook, the carpenter, the farmer, and the plumber, each has a role which must be played without hugging the center of the stage, which belongs to the young person in need of rehabilitation. In studying an institution, therefore, one begins with an appraisal of the climate of the relationships.

Intake Policy

But regardless of the rehabilitative philosophy, the administrative skill of the director, and the quality of staff rapport, to be effective an institution must be permitted to select its wards. We discussed earlier the pressures on public training schools to admit youths whom they may not be geared to serve. There is often also pressure to keep wards longer than their progress warrants because of the hesitancy to take a chance on their release to the community. Our next question in studying an institution, then, is:

2. *Does the institution select its inmates in the light of the program that it is able to offer in view of the needs of the prospective ward?*

Living Arrangements and Nontreatment Staff

Our descriptions in preceding chapters of the different institutions showed a fairly wide range in living arrangements, i.e., big dormitories, small ones, cottage plans, camps, and occasionally some provision for individual rooms, particularly for girls. We noted that in the treatment centers under both public and private auspices, some directors preferred cottage parents, others a house mother or house father. Still others, like Wiltwyck, employed trained counselors, or, like the Orthogenic School in Chicago, a three-shift arrangement of young college students. Each plan apparently has advantages and disadvantages; so far, the literature offers no proof of the *superiority* of any one plan. Whatever the plan, however, a relevant question is:

3. *Are the living arrangements designed with an awareness of the effects of group living on disturbed children?*

All institutions, with the exception of those such as Lincoln Hall, run by religious orders, apparently agree that the problem of recruiting and holding well-adjusted and properly qualified residential personnel calls for more study and attention. Training is a problem that faces every institution. There is no guarantee that the holder of a college degree automatically has the necessary personality or experience to work constructively with young people in trouble. As MacCormick says of the probation officer (see Chapter 16), faith in young people is a necessary ingredient. In appraising the success of the Borstal system, Healy and Alper note[1] that the devotion and dedication of the staff appear to have some relation to the outcome of treatment. Too often in the United States formal training is evaluated more highly than these personal qualities. The Ralston boys (Chapter 23) were quite astute in sizing up the staff in these respects.

One staff member who is more readily recruited, probably because of the dedicated nature of his calling, is the chaplain. As Tony's story revealed (Chapter 22), and Butch's (Chapter 24), a clergyman can be an effective member of the team if he is prepared to follow the team lead in matters which are outside his purely religious duties, which must obviously conform with the beliefs and practices of his religion.

While the provisions for health—i.e., medical, dental, and nursing care—are important, in most institutions these aspects meet the standards of the state or the locality. Recreation likewise is no longer confined to the provision of physical exercise, but has an important place in the rehabilitative process. The proper provision of food, the subject of much tension in Ralston, is gaining increasing recognition as a means for doing more than satisfying hunger.

[1] William Healy and Benedict Alper, *Criminal Youth and the Borstal System*, New York, The Commonwealth Fund, 1941.

Another question the investigator seeks to answer is, therefore:

4. *Do all the members of the staff, be they cottage parents, teachers, shop supervisors, chaplains, dietitians, physicians, nurses, or group leaders, consider themselves part of a team working together with the treatment staff for the best interest of the child?*

Treatment Staff

The word "treatment" is often used indiscriminately to refer to any activity on behalf of a delinquent regardless of the role of the staff member in the institutional set-up. We have noted above the obvious necessity for *all* staff members to cooperate in the interests of the institutionalized delinquent without trying, consciously or unconsciously, to hug the center of the stage.

The *responsibility for planning treatment* must rest with the clinical staff. The usual members of the clinic team are a psychiatrist, a psychologist, a psychiatrically trained social worker, and sometimes a physician. While the size and the composition of the clinic team may differ, it should retain the responsibility for diagnosis, treatment plan, evaluation of progress, and need for changes in the plan.

This responsibility is properly lodged in the clinical team because their education and training equips them to determine the meaning and significance of behavior in each individual case. They understand also the meaning of their own reactions as conditioned by their personal experiences and attitudes. They have been taught to understand the differential effect of their responses on the behavior of others, in this case the delinquent and other staff members.

The question which the investigator asks about the treatment staff, then, is:

5. *Does the institution provide clinical, psychological, and social work facilities for initially determining the needs of the individual young person so that the program will correspond to his needs? And as he progresses will the necessary changes be made on the basis of professional study rather than hunches?*

Educational Program and Work Experience

There is general agreement that the educational program in a training school should be at least as good as that offered in the community. No subject should be taught for its own sake, but rather because it will assist the young person's return to his own community.

The surveyor will therefore ask:

6. *Does the institution modify its educational methods and curriculum*

to serve children who are initially unresponsive to ordinary methods of academic instruction?

To be adequate, the vocational program should include experience in a variety of occupations, integrated with the academic program. For girls, cosmetology as well as laundry and cooking are fairly constant vocational fare. Although cosmetology would have been frowned upon in the past, today it is recognized as an aid in rehabilitation which gives the girl a sense of her own worth as well as a means of earning a steady livelihood—provided of course she can bring in and hold her clientèle.

Occasionally, vocational programs reflect the opinions of the members of the board of directors or the superintendent, without considering whether the young person is likely to find a job in the community to which he will return. For example, some Michigan institutions provide no training in auto mechanics despite the fact that Detroit is a center of the automotive industry. Contrariwise, in Michigan and in many other states, training in farming and agriculture is stressed for boys and sometimes for girls who come from urban communities and who will have no opportunity to use the training.

Training programs in some institutions for girls take no note of changes in eating habits, in serving, in diet, or in readily available products on the market today. These institutions still train girls for serving four- or five-course meals, with homemade hot bread and jam at each meal. Nor do the training programs incorporate the use of labor-saving devices which the girls themselves will probably buy on the installment plan when they set up their own households. Occasionally, too, a vocational program is a two-edged sword. It may limit Negroes to work in kitchens and laundries on the assumption that there are more opportunities for them in those fields. By doing so it closes wider occupational fields to them.

Often the academic and vocational training in an institution fails to stress the need for the young person to involve himself actively in the process. He studies "for the teacher, not for himself." He makes his bed, like the GI, because it is the rule and not because he gets satisfaction from contemplating a task well done. Intellectual interests as well as habits of study and neatness enforced in the institution unfortunately do not carry over when the inmates return to the community. Educators believe that if good habits are to survive, the individual's controls must come from within, and ordinarily the good teacher aids this process not by physical discipline but by encouragement.[2]

A pertinent question concerning vocational and work experience provided by the institution, is:

[2] Percival M. Symonds, "Characteristics of the Effective Teacher Based on Pupil Evaluation," *Journal of Experimental Education,* Vol. 23 (June 1955), pp. 289-311; and *idem.,* "What Education Has to Learn from Psychology," *Teachers College Record,* Vol. 57, no. 7 (April 1956), pp. 449-62.

7. Is the allocation of work responsibility based on the needs of the young person, and arranged so that he will profit by the assignment? Or is it determined by the needs of the institution, i.e., to have the laundry done, the gardens weeded, the kitchens cleaned, the meals served, and the dishes washed in the most economical and efficient way?

Disciplinary Measures

One of the main problems in any institution in which the inmates are not there by choice, and are not to be just "contained" but rather rehabilitated for return to a useful life in the community, is the matter of maintaining discipline. Recognition of the crucial role of disciplinary measures in an institutional program is demonstrated by the fact that the U.S. Children's Bureau pamphlet—*Tentative Standards for Training Schools*[3]—devotes three times as much space to discipline as to other topics.

The manner in which an institution handles young people who do not conform to the program requirements is not only crucial to the success of the program but indicative of the staff's understanding of the purpose of the institution. Judgment of the adequacy of the institution's use of discipline depends upon reconciling three points of view:

The community wants the institution to prevent further delinquent behavior and to protect it from such infractions of institutional discipline as escapes or forays into the community.

The young person, who usually arrives in a mood of fear or suspicion— as indicated in the study of Ralston and the story of Tony—regards the institution as his enemy rather than his tutor. While he may recognize that conformity is the price of his release, he rarely acknowledges his need for help in changing his attitudes. Thus he is greatly tempted to disobey the rules.

The staff of the institution, convinced that repression or suppression of delinquent behavior does not mean reform, are often hard put to it, with our present lack of knowledge of results, to devise appropriate educational means to control aggressive behavior. They know that the way in which violations of rules are met is an important factor in determining the institution's success in convincing the young offender that it is concerned with helping rather than punishing him. The "it hurts me more than it does you" approach is like the dentist's comfort to the squirming patient. Perhaps the most important attribute of the staff is the ability to control hostile impulses in the face of aggression, and an awareness of the ever-present temptation to meet aggression with aggression. Some of the formal disciplinary measures in current use

[3] *Tentative Standards for Training Schools*, No. 351, Washington, U.S. Children's Bureau, 1954. Report of the Bureau's November 1952 Conference on Training School Standards with a statement on "A Philosophy for Training Schools."

suggest that the staff member, like the parent, often does not know what else to do.

One must ask, then:

8. *Is discipline used sparingly, as a means of helping the child to understand the natural consequences of his own actions, or is it used as an instrument of revenge or simply to keep order in the institution?*

The members of the 1952 Conference on Training School Standards agreed that while there must be some control and limitation both for the protection of others and for that of the young person unable to master himself, one way to avoid infractions and the implicit flouting of authority is to set up as few regulations as possible. Among the generally accepted taboos are those against hitting institutional employees, running away, or ignoring the general time schedule. Some staff members are developing skill in recognizing ways to avoid crisis situations.

In discussing the various common devices for control, the institutional representatives agreed that deprivation of privileges, assignment of unpleasant chores, the use of demerits, and group punishment are questionable in view of the institution's goals. If privileges are few and far between, deprivation will not be very effective. To regard chores as punishment conveys an unwholesome attitude toward necessary but unexciting work. Labeling work as punishment is reminiscent of the teacher who keeps pupils after school and makes them write the same sentence one hundred times. Learning acquires a disagreeable instead of a pleasant association.

The use of demerits may be disadvantageous from a treatment standpoint if the system deprives a young person from going home when he needs to (see Monsignor Furfey's comment on the Barnabas System in Chapter 24). Furthermore, after a certain number of demerits the assurance of failure, as the Ralston boys noted, discourages striving for better behavior. Institutions might take a leaf from the progressive educator's book, which recommends rewards in accordance with effort expended rather than absolute accomplishment, holding that there is little point in prizes to those whose capacity and work habits make the acquisition of the prize almost inevitable.

It was pointed out at the conference that to punish the group because one cannot identify the culprit is also unsound because it goes counter to the group mores, which do not permit informing on a comrade; it is apt to increase the feeling of resentment against the authorities; and there is a possibility that it will boomerang on the culprit when the group gets him alone.

Segregation is another device that needs to be carefully scrutinized to assure that it is used only as a therapeutic cooling-off process, and that it does not intensify hostile attitudes. Solitary confinement over long periods of time, often with cuts in food rations and lack of access to physical or intellectual activities, will only reinforce the offender's belief in the hostility of the authorities.

The aspect of discipline about which there is and has been the greatest difference of opinion is the use of corporal punishment. The National Conference of Juvenile Agencies and the National Association of Training Schools[4] stated that corporal punishment could not be condoned in any form or fashion. It could not be controlled, and it fitted in too neatly with the delinquent's concept of the hostile adult world. This point has also been made by psychiatrists and sociologists.

The deliberators disagreed as to where the responsibility for administering disciplinary measures was appropriately lodged. They did agree, however, that the practice of permitting the children themselves to determine the punishment and apply it reflected a misunderstanding of the principle that punishment should correspond to the individual's needs. Obviously children are not aware of the psychological implications of conduct. Their suggestions therefore usually reflect the disciplinary habits and practices of their parents or teachers. If these procedures had been psychologically sound, some of these children would have had less trouble with authority than their delinquent behavior reveals. Furthermore, putting the responsibility in the hands of their peers encourages the kangaroo court system, which plays into the destructive needs of the more aggressive members in the group.

At the other extreme is the practice of not permitting any but the superintendent or his deputy to carry out or to administer the punishment. Among its disadvantages is the lapse of time between the deed and its consequence. This lapse, as Fritz Redl points out, removes punishment from its role as a normal part of daily living. It is similar to the mother who tells her disobedient child that he may anticipate punishment for his misdeeds "when Papa comes home." There is a parallel also in the school where the classroom teacher sends the child to the principal's office for disciplining. Sometimes the child sits in the principal's office, all ears for conversations which were not designed for his edification; or, if the principal has to leave the office, the child may be seen trailing him in a school corridor. Another disadvantage is that this method prevents the staff member from learning to deal with disciplinary problems himself.

Some of the conferees suggested that a special committee be given responsibility for deciding on appropriate discipline. A more productive function of the committee, however, appeared to be to review the results and the effectiveness of certain disciplinary measures. This is a practice similar to that in some county medical associations or teaching hospitals which examine the possible reasons for higher than usual maternal mortality rates. Such a pro-

---

[4] Now known as National Association of Training Schools and Juvenile Agencies.

ceeding is not regarded as necessarily critical of the individual obstetrician. By revealing examples of human fallibility, it provides an opportunity to learn by reviewing one's mistakes.

Preparation for Return to the Community

The final question concerning the institution is:

9. *Is the institution's goal the preparation of the young person for return to the community, or is its main emphasis on training him to adjust to the institution's routine, on the assumption that the two are identical?*

Put another way, does the institution aim to instill in each of its charges a desire to be an independent, productive citizen, with confidence in his own capacity to achieve his maximum potentiality? If the goal is his return to the community, does the institutional staff keep in touch with the family and the community and arrange for weekend or holiday visits, or possibly for work assignments in the community? Upon his return, does the institution provide competent and flexible parole supervision (see Berg's description of Baltimore plan, Chapter 22)?

Appraisals of Institutional Programs

As we proceed to present the findings of studies of various institutional programs, we will note only general references to the specific criteria implied in the questions above. Nevertheless every responsible investigator balances his findings on each of these points in arriving at his estimate of effectiveness. The best test, of course, would be what happens to the wards of the institution after they leave. But only rarely do the studies, regardless of their auspices, provide this sort of definitive data. It is hard to secure because it means follow-up studies which are expensive and time consuming. Furthermore, it is not simple, requiring the reconciliation of many different points of view.

Obstacles to Evaluation

Some obstacles in the evaluation of treatment results are pointed out in an article by Blum.[5] By and large, Blum suggests, correctional policy is based upon a philosophy of revenge, retribution, and reformation as embodied in various systems of law—tribal, Roman, Semitic, and common—in combination with hedonism and Christian doctrine. Thus, an inevitable schism exists between the orientation of the administrator and the evaluator whose approach must be scientific. Rules, structure, and practice are taken for granted by the administrator as the "rock upon which he has built his grey-walled temples,"

[5] Richard H. Blum, "Overcoming Impediments to Research in the Correctional Field," *Journal of Correctional Psychology*, Vol. 2, no. 1 (March 1955), pp. 7-9, 16.

and perforce he makes his daily decisions on this basis. The evaluator, on the other hand, takes nothing for granted, usually having no immediate decisions to make. The administrator is apt to look for results immediately useful to him in practice, and he expects naturally to enhance rather than diminish the prestige of his institution—a demand often difficult to fulfill.

There are also the limitations of the researcher himself. He may be insufficiently trained, and ineffective in gaining the necessary cooperation of other members of the staff. Sometimes the pressure of work is too much for him, and occasionally he may be tempted to engage in therapy.

A third obstacle, the nature of the data available to the researcher who attempts to evaluate an institutional program, constitutes perhaps the most formidable of all. Before his institutionalization, the delinquent or criminal has usually run the gamut of the entire penal treatment program—apprehension, trial or hearing, and commitment. As Michael and Adler and Sellin have pointed out (see Chapter 12), true experiments directed at measuring the results of treatment are too difficult to carry out. In consequence, studies have yielded descriptions rather than tests of hypotheses.

According to Blum, Alexander and Healy's *Roots of Crime*[6] exposes the failure of psychoanalytic therapy for prison inmates. Since no one has succeeded in designing an appropriate control group, questions as to whether psychoanalysis aids the rehabilitation of offenders, and whether it is likewise efficacious with nonoffenders, still await definitive answers.

The Gluecks' follow-up of criminal careers of both men and women committed to reformatories showed discouraging results.[7] Cabot's introduction suggests that the *maturation* process rather than the *treatment* in the institution may be responsible for the lower incidence of the older age group in prison populations. Increasing ability to avoid detection and pursuit may also be a factor.

Aware of these limitations we proceed now to present the findings of several investigations (1) of public correctional institutions; and (2) of certain special institutions, both public and private, with treatment programs.

Public Correctional Institutions

PUBLIC HEARINGS. The recent Senate hearings on delinquency[8] illustrate the process of a public investigation in which there were probably political implications in choosing the aspects of the problem on which public

[6] Franz Alexander and William Healy, *Roots of Crime*; New York, Alfred Knopf, 1935.

[7] Sheldon and Eleanor T. Glueck, *Five Hundred Criminal Careers*, New York, Knopf, 1930.

[8] Hearings before the Subcommittee to Investigate Delinquency of the Committee on the Judiciary, U.S. Senate, 84th Congress, April 6 and 7, 1955; April 20, May 11 and 12, 1955; June 15-18, 1955; Report No. 62, March 14, 1955.

hearings were held. The major portion of the subcommittee report caters to the spectacular interest of the public in the effect on delinquency of motion pictures, comic books, television, and jobs for youth. *Less than one page* is devoted to evaluating training schools for delinquent children. In commenting on the widespread lack of facilities and insufficient staff for an individualized treatment program, it is noted that public institutions "are faced with pressure to expand their population capacities as the most economical means in which to accommodate more children." This is clearly in disregard of the upper limit of 200 set by national standard-setting organizations if individualized treatment is to be undertaken.

Doubtless because of their public auspices, state training schools are especially subject to attack or public investigation of their practices. Often the political use of such disclosures interferes with implementation of the objective recommendations. Sometimes the superintendents and the boards of directors of these schools are unable or unwilling to admit publicly that anything is wrong. Occasionally, such abuses as cruel treatment, deprivation of food and exercise, solitary confinement, may be at least temporarily corrected. Often the investigations serve as springboards for requests for more appropriations for the support of programs advertised as key solutions, without proof of their validity.

EARLIER FINDINGS. It is perhaps somewhat disappointing to discover the same revelations of shortcomings and similar recommendations for improvement made again and again. Almost three decades ago the Bowler and Bloodgood studies under the auspices of United States Children's Bureau[9] revealed the abuses and the failure in institutions in states which represented the *avant garde* in the 1930s. They found that at least 70 per cent of the paroled delinquents received no specific services from the parole officers. Thirteen per cent were never seen, and 10 per cent were seen only once. The visits, even in the cases in which there were six or more (slightly less than a third of the total), were obviously perfunctory. In the opinion of the authors, California, New Jersey, and New York were the only three states at that time that were increasing their efforts to improve after-care or parole service.

The 1940 studies of Hopkirk, based on his first-hand observations as an experienced institutional manager and child-care expert, came to the dismal conclusion that practice in only one third of the better training schools conformed to high standards or manifested a continuing interest in improvement. One third were so deficient that in Hopkirk's opinion they should be eliminated.[10]

[9] Alida C. Bowler and Ruth Salter Bloodgood, *Institutional Treatment of Delinquent Boys*, Parts I and II, Nos. 228 and 230, Washington, U.S. Children's Bureau, 1935 and 1936.
[10] Howard W. Hopkirk, *Institutions Serving Children*, New York, Russell Sage, 1944, pp. 207-209.

Even when changes are made following studies, they are often as evanescent as the results of reform administrations in city politics. Like the march of the Beautiful Sabine Women, the changes sometimes represent one step forward for each two steps backward. The reason may be that reformers do not keep their shoulder at the wheel of progress, which in turn does not automatically move in a forward direction. Having won the first round, throwing "the scoundrels" out, the reformers leave the tasks of everyday business to people who may be, and usually are, subject to all kinds of pressures to maintain the status quo. This does not mean that all officials and administrators are against change, but rather that—as with the preservation of liberty—the vigilance of the public, or its representatives on boards of directors, is essential if institutions for delinquents are to be held to the standards and goals recommended in the light of today's best knowledge.

DEUTSCH'S STUDY. Findings similar to those of Bloodgood and of Hopkirk were repeated and reported by Albert Deutsch in *Our Rejected Children*.[11] That credence should be given this journalist's findings was the burden of MacCormick's introduction to the book. As a responsible reporter, trained to get the facts but without obligation to buttress them with voluminous footnotes, Deutsch knew how to avoid libelous statements in pursuit of his goal, i.e., reaching the general public to do something about the scandalous conditions.

In Part I, "They Call It Reform," Deutsch reported the findings of his coast-to-coast survey of state training schools and a few private institutions, located in the wealthy states, which advocated good social welfare programs. Whittier School in California, at one time considered one of the outstanding schools in the country, and the Lancaster School for Boys in Ohio, the first reformatory to adopt the cottage plan, came in for major criticism. The prevailing atmosphere, as Deutsch perceived it, was, like that described by Tony, one of fear and repression.

Although in some institutions parts of the program were good, others were often backward. The good, in Deutsch's words, was "what one had a right to expect in institutions for child-care in a rich and civilized community. The bad was inexcusable. The very bad was intolerable."

In spite of the efforts of many officials and staff members to give "kindly and intelligent guidance to their juvenile wards," the following were the most patent sins:

1. Regimentation which means mass treatment.
2. Monotony with respect to food, work, recreation.
3. Enforced idleness and isolation, both spiritual and physical.
4. Excessive use of both physical and mental punishment. (This is an

---

[11] Albert Deutsch, *Our Rejected Children*, Boston, Little, Brown, 1950.

interesting comment because it reveals that not all punishment is physical; sharp tongues and refusal to pay attention may be experienced as severely as physical assault.)

5. Babelism—"the profusion of neologisms that sound impressively modern while hiding an ugly reality."

Deutsch referred to the use of euphemistic terms to cover negative purposes: "meditation" to describe solitary confinement; "lost privilege cottages," a new name for cell blocks; kitchen drudgery and other forms of industrial exploitation rechristened "vocational rehabilitation"; whips and paddles relabeled as "tools of control."

Partisan political influence combined with public penury and complacency were responsible, Deutsch believed, for the existence of the shocking conditions which were primarily found in the state institutions.

As MacCormick predicated, the directors of many of these institutions denied the accusations. With rare exceptions, at meetings like those of the Association of Training School Superintendents, the directors of these institutions attempted to point to flaws in Deutsch's procedure. Only one or two saw the exposure as an opportunity to elicit more public support for better programs.

ELMIRA AND COXSACKIE.   Ten years after the publication of *Youth in the Toils*,[12] the study which led to the establishment of the Youth Correction Authority, described in Chapter 19, the sponsoring committee launched another study to determine whether the disgraceful conditions in New York State's facilities for the convicted 16- to 21-year-old male offender had improved. New York State had not adopted the Youth Authority Plan, but instead had made several notable changes in its program. Specifically, it had established a reception center at Elmira to screen the male offender sentenced to confinement in state institutions; and had introduced a program of social education in Elmira and at the New York State Vocational Institution at West Coxsackie. A study published in 1950[13] disclosed the following:

The reception center, established in 1945, processed between 1200 and 1300 youths a year. In this study process each discipline contributed its own description of "what the youngster appears to be, but very little idea of how he came to be that way." There was no indication, therefore, of the psychological roots of much delinquent behavior and little in the study that could be effectively used in treatment.

The two institutions to which it was possible to send young people who were processed in the center were too large and too crowded and inevitably

12 Leonard V. Harrison and Pryor McNeill Grant, *Youth in the Toils,* New York, Macmillan, 1935.

13 Bertram M. Beck, *Youth Within Walls,* New York, Community Service Society, 1950.

over-regimented. Elmira's capacity was almost 1400, Coxsackie's a little over 800. Both were not only full most of the time but there was overcrowding in the dormitories and doubling up in the cells.

Their appearance was forbidding. Elmira was partly walled and its towers were manned with armed custodial officers. Although Coxsackie had no walls, its limited outdoor recreation space was fenced in with barbed wire, and during the winter months most of the population was confined indoors.

The recreational programs did not provide outlets for the pent-up emotions and the particularly aggressive impulses characteristic of adolescents in custody. The aim of the vocational programs was, as in many custodial institutions, chiefly to cut down institutional costs rather than to train inmates to be self-supporting. Nor was the staff in charge of the vocational programs trained in educational methods. The largest contingents on the staffs of both institutions, approximately 190 at Elmira and 110 at Coxsackie, were custodial officers, who wore policeman-like uniforms. At Elmira the officers carried clubs.

In describing the treatment program, Beck suggested that the terms "treatment," "diagnosis," and "casework" had been borrowed from other professions "without borrowing knowledge."[14] Both Elmira and Coxsackie had a unit called "guidance service" whose stated primary objective was "to obtain the participation of the inmate in a plan of institutional treatment that will prepare him for parole and to stimulate him, as well as his relatives and friends, to work toward the formulation of an effective parole program related as closely as possible to the institutional treatment program. The service unit is both the caseworking agency and the central coordinating agency of the institution."[15] But although New York State had introduced a program of social education, it had not provided leaders trained in the group process. There were no caseworkers on the staff and the program of group therapy fell far short of what is ordinarily understood to be effective group leadership. Since participation in the group therapy program was required of those who were homosexuals or who had been disciplinary problems, it carried the taint of punishment. In short, neither the atmosphere nor the program at either institution was conducive to effective treatment of delinquent youths. The best that could be said of them was that the various staff members manifestly strove to do an effective job of rehabilitation.[16]

The effectiveness of an institution's program is usually based on the parole statistics. Those quoted by Beck revealed that over one half of the

[14] *Ibid.*, p. 24.
[15] Edward Murphy, "Service Units—What They Are and How They Function," *Correction*, Vol. 24, no. 8 (Nov. 1949), p. 8.
[16] Beck, *op. cit.*, p. 30.

youths released from Elmira on parole were unable to complete their initial parole period without getting into further trouble.[17] These discouraging results from the institutions for the younger offender in comparison with those in prisons (32 per cent of the violators in the same time period) may be related to what Dr. Richard Cabot described as "the hardening of the criminal artery which occurs sometime after 25."

In Beck's opinion New York State's facilities for treating youthful offenders would be improved if:[18]

1. Commitment of youths was made to the youth division of the State Department of Correction instead of to the individual institution, and a treatment plan were made by qualified individuals after full study.

2. There was full use of a diversified range of facilities including camps, clinical facilities, and security institutions.

3. Treatment terminated after consideration by the youth division in cooperation with the parole board, instead of on an arbitrary date as at present.

4. There was a psychiatric treatment center providing care for about 20 per cent of the youths annually processed at the reception center.

And, as an essential preliminary, Beck pointed to the need for revision of the chaotic process of sentencing.

To put these proposals into operation, as Beck noted, would probably require many staff changes. There would be strong opposition to the new program from many of those currently employed, as there is from judges faced by the proposals of court reform.[19]

Institutions with Treatment Programs[20]

Sometimes the impetus for appraisal comes from within the institution itself. Often the findings of such studies are available only to the boards of directors of the institutions that requested them. Three exceptions, however, are the studies cited below of Hawthorne Cedar Knolls, Wiltwyck, and Highfields.

HAWTHORNE CEDAR KNOLLS. A study of particular interest from the

[17] New York State Division of Parole, Executive Department, 19th Annual Report, 1948, pp. 132-38.

[18] Beck, op. cit., pp. 65-70.

[19] Note, for example, the opposition to the Tweed Commission, "Report and Proposals for Court Reform in New York State," voiced in the New York State Legislature during the spring of 1958. A forthcoming report of the Juvenile Deliquency Evaluation Project of New York City discloses little change in the program of the Reception Center since Beck's study, and little or no improvement in the recidivist rate.

[20] See Chapter 24 for descriptions of the three institutions covered in this section.

sociological point of view because it was made by two participant observers[21] employs a more sophisticated technique than that used by Robin at Ralston. The authors were concerned with the peer group dynamics in one of the cottages (No. 19) to which the older and more aggressive boys were transferred. In describing their approach the authors state:

> The lack of an explicitly worked out methodology was related to the looseness of our conceptions as to what really constituted "delinquent" values and behavior. We needed to translate the pictures that had been created in our head of the cottage functioning into objective and operational terms. We knew the three main group variables that we wanted to tie down: (1) the social organization, (2) the culture and the dominant norms and values that pervaded the cottage, and (3) the roles that individual youngsters played in the cottage organization.

They used Bales' twelve categories of interaction[22] to note and score critical incidents around serving and eating meals. The dining room offered special advantages because all the boys in the cottage were together there, and because the observer's questions and activities at the table with the boys would be accepted more naturally than they would be in some other group situations. Checking their observations, they agreed as follows with regard to:

> 1. *The cottage culture:* In the relationships to each other, the boys who are at the bottom of the status ladder are highly conscious and fearful of approaching the older, more experienced boys; on the other hand, high-status individuals are very sensitive to low-status members' feelings and rarely interact in neutral ways but in a highly dictatorial manner. The most simple directions or requests are frequently weighted with challenge, ranking and deflating the other person's status.
> 2. *The cottage social organization:* The critical incident observation confirmed previous observations of the cottage hierarchy, that high-status members were relatively frequent initiators, low-status members relatively frequent targets.
> 3. *The role the individual plays in the group:* The profiles of the cottage as revealed by the Gross Incidents point up its truncated character, the extreme negativism and hostility between different clique members and the predominant pecking order.

The questions to which it is hoped further refinement and application of this method will provide answers are:

[21] Howard Polsky and Martin Kohn, "The Study of Interaction Processes in a Delinquent Subculture," paper read at Fifty-third Annual Meeting of the American Sociological Society, University of Washington, Seattle, August 29, 1958. Howard Polsky is a Russell Sage Resident at Hawthorne Cedar Knolls School; Martin Kohn is former director of research.

[22] Robert F. Bales, *Interaction Process Analysis,* Cambridge, Addison-Wesley Press, 1951.

To what extent does the individual play a role in the group similar to the one which he has played in the past, in his home and community? To what extent does the individual create a micro-social world in which he perpetuates his past patterns of integration? To what extent does the social context impose certain ways of relating? Is the individual forced to operate within the available niches? In what ways does the individual change as he ascends the status hierarchy? To what extent does he change as a function of involvement with adults, therapy, etc.? To answer these questions we must know how the individual functions within the group.

The boys are at Hawthorne because of anti-social activity which could not be dealt with in the community. The responsible intake people have come to the conclusion that they need institutional help. Once they arrive, however, they are placed in cottages and their subsequent development is greatly influenced by the cultural and social peer organization they evolve.

When one boy is acting-out against another, he is fulfilling needs which are traceable to his unique development history. If he has difficulty containing his impulses and is sensitive about rejection or insults, he will trigger hostility toward alleged challengers. The specific action of one individual against another takes place in the context of eighteen other members who are not passive spectators. They are actively reacting to the situation. Group culture and atmosphere are being created. In the short-term sense, one individual may be reducing tensions, but at the same time he sets up a circular process which interferes with the integration of the group as a whole and often reenforces the pathological mode of reaction.

We are told that the administration of the Jewish Board of Guardians has already acted on these findings and instituted some changes in the transfer process and in the cottage parents' role in Cottage 19.

One would like to know whether other cottages will be studied in a similar fashion. If so, and if the findings for Cottage 19 apply also, though with less intensity, to the others, there are important implications for evaluating the effectiveness of any institutional program, however well staffed, for rehabilitating hostile aggressive adolescents. Apparently, more psychiatric service is not the total answer. Currently the Jewish Board of Guardians, which has had several unpublished studies of its institutions, is said to be considering a scientifically planned study of this question.[23]

In presenting below the evidence on the effectiveness of the program at Wiltwyck, it is necessary to recall that the boys whom it serves are in general younger than those at Hawthorne and come from a more disadvantaged back-

---

[23] Donald H. Block, M.D., *A Prospectus for a Research Program for the Jewish Board of Guardians*, New York, Jewish Board of Guardians, 1957, pp. 1-48.

ground educationally and socio-economically. Except perhaps that they are younger and less aggressive, they resemble the population at Ralston more than they do that at Hawthorne Cedar Knolls.

WILTWYCK. In 1954, at the request of Dr. Ernest Papanek, the director at the time, a study was made of the Wiltwyck School for Boys, based on the records of approximately all of the 400 boys who had been committed to the institution from the time of its inception in 1937 through 1952.[24] The object of the study was to see whether the outcome of the treatment differed with the direction of the program whether it was under a minister (its first director), or any of his three successors, the last of whom, Papanek, combined training in psychology, education, and social work. The method used in the study was a content analysis of the boys' records, supplemented by evidence of the subsequent contacts of the boys with the court or other correctional agencies.

Despite the much more elaborate provision of staff and psychiatric service in the later years, the major findings indicated little difference in the rate of success in the four periods. In each period, at least half the boys were subsequently in trouble, although at their release from the institution they were considered well enough adjusted to warrant their return to the community.

The explanation may be the nature of the problem which brought the majority of the boys from Negro Harlem to the institution in the first place. The psychiatric diagnoses showed that a little over half of the boys had difficulties traceable to *situational deprivations* (bad living conditions, and so forth) rather than to character disorders or psychoneurotic traits. To be sure, there were some boys who required and received intensive psychiatric therapy. This did not, however, compensate for the deprivation in the home community.

The disturbing conclusion appears to be that for members of deprived minority groups no institutional program, even when carefully designed or adequately staffed, can be expected to compensate for the community's lack of provision of decent living and working conditions.

In the period since this study was completed, Wiltwyck's program has been extended through the allocation of higher rates of board by New York City for treatment centers. The additional therapeutic staff includes psychologists, art therapists, and group workers. To speed the process of readjustment back into the community, a halfway house has been set up in St. Albans, Long Island. The likelihood of a site for the institution much nearer to New

[24] Student thesis, No. 4371, at the New York School of Social Work, May 1954, supervised by Sophia M. Robison, Alvan Martin, and Isabel Stamm; see also William and Joan McCord, *Psychopathy and Delinquency*, New York, Grune & Stratton, 1956. This volume includes considerable material on the effects of Wiltwyck treatment, pp. 123-71.

York City has increased. A further follow-up of the boys, none of whom was over 11 at the time of his original commitment, is contemplated.

HIGHFIELDS. This institution is exceptional in that it incorporated at its initiation provision for studying the effects of the program stressing group therapy. The program was established by the State of New Jersey in 1950 as an alternative to commitment to the State Institution for Delinquent Boys at Annandale.[25]

The advisory committee responsible for evaluation[26] sought answers to the following three questions:

1. Do the boys undergoing the Highfields experience have lower, higher, or the same recidivist rates as boys undergoing other forms of treatment?

2. Do they change in their attitudes toward their families, toward law and order, and in their own outlook?

3. Is there any change in personality manifestations?

The research design called for a five-year study. It included a control group of boys similar in age and eligible for Highfields but committed to Annandale. Detailed case histories for each boy prior to, during, and subsequent to his stay at Highfields were assembled. Interviews with each boy and with people in the community whom he designated, constituted the sources of information about his adjustment immediately subsequent to, and at stated intervals following, his release from Highfields.

Two studies report the results of the program for the 226 boys who completed the training period at Highfields.[27] About one fifth of the boys who were referred by the court to Highfields in the five-year period did not go through with the program. Some boys ran away immediately and others were too disturbed to fit into the program. Approximately one third of the boys who did remain for the four-month program were judged as successfully adjusted in the year following their release. In comparing them with the control, boys who were committed to Annandale, almost twice the number of boys committed to Annandale (33 per cent) were in trouble again during the first year of their return to the community in comparison with 18 per cent of the Highfields boys.[28]

About one fourth of the Highfields group were Negroes. The follow-up

[25] F. Lovell Bixby and Lloyd W. McCorkle, "Guided Group Interaction in Correctional Work," *American Sociological Review*, Vol. 16, no. 4 (Aug. 1951), pp. 455-61.

[26] Professor Ernest W. Burgess, Chairman; Dr. J. Quinter Holsopple, Dr. Richard L. Jenkins, Dr. Walter C. Reckless, Mr. G. Howland Shaw, and Prof. Wellman J. Warner, of New York University.

[27] H. Ashley Weeks, *Youthful Offenders at Highfelds: An Evaluation of the Effects of the Short-Term Treatment of Delinquent Boys*, The University of Michigan Press, 1958; and Lloyd W. McCorkle, Albert Ellis, and F. Lovell Bixby, *The Highfields Story: An Experimental Treatment Project for Youthful Offenders*, New York, Henry Holt, 1958.

[28] Lloyd McCorkle *et al.*, *op. cit.*, p. 143, Table 9.

results indicated that Highfields was twice as successful with Negro boys—three in every five—in contrast with Annandale (three out of every ten). The research staff suggests that the reason for the greater success with the Negro than with the white boys is probably related to their small proportion of the total (never more than one fourth or one fifth) and their feeling of acceptance by the group. To increase the number of Negro boys, however, might reduce the chances of success.[29]

Guttman Scale Analysis which was used to estimate changes in the morale and in the attitudes of the boys toward their families and toward law and order, indicated little change for either the Negro or the white group as a result of their stay in Highfields. Likewise, the screening test for psychoneurosis showed little change in the pre- and post-tests of the Highfields boys. The major finding was an increase in anxiety which is considered a good sign in the rehabilitation of delinquent boys. On the other hand, the scores of the Annandale boys show considerable reduction. Dr. Jenkins' explanation of this reduction in anxiety in a comment to Dr. Weeks in September 1952, was as follows, and was equally applicable in 1955.

> To me the obvious interpretation of the reduction in the scores of the Annandale boys on the psychoneurotic screening adjunct during their stay at Annandale is that in the delinquent processing which goes on at an institution like Annandale, they become increasingly accepting of themselves as delinquents and any conflicts which they may have about it diminish. They become more at peace within themselves, more content to blame society for their failures, and have fewer obstacles of conscience to the continuance of a predatory pattern.

The general conclusion, therefore, appears to be that Highfields accomplished as much, if not more, in its four-month residential treatment as the reformatory at Annandale in its more than twelve-month confinement. Definitive results, however, on why they were more successful with some boys than with others await further analysis.[30]

On the basis of the Highfields project, one might be inclined to be optimistic about the results of institutional treatment. Unfortunately, however, studies like that of Highfields are rare. Across America, the results of institutional care, whether under private or public auspices, are inconclusive and somewhat discouraging in comparison with the results reported by English institutions quoted in Chapter 25. There is a ray of hope, however, in Gardner's suggestion[31] that it is possible for institutions to be therapeutic

---

[29] H. Ashley Weeks, *op. cit.*, p. 122.
[30] *Ibid.*, p. 128.
[31] George E. Gardner, Ph.D., M.D., "The Institution as Therapist," *The Child*, Vol. 16, no. 5 (Jan. 1952), Washington, U.S. Children's Bureau, p. 70.

instruments. He does more than utter pious wishes; he lists the necessary precedent conditions for the institutions of the future.

Institutions of the Future

Instead of the punitive hostile role which, McCorkle suggests, prevails so frequently in American institutions, and which Deutsch's investigations in the juvenile field confirm, Gardner sees the institution of the future in the role of therapist. A psychiatrist with wide experience, and training in psychology as well, working with delinquent boys and girls at the Judge Baker Guidance Center in Boston, Gardner outlines the necessary general principles for the success of specific methods of therapy, regardless of the setting. He follows clinical procedure in his analysis, i.e., (1) an outline of the chief complaint from the point of view of the community and the child; (2) the treatment goal; and (3) the therapeutic process as it evolves. Below we present each of these steps.

Recognition of the Problem

The community's chief complaint is that 90 per cent of delinquent children are hostile and aggressive. They break and enter, they steal other people's property, they assault and damage, they refuse to go to school, they resent the authority of the community and the home. Society responds by applying corrective and punishing restraints.

The chief complaint of the child himself (obviously the one with which "the therapist institution" is primarily concerned) is not nearly so apparent. To the delinquent, the external world appears at all points to be "aggressive, destructive and primitive." The delinquent conceives of human beings as predatory animals. As accounts of gang members confirm, from their early childhood, these children have become highly sensitized both to the expressed and to the unexpressed hostility of which all human beings are capable. Psychiatrists believe that if these children had been reared in homes where they were loved and wanted, these negative experiences would have receded into the background. The majority of the boys whom Gardner has seen in treatment have been able to recognize that their initial cold response reflected the rejection which they had experienced as children.

A second disabling factor is the delinquent's own conception of himself, "again usually unconscious and unexpressed, save in the treatment setting."

He is a hostile, aggressive predatory animal, driven by urges he does not completely understand to wrest from this environment of humans whatever he can—either through mutilative or destructive methods or by a process of leechlike osmosis—or by both methods.

How he arrives at such a concept of self we in psychiatry are only now beginning dimly to envision; but we are convinced that this is a very prevalent concept, that it is due to development faults or arrests in what usually is orderly personality growth, and that it is just at this point (in relation to the concept of self) that the commonality between delinquent behavior and neurotic behavior is beginning to become apparent.

Punishment, Gardner claims, confirms the delinquent's conception of himself which generated his antisocial behavior. And, as Erikson pointed out (Chapter 6), if one's self-concept is continually bombarded by the adult world's hostile treatment, one cannot be expected to consider oneself a worthwhile individual.

The Treatment Goal

The goal of treatment is to alter the delinquent's views of the world and himself. With its collective personnel the institution can initiate the necessary changes in the youth's conceptions through the conscious use of the principles and steps which are basic in all psychotherapy.

The Therapeutic Process

The four steps in the psychotherapeutic process, whether in or out of an institution, as we saw in the stories of Carol on Probation, John at Hawthorne, and Butch at Berkshire Farm, are:

1. *Establishing positive transference:* "A noncombative, nonaggressive relationship which is accepting and permissive. It sets reasonable limits in the expression of aggressive impulses of the child and controls the aggressiveness of his associated colleagues and superiors which he also fears."

2. *Revealing to the individual the mechanisms which govern his responses:* Even if a psychoanalytic procedure is not available, continued inevitable contacts with other people in groups will help individuals to arrive at an appreciable degree of insight as to their own underlying motives.

3. *Confronting the individual with and interpreting to him his behavioral patterns:* This process, which makes clear to the delinquent just what he seems to be trying to do, goes on apace in institutional living, as well as in individual therapy situations. Wittingly or unwittingly the child's adult associates at all times—housemasters, teachers, and administrators—each in his own way, is constantly confronting the boy and girl with what seems to be the reason for his or her behavior.

4. *Providing opportunity for trial-and-error learning:* If the individual child makes the first tentative attempts to change his behavior, modifying his previous concept of himself and others, the educational, social, athletic, vocational, and other programs provide numerous opportunities for such trials, and the institution's personnel should be alert to the initial endeavors of the child to change.

The institution offers abundant opportunities to apply the therapeutic devices of suggestion, advice, encouragement, sympathy at the time of failure, as well as approval, prestige, and citation through work or house assignments. The institution also has ample opportunity to provide and guide the first outward expression of such changes in trial behavior.

If we can add to Gardner's provocative ideas about the therapeutically oriented institutions of the future, the new awareness of the structure of formal and informal relationships, of ingroup and outgroup responses—i.e., of the setting of the institution on which the sociologist is laying more and more emphasis—we can hope for a more successful institution in the not too distant future.

Acting on Lawrence Frank's concept of "Society as the Patient"[32] the Belmont Social Rehabilitation Unit in England, of which Maxwell Jones is director, is attempting to create a different type of institutional setting. The rehabilitative process for adults with acting-out disorders is accomplished through setting up a situation in which, like Aichorn's in Vienna, the patients are permitted to play their everyday roles instead of being ordered about as in the usual institutional hierarchy.[33] In our opinion this approach invites more consideration from those concerned with rehabilitating juvenile delinquents who have been removed from their homes.[34]

In view of what we have learned about the differential nature of the referral of cases to court, as well as of court action with respect to children from different strata of our society, it is doubtful whether all the young people described as delinquent actually need to be removed from their homes—quarantined so to speak—either for their own or the community's protection. Apart from the human costs, the annual material costs of this type of care are estimated to be $65 million in public institutions alone, almost 80 per cent of it spent for operating costs.

Perhaps we need to reconsider the whole process of institutionalization

[32] Lawrence K. Frank, "Society as the Patient," *Essays on Culture and Personality*, New Brunswick, Rutgers University Press, 1950.

[33] Robert and Rhona Rapoport, "Community as the Doctor," *Human Organization*, Vol. 16, no. 4 (April 1958), pp. 28-31.

[34] Seymour Parker, "Role Theory and the Treatment of the Social Acting-Out Disorders," *The British Journal of Delinquency*, Vol. 7, no. 4 (April 1957), pp. 285-300.

of delinquents, both temporary and long-term. Is it being resorted to only for those who cannot or should not remain in the community, i.e., those young people whose behavior has smallpox implications, or is it being used to confine those whose misbehavior is no more serious than chicken pox? The unanswered questions are:

1. To what extent does the highly selective nature of the whole correctional process—apprehension by the police, referral to the juvenile court, and action of the court—unsoundly reflect the biases of the dominant group in a multi-cultural population?

2. What can we do about it?

A gleam of hope for the gallant effort of those institutional staff members who are working to bring about rehabilitation is that public interest has been aroused. Once it is aroused ways will be found to counteract the apathy which consigns these nonconforming children to the care of institutions and then either washes its hands of any further responsibility, or demands stricter punishment when the community is bothered by runaways or other invasions of its privacy.

Summary

In evaluating the effectiveness of an institution for delinquents, the standards set by conferences of directors of training schools and juvenile institutions provide convenient yardsticks. They cover physical plant, administrative policies, and the responsibilities of residential, educational, and treatment staffs. With humility, the superintendents label their descriptions as *aspirations* rather than goals.

The goal of the institution should be to equip its wards for resuming a healthy and constructive life back in the community, rather than to impose conformity with the institution's rules. It is agreed that unnecessary rules invite the hostile young person to break them. The inmate who feels that society, represented by the authorities, has rejected him regards the administration as the enemy.

Discipline in the institution is always a challenge. The community's demands, and the needs of the young person as a result of his early life history, usually place conflicting pressures on the institutional staff. The measures taken to enforce discipline reveal a great deal about the philosophy of the institution. Such current practices as deprivation of privileges, assignment of unpleasant chores, demerits, group punishment, and segregation have unsound psychological implications. Moreover, there are drawbacks in permitting disciplinary measures to be carried out by the children, by a special committee, or by the director of the institution.

Despite the availability of standards, the researcher may lack the necessary skill and must always remember that since the institutional inmate has usually run the gamut of the entire penal treatment program the effect of any particular program is hard to measure.

While the literature provides accounts of individual experiences and descriptions of institutional programs from the viewpoint of the inmate protagonists, we only occasionally find an objective observer's judgment of our institutions. Public hearings and other studies over the last three decades have pointed out the all-too-frequent regimentation, monotony, and excessive use of physical and mental punishment. Many of these practices, vividly described by Deutsch, are obviously vestiges of the prison roots of reform schools.

Juvenile institutions under private auspices, which in the main are able to restrict their intake, are in a more favorable position than institutions under public auspices. Nevertheless, a realistic *appraisal* of the source and degree of their effectiveness is rare. The study of Wiltwyck, a treatment center which accommodates 100 boys between the ages of 8 and 12, shows little difference in the outcome of treatment regardless of the orientation of the director and the staff. The explanation for the failure of half the boys to maintain the gains registered while in the institution is no doubt related to the conditions in the Harlem ghetto to which most of them must return.

A refreshing exception, from the research point-of-view, is the small state-supported institution at Highfields, which from the beginning incorporated plans for studying its process and results. The purpose was to test the efficacy of participation in group therapy sessions and a work program for 20 boys at a time, for whom the alternative was commitment to the New Jersey State Institution for Delinquent Boys at Annandale. To date the results are decidedly in favor of Highfields.

Without suggesting a plan for testing the results, Dr. Gardner of the Judge Baker Guidance Center in Boston is hopeful that future institutions for delinquents will be able to provide a therapeutic group setting in which the traditional four steps of individual psychotherapy can be followed. Dr. Gardner believes that the institution itself offers advantages for certain types of children over and above the very limited number of delinquent young people whom individual therapy can now help.

Sociologists might add considerably to our knowledge of an effective institution if they were concerned, as Polsky and Kohn were in their study of Hawthorne, with applying sociological theory to the understanding of group relationships and group process.

PART FIVE

PROGRAMS FOR PREVENTING DELINQUENCY

CHAPTER 27

Prevention Through Punishment and Community Planning

What Is Prevention?

PREVENTION APPLIED TO DELINQUENCY HAS AT LEAST TWO FRAMES OF REFER-
ence: (1) forestalling delinquent activity, and (2) halting the antisocial behavior of those already labeled delinquent. Although their sponsors frequently
call them experiments, programs advertised as preventing delinquency rarely
incorporate devices either for measuring the effectiveness of the proposals or
for defining precisely whom the programs will attempt to reach. Instead, the
programs reflect the strongly held beliefs of the sponsors about the cause or
causes of delinquency and the way to deal with it.

There are four major approaches to delinquency prevention: Those who
believe that in the main, parents and children are masters of their own des-
tiny and hence deserve to be punished for wrongdoing, call for stricter measures of control and law enforcement. A second group, which in contrast to
the first regards delinquency as a reaction to certain community inadequacies,
seeks better community organization and increased services to diminish the
chances of delinquent behavior. The third group—perhaps the smallest—
believes that delinquent behavior stems from psychological disturbances, and
advocates the application of clinical facilities, such as those described in
Chapter 17 but not court-connected, to the prevention of delinquency. The
fourth approach, centering on the antisocial gang, is just beginning to be
articulated by sociologists who, like Cohen and Whyte, Ohlin and Cloward,
point to the need to pay more attention to the social structure to which delin-

quent behavior is one response. In Chapter 29 we shall discuss some aspects of the fourth approach, concerned with programs for controlling gang behavior. This chapter and the following one examine the general proposals for prevention offered by the first two groups mentioned above.

Programs Accenting Repression and Control

Perhaps the reason for the major emphasis on repression and control in crime and delinquency prevention is because, as Lukas says, to learn how to prevent them is "unromantic, unspectacular and not susceptible to headlines and Senate inquiries."[1] Despite the evidence that almost 75 per cent of the crime and delinquency committed is not reported, and that apprehended offenders report many previous offenses for which they were not caught, there is constant pressure for more severe punishment as a means of prevention. Offenses are often committed in such a way that the chances of their being reported to law enforcement officials are slight. When an offense is detected, unless it happens to be of a spectacular nature,[2] little publicity is given to the punishment of the offender. Furthermore, young people who live in the so-called delinquency areas know very well that the majority of those who indulge in criminal behavior are not usually caught. They may well have seen collusion between criminals and some police officials which seems to "spread a blanket of immunity over offenders."

Popular but ineffective measures, advocated by many cities and towns to control crime and delinquency, are bright lights on street corners and in parks, and the enforcement of curfew regulations. One currently advocated measure of delinquency control provides for fining and imprisoning parents of delinquent children. Those who insist on the use of the parental rod assume that all wisdom inheres in parents; that discipline is the surest protection for society; and that nonconformity to parental standards is sin.

Despite the pyramiding of such programs for curbing delinquency and the increasingly larger expenditures, in Lukas' words, "the ebb and flow of the enormous body of crime maintains the inexorable constancy of the tides. . . . The trends of prison populations, the rates of recidivism and criminal court calendars show no sign of abatement."[3] It is clearly impossible to evaluate the effectiveness of such broad catch-all programs without an agreement on the nature of the problem, the underlying assumptions as to its cause, and a clear definition of terms.

[1] Edwin J. Lukas, "Limitations in the Traditional Approach to Delinquency," *Yearbook*, National Probation and Parole Association, 1951, p. 159.
[2] *Ibid.*, p. 160.
[3] *Ibid.*, p. 154.

Programs Accenting Community Organization

Coordinating Councils

August Vollmer, the chief of police in Berkeley, California, is credited with establishing the first coordinating council in the early 1920s.[4] A decade later, at the request of a juvenile court judge who was beset by an increase in antisocial activities of young people in Los Angeles, Kenneth S. Beam launched the first council in that city.

The assumptions on which the council idea rests are: (1) that citizens have a common interest in the welfare of their immediate neighborhood, and (2) that the available and appropriate services are not always marshaled to serve individuals who may be in trouble.

With the encouragement of the California Youth Authority (see Chapter 19) the coordinating council idea spread like wildfire in the 1940s. From a total of 250 surveyed in twenty states in 1936, presently more than 700 councils have been identified in the eight states of California, Illinois, Iowa, Michigan, Minnesota, Missouri, New York, and Wisconsin.[5]

Sponsorship of these councils includes state organizations, universities and colleges, county and city governments, and local civic, fraternal, and business organizations. The usual community council is made up of representatives of official as well as unofficial agencies, including city or county officials, police, parent-teacher organizations, women's clubs, church organizations and the clergy, social agencies, character-building and service clubs. The major emphasis in a coordinating council is to prevent delinquency by coordinating services already existing instead of attempting to provide new ones. The members of the council meet to discuss problem situations. They try to arrive at solutions as a joint rather than as a competitive service.

As Beam points out, it is not sufficient to organize a council. To be effective, the council requires the services of adequately trained personnel. To illustrate the coordinating council as a device which both prevents and treats delinquency, we describe below programs in such widely different states as Minnesota, Virginia, and Pennsylvania.

ST. PAUL, MINNESOTA. In St. Paul, the U.S. Children's Bureau staff studied the provision of social services within a restricted area.[6] In collabora-

---

[4] Kenneth S. Beam, "Community Organization," Report of a National Survey of Coordinating and Neighborhood Councils, *Yearbook,* National Probation Association, 1937 and Kenyon J. Scudder, "The Coordinating Council at Work," *Yearbook,* National Probation Association, 1936, pp. 67-77.

[5] Kenneth S. Beam, *Organization of the Community for Delinquency Prevention.* San Diego Coordinating Councils, San Diego, Calif., 1957.

[6] *Children in the Community,* "The St. Paul Experiment in Child Welfare." No. 317, Washington, U.S. Children's Bureau, 1947.

tion with the schools, courts, public and private casework and group work agencies, the community council staff attempted to discover what prevented these community agencies from dealing effectively with delinquents. To identify children in need of help, several staff members were assigned to work closely with the schools and the police—the two agencies most likely to come in contact with children in difficulty. To broaden the community's understanding of behavior difficulties, discussion groups were organized for those interested in learning to recognize emotionally maladjusted children. And after children had been referred for treatment to the project staff, conferences were held with the referring agency to interpret the meaning of the behavior and what the project personnel thought might be done about it.

Initially two types of children were referred to the project for help: those with whom all previous efforts had failed, and those whose behavior was extremely annoying, regardless of the nature of their difficulties. Gradually children whose problems were less severe, and who were also more amenable to the services provided, were referred for help. The project staff included a psychiatrist, a psychologist, two psychiatric social workers, a school social worker, and a group worker. The major services included not only intensive psychiatric therapy but environmental changes—foster care, group recreational facilities, tutoring, and special health services.

The first step in the new plan was to clear the family with the Social Service Exchange to find out whether any agencies in the community already knew any member of the family, and if so, in what connection. If on the basis of these facts the child appeared to need the project's assistance, a social worker visited the parents. If the parents were reluctant to ask for help in dealing with an emotional problem, the social worker suggested that the project would be glad to help with an academic or health problem, or in securing recreational opportunities.

During the six and a half years of the St. Paul project's existence, almost 1500 children living in an area characterized by a fairly high delinquency rate and served by many agencies came to the project. About half of these children were given individualized service.

At the project's termination staff members estimated the extent of improvement in each case. Major improvement in behavior, or factors affecting behavior, was reported for 18 per cent of the children; 65 per cent were rated as partly improved; and in 17 per cent no improvement was noted. The amount of improvement did not appear to be related either to the characteristics of the children, the types of problems, or methods of work. The proportion of failure was similar to that noted in the treatment services of the Judge Baker Guidance Center. Witmer and Tufts comment: "Whether this plan of going out in search of patients succeeded in locating and helping the kinds of children who were not usually reached by a conventional child guidance clinic is not known."[7] Unfortunately from a research point of view, the project kept no record of the children whom they did not consider in need of treatment, those already under care by other agencies, or those whose parents refused the services offered.

NEWPORT NEWS, VIRGINIA. Basing this project essentially on the California plan, the Bureau of Public Assistance and the U.S. Children's Bureau cooperated with the Virginia State Department of Public Welfare to sponsor a community council in Newport News in the 1940s. With the influx of Army and Navy personnel, community facilities were tapped beyond their capacity and simultaneously there was an upsurge of delinquent behavior. The project called attention to the need for health, education, and recreation services as well as for housing for both residents and transients. Reports indicate success in welding the efforts of community agencies and individuals which formerly were working at cross-purposes or duplicating each other's efforts.[8]

PHILADELPHIA NEIGHBORHOOD COMMITTEES. A somewhat different type of community council is exemplified in the neighborhood committees organized by the Philadelphia Crime Prevention Association in 1942. The concern of the committees was with boys who had been formally adjudicated as delinquents as well as with those against whom informal complaints had been filed. A member of a committee is assigned as a Big Brother to each boy under care. If the boy requires the services of a specialized agency, the appropriate arrangements are made. In 1949 there were 77 neighborhood committees affiliated with an advisory coordinating body.[9] In 1958 the Philadelphia Youth Commission put into operation, in cooperation with the Health and Welfare Council, a plan called Operation Poplar which is providing a variety of services in Philadelphia's most disadvantaged areas.[10]

EVALUATING COMMUNITY COUNCILS. Sometimes coordinating operations are viewed with disfavor by the administrators of established social agencies. One objection is the competition such projects offer in appealing for financial support. Another objection, which is perhaps less mercenary, is the possible harm to a family's morale in a public discussion of its problems. In a bona fide social agency, the client's affairs are treated as confidentially as they would be by a doctor, a lawyer, or a minister. Despite these objections, in principle community councils with proper leadership represent a useful com-

[7] Helen L. Witmer and Edith Tufts, "The Effectiveness of Delinquency Prevention Programs," No. 350, Washington, U.S. Children's Bureau, 1954, p. 44.

[8] A Community Plans for Its Children, Final Report on Newport News, Va. Project, No. 321, Washington, U.S. Children's Bureau, 1947.

[9] Negley Teeters and John Reinemann, The Challenge of Delinquency, New York, Prentice Hall, 1950, p. 667.

[10] Stephan H. Kneisel, executive director, Philadelphia Crime Prevention Association, Annual Report, 1957.

munity effort to fill in the gaps by making services available to all persons who need them.

Area Projects

Another form of community effort to deal with delinquency is the area project. In the area project, the neighborhood center is the central point of the program. It provides recreational and educational opportunities, and is staffed by persons recruited from the community. The program aims to develop social relations which will result in the acceptance of standards of conduct more nearly like those of a middle-class community. Groups are organized in which parents can discuss with one another their common problems in the rearing of their children. For young people recognized as delinquents, and more specifically for those on parole from the state institutions, individual service is provided. The attempt is to compensate for the usual community rejection of their disapproved behavior and, by accepting them as worthwhile individuals, to increase the deviants' potential regard for conventional values.

Supporters of the area project idea believe that the young people of the community can identify more satisfactorily with so-called "big shots" in the neighborhood than they can with professionally trained workers who come from outside the community and who often do not share its standards.

On the assumption that the majority of these young people are *socially* rather than *emotionally* maladjusted, the area project seeks to provide them with opportunities for attachments to adults who will recognize their attempts to conform to more conventional standards of conduct. If these attachments develop, associations with delinquents and criminals may be relinquished. From the point of view of the area committee, this helping role can be played effectively by a neighbor, the corner grocer, local social leader, ward or precinct official.

The theory behind these cooperative self-help units is that if the community initiates, finances, and manages its own program of social and educational activities, local institutions and public officials will feel responsible for making their services more effective. They will then suppress or eliminate harmful community conditions and practices contributing to delinquency. This will facilitate the eventual absorption of the delinquent into the more conventional life of the community.

The implicit assumptions behind this program are: (1) that delinquency in low-income areas is frequently the result of exposure to destructive social experiences; (2) that effective treatment and prevention can result only from constructive changes in the life of the community; and (3) that these changes can be brought about only if the local community assumes the responsibility for: (a) defining its objectives, (b) formulating its policies, (c) providing financial support and exercising the necessary control over budgets, personnel, and programs.

These assumptions and procedures contrast with the usual prescriptions for "doing things *for* the community." In regarding residents as of inferior status and incapable of providing for their own welfare, the programs of many of the established social agencies disregard the community's own potentialities.

CHICAGO. The first area project, called "back-of-the-yards," was established in Chicago by Clifford Shaw and his associates (see Chapter 7), when their delinquency area studies revealed gang associations closely tied in with neighborhood activities.[11] With the help of local leaders, committees on which clergymen and merchants served were augmented by local politicians, some of whom would doubtlessly have been viewed with suspicion by orthodox social agencies.

Since the initiation of this first Chicago area project, six other communities in Chicago (Hegewisch, Russell Square, South Side, Near West Side, Near Northwest Side, and Near North Side) have organized area projects. The twenty-two centers in these communities, which provide activities for at least 7500 children, are proof of public interest and effort, and of the willingness of the local residents to work for their children's welfare. Individual service has also been given to at least 575 juvenile delinquents and offenders. Some of the gains credited to the Chicago area projects are:

1. Previously untapped resources of local talent and leadership for welfare programs have been discovered.

2. An unanticipated ability not only to raise money but to spend it carefully and wisely has developed.

3. Committees have functioned continuously and effectively, despite turnover and diversity in the backgrounds and social class of their members.

4. Land has been secured for the building of summer camps, and although the leadership is in many instances untutored, effective contacts have been made by parent-teacher associations with school authorities.

5. Action has been taken against junk dealers who receive stolen property, tavern owners who sell liquor to minors, and others who contribute to the delinquency of children.

6. Some parolees have been successfully incorporated into community groups.

The sponsors of these projects are encouraged by the downward trend in delinquency rates since the initiation of the projects, especially in the Russell Square and Near West Side neighborhoods. They believe that if the

[11] See also Saul Alinsky, *Reveille for Radicals,* Chicago, Chicago University Press, 1946.

residents of a community participate in a program for its improvement, their activity, in and of itself, will help to change the community and make it a better place in which to rear children. They believe also that if attempts are made to incorporate the offender into his neighborhood group he is more likely to conform to the conventional standards of behavior.

Assessing the twenty-five-year operation of the Chicago area project, Kobrin[12] comments that the project "embodied Clifford Shaw's philosophy of keeping preventional work focused upon its proper object, the delinquent as a person in his milieu." In Kobrin's opinion it is sociologically sound to expect that if the community in which the adolescent male lives does not provide adequate adult controls, delinquent patterns are likely to prevail. To counteract these patterns, the structure of the community must be altered so that the family, the peer group, and the neighbors offer the adolescent an example of approved behavior.

Kobrin does not claim that over-all favorable changes noted in the delinquency rate are directly attributable to the effects of the area project alone. Nor does he think that it is possible to measure precisely how much improvement has taken place. He does believe, however, that the area project indicates that the efforts of teachers, police, social workers, and court officials are most effective when they plan jointly with the area residents to meet their specific problems and needs.[13]

WASHINGTON, D.C. Basing its program on the experience of a pilot project under the joint sponsorship of the Citizens Council and the United Community Services, Washington, D.C., is currently providing the staff for area councils to prevent delinquency.[14] One half-time and two full-time community organizers have been assigned to each of the twenty-six areas into which the District of Columbia has been divided. A manual is available for guiding organization procedures.

Simultaneously, the Youth Council is sponsoring a school demonstration project to bring maximum services to the 1000 children in two specially selected elementary schools located in Washington's "wickedest precinct." Class size is to be limited to 30 pupils. Provision is made for remedial reading and special classes as needed.

The agenda also includes additional protective services to children in families under care of the Welfare Department, better health service, more effective recreational programs, better liaison between schools and the Welfare

[12] Solomon Kobrin, "The Chicago Area Project—a 25 Year Assessment," *The Annals*, American Academy of Political and Social Science, No. 322 (March 1959), pp. 19-29.

[13] *Ibid.*, pp. 28-29.

[14] *News Notes on Juvenile Delinquency*, Washington, U.S. Children's Bureau, Oct. 14, 1954.

Department for children released from institutions, and better police-juvenile court cooperation.

A Juvenile Control Unit has been organized in the metropolitan police department of the District of Columbia. Arrangements for an intensive in-service training program include enrollment of members of the police force for special courses at the Delinquency Control Institute of the University of Southern California. Simultaneously, the District Public Housing and Re-development Authority is improving the deteriorated neighborhoods by lo-cating small blocks of public housing units in each area.

EVALUATING AREA PROJECTS. In general then, the area project is a democratic device for bringing together representative citizens to improve conditions affecting home and community living. In broadening the horizon of the local citizenry and extending their interest from the people on the block to the community as a whole, no one pattern is followed. The programs evolve out of the needs of the people and their concern with the problems closest to them. If they have had little experience in democratic processes, they may need to work together in small groups before joining with repre-sentatives of more sophisticated agencies. To a considerable degree, the settle-ment house movement has, in the past, performed this role in many com-munities.

Such delinquency prevention programs in low-income communities are handicapped, however, by several conditions both within and without the community. One can distinguish three limiting factors *within* the community.

1. Parents in the low-income bracket cannot provide their children with the means for effective competition with their contemporaries in the more privileged sections of the city. While there is not obviously a one-to-one relationship between poverty and delinquency, continued economic depriva-tion in a highly competitive society in which wealth is both the source of power and prestige and the symbol of success means less regard for members in the low-income group. With success theoretically available to all in a democratic society, poverty is apt to be associated with inferiority, or even perversity of character.

2. In low-income areas the prestige of the powerful criminal and political organization, well-known to the children, may be one of the most direct social factors contributing to the delinquency of both children and adults. Attempts to deal with these forces from outside the community have been generally un-successful for any prolonged period.

3. The constant change of population in the low-income areas can easily interfere with the development of common interests and collective action on the part of local residents.

The forces *outside* of the community which militate against the applica-tion of the principle of the self-help project are:

1. There is difficulty in raising money from the usual sources unless speedy success can be guaranteed. This particular field of work has no "financial pull."

2. The prevailing administrative pattern in the community invests authority in a central board which delegates it to an administrative staff. This "front-office" psychology generally subordinates the very persons whom the organization is supposed to serve, and therefore tends to resist the self-help or area plan that places the responsibilities squarely on the people in the community themselves rather than on the professional staff.

3. The usual procedure of working with the "good" elements of the community fails to recognize, as the area projects do, that the "bad" elements are equally a part of the community, and that to disregard them will not help them to conform to accepted moral standards.

4. Professionally trained social workers often object to the use of the untrained worker. In the opinion of the area project sponsors, however, professional training is *secondary* to the manifest interest in the welfare of the delinquent, identification with the community, and the approach to the individual on a natural basis.

5. Because the local leadership of institutions and agencies has not been invited to assume responsibility for either management or operation, it is difficult to establish good working relations with them in the area project. As a consequence, many residents of low-income communities have developed resistance to what appears to them to be the "agency" attitudes that prevail in American society. In the opinion of residents of these areas, the emphasis upon agency reputation and self-perpetuation should be secondary to a critical re-examination of methods and program.

Summary

As preventive methods have more definitely focused on services rather than on programs of repression and punishment, *community councils* have developed as attempts to coordinate available services so that they will bear more directly and efficiently on the needs of young persons in trouble. Beginning in California in the 1930s, the community councils have assumed various forms in the large cities across the country, and today are found in many communities under many auspices. The diffuse nature of their operations, however, makes it difficult to estimate their effectiveness in any but descriptive terms.

Area projects, on the other hand, are usually more specifically focused. Their goal is to broaden the horizon of a local citizen and extend his interest from his neighbors on the block to the community as a whole. Programs vary, depending upon the needs as defined by the community and upon the experience of the citizens in working through the democratic process. We have descriptions of area projects in Washington, D.C., Philadelphia, and a half-dozen communities in Chicago, where they have been most highly developed. The philosophy of an area pulling itself up by its own boot straps was initiated in the back-of-the-yards project of Shaw and Alinsky.

Obstacles faced by these area projects include the resistance of some organized agencies, the difficulty of securing funds, the necessity of combatting the prestige of some of the powerful criminal and political organizations which operate in many of the lower-income communities. In spite of these negative factors, however, the efforts of the community councils and the area projects are in line with the social casework theory that help is most likely to be effective if the individuals needing it participate actively in searching for it and putting it into operation.

CHAPTER 28

Prevention Through Increased Services to Individuals

THIS CHAPTER PRESENTS THE MAJOR EFFORTS AT PREVENTION THROUGH such special programs focused on the individual delinquent as: (1) opportunities for recreation; (2) additional services in schools; (3) a combination of services to school children and their families; and (4) "aggressive casework" for reaching families reluctant to accept help with their erring children.

Leisure-Time Activities

As with the Police Athletic League program in New York (see Chapter 14), the proverb "Satan finds mischief for idle hands to do" is undoubtedly the rationale behind most proposals for providing recreational opportunities to prevent and to cure delinquency. Some programs, such as PAL's, have the broad aims of developing good character, instilling a sense of responsibility, and promoting a friendly relationship between girls and boys and police officers; and the hope is that if those who enforce the law are respected, the law itself will be respected.[1] Other leisure-time programs have the more specific goal of modifying the behavior of the delinquent or the potential delinquent, and several studies have claimed that providing expanded recreational opportunities could make a serious dent on the delinquency problem.

In assessing the effectiveness of these services it is essential to state

[1] Speech by Deputy Police Commissioner James B. Nolan, annual meeting of the New York State Welfare Conference, Nov. 1950.

476

whether change will be measured in terms of a decrease in the rate of delinquency or by means of perceived changes in the individual's behavior. In any event, whether recreational activities will check delinquency depends in part on the delinquent's interest in the activities. In some neighborhoods, despite the community's disapproval, delinquency *is* recreation. The alternatives offered by playgrounds and settlements meet stiff competition from the frequently more exciting activities initiated by the boys themselves. Nor can it be assumed that a young person's avoidance of supervised recreational activities implies that he is engaged in delinquent behavior. Many so-called "normal" boys share the delinquent's preference for self-initiated leisure-time activities.

Truxal Study

In 1925 Truxal carried out an elaborate study in New York City for the National Recreation Commission.[2] He tabulated juvenile court cases by health area of residence in the Borough of Manhattan in New York City, and compared them with the provision of recreational centers. Contrary to the expectation of the sponsors, the statistics did not demonstrate that in areas with playgrounds and parks the rate of delinquents was lower than in areas without these facilities. The obvious shortcomings of this study were:

1. It assumed that all delinquents need recreational opportunities.

2. No study was made of the nature of the recreational provisions. As noted in previous chapters, qualified leaders as well as adequate play space are both necessary for a constructive experience.

Only three studies of the relation between delinquency prevention and recreation, in the opinion of Witmer and Tufts,[3] meet the criteria for adequate evaluation. The first of these studies was carried out by Thrasher in New York City in 1927; the second was that of Shanas and Dunning in Chicago in 1938; and the third by Ellery Reed in Cincinnati in 1942. Below we discuss the methods and the findings of each of these three studies, along with a more recent study in Louisville, Kentucky.

New York City Boys' Club Study

A famous investigation relating recreational activity to delinquency is the Boys' Club Study of 1927,[4] conducted by Frederic Thrasher, known for

[2] Andrew G. Truxal, *Outdoor Recreation Legislation and Its Effectiveness,* New York, Columbia University Press, 1929.

[3] Helen L. Witmer and Edith Tufts, *The Effectiveness of Delinquency Prevention Programs,* No. 350, Washington, U.S. Children's Bureau, 1954.

[4] Frederic M. Thrasher, "The Boys' Clubs and Juvenile Delinquency," *American Journal of Sociology,* Vol. 42 (July 1936), pp. 66-80.

his pioneering study of the gangs in Chicago (see Chapter 9). The Boys' Club Study was concerned with the effect of membership in the clubs on the incidence of juvenile delinquency in the East Harlem area where the program was initiated.

The club members were predominantly children of poor foreign-born parents with little formal education. An intensive study of 60 problem boys disclosed extreme disorganization and poverty—factors which were obviously beyond the power of a boys' club program to neutralize in the short time spent each week in a club's mass activity program.

The club apparently never attracted more than 60 per cent of its capacity—4000 boys—and only half of those who were members had been identified as delinquents. Furthermore, there was a 33 per cent turnover in club membership in each of the four years covered. And, most discouraging, while 18 per cent of the numbers were known as delinquents when they first joined the club, after participation in club activities, the percentage of delinquents rose to 28. Thus, with each year of continued membership, the proportion of delinquents increased. Thrasher's conclusion that "the Boys' Club program is one of the most important and essential elements in any crime prevention program . . . and we shall need many more boys' clubs to perform the function of crime prevention adequately," appears to be a non-sequitur.

One explanation for the increase in the percentage of delinquents among the older members is that with each year of membership and corresponding increase in age, the chance of being apprehended as a delinquent appears to increase. The community's reaction to the behavior of an 11-year-old is more apt to be punitive than in the case of an 8-, 9-, or 10-year-old. As the boy grows older the community assumes that his behavior is intentional and he could have controlled it if he had so wished. Increasing age also tends to bring increasingly threatening forms of delinquency.

To prove or disprove any causal relationship between membership in a boy's club and delinquency would require a very different kind of study design than that employed by Thrasher.

Louisville Boys' Club Study

New York University Center for Community and Field Services has released a more sophisticated study of the effect of a boys' club in Louisville, Kentucky.[5] The method used was a comparison of the changes in the official delinquency rates among boys of comparable age in the area served by the

[5] Roscoe C. Brown, Jr., *A Boys' Club and Delinquency, a Study of the Statistical Incidence of Juvenile Delinquency in Three Areas in Louisville, Kentucky,* New York, New York University Center for Community and Field Services, Monograph 2, 1956.

boys' club with those in two other areas which differed from it chiefly with respect to the provision of services for boys. Although the ratio of delinquents in the boys' club area did decline appreciably in comparison with the control areas, the authors of the study refrain from claiming that the boys' club was responsible. And they do not advocate further replication of statistical studies. Instead they suggest a plan that appears to us to offer more hope, i.e., psychosocial observation of 500 matched pairs of boys, from several cities, in which one set of boys belongs to a boys' club and the other does not.

Chicago Study

Shanas and Dunning[6] studied records of participation in recreational facilities in Chicago during the years 1938-39 for approximately 15,000 boys and 8000 girls, 10 to 17 years old, and resident in five areas, four of them slums. "Official delinquents" were considered to be those who had been known to the police or the juvenile court in the five years preceding the study. "Unofficial delinquents" were young people described by the personnel of the cooperating agencies as addicted to stealing, truancy, malicious mischief, and so forth, even if they were not known to the police or the court.

In distinguishing the official and unofficial delinquents with respect to their use of the facilities, the conclusions were as follows:

1. Regardless of the area of residence, recreational facilities were used by larger proportions of nondelinquents (95 per cent) than delinquents (63 per cent).

2. In the area with the lowest delinquency rate, however, participation in agency activities was more nearly equal in the two groups.

3. There was more participation in the agency's program by younger than by older boys.

Describing the nature of the activities and the participation of delinquents and nondelinquents, the authors concluded:

1. Delinquent boys who participated in recreational activities spent more time in them than did the nondelinquent boys. The total amount of time spent in the agency by either official or unofficial delinquents ranged from 43 to 88 hours a year. Translated into number of sessions, this meant from 20 to 40 sessions a year. In the *supervised activities,* however, between a third and a half of all participants spent less than 10 hours annually.

2. Official delinquents, in comparison with unofficial delinquents, chose the less closely supervised activities, i.e., games and competitive sports rather than club activities. This choice was most marked in the slum areas.

3. About one third of the delinquents in the more advantaged neigh-

6 Ethel Shanas and Catherine Dunning, *Recreation and Delinquency,* Chicago, Recreation Commission, 1942.

borhoods, in contrast to two thirds in the slum areas, participated in the activities.

4. Both delinquent and nondelinquent boys said they spent about twice as much time in the movies as they did in supervised recreation.

The finding with respect to the changing incidence of official delinquency during the period of study and the use of recreational facilities disclosed that approximately 2 per cent of those participating in the recreational program, in comparison with 5 per cent of the nonparticipants, were known to the court. Some 10 per cent of the official delinquents using the recreational facilities persisted in their delinquent acts, in comparison with 16 per cent of those who did not use the recreational facilities.

If these findings are typical of other communities, not much can be expected of recreational programs in preventing delinquency. In the first place, they attract relatively few children and, in the second place, the children who come spend so little time in the activities that it is unlikely that changes in behavior patterns will result. The difference in the official delinquency rate between the users and nonusers of the recreational facilities might appear to suggest that recreational activities prevent delinquency. As Witmer and Tufts note, however, "unless these two groups of boys were fairly much alike in other respects, it may well be that the figures only show that the delinquents and near-delinquents who use recreational facilities are the ones who are less likely to commit offenses.[7]

Cincinnati Study

To determine how the characteristics of delinquent children differ from those of children who attend group work agencies, Ellery Reed examined the records of fifty young people chosen at random from the April 1940 docket of the Cincinnati Juvenile Court.[8] He found that fewer than one fourth of those known to the court had been in contact with group work agencies prior to their court appearance.

In comparing the two groups, i.e., those known to the agencies and those known to the court, Reed concludes that:

1. The children in the court series came in significantly larger proportions from underprivileged areas (51 per cent), in comparison with those known to the group work agencies (37 per cent).

2. Families with children before the court were the more disorganized, as measured by the number of social agencies to which they were known.

[7] Witmer and Tufts, op. cit., p. 20.

[8] Ellery Reed, "How Effective are Group Work Agencies in Preventing Delinquency?" The Social Service Review, Vol. 22 (Sept. 1948), pp. 340-48; and idem, Focus, Vol. 28, no. 6 (Nov. 1949), pp. 170-76.

3. Among the young people known to the court there were smaller proportions of Caucasians, of girls, and of children under 15 than among those known to the group work agencies.

According to these findings the Cincinnati group work agencies were serving children who differed in a considerable number of respects from those identified as delinquents by the court.

As a second phase of his study, Reed sought to determine whether the clientèle of the group work agencies included children whose behavior was similar to that of the official delinquents. When he checked the names of the 1700 group work agency members against the juvenile court file for the year 1944, he found that slightly less than 10 per cent of the members had court records before they participated in the group work activities. The older the child, the more likely was a registration of official delinquency.

Reed concluded that although the rate of delinquency among the clientèle of the group work agency was not as high as it was in the city as a whole for each age group, regardless of the economic status of the neighborhood, one could not claim that the group work program was the preventive agent. The sound inference appeared to be that since the clientèle of the group work agencies, in comparison with that of the court, contained larger proportions of young children, and smaller proportions of the underprivileged and insecure elements in the population, there was an unintended predominance of nondelinquents in the group work agencies.

In summary, if the group work agencies in other cities are similar to those in Cincinnati, they serve fewer boys and girls in danger of becoming delinquents. And, as Witmer and Tufts put it, the very nature of their programs appears to screen out "the boys and girls who are handicapped physically, mentally, economically or racially, or who are emotionally maladjusted or have an unfortunate or unhappy family background."[9]

School Programs

We turn now to the second set of juvenile delinquency programs—those focused on the school. Since, as we noted in Chapter 10, many people credit the school with considerable responsibility both for causing and for controlling delinquency, it is no surprise to find that the school is the locale of services to prevent delinquency. The three programs described below—in Passaic, New Jersey; Gary, Indiana; and New York City—include some evaluation of the results. In each, the school plays a *central* but *different* role in the program for delinquency prevention.

[9] Witmer and Tufts, *op. cit.*, p. 24, fn. 20.

Passaic, New Jersey

The Passaic, New Jersey, Children's Bureau was modeled after the bureau initiated originally by Mayor Hague of Jersey City in the early 1930s to forestall the referral of children to the juvenile court (see Chapter 2). The Passaic Bureau still investigates all complaints made to the police, all children apprehended by the police, and all children whom the teachers, social workers, or others in the community believe to be in need of help. Psychiatric, psychological, and other clinical studies are made, and social treatment provided as needed. The staff consists of the director of the school's guidance program, counselors, attendance officers, a social worker, a remedial reading instructor, four police officers, and a psychiatrist.[10]

In testing the efficacy of this program in 1945 its director checked subsequent police arrests of all clients of the bureau who had then reached the age of 16.[11] He found that only 15 per cent of the boys and girls had been arrested for any violation other than that of motor vehicle ordinances. He did not, however, as we believe was necessary, compare these figures with the incidence of arrest for the different age and sex groups in the comparable general population at the time.

Gary, Indiana

Unlike the general goal of the Passaic program, that in Gary, Indiana, was to alleviate and prevent a specific form of delinquency—truancy from school. In this experiment, initiated by the director of the Department of Child Welfare in the Public Schools of Gary, truancy was redefined as school resistance.[12]

According to Mark Roser, an efficient school, i.e., one sensitive to all a child's needs, seeks through cooperative efforts with the child's family and the community to achieve those values which are the foundation of the good life: "... the process is democratic in nature, expanding in contact, exploratory in approach, and flexible in operation."[13] Obviously the operations of the school are circumscribed by the culture in which it functions. A disorganized, socially unhealthful home or neighborhood probably adds to the difficulty of bringing up and educating healthy children.

[10] Benjamin Fine, 1,000,000 *Delinquents*, New York, World, 1955. Chapter 9, "Guidance for Delinquents," gives a fairly complete description of the Passaic and other school programs, pp. 179-86.

[11] William C. Kvaraceus, *Juvenile Delinquency and the School*, New York, World, 1945, p. 16.

[12] Mark Roser, "The Role of the Schools in Heading Off Delinquency," *Yearbook*, National Probation and Parole Association, 1951; see also Chapter 10 for discussion of Roser's theory.

[13] Roser, *op. cit.*, p. 169.

To expect the school to cure truancy is about as effective as treatment would be in a hospital in which all patients were placed in the same kind of ward, given the same medication, and told that if they didn't get well they would be punished. To help truants effectively requires an understanding of why each child behaves as he does. Assigning them to special classes often precipitates fights in the hallways and playgrounds—additional evidence to the truant that the school rejects him. The nonlearner in an average class, unless he receives special help, is usually the most completely rejected child in the group. We agree with Roser that referral to the court to force boys and girls to remain in school and to experience continued failure is illogical, harmful, and socially wasteful.

The Gary experiment included approximately 100 children who attended school irregularly—one fourth of them were chronic truants. About 30 continually misbehaved, fought, or quarreled. A special school setting was designed for these 100 children, who were placed in classes of not more than 15 members. Attendance was not compulsory. Sessions were a half day in length, to allow "these anxious and fear-ridden children more freedom and an experience of time-free activity." While they were taught to read and write, free play, drawing, and related activities were also emphasized. The plan sought to provide experiences which would give the children a feeling of success each day. "These children were given an extra dose of 'nurture'; the learning process was restarted on their own level; additional freedom and like-grouping resulted in a reduction of hostility and rejection."[14] Casework counseling was provided for the parents to counteract their negative attitudes toward their children.

After two years in this special setting, truancy was no longer a problem. One fourth of the children who participated gained more than 10 points in their IQ tests, and the majority of parents commented on their improved behavior at home.

The Harlem Project[15]

Because a single junior high school in the Harlem area of New York City was contributing an undue proportion of children to the juvenile court, in 1943 the New York Foundation persuaded the Board of Education to cooperate in providing additional services and facilities to three schools in the area. The sponsors believed that even if they could not change the social

14 *Ibid.*, p. 177.
15 *The Role of the School in Preventing and Correcting Maladjustment and Delinquency, A Study in Three Schools*, report on the Harlem Project, sponsored jointly by the New York Foundation and the Board of Education of the City of New York, Sept. 1943 to June 1945. See also Chapter 15, in which the School Services are described, and Chapter 9, in which the gang aspects in the Harlem area are discerned.

and economic conditions under which the Harlem children lived, the quality of their school experience could be improved. Sympathetic and understanding teachers, an interesting curriculum, a well-staffed and well-equipped after-school recreational program might, they argued, offset some of the handicaps of living in a rapidly deteriorating area. Psychiatric and medical services as well as remedial tutoring and vocational guidance were provided.

The three schools selected were: Junior High School No. 120 for boys, located in a new building across the street from Mount Morris Park, and accommodating about 1400; Junior High School No. 101 for girls, located in an old building on Lexington Avenue and 111th Street; and Public School No. 10, an elementary 6-B school located on St. Nicholas Avenue and 116th Street, many of whose pupils continued their education in these junior high schools. The results in the two junior high schools are detailed here.

JHS 120

THE RESULTS. The fluctuation in the statistics for truancy and delinquency in the two-year period in this school did not reveal a decrease in the actual incidence of antisocial behavior. The project did, however, provide clear evidence of the needs of the boys, and their attitudes toward the curriculum and toward the teachers. Yet, although the skills of the teachers and their attitudes toward students were also documented, it could not be claimed that the clinical services in this school were to any large degree effective in changing either the boys' behavior or the attitudes of the teachers to the boys.

THE BOYS' ATTITUDES TOWARD SCHOOL. The boys who were referred to the school clinic talked about their school life without rancor. They said they preferred the departmental system of the junior high school to the elementary school home room system because, in the latter, if you got mad at the teacher and stayed there all day, you stayed mad. When you changed classes, as you did in junior high, you got pleased by the time you moved to the next teacher.[16]

In describing their attitude toward the teachers, more than two thirds of the boys voluntarily mentioned being hit by the teacher, the class president, or the monitor. Describing disciplinary practices, they said:

"She's nice. She don't yell at you, just kicks you in the shins and makes you get back in line."

"He even gets at your notebook. If it ain't neat, he rips it up."

"He makes like he's going to slap you; you duck and he don't hit you."

"He makes you go through the mill" (a line-up in which a boy gets a lick from each classmate and a final whack from the teacher).

[16] *The Role of the School in Preventing and Correcting Maladjustment and Delinquency*, p. 30.

"He sprays you with water if you talk after the bell."

"He sets a curfew, and if you talk you have to bend over and let the monitor hit you."

"He's fair, he cracks your knuckles; then you can explain whether or not you deserved it and he takes off your demerits."[17]

Apparently, the boys neither questioned nor strongly resented this kind of treatment. What happened at school may possibly have been similar to what happened at home. The clinic staff was, in fact, surprised by the boys' passive acceptance of the school discipline. Apparently, no boy considered discussing his experience with any member of the school faculty.

The study revealed startling gaps between the boys' capacities, as measured by their IQ's, and their accomplishments. Although the median IQ was 99 for the group studied, only one tenth of the boys read at their grade level, and all were retarded in arithmetic.

The boys saw no relation between their school accomplishments and job opportunities. None of them had discussed their vocational ambitions with anyone at the school, and few of their parents had ever come to the school to discuss their children's progress.

TEACHER SKILL. In order to appraise any effect which the presence of the project might have on the atmosphere in the classroom, arrangements were made for observations of the teachers during the first and second year. The observers were members of the departments of education of New York City's municipal colleges. In their opinion 40 per cent of the lessons they observed had been inadequately planned. The teaching methods of 20 per cent of the teachers were described as formal and routine. The approach of the teachers to the pupils was described as "poor," "patronizing," or "listless" in one fifth of the observations, and "authoritative" or "scolding" in another fifth. The pupils' response to the teaching was described as "uninterested" in more than one third of the classes. And there was no appreciable difference between the observations at the end of the first and second years with respect to the quality of classroom instruction or the nature of the boys' response.

The over-all appraisal of the teachers in this school by people responsible for training teachers in the city system rated about one quarter (23 per cent) as below the city's average.[18]

Explanations for the low ratings included: the number of teachers assigned to the school who were unsympathetic or hostile to Negroes; the excessively high proportion of substitute teachers and the consequent shifting of teacher personnel; the lack of training or preparation of teachers to meet

17 *Ibid.*, p. 31.
18 *Ibid.*, p. 57.

the problems of an underprivileged community, and the school system's failure to provide in-service training.

The sponsoring committee of the project concluded that no school could be expected to meet and handle problems of so many disturbed adolescents. Too many of these children had been so repeatedly knocked about, rejected, and punished that their rebellion and aggression seemed a reasonable response.

J H S 101

THE PROJECT. In contrast to the project in the junior high school for boys, the program in J H S 101 for girls achieved its goal: a demonstration that, given special services, most "unmanageable" girls can be adjusted in the regular school. The assets in this girls' junior high school were a cooperative principal and a relatively stable faculty of more than average ability.

The project enriched the academic school program by providing for remedial reading, instruction in arithmetic, speech correction, and health work. Additional staff was made available for group and individual guidance as well as for classes in dramatics, pottery, child care, art, and Spanish dancing. The after-school recreation program was staffed by five specially equipped workers who cooperated with the day-school staff.

THE CLIENTÈLE. During the two years of the project's operation, 100 girls who had been designated as unmanageable were referred by the elementary schools in the district. Of these 67 were accepted. The 33 whose parents refused to cooperate provided a control group.

The label "unmanageable" included girls whose behavior was aggressive or disruptive toward teachers or students, ranging all the way from clowning to violent outbursts of temper. In the reports of their elementary school teachers these girls were described as obstinate, uncontrolled, quarrelsome, tough, rebellious, uncooperative, resentful. Some refused to work, some resented correction or authority. A few had threatened the teacher or indulged in temper tantrums. Some teachers who "diagnosed" the girls saw evidence of "persecution complex, psychopathic traits, emotional instability," exhibitionism, and antisocial attitudes.[19]

The majority of the girls accepted in the project were Negroes. The remainder were Spanish, Italian, and Puerto Rican. Two thirds were retarded one or more terms. About half of the girls had IQ's ranging from 75 to 90; 5 were in the above-normal range, from 110 to 130. The average IQ was 89. Thus, the referring schools were not associating difficult behavior exclusively with subnormal intelligence, nor was truancy the major problem. On the other hand, unmanageability was associated with poor work marks.

An analysis of the school record cards for each girl showed that failures

[19] *Ibid.*, p. 71.

increased as these girls moved from the elementary to the junior high school. Practically all those for whom data were available had experienced several shifts in school, rarely remaining long enough in any one elementary school to feel they belonged to it. In the six years before they entered junior high school 40 per cent had attended three or four schools, and another 40 per cent had been in five or more schools.

The families of the girls, like those of the boys in J H S 120, had felt the effects of the depression years, and many had received some form of public aid. At the time the girls were referred to the project, about half of the families were on the active list of one or more social agencies. Those who were not receiving financial aid were perhaps living on a more marginal level than if they had been receiving relief. Forty per cent of the girls were living with their mothers only; and in some homes in which the father was present, there was severe conflict. The clinic records revealed "gross social pathology," as well as other sociological factors which might create unmanageability.[20]

The project provided the usual type of child guidance service, i.e., treatment either in cooperation with other agencies or by the clinic staff. The clinic goal was real improvement, not superficial compliance with the rules and regulations of the school. Suggestions were made to the teachers for direct help in the classroom. Although the control group was not accepted for care by the clinic, some suggestions were made to their teachers as to ways in which their problems might be adjusted.

THE OUTCOME. At the end of the two-year period, the teachers of the 67 girls reported five indices of improvement:

More than 70 per cent of the project cases, in comparison with one third of the control girls, were rated as having improved in school behavior since the time of referral.

The teachers' criteria for improvement of the girls under care were: decrease in disturbing behavior, better attendance, greater effort in school work, and better conduct. The teachers used a rating scale designed by the project staff to cover group relations, teacher-pupil relations, work habits, adjustment to school routine, and also over-all adjustment. While the clinic was concerned not only with the girls' adjustment in school but with their home and community life, the clinic staff agreed that *the teachers' judgment of improvement meant real adjustment.*

To estimate the adjustment of the 33 girls in the control group, data were gathered by the clinic social worker with student assistants from the New York School of Social Work. Visits were made to the referring schools; principals, guidance workers, and sometimes the individual teachers were interviewed. Their replies, recorded on special observation schedules, were

---

[20] "Gross social pathology" had been reported in January 1939 by a committee of principals on the conditions in the schools of Harlem, *ibid.*, p. 71.

discussed with the psychiatric social worker and the project staff member who had originally investigated the girls' eligibility for inclusion in the project. (In the opinion of the research director, the author of this textbook, the study would have been improved if all the girls and their families had been re-interviewed and revisited; this, however, did not prove possible because of time limitations.)

The second conclusion was that *poor home conditions did not appear to be an insurmountable obstacle to behavior adjustment.* Given individual and special help, girls from these homes were strengthened to withstand the impact of home difficulties.

In the third place, *the type of emotional maladjustment had no relation to the outcome,* i.e., whether the diagnosis was psychoneurotic (10 cases), reactive behavior type (25), or schizoid (6).

In the fourth place, *the most important factor in the improvement in teacher-pupil relationship was teacher effectiveness.* On the basis of the ratings of teacher effectiveness referred to above, after testing the findings for significant difference, the chances for adjustment of unmanageable girls were greater when they were placed in the classes of the above-average teachers.[21]

And finally, *the effort of the school to carry out the suggestions was an additional positive factor in the girls' adjustment.*

It should be recalled that at the time of the original referral, all 100 girls had manifested some type of aggressive behavior toward their teachers or their classmates. The only evident original difference between the *project* and the *control* girls was the willingness of the former's parents to accept the project's services. At the termination of the project, adjustment was regarded as good for about *three fourths* of the project girls (in those cases in which the school undertook to carry out the clinic recommendations), in comparison with *one half* of the control girls.

The project staff, as well as the teachers in the school, considered that the project had been successful; more so, perhaps, in its first goal, i.e., adjustment of unmanageable girls, than in the second, i.e., "to spread the mental hygiene approach towards all pupils." Truancy and lateness were reduced to a minimum; and school officials were convinced that the so-called problem girls could continue to be referred to J H S 101 from other schools with a good chance of ceasing to be problems. The deprived home and community lives of these underprivileged children had apparently not twisted all of them beyond straightening. "Without waiting for the day when economic and social problems may be solved on a broad scale," the project staff believed that "the public schools can begin now to reduce the amount of anti-social behavior so often associated with such problems."[22]

---

[21] *Ibid.*, p. 85.
[22] *Ibid.*, p. 95.

EFFECT ON TEACHERS. There was a change in teacher attitude as the clinic and teaching staff came to understand each other better. A specially designed questionnaire distributed to 52 teachers and returned by 44, without signatures, yielded the following results:

1. 63 per cent said they had gained *professionally* from the project;

2. 70 per cent said they had gained *personally* from the project, i.e., they had learned to attach greater importance to the need for friendship between teacher and child;

3. 71 per cent considered the project successful.

Asked for their recommendations for the school system as a result of the experience, however, slightly less than half said they thought the project had value for the school system. Slightly more than one third of those who were critical believed that the girls set a bad example; and some felt that the project demanded too much time.

The clinic experience indicated that often it was difficult for a teacher to accept suggestions about behavior that threatened her feeling of security in the classroom or implied lack of respect for her authority. Not until the recommendation was interpreted as the child's need for an accepting and affectionate parent-substitute were most teachers able to accede to the suggestion.

FOLLOW-UP OF PROJECT GIRLS. To determine whether the adjustment achieved in the junior high school was maintained after the girls left the project school, the careers of the girls who attended senior high school were followed.[23] Unhappily, however, the good results did not carry over in their subsequent school careers, possibly because "of the withdrawal of the mother substitutes provided by the social worker or teacher of the Junior High School 101, in the case of girls whose problems stemmed so clearly from the emotional deprivations in the mother-child relationship."[24]

The sponsoring committee recommended that the type of additional services provided through the project in J H S 101 should begin in the ele-

[23] Master theses in New York School of Social Work: Helen Terry, "Follow-up study of the girl referred to but not accepted by special project in Public School 101," Project No. 1912; Jacqueline Hariston, "Follow-up study of girls receiving special services at Public School 101," Project No. 1934; Virginia O'Neill, "A follow-up study of 12 girls from two Junior High Schools who were not accepted for experimental project in Junior High School 101, Manhattan," Project No. 1951; Edith Eisner, "The present adjustment of 15 girl graduates of Junior High School 101 who were served by the experimental treatment program in the school," Project No. 2025; Joan Barnert, "A second follow-up study of the girls referred to but not accepted by special project in Public School 101," Project No. 2063; Marian Thurman, "Study of the 8 girls who were committed to institutions after being under full care of the Harlem Project in Junior High School 101," Project No. 2127; Betty Feldman, "A comparative study of the results obtained in a 1945 and 1946 follow-up study of the adjustment of 27 girls graduated from the Harlem Project at Manhattan Junior High School 101," Project No. 2275.

[24] *The Role of the School in Preventing and Correcting Maladjustment and Delinquency*, p. 90.

mentary schools and extend to the high schools, trade schools, and vocational schools. If the unmanageable girl is to adjust and hold her own within the regular school setting, she must receive help as soon as she needs it, and until she can stand alone.[25]

Combinations of Services to Children and Their Families

Cambridge-Somerville Youth Study[26]

Unlike the Harlem Project, which concentrated on services provided by the school to prevent delinquency, the Cambridge-Somerville Youth Study undertook to provide a variety of services to young people who were rated by teachers and clinicians as to the likelihood of their becoming delinquents. The initiative and financing for the Cambridge-Somerville study was provided by Dr. Richard Cabot who, at the National Conference of Social Work in Boston in 1931, had stated his conviction that the time had come for social agencies to *demonstrate* and not just to *acclaim* their positive results.

Cabot hypothesized that the way to prevent delinquency was to build character during the formative years. To test this hypothesis, 750 boys attending the Cambridge and Somerville, Massachusetts, schools were classified as to the likelihood of their becoming delinquent. This was done through interviews with teachers, physical and psychological tests, and psychiatric interviews. After classification, a flip of the coin determined which was to be the treatment and which the control boy. The caseload of each counselor included some boys for whom the delinquency prediction was negative, but none of the counselors knew the predictive rating of the boys.

The project provided individual counseling, tutoring, camp and recreational facilities, correction of health defects, medical care and, when necessary, financial assistance from family or community agencies. The services began in 1936 and terminated in 1945.

The first two evaluations of the project upon its termination yielded no significant findings with respect to the incidence of overt and apprehended delinquency or improvement in the treatment group in comparison with the control group. The chief value of these evaluation attempts was in pointing out the difficulties of appraising psychological growth and maturity by tests and rating scales that rely heavily on subjective interpretations.

Because the sponsors of the project and the staff were dissatisfied with these negative results, Powers and Witmer were asked to try their hands at an evaluation. They began by questioning Cabot's hypothesis that the control

[25] *Ibid.*, p. 99.
[26] Edwin Powers and Helen L. Witmer, *An Experiment in the Prevention of Delinquency*, New York, Columbia University Press, 1951.

method was an appropriate way to study the problem. In their opinion, comparisons in terms of averages not only frequently obliterate wide differences in individual reactions but fail to provide answers which are useful to those who work with individuals. The control method does not reveal whether it was the new factor—in this case, counseling service—or one or more of the old factors that produced the results. Conversely, even if no significant differences appear between the control and the treatment group, there is no certainty that the new factor has not been important.

Their second assumption was that a medical analogy was inappropriate, because the concepts of delinquency and of good character lack the definiteness of a disease, and social services lack the specificity of a medical remedy. As a result, the Cambridge-Somerville experiment was, in their opinion, as scientific as "a medical one would be in which different kinds of medicine were given to patients suffering from different kinds of disorders by doctors who hold different theories as to the cause of illness."[27] A third difficulty lay in measuring success or failure in crime prevention in terms of the young person's development of social responsibility and character.

Powers and Witmer proposed a more modest alternative for evaluation, i.e., to determine whether the boys appeared to benefit from the counselor's service, and whether those who benefited were better "adjusted" than their controls. This process involved:

1. Grouping the boys according to their characteristics and those of their families.

2. Classifying the kind of treatment that each boy was given.

3. Determining whether there were results from any combination of boy types and treatment methods that could be regarded as fairly uniform.

Despite the impressionistic nature of the appraisal and the absence of an independent check of the records or a recheck of the objective tests used in the two interim evaluations, Powers and Witmer's findings are of interest.

THE BOYS AND THEIR HOMES. In the main, the boys accepted in the program were in good health, had fairly normal intelligence, and lived under poor or relatively poor financial conditions, with corresponding housing and neighborhood situations. A large proportion had foreign-born or culturally foreign parents.

In the matter of the boys' behavior, the majority appeared to be only mildly maladjusted, if at all. Only one seventh revealed extreme problems of emotional or social maladjustment. More than half showed no evidence of either official or unofficial delinquent behavior. About 17 per cent had engaged in such delinquent conduct as stealing or persistent truancy. Thus, by either classification—official delinquency or problem behavior—at least half the boys appeared to have little wrong with them. A considerable pro-

27 *Ibid.*, p. 343.

portion of those who were considered delinquent did not seem to be headed for official delinquency, as far as could be judged by their conduct at the time that the experiment began.

Classification of the boys' homes revealed that none of the well-adjusted boys and only about one in 15 of those judged to be slightly maladjusted came from homes which were graded "C" in respect to the emotional atmosphere, i.e., with parents who were overprotective or overindulgent. On the other hand, all but three of the extremely maladjusted boys came from "C" homes. More striking perhaps is the finding that 80 per cent of the boys who were judged to be well-adjusted came from homes that were rated "A" with respect to the emotional climate, i.e., with good parent-child relations.

The "A," "B," "C" classification of the emotional climate of the homes corresponds to the "Good," "Fair," "Poor" designations which concentrated on the social situation. The ratings were arrived at as follows:

> Each family situation was looked at from the viewpoint of the prevailing mores, and we considered to what extent the parents behaved toward each other and their children as custom prescribes. Such a way of viewing the matter permitted some latitude when foreign-born families or those of some definite American sub-culture were under consideration. In general, however, the families were rated on the assumption that parents shall be "faithful" to each other, shall not quarrel excessively, shall provide adequate food, shelter, and clothing for the children, shall care for the children's physical needs and instruct them, without harsh discipline, in social rules and customs, that they shall supervise their conduct, guide their development, and handle them with at least a reasonable degree of kindliness.[28]

THE NATURE OF THE SOCIAL SERVICES PROVIDED. The choice of counselors was not limited to those with formal social work training. Among the nineteen who served for various periods of time (World War II interrupted the service) eight had professional social work training, two were psychologists, one was a trained nurse, and the remaining eight had had some social work courses. Cabot's aim was to secure the services of men and women who expressed an interest in working with difficult boys, could presumably establish friendly relations with them, and would bring energy and imagination to the job. Halfway through the project a supervisor was added to the staff. Prior to that, each staff member had worked independently, using his native skills, his personality, and the available resources.

Analysis of working methods revealed that they ranged from what might be called "Big Brother" activities, conducted on a full-time paid basis, to various forms of social casework. Some counselors saw their boys frequently, a few made no home visits, some paid a great deal of attention to members

---

[28] *Ibid.,* p. 358.

of the family, while others concentrated on the boy. In Witmer's opinion the variation in the kind and the amount of service appeared to be related to the circumstances of the boy's situation rather than to the difference in the counselor's approach.

MEASURING THE RESULTS. Since at the termination of the services in 1945, equal proportions of the treatment and control groups appeared to be well-adjusted, it was concluded that "delinquency and social maladjustment are not prevented by programs under which hard-working, well-disposed individuals do all that they can to offset the disadvantages under which boys live."[29]

Searching for more definitive tests of the effectiveness of the program, Powers and Witmer reversed the control group method to determine, case by case, whether or not the treated boy had benefited, and compared his adjustment with that of his control. Their aim was to see whether the services of the counselor had made any perceptible difference in the long run; and if so, under what circumstances in the boy's life, and which treatment method appeared to have helped.

"Help" was defined in a social work sense as help to the individual in dealing with the difficulties that stood in the way of his playing his required roles in organized social groups. If, for example, a reading disability appeared to be interfering with the boy's social adjustment, the value of the tutoring that he received would be judged in relation to his subsequent behavior.

Classification of the boys on the basis of the extent to which they appeared to be benefited yielded five groups:

1. Those clearly aided by the services (21 per cent).

2. Those to whom the services were possibly of some assistance, although not much change in behavior was noted (16 per cent).

3. Those for whom little was accomplished in spite of friendly relations (9 per cent).

4. Those for whom the services were ineffectual, either because the boys or their parents refused help, or because the work of the counselor was slight or of poor quality, or for other reasons (37 per cent).

5. Those who did not need help (17 per cent).

IMPLICATIONS OF THE STUDY. Replying to Allport's question[30] with respect to Cabot's original hypothesis that the contagion of personality can be effectively replaced by skill applied to specific needs, Powers and Witmer state that it is important to know whether the situations with which the counselor deals are all equally amenable to his skills. Their analysis suggested that in a considerable group of cases the negative outcome was probably related to lack of skill in the social worker, especially in dealing with neu-

29 *Ibid.*, p. 419.
30 *Ibid.*, Foreword, p. x.

rotics. (Most of the boys who persisted in delinquency despite all efforts made to help them appeared to be seriously neurotic youngsters from homes which were unsatisfying emotionally.)

Neither the age of the boy, his IQ, the neighborhood, nor the duration of the services appeared to be crucial factors in the outcome. The widespread acceptance of the counselor's offer of help was due to its explicit rather than to its implicit aim. Disadvantaged parents are usually willing to let their children have the services such as the study successfully afforded, and children can benefit from such services "if what they need is advice, encouragement, backing, ethical precepts, scientific information, as well as access to good recreational, educational, and medical facilities which competent, affectionate parents usually give.[31] The fact that the largest number of successes (21 per cent) was credited to the nurse suggests that there is more than one way to help young people with certain kinds of problems. The personal factor in the relationship is significantly related to successful outcome.

Powers and Witmer concluded that the study was not useless but revealed the limitations of the method. In their words: "No such generous, ambitious but professionally rather naive program can diminish to any considerable extent that persistent problem, juvenile delinquency.[32] We would add that one of the main reasons the experiment did not provide definitive answers is that the concepts of delinquency and treatment had not been clarified.

In 1956 the Cabot Foundation financed another follow-up of the 750 boys in the original Cambridge-Somerville Youth Study. The research team[33] decided that the criterion for success of the services provided to the 325 boys chosen for active help would be the absence of criminal behavior as recorded in official court convictions. They acknowledge the shortcomings of this criterion. Because, however, they had no satisfactory and convenient alternative, they felt justified because (1) it is unlikely that a confirmed criminal would pass through the first thirty years of his life without being apprehended at least once; and (2) since most of the boys were residents of deteriorated neighborhoods, they were more likely than the residents of middle-class neighborhoods to be apprehended for wrongdoing. The 506 boys who could be located in 1956 were predominantly of lower- or lower-middle-class backgrounds. Their median IQ during the period of the original study had been 98 and their median age when treatment began had been 11.

The findings revealed no statistically significant difference in the outcome between the treated and the untreated group with respect to the number of criminal convictions, the age at conviction—i.e., before or after 18—in-

[31] *Ibid.*, p. 581.
[32] *Ibid.*, p. 577.
[33] William and Joan McCord, *Origins of Crime, A New Evaluation of the Cambridge-Somerville Study*, New York, Columbia University Press, 1959.

telligence, or personality. The authors were forced, therefore, to conclude that the treatment program in its *totality* had been ineffective as a preventive of crime.

Detailed comparisons were made with respect to the relative effect of differences in treatment process, i.e., the background of the staff, the number of changes in staff (due to the interruption of war service), the length of treatment by the first counselor, the duration of treatment. Again the results were discouraging: 53 per cent of those treated for more than six years had records of subsequent convictions in comparison with 35 per cent of those under care for less than four years.

The significant findings were, first, with regard to frequency of contact. Among the boys seen twice a week for at least six months, 25 per cent were convicted of crimes in comparison with 51 per cent of those who were seen less frequently. But among the 82 who were seen less than once a month, one third were subsequently convicted of crime.

The second significant finding relates to the youngest age group. For those under 10, when the treatment first began, the percentage convicted of crimes was less than 30, in contrast to 66 for those who began at age 10. It was suggested that the drop in the crime rate for older boys—i.e., to 45 per cent at age 11 and 37 per cent for those between 12 and 13 when treatment began—may be explained by the fact that a higher proportion continued to have guidance through the difficult adolescent period.

The third finding was that regardless of the age of the boy, a significantly lower crime rate, 29 per cent, resulted when the first counselor was a woman than when the first counselor was male (46 per cent). The authors state that this difference may be the result of an independent variable that was not measured.

It was decided to test the effect of intensive treatment offered to certain boys in the Cambridge-Somerville study. The records were analyzed to find cases where the counselor had maintained a relationship with the boy for at least two years, visited at least once a week, recorded his concern with the boy's basic personality problem in the area of parental relations, feelings about sex, attitudes toward authority and peers, or feelings of guilt, anxiety, or aggression. Unfortunately, only 12 of the 253 boys followed up had records which satisfied these requirements. The matching process in this part of the study was the selection of *another treated boy* rather than a *control*, since obviously the information on the control boys was much less complete.

The next step was to equate each pair on eight factors: the mother's attitude and the father's attitude toward the boy, the type of parental discipline, the general home atmosphere, the neighborhood, and the child's personality, intelligence, and delinquency prognosis score which had been assigned at the beginning of the experiment. While the matching was not perfect, it was reasonably close.

The results favored the boys receiving the most intensive treatment. Only 6 of the 12 committed at least one crime in comparison with 11 of their matched comrades. However, as the researchers acknowledge, the sample is so small that generalizations are of uncertain validity.

Commenting on the results of the study, Dr. Allport writes that, in his opinion, results of the McCord study justify the large expenditure of time and money that the Cambridge-Somerville study entailed.

> I think [he continues] that Richard Cabot would be deeply gratified. In part the results confirm his hypothesis. Children worked with frequently, if they are young enough, and if some substitute for parental neglect can be provided, seem to benefit. At the same time the parental situation turns out to be the major (and most stubborn) factor. Cabot would like such confirmation as exists for his hypothesis, also such disconfirmation. (The trouble, of course, was that the GSYS counseling program could not completely carry through his high ideals of treatment.) He would also approve the new light that the research has shed on this most difficult problem.[34]

Maximum Benefits Project

The Maximum Benefits Project is a research and service activity under the auspices of the Washington, D.C. Youth Council, designed to forestall delinquency through preventive services to elementary school children and their families.[35] The program has three aims: (1) to offer service, including clinical services, if necessary, to individual children with severe behavior problems; (2) to identify the predelinquent; and (3) to demonstrate how increased services can help the elementary school to prevent delinquency.

The area selected as "The Wickedest Precinct," Washington's Second Police Precinct, has witnessed, in common with other cities, a recent rapid shift of its economically privileged residents to the suburbs. In the Taylor School, where services were set up, the pupils, both white and Negro, have moved more frequently than Washington school children in general. The records for attendance and for scholastic readiness are well below the average. A variety of classifying and rating scales have been used for both individuals and families. Among the devices are the Glueck prediction scores, Healy's method of classifying families as well as Bradley Buell's, and a rating scale developed in a Dutch housing study.

To help these children and these families, more than service to the individual child in the school and the traditional methods of working with

[34] Personal communication from Gordon W. Allport, Executive Secretary of the Ella Lyman Cabot Trust, Cambridge, May 18, 1959.
[35] A mimeographed report prepared for the Eugene and Agnes E. Meyer Foundation by Dr. Emory F. Hodges, Dr. C. Downing Tait, Jr., and Nina B. Trevett summarizes the results to date of service to 179 problem children, 1959.

hard-core families was needed. Almost all of the 179 families had had contact with many of the agencies offering financial or other services, and almost two thirds of them were known to agencies in the correctional field even before the child entered school. The children were academically retarded and had high delinquency prediction scores.

A project social worker or a caseworker designated by one of the other agencies interested in the family was responsible for helping the family. Financial aid was provided in 157 cases, suggestions to school personnel in 103. Psychotherapy was recommended for the child or the parent in 33 cases (approximately 20 per cent). In 10 per cent, the recommendation was placement away from home. Other services included legal aid, health services, group activities, more adequate housing—the whole gamut of welfare services.

FOLLOW-UP RESULTS. In February 1956 and again in Febuary 1958, follow-up surveys estimated changes in academic performance and in referrals to court or police in the treated as compared with the control group—half of the referrals who were not given service. In 1956 the school follow-up showed more improvement among the treated than the untreated group. Two years later, however, there was no difference between the groups. Thus, from the teachers' point of view, the treatment program yielded negligible results.

The court follow-ups revealed slightly more convictions in the treated than in the untreated group. Thus the program could not be considered successful on that score either. The one encouraging factor from the sponsors' viewpoint was the validation of the Glueck scores in detecting potential delinquents.

In view of the failure of the remedial efforts the sponsors now recommend (1) stationing a social worker in each elementary school in a slum area to *detect the beginning* of problem behavior and to initiate appropriate services; (2) providing medical, psychological, and psychiatric services *in addition to the usual social casework service* to avoid the damage of continued unfavorable conditions; (3) *enriching the school curriculum* through provision of opportunities for extending the social and cultural horizons beyond those of the sordid neighborhood to compensate for the preponderance of damaging social experience; (4) concerted community effort to plan for the total needs of the families which are *socially incompetent;* and (5) possibly establishing an experimental subcommunity with a therapeutic goal for the families willing to cooperate, an idea suggested by the Dutch report on housing problem families.

Special Services to Hard-Core Families

We come now to the third approach to delinquency prevention as well as treatment, i.e., the newly advocated method of persisting in offering social work services to "hard-core" families. In the main these are multi-problem families who are reluctant to ask for or to accept help.

As we noted in Chapter 17, since the outcome of child guidance work appeared to be unsuccessful in many cases because the parents would not or could not cooperate, the child guidance clinics early decided to limit their services to children whose parents were not only willing to ask for help but prepared to make the personal investment of time and energy necessary to secure it. Recently, however, a reversal of this tendency has been in evidence. A technique called "aggressive casework" was developed in a special project beginning in July 1949, under the joint auspices of the Bureau of Child Welfare of the New York City Department of Public Welfare and the Youth Board.[36] It is termed "aggressive" because it seeks out the client instead of waiting for him to come to the agency for help.

This technique, with some variations, is currently used not only in New York City but in St. Paul. The assumptions underlying this approach are as follows:

1. The family as a social unit is responsible for bringing up and training its children.

2. An individual social worker can serve as a more effective liaison between the family and the various community resources than a half dozen social workers each offering a different service.

3. Since adjustment is a two-way process, it involves change not only in the family's reaction but in the attitudes of the community's institutions, and in the community's willingness to provide additional resources.

By the New York City Youth Board

The goal of the program of the Youth Board of New York City to persuade resistive families to accept service was to identify problem children *before* their difficulties became too serious, and to mobilize all the community's resources to help them.

The Youth Board chose as its field of operation the eleven areas in New York City which, according to the Central Register (see Chapter 4), showed the highest rates of official and unofficial delinquents. The first step was to establish what were designated as referral units in elementary schools in the geographic areas selected for service. Ideally the staff of a unit consisted of a supervisor and four social caseworkers.[37] Instead of providing direct service, the staff of the referral unit contracted with designated oper-

[36] *Reaching the Unreached*, and *How They Were Reached*, New York City Youth Board, 1952 and 1954.

[37] There has been continued difficulty in securing and retaining staff. And the auspices of this project has changed hands; currently it is financed by the New York City Mental Health Board, but under the jurisdiction of the Board of Education.

ating agencies to undertake responsibility for treatment on a per capita payment basis. If there was no agency to which the client could be referred, the referral unit assumed responsibility for treatment until the services of another agency might be made available.

As in the case of the St. Paul area project, described in Chapter 27, the first step in dealing with an applicant is to determine through the Social Service Exchange whether or not any member is currently under care of a social agency. If no one in the family is now on the active list of any social agency, the parent is asked to come for an office interview at the referral unit. If there is no response, the social worker visits the home to arouse the parent's interest in at least discussing his child's problem and ways in which a social agency might help. Because families are frequently unwilling to ask for help, the social worker may have to make repeated visits, listening patiently and sympathetically to their complaints about their previous experiences with social agencies. What the social worker is trying to accomplish is to help the family see that an agency might be helpful, even though its former experience with agencies has seemed unsatisfactory.

If the family appears willing to proceed, more than one interview is usually necessary to decide which social agency is best equipped to help. To make sure that the family will follow through once the decision has been made, the social worker prepares its members for the necessary steps. Social workers know well that an ostensible verbal acquiescence is no guarantee that a plan will be carried through. Appointments are often broken, with or without plausible reasons, and some clients who show up for the initial interview do not return.

An analysis of the recent case loads of the referral units showed that about one third of the families live in deteriorated neighborhoods, are inadequately housed, and are trying to get along on marginal incomes. Some of them display a feeling of hopelessness, and others appear disinterested in suggestions for improving their lot. To help them calls for special skills.

The story of John Raymond below illustrates the aggressive casework approach initiated in the Youth Board by Alice Overton, from whose account the excerpts are taken.[38]

> JOHN RAYMOND. John, age 8, was referred to the Youth Board referral unit because he was troublesome in class, often truant, stammered and stole. He stole not only in school but in downtown stores. Because of his youth, he had not been referred to court.
>
> The fourth in a family of seven children, John was a fidgety, pale, thin, undersized boy who bit his nails. The youngest child, the only girl

---

[38] Alice Overton, "Serving Families 'Who don't want help,' " speech at the 80th Annual Meeting of the National Conference of Social Work, Cleveland, June 3, 1953. Italics added.

in the family, was mongoloid. All the children had made poor school adjustments and the older boys had been involved in delinquent acts.

The previous efforts of the community agencies to help the Raymonds had been as follows: On several occasions between 1943 and 1950 a family agency had offered various kinds of help, which the family had refused maintaining that all they needed was financial aid. In 1946 the father had served a 30-day sentence in the workhouse for larceny, and the Prison Association of New York had offered help. When the older children were referred to the children's court for delinquent behavior, the family and the children's division of the domestic relations court tried to help the family. In the last few years they had been on and off the public assistance rolls.

When the social worker from the referral unit made the first home visit, John's father slammed the door in her face. Mrs. Raymond, however, persuaded her husband to let the social worker come in, since the agency had written to ask for an appointment. When the worker gained entrance to the apartment, she observed a four-room apartment, dirty and poorly furnished. Mr. Raymond insisted that the family had no problems; that he had *"whipped the stealing"* out of John, and there was nothing that a social agency could do. He claimed that the school system and the teachers were responsible for the poor record of his children; that the teachers should have been able to discipline his children; and, furthermore, that social agencies had pried into his affairs, trying to tell him how to run his family. He felt that he had been pushed around enough. He just wanted to be let alone.

In an initial inventory of the liabilities and the assets of the Raymond family, the social worker saw some serious elements of neglect and rejection in this family setting. The father was an impulsive, hot-tempered, bossy kind of man who frequently drank to excess, and was usually disheveled in his appearance. A tentative diagnosis was that he was compensating for his inadequacy by acting the tyrant, beating the children, and demanding complete silence at home. The mother, who was in very poor health, avoided the overwhelming responsibilities which she faced by indirect and evasive tactics. The children looked to her for protection, which she was not always able to provide. The assets in the situation were implicit in the family's cohesion, and the mother's underlying wish to help her children.

The plan for treatment of this family was to begin with the mother, because she appeared more capable of accepting help in meeting the health and emotional needs of the children. Although she cooperated in arranging for the medical checkups and the psychological studies, she was unable to go through with the plans. Her husband's role in the home and her fear of him made complete cooperation with the agency, in her eyes, disloyalty to him. This attitude made it difficult to achieve positive changes in the family situation. When the social worker said

that she would like to talk over the plans with her husband, Mrs. Raymond cautioned care because of his excitable nature. Reluctantly, however, she arranged the appointment with her husband. Since the philosophy of the process is that all members of the family are important
in the treatment process, work with all members of the family went on
simultaneously.

Excerpts from the case record reveal the investment of time and the
skill of the social worker in bringing about changes in Mr. Raymond's *attitude
toward authority*. This attitude, the social worker assumed, was the major
obstacle to the family's acceptance of help.

> The father's resistance to help was evidenced in his failure to keep the
> first appointments. On subsequent occasions he would come into the
> kitchen of his apartment while the social worker was talking with his
> wife there. At the beginning he stayed for brief intervals, but gradually
> extended his stay.

In appearing on occasions when he was intoxicated, Mr. Raymond was
testing the social worker's acceptance of him as an individual regardless of
his behavior. When he was sure that the social worker's respect for him as
a parent was genuine and unwavering, these tactics and others were no
longer necessary. His first harsh reference to his own criminal record was a
trial balloon to see whether the social worker would still be willing to help
him.

> Mr. Raymond made two requests when he began to be assured of the
> worker's acceptance. The first concerned how to facilitate his brother's
> release from prison, which appeared to be dependent upon the assur-
> ance that a job was waiting for him. The second request was for help
> in getting a part-time job for his son in high school. The social worker
> acted promptly on both requests, as she did in making arrangements
> to send three of the children to camp, and also in securing an extension
> of time for clearing up the eligibility requirements for public assistance.

To prove to the client that social service is of practical value, any reasonable requests of the client must be met as quickly as possible.

> The social worker then began to help the father to see that his previous
> methods—fighting with the public assistance worker, failing to keep an
> employment interview—resulted only in hurt to his family. He began
> to talk about fears for his health, and it became clear that he broke
> clinic appointments because he was afraid to go to the clinic for fear he
> might find out that his illness might have serious consequences. After
> the social worker assured him that the disability he suffered from in his
> arms, as well as a diabetic condition, were not fatal, he began to attend
> the clinic regularly. Subsequently, he also took steps to deal with the
> health problems of his children.

In the course of the social worker's many visits, Mr. Raymond's remarks suggested some of the source of his hostility toward social agencies, and his feeling that it was necessary to resist their offers of help. He indicated that he had had a hard time in life; that his own father had never fully supported the family, and had always been very strict. There was also a history of imprisonment involving several members of the family, an experience which intensified his distrust for persons in authority. "If you want something," he stated, *"you have to fight for it."*

As Mr. Raymond learned to trust the social worker, he was able to consider the meaning of his behavior. For example, he assented to the social worker's comment that his display of temper toward John's school principal had netted him little advantage, but, on the contrary, had made the situation more difficult for his children.

There were encouraging signs of change in his behavior, such as the repainting of the apartment, improvement in his personal appearance, and a decrease in his drinking. When the school principal complained that he would have to suspend John, Mr. Raymond's first response was anger. He quickly calmed down, however, and accepted, instead, John's transfer to another school.

Mr. Raymond later reported with satisfaction that he could talk at length with the new principal without losing his temper. He was especially impressed at the courtesy shown him in introducing him to John's new teacher, who showed him the boy's work and made suggestions for encouraging John. Mr. Raymond was also very pleased when the school principal wrote him of John's improvement. In the past, he said, *he only heard from the school when his boys were in trouble.* If he had had praise occasionally, he felt he might have had less difficulty in accepting the criticisms.

A good deal of time was invested in explaining to the principal and to John's new teacher why it was necessary for them to adopt a special attitude toward Mr. Raymond, and why a sympathetic approach, which accorded him status as a father, would help him overcome some of his former hostility and anger.

Just as the Youth Board social worker prepared the school principal for contacts with Mr. Raymond, so she prepared the "Y," the clinics, and the remedial reading center for effective work with the family. When the clients cannot easily adjust to the many pressures in their lives, it is not effective to follow the formal procedures of large organizations. Special efforts are required to avoid the points of friction which, in the past, have frequently caused families most in need of help to refuse it. Instead of merely requesting information from the school about the family, the social worker regards the school as a partner whose active cooperation is essential if the family is to be helped. Children spend much more time with their teachers than with their social workers. The support, the attention, and the remedial help which the teacher can give are not likely to be forthcoming if all that the school gets from the social worker is a written statement containing information which the agency thinks it is wise for the school to have.

To establish a constructive relationship with the school the social worker must recognize the stresses and the strains on the teacher, and what she can and cannot do. Teachers, public assistance workers, probation officers, and even other professional social workers are human beings with feelings, as well as limitations imposed by the agency's structure. Many of the practices of modern child care agencies, for example, are built on the assumption that permissiveness is more effective than parental controls. The need for consistency in parental behavior and for the setting of limits appears to have had little emphasis in social work practice, which often expects more of most parents than they can achieve.

The experience of the referral units in Miss Overton's opinion, with which we agree, reveals that change in behavior is possible even when the clients cannot verbalize their changed attitudes. The actions of some of these inarticulate families demonstrate a modification of their behavior. They often do more in behalf of their children than people who "can talk a good line of insight." In offering service to families with less to say, the social worker must sharpen her powers of observation.

By the St. Paul Family-Centered Unit

Building on the experience of the New York City Youth Board demonstration project, a family-centered service unit was set up in St. Paul, Minnesota, in 1954. The criteria for the selection of the participating families were as follows:

1. The family must be known to the Board of Child Welfare, have at least one child under 18, and at least one parent must be interested in the children.

2. The services offered in the past must have been obviously inadequate in the light of the family's needs.

The staff consisted of the director, the same Alice Overton who had spearheaded the application of the new method in the New York City Youth Board project; eight social workers; and five supervisors, all on loan from the social casework agencies in the community. No case load exceeded 20 families.

Some of the questions to which answers were sought were:

1. If the approach is family-centered, in what way are the relationships between the social worker and the *individual* members of the family established and dealt with?

2. What consideration is given by the social worker to environmental factors and their influence on the family situation?

3. What psychiatrically oriented formulations about delinquency are consciously applied in the casework process and being tested for their effectiveness?

4. With a professional staff drawn from social agencies with diverse points of view about treatment, what provisions are made for their training to assure a unified approach to understanding delinquency and dealing with it, consistent with the underlying theory and the corresponding practice?

According to the executive director of the Greater St. Paul Community Chest and Council, the project was a unique effort to meet the needs of the 6 per cent of families so beset by problems that they had required a large share of all the community's welfare services.[39] Instead of creating a new service, the St. Paul Project set about coordinating the efforts of the existing health and welfare services in the case of each of these families. Discussions among and between the agencies revealed the necessity to modify usual agency practices. In the process, many gaps and inconsistencies in the St. Paul services were disclosed.

In 1956 a sample study of 50 families under care in the project revealed moderate or marked improvement in seven areas of social functioning in more than half of the families (58 per cent). In another 30 per cent there was slight improvement. Of the remainder, 4 per cent appeared to get worse instead of better. An encouraging result of the efforts was that almost two thirds of the families were accepting services which they had formerly refused.

With additional grants by the Hill Family Foundation the life of the project, originally planned to terminate in June 1956, was extended to July 1, 1959, and the number of hard-core families to be served was increased to 350. Probation officers, school social workers, and the public assistance staff agreed to join efforts with the representatives of the private agencies who initiated the project.

Summing up the results in 1959, Overton reports[40] that about two thirds of the families under care showed gains. These ranged from improvement in housekeeping to marked progress in family unity. The worst failures were found "among families where pervasive and persistent marital conflict seemed to yield satisfaction or buttress resistance to change." Among the results of particular interest to those concerned with ways of helping the families of

---

[39] Charles J. Birt, "Family-Centered Project of St. Paul," *Social Work,* Journal of the National Association of Social Workers, Vol. 1, no. 4 (Oct. 1956), pp. 41-47.

[40] Alice Overton, Katherine H. Tinker and Associates, *Casework Notebook,* 2nd ed., Family Centered Project, St. Paul, Minn., Greater St. Paul Community Chest and Councils, Inc., March 1959, pp. 157-66. For a full report on the research findings see Ludwig L. Geismar and Beverly Ayres, *Families in Trouble,* and *idem, Patterns of Change in Problem Families,* 1959.

delinquents, the St. Paul Project reveals that multi-problem families are far better treatment risks than had been assumed. Improvement in social functioning is possible even when there are serious personality limitations.

A second finding is that social workers should no longer be afraid to tell parents about the danger they see, nor should they gloss over the realities.

The still unsolved problem in the effective operation of the family-centered unit is how to devise ways of keeping the focus of treatment on the *family group* rather than on an *individual* with specific needs. Overton suggests that (1) closer observation of family relations in the home may be better than dependence on office interviews; (2) Emphasis should be on joint planning with the parents and concern with their honest evaluation of the negative as well as the positive aspects of the service; (3) there must be more concern with the values and goals of the deprived families and their capacities for growth; (4) For more effective prognosis, it is important to uncover the potential health in the multi-problem family rather than depending on the description of the problems themselves.

Obviously, the project sponsors are searching for hypotheses which are not based solely on the relationship between descriptive factors (see Chapter 13). To date, the St. Paul findings support Mack, Jephcott, and Carter's postulate that "rough" families are *sui generis*. If we are going to help them accept the positive aspects of middle-class standards for their children's behavior, we need to understand them better than we now do.

Summary

There is some evidence that delinquents and potential delinquents use the mass recreation facilities which have been provided in some neighborhoods. The fact that there is slightly less official delinquency among those who use the facilities than among those who do not may only mean, however, that delinquents who use the facilities are less confirmed in their delinquent behavior. While there is general agreement that all children do need opportunities for healthy recreation, it cannot be proved that the provision of these facilities alone will prevent delinquency, any more than that access to fresh air alone is sufficient protection against disease.

Preventive programs centered in the school, like Roser's program for dealing with truants in Gary, Indiana, or the Harlem project in J H S 101 for dealing with unmanageable girls, appear to have some support for their claims of success. The latter program, however, draws attention to the community's failure to continue supportive efforts, and to the dependence of success on teachers who are prepared to provide more than just competent instruction. The Maximum Benefits Program in Washington, D.C., points to the need for earlier detection.

The Cambridge-Somerville Youth Survey provided friendly counseling and a variety of tangible services to 375 boys over a period of years and withheld these services from the matched controls. A comparison by Powers and Witmer of the subsequent records of the treated and the control groups revealed that the rate of official delinquency was similar in both groups. However, the services were helpful for certain types of boys, i.e., those whose parents were not only affectionate but interested in the welfare of their children. The services, on the other hand, were ineffectual for young people who came from homes which did not provide adequate affection, and for youngsters who evidenced serious personality disorders. The results of the McCord follow-up, beginning in 1956, and tracing the subsequent criminal careers of 506 of the 750 original subjects did not materially change these conclusions. The suggestion that success was associated with long-term supportive treatment was based on too slight a statistical sample to be conclusive.

The aggressive casework technique applied first to hard-core families in New York City and currently in St. Paul, Minnesota, builds on the assets of families ordinarily not accepted for care by agencies who insist, as a prerequisite of service, that the families be sufficiently cooperative to ask for help. This service calls for special skill and perseverance on the part of the social worker. The assumption that the community has a responsibility to help all families whose children are in danger of growing up as delinquents underlies this approach. It implies that adjustment is a two-way process involving change in family attitudes through patient demonstration of the social worker's concern for all members of the family. It implies also that the community agencies need to modify their efforts in order to help such families use the proffered services in a more productive fashion.

CHAPTER 29

Community Efforts to Deal with the Gang Problem

The Eagles

The Eagles were led by a boy named "Buzz-saw," a well-built, utterly fearless but wild boy. His father was a drunkard, and his mother was too busy working and looking after the other children to pay much attention to him. Buzz-saw was a violent dictator who hated all adults. He kept his gang embroiled in constant warfare, inside school as well as out. Other gangs would be ready to quit street-fighting, but attacks by Buzz-saw and the Eagles kept them fighting. Among the Rajahs, the High Hats, the Ramblers and the Skulls, he was like a great czar, deferred to by other gang leaders. He sneered with contempt at the settlement house. Going in a "rumble," his war-cry was: "All I wanna see is blood!"

Then one day Buzz-saw was seized by the police, allegedly for creating a near-riot in a candy store, on complaint of the owner. Buzz-saw actually was innocent, mistakenly identified, and when picked up by the police, he was wildly defiant. The police promptly slapped him down.

Meanwhile, the street worker [Kurahara] investigated the actual incident and showed up in police court with the candy store owner and proved that Buzz-saw, however obnoxious, was actually innocent of this particular offence. The police let Buzz-saw go.

"From that point on," says Kurahara, "Buzz-saw changed his attitude toward the settlement house. He instructed his gang to listen to the street worker. . . . In a short time the whole gang changed from being a vicious, war-ring into a social club. Later, with the help of the street worker, Buzz-saw got a job. After that he really settled down."[1]

This story of Buzz-saw and its happy ending is not a fairy tale. Behind it lie the efforts of many people who believe that it is possible to redirect even such hostile and deprived adolescents as Buzz-saw and his gang to a new view of life. This new approach to the gang, called the street club project, like that of its first cousin, the detached worker, is based on the conviction that even the most hostile youngster has within himself the possibilities for redirection if he is offered help by an understanding and accepting adult instead of the customary slapping down to which in his early years he has too often been subjected by the representatives of authority—the police, the teacher, and his father.

In this chapter we examine the newer concepts and methods of dealing with the antisocial gang which recognize its positive potentialities. The gang is regarded as a form of autonomous group with many positive connotations if the activities and attitudes of the members can be redirected into socially acceptable channels. Earlier efforts to disperse the gang in the hope that it will not reassemble have had little success because, as indicated in Chapter 9, the gang usually fills a need for the support of the peer group for many young people in the process of growth from childhood to adulthood.

Area programs and community councils for redirecting gang activities by focusing on the so-called natural groupings of teenage boys were described in Chapter 27. Since there was no provision for formal research connected with these programs, there is no measure of their success. More useful knowledge of the day-to-day activities of gang members and the ways in which the community has attempted to redirect their energy derives from four sources: (1) the cellar club projects of the National Youth Administration of the 1930s, which are the antecedents of (2) the street club projects, (3) the detached worker projects, and (4) a unique development in a disorganized area near San Francisco.

The Cellar Clubs

In General

The depression years witnessed the rise and growth of the cellar clubs. Recognizing that at the worst of the 1930 depression almost one third of the young people in cities were attached in one way or another to youth groups, youth congresses, street corner gangs, social or cellar clubs, the National Youth Administration with the WPA Adult Education Program organized

---

[1] Harry Henderson, "If You Can't Lick 'Em." Reprinted by permission of *Pageant* Magazine. Copyright 1956 by Hillman Periodicals, Inc.

a program to serve them. The directors respected the autonomy of the groups, regarding group life as appropriate for these youngsters faced with problems created by the exigencies of modern living. No attempt was made to persuade the groups to change their meeting places.

In New York City

In New York, as in other metropolitan areas, the cellar club staff met the groups in their natural habitats: bedrooms in a Harlem flat; stores in Williamsburg, Brooklyn; a cellar on the lower East Side of Manhattan. The urge to be free of home restrictions (common to all youth regardless of socio-economic class) was particularly strong with these youngsters from poor, drab homes. By pooling their meager resources they secured meeting places which they decorated to suit their own taste. There were hundreds of such groups, "many of them too small for effective group activity because of the physical limitations of the rooms in which they met. . . . Nevertheless, each possessed an individuality of its own, was jealous of its prestige, and proud of its name, 'Aristocrats,' 'Commodores,' 'Falcons,' 'Manhattan Knights,' 'Clarions,' etc."[2]

As reactions to the deprivations of the individual homes, the poverty of community resources, the cellar clubs were protests against the paternalistic restrictions of the usual social agency programs. They were similar to gangs in that they were not affiliated with fraternal, patriotic, or political organizations. Like the members of the gang, the boys lived in the neighborhood and congregated in candy stores or pool parlors. Although a certain amount of antisocial behavior and a cynical outlook were not considered insurmountable obstacles, groups which were deeply affected by social disintegration were not included in the youth service program.[3]

THE APPROACH AND THE STAFF. The staff played largely by ear. Aware that attempts to preach or to attach the group to an organized agency would meet with resistance, the first essential in winning their confidence was to accept the members as they were. In identifying himself with the neighborhood standards, the youth leader concerned himself with problems confronting the group—i.e., what to do about impending police raids, how to keep out racketeers, how to pay the rent, how to find jobs, or how to make dances more attractive. To deal with these problems the youth leader needed a variety of skills above and beyond the usual formal educational techniques. He virtually lived in the club room, sat around the radio with the boys, joined

---

2 Frank Caplan, "Extending Educational Services to Autonomous Groups of Unemployed Youth," *The Journal of Educational Sociology*, Vol. 19, no. 9 (May 1946), p. 548.
3 *Ibid.*, p. 549.

in their bull sessions, hoping to help the members make intelligent choices for action.

EFFECTIVENESS OF THE PROGRAM.   Although it lacked any formal evaluation, Caplan believed that this program aided many young people to survive the unusual vicissitudes of life in the depression period. The club members developed talents for leadership, undertook responsibility, and met their problems effectively. As loyalties were strengthened, the prestige of the group became a matter of common concern. Their programs included more and more educational content, and the responsibilities for club activities were distributed more widely among the members.

Gradually the club endorsed the community's demands for new housing, additional playgrounds, or a new school. In turn, the community participated in the leisure-time programs of the clubs and minimized the segregating aspects which are so often a community's response to the gang. The formation of a community council representing individual groups signalized the culmination of the socialization process. To quote Caplan: "The educational improvement of the autonomous youth club lies in its being the most spontaneous and uncontrolled form in which young people gather. Its contribution to educational theory stems from the contradictory fact that it is also a highly self-regulated and constantly developing group, which is the perfect example of a self-regulating unit exposed to the endless influences of group and community life."[4]

The youth leader's success, as described in the cellar club project, may be partly attributable to the large number of young people affected by the depression. In the widened gap between the gang and the public in today's more favorable economic situation, hostile gangs appear less accessible, even to the nondirective methods of the youth leader of yesterday.

The Street Club Projects

The end of World War II witnessed the rise of the street club projects. As these have developed in New York, Chicago, Roxbury, Massachusetts, and Cleveland, they have taken a variety of forms. Projects in the first two cities are discussed below.

Manhattanville Community Center

Street workers are usually associated with settlement or neighborhood houses. Kurahara, the trained group worker who worked with Buzz-saw, is on the staff of Manhattanville Community Center, which serves an area in

4 *Ibid.,* p. 554.

which Puerto Ricans and American Negroes live side by side with the old-time Irish inhabitants of run-down tenements in the shadow of Columbia University, Grant's Tomb, and Riverside Church.[5]

In describing his job Kurahara, who supervises a staff of five street workers, says "it requires the patience of a saint and the courage of an infantryman." Getting acquainted means sticking around in the gang's hangout and trying to make friends no matter what happens. At first the boys are suspicious of an adult who says that he likes them and wants to help them make use of the facilities offered by the community center. The more garrulous boys are often shushed with the admonition: "raisin bread," which means: "be quiet!"

The street worker bides his time and persists in his offers of friendliness. He treats the boys to a cup of coffee, to cigarettes, or to a game of pool. Like buddies in the army, he gets to know each boy as an individual. One boy doesn't go home evenings because ten people occupy three rooms. Harry's mother is often drunk. John is always hungry, and there is never enough food in the house. Jim is a poor reader whose teacher makes fun of him in front of the class. As Kurahara says, one begins to understand the hostility that surrounds these kids and why the gang represents a retreat which offers security, warmth, and sometimes affection. The street worker comes to feel the full effect on the boys of "the long tedious winter nights with nothing to do and nowhere to go to get out of the cold."

Adults in the area regard the gangs with bitter contempt, commenting, "this used to be a decent neighborhood." The police keep the gang moving. And because he hangs out with the gang, the street worker may be put on the spot if he appears to sanction law-breaking. Sometimes the boys planning a rumble implore the street worker to go away. Usually, however, he stays with them and tries to suggest other ways to settle the dispute. Most of the boys don't really want to fight. However, although few are as violent as Buzz-saw, no one wants to be called "chicken."

The street worker's first aim is to get close to the leader, who is often a boy with superior ability, but like Buzz-saw, eaten up with resentment which pushes him into indiscriminate hating. As a substitute for the hostile patterns of attack, the street worker suggests that it is not "chicken" to settle disputes peaceably or even by a fair fight in a boxing match in the gym.

The program offered these boys when, like Buzz-saw's gang, they eventually move into the community center, is one designed to meet practical as well as leisure-time needs. It may be a brief course in how to prepare for a job, how to fill out applications, or how to make up for deficiencies in their school work. In 1956 only 5 per cent of the gang members in Manhattanville

[5] A new development known as Morningside Gardens has recently replaced some of the slums in this area.

had completed high school. Most of them were slow learners and slow readers. The majority had quit school to earn money but usually landed in dead-end jobs.

According to Clyde E. Murray, Manhattanville's director at the time, the street workers successfully redirected the gang's energies. Instead of the wreckage and the destruction in the center, which were common before the street worker program began, the boys cooperated to build a lounge on the fifth floor. This involved carrying everything, including the cement and the lumber, by hand up five flights of stairs. They plastered the walls, built the settees, and even painted a mural showing the dances of all nations. Part of the magic, says Murray, is "faith that the kids can change."[6]

Hyde Park Youth Project

In Chicago, Fertig, a street worker who is trained as a sociologist rather than as a group worker, was assigned in 1955 to work with four teenage street clubs known as the Dorchester Gang.[7] Some of the gang members have been regular attendants at the Friday night dances at the Hyde Park neighborhood club.

Since the project began, the membership of the groups has shifted considerably. Some have moved away because their families could not afford the higher rentals of the new buildings in the redevelopment project. Some have been inducted into the Army and some have been committed to correctional institutions. Less than half of the boys live with both their parents and the absence of the father in the home is most noticeable among the aggressively antisocial boys. Many fathers are described as weak or as alcoholics.

Every one of these boys had previously engaged in some kind of delinquency, the majority in drinking, and in sex offenses. Half of them had participated in gang fights. Some of the most frequent violations of city ordinances were obstructing the passage of street cars or buses and defacing store signs. Among the more conspicuous offenses were beating up children, throwing eggs at adults, urinating on a policeman.

The groups that Fertig has worked with included one which was known as the "white boys protective association"—active against the invasion, as they described it, of Negroes into the neighborhood. A signal for a fight was the response of a Negro boy to the "come-on" tactics of a white girl sitting near him in a bar frequented by the members of the gang. Challenged to fight,

[6] Henderson, op. cit.

[7] Ralph Fertig, "Hyde Park Youth Project, Summary," June 30 to December 31, 1955; Welfare Council of Metropolitan Chicago, mimeographed report. See also *Hard-to-Find Youth Project*, Report of Welfare Council of Metropolitan Chicago, Operating Bulletin 7, Sept. 17, 1958, for some provocative ideas on youth culture drawn from the Hyde Park Project.

the Negro left the bar to gather his cohorts and the white group did the same. Informed of the impending rumble, the street worker appeared at the scene of the fight and headed it off by suggesting that the opposing groups sit down and discuss the issues. The white boys agreed, when they had cooled down, that the Negro had only reacted as any normal male would to the provocative behavior of the girl.

As Fertig has worked with the boys he has observed a gradual change in the attitudes toward the Negroes who have moved into the neighborhood as the whites moved out. Instead of the initial automatic rejection on the basis of skin color, he senses growing acceptance of individuals. Discriminatory feelings are less openly expressed than they were formerly.

The South Americans and the Mexicans in the neighborhood have a special status. They apparently are attractive to the Italian and Irish girls. The Latin girls in this group are popular with the non-Latin boys. The highest prestige is accorded four Oriental boys and three Oriental girls whose parents have encouraged them to associate with the white community. They attend the university.

The role of the street club worker in this project has been to try to "sell" middle-class standards of behavior. Fertig has arranged fishing trips, bicycle excursions, swimming outings, and picnics. He helped to organize a baseball team and a variety of entertainments. For the boys old enough to work, he has arranged contact with employers. For younger ones, there is a group called the "young workmen" who answer the calls of the neighborhood for casual labor, cutting grass, small paint or repair jobs. For the older boys who have driving licenses, the street club worker has enlisted the interest of some mechanics in the neighborhood who helped the boys start a garage and repair shop. Eight boys have assumed responsibility for the $50 a month rental. They offer minor services to other car owners and keep their own cars running.

The street worker describes his role as that of a catalyst who makes it possible for the boys to take advantage of the opportunities offered by the neighborhood center. He sees them gradually accepting the socially approved forms of boy-girl relationships and substituting the peace table for the street fight to settle disputes. Boys who need more intensive casework service are referred to the special services offered by the project. In the majority of cases, however, the group itself is the medium through which the street worker functions.

In Fertig's opinion, fighting incidents as well as illicit sex affairs have markedly decreased. He believes the club serves as a primary means of gaining status through greater conformity with the standards of the wider community. Only boys in the lowest-status level use the group to express generally hostile behavior. The group activity of the middle-status boys is more practically oriented to the theft of bicycles or automobiles—symbols of high status. The members of this middle-status group are less apt to truant than to cheat, because they share the aspirations of the highest-status group to get ahead in school. This high-status group has elected "the professor" as its leader and a girl as its vice-chairman.

Gandy, the research director of the Hyde Park Project from 1955 to 1958, has recently reported on the effect of the program in forestalling or curbing anti-social behavior.[8] Less sanguine than Fertig, he comes to the reluctant conclusion that the intensive services provided for varying periods of time (6 to 18 months) have had little or no effect on the youths who, at the time of first contact with the project, had already had a history of anti-social behavior.

These descriptions of the Manhattanville and Hyde Park projects, illustrated by the accounts of Kurahara in New York and Fertig in Chicago, reveal little standardization in the role of the street worker. Although their responsibility and their training is different, both workers have an intense interest in the young people with whom they are working, and communicate to them their genuine concern. They are both tirelessly energetic and in very different ways offer ideals for the members to emulate. Though they do not censure or blame, they do not share the boys' standards of behavior. The goal in this type of activity is to attach these young people in a constructive way to the neighborhood or the community center.

The Detached Worker Programs

The detached worker approach, also a product of World War II, represents an organized effort to cope with the aggressive behavior of the anti-social gang *without* attempting to attach the gang members to the settlement or community center. The detached worker is so called because, unlike Kurahara and Fertig, he is not affiliated with a settlement or group work organization, and does not attempt to bring the gang within the orbit of the organized agency. Like the youth leader of cellar club days, the detached worker seeks out the gang; he avoids preaching, and identifies himself with gang members, assuring them at the same time that he likes them as individuals, even though he may disapprove of some of their actions. The basic assumptions in the detached worker approach are:

1. The negative behavior of gangs is an expression of hostility toward adult authority, stemming from early childhood rejection by parents or parent

[8] John M. Gandy, "Preventive Work with Street-Corner Groups: Hyde Park Youth Project, Chicago," *The Annals,* American Academy of Political and Social Science, No. 322 (March 1959), pp. 107-16.

substitutes. The aggression, from the gang member's point of view, is, therefore, an appropriate response to the hostile adult world.

2. Change in behavior can occur only when the individual is motivated to change through the establishment of a meaningful relationship with someone who accepts him for his own sake and supports him in his efforts to change.

While this approach makes some use of the facilities provided by the community, its major emphasis is on meeting the basic psychological needs expressed in all behavior.

Preceding the present detached worker programs in New York, Chicago, and Boston, there were three projects in New York City which attempted to put this technique into practice. The name "street club" is also used in connection with these detached worker projects. The Harlem Project of 1943-45, the Street Club Project of the Welfare Council, and the New York City Youth Board Program initiated in 1950, have each added somewhat to our knowledge of gang composition and structure.

The Harlem Project

The Harlem Project[9] sharpened the community's awareness that gangs were not being reached by the group work agencies, regardless of their efforts to extend their facilities and programs. At the same time the Project established the feasibility of the street club approach. Upon its termination, the attention of the Welfare Council of New York City, now known as the Community Council of Greater New York, was drawn to the need for taking some responsibility for a problem whose significance was not purely local. Concurrent pressure from the Prison Association of New York (concerned with the increasing gang warfare and the resultant killings and injuries) resulted in the organization of the Committee on Street Clubs, which in September 1945 set up the experimental project described in the publication *Working with Teen-age Gangs*,[10] from which the following report is drawn.

Welfare Council Committee on Street Clubs

The Welfare Council Committee on Street Clubs decided to concentrate on the Central Harlem area which had been served by the Harlem Project. The majority of the tenements, built prior to 1900, were dilapidated,

[9] See Chapters 9, 10, and 28 for descriptions of various aspects of the Harlem Project.
[10] Paul L. Crawford, Daniel I. Malamud, and James R. Dumpson, *Working with Teen-age Gangs, A Report on the Central Harlem Street Clubs Project*, New York, Welfare Council, 1950. Mr. G. Howland Shaw, then president of the Welfare Council, was the prime mover in obtaining support for the project.

rat-infested, and without proper lighting or ventilation. The rates for infant mortality, tuberculosis, public assistance, neglected and dependent children, and family court cases were more than double those in the rest of the city. Interspersed among the dwellings were bars, poolrooms, and candy stores, where numbers rackets and narcotics salesmen plied their trades. Hospital beds were insufficient and facilities inadequate. Schools were old and, as revealed in Chapter 28, the teacher turnover considerable. The vast majority of the inhabitants of Central Harlem were Negroes whose limited opportunities for work were chiefly in unskilled and low pay occupations. "Such harmful conditions unfavorably leave their imprint on children who live under them. Frustration and boredom pile up, until many boys are ready to do anything in order to snatch some fun and excitement from life. Tensions mount until they explode in hostile and aggressive acts. This is the soil from which anti-social gangs spring."[11]

THE STAFF. The street club project established headquarters in a loft building on the corner of 116th Street and Seventh Avenue. All but one of the staff members were Negroes who either lived in Harlem or were well acquainted with the area. Their educational and experience backgrounds differed. Some had majored in recreation and physical education; one had a background in anthropology and some experience in recreation work and administered psychological tests in the Army; another who had majored in psychology had worked in a public welfare agency. The one white member of the staff had taught in high school, was a good athlete, and was actively interested in social and political problems. One woman member of the staff had been a college instructor with experience in group work and community organization. A director of research was appointed several months after the project had started. The common characteristics of the staff were a liking for and ability to attract young people, and a nonauthoritative attitude.

THE APPROACH TO THE GANG. Initially gang members, as later in Manhattanville, appeared puzzled by the workers, and eyed them with suspicion. Each worker, in making it clear to the boys that he did not reject them because of their illegal behavior, nevertheless drew a clear line at engaging in illegal acts with them. He also set limits in discussing his own personal life, about which the boys questioned him. In dealing with them, the street club worker had to distinguish between a friendly and a professional relationship —one which emphasizes skilled help more than kindness.

While the methods of the individual workers varied, the aim was to permit the group to make its own decisions and to offer little specific direction, so that the members would become self-reliant. Programs were not ends in themselves, but means for developing better interpersonal and social adjustments.

[11] *Ibid.*, p. 16.

Some evidence of the effectiveness of this approach was noted as the officers of clubs gradually began to see the advantages of mediation in settling disputes. Awareness of the rights and needs of others was also revealed in a recorded comment of one of the boys: "There are a lot of fellows living on the block who can play better than some of the players we have. If we got them on the team, we could win more games, but we'd rather not win quite so many games, and have a team for those who do play than leave them out."[12] Gradually cooperation with other groups in the community, as in the case of the cellar clubs, began to replace former enmity. Members of different gangs joined in camping trips and block parties. And also as with the cellar clubs, the community agencies, with the help of the Precinct Coordinating Council of the Police Department (see Chapter 13), collected money and helped in other ways to make the boys realize "that there were adults in the community concerned with their welfare and willing to lend a helping hand."

The occasions when the gangs planned fights put the worker's skill to the severest test. He was neutral whenever there seemed a possibility that taking sides would threaten his relationship with the boys. On other occasions, when antisocial actions seemed imminent, he attempted to redirect the attitudes or activities. Sometimes, in order to stimulate change in behavior, reasoning or example-setting techniques seemed appropriate. Occasionally, delaying techniques such as changing the subject, a suggestion that decisions be postponed, or proposing more socially acceptable courses of action were used. For a boy with severe personal problems—a chronic truant or narcotic user—insight-inducing techniques were employed in individual sessions with the boy.

ASSESSING CHANGES IN GANG BEHAVIOR. The chief source for studying change was the records in which the staff recorded the day-by-day process of working with the boys. Recognizing such obvious limitations as the selective process in recording, and the fact that antisocial behavior of which the worker was unaware could undoubtedly have occurred, the records at the time the project terminated revealed on the positive side:

1. Gang fights had decreased.
2. Most of the boys had given up carrying weapons.
3. The post of War Counselor had been abolished.
4. The Gay Blades had moved to a new hangout in order to avoid rumbles with the neighboring Politicos.
5. The Jay-Bees had negotiated a situation which at the beginning of the project would certainly have exploded into a gang fight.
6. The members attended school more regularly.
7. While there was no marked decrease in stealing, the detached work-

12 *Ibid.*, p. 55.

ers noted an increase in feeling of guilt and anxiety in three of the gangs with respect to their stealing activities.

8. There was a surface change in the attitude toward girls.

On the red side of the ledger there appeared to be no decrease in the use of liquor or narcotics.

The report did not claim that the success in reducing acts of aggression was entirely due to the efforts of the detached worker. It was recognized that increased maturity, changing socio-economic influences, and the boys' desire to win approval through socially more acceptable behavior may also have been important factors. The failure to change drinking habits and dope addiction possibly reflected either deep-seated personality problems or community sanction for such activities.

GUIDES TO WORKING WITH GANGS. The report outlined the initial steps in establishing relations with the boys. The approach is the first stage. In the second stage, i.e., stimulating change, the worker needs to individualize his approach, understand the meaning of the boys' behavior in specific situations, and learn to control his own need to direct the boys. Overnight hikes and other outlets for legitimate fun and enjoyment appeared to be particularly helpful in the Welfare Council project.

The effectiveness of any of the techniques to prevent antisocial behavior depends mainly on the quality of the relationship with the boys. Manipulation was usually not as successful as insistence on the boys' working out their own solutions. "Even mistaken decisions, if they are independently made, may stimulate growth in some boys."[13]

In the opinion of the project workers, it is not feasible to work with more than one gang at a time; and if there can be an area team of detached workers, each assigned to a particular gang, friendlier intergang relations, they believe, will ensue.

Since it is impossible to work intensively with all the boys, the detached worker must decide with which boys he will work, and whether his goals will be modification of surface behavior or attempting more fundamental personality change. He also needs to know the varying roles and techniques that he will use to achieve these goals, and the relative importance of similarity in race and religious affiliation between the worker and the gang members.

LIMITATIONS OF THE PROJECT. The major limitation of the Welfare Council street club project was noted in the report: despite changes in the surface behavior as a result of the relationships with the detached worker, no basic changes in the boys' ideology occurred:

> To these boys the world is still a dangerous jungle. Yes, they may grant the presence of sympathetic allies in this jungle but a jungle it is none-

[13] *Ibid.*, p. 135, fn. 6.

theless. It is still important to them to be tough; fearfulness and weakness are still despised traits.

The exaggerated need for status, the contempt for the law, the exploitative attitudes towards girls—these and other trends still operate virtually unmodified in most of the boys. . . .

There is no answer to the question whether more basic changes in ideology would have occurred if the workers had been more skilled, if the operations had continued for a longer period of time, if more psychiatric help had been available, or if there had been a more active area committee. *Our failure to achieve such basic changes should serve as a challenge to future projects.*[14]

With respect to the research program, the handicaps were:

1. Failure to plan in advance and to engage the research director at the initiation of the project.

2. Insufficient funds allocated for research.

3. Relations between the research director, the staff, and the research committee not clearly defined at the outset.

Because the program involved both service and research, the area workers felt some pressure to prove they were successful in helping the boys, in order to assure continued financial support.

New York City Youth Board Program

A detached worker program was incorporated in 1950 as part of the Youth Board effort to deal directly with juvenile delinquency. Established by local law in 1947, and financed by the city and state on a fund-matching basis, the Youth Board's program had been initially concerned with recreational activities for delinquents.[15]

The detached worker project in 1950 actually represented a continuation of the Welfare Council street club project, re-engaging the services of as many members of the street club staff as were available. According to *Perspectives on Delinquency Prevention:*

> The New York City Youth Board has been doing a notable job with predelinquent and delinquent youth who seemed too tough for any other agency to handle. Developing from a pilot project sponsored by Welfare Council, the "Council of Street Clubs" now provides a corps of specially

[14] *Ibid.*, pp. 149-50. Italics added.

[15] By 1949, the Youth Board program included referral units in high delinquency areas, demonstration programs in three Bronx schools, psychiatric service for the magistrates' and children's courts, a year-round community center and recreation program including play streets and game placements, a group work pilot center in the Bedford-Stuyvesant district of Brooklyn, and research activities involved in setting up the Central Register described in Chapter 4. Since 1957 some of these activities have been terminated or transferred to other auspices, and others such as central planning have been expanded.

trained, highly skilled group workers who maintain a continuing contact with some 22 teen-age gangs.

As a result of the patient efforts of the social group workers, youths who were prone to street fighting and even more serious crime are now moving in the direction of running successful social affairs and building their reputation in a more socially acceptable fashion.

Make no mistake, this work *is difficult and sometimes disappointing. Boys who have been embittered by school failure, poverty and social discrimination, who have acquired their learning from hard tutors in the streets, do not become little gentlemen overnight.* It is just as well we recognize this, so that no impossible demands for window dressing "progress" reports confront this staff. They are walking a tortuous road, but there have been some notable achievements.[16]

In initiating and extending its detached worker project, however, the Youth Board apparently was more concerned with making services available than it was with standardizing the qualifications necessary for this type of work or evaluating the effectiveness of the individual worker's approach. As far as published reports indicate, the questions raised by the Welfare Council street club project in regard to goals, techniques, and staff were not considered. Although with funds leftover from the street club project, the research division of the Youth Board employed a social scientist to design a project evaluating its operations, the project was not carried out.

A three-day conference called by the Children's Bureau in the spring of 1957 attracted the attendance of 200 practitioners, administrators, and theoreticians from twenty-two states, who wished to take an objective look at the widely advertised methods in street club and detached worker projects which claimed success in preventing antisocial gang behavior. Those who participated were impressed by the frankness of the discussions and the willingness to admit how little was positively known. Some of the problems were presented in addresses by Dr. Albert K. Cohen on "Youth Subcultures" (see Chapters 8 and 9); "The Nature of the Groups," by Elliot Studt; "Goals and Objectives," by David Austin, formerly of the Roxbury Special Youth Program,[17] and currently executive secretary of the Group Work Council of the Cleveland Welfare Federation.[18] A summary of the reactions and comments of the participants[19] underscores the highlights in advance of a full report of the conference which will be issued later. It raised more questions than it settled.

[16] Henry Epstein, *Perspectives on Delinquency Prevention*, City of New York, May 1955, pp. 5-65. Italics added.
[17] See Walter B. Miller, "The Impact of a Community Group Work Program on Delinquent Corner Groups," *The Social Service Review*, Vol. 31, no. 4 (Dec. 1957), pp. 390-406.
[18] David Austin, "Goals for Gang Workers," *Social Work*, Journal of the National Association of Social Workers, Vol. 2, no. 4 (Oct. 1957), pp. 43-50.
[19] *Social Legislation Information Service*, No. 20, Washington, 85th Congress, May 27, 1957.

Bringing the Police into the Agency

A California Project

A neighborhood center in Oakland, California (a suburb of San Francisco), brings the police directly into the agency setup.[20] This approach flies in the face of the currently popular theory that effective service to delinquents requires the withdrawal of the group worker from open association with the authoritative representatives of other official agencies in the community.

The Oakland Recreation Department has sponsored a group work program in an extremely disorganized neighborhood populated largely by newcomer Negro and Mexican families. Extreme transiency, very poor housing, and high tuberculosis, venereal disease, and delinquency rates prevail. When the project began, in one club of 15 boys, only 2 had never been on probation; and 28 of 35 registered members in one co-ed dance group either had been or were under some kind of supervision from the probation department. Whether they were officially classified as delinquent or not, however, a high proportion of the children had indulged in aggressive behavior.

In addition to the usual program in the agency, the staff is free to move about the neighborhood and spend time with the young people wherever they congregate. If things are slow at the center, the staff visits the local ice-cream parlors and candy stores to mobilize groups, proceeding in a fashion similar to the street club and Youth Board worker.

The distinguishing feature of the Oakland project is that it gathers together, in an autonomous and informal group, staff members of all the agencies serving the area. Public health nurses, public assistance workers, school guidance personnel, the school principal, recreation directors, and group workers, sit in council with clergymen from the neighboring churches, patrolmen and members of the juvenile detail of the police department. In contrast, however, to the usual police coordinating council, this is *not* an action group. Its informal nature makes it possible to talk informally about problem situations. Programs or problems in which several agencies share are discussed, and as a result, a group conscience is promoted which facilitates teamwork among all participants.

Patrolmen assigned to the area are encouraged to drop in at the center, on the assumption that as the young people become accustomed to seeing them, antagonism will decrease.

> . . . after the first ripple of apprehension, . . . the tradition became well established . . . and some of its results impressed us as being positive.

[20] Evelio Grillo, "Social Group Work in Community Programs for the Prevention and Treatment of Juvenile Delinquency," Group Work and Community Organization, papers published for The National Conference of Social Work, New York, Columbia University Press, 1955, pp. 77-86.

The squad car would park in front of the center, younger children would scamper up to it to have their curiosity satisfied about the gadgets, the sirens and the lights. It was regular practice for the older boys and the patrolmen to talk to each other informally for a considerable length of time, both elements apparently accepting the fact that subsequent contacts might occur under less pleasant circumstances.[21]

At large dances the police often drop in. When the dance is over, the squad car, which circulates slowly and quietly throughout the neighborhood, encourages compliance with curfew regulations and inhibits the boisterousness which might lead to more destructive behavior. "Serious trouble was averted on two occasions by the pre-arranged simple expedient of calling the Police Department and asking for a squad car to park in front of the center in case we needed the help of the police and then telling the children that this was what we had done."[22]

On one occasion a group made up largely of delinquents decided to sponsor a boxing show to raise funds for the center's Christmas celebration for younger children. The priest helped the boys arrange for the use of the social hall in the church, the boxing ring and equipment. When the priest suggested that a police officer friend of his would help secure the posters and get the tickets printed, the boys visited the officer at City Hall. At the suggestion of the settlement director a committee of boys asked the police captain to be the timekeeper, and two probation officers to act as judges. The use of church facilities, the cooperation of the probation officers and the police in a successful public function symbolized a united community in which the center was "working with the police, not in spite of it."

The staff members are not embarrassed to ask the police to help them control a situation. The police know that there are many ways in which they can collaborate with the group workers. Despite their occasional jibes at the police, the young people appear relieved when they know that the police will keep order and they can have fun. The children know that the staff never informs on any of them, and consequently there is no need for the staff to act defensively in relation to them.

Grillo does not think that dissociation from the police is a necessary condition for establishing rapport with delinquent groups. On the contrary, he believes that such dissociation is a "seductive process which plays directly into that part of the delinquent symptoms which lie in the area of authority conflicts." To dissociate the agency from the police is equivalent to saying, "In order to help, we will join you in your separation from society." Rapport established with someone officially representing society may be more effective in convincing young people that society does care about them.

21 *Ibid.*, pp. 82-83.
22 *Ibid.*, p. 83.

The Oakland approach, according to Grillo, is important because delinquency represents, among other things, "a psychological separation from society manifested by behavior consistently unacceptable to society, by rejection of its service institutions, and by non-involvement in many of the processes by which society formally organizes itself."[23] These separating processes are exaggerated in disorganized neighborhoods in which broken families of varying ethnic groups congregate and are discriminated against by the rest of the community. In other words, "disintegrating forces in the community operate to reinforce the separation forces." As a counter agent, it is necessary that the social agencies serving such an area use an approach which includes the police as representatives of the community, so that they will represent an integrating force rather than a threat.

In evaluating these various approaches—youth leader, street worker, detached worker, and ordinary group worker—to helping redirect the antisocial gang, one is reminded of Albert Cohen's thesis (see Chapter 9) that the gang offers status to boys in working-class families who are unable, because of their socio-economic position, to share the aspirations of middle-class families. Cohen suggests that the gang provides the possibility of satisfaction in *reversing* middle-class standards of thrift, orderliness, and postponement of present pleasure in favor of future gain. If this is true, then the community efforts to control gang behavior by attempting to persuade the gang to accept middle-class standards face an almost insurmountable barrier.

Even assuming that Cohen's theory is correct, however, knowing the cause does not suggest the immediate or the best method of control. If much of the antisocial gang behavior is a logical consequence of the very forces and values which have promoted American progress we indeed face a dilemma. The attempts of the youth worker, attached or unattached, to redirect the energies of the more antisocial gang member into socially acceptable activities face great obstacles unless there is a change in the predominant value system and the structures and interrelationships of our society which support it. Two sociologists, Barron and Mills, underscore attention to this aspect of American life.[24]

Summary

Community efforts to deal constructively with the persistent problem of the antisocial or conflict gang have assumed various forms. Such projects as the cellar club program under the National Youth Administration's auspices

[23] *Ibid.*, p. 86.
[24] Milton L. Barron, *The Juvenile in Delinquent Society*, New York, Alfred A. Knopf, 1954; and C. Wright Mills, *The Sociological Imagination*, New York, Oxford University Press, 1959.

in the depression years initiated the pattern of respecting the autonomous nature of the gang and working with it outside the confines of the settlement.

The Harlem Project in 1945 applied the nondirective approach in an attempt to reach the boy who would not make use of the increased after-school facilities supplied by a special project in a local junior high school.

The street club project of the New York City Welfare Council in 1947 formalized the detached worker approach initiated by the Harlem Project. More attention was paid to the qualifications of the workers, to the staff, and to the day-by-day contacts of the four detached workers, each assigned to his special gang. Some provision was made for research in order to see what did and what did not work.

The New York City Youth Board in 1950 instituted a similar program shortly after the termination of the street club project, extending it to additional areas. Other programs in Chicago, Roxbury, Massachusetts, and Cleveland have incorporated or adapted various aspects of the street club approach.

Some of the issues in working with the gangs and attempting to redirect their energies into more constructive and socially approved channels are the extent to which the worker can maintain his role with the gang and at the same time call in the police if he believes that a rumble is likely to have harmful results. The worker cannot give up his own standards even though he does not try to force them on the gang members.

Whether the detached worker or the street worker is successful in doing more than changing some of the superficial behavior of the gang members with respect to girls, destruction of property, and so forth, is a question which the accounts of the Welfare Council Project, those under the auspices of the Youth Board of New York City and those in other communities have not yet answered.

A neighborhood center in a disorganized area of Oakland has developed a different approach to the delinquents who live in the area and belong to some of the clubs in the settlement. Instead of emphasizing the separation of the delinquent or his rejection by the community by subtly siding with him in regarding the police as the enemy, Grillo's program is based on bringing representatives of all the social, religious, and protective forces in the community into direct contact with the agency's program. The aim is to show the delinquent that the authoritative representatives of society are concerned with his welfare and not necessarily his antagonists. This approach appears to have constructive possibilities. It does not explain, however, how the youths who have not participated in the program are persuaded to join it.

PART SIX

CONCLUSION

CHAPTER 30

The Road Ahead

IN STUDYING THE NATURE AND CONTROL OF DELINQUENCY THIS TEXT ASSUMES that the way in which any field of knowledge has been staked out largely reflects the conditioning of those who work in the field. In turn, this conditioning is determined by the indoctrination of the workers and by the theories in vogue at the time. The rapidly changing aspects of the physical sciences illustrate the impossibility of considering all the relevant factors in the explanation of any phenomenon at any one time. As contiguous fields develop and instruments extend our capacities for observation, the subject matter of any field changes its emphasis. In consequence, both definitions and concepts are sharpened. So let us review where we stand today with respect to our knowledge of the nature of delinquency and how best to control it.

1. In re-examining the configurations of the territory embraced by the concept of delinquency the evidence shows that: (a) the field is not as clearly delineated as that of other sciences or aspects of knowledge which have been separated for convenience in study; and (b) there is no agreement as to the meaning or significance of the term "delinquency."

We are forced to ask how far our undifferentiated concept of delinquency includes adolescent behavior which more self-contained societies recognized as a symptom of the growing up process. Such societies made very special provisions for the gradual induction of youth into adulthood.

Perhaps our American attitudes toward children and youth and our struggles to reconcile conflicting philosophies of child rearing in our multi-ethnic society have precipitated responses which we disapprove and deplore. The antisocial gang may be an unintended consequence of our American concern with the "Rights of Infants" (Dr. Margaret Ribble's phrase), as well as of our relentless pursuit of the material symbols of status. Have we, as

527

some sociologists suggest, failed to recognize that the American dream of equal opportunity for all cannot be realized? As they try to find their place in middle-class society we do not provide youth in each of the many ethnic, socio-economic subcultures with equal access to approved and satisfying means for acquiring the highly coveted and well-advertised status symbols.

Investigators suggest that Americans, in comparison with adults in many foreign countries, are hostile, impatient, and rejecting of nonconforming youth. We have too often forgotten our own adolescent rebellion and do not provide the proper controls without overtones of hostility. Instead we over-reach ourselves to give our youth the material advantages that our abundant resources make possible. And we are apt to be impatient when our children do not reward us with their good behavior. In attempting to buy love and good conduct with the coin of the realm we forget the insights provided by psychiatry that to give love, as a peer, a spouse, or a parent, one must have experienced it as a child. At the same time, the very traits that we deplore in our delinquents are often those that we admire in our captains of industry, our financiers, and our generals.

In another respect we serve our children less well than our European neighbors. Although we know that, as Erikson says, useful work is important in the development of a sense of ego-identity, we have been less successful than many European countries in providing our youth with meaningful work opportunities. In America, a variety of influences, including the regulations of labor supply and increased automation, have curtailed and postponed the opportunities for adolescents to engage in real work. They are curtailed because the mechanization of city life has replaced tasks which utilized the energies of every member of the family. Even recreational outlets today are more apt to be in the form of vicarious participation of the spectator than the direct action of the participant.

In the name of equality of opportunity we have insisted that young people remain in school longer than they do in Europe. The child may be, as Shapiro says, a reluctant scholar; but regardless of his educational motivation, unless he is definitely feeble-minded, he must attend school until he is 16 and often 17. If he is truant he is a delinquent. Yet his physiological development has not slowed down to keep pace with the lengthening of his period of economic dependency. As a matter of fact, recent studies indicate that puberty occurs at an earlier age in well-fed populations than in those which have long experienced scarcities of food and poor living conditions. Although young people today often acquire the bodies and the emotional needs of adults at an earlier age than formerly, the mores of our current American society require them to remain dependent as economic units and to defer the gratification of their sex impulses, especially if they might result in pregnancy, until they are 18 or older.

Students of delinquency, viewing it as an entity analogous to illness, have in the main focused their attention on the characteristics of delinquents, and have not differentiated its various forms, which may have very different causes and consequences. For example, as Albert Cohen suggests, they have not sufficiently distinguished between individual delinquent behavior and gang behavior. This creates a dilemma of the sort that would confront the public health field if it were unable to differentiate between types of illness and had to depend upon diagnoses based on the superficial symptoms or characteristics of ailing people.

Regardless of the reaction of the "victim," if we wish to rehabilitate the offender we must understand the meaning the antisocial behavior has for him. It may, as Dr. David Levy points out, be customary behavior in the neighborhood in which the delinquent lives; or it may be an unconscious effort to punish his parents for what he feels are their "delinquencies" toward him; or the young person may be so confused and sick that he needs to be removed from the community for its protection and his own. These differences in meaning with their consequent different treatment approaches can only be determined after study of the relevant factors by people who understand the dynamics of behavior.

2. We have reviewed the various concepts of cause. Parents, social workers, teachers, judges, ministers, psychiatrists, police, biologists, each approach the problem from a different vantage point and with a different stake in it. Each of these, feeling partly responsible, offers his own explanation, tending simultaneously to project the blame onto the others. Because their solutions reflect their indoctrination, the explanations of delinquency as well as the proposals for its cure not only vary widely but conflict each with the other. None of the explanations of cause is satisfactory to any large group of people. Each of the attempted explanations of delinquency—in terms of individual characteristics, family types, community conditions, or culture conflicts—has been inconclusive.

The area in which today the various disciplines most nearly agree is that *some form of family disorganization* is a factor in delinquency—usually the failure of parents to give their children the two things that they need most: the *assurance of continuing love, and moral discipline made acceptable by love.*

Much of the failure of the studies that have tried to establish the relationship of various characteristics to the phenomena of delinquency is due to their authors' misunderstanding of the function of statistical techniques. Statistics provide descriptive but not causal explanations. As Albert Pierce points out, there is a difference between arriving at definitions and establishing propositions empirically.

3. In describing and checking the programs, theories, and formulas for

remedy and treatment against the re-examined behavior of those who have been labeled delinquent, we have found little evidence of the effectiveness of most of the devices that have been advocated for controlling or treating delinquency.

Since a social problem is usually a matter of degree, it is hardly likely that any system of treatment or prevention will entirely eliminate it. The best that we can hope for is to contain it within the limits that the social system can tolerate. To do this means to achieve a state of equilibrium between the needs of individuals, as we understand them, and their access to satisfactions which our social system tries to provide. In the absence of final definitions or causal theories we must continue to distinguish what we do and what we do not know, on the basis of the facts as defined by sociologists, psychologists, anthropologists, lawyers, social workers, and so forth. While each of the proposed programs has some scientifically based roots, the problems of delinquency, like those of other social problems, will not be solved independently by any one discipline.

Although our negative findings underscore how far we are from the goal of understanding and controlling delinquency, there are some signs of progress—not the least of which is the acknowledgment of our ignorance. Five proposals emerge from the findings in this review:

1. To redefine delinquency.

The questions to be answered are: Is there such an entity as a "delinquent"—a person who differs markedly from other young people because *one* aspect of his behavior has merited the community's disapproval? Is there agreement that certain behavior can be uniformly labeled delinquent regardless of color, ethnic identification, or area of residence?

2. To apply the sociological principle of clear definition of appropriate role to each of the institutions charged with some responsibility for controlling or preventing delinquency.

While the family's primary responsibility is to rear the child in the way he should go, the diversification of society's expectations requires today that the church and the school, as well as the protective system of police and courts and the many other community services, each play an appropriate and distinctive auxiliary role. Duplication and confusion result unless each institution confines its services to those which the competence of its staff equips it to perform. For example, the police are not equipped for casework or recreation service, the judges are not trained to decide on treatment procedures, and social workers should not assume the judicial functions. Institutions need to be clear about what kinds of children they can help in view of their equipment and their personnel. If we apply these principles in examining the community's provisions for dealing with delinquents, we shall be better able to judge their effectiveness.

3. To replace invalidated theories and treatment processes *by implementing those for which the evidence appears to be most promising.*

Those who feel that the already available knowledge needs only to be put to work rarely inquire into the assumptions on which the programs have been built. Those who refuse to act because they have no certainty as to the effectiveness of the proposed action err perhaps in the opposite direction. They fail to recognize that cures sometimes have been hit upon before the reasons for their effectiveness are known. For example, today medicine is both rediscovering and explaining the effectiveness of antibiotics, which apparently the simple peasant sensed but did not understand when he put mud on a wound.

Similarly, if evidence has been accumulated that love and acceptance produce constructive changes, whereas punishment for its own sake and rejection seem only to increase the delinquent's aggression, regardless of whether there is a satisfactory explanation they merit wider application. The experience of carefully organized treatment centers is beginning to show that, slow as the process may be, the building of a young person's confidence in himself and a feeling of his own worth can pay off if we apply proper "controls from without" to supplement "controls from within." The Highfields results with guided group therapy for small groups of boys certainly merit further consideration.

4. To reconsider our use of personnel and physical plant.

There is telling evidence, in the high recidivist rate, of the ineffectiveness of *most* of our reformatories and institutions when compared with institutions abroad. One reason may be our failure to draw on many sources of personnel which the Europeans have tapped. There is an amazing range of background experience among those who act as judges, probation officers, or heads of institutions in England, France, and Sweden. In these countries the tradition of service and concern even in the so-called upper classes has provided a resource for personnel which we have not tapped. Although we know it will take years to get fully trained staff, we continue to insist that we cannot operate without them. As a result, we too often have to make do with inadequate staff. Our very high turnover in youth work, probation, and institutional staff gives little hope of successful treatment.

We must experiment boldly to make more creative use of our human resources as well as our physical plant. If we sorted out our misbehaving young people in accordance with Dr. Levy's classification, we would assign the third group who require deep therapy to highly trained psychiatrists, probably in an institutional setting. Those in the first group, whose behavior is a reflection of the community in which they live, might be helped by area projects and other types of service which (1) make the community a better place to live; (2) provide examples of approved behavior that open up roads to status more acceptable to society than the way of the gangster. The second group, whose problem is one of relationship, might best be guided to family agencies or mental-hygiene clinics in which social caseworkers are trained to deal with the interrelations of parents and children.

5. Our fifth proposition concerns research.

Before we can deal intelligently with any aspect of delinquency we need to know its extent and its areas of impact. A Central Register of delinquents to which both official and unofficial agencies reported would: (1) provide an unduplicated case count; (2) point out neighborhoods of high hazard and the types of families most likely to be involved. If properly used the register would make it possible for any community to know which agencies are most effective in dealing with the various types of delinquents for whom they undertake to provide services. From a research standpoint the register would provide a pool from which to select a variety of random and representative families for testing various appropriate hypotheses.

Meanwhile we must revise the haphazard structure, from a research standpoint, of many programs which claim that they deal effectively with delinquents. In designing our programs in *treatment and prevention,* we should apply criteria such as those outlined by Herzog.[1] This means stating our objectives, describing our methods, specifying those to whom we are directing our services, and stating the criteria we intend to apply in judging the effectiveness of the undertaking.

In attempts to *explain* delinquency we propose that scientifically designed research projects replace the usual search for association of descriptive characteristics. Instead we need to study the relative roles of the physical environment, the subculture, and the family pattern, as well as the special needs of the individual or individuals designated delinquent.

Toward this end we urge a study of the dynamics of delinquent behavior as experienced in interrelationships—both psychological and structural-functional—giving consideration to the technology and the culture of the family setting. For example, the approach of the ten-year Newcastle-on-Tyne study of the medical needs of a thousand English families could be adapted to examine how ordinary families, in different settings and with different ethnic backgrounds, manage to bring up their children despite the stresses and strains to which they, like their problem neighbors, are subject.

With this approach we recognize that the efforts we make to understand delinquency are only a part of the rewarding and continuing effort to understand ourselves and our society.

[1] Elizabeth Herzog, *Some Guide Lines for Evaluative Research: Assessing Psychosocial Change in Individuals,* No. 375, Washington, U.S. Children's Bureau, 1959.

INDEXES

Index of Authors

Index of Subjects

559

TEXAS A&M UNIVERSITY-TEXARKANA